Benchmark Series

Levels 1 & 2

Microsoft® Word 2010

Nita Rutkosky

Pierce College at Puyallup
Puyallup, Washington

Audrey Rutkosky Roggenkamp

Pierce College at Puyallup
Puyallup, Washington

Paradigm PUBLISHING

St. Paul • Indianapolis

Managing Editor	Sonja Brown
Senior Developmental Editor	Christine Hurney
Production Editor	Donna Mears
Copy Editor	Susan Capecchi
Cover and Text Designer	Leslie Anderson
Desktop Production	Ryan Hamner, Julie Johnston, Jack Ross
Proofreader	Laura Nelson
Indexer	Sandi Schroeder

Acknowledgements: The authors, editors, and publisher thank the following instructors for their helpful suggestions during the planning and development of the books in the Benchmark Office 2010 Series: Somasheker Akkaladevi, Virginia State University, Petersburg, VA; Ed Baker, Community College of Philadelphia, Philadelphia, PA; Lynn Baldwin, Madison Area Technical College, Madison, WI; Letty Barnes, Lake Washington Technical College, Kirkland, WA; Richard Bell, Coastal Carolina Community College, Jacksonville, NC; Perry Callas, Clatsop Community College, Astoria, OR; Carol DesJardins, St. Clair County Community College, Port Huron, MI; Stacy Gee Hollins, St. Louis Community College--Florissant Valley, St. Louis, MO Sally Haywood, Prairie State College, Chicago Heights, IL; Dr. Penny Johnson, Madison Technical College, Madison, WI; Jan Kehm, Spartanburg Community College, Spartanburg, SC; Jacqueline Larsen, Asheville Buncombe Tech, Asheville, NC; Sherry Lenhart, Terra Community College, Fremont, OH; Andrea Robinson Hinsey, Ivy Tech Community College NE, Fort Wayne, IN; Bari Siddique, University of Texas at Brownsville, Brownsville, TX; Joan Splawski, Northeast Wisconsin Technical College, Green Bay, WI; Diane Stark, Phoenix College, Phoenix, AZ; Mary Van Haute, Northeast Wisconsin Technical College, Green Bay, WI; Rosalie Westerberg, Clover Park Technical College, Lakewood, WA.

The publishing team also thanks the following individuals for their contributions to this project: checking the accuracy of the instruction and exercises—Robertt (Rob) W. Neilly, Traci Post, and Lindsay Ryan; developing lesson plans, supplemental assessments, and supplemental case studies—Jan Davidson, Lambton College, Sarina, Ontario; writing rubrics to support end-of-chapter and end-of-unit activities—Robertt (Rob) W. Neilly, Seneca College, Toronto, Ontario; writing test item banks—Jeff Johnson; writing online quiz item banks—Trudy Muller; and developing PowerPoint presentations—Janet Blum, Fanshawe College, London, Ontario.

Trademarks: Access, Excel, Internet Explorer, Microsoft, PowerPoint, and Windows are trademarks or registered trademarks of Microsoft Corporation in the United States and/or other countries. Some of the product names and company names included in this book have been used for identification purposes only and may be trademarks or registered trade names of their respective manufacturers and sellers. The authors, editors, and publisher disclaim any affiliation, association, or connection with, or sponsorship or endorsement by, such owners.

We have made every effort to trace the ownership of all copyrighted material and to secure permission from copyright holders. In the event of any question arising as to the use of any material, we will be pleased to make the necessary corrections in future printings. Thanks are due to the aforementioned authors, publishers, and agents for permission to use the materials indicated.

Paradigm Publishing is independent from Microsoft Corporation, and not affiliated with Microsoft in any manner. While this textbook may be used in assisting end users to prepare for a Microsoft Office Specialist exam, Microsoft, its designated program administrator, and Paradigm Publishing do not warrant that use of this textbook will ensure passing a Microsoft Office Specialist exam.

ISBN 978-0-76384-296-3 (Text)
ISBN 978-0-76384-299-4 (Text + CD)

© 2011 by Paradigm Publishing, Inc.
875 Montreal Way
St. Paul, MN 55102
Email: educate@emcp.com
Website: www.emcp.com

Printed in the United States of America

19 18 17 16 15 14 13 12 11 10   1 2 3 4 5 6 7 8 9 10

Contents

Microsoft Word 2010 Level 2

Contents   v

Benchmark Microsoft Word 2010 is designed for students who want to learn how to use this powerful word processing program to create professional-looking documents for workplace, school, and personal communication needs. No prior knowledge of word processing is required. After successfully completing a course using this textbook, students will be able to

- Create and edit memos, letters, fliers, announcements, and reports of varying complexity
- Apply appropriate formatting elements and styles to a range of document types
- Add graphics and other visual elements to enhance written communication
- Plan, research, write, revise, and publish documents to meet specific information needs
- Given a workplace scenario requiring a written solution, assess the communication purpose and then prepare the materials that achieve the goal efficiently and effectively

In addition to mastering Word skills, students will learn the essential features and functions of computer hardware, the Windows 7 operating system, and Internet Explorer 8.0. Upon completing the text, they can expect to be proficient in using Word to organize, analyze, and present information.

Achieving Proficiency in Word 2010

Since its inception several Office versions ago, the Benchmark Series has served as a standard of excellence in software instruction. Elements of the book function individually and collectively to create an inviting, comprehensive learning environment that produces successful computer users. The following visual tour highlights the text's features.

UNIT OPENERS display the unit's four chapter titles. Each level has two units, which conclude with a comprehensive unit performance assessment.

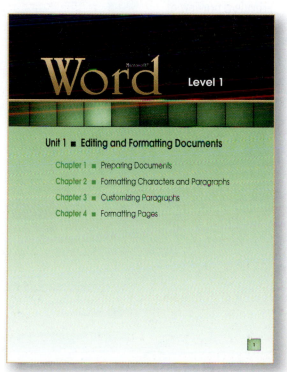

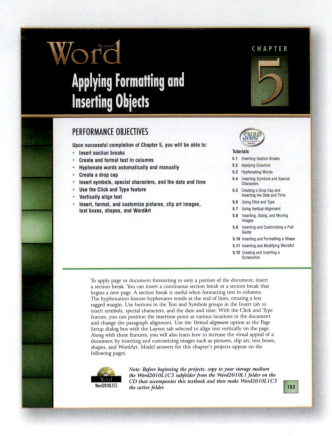

CHAPTER OPENERS present the performance objectives and an overview of the skills taught.

SNAP interactive tutorials are available to support chapter-specific skills at www.snap2010.emcp.com.

DATA FILES are provided for each chapter. A prominent note reminds students to copy the appropriate chapter data folder and make it active.

PROJECT APPROACH: Builds Skill Mastery within Realistic Context

MODEL ANSWERS provide a preview of the finished chapter projects and allow students to confirm they have created the materials accurately.

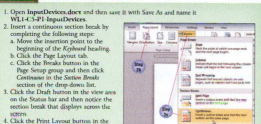
MULTIPART PROJECTS provide a framework for the instruction and practice on software features. A project overview identifies tasks to accomplish and key features to use in completing the work.

STEP-BY-STEP INSTRUCTIONS guide students to the desired outcome for each project part. Screen captures illustrate what the student's screen should look like at key points.

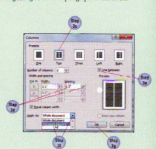
Between project parts, the text presents instruction on the features and skills necessary to accomplish the next section of the project.

Typically, a file remains open throughout all parts of the project. Students save their work incrementally.

MAGENTA TEXT identifies material to type.

At the end of the project, students save, print, and then close the file.

QUICK STEPS provide feature summaries for reference and review.

HINTS provide useful tips on how to use features efficiently and effectively.

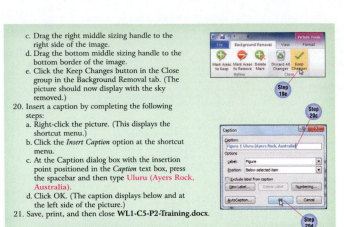

c. Drag the right middle sizing handle to the right side of the image.
d. Drag the bottom middle sizing handle to the bottom border of the image.
e. Click the Keep Changes button in the Close group in the Background Removal tab. (The picture should now display with the sky removed.)

20. Insert a caption by completing the following steps:
   a. Right-click the picture. (This displays the shortcut menu.)
   b. Click the *Insert Caption* option at the shortcut menu.
   c. At the Caption dialog box with the insertion point positioned in the *Caption* text box, press the spacebar and then type Uluru (Ayers Rock, Australia).
   d. Click OK. (The caption displays below and at the left side of the picture.)

21. Save, print, and then close **WL1-C5-P2-Training.docx**.

Project 3   Customize a Report on Robots   2 Parts

You will open a report on robots and then add visual appeal to the report by inserting and formatting a clip art image and a built-in text box.

Inserting a Clip Art Image

Microsoft Office includes a gallery of media images you can insert in a document such as clip art, photographs, and movie images, as well as sound clips. To insert an image in a Word document, click the Insert tab and then click the Clip Art button in the Illustrations group. This displays the Clip Art task pane at the right side of the screen as shown in Figure 5.7.

To view all picture, sound, and motion files, make sure the *Search for* text box in the Clip Art task pane does not contain any text and then click the Go button. When the desired image is visible, click the image to insert it in the document. Use buttons in the Picture Tools Format tab to format and customize the clip art image.

Unless the Clip Art task pane default settings have been customized, the task pane displays all illustrations, photographs, videos, and audio files. The *Results should be* option has a default setting of *Selected media file types*. Click the down-pointing arrow at the right side of this option to display media types. To search for a specific media type, remove the check mark before all options at the drop-down list except for the desired type. For example, if you are searching only for photograph images, remove the check mark before *Illustrations*, *Videos*, and *Audio*.

▼ **Quick Steps**

Insert Clip Art Image
1. Click Insert tab.
2. Click Clip Art button.
3. Type search word or topic.
4. Press Enter.
5. Click desired image.

HINT

You can drag a clip art image from the Clip Art task pane to your document.

Clip Art

CHAPTER REVIEW ACTIVITIES: A Hierarchy of Learning Assessments

Chapter Summary

- Group Word documents logically into folders. Create a new folder at the Open or Save As dialog box.
- You can select one or several documents at the Open dialog box. Copy, move, rename, delete, or open a document or selected documents.
- Use the *Cut*, *Copy*, and *Paste* options from the Organize button drop-down list or the Open dialog box shortcut menu to move or copy a document from one folder to another.
- Delete documents and/or folders with the *Delete* option from the Organize button drop-down list or shortcut menu.
- With options at the Save & Send tab Backstage view, you can send a document as an email attachment, save your document to SkyDrive and SharePoint, save your document in a different file format, and post your document to a special location such as a blog.
- Click the Change File Type button in the File Types category at the Save & Send tab Backstage view, and options display for saving the document in a different file format. You can also save documents in a different file format with the *Save as type* option box at the Save As dialog box.
- Move among the op[...] representing the des[...] Switch Windows bu[...] document name.
- View a portion of al[...] clicking the Arrange[...]
- Use the Minimize, [...] corner of the windo[...]
- Divide a window in[...] Split button in the [...] the same document[...]
- View the contents o[...] and then clicking th[...]
- Insert a document i[...] the Object button a[...] At the Insert File di[...]
- Preview a document[...] in the document wi[...] below the preview p[...] display size of the p[...]
- At the Print tab Bac[...] the page orientatio[...] to print on one pag[...] pages; and specify t[...]
- With Word's envel[...] Envelopes and Labe[...]

232   Word Level 1 ■ Unit 2

CHAPTER SUMMARY captures the purpose and execution of key features.

- If you open the Envelopes and Labels dialog box in a document containing a name and address (with each line ending with a press of the Enter key), that information is automatically inserted in the *Delivery address* text box in the dialog box.
- Use Word's labels feature to print text on mailing labels, file labels, disc labels, or other types of labels.
- Word includes a number of template documents you can use to create a variety of documents. Display the list of template documents by clicking the File tab, clicking the New tab, and then clicking the Sample templates button.

Commands Review

COMMANDS REVIEW summarizes visually the major features and alternative methods of access.

FEATURE	RIBBON TAB, GROUP	BUTTON, OPTION	KEYBOARD SHORTCUT
Open dialog box	File	Open	Ctrl + O
Save As dialog box	File	Save As	
Print tab Backstage view	File	Print	Ctrl + P
Arrange all documents	View, Window		
Minimize document			
Maximize document			
Restore			
Split window	View, Window		
View documents side by side	View, Window		
Insert file	Insert, Text		
Envelopes and Labels dialog box with Envelopes tab selected	Mailings, Crea[...]		
Envelopes and Labels dialog box with Labels tab selected	Mailings, Cre[...]		
New tab Backstage view	File		

Concepts Check   Test Your Knowledge

Completion: In the space provided at the right, indicate the correct term, command, or number.

1. Create a new folder with this button at the Open or Save As dialog box.

2. At the Open dialog box, the current folder path displays in this.

3. Using the mouse, select nonadjacent documents at the Open dialog box by holding down this key while clicking the desired documents.

4. Documents deleted from the hard drive are automatically sent here.

5. Copy a document to another folder without opening the document at the Open or Save As dialog box with the Organize button drop-down list or this menu.

6. The letters PDF stand for this.

7. Saving a document in this format strips out all formatting.

8. Click this button in the Window group in the View tab to arrange all open documents so a portion of each document displays.

9. Click this button and the active document fills the editing window.

10. Click this button to reduce the active document to a button on the Taskbar.

11. To display documents side by side, click this button in the Window group in the View tab.

12. Display the Insert File dialog box by clicking the Object button arrow in the Insert tab and then clicking this option.

13. Type this in the *Pages* text box at the Print tab Backstage view to print pages 3 through 6 of the open document.

14. Type this in the *Pages* text box at the Print tab Backstage view to print pages 4 and 9 of the open document.

15. The Envelopes button is located in the Create group in this tab.

16. Click the Sample templates button at this Backstage view to display a list of templates.

234   Word Level 1 ■ Unit 2

CONCEPTS CHECK questions assess knowledge recall.

Skills Check — Assess Your Performance

Assessment

1 APPLY CHARACTER FORMATTING TO A LEASE AGREEMENT DOCUMENT

1. Open **LeaseAgrmnt.docx**.
2. Save the document with Save As and name it **WL1-C2-A1-LeaseAgrmnt**.
3. Press Ctrl + End to move the insertion point to the end of the document and then type the text shown in Figure 2.8. Bold, *italicize*, and underline text as shown.
4. Select the entire document and then change the font to 12-point Candara.
5. Select and then bold *THIS LEASE AGREEMENT* located in the first paragraph
6. Select an
7. Select an
8. Select an
9. Select th Corbel a formatti
10. Select th caps forr
11. Use Forr for the r *Premises, Default, ;*
12. Save, pri

Figure 2.8 Assessment 1

Inspection of Premises

Lessor shall have the exhibit the Premises Premises at any time

Default

If Lessee fails to pay Lessor may declare th and all rights and rem

Late Charge

In the event that any of the month, Lessee

SKILLS CHECK exercises ask students to create a variety of documents using multiple features without how-to directions.

Visual Benchmark — Demonstrate Your Proficiency

1 CREATE A SHAPE

1. At a blank document create the document shown in Figure 5.10 with the following specifications:
   a. Draw the shape using the *Quad Arrow Callout* located in the *Block Arrows* section.
   b. Apply the *Subtle Effect – Olive Green, Accent 3* shape style to the shape.
   c. Change the shape effect to *Soft Round* bevel.
   d. Change the height and width of the shape to 5 inches.
   e. Type the text in the shape as shown and set the text in 16-point Copperplate Gothic Bold and change the text color to dark green.
   f. Insert the truck clip art image and size and position it as shown in Figure 5.10. (If this truck clip art image is not available, choose another truck clip art image. Change the text wrap to *In Front of Text*.)
2. Center the shape on the page.
3. Save the document and name it **WL1-C5-VB1-FourCorners**.
4. Print and then close the document.

Figure 5.10 Visual Benchmark 1

VISUAL BENCHMARK assessments test students' problem-solving skills and mastery of program features.

Case Study — Apply Your Skills

Part 1

You are the office manager for the real estate company, Macadam Realty, and have been asked by the senior sales associate, Lucy Hendricks, to organize contract forms into a specific folder. Create a new folder named *RealEstate* and then copy into the folder documents that begin with the letters "RE." Ms. Hendricks has also asked you to prepare mailing labels for Macadam Realty. Include the name, Macadam Realty, and the address 100 Third Street, Suite 210, Denver, CO 80803, on the labels. Use a decorative font for the label and make the *M* in *Macadam* and the *R* in *Realty* larger and more pronounced than surrounding text. ***Hint: Format text in the label by selecting text, right-clicking in the selected text, and then choosing the desired option at the shortcut menu.*** Save the completed document and name it **WL1-C6-CS-P1-RELabels**. Print and then close the document.

Part 2

One of your responsibilities is to format contract forms. Open the document named **REConAgrmnt.docx** and then save it and name it **WL1-C6-CS-P2-REConAgrmnt**. The sales associate has asked you to insert signature information at the end of the document and so you decide to insert at the end of the document the file named **RESig.docx**. With **WL1-C6-CS-P2-REConAgrmnt.docx** still open, open **REBuildAgrmnt.docx**. Format the **WL1-C6-CS-P2-REConAgrmnt.docx** document so it is formatted in a manner similar to the **REBuildAgrmnt.docx** document. Consider the following when specifying formatting: margins, fonts, and paragraph shading. Save, print, and then close **WL1-C6-CS-P2-REConAgrmnt.docx**. Close **REBuildAgrmnt.docx**.

Part 3

As part of the organization of contracts, Ms. Hendricks has asked you to insert document properties for the **REBuildAgrmnt.docx** and **WL1-C6-CS-P2-REConAgrmnt.docx** documents. Use the Help feature to learn how to insert document properties. With the information you learn from the Help feature, open each of the two documents separately, display the Info tab Backstage view, click the Show All Properties hyperlink, and then insert document properties in the following fields (you determine the information to type): *Title, Subject, Categories,* and *Company*. Print the document properties for each document (change the first gallery in the Settings category in the Print tab Backstage view to *Document Properties*). Save each document with the original name and close the documents.

Part 4

A client of the real estate company, Anna Hurley, is considering purchasing several rental properties and has asked for information on how to locate real estate rental forms. Using the Internet, locate at least three websites that offer real estate rental forms. Write a letter to Anna Hurley at 2300 South 22nd Street, Denver, CO 80205. In the letter, list the websites you found and include information on which site you thought offered the most resources. Also include in the letter that Macadam Realty is very interested in helping her locate and purchase rental properties. Save the document and name it **WL1-C6-CS-P4-RELtr**. Create an envelope for the letter and add it to the letter document. Save, print, and then close **WL1-C6-CS-P4-RELtr.docx**. (You may need to manually feed the envelope in the printer.)

CASE STUDY requires analyzing a workplace scenario and then planning and executing multipart projects.

Students search the Web and/or use the program's Help feature to locate additional information required to complete the Case Study.

System Requirements ■■■■■■■■■■■■■■■■■■■■■■■■■

This text is designed for the student to complete projects and assessments on a computer running a standard installation of Microsoft Office 2010, Professional Edition, and the Microsoft Windows 7 operating system. To effectively run this suite and operating system, your computer should be outfitted with the following:

- 1 gigahertz (GHz) processor or higher; 1 gigabyte (GB) of RAM
- DVD drive
- 15 GB of available hard-disk space
- Computer mouse or compatible pointing device

Office 2010 will also operate on computers running the Windows XP Service Pack 3 or the Windows Vista operating system.

Screen captures in this book were created using a screen resolution display setting of 1280 × 800. Refer to the *Customizing Settings* section of *Getting Started in Office 2010* following this preface for instructions on changing your monitor's resolution. Figure G.10 on page 10 shows the Microsoft Office Word ribbon at three resolutions for comparison purposes. Choose the resolution that best matches your computer; however, be aware that using a resolution other than 1280 × 800 means that your screens may not match the illustrations in this book.

About the Authors ■■■■■■■■■■■■■■■■■■■■■■■■■

Nita Rutkosky began teaching business education courses at Pierce College in Puyallup, Washington, in 1978. Since then she has taught a variety of software applications to students in postsecondary Information Technology certificate and degree programs. In addition to *Benchmark Office 2010*, she has co-authored *Marquee Series: Microsoft Office 2010, 2007*, and *2003; Signature Series: Microsoft Word 2010, 2007*, and *2003*; and *Using Computers in the Medical Office: Microsoft Word, Excel, and PowerPoint 2007* and *2003*. She has also authored textbooks on keyboarding, WordPerfect, desktop publishing, and voice recognition for Paradigm Publishing, Inc.

Audrey Rutkosky Roggenkamp has been teaching courses in the Business Information Technology department at Pierce College in Puyallup since 2005. Her courses have included keyboarding, skill building, and Microsoft Office programs. In addition to this title, she has co-authored *Marquee Series: Microsoft Office 2010* and *2007; Signature Series: Microsoft Word 2010* and *2007*; and *Using Computers in the Medical Office 2007* and *2003* for Paradigm Publishing, Inc.

What is the Microsoft® Office Specialist Program?

The Microsoft Office Specialist Program enables candidates to show that they have something exceptional to offer—proven expertise in certain Microsoft programs. Recognized by businesses and schools around the world, over 4 million certifications have been obtained in over 100 different countries. The Microsoft Office Specialist Program is the only Microsoft-approved certification program of its kind.

What is the Microsoft Office Specialist Certification?

The Microsoft Office Specialist certification validates through the use of exams that you have obtained specific skill sets within the applicable Microsoft Office programs and other Microsoft programs included in the Microsoft Office Specialist Program. Candidates can choose which exam(s) they want to take according to which skills they want to validate.

The available Microsoft Office Specialist Program exams* include:

Using Windows Vista®	Using Microsoft® Office PowerPoint® 2007
Using Microsoft® Office Word 2007	Using Microsoft® Office Access® 2007
Using Microsoft® Office Word 2007 - Expert	Using Microsoft® Office Outlook® 2007
Using Microsoft® Office Excel® 2007	Using Microsoft SharePoint® 2007
Using Microsoft® Office Excel® 2007 - Expert	

The Microsoft Office Specialist Program 2010 exams* include:

Microsoft Word 2010	Microsoft PowerPoint® 2010
Microsoft Word 2010 Expert	Microsoft Access® 2010
Microsoft Excel® 2010	Microsoft Outlook® 2010
Microsoft Excel® 2010 Expert	Microsoft SharePoint® 2010

What does the Microsoft Office Specialist Approved Courseware logo represent?

The logo indicates that this courseware has been approved by Microsoft to cover the course objectives that will be included in the relevant exam. It also means that after utilizing this courseware, you may be better prepared to pass the exams required to become a certified Microsoft Office Specialist.

For more information:

To learn more about Microsoft Office Specialist exams, visit www.microsoft.com/learning/msbc. To learn about other Microsoft approved courseware from Paradigm Publishing, Inc., visit www.ParadigmCollege.com.

*The availability of Microsoft Office Specialist certification exams varies by Microsoft program, program version, and language. Visit www.microsoft.com/learning for exam availability.

Microsoft, Access, Excel, the Office Logo, Outlook, PowerPoint, SharePoint, and Windows Vista are either registered trademarks or trademarks of Microsoft Corporation in the United States and/or other countries. The Microsoft Office Specialist logo and the Microsoft Office Specialist Approved Courseware logo are used under license from Microsoft Corporation.

Getting Started in Office 2010

In this textbook, you will learn to operate several computer application programs that combine to make an application "suite." This suite of programs is called Microsoft Office 2010. The programs you will learn to operate are the software, which includes instructions telling the computer what to do. Some of the application programs in the suite include a word processing program named Word, a spreadsheet program named Excel, a database program named Access, and a presentation program named PowerPoint.

Identifying Computer Hardware

The computer equipment you will use to operate the suite of programs is referred to as hardware. You will need access to a microcomputer system that should consist of the CPU, monitor, keyboard, printer, drives, and mouse. If you are not sure what equipment you will be operating, check with your instructor. The computer system shown in Figure G.1 consists of six components. Each component is discussed separately in the material that follows.

Figure G.1 Microcomputer System

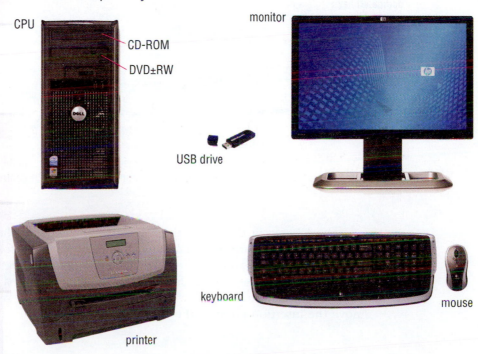

CPU
CD-ROM
DVD±RW
USB drive
monitor
printer
keyboard
mouse

CPU

CPU stands for Central Processing Unit and it is the intelligence of the computer. All the processing occurs in the CPU. Silicon chips, which contain miniaturized circuitry, are placed on boards that are plugged into slots within the CPU. Whenever an instruction is given to the computer, that instruction is processed through circuitry in the CPU.

Monitor

The monitor is a piece of equipment that looks like a television screen. It displays the information of a program and the text being input at the keyboard. The quality of display for monitors varies depending on the type of monitor and the level of resolution. Monitors can also vary in size—generally from 15-inch size up to 26-inch size or larger.

Keyboard

The keyboard is used to input information into the computer. Keyboards for microcomputers vary in the number and location of the keys. Microcomputers have the alphabetic and numeric keys in the same location as the keys on a typewriter. The symbol keys, however, may be placed in a variety of locations, depending on the manufacturer. In addition to letters, numbers, and symbols, most microcomputer keyboards contain function keys, arrow keys, and a numeric keypad. Figure G.2 shows an enhanced keyboard.

Figure G.2 Keyboard

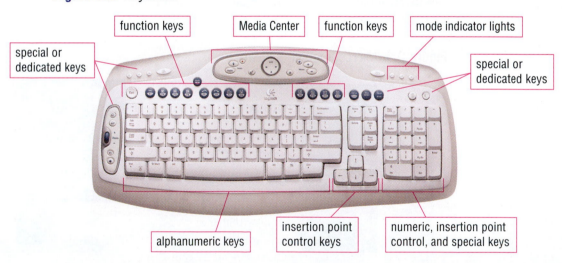

The 12 keys at the top of the keyboard, labeled with the letter F followed by a number, are called *function keys*. Use these keys to perform functions within each of the suite programs. To the right of the regular keys is a group of *special* or *dedicated keys*. These keys are labeled with specific functions that will be performed when you press the key. Below the special keys are arrow keys. Use these keys to move the insertion point in the document screen.

A keyboard generally includes three mode indicator lights. When you select certain modes, a light appears on the keyboard. For example, if you press the Caps Lock key, which disables the lowercase alphabet, a light appears next to Caps Lock. Similarly, pressing the Num Lock key will disable the special functions on the numeric keypad, which is located at the right side of the keyboard.

Disk Drives

Depending on the computer system you are using, Microsoft Office 2010 is installed on a hard drive or as part of a network system. Whether you are using Office on a hard drive or network system, you will need to have available a DVD or CD drive and a USB drive or other storage medium. You will insert the CD (compact disc) that accompanies this textbook in the DVD or CD drive and then copy folders from the CD to your storage medium. You will also save documents you complete at the computer to folders on your storage medium.

Printer

A document you create in Word is considered soft copy. If you want a hard copy of a document, you need to print it. To print documents you will need to access a printer, which will probably be either a laser printer or an ink-jet printer. A laser printer uses a laser beam combined with heat and pressure to print documents, while an ink-jet printer prints a document by spraying a fine mist of ink on the page.

Mouse

Many functions in the suite of programs are designed to operate more efficiently with a mouse. A mouse is an input device that sits on a flat surface next to the computer. You can operate a mouse with the left or the right hand. Moving the mouse on the flat surface causes a corresponding mouse pointer to move on the screen. Figure G.1 shows an illustration of a mouse.

Using the Mouse ■■■■■■■■■■■■■■■■■■■■■■■■■■■■■■■■■

The programs in the Microsoft Office suite can be operated with the keyboard and a mouse. The mouse may have two or three buttons on top, which are tapped to execute specific functions and commands. To use the mouse, rest it on a flat surface or a mouse pad. Put your hand over it with your palm resting on top of the mouse and your wrist resting on the table surface. As you move the mouse on the flat surface, a corresponding pointer moves on the screen.

When using the mouse, you should understand four terms — point, click, double-click, and drag. When operating the mouse, you may need to point to a specific command, button, or icon. Point means to position the mouse pointer on the desired item. With the mouse pointer positioned on the desired item, you may need to click a button on the mouse. Click means quickly tapping a button on the mouse once. To complete two steps at one time, such as choosing and then executing a function, double-click a mouse button. Double-click means to tap the left mouse button twice in quick succession. The term drag means to press and hold the left mouse button, move the mouse pointer to a specific location, and then release the button.

Using the Mouse Pointer

The mouse pointer will change appearance depending on the function being performed or where the pointer is positioned. The mouse pointer may appear as one of the following images:

- The mouse pointer appears as an I-beam (called the I-beam pointer) in the document screen and can be used to move the insertion point or select text.

- The mouse pointer appears as an arrow pointing up and to the left (called the arrow pointer) when it is moved to the Title bar, Quick Access toolbar, ribbon, or an option in a dialog box.

- The mouse pointer becomes a double-headed arrow (either pointing left and right, pointing up and down, or pointing diagonally) when performing certain functions such as changing the size of an object.

- In certain situations, such as moving an object or image, the mouse pointer displays with a four-headed arrow attached. The four-headed arrow means that you can move the object left, right, up, or down.

- When a request is being processed or when a program is being loaded, the mouse pointer may appear with a circle beside it. The moving circle means "please wait." When the process is completed, the circle is removed.

- The mouse pointer displays as a hand with a pointing index finger in certain functions such as Help and indicates that more information is available about the item. The mouse pointer also displays as a hand when you hover the mouse over a hyperlink.

Choosing Commands ■■■■■■■■■■■■■■■■■■■■■■■■■■■■

Once a program is open, you can use several methods in the program to choose commands. A command is an instruction that tells the program to do something. You can choose a command using the mouse or the keyboard. When a program such as Word or PowerPoint is open, the ribbon contains buttons for completing tasks and contains tabs you click to display additional buttons. To choose a button on the Quick Access toolbar or in the ribbon, position the tip of the mouse arrow pointer on a button and then click the left mouse button.

The Office suite provides access keys you can press to use a command in a program. Press the Alt key on the keyboard to display KeyTips that identify the access key you need to press to execute a command. For example, press the Alt key in a Word document with the Home tab active and KeyTips display as shown in Figure G.3. Continue pressing access keys until you execute the desired command. For example, if you want to begin spell checking a document, you would press the Alt key, press the R key on the keyboard to display the Review tab, and then press the letter S on the keyboard.

Choosing Commands from Drop-Down Lists

To choose a command from a drop-down list with the mouse, position the mouse pointer on the desired option and then click the left mouse button. To make a selection from a drop-down list with the keyboard, type the underlined letter in the desired option.

Figure G.3 Word Home Tab KeyTips

Some options at a drop-down list may be gray-shaded (dimmed), indicating that the option is currently unavailable. If an option at a drop-down list displays preceded by a check mark, that indicates that the option is currently active. If an option at a drop-down list displays followed by an ellipsis (…), a dialog box will display when that option is chosen.

Choosing Options from a Dialog Box

A dialog box contains options for applying formatting to a file or data within a file. Some dialog boxes display with tabs along the top providing additional options. For example, the Font dialog box shown in Figure G.4 contains two tabs — the Font tab and the Advanced tab. The tab that displays in the front is the active tab. To make a tab active using the mouse, position the arrow pointer on the desired tab and then click the left mouse button. If you are using the keyboard, press Ctrl + Tab or press Alt + the underlined letter on the desired tab.

Figure G.4 Word Font Dialog Box

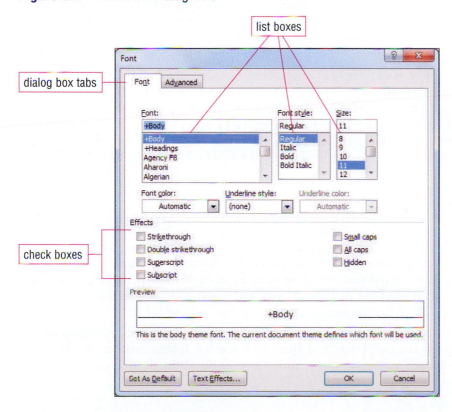

To choose options from a dialog box with the mouse, position the arrow pointer on the desired option and then click the left mouse button. If you are using the keyboard, press the Tab key to move the insertion point forward from option to option. Press Shift + Tab to move the insertion point backward from option to option. You can also hold down the Alt key and then press the underlined letter of the desired option. When an option is selected, it displays with a blue background or surrounded by a dashed box called a marquee. A dialog box contains one or more of the following elements: text boxes, list boxes, check boxes, option buttons, measurement boxes, and command buttons.

List Boxes

Some dialog boxes such as the Word Font dialog box shown in Figure G.4 may contain a list box. The list of fonts below the *Font* option is contained in a list box. To make a selection from a list box with the mouse, move the arrow pointer to the desired option and then click the left mouse button.

Some list boxes may contain a scroll bar. This scroll bar will display at the right side of the list box (a vertical scroll bar) or at the bottom of the list box (a horizontal scroll bar). You can use a vertical scroll bar or a horizontal scroll bar to move through the list if the list is longer than the box. To move down through a list on a vertical scroll bar, position the arrow pointer on the down-pointing arrow and hold down the left mouse button. To scroll up through the list in a vertical scroll bar, position the arrow pointer on the up-pointing arrow and hold down the left mouse button. You can also move the arrow pointer above the scroll box and click the left mouse button to scroll up the list or move the arrow pointer below the scroll box and click the left mouse button to move down the list. To move through a list with a horizontal scroll bar, click the left-pointing arrow to scroll to the left of the list or click the right-pointing arrow to scroll to the right of the list.

To make a selection from a list using the keyboard, move the insertion point into the box by holding down the Alt key and pressing the underlined letter of the desired option. Press the Up and/or Down Arrow keys on the keyboard to move through the list.

In some dialog boxes where enough room is not available for a list box, lists of options are inserted in a drop-down list box. Options that contain a drop-down list box display with a down-pointing arrow. For example, the *Underline style* option at the Word Font dialog box shown in Figure G.4 contains a drop-down list. To display the list, click the down-pointing arrow to the right of the *Underline style* option box. If you are using the keyboard, press Alt + U.

Check Boxes

Some dialog boxes contain options preceded by a box. A check mark may or may not appear in the box. The Word Font dialog box shown in Figure G.4 displays a variety of check boxes within the *Effects* section. If a check mark appears in the box, the option is active (turned on). If the check box does not contain a check mark, the option is inactive (turned off). Any number of check boxes can be active. For example, in the Word Font dialog box, you can insert a check mark in any or all of the boxes in the *Effects* section and these options will be active.

To make a check box active or inactive with the mouse, position the tip of the arrow pointer in the check box and then click the left mouse button. If you are using the keyboard, press Alt + the underlined letter of the desired option.

Text Boxes

Some options in a dialog box require you to enter text. For example, the boxes below the *Find what* and *Replace with* options at the Excel Find and Replace dialog box shown in Figure G.5 are text boxes. In a text box, you type text or edit existing text. Edit text in a text box in the same manner as normal text. Use the Left and Right Arrow keys on the keyboard to move the insertion point without deleting text and use the Delete key or Backspace key to delete text.

Option Buttons

The Word Insert Table dialog box shown in Figure G.6 contains options in the *AutoFit behavior* section preceded by option buttons. Only one option button can be selected at any time. When an option button is selected, a blue circle displays in the button. To select an option button with the mouse, position the tip of the arrow pointer inside the option button and then click the left mouse button. To make a selection with the keyboard, hold down the Alt key and then press the underlined letter of the desired option.

Measurement Boxes

Some options in a dialog box contain measurements or numbers you can increase or decrease. These options are generally located in a measurement box. For example, the Word Paragraph dialog box shown in Figure G.7 contains the *Left*, *Right*, *Before*, and *After* measurement boxes. To increase a number in a measurement box, position the tip of the arrow pointer on the up-pointing arrow to the right of the desired option and then click the left mouse button. To decrease the number, click the down-pointing arrow. If you are using the keyboard, press Alt + the underlined letter of the desired option and then press the Up Arrow key to increase the number or the Down Arrow key to decrease the number.

Command Buttons

In the Excel Find and Replace dialog box shown in Figure G.5, the boxes along the bottom of the dialog box are called command buttons. Use a command button to execute or cancel a command. Some command buttons display with an ellipsis (...). A command button that displays with an ellipsis will open another dialog box. To choose a command button with the mouse, position the arrow pointer on the desired button and then click the left mouse button. To choose a command button with the keyboard, press the Tab key until the desired command button contains the marquee and then press the Enter key.

Figure G.5 Excel Find and Replace Dialog Box

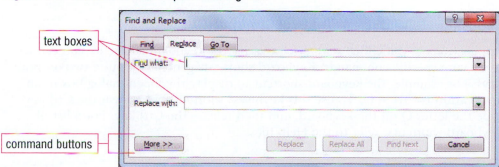

Figure G.6 Word Insert Table Dialog Box

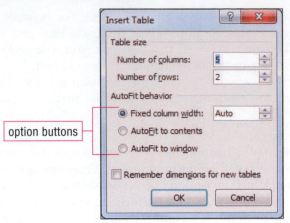

option buttons

Figure G.7 Word Paragraph Dialog Box

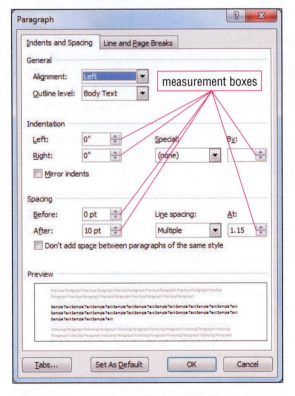

Choosing Commands with Keyboard Shortcuts

Applications in the Office suite offer a variety of keyboard shortcuts you can use to execute specific commands. Keyboard shortcuts generally require two or more keys. For example, the keyboard shortcut to display the Open dialog box in an application is Ctrl + O. To use this keyboard shortcut, hold down the Ctrl key, type the letter O on the keyboard, and then release the Ctrl key. For a list of keyboard shortcuts, refer to the Help files.

Choosing Commands with Shortcut Menus

The software programs in the suite include menus that contain commands related to the item with which you are working. A shortcut menu appears in the file in the location where you are working. To display a shortcut menu, click the right mouse button or press Shift + F10. For example, if the insertion point is positioned in a paragraph of text in a Word document, clicking the right mouse button or pressing Shift + F10 will cause the shortcut menu shown in Figure G.8 to display in the document screen (along with the Mini toolbar).

To select an option from a shortcut menu with the mouse, click the desired option. If you are using the keyboard, press the Up or Down Arrow key until the desired option is selected and then press the Enter key. To close a shortcut menu without choosing an option, click anywhere outside the shortcut menu or press the Esc key.

Working with Multiple Programs

As you learn the various programs in the Microsoft Office suite, you will notice how executing commands in each is very similar. For example, the steps to save, close, and print are virtually the same whether you are working in Word, Excel, or PowerPoint. This consistency between programs greatly enhances a user's ability to transfer knowledge learned in one program to another within the suite. Another appeal of Microsoft Office is the ability to have more than one program open at the same time. For example, you can open Word, create a document, and then open Excel, create a spreadsheet, and copy the spreadsheet into Word.

Figure G.8 Word Shortcut Menu

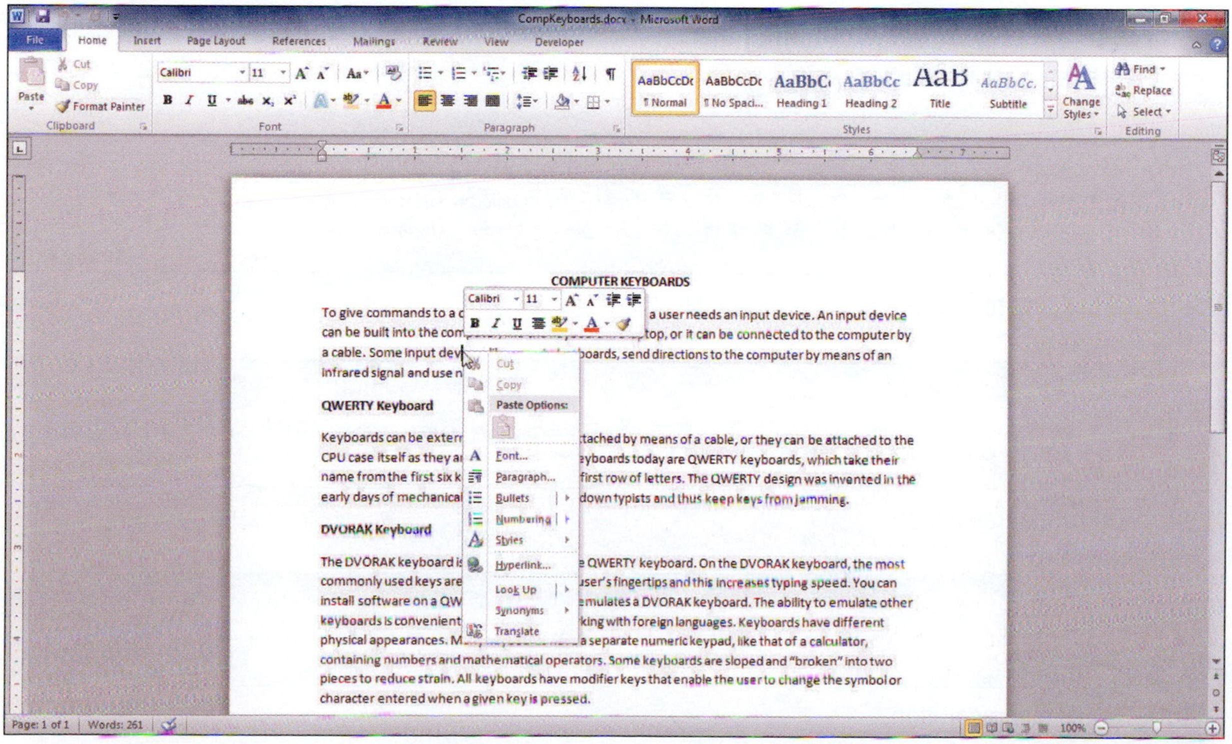

Figure G.9 Taskbar with Word, Excel, and PowerPoint Open

When you open a program, a button displays on the Taskbar containing an icon representing the program. If you open another program, a button containing an icon representing the program displays to the right of the first program button. Figure G.9 shows the Taskbar with Word, Excel, and PowerPoint open. To move from one program to another, click the button on the Taskbar representing the desired program file.

Customizing Settings

Before beginning computer projects in this textbook, you may need to customize the monitor settings and turn on the display of file extensions. Projects in the chapters in this textbook assume that the monitor display is set at 1280 by 800 pixels and that the display of file extensions is turned on.

Changing Monitor Resolutions

Before you begin learning the applications in the Microsoft Office 2010 suite, take a moment to check the display settings on the computer you are using. The ribbon in the Microsoft Office suite adjusts to the screen resolution setting of your computer monitor. Computer monitors set at a high resolution will have the ability to show more buttons in the ribbon than will a monitor set to a low resolution. The illustrations in this textbook were created with a screen resolution display set at 1280 × 800 pixels. In Figure G.10 the Word ribbon is shown three ways: at a lower screen resolution (1024 × 768 pixels), at the screen resolution featured

Figure G.10 Monitor Resolution

1024 × 768 screen resolution

1280 × 800 screen resolution

1440 × 900 screen resolution

throughout this textbook, and at a higher screen resolution (1440 × 900 pixels). Note the variances in the ribbon in all three examples. If possible, set your display to 1280 × 800 pixels to match the illustrations you will see in this textbook.

Project 1 Setting Monitor Display to 1280 by 800

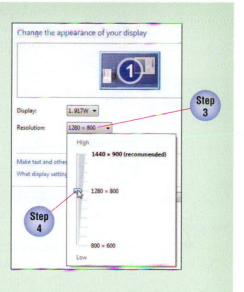

1. At the Windows 7 desktop, click the Start button and then click *Control Panel*.
2. At the Control Panel dialog box, click the *Adjust screen resolution* option in the Appearance and Personalization category.
3. At the Control Panel Screen Resolution window, click the Resolution option button. (This displays a drop-down slider bar. Your drop-down slider bar may display differently than what you see in the image at the right.)
4. Drag the slider bar button on the slider bar until *1280 × 800* displays to the right of the slider button.
5. Click in the Control Panel Screen Resolution window to remove the slider bar.
6. Click the Apply button.
7. Click the Keep Changes button.
8. Click the OK button.
9. Close the Control Panel window.

Project 2 Displaying File Extensions

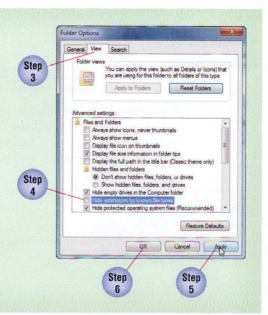

1. At the Windows 7 desktop, click the Start button and then click *Computer*.
2. At the Computer window, click the Organize button on the toolbar and then click *Folder and search options* at the drop-down list.
3. At the Folder Options dialog box, click the View tab.
4. Click the *Hide extensions for known file types* check box to remove the check mark.
5. Click the Apply button.
6. Click the OK button.
7. Close the Computer window.

Completing Computer Projects ■■■■■■ ■■■■ ■■■■■ ■■■

Some computer projects in this textbook require that you open an existing file. Project files are saved on the Student Resources CD that accompanies this textbook. The files you need for each chapter are saved in individual folders. Before beginning a chapter, copy the necessary folder from the CD to your storage medium (such as a USB flash drive) using the Computer window. If storage capacity is an issue with your storage medium, delete any previous chapter folders before copying a chapter folder onto your storage medium.

Project 3   Copying a Folder from the Student Resources CD

1. Insert the CD that accompanies this textbook in the CD drive. At the AutoPlay window that displays, click the Close button located in the upper right corner of the window.
2. Insert your USB flash drive in an available USB port. If an AutoPlay window displays, click the Close button.
3. At the Windows desktop, open the Computer window by clicking the Start button and then clicking *Computer* at the Start menu.
4. Double-click the CD drive in the Content pane (displays with the name *BM10StudentResources* preceded by the drive letter).
5. Double-click the desired program folder name in the Content pane.
6. Click once on the desired chapter subfolder name to select it.
7. Click the Organize button on the toolbar and then click *Copy* at the drop-down list.
8. In the Computer window Content pane, click the drive containing your storage medium.
9. Click the Organize button on the toolbar and then click *Paste* at the drop-down list.
10. Close the Computer window by clicking the Close button located in the upper right corner of the window.

Project 4   Deleting a Folder

Note: Check with your instructor before deleting a folder.

1. Insert your storage medium (such as a USB flash drive) in the USB port.
2. At the Windows desktop, open the Computer window by clicking the Start button and then clicking *Computer* at the Start menu.
3. Double-click the drive letter for your storage medium (drive containing your USB flash drive such as *Removable Disk (F:)*).
4. Click the chapter folder in the Content pane.
5. Click the Organize button on the toolbar and then click *Delete* at the drop-down list.
6. At the message asking if you want to delete the folder, click the Yes button.
7. Close the Computer window by clicking the Close button located in the upper right corner of the window.

Using Windows 7

A computer requires an operating system to provide necessary instructions on a multitude of processes including loading programs, managing data, directing the flow of information to peripheral equipment, and displaying information. Windows 7 is an operating system that provides functions of this type (along with much more) in a graphical environment. Windows is referred to as a *graphical user interface* (GUI—pronounced *gooey*) that provides a visual display of information with features such as icons (pictures) and buttons. In this introduction, you will learn these basic features of Windows 7:

- Use desktop icons and the Taskbar to launch programs and open files or folders
- Add and remove gadgets
- Organize and manage data, including copying, moving, creating, and deleting files and folders; and create a shortcut
- Explore the Control Panel and personalize the desktop
- Use the Windows Help and Support features
- Use search tools
- Customize monitor settings

Before using one of the software programs in the Microsoft Office suite, you will need to start the Windows 7 operating system. To do this, turn on the computer. Depending on your computer equipment configuration, you may also need to turn on the monitor and printer. If you are using a computer that is part of a network system or if your computer is set up for multiple users, a screen will display showing the user accounts defined for your computer system. At this screen, click your user account name and, if necessary, type your password and then press the Enter key. The Windows 7 operating system will start and, after a few moments, the desktop will display as shown in Figure W.1. (Your desktop may vary from what you see in Figure W.1.)

Exploring the Desktop

When Windows is loaded, the main portion of the screen is called the *desktop*. Think of the desktop in Windows as the top of a desk in an office. A business person places necessary tools—such as pencils, pens, paper, files, calculator—on the desktop to perform functions. Like the tools that are located on a desk, the desktop contains tools for operating the computer. These tools are logically grouped and placed in dialog boxes or panels that you can display using icons on the desktop. The desktop contains a variety of features for using your computer and software programs installed on the computer. The features available on the desktop are represented by icons and buttons.

Figure W.1 Windows 7 Desktop

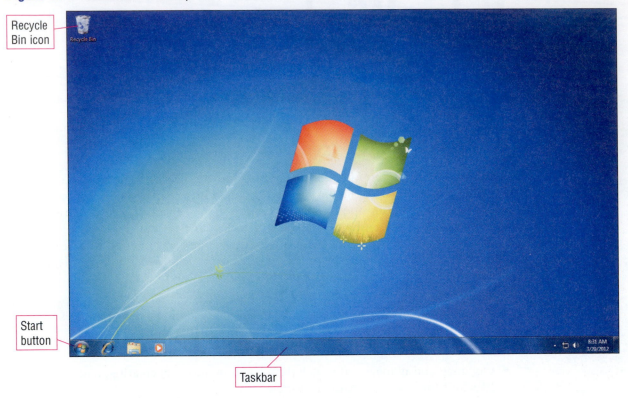

Recycle Bin icon

Start button

Taskbar

Using Icons

Icons are visual symbols that represent programs, files, or folders. Figure W.1 identifies the Recycle Bin icon located on the Windows desktop. The Windows desktop on your computer may contain additional icons. Programs that have been installed on your computer may be represented by an icon on the desktop. Also, icons may display on your desktop representing files or folders. Double-click an icon and the program, file, or folder it represents opens on the desktop.

Using the Taskbar

The bar that displays at the bottom of the desktop (see Figure W.1) is called the Taskbar. The Taskbar, shown in Figure W.2, contains the Start button, pinned items, a section that displays task buttons representing active tasks, the notification area, and the Show Desktop button.

Figure W.2 Windows 7 Taskbar

Show desktop button

pinned items

buttons for active tabs

notification area

Click the Start button, located at the left side of the Taskbar, and the Start menu displays as shown in Figure W.3 (your Start menu may vary). You can also display the Start menu by pressing the Windows key on your keyboard or by pressing Ctrl + Esc. The left side of the Start menu contains links to the most recently and frequently used programs. The name of the currently logged on user displays at the top of the darker right portion of the menu followed by the user's libraries. The two sections below the personal libraries provide links to other Windows features, such as games, the Control Panel, and Windows Help and Support. Use the Shut down button to put the system in a power-conserving state or into a locked, shut down, or sleep mode.

To choose an option from the Start menu, drag the arrow pointer to the desired option (referred to as *pointing*) and then click the left mouse button. Pointing to options at the Start menu that are followed by a right-pointing arrow will cause a side menu to display with additional options. When a program is open, a task button representing the program appears on the Taskbar. If multiple programs are open, each program will appear as a task button on the Taskbar (a few specialized tools may not).

Manipulating Windows

When you open a program, a defined work area displays on the screen, which is referred to as a *window*. A Title bar displays at the top of a window and contains buttons at the right side for closing the window and minimizing, maximizing, and restoring the size of the window. You can open more than one window at a time and the open windows can be cascaded or stacked. Windows 7 contains a Snap feature that causes a window to "stick" to the edge of the screen when the window

Figure W.3 Start Menu

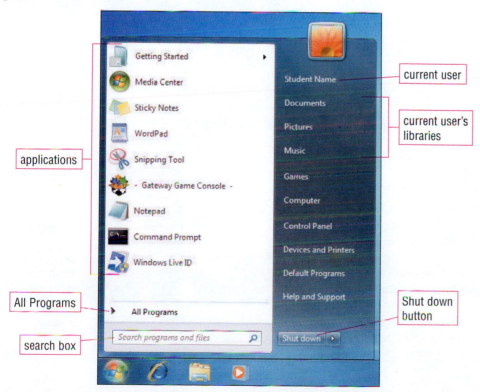

is moved to the left or right side of the screen. Move a window to the top of the screen and the window is automatically maximized. If you drag down a maximized window, the window is automatically restored down.

In addition to moving and sizing a window, you can change the display of all open windows. To do this, position the mouse pointer on the Taskbar and then click the right mouse button and a pop-up list displays with options for displaying multiple open windows. You can cascade the windows, stack the windows, and display the windows side by side.

Project 1   Opening Programs, Switching between Programs, and Manipulating Windows

1. Open Windows 7. (To do this, turn on the computer and, if necessary, turn on the monitor and/or printer. If you are using a computer that is part of a network system or if your computer is set up for multiple users, you may need to click your user account name and, if necessary, type your password and then press the Enter key. Check with your instructor to determine if you need to complete any additional steps.)

2. When the Windows 7 desktop displays, open Microsoft Word by completing the following steps:
   a. Position the arrow pointer on the Start button on the Taskbar and then click the left mouse button.
   b. At the Start menu, click *All Programs* and then click *Microsoft Office* (this displays programs in the Office suite below Microsoft Office).
   c. Drag the arrow pointer down to *Microsoft Word 2010* and then click the left mouse button.
   d. When the Microsoft Word program is open, notice that a task button representing Word displays on the Taskbar.

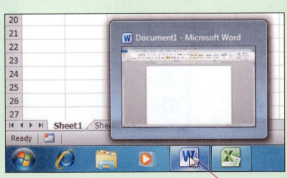

Step 2d

3. Open Microsoft Excel by completing the following steps:
   a. Position the arrow pointer on the Start button on the Taskbar and then click the left mouse button.
   b. At the Start menu, click *All Programs* and then click *Microsoft Office*.
   c. Drag the arrow pointer down to *Microsoft Excel 2010* and then click the left mouse button.
   d. When the Microsoft Excel program is open, notice that a task button representing Excel displays on the Taskbar to the right of the task button representing Word.

4. Switch to the Word program by clicking the task button on the Taskbar representing Word.

5. Switch to the Excel program by clicking the task button on the Taskbar representing Excel.

Step 4

6. Restore down the Excel window by clicking the Restore Down button that displays immediately left of the Close button in the upper right corner of the screen. (This reduces the Excel window so it displays along the bottom half of the screen.)

7. Restore down the Word window by clicking the Restore Down button located immediately left of the Close button in the upper right corner of the screen.

8. Position the mouse pointer on the Word window Title bar, hold down the left mouse button, drag to the left side of the screen until an outline of the window displays in the left half of the screen, and then release the mouse button. (This "sticks" the window to the left side of the screen.)

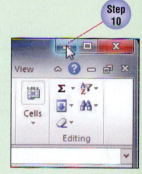

9. Position the mouse pointer on the Excel window Title bar, hold down the left mouse button, drag to the right until an outline of the window displays in the right half of the screen, and then release the mouse button.

10. Minimize the Excel window by clicking the Minimize button that displays in the upper right corner of the Excel window Title bar.

11. Hover your mouse over the Excel button on the Taskbar and notice the Excel window thumbnail that displays above the button and then click the thumbnail. (This displays the Excel window at the right side of the screen.)

12. Cascade the Word and Excel windows by positioning the arrow pointer on an empty area on the Taskbar, clicking the right mouse button, and then clicking *Cascade windows* at the pop-up list.

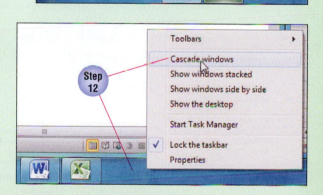

13. After viewing the windows cascaded, display them stacked by right-clicking an empty area on the Taskbar and then clicking *Show windows stacked* at the pop-up list.

14. Display the desktop by right-clicking an empty area on the Taskbar and then clicking *Show the desktop* at the pop-up list.

15. Display the windows stacked by right-clicking an empty area on the Taskbar and then clicking *Show open windows* at the pop-up list.

16. Position the mouse pointer on the Word window Title bar, hold down the left mouse button, drag the window to the top of the screen, and then release the mouse button. This maximizes the Word window so it fills the screen.

17. Close the Word window by clicking the Close button located in the upper right corner of the window.

18. At the Excel window, click the Maximize button located immediately left of the Close button in the upper right corner of the Excel window.

19. Close the Excel window by clicking the Close button located in the upper right corner of the window.

Using the Pinned Area

The icons that display immediately right of the Start button are pinned programs. Clicking an icon opens the program associated with the icon. Click the first icon to open the Internet Explorer web browser, click the second icon to open a window containing Libraries, and click the third icon to open the Windows media player window.

Exploring the Notification Area

The notification area is located at the right side of the Taskbar and contains icons that show the status of certain system functions such as a network connection or battery power. It also contains icons you can use to manage certain programs and Windows 7 features. The notification area also contains the system clock and date. Click the time or date in the notification area and a window displays with a clock and a calendar of the current month. Click the Change date and time settings hyperlink that displays at the bottom of the window and the Date and Time dialog box displays. To change the date and/or time, click the Change date and time button and the Date and Time Settings dialog box displays similar to the dialog box shown in Figure W.4. (If a dialog box displays telling you that Windows needs your permission to continue, click the Continue button.)

Change the month and year by clicking the left-pointing or right-pointing arrow at the top of the calendar in the *Date* section. Click the left-pointing arrow to display the previous month(s) and click the right-pointing arrow to display the next month(s).

To change the day, click the desired day in the monthly calendar that displays in the dialog box. To change the time, double-click either the hour, minute, or seconds and then type the appropriate time or use the up- and down-pointing arrows in the spin boxes to adjust the time.

Some programs, when installed, will add an icon to the notification area of the Taskbar. Display the name of the icon by positioning the mouse pointer on the icon and, after approximately one second, the icon label displays. If more icons have been inserted in the notification area than can be viewed at one time, an up-pointing arrow button displays at the left side of the notification area. Click this up-pointing arrow button and the remaining icons display.

Setting Taskbar Properties

You can customize the Taskbar with options from the Taskbar shortcut menu. Display this menu by right-clicking on an empty portion of the Taskbar. The Taskbar shortcut menu contains options for turning on or off the display of specific toolbars, specifying the display of multiple windows, displaying the Start Task Manager dialog box, locking or unlocking the Taskbar, and displaying the Taskbar and Start Menu Properties dialog box.

With options in the Taskbar and Start Menu Properties dialog box shown in Figure W.5, you can change settings for the Taskbar as well as the Start menu. Display this dialog box by right-clicking on an empty area on the Taskbar and then clicking *Properties* at the shortcut menu.

Each property is controlled by a check box. Property options containing a check mark are active. Click the option to remove the check mark and make the option inactive. If an option is inactive, clicking the option will insert a check mark in the check box and turn on the option (make it active).

Figure W.4 Date and Time Settings Dialog Box

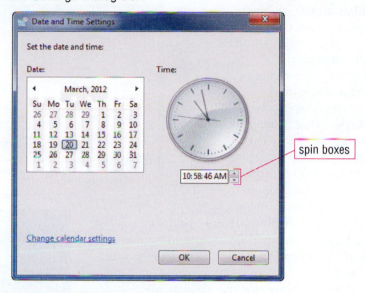

spin boxes

Figure W.5 Taskbar and Start Menu Properties Dialog Box

Insert a check mark in this option to hide the Taskbar unless you move the mouse pointer over the location where the Taskbar should display.

Insert a check mark in this option to display icons in a reduced manner on the Taskbar.

Use this option to change the location of the Taskbar from the bottom of the desktop to the left side, right side, or top of the desktop.

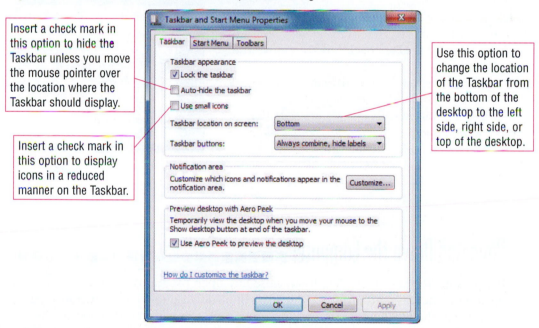

Project 2 | **Changing Taskbar Properties**

1. Make sure the Windows 7 desktop displays.
2. Change Taskbar properties by completing the following steps:
   a. Position the arrow pointer on any empty area on the Taskbar and then click the right mouse button.
   b. At the shortcut menu that displays, click *Properties*.

c. At the Taskbar and Start Menu Properties dialog box, click the *Auto-hide the taskbar* check box to insert a check mark.

d. Click the *Use small icons* check box to insert a check mark.

e. Click the button (displays with the word *Bottom*) that displays at the right side of the *Taskbar location on screen* option and then click *Right* at the drop-down list.

f. Click OK to close the dialog box.

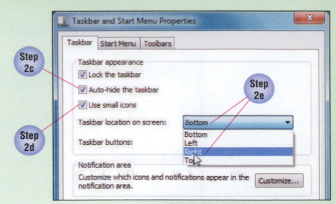

3. Since the *Auto-hide the taskbar* check box contains a check mark, the Taskbar does not display. Display the Taskbar by moving the mouse pointer to the right side of the screen. Notice that the icons on the Taskbar are smaller.

4. Return to the default settings for the Taskbar by completing the following steps:

a. Move the mouse pointer to the right side of the screen to display the Taskbar.

b. Right-click any empty area on the Taskbar and then click *Properties* at the shortcut menu.

c. Click the *Auto-hide the taskbar* check box to remove the check mark.

d. Click the *Use small icons* check box to remove the check mark.

e. Click the button (displays with the word *Right*) that displays at the right side of the *Taskbar location on screen* option and then click *Bottom* at the drop-down list.

f. Click OK to close the dialog box.

Powering Down the Computer ▪▪▪▪▪▪▪▪▪▪▪▪▪▪▪▪▪▪▪▪▪▪▪

If you want to shut down Windows, close any open programs, click the Start button on the Taskbar, and then click the Shut down button as shown in Figure W.6. Click the button containing a right-pointing triangle that displays at the right side of the Shut down button and a drop-down list displays with options for powering down the computer.

In a multi-user environment, click the *Switch user* option to change users or click the *Log off* option to log off your computer, which shuts down your applications and files and makes system resources available to other users logged on to the system. If you need to walk away from your computer and you want to protect your work, consider locking the computer by clicking the *Lock* option. When you lock the computer, the desktop is hidden but the system is not shut down and the power is not conserved. To unlock the computer, click the icon on the desktop representing your account, type your password, and then press Enter. Click the *Restart* option to shut down and then restart the computer and click

Figure W.6 Shut Down Button and Power Options Button

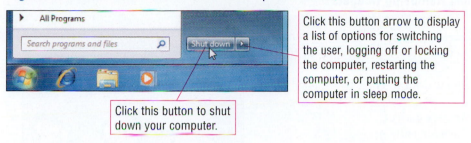

Click this button arrow to display a list of options for switching the user, logging off or locking the computer, restarting the computer, or putting the computer in sleep mode.

Click this button to shut down your computer.

the *Sleep* option to save power without having to close all files and applications. In sleep mode, Windows saves files and information about programs and then powers down the computer to a low-power state. To "wake" the computer back up, quickly press the computer's power button.

Using Gadgets

You can add gadgets to your desktop. A gadget is a mini program providing information at a glance and easy access to frequently used tools. For example, you can add a Clock gadget to your desktop that shows the current time, a Weather gadget that displays the current temperature where you live, or a Calendar gadget that displays the current date. Gadgets are added to the Sidebar, which is a location at the right side of the Windows 7 desktop.

To view available gadgets, right-click in a blank area on the desktop and then click *Gadgets* at the shortcut menu. This displays the gadget gallery similar to what you see in Figure W.7. To add a gadget to the Sidebar, double-click the desired gadget. To remove a gadget from the Sidebar, hover the mouse pointer over the gadget and then click the Close button that displays at the upper right side of the gadget. ***Note: The Gadget option on the shortcut menu may be missing if the computer you are using is located in a school setting where customization options have been disabled. If you do not see* Gadget *on the shortcut menu, please skip Project 3.***

Figure W.7 Gadget Gallery

1. At the Windows 7 desktop, right-click in a blank area on the desktop and then click *Gadgets* at the shortcut menu.
2. At the Gadgets Gallery, double-click the *Clock* gadget.
3. Double-click the *Weather* gadget.
4. Double-click the *Calendar* gadget.
5. Close the Gadget Gallery by clicking the Close button located in the upper right corner of the gallery.
6. Hover your mouse over the Calendar gadget until buttons display at the right side of the gadget and then click the Larger size button. (This expands the calendar to display the days of the month.)
7. Hover your mouse over the Weather gadget and then click the Options button.
8. At the Weather dialog box that displays, type in the *Select current location* text box the name of your city followed by your state (or province) and then press Enter.
9. If a drop-down list displays with city names, scroll down the list to display your city and then click your city and state (or province).
10. Click OK to close the Weather dialog box.
11. After viewing the gadgets, remove the Clock gadget by hovering the mouse over the clock and then clicking the Close button that displays at the upper right side of the clock.
12. Close the Weather gadget by hovering the mouse over the gadget and then clicking the Close button that displays.
13. Close the Calendar gadget by hovering the mouse over the gadget and then clicking the Close button that displays.

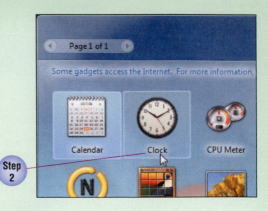

Step 2

Step 6

Step 7

Step 11

Managing Files and Folders

As you begin working with programs in Windows 7, you will create files in which data (information) is saved. A file might contain a Word document, an Excel workbook, or a PowerPoint presentation. As you begin creating files, consider creating folders into which those files will be stored. You can complete file management tasks such as creating a folder and copying and moving files and folders at the Computer window. To display the Computer window shown in Figure W.8, click the Start button on the Taskbar and then click *Computer*. The various components of the Computer window are identified in Figure W.8.

Figure W.8 Computer Window

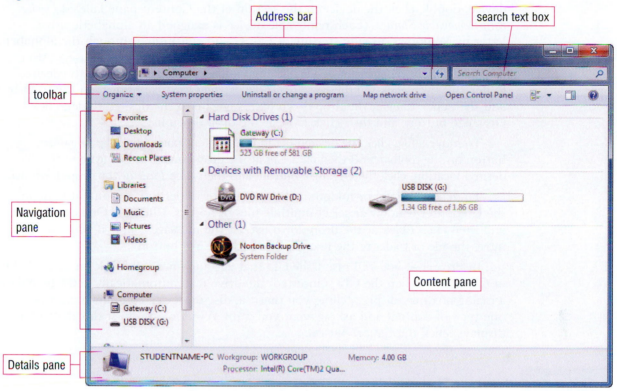

In the Content pane of the Computer window, icons display representing each hard disk drive and removable storage medium such as a CD, DVD, or USB device connected to your computer. Next to each storage device icon, Windows provides the amount of storage space available as well as a bar with the amount of used space shaded with color. This visual cue allows you to see at a glance the proportion of space available relative to the capacity of the device. Double-click a device icon in the Content pane to change the display to show the contents stored on the device. You can display contents from another device or folder using the Navigation pane or the Address bar on the Computer window.

Copying, Moving, and Deleting Files and Folders

File and folder management activities might include copying and moving files or folders from one folder or drive to another, or deleting files or folders. The Computer window offers a variety of methods for copying, moving, and deleting files and folders. This section will provide you with steps for copying, moving, and deleting files and folders using options from the Organize button on the toolbar and the shortcut menu.

To copy a file to another folder or drive, first display the file in the Content pane by identifying the location of the file. If the file is located in the Documents folder, click the *Documents* folder in the *Libraries* section in the Navigation pane and then click the file name in the Content pane that you want to copy. Click the Organize button on the toolbar and then click *Copy* at the drop-down list. In the Navigation pane, click the location where you want to copy the file. Click the Organize button and then click *Paste* at the drop-down list. You would complete similar steps to copy and paste a folder to another location.

If the desired file is located on a storage medium such as a CD, DVD, or USB device, double-click the device in the section of the Content pane labeled *Devices with Removable Storage*. (Each removable device is assigned an alphabetic drive letter by Windows, usually starting at F or G and continuing through the alphabet depending on the number of removable devices that are currently in use.) After double-clicking the storage medium in the Content pane, navigate to the desired folder and then click the file to select it. Click the Organize button on the toolbar and then click *Copy* at the drop-down list. Navigate to the desired folder, click the Organize button, and then click *Paste* at the drop-down list.

To move a file, click the desired file in the Content pane, click the Organize button on the toolbar, and then click *Cut* at the drop-down list. Navigate to the desired location, click the Organize button, and then click *Paste* at the drop-down list.

To delete a file(s) or folder(s), click the file or folder in the Content pane in the Computer window or select multiple files or folders. Click the Organize button and then click *Delete* at the drop-down list. At the message asking if you want to move the file or folder to the Recycle Bin, click the Yes button.

In Project 4, you will insert the CD that accompanies this book into the DVD or CD drive. When the CD is inserted, the drive may automatically activate and a dialog box may display telling you that the disc or device contains more than one type of content and asking what you want Windows to do. If this dialog box displays, click the Cancel button.

Project 4 Copying a File and Folder and Deleting a File

1. Insert the CD that accompanies this textbook into the appropriate drive. If a dialog box displays telling you that the disc or device contains more than one type of content and asking what you want Windows to do, click the Cancel button.
2. Insert your storage medium (such as a USB flash drive) in the USB port (or other drive). If an AutoPlay window displays, click the Close button.
3. At the Windows 7 desktop, click the Start button and then click *Computer* located at the right side of the Start menu.
4. Copy a file from the CD that accompanies this textbook to the drive containing your storage medium by completing the following steps:
   a. Double-click the CD drive in the Content pane containing the CD from the book.
   b. Double-click the *StudentDataFiles* folder in the Content pane.
   c. Double-click the *Windows7* folder in the Content pane.
   d. Click **WordDocument01.docx** in the Content pane.
   e. Click the Organize button on the toolbar and then click *Copy* at the drop-down list.

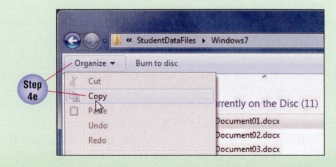

f. In the Computer section in the Navigation pane, click the drive containing your storage medium. (You may need to scroll down the Navigation pane.)

g. Click the Organize button and then click *Paste* at the drop-down list.

5. Delete **WordDocument01.docx** from your storage medium by completing the following steps:

a. Make sure the contents of your storage medium display in the Content pane in the Computer window.

b. Click **WordDocument01.docx** in the Content pane to select it.

c. Click the Organize button and then click *Delete* at the drop-down list.

d. At the message asking if you want to permanently delete the file, click the Yes button.

6. Copy the Windows7 folder from the CD to your storage medium by completing the following steps:

a. With the Computer window open, click the drive in the *Computer* section in the Navigation pane that contains the CD that accompanies this book.

b. Double-click *StudentDataFiles* in the Content pane.

c. Click the *Windows7* folder in the Content pane.

d. Click the Organize button and then click *Copy* at the drop-down list.

e. In the *Computer* section in the Navigation pane, click the drive containing your storage medium.

f. Click the Organize button and then click *Paste* at the drop-down list.

7. Close the Computer window by clicking the Close button located in the upper right corner of the window.

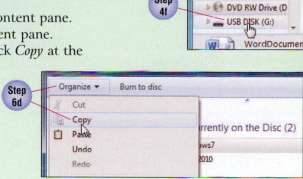

In addition to options in the Organize button drop-down list, you can use options in a shortcut menu to copy, move, and delete files or folders. To use a shortcut menu, select the desired file(s) or folder(s), position the mouse pointer on the selected item, and then click the right mouse button. At the shortcut menu that displays, click the desired option such as Copy, Cut, or Delete.

Selecting Files and Folders

You can move, copy, or delete more than one file or folder at the same time. Before moving, copying, or deleting files or folders, select the desired files or folders. To make selecting easier, consider changing the display in the Content pane to List or Details. To change the display, click the Views button arrow on the toolbar in the Computer window and then click *List* or *Details* at the drop-down list. You can also cycle through the various views by clicking the Views button. Hover your mouse over the Views button and the ScreenTip *Change your view* displays.

To select adjacent files or folders, click the first file or folder, hold down the Shift key, and then click the last file or folder. To select nonadjacent files or folders, click the first file or folder, hold down the Ctrl key, and then click any other files or folders.

1. At the Windows 7 desktop, click the Start button and then click *Computer*.
2. Copy files from the CD that accompanies this textbook to the drive containing your storage medium by completing the following steps:

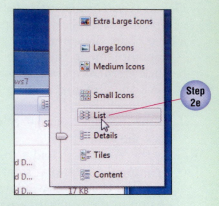

   a. Make sure the CD that accompanies this textbook and your storage medium are inserted in the appropriate drives.
   b. Double-click the CD drive in the Content pane in the Computer window.
   c. Double-click the *StudentDataFiles* folder in the Content pane.
   d. Double-click the *Windows7* folder in the Content pane.
   e. Change the display to List by clicking the Views button arrow on the toolbar and then clicking *List* at the drop-down list.
   f. Click **WordDocument01.docx** in the Content pane.
   g. Hold down the Shift key, click **WordDocument05.docx**, and then release the Shift key. (This selects five documents.)
   h. Click the Organize button and then click *Copy* at the drop-down list.

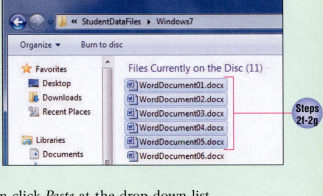

   i. In the *Computer* section in the Navigation pane, click the drive containing your storage medium.
   j. Click the Organize button and then click *Paste* at the drop-down list.
3. Delete the files from your storage medium that you just copied by completing the following steps:

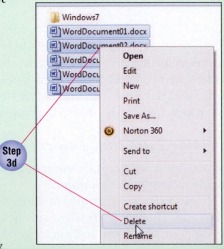

   a. Change the view by clicking the Views button arrow bar and then clicking *List* at the drop-down list.
   b. Click **WordDocument01.docx** in the Content pane.
   c. Hold down the Shift key, click **WordDocument05.docx**, and then release the Shift key.
   d. Position the mouse pointer on any selected file, click the right mouse button, and then click *Delete* at the shortcut menu.
   e. At the message asking if you are sure you want to permanently delete the files, click Yes.
4. Close the Computer window by clicking the Close button located in the upper right corner of the window.

Manipulating and Creating Folders

As you begin working with and creating a number of files, consider creating folders in which you can logically group the files. To create a folder, display the Computer window and then display in the Content pane the drive or folder where you want to create the folder. Position the mouse pointer in a blank area in the Content pane, click the right mouse button, point to *New* in the shortcut menu, and then click *Folder* at the side menu. This inserts a folder icon in the Content pane and names the folder *New folder*. Type the desired name for the new folder and then press Enter.

Project 6 **Creating a New Folder**

1. At the Windows 7 desktop, open the Computer window.
2. Create a new folder by completing the following steps:
   a. Double-click in the Content pane the drive that contains your storage medium.
   b. Double-click the Windows7 folder in the Content pane. (This opens the folder.)
   c. Click the Views button arrow and then click *List* at the drop-down list.
   d. Position the mouse pointer in a blank area in the Content pane and then click the right mouse button.
   e. Point to *New* in the shortcut menu and then click *Folder* at the side menu.

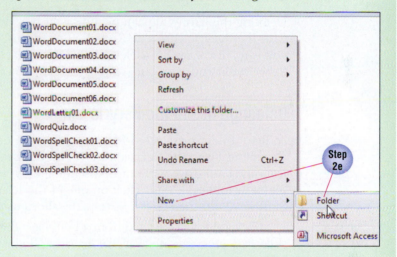

   f. Type **SpellCheckFiles** and then press Enter. (This changes the name from *New folder* to *SpellCheckFiles*.)
3. Copy **WordSpellCheck01.docx**, **WordSpellCheck02.docx**, and **WordSpellCheck03.docx** into the SpellCheckFiles folder you just created by completing the following steps:
   a. Click the Views button arrow and then click *List* at the drop-down list. (Skip this step if *List* is already selected.)
   b. Click once on the file named **WordSpellCheck01.docx** located in the Content pane.
   c. Hold down the Shift key, click once on the file named **WordSpellCheck03.docx**, and then release the Shift key. (This selects three documents.)
   d. Click the Organize button and then click *Copy* at the drop-down list.
   e. Double-click the *SpellCheckFiles* folder in the Content pane.
   f. Click the Organize button and then click *Paste* at the drop-down list.

4. Delete the SpellCheckFiles folder and its
   contents by completing the following steps:
   a. Click the Back button (contains a left-
      pointing arrow) located at the left side
      of the Address bar.
   b. With the SpellCheckFiles folder selected in
      the Content pane, click the Organize button
      and then click *Delete* at the drop-down list.
   c. At the message asking you to confirm the
      deletion, click Yes.
5. Close the window by clicking the Close button located in the upper right corner of the window.

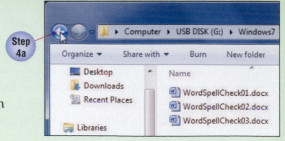

Using the Recycle Bin ■■■■■■■■■■■■■■■■■■■■■■■■■■■

Deleting the wrong file can be a disaster but Windows 7 helps protect your work
with the Recycle Bin. The Recycle Bin acts just like an office wastepaper basket;
you can "throw away" (delete) unwanted files, but you can "reach in" to the
Recycle Bin and take out (restore) a file if you threw it away by accident.

Deleting Files to the Recycle Bin

A file or folder or selected files or folders you delete from the hard drive are sent
automatically to the Recycle Bin. If you want to permanently delete files or folders
from the hard drive without first sending them to the Recycle Bin, select the desired
file(s) or folder(s), right click on one of the selected files or folders, hold down the
Shift key, and then click *Delete* at the shortcut menu.

Files and folders deleted from a USB flash drive or disc are deleted permanently.
(Recovery programs are available, however, that will help you recover deleted files or
folders. If you accidentally delete a file or folder from a USB flash drive or disc, do
not do anything more with the USB flash drive or disc until you can run a recovery
program.)

You can delete files in the manner described earlier in this section and you
can also delete a file by dragging the file icon to the Recycle Bin. To do this, click
the desired file in the Content pane in the Computer window, drag the file icon
on top of the Recycle Bin icon on the desktop until the text *Move to Recycle Bin*
displays, and then release the mouse button.

Restoring Files from the Recycle Bin

To restore a file from the Recycle Bin, double-click the Recycle Bin icon on the
desktop. This opens the Recycle Bin window shown in Figure W.9. (The contents
of the Recycle Bin will vary.) To restore a file, click the file you want restored and
then click the Restore this item button on the toolbar. This removes the file from
the Recycle Bin and returns it to its original location. You can also restore a file
by positioning the mouse pointer on the file, clicking the right mouse button, and
then clicking *Restore* at the shortcut menu.

Figure W.9 Recycle Bin Window

toolbar

Navigation pane

Content pane

Details pane

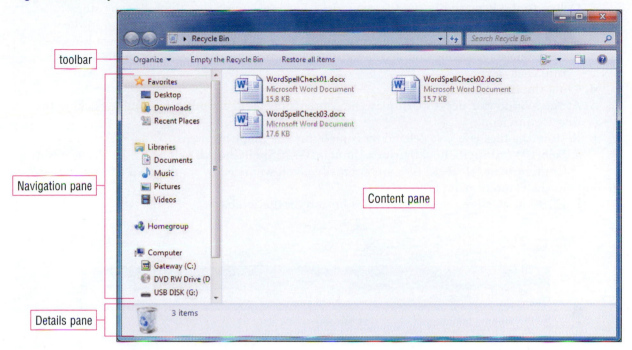

Project 7   Deleting Files to and Restoring Files from the Recycle Bin

Before beginning this project, check with your instructor to determine if you can copy files to the hard drive.

1. At the Windows 7 desktop, open the Computer window.
2. Copy files from your storage medium to the Documents folder on your hard drive by completing the following steps:
   a. Double-click in the Content pane the drive containing your storage medium.
   b. Double-click the *Windows7* folder in the Content pane.
   c. Click the Views button arrow and then click *List* at the drop-down list. (Skip this step if *List* is already selected.)
   d. Click **WordSpellCheck01.docx** in the Content pane.
   e. Hold down the Shift key, click **WordSpellCheck03.docx**, and then release the Shift key.
   f. Click the Organize button and then click *Copy* at the drop-down list.
   g. Click the *Documents* folder in the *Libraries* section in the Navigation pane.
   h. Click the Organize button and then click *Paste* at the drop-down list.

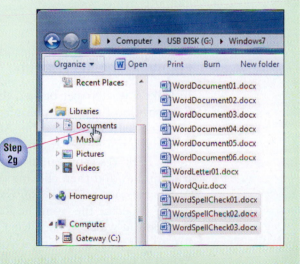

Step 2g

3. Delete to the Recycle Bin the files you just copied by completing the following steps:
   a. With **WordSpellCheck01.docx** through **WordSpellCheck03.docx** selected in the Content pane, click the Organize button and then click *Delete* at the drop-down list.
   b. At the message asking you if you are sure you want to move the items to the Recycle Bin, click Yes.
4. Close the Computer window.
5. At the Windows 7 desktop, display the contents of the Recycle Bin by double-clicking the Recycle Bin icon.
6. Restore the files you just deleted by completing the following steps:
   a. Select **WordSpellCheck01.docx** through **WordSpellCheck03.docx** in the Recycle Bin Content pane. (If these files are not visible, you will need to scroll down the list of files in the Content pane.)
   b. Click the Restore the selected items button on the toolbar.

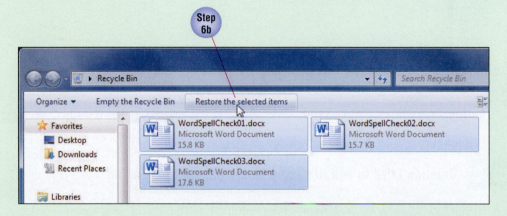

7. Close the Recycle Bin by clicking the Close button located in the upper right corner of the window.
8. Display the Computer window.
9. Click the *Documents* folder in the *Libraries* section in the Navigation pane.
10. Delete the files you restored.
11. Close the Computer window.

Emptying the Recycle Bin

Just like a wastepaper basket, the Recycle Bin can get full. To empty the Recycle Bin, position the arrow pointer on the Recycle Bin icon on the desktop and then click the right mouse button. At the shortcut menu that displays, click the *Empty Recycle Bin* option. At the message asking if you want to permanently delete the items, click Yes. You can also empty the Recycle Bin by displaying the Recycle Bin window and then clicking the Empty the Recycle Bin button on the toolbar. At the message asking if you want to permanently delete the items, click Yes. To delete a specific file from the Recycle Bin window, click the desired file in the Recycle Bin window, click the Organize button, and then *Delete* at the drop-down list. At the message asking if you want to permanently delete the file, click Yes. When you empty the Recycle Bin, the files cannot be recovered by the Recycle Bin or by Windows 7. If you have to recover a file, you will need to use a file recovery program.

Before beginning this project, check with your instructor to determine if you can delete files/folders from the Recycle Bin.

1. At the Windows 7 desktop, double-click the Recycle Bin icon.
2. At the Recycle Bin window, empty the contents by clicking the Empty the Recycle Bin button on the toolbar.
3. At the message asking you if you want to permanently delete the items, click Yes.
4. Close the Recycle Bin by clicking the Close button located in the upper right corner of the window.

Creating a Shortcut

If you use a file or program on a consistent basis, consider creating a shortcut to the file or program. A shortcut is a specialized icon that represents very small files that point the operating system to the actual item, whether it is a file, a folder, or an application. If you create a shortcut to a Word document, the shortcut icon is not the actual document but a path to the document. Double-click the shortcut icon and Windows 7 opens the document in Word.

One method for creating a shortcut is to display the Computer window and then make active the drive or folder where the file is located. Right-click the desired file, point to *Send To,* and then click *Desktop (create shortcut).* You can easily delete a shortcut icon from the desktop by dragging the shortcut icon to the Recycle Bin icon. This deletes the shortcut icon but does not delete the file to which the shortcut pointed.

1. At the Windows 7 desktop, display the Computer window.
2. Double-click the drive containing your storage medium.
3. Double-click the *Windows7* folder in the Content pane.
4. Change the display of files to a list by clicking the Views button arrow and then clicking *List* at the drop-down list. (Skip this step if *List* is already selected.)
5. Create a shortcut to the file named **WordLetter01.docx** by right-clicking **WordLetter01.docx**, pointing to *Send to,* and then clicking *Desktop (create shortcut).*

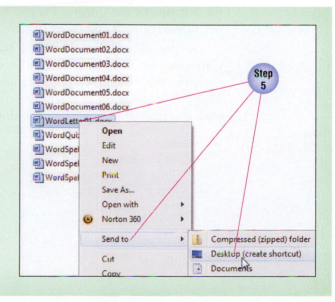

6. Close the Computer window.
7. Open Word and the file named **WordLetter01.docx** by double-clicking the *WordLetter01.docx* shortcut icon on the desktop.
8. After viewing the file in Word, exit Word by clicking the Close button that displays in the upper right corner of the window.
9. Delete the *WordLetter01.docx* shortcut icon by completing the following steps:
   a. At the desktop, position the mouse pointer on the *WordLetter01.docx* shortcut icon.
   b. Hold down the left mouse button, drag the icon on top of the Recycle Bin icon, and then release the mouse button.

Exploring the Control Panel

The Control Panel, shown in Figure W.10, contains a variety of icons you can use to customize the appearance and functionality of your computer as well as access and change system settings. Display the Control Panel by clicking the Start button on the Taskbar and then clicking *Control Panel* at the Start menu. The Control Panel organizes settings into categories to make them easier to find. Click a category icon and the Control Panel displays lower-level categories and tasks within each of them.

Hover your mouse over a category icon in the Control Panel and a ScreenTip displays with an explanation of what options are available. For example, if you hover the mouse over the Appearance and Personalization icon, a ScreenTip displays with information about the tasks available in the category such as changing the appearance of desktop items, applying a theme or screen saver to your computer, or customizing the Start menu and Taskbar.

If you click a category icon in the Control Panel, the Control Panel displays all of the available subcategories and tasks in the category. Also, the categories display in text form at the left side of the Control Panel. For example, if you click the Appearance and Personalization category icon, the Control Panel displays as shown in Figure W.11. Notice how the Control Panel categories display at the left side of the Control Panel and options for changing the appearance and personalizing your computer display in the middle of the Control Panel.

By default, the Control Panel displays categories of tasks in what is called Category view. You can change this view to *Large icons* or *Small icons*. To change the view, click the down-pointing arrow that displays at the right side of the text *View by* that displays in the upper right corner of the Control Panel, and then click the desired view at the drop-down list (see Figure W.10).

Figure W.10 The Control Panel

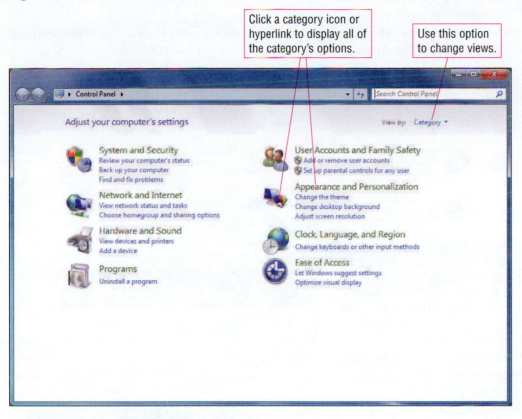

Click a category icon or hyperlink to display all of the category's options.

Use this option to change views.

Figure W.11 Appearance and Personalization Window

lower-level categories

task hyperlinks

Click this option to return to the main Control Panel.

Click a category to display category options.

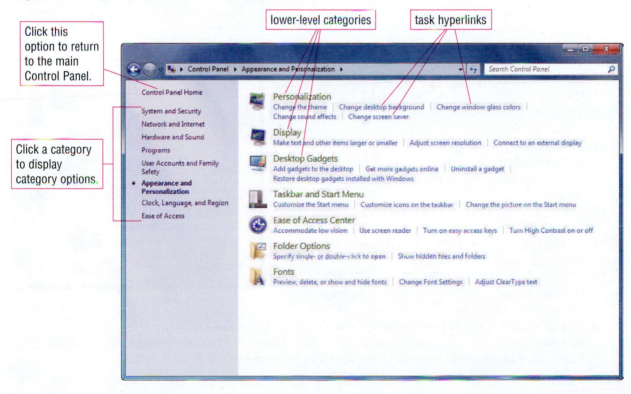

Project 10   Changing the Desktop Theme

1. At the Windows 7 desktop, click the Start button and then click *Control Panel* at the Start menu.
2. At the Control Panel, click the Appearance and Personalization category icon.

3. Click the <u>Change the theme</u> hyperlink that displays below the Personalization category in the panel at the right in the Control Panel.
4. At the window that displays with options for changing visuals and sounds on your computer, click the *Landscapes* theme.

5. Click the <u>Desktop Background</u> hyperlink that displays in the lower left corner of the panel at the right.
6. Click the button that displays below the text *Change picture every* and then click *10 Seconds* at the drop-down list. (This tells Windows to change the picture on your desktop every 10 seconds.)
7. Click the Save changes button that displays in the lower right corner of the Control Panel.
8. Click the Close button located in the upper right corner to close the Control Panel.
9. Look at the picture that displays as the background at the desktop. Wait for 10 seconds and then look at the second picture that displays.
10. Click the Start button and then click *Control Panel* at the Start menu.
11. At the Control Panel, click the Appearance and Personalization category icon.
12. Click the <u>Change the theme</u> hyperlink that displays below the Personalization category in the panel at the right.

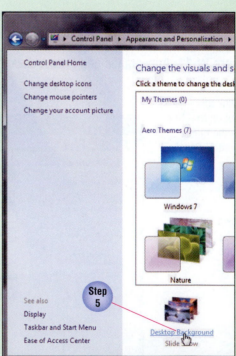

13. At the window that displays with options for changing visuals and sounds on your computer, click the *Windows 7* theme in the *Aero Themes* section. (This is the default theme.)
14. Click the Close button located in the upper right corner of the Control Panel.

Searching in the Control Panel

The Control Panel contains a large number of options for customizing the appearance and functionality of your computer. If you want to customize a feature and are not sure where the options for the feature are located, search for the feature. To do this, display the Control Panel and then type the name of the desired feature. By default, the insertion point is positioned in the *Search Control Panel* text box. When you type the feature name in the Search Control Panel, options related to the feature display in the Control Panel.

Project 11   Customizing the Mouse

1. Click the Start button and then click *Control Panel*.
2. At the Control Panel, type **mouse**. (The insertion point is automatically located in the *Search Control Panel* text box when you open the Control Panel. When you type *mouse*, features for customizing the mouse display in the Control Panel.)
3. Click the Mouse icon that displays in the Control Panel.
4. At the Mouse Properties dialog box, notice the options that display. (The *Switch primary and secondary buttons* option might be useful, for example, if you are left-handed and want to switch the buttons on the mouse.)
5. Click the Cancel button to remove the dialog box.
6. At the Control Panel, click the <u>Change the mouse pointer display or speed</u> hyperlink.

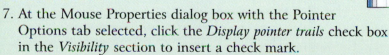

7. At the Mouse Properties dialog box with the Pointer Options tab selected, click the *Display pointer trails* check box in the *Visibility* section to insert a check mark.
8. Drag the button on the slider bar (located below the *Display pointer trails* check box) approximately to the middle of the bar.
9. Click OK to close the dialog box.
10. Close the Control Panel.
11. Move the mouse pointer around the screen to see the pointer trails as well as the speed at which the mouse moves.

Displaying Personalize Options with a Shortcut Command

In addition to the Control Panel, you can display customization options with a command from a shortcut menu. Display a shortcut menu by positioning the mouse pointer in the desired position and then clicking the right mouse button. For example, display a shortcut menu with options for customizing the desktop by positioning the mouse pointer in an empty area on the desktop and then clicking the right mouse button. At the shortcut menu that displays, click the desired shortcut command.

Project 12   Customizing with a Shortcut Command

1. At the Windows 7 desktop, position the mouse pointer in an empty area on the desktop, click the right mouse button, and then click *Personalize* at the shortcut menu.
2. At the Control Panel Appearance and Personalization window that displays, click the <u>Change mouse pointers</u> hyperlink that displays at the left side of the window.
3. At the Mouse Properties dialog box, click the Pointer Options tab.
4. Click in the *Display pointer trails* check box to remove the check mark.
5. Click OK to close the dialog box.
6. At the Control Panel Appearance and Personalization window, click the <u>Screen Saver</u> hyperlink that displays in the lower right corner of the window.
7. At the Screen Saver Settings dialog box, click the option button below the *Screen saver* option and then click *Ribbons* at the drop-down list.
8. Check the number in the *Wait* text box. If a number other than *1* displays, click the down-pointing arrow in the spin box at the right side of the text box until *1* displays. (This tells Windows to display the screen saver after one minute of inactivity.)
9. Click OK to close the dialog box.
10. Close the Control Panel by clicking the Close button located in the upper right corner of the window.

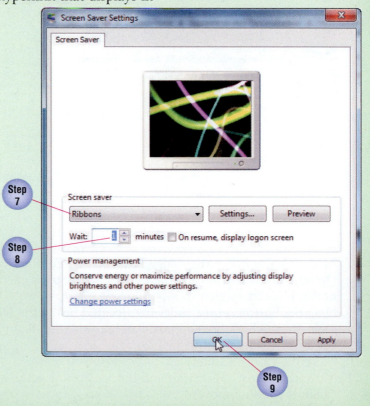

11. Do not touch the mouse or keyboard and wait over one minute for the screen saver to display. After watching the screen saver, move the mouse. (This redisplays the desktop.)
12. Right-click in an empty area on the desktop and then click *Personalize* at the shortcut menu.
13. At the Control Panel Appearance and Personalization window, click the <u>Screen Saver</u> hyperlink.
14. At the Screen Saver Settings dialog box, click the option button below the *Screen saver* option and then click *(None)* at the drop-down list.
15. Click OK to close the dialog box.
16. Close the Control Panel Appearance and Personalization window.

Exploring Windows Help and Support ▪▪▪▪▪▪▪▪▪▪▪▪▪▪

Windows 7 includes an on-screen reference guide providing information, explanations, and interactive help on learning Windows features. Get help at the Windows Help and Support window shown in Figure W.12. Display this window by clicking the Start button and then clicking *Help and Support* at the Start menu. Use buttons in the window toolbar to display the opening Windows Help and Support window, print the current information, display a list of contents, get customer support or other types of services, and display a list of Help options.

Figure W.12 Windows Help and Support Window

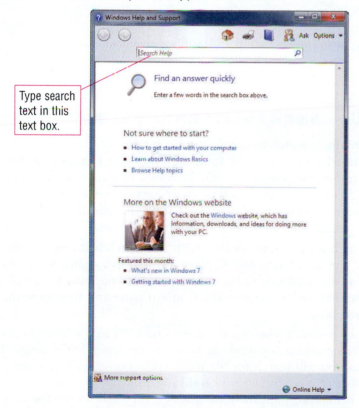

Type search text in this text box.

1. At the Windows 7 desktop, click the Start button and then click *Help and Support* at the Start menu.
2. At the Windows Help and Support window, click the <u>Learn about Windows Basics</u> hyperlink.
3. Click a hyperlink that interests you, read the information, and then click the Back button on the Windows Help and Support window toolbar. (The Back button is located in the upper left corner of the window.)
4. Click another hyperlink that interests you and then read the information.
5. Click the Help and Support home button that displays on the window toolbar. (This returns you to the opening Windows Help and Support window.)
6. Click in the *Search Help* text box, type **delete files**, and then press Enter.
7. Click the <u>Delete a file or folder</u> hyperlink that displays in the window.
8. Read the information that displays about deleting files or folders and then click the Print button on the window toolbar.
9. At the Print dialog box, click the Print button.
10. Click the Close button to close the Windows Help and Support window.

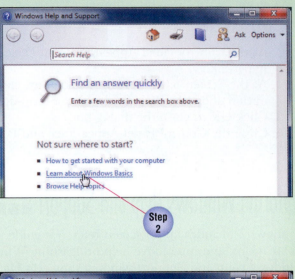

Step 2

Step 5

Using Search Tools

The Start menu contains a search tool you can use to quickly find a program or file on your computer. To use the search tool, click the Start button and then type the first few characters of the program or file for which you are searching in the *Search programs and files* text box. As you type characters in the text box, a pop-up list displays with program names or file names that begin with the characters. As you continue typing characters, the search tool refines the list.

You can also search for programs or files with the search text box in the Computer window. The search text box displays in the upper right corner of the Computer window at the right side of the Address bar. If you want to search a specific folder, make that folder active in the Content pane and then type the search text in the text box.

When conducting a search, you can use the asterisk (*) as a wildcard character in place of any letters, numbers, or symbols within a file name. For example, in the following project you will search for file names containing *check* by typing ***check** in the search text box. The asterisk indicates that the file name can start with any letter but it must contain the letters *check* somewhere in the file name.

Project 14 **Searching for Programs and Files**

1. At the Windows 7 desktop, click the Start button.
2. With the insertion point positioned in the *Search programs and files* text box, type **paint**. (Notice as you type the letters that Windows displays programs and/or files that begin with the same letters you are typing or that are associated with the same letters in a keyword. Notice that the Paint program displays below the heading *Programs* at the top of the list. Depending on the contents stored in the computer you are using, additional items may display below Paint.)

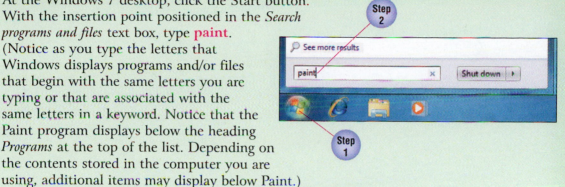

Step 2

Step 1

3. Click *Paint* that displays below the *Programs* heading.
4. Close the Paint window.
5. Click the Start button and then click *Computer*.
6. At the Computer window, double-click the icon representing your storage medium.
7. Double-click the *Windows7* folder.
8. Click in the search text box located at the right of the Address bar and then type **document**. (As you begin typing the letters, Windows filters the list of files in the Content pane to those that contain the letters you type. Notice that the Address bar displays *Search Results in Windows7* to indicate that the files that display matching your criteria were limited to the current folder.)

Step 8

9. Select the text *document* that displays in the search text box and then type ***check**. (Notice that the Content pane displays file names containing the letters *check* no matter how the file name begins.)
10. Double-click ***WordSpellCheck02.docx*** to open the document in Word.
11. Close the document and exit Word by clicking the Close button located in the upper right corner of the window.
12. Close the Computer window.

Step 9

Step 10

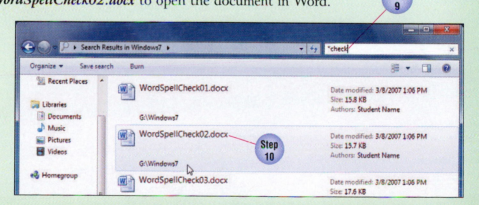

Browsing the Internet Using Internet Explorer 8.0

Microsoft Internet Explorer 8.0 is a web browser program with options and features for displaying sites as well as navigating and searching for information on the Internet. The **Internet** is a network of computers connected around the world. Users access the Internet for several purposes: to communicate using instant messaging and/or email, to subscribe to newsgroups, to transfer files, to socialize with other users around the globe in chat rooms, and also to access virtually any kind of information imaginable.

Using the Internet, people can find a phenomenal amount of information for private or public use. To use the Internet, three things are generally required: an Internet Service Provider (ISP), a program to browse the Web (called a **web browser**), and a **search engine**. In this section, you will learn how to:

- Navigate the Internet using URLs and hyperlinks
- Use search engines to locate information
- Download web pages and images

You will use the Microsoft Internet Explorer web browser to locate information on the Internet. Uniform Resource Locators, referred to as URLs, are the method used to identify locations on the Internet. The steps for browsing the Internet vary but generally include: opening Internet Explorer, typing the URL for the desired site, navigating the various pages of the site, navigating to other sites using links, and then closing Internet Explorer.

To launch Internet Explorer 8.0, click the Internet Explorer icon on the Taskbar at the Windows desktop. Figure IE.1 identifies the elements of the Internet Explorer, version 8.0, window. The web page that displays in your Internet Explorer window may vary from what you see in Figure IE.1.

If you know the URL for the desired website, click in the Address bar, type the URL, and then press Enter. The website's home page displays in a tab within the Internet Explorer window. URLs (Uniform Resource Locators) are the method used to identify locations on the Internet. The format of a URL is *http://server-name.path*. The first part of the URL, *http*, stands for HyperText Transfer Protocol, which is the protocol or language used to transfer data within the World Wide Web. The colon and slashes separate the protocol from the server name. The server name is the second component of the URL. For example, in the URL http://www.microsoft.com, the server name is *microsoft*. The last part of the URL specifies the domain to which the server belongs. For example, *.com* refers to "commercial" and establishes that the URL is a commercial company. Examples of other domains include *.edu* for "educational," *.gov* for "government," and *.mil* for "military."

Figure IE.1 Internet Explorer Window

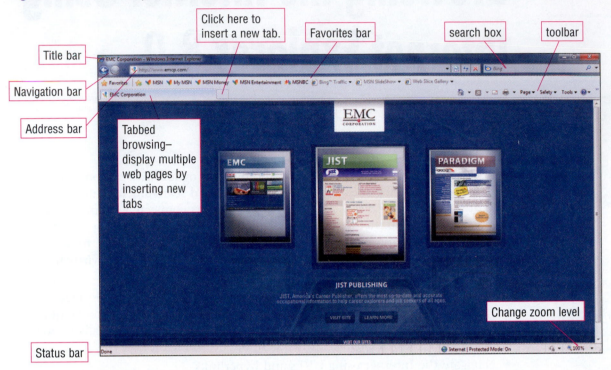

Title bar

Navigation bar

Address bar

Click here to insert a new tab.

Favorites bar

search box

toolbar

Tabbed browsing–display multiple web pages by inserting new tabs

Change zoom level

Status bar

Project 1   Browsing the Internet Using URLs

1. Make sure you are connected to the Internet through an Internet Service Provider and that the Windows desktop displays. (Check with your instructor to determine if you need to complete steps for accessing the Internet such as typing a user name and password to log on.)
2. Launch Microsoft Internet Explorer by clicking the Internet Explorer icon located on the Taskbar located at the bottom of the Windows desktop.
3. At the Internet Explorer window, explore the website for Yosemite National Park by completing the following steps:
    a. Click in the Address bar, type **www.nps.gov/yose**, and then press Enter.
    b. Scroll down the home page for Yosemite National Park by clicking the down-pointing arrow on the vertical scroll bar located at the right side of the Internet Explorer window.
    c. Print the home page by clicking the Print button located on the Internet Explorer toolbar. (Some websites have a printer friendly button you can click to print the page.)

Step 3b

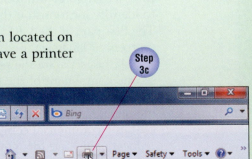

Step 3c

4. Explore the website for Glacier National Park by completing the following steps:
   a. Click in the Address bar, type **www.nps.gov/glac**, and then press Enter.
   b. Print the home page by clicking the Print button located on the Internet Explorer toolbar.
5. Close Internet Explorer by clicking the Close button (contains an X) located in the upper right corner of the Internet Explorer window.

Navigating Using Hyperlinks ▪▪▪▪▪▪▪▪▪▪▪▪▪▪▪▪▪▪▪▪

Most web pages contain "hyperlinks" that you click to connect to another page within the website or to another site on the Internet. Hyperlinks may display in a web page as underlined text in a specific color or as images or icons. To use a hyperlink, position the mouse pointer on the desired hyperlink until the mouse pointer turns into a hand, and then click the left mouse button. Use hyperlinks to navigate within and between sites on the Internet. The navigation bar in the Internet Explorer window contains a Back button that, when clicked, takes you to the previous web page viewed. If you click the Back button and then want to return to the previous page, click the Forward button. You can continue clicking the Back button to back your way out of several linked pages in reverse order since Internet Explorer maintains a history of the websites you visit.

Project 2   Navigating Using Hyperlinks

1. Make sure you are connected to the Internet and then click the Internet Explorer icon on the Taskbar.
2. At the Internet Explorer window, display the White House web page and navigate in the page by completing the following steps:
   a. Click in the Address bar, type **whitehouse.gov**, and then press Enter.
   b. At the White House home page, position the mouse pointer on a hyperlink that interests you until the pointer turns into a hand, and then click the left mouse button.
   c. At the linked web page, click the Back button. (This returns you to the White House home page.)
   d. At the White House home page, click the Forward button to return to the previous web page viewed.
   e. Print the web page by clicking the Print button on the Internet Explorer toolbar.
3. Display the website for Amazon.com and navigate in the site by completing the following steps:
   a. Click in the Address bar, type **www.amazon.com**, and then press Enter.

b. At the Amazon.com home page, click a hyperlink related to books.

c. When a book web page displays, click the Print button on the Internet Explorer toolbar.

4. Close Internet Explorer by clicking the Close button (contains an X) located in the upper right corner of the Internet Explorer window.

Searching for Specific Sites

If you do not know the URL for a specific site or you want to find information on the Internet but do not know what site to visit, complete a search with a search engine. A search engine is a software program created to search quickly and easily for desired information. A variety of search engines are available on the Internet, each offering the opportunity to search for specific information. One method for searching for information is to click in the search box located to the right of the Address bar, type a keyword or phrase related to your search, and then click the Search button or press Enter. Another method for completing a search is to visit the website for a search engine and use options at the site.

Bing is Microsoft's online search portal and is the default search engine used by Internet Explorer. Bing organizes search results by topic category and provides related search suggestions.

Project 3   Searching for Information by Topic

1. Start Internet Explorer.
2. At the Internet Explorer window, search for sites on bluegrass music by completing the following steps:
   a. Click in the search box (may display *Bing*) located at the right side of the Address bar.
   b. Type **bluegrass music** and then press Enter.
   c. When a list of sites displays in the Bing results window, click a site that interests you.
   d. When the page displays, click the Print button.
3. Use the Yahoo! search engine to find sites on bluegrass music by completing the following steps:
   a. Click in the Address bar, type **www.yahoo.com**, and then press Enter.
   b. At the Yahoo! website, with the insertion point positioned in the search text box, type **bluegrass music** and then press Enter. (Notice that the sites displayed vary from sites displayed in the earlier search.)
   c. Click hyperlinks until a website displays that interests you.
   d. Print the page.

4. Use the Google search engine to find sites on jazz music by completing the following steps:

   a. Click in the Address bar, type **www.google.com**, and then press Enter.

   b. At the Google website, with the insertion point positioned in the search text box, type **jazz music** and then press Enter.

   c. Click a site that interests you.

   d. Print the page.

5. Close Internet Explorer.

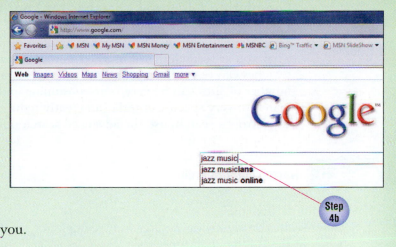

Using a Metasearch Engine

Bing, Yahoo!, and Google are search engines that search the Web for content and display search results. In addition to individual search engines, you can use a metasearch engine, such as Dogpile, that sends your search text to other search engines and then compiles the results in one list. With a metasearch engine, you type the search text once and then access results from a wider group of search engines. The Dogpile metasearch engine provides search results from Google, Yahoo!, Bing, and Ask.

Project 4   **Searching with a Metasearch Search Engine**

1. At the Windows desktop, click the Internet Explorer icon on the Taskbar.

2. Click in the Address bar.

3. Type **www.dogpile.com** and then press Enter.

4. At the Dogpile website, type **jazz music** in the search text box and then press Enter.

5. Click a hyperlink that interests you.

6. Close the Internet Explorer window.

Completing Advanced Searches for Specific Sites ■■■■■■■■■ ■

Web Search

The Internet contains an enormous amount of information. Depending on what you are searching for on the Internet and the search engine you use, some searches can result in several thousand "hits" (sites). Wading through a large number of sites can be very time-consuming and counterproductive. Narrowing a search to very specific criteria can greatly reduce the number of hits for a search. To narrow a search, use the advanced search options offered by the search engine.

Project 5   Narrowing a Search

1. Start Internet Explorer.
2. Search for sites on skydiving in Oregon by completing the following steps:
   a. Click in the Address bar, type **www.yahoo.com**, and then press Enter.
   b. At the Yahoo! home page, click the Web Search button next to the search text box.
   c. Click the <u>more</u> hyperlink located above the search text box and then click Advanced Search at the drop-down list.

   Step 2c

   Web | Images | Video | Local | Shopping | more ˅
   Answers
   Directory
   Jobs
   News
   Sports
   All Search Services
   Advanced Search
   Preferences
   Advertising Programs
   © 2010 Yahoo! | Page Tour | P | Subm

   d. At the Advanced Web Search page, click in the search text box next to *all of these words*.
   e. Type **skydiving Oregon tandem static line**. (This limits the search to web pages containing all of the words typed in the search text box.)
   f. Click the Yahoo! Search button.
   g. When the list of websites displays, click a hyperlink that interests you.
   h. Click the Back button until the Yahoo! Advanced Web Search page displays.
   i. Click in the *the exact phrase* text box and then type **skydiving in Oregon**.
   j. Click the *Only .com domains* in the *Site/Domain* section.
   k. Click the Yahoo! Search button.
   l. When the list of websites displays, click a hyperlink that interests you.
   m. Print the page.
3. Close Internet Explorer.

   Step 2e

   YAHOO! SEARCH   Yahoo! - Search Home - Help
   Advanced Web Search
   You can use the options on this page to create a very specific search. Just fill in the fields you need for your current search.   Yahoo! Search

   Show results with   all of these words   skydiving Oregon tandem static line   any part of the page ˅
                        the exact phrase   any part of the page ˅
                        any of these words   any part of the page ˅
                        none of these words   any part of the page ˅

   Step 2i

   Step 2j

   Step 2k

   YAHOO! SEARCH   Yahoo! - Search Home - Help
   Advanced Web Search
   You can use the options on this page to create a very specific search. Just fill in the fields you need for your current search.   Yahoo! Search

   Show results with   all of these words   skydiving Oregon tandem static line   any part of the page ˅
                        the exact phrase   skydiving in Oregon   any part of the page ˅
                        any of these words   any part of the page ˅
                        none of these words   any part of the page ˅
   Tip: Use these options to look for an exact phrase or to exclude pages containing certain words. You can also limit your search to certain parts of pages.

   Updated   anytime ˅
   Site/Domain   ○ Any domain
                  ◉ Only .com domains ○ Only .edu domains
                  ○ Only .gov domains ○ Only .org domains

Downloading Images, Text, and Web Pages from the Internet ▪■■■

The image(s) and/or text that display when you open a web page as well as the web page itself can be saved as a separate file. This separate file can be viewed, printed, or inserted in another file. The information you want to save in a separate file is downloaded from the Internet by Internet Explorer and saved in a folder of your choosing with the name you specify. Copyright laws protect much of the information on the Internet. Before using information downloaded from the Internet, check the site for restrictions. If you do use information, make sure you properly cite the source.

Project 6   Downloading Images and Web Pages

1. Start Internet Explorer.
2. Download a web page and image from Banff National Park by completing the following steps:
   a. Search for sites on the Internet for Banff National Park.
   b. From the list of sites that displays, choose a site that contains information about Banff National Park and at least one image of the park.
   c. Save the web page as a separate file by clicking the Page button on the Internet Explorer toolbar and then clicking *Save As* at the drop-down list.
   d. At the Save Webpage dialog box, type **BanffWebPage**.

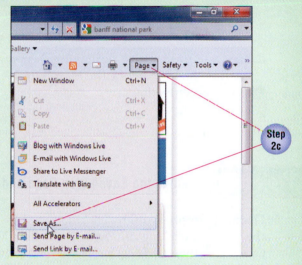

Step 2c

   e. Navigate to the drive containing your storage medium and then click the Save button.

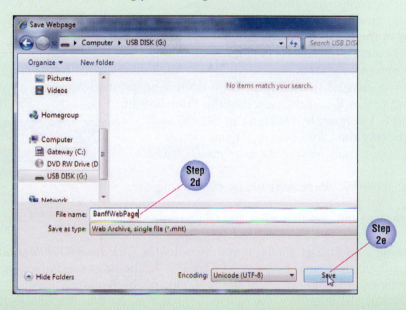

Step 2d

Step 2e

3. Save an image file by completing the following steps:
   a. Right-click an image that displays at the website. (The image that displays may vary from what you see below.)
   b. At the shortcut menu that displays, click *Save Picture As*.
   c. At the Save Picture dialog box, type **BanffImage** in the *File name* text box.

Step
3b

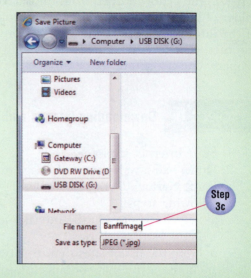

Step
3c

   d. Navigate to the drive containing your storage medium and then click the Save button.
4. Close Internet Explorer.

Project 7   Opening the Saved Web Page and Image in a Word Document

1. Open Microsoft Word by clicking the Start button on the Taskbar, clicking *All Programs*, clicking *Microsoft Office*, and then clicking *Microsoft Word 2010*.
2. With Microsoft Word open, insert the image in a document by completing the following steps:
   a. Click the Insert tab and then click the Picture button in the Illustrations group.
   b. At the Insert Picture dialog box, navigate to the drive containing your storage medium and then double-click *BanffImage.jpg*.
   c. When the image displays in the Word document, print the document by pressing Ctrl + P and then clicking the Print button.
   d. Close the document by clicking the File tab and then clicking the Close button. At the message asking if you want to save the changes, click *Don't Save*.
3. Open the **BanffWebPage.mht** file by completing the following steps:
   a. Click the File tab and then click the Open button.
   b. At the Open dialog box, navigate to the drive containing your storage medium and then double-click *BanffWebPage.mht*.
   c. Preview the web page(s) by pressing Ctrl + P. At the Print tab Backstage view, preview the page shown at the right side of the Backstage view.
4. Close Word by clicking the Close button (contains an X) that displays in the upper right corner of the screen.

Step
2b

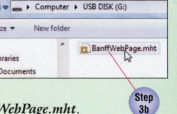

Step
3b

Microsoft® Word

Level 1

Unit 1 ▪ Editing and Formatting Documents

Word

Microsoft®

CHAPTER 1

Preparing Documents

PERFORMANCE OBJECTIVES

Upon successful completion of Chapter 1, you will be able to:

- Open Microsoft Word
- Create, save, name, print, open, and close a Word document
- Exit Word
- Edit a document
- Move the insertion point within a document
- Scroll within a document
- Select text in a document
- Use the Undo and Redo buttons
- Check spelling and grammar in a document
- Use the Help feature

Tutorials

1.1 Creating, Saving, and Printing a Document
1.2 Using the AutoCorrect Feature
1.3 Previewing and Printing Documents
1.4 Opening and Pinning a Document
1.5 Editing a Document
1.6 Using the Spelling and Grammar Feature
1.7 Using the Help Feature

In this chapter, you will learn to create, save, name, print, open, close, and edit a Word document as well as complete a spelling and grammar check. You will also learn about the Help feature, which is an on-screen reference manual providing information on features and commands for each program in the Office suite. Before continuing, make sure you read the *Getting Started* section presented at the beginning of this book. This section contains information about computer hardware and software, using the mouse, executing commands, and exploring Help files. Model answers for this chapter's projects appear on the following page.

Word2010L1C1

Note: Before beginning the projects, copy to your storage medium the Word2010L1C1 subfolder from the Word2010L1 folder on the CD that accompanies this textbook. Steps on how to copy a folder are presented on the inside of the back cover of this textbook. Do this every time you start a chapter's projects.

The traditional chronological resume lists your work experience in reverse-chronological order (starting with your current or most recent position). The functional style deemphasizes the "where" and "when" of your career and instead groups similar experience, talents, and qualifications regardless of when they occurred.

Like the chronological resume, the hybrid resume includes specifics about where you worked, when you worked there, and what your job titles were. Like a functional resume, a hybrid resume emphasizes your most relevant qualifications in an expanded summary section, in several "career highlights" bullet points at the top of your resume, or in project summaries.

Created:
Thursday, December 6, 2012
Note: The two paragraphs will become the 2nd and 3rd paragraphs in the 5th section.

Project 1 Prepare a Word Document
WL1-C1-P1-Computers.docx

The majority of new jobs being created in the United States today involve daily work with computers. Computer-related careers include technical support jobs, sales and training, programming and applications development, network and database administration, and computer engineering.

A technician is an entry-level worker who installs and maintains hardware and/or software. Technical sales and technical training jobs emphasize interpersonal skills as much as they do technical skills. Programming is one of the most difficult and highly skilled jobs in the industry. Programmers create new software, such as Microsoft Windows or computer games, and often have college degrees. Software engineers are programmers trained to create software in teams with other programmers. Application developers are similar to programmers, but they use existing software such as a database to create applications for business solutions. Application development jobs include database administration, network administration, and systems analysis. Database and network administration involve overseeing and maintaining databases and networks, respectively. Systems analysts design information systems or evaluate and improve existing ones.

Project 2 Save and Edit a Word Document
WL1-C1-P2-CompCareers.docx

COMPUTER KEYBOARDS

To enter commands into a computer or to enter data into it, a user needs an input device. An input device can be built into the computer, like the keyboard in a laptop, or it can be connected to the computer by a cable. Some input devices, like remote keyboards, send directions to the computer by means of an infrared signal.

Keyboards can be external devices that are attached by a cable, or they can be attached to the CPU case itself as they are in laptops. Most keyboards today are QWERTY keyboards, which take their name from the first six keys at the left of the first row of letters. The QWERTY design was invented in the early days of mechanical typewriters to slow down typists and thus keep keys from jamming.

The DVORAK keyboard is an alternative to the QWERTY keyboard. On the DVORAK keyboard, the most commonly used keys are placed close to the user's fingertips and this increases typing speed. You can install software on a QWERTY keyboard that emulates a DVORAK keyboard. The ability to emulate other keyboards is convenient especially when working with foreign languages.

Project 4 Insert and Delete Text
WL1-C1-P4-CompKeyboards.docx

ON THE HORIZON

The march of computer technology continues to change the nature of our jobs and workplaces. Considering the global economic and technology scene, some major changes in occupations involve changes in communications media, work locations, and communications tools.

Communications Media

One key to being successful in our modern, technological world is spotting a trend early and adjusting one's career direction accordingly. For example, 80 percent of daily newspaper readers are over 50 years old. Young readers are not as interested in the printed word, and each year the industry suffers from a shrinking number of subscriptions. The young are still reading, but they are reading online media sites rather than the printed page. Websites make excellent dynamic newspapers, as they can be changed at will, they require no printing or distribution costs, and they do not require the newspaper delivery person to go door to door asking for payment. This gradual switch to the new media is causing many jobs to change. The number of printing and lithography jobs is shrinking, but web developers and graphic artists are in demand.

Industry-morphing trends are sweeping away many traditional approaches to the marketing and distribution of products. Increasingly, music and movies are being downloaded versus being bought on a disc. Fewer movies are being rented, while more people are watching them on-demand through their cable systems. Once a successful approach is discovered, every type of media that can be digitized rather than produced and distributed in physical form will come under increasing pressure to modernize in order to match the competition. Individuals managing career paths need to be aware of these trends and avoid becoming part of a downsizing effort.

Telecommuting

Telecommuting, sometimes called telework, involves working via computer from home or while traveling rather than going to the office on a daily basis. Approximately 25 million Americans telecommute at least one day per week. Telework plans have been especially successful for commissioned salespeople, who are often more productive when away from the office environment.

Project 5 Complete a Spelling and Grammar Check
WL1-C1-P5-TechOccTrends.docx

Project 1 — Prepare a Word Document — 2 Parts

You will create a short document containing information on computers and then save, print, and close the document.

Opening Microsoft Word ■■■■■■■■■■■■■■■■■■

Microsoft Office 2010 contains a word processing program named Word that you can use to create, save, edit, and print documents. The steps to open Word may vary depending on your system setup. Generally, to open Word, you would click the Start button on the Taskbar at the Windows desktop, point to *All Programs*, click *Microsoft Office*, and then click *Microsoft Word 2010*.

Start

▼ **Quick Steps**

Open Word
1. Click Start button.
2. Point to *All Programs*.
3. Click *Microsoft Office*.
4. Click *Microsoft Word 2010*.

Creating, Saving, Printing, and Closing a Document ■■■

When Microsoft Word is open, a blank document displays as shown in Figure 1.1. The features of the document screen are described in Table 1.1.

At a blank document, type information to create a document. A document is any information you choose — for instance, a letter, report, term paper, table, and so on. Some things to consider when typing text are:

- **Word Wrap:** As you type text to create a document, you do not need to press the Enter key at the end of each line because Word wraps text to the next line. A word is wrapped to the next line if it begins before the right margin and continues past the right margin. The only times you need to press Enter are to end a paragraph, create a blank line, or end a short line.

- **AutoCorrect:** Word contains a feature that automatically corrects certain words as you type them. For example, if you type the word *adn* instead of *and*, Word automatically corrects it when you press the spacebar after the word. AutoCorrect will also superscript the letters that follow an ordinal number (a number indicating a position in a series). For example, if you type *2nd* and then press the spacebar or Enter key, Word will convert this ordinal number to 2nd.

- **Automatic Spell Checker:** By default, Word will automatically insert a red wavy line below words that are not contained in the Spelling dictionary or automatically corrected by AutoCorrect. This may include misspelled words, proper names, some terminology, and some foreign words. If you type a word not recognized by the Spelling dictionary, leave it as written if the word is correct. However, if the word is incorrect, you have two choices — you can delete the word and then type it correctly, or you can position the I-beam pointer on the word, click the right mouse button, and then click the correct spelling in the pop-up list.

- **Automatic Grammar Checker:** Word includes an automatic grammar checker. If the grammar checker detects a sentence containing a grammatical error, a green wavy line is inserted below the sentence. You can leave the sentence as written or position the mouse I-beam pointer on the sentence, click the *right* mouse button, and a pop-up list will display with possible corrections.

- **Spacing Punctuation:** Typically, Word uses Calibri as the default typeface, which is a proportional typeface. (You will learn more about typefaces in Chapter 2.) When typing text in a proportional typeface, space once (rather than twice) after

HINT

To avoid opening the same program twice, use the Taskbar to see which programs are open.

HINT

A book icon displays in the Status bar. A check mark on the book indicates no spelling errors detected in the document by the spell checker, while an X in the book indicates errors. Double-click the book icon to move to the next error. If the book icon is not visible, right-click the Status bar and then click the *Spelling and Grammar Check* option at the pop-up list.

Figure 1.1 Blank Document

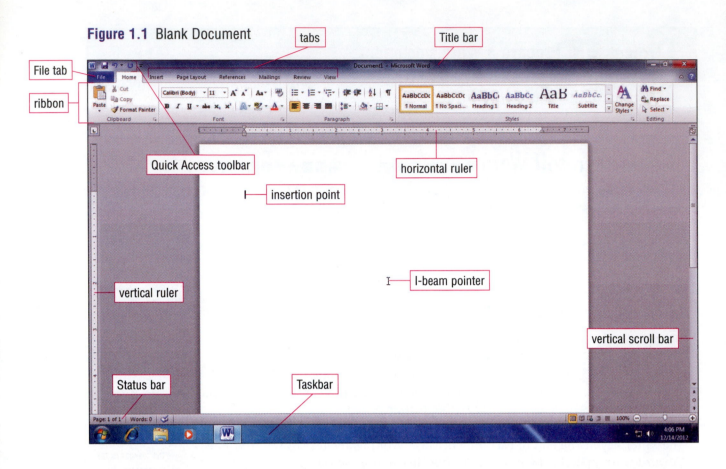

Table 1.1 Microsoft Word Screen Features

Feature	Description
File tab	Click the File tab and the Backstage view displays containing buttons and tabs for working with and managing documents.
Horizontal ruler	Used to set margins, indents, and tabs.
I-beam pointer	Used to move the insertion point or to select text.
Insertion point	Indicates location of next character entered at the keyboard.
Quick Access toolbar	Contains buttons for commonly used commands.
Ribbon	Area containing the tabs and commands divided into groups.
Status bar	Displays number of pages and words, View buttons, and the Zoom slider bar.
Title bar	Displays document name followed by program name.
Tabs	Contains commands and features organized into groups.
Taskbar	Divided into three sections—the Start button, the task buttons area, and the notification area.
Vertical ruler	Used to set top and bottom margins.
Vertical scroll bar	Used to view various parts of the document.

end-of-sentence punctuation such as a period, question mark, or exclamation point, and after a colon. Proportional typeface is set closer together, and extra white space at the end of a sentence or after a colon is not needed.

- **Option Buttons:** As you insert and edit text in a document, you may notice an option button popping up in your text. The name and appearance of this option button varies depending on the action. If a word you type is corrected by AutoCorrect, if you create an automatic list, or if autoformatting is applied to text, the AutoCorrect Options button appears. Click this button to undo the specific automatic action. If you paste text in a document, the Paste Options button appears near the text. Click this button to display the Paste Options gallery with buttons for controlling how the pasted text is formatted.

- **AutoComplete:** Microsoft Word and other Office applications include an AutoComplete feature that inserts an entire item when you type a few identifying characters. For example, type the letters *Mond* and *Monday* displays in a ScreenTip above the letters. Press the Enter key or press F3 and Word inserts *Monday* in the document.

Using the New Line Command

A Word document is based on a template that applies default formatting. Some basic formatting includes 1.15 line spacing and 10 points of spacing after a paragraph. Each time you press the Enter key, a new paragraph begins and 10 points of spacing is inserted after the paragraph. If you want to move the insertion point down to the next line without including the additional 10 points of spacing, use the New Line command, Shift + Enter.

Project 1a	Creating a Document	Part 1 of 2

1. Follow the instructions in this chapter to open Microsoft Word or check with your instructor for specific instructions.
2. At a blank document, type the information shown in Figure 1.2 with the following specifications:
   a. Correct any errors highlighted by the spell checker as they occur.
   b. Space once after end-of-sentence punctuation.
   c. After typing *Created:* press Shift + Enter to move the insertion point to the next line without adding 10 points of additional spacing.
   d. To insert the word *Thursday* located towards the end of the document, type **Thur** and then press F3. (This is an example of the AutoComplete feature.)
   e. To insert the word *December*, type **Dece** and then press the Enter key. (This is another example of the AutoComplete feature.)
   f. Press Shift + Enter after typing *December 6, 2012*.
   g. When typing the last line (the line containing the ordinal numbers), type the ordinal number text and AutoCorrect will automatically convert the letters in the ordinal numbers to superscript.
3. When you are finished typing the text, press the Enter key once.

Figure 1.2 Project 1a

The traditional chronological resume lists your work experience in reverse-chronological order (starting with your current or most recent position). The functional style deemphasizes the "where" and "when" of your career and instead groups similar experience, talents, and qualifications regardless of when they occurred.

Like the chronological resume, the hybrid resume includes specifics about where you worked, when you worked there, and what your job titles were. Like a functional resume, a hybrid resume emphasizes your most relevant qualifications in an expanded summary section, in several "career highlights" bullet points at the top of your resume, or in project summaries.

Created:
Thursday, December 6, 2012
Note: The two paragraphs will become the 2nd and 3rd paragraphs in the 5th section.

▼ Quick Steps

Save a Document
1. Click Save button.
2. Type document name.
3. Click Save button in dialog box.

H I N T

Save a document approximately every 15 minutes or when interrupted.

Save

Saving a Document

Save a document if you want to use it in the future. You can use a variety of methods to save a document such as clicking the Save button on the Quick Access toolbar, clicking the File tab and then clicking the Save As button, or using the keyboard shortcut Ctrl + S. To save a document, click the Save button on the Quick Access toolbar. At the Save As dialog box shown in Figure 1.3, type the name of the document and then press Enter or click the Save button located in the lower right corner of the dialog box.

Figure 1.3 Save As Dialog Box

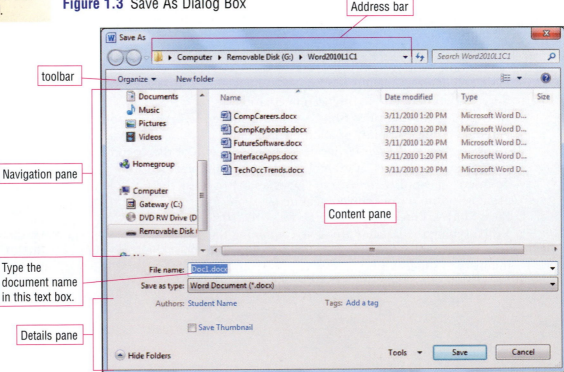

Naming a Document

Document names created in Word and other applications in the Office suite can be up to 255 characters in length, including drive letter and any folder names, and may include spaces. File names cannot include any of the following characters:

forward slash (/)   question mark (?)

backslash (\)   quotation mark (")

greater than sign (>)   colon (:)

less than sign (<)   semicolon (;)

asterisk (*)   pipe symbol (|)

Printing a Document

Click the File tab and the Backstage view displays as shown in Figure 1.4. Use buttons and tabs at this view to work with and manage documents such as opening, closing, saving, and printing a document. If you want to remove the Backstage view without completing an action, click the File tab, click any other tab in the ribbon, or press the Esc key on your keyboard.

Many of the computer exercises you will be creating will need to be printed. A printing of a document on paper is referred to as ***hard copy*** and a document displayed in the screen is referred to as ***soft copy***. Print a document with options at the Print tab Backstage view shown in Figure 1.5. To display this view, click the File tab and then click the Print tab. You can also display the Print tab Backstage view by pressing the keyboard shortcut, Ctrl + P.

The left side of the Print tab Backstage view displays three categories—Print, Printer, and Settings. Click the Print button in the Print category to send the

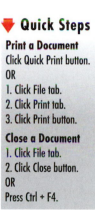

▼ Quick Steps

Print a Document
Click Quick Print button.
OR
1. Click File tab.
2. Click Print tab.
3. Click Print button.

Close a Document
1. Click File tab.
2. Click Close button.
OR
Press Ctrl + F4.

Figure 1.4 Backstage View

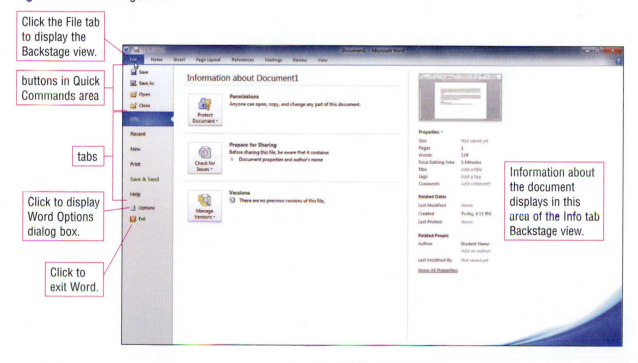

Click the File tab to display the Backstage view.

buttons in Quick Commands area

tabs

Click to display Word Options dialog box.

Click to exit Word.

Information about the document displays in this area of the Info tab Backstage view.

Figure 1.5 Print Tab Backstage View

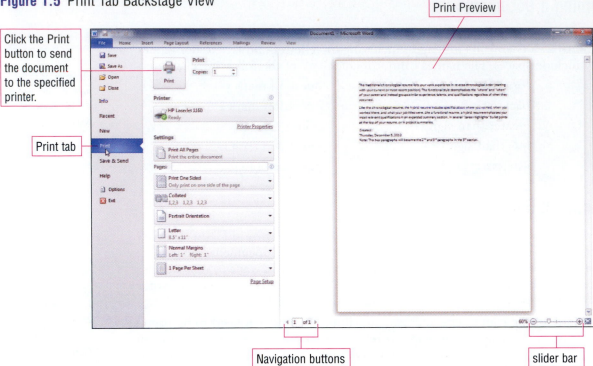

Click the Print button to send the document to the specified printer.

Print tab

Print Preview

Navigation buttons

slider bar

document to the printer and specify the number of copies you want printed with the *Copies* option. Use the gallery in the Printer category to specify the desired printer. The Settings category contains a number of galleries, each with options for specifying how you want your document printed such as whether or not you want the pages collated when printed; the orientation, page size, and margins of your document; and how many pages of your document you want to print on a page.

Quick Print

Another method for printing a document is to insert the Quick Print button on the Quick Access toolbar and then click the button. This sends the document directly to the printer without displaying the Print tab Backstage view. To insert the button on the Quick Access toolbar, click the Customize Quick Access Toolbar button that displays at the right side of the toolbar and then click *Quick Print* at the drop-down list. To remove the Quick Print button from the Quick Access toolbar, right-click on the button and then click the *Remove from Quick Access Toolbar* option that displays in the drop-down list.

Closing a Document

When you save a document, it is saved on your storage medium and remains in the document screen. To remove the document from the screen, click the File tab and then click the Close button or use the keyboard shortcut, Ctrl + F4. When you close a document, the document is removed and a blank screen displays. At this screen, you can open a previously saved document, create a new document, or exit the Word program.

1. Save the document you created for Project 1a and name it **WL1-C1-P1-Computers** (for Word Level 1, Chapter 1, Project 1 and the document refers to computers) by completing the following steps:

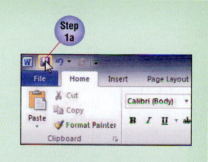

   a. Click the Save button on the Quick Access toolbar.
   b. At the Save As dialog box, navigate to the Word2010L1C1 folder on your storage medium. (To do this, click the drive representing your storage medium in the Navigation pane and then double-click the Word2010L1C1 folder.)
   c. Click in the *File name* text box (this selects any text in the box), type **WL1-C1-P1-Computers**, and then press Enter.

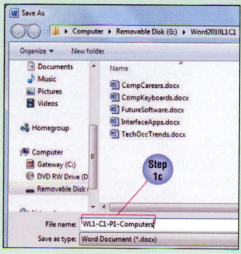

2. Print the document by clicking the File tab, clicking the Print tab, and then at the Backstage view, clicking the Print button.

3. Close the document by clicking the File tab and then clicking the Close button.

Project **2**   **Save and Edit a Word Document**   **2 Parts**

You will open a document located in the Word2010L1C1 folder on your storage medium, add text to the document, and then save the document with a new name.

Creating a New Document ■■■■■■■■■■■■■■■■■■■■■■

When you close a document, a blank screen displays. If you want to create a new document, display a blank document. To do this, click the File tab, click the New tab, and then click the Create button that displays below the image of the blank document at the right side of the New tab Backstage view. You can also open a new document using the keyboard shortcut, Ctrl + N, or by inserting a New

▼ **Quick Steps**

Create a New Document
1. Click File tab.
2. Click New tab.
3. Click Create button.

button on the Quick Access toolbar. To insert the button, click the Customize Quick Access Toolbar button that displays at the right side of the toolbar and then click *New* at the drop-down list.

Opening a Document ■■■■■■■■■■■■■■■■■■■■■■■

Quick Steps

Open a Document
1. Click File tab.
2. Click Open button.
3. Double-click document name.

After you save and close a document, you can open it at the Open dialog box shown in Figure 1.6. To display this dialog box, click the File tab and then click the Open button. You can also display the Open dialog box using the keyboard shortcut, Ctrl + O, or by inserting an Open button on the Quick Access toolbar. To insert the button, click the Customize Quick Access Toolbar button that displays at the right side of the toolbar and then click *Open* at the drop-down list. At the Open dialog box, open a document by double-clicking the document name.

If you want to see a list of the most recently opened documents, click the File tab and then click the Recent tab. This displays the Recent tab Backstage view containing a list of the most recently opened documents. To open a document from the list, scroll down the list and then click the desired document.

The Recent tab Backstage view contains the *Quickly access this number of Recent Documents* option that displays at the bottom of the screen. Click the option to insert a check mark in the check box and the four most recently opened document names display below the four options (*Save, Save As, Open,* and *Close*) in the Quick Commands area. By default, four document names display. You can change this number with the option box that displays at the right side of the *Quickly access this number of Recent Documents* option.

Figure 1.6 Open Dialog Box

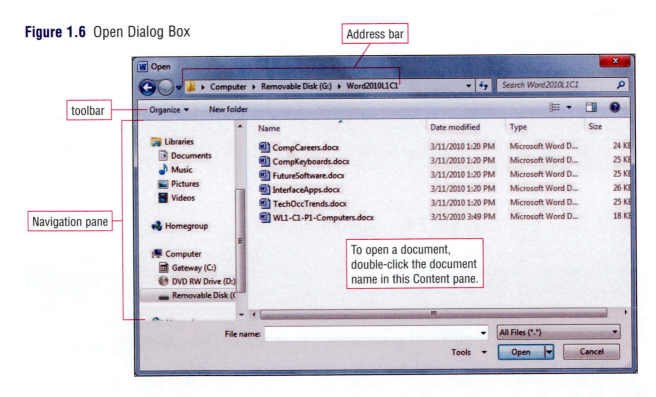

Pinning a Document ■■■■■■■■■■■■■■■■■■■■■■

When you click the File tab and then click the Recent tab, the Recent Documents list displays with the most recently opened documents. If you want a document to remain in the list, "pin" the document to the list by clicking the pin button that displays at the right side of the document name. This changes the dimmed gray stick pin to a blue stick pin. The next time you display the Recent Documents list, the document you "pinned" displays at the top of the list. To "unpin" the document, click the pin button to change it from a blue pin to a dimmed gray pin. You can pin more than one document to the list.

| Project 2a | Opening and Pinning/Unpinning a Document | Part 1 of 2 |

1. Open the **CompCareers.docx** document by completing the following steps:
   a. Click the File tab and then click the Open button in the Quick Commands area.
   b. At the Open dialog box, make sure the Word2010L1C1 folder on your storage medium is the active folder.
   c. Double-click *CompCareers.docx* in the Content pane.
2. Close **CompCareers.docx**.
3. Open **FutureSoftware.docx** by completing steps similar to those in Step 1.
4. Close **FutureSoftware.docx**.
5. Pin the **CompCareers.docx** document to the Recent Documents list by completing the following steps:
   a. Click the File tab. (If the Recent tab Backstage view does not display, click the Recent tab.)
   b. Click the dimmed gray stick pin that displays at the right side of the document

   CompCareers.docx. (This moves the document to the top of the list and changes the dimmed gray stick pin to a blue stick pin.)
6. Click *CompCareers.docx* at the top of the Recent Documents list to open the document.
7. With the insertion point positioned at the beginning of the document, type the text shown in Figure 1.7.
8. Unpin the **CompCareers.docx** from the Recent Documents list by completing the following steps:
   a. Click the File tab and then click the Recent tab.
   b. At the Recent Documents list, click the blue stick pin that displays at the right of the **CompCareers.docx** document name. (This changes the pin from a blue stick pin to a dimmed gray stick pin.)
   c. Click the File tab to return to the document.

Figure 1.7 Project 2a

The majority of new jobs being created in the United States today involve daily work with computers. Computer-related careers include technical support jobs, sales and training, programming and applications development, network and database administration, and computer engineering.

▼ **Quick Steps**

Save a Document with Save As
1. Click File tab.
2. Click Save As button.
3. Navigate to desired folder.
4. Type document name.
5. Press Enter.

Exit Word
1. Click File tab.
2. Click Exit button.
OR
Click Close button.

Saving a Document with Save As ▪▪▪▪▪▪▪▪▪▪▪▪▪▪▪▪

If you open a previously saved document and want to give it a new name, use the Save As button at the Backstage view rather than the Save button. Click the File tab and then click the Save As button and the Save As dialog box displays. At this dialog box, type the new name for the document and then press Enter.

Exiting Word ▪▪▪▪▪▪▪▪▪▪▪▪▪▪▪▪▪▪▪▪▪▪▪▪▪

Save any open documents before exiting Word.

When you are finished working with Word and have saved all necessary information, exit Word by clicking the File tab and then clicking the Exit button located below the Help tab. You can also exit the Word program by clicking the Close button located in the upper right corner of the screen.

Project 2b Saving a Document with Save As   Part 2 of 2

1. With **CompCareers.docx** open, save the document with a new name by completing the following steps:
   a. Click the File tab and then click the Save As button.
   b. At the Save As dialog box, press the Home key on your keyboard to move the insertion point to the beginning of the file name and then type **WL1-C1-P2-**. (Pressing the Home key saves you from having to type the entire document name.)
   c. Press the Enter key.
2. Print the document by clicking the File tab, clicking the Print tab, and then clicking the Print button at the Print tab Backstage view. (If your Quick Access toolbar contains the Quick Print button, you can click the button to send the document directly to the printer.)
3. Close the document by pressing Ctrl + F4.

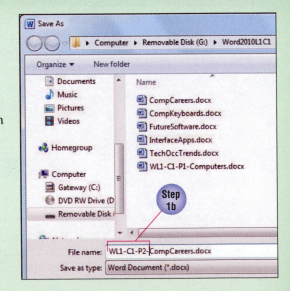

You will open a previously created document, save it with a new name, and then use scrolling and browsing techniques to move the insertion point to specific locations in the document.

Editing a Document ⬛■⬛■⬛■⬛■⬛■⬛■⬛■⬛■⬛■⬛■⬛■⬛■⬛■⬛

When editing a document, you may decide to insert or delete text. To edit a document, use the mouse, the keyboard, or the mouse combined with the keyboard to move the insertion point to specific locations in the document. To move the insertion point using the mouse, position the I-beam pointer where you want the insertion point located and then click the left mouse button.

You can also scroll in a document, which changes the text display but does not move the insertion point. Use the mouse with the *vertical scroll bar*, located at the right side of the screen, to scroll through text in a document. Click the up scroll arrow at the top of the vertical scroll bar to scroll up through the document and click the down scroll arrow to scroll down through the document. The scroll bar contains a scroll box that indicates the location of the text in the document screen in relation to the remainder of the document. To scroll up one screen at a time, position the arrow pointer above the scroll box (but below the up scroll arrow) and then click the left mouse button. Position the arrow pointer below the scroll box and click the left button to scroll down a screen. If you hold down the left mouse button, the action becomes continuous. You can also position the arrow pointer on the scroll box, hold down the left mouse button, and then drag the scroll box along the scroll bar to reposition text in the document screen. As you drag the scroll box along the vertical scroll bar in a longer document, page numbers display in a box at the right side of the document screen.

Project 3a   Scrolling in a Document   Part 1 of 2

1. Open **InterfaceApps.docx** (from the Word2010L1C1 folder you copied to your storage medium.)
2. Save the document with Save As and name it **WL1-C1-P3-InterfaceApps**.
3. Position the I-beam pointer at the beginning of the first paragraph and then click the left mouse button.
4. Click the down scroll arrow on the vertical scroll bar several times. (This scrolls down lines of text in the document.) With the mouse pointer on the down scroll arrow, hold down the left mouse button and keep it down until the end of the document displays.
5. Position the mouse pointer on the up scroll arrow and hold down the left mouse button until the beginning of the document displays.
6. Position the mouse pointer below the scroll box and then click the left mouse button. Continue clicking the mouse button (with the mouse pointer positioned below the scroll box) until the end of the document displays.
7. Position the mouse pointer on the scroll box in the vertical scroll bar. Hold down the left mouse button, drag the scroll box to the top of the vertical scroll bar, and then release the mouse button. (Notice that the document page numbers display in a box at the right side of the document screen.)
8. Click in the title at the beginning of the document. (This moves the insertion point to the location of the mouse pointer.)

Moving the Insertion Point to a Specific Page

Previous
Page

Select Browse
Object

Next Page

Along with scrolling options, Word also contains navigation buttons for moving the insertion point to specific locations. Navigation buttons display toward the bottom of the vertical scroll bar and include the Previous Page button, the Select Browse Object button, and the Next Page button. The full names of and the tasks completed by the Previous and Next buttons vary depending on the last navigation completed. Click the Select Browse Object button and a palette of browsing choices displays. You will learn more about the Select Browse Object button in the next section.

Word includes a Go To option you can use to move the insertion point to a specific page within a document. To move the insertion point to a specific page, click the Find button arrow located in the Editing group in the Home tab and then click *Go To* at the drop-down list. At the Find and Replace dialog box with the Go To tab selected, type the page number in the *Enter page number* text box and then press Enter. Click the Close button to close the dialog box.

Browsing in a Document

The Select Browse Object button located toward the bottom of the vertical scroll bar contains options for browsing through a document. Click this button and a palette of browsing choices displays. Use the options on the palette to move the insertion point to various features in a Word document. Position the arrow pointer on an option in the palette and the option name displays above the options (the option name may display below the options). The options on the palette and the location of the options vary depending on the last function performed.

Moving the Insertion Point with the Keyboard

To move the insertion point with the keyboard, use the arrow keys located to the right of the regular keyboard. You can also use the arrow keys on the numeric keypad. If you use these keys, make sure Num Lock is off. Use the arrow keys together with other keys to move the insertion point to various locations in the document as shown in Table 1.2.

When moving the insertion point, Word considers a word to be any series of characters between spaces. A paragraph is any text that is followed by a stroke of the Enter key. A page is text that is separated by a soft or hard page break. If you open a previously saved document, you can move the insertion point to where the insertion point was last located when the document was closed by pressing Shift + F5.

Table 1.2 Insertion Point Movement Commands

To move insertion point	Press
One character left	Left Arrow
One character right	Right Arrow
One line up	Up Arrow
One line down	Down Arrow

continues

Table 1.2 Insertion Point Movement Commands, continued

To move insertion point	Press
One word to the left	Ctrl + Left Arrow
One word to the right	Ctrl + Right Arrow
To end of a line	End
To beginning of a line	Home
To beginning of current paragraph	Ctrl + Up Arrow
To beginning of next paragraph	Ctrl + Down Arrow
Up one screen	Page Up
Down one screen	Page Down
To top of previous page	Ctrl + Page Up
To top of next page	Ctrl + Page Down
To beginning of document	Ctrl + Home
To end of document	Ctrl + End

Project 3b **Moving the Insertion Point and Browsing in a Document** **Part 2 of 2**

1. With **WL1-C1-P3-InterfaceApps.docx** open, move the insertion point to page 3 by completing the following steps:
   a. Click the Find button arrow located in the Editing group in the Home tab and then click *Go To* at the drop-down list.
   b. At the Find and Replace dialog box with the Go To tab selected, type 3 in the *Enter page number* text box and then press Enter.
   c. Click the Close button to close the Find and Replace dialog box.

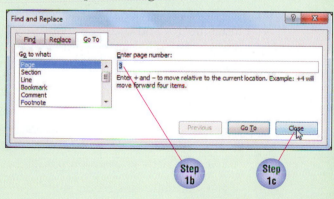

2. Click the Previous Page button located immediately above the Select Browse Object button on the vertical scroll bar. (This moves the insertion point to page 2.)

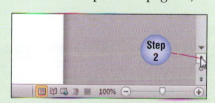

3. Click the Previous Page button again. (This moves the insertion point to page 1.)
4. Click the Next Page button located immediately below the Select Browse Object button on the vertical scroll bar. (This moves the insertion point to the beginning of page 2.)

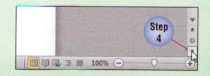

5. Move to the beginning of page 3 by completing the following steps:
   a. Click the Select Browse Object button.
   b. At the palette of browsing choices, click the last choice in the bottom row (*Browse by Page*). (This moves the insertion point to page 3.)
6. Press Ctrl + Home to move the insertion point to the beginning of the document.
7. Practice using the keyboard commands shown in Table 1.2 to move the insertion point within the document.
8. Close **WL1-C1-P3-InterfaceApps.docx**.

Step 5b

Step 5a

Project 4 — Insert and Delete Text

2 Parts

You will open a previously created document, save it with a new name, and then make editing changes to the document. The editing changes include selecting, inserting, and deleting text.

Inserting and Deleting Text

Editing a document may include inserting and/or deleting text. To insert text in a document, position the insertion point in the desired location and then type the text. Existing characters move to the right as you type the text. A number of options are available for deleting text. Some deletion commands are shown in Table 1.3.

Selecting Text ■■■■■■■■■■■■■■■■■■■■■■■■■■

You can use the mouse and/or keyboard to select a specific amount of text. Once selected, you can delete the text or perform other Word functions involving the selected text. When text is selected, it displays with a blue background as shown in Figure 1.8 and the Mini toolbar displays in a dimmed fashion and contains options for common tasks. Move the mouse pointer over the Mini toolbar and it becomes active. (You will learn more about the Mini toolbar in Chapter 2.)

Table 1.3 Deletion Commands

To delete	Press
Character right of insertion point	Delete key
Character left of insertion point	Backspace key
Text from insertion point to beginning of word	Ctrl + Backspace
Text from insertion point to end of word	Ctrl + Delete

Figure 1.8 Selected Text and Mini Toolbar

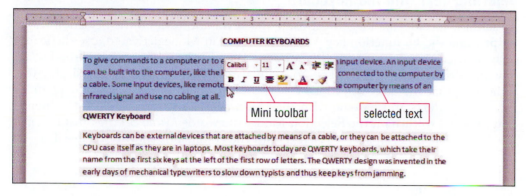

Selecting Text with the Mouse

Use the mouse to select a word, line, sentence, paragraph, or the entire document. Table 1.4 indicates the steps to follow to select various amounts of text. To select a specific amount of text such as a line or a paragraph, the instructions in the table tell you to click in the selection bar. The selection bar is the space located toward the left side of the document screen between the left edge of the page and the text. When the mouse pointer is positioned in the selection bar, the pointer turns into an arrow pointing up and to the right (instead of to the left).

To select an amount of text other than a word, sentence, or paragraph, position the I-beam pointer on the first character of the text to be selected, hold down the left mouse button, drag the I-beam pointer to the last character of the text to be selected, and then release the mouse button. You can also select all text between the current insertion point and the I-beam pointer. To do this, position the insertion point where you want the selection to begin, hold down the Shift key, click the I-beam pointer at the end of the selection, and then release the Shift key. To cancel a selection using the mouse, click anywhere in the document screen outside the selected text.

HINT
To select text vertically, hold down the Alt key while dragging with the mouse.

Table 1.4 Selecting with the Mouse

To select	Complete these steps using the mouse
A word	Double-click the word.
A line of text	Click in the selection bar to the left of the line.
Multiple lines of text	Drag in the selection bar to the left of the lines.
A sentence	Hold down the Ctrl key, then click anywhere in the sentence.
A paragraph	Double-click in the selection bar next to the paragraph or triple-click anywhere in the paragraph.
Multiple paragraphs	Drag in the selection bar.
An entire document	Triple-click in the selection bar.

Selecting Text with the Keyboard

If text is selected, any character you type replaces the selected text.

To select a specific amount of text using the keyboard, turn on the Selection Mode by pressing the F8 function key. With the Selection Mode activated, use the arrow keys to select the desired text. If you want to cancel the selection, press the Esc key and then press any arrow key. You can customize the Status bar to display text indicating that the Selection Mode is activated. To do this, right-click any blank location on the Status bar and then click *Selection Mode* at the pop-up list. When you press F8 to turn on the Selection Mode, the words *Extend Selection* display on the Status bar. You can also select text with the commands shown in Table 1.5.

Project 4a   Editing a Document

Part 1 of 2

1. Open **CompKeyboards.docx**. (This document is located in the Word2010L1C1 folder you copied to your storage medium.)
2. Save the document with Save As and name it **WL1-C1-P4-CompKeyboards**.
3. Change the word *give* in the first sentence of the first paragraph to *enter*.
4. Change the second *to* in the first sentence to *into*.
5. Delete the words *means of* in the first sentence in the *QWERTY Keyboard* section.
6. Select the words *and use no cabling at all* and the period that follows located at the end of the last sentence in the first paragraph, and then press the Delete key.
7. Insert a period immediately following the word *signal*.
8. Delete the heading line containing the text *QWERTY Keyboard* using the Selection Mode by completing the following steps:
   a. Position the insertion point immediately before the *Q* in *QWERTY*.
   b. Press F8 to turn on the Selection Mode.
   c. Press the Down Arrow key.
   d. Press the Delete key.
9. Complete steps similar to those in Step 8 to delete the heading line containing the text *DVORAK Keyboard*.
10. Begin a new paragraph with the sentence that reads *Keyboards have different physical appearances.* by completing the following steps:
    a. Position the insertion point immediately left of the *K* in *Keyboards* (the first word of the fifth sentence in the last paragraph).
    b. Press the Enter key.
11. Save **WL1-C1-P4-CompKeyboards.docx**.

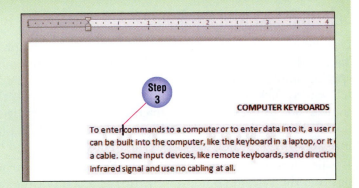

Table 1.5 Selecting with the Keyboard

To select	Press
One character to right	Shift + Right Arrow
One character to left	Shift + Left Arrow
To end of word	Ctrl + Shift + Right Arrow
To beginning of word	Ctrl + Shift + Left Arrow
To end of line	Shift + End
To beginning of line	Shift + Home
One line up	Shift + Up Arrow
One line down	Shift + Down Arrow
To beginning of paragraph	Ctrl + Shift + Up Arrow
To end of paragraph	Ctrl + Shift + Down Arrow
One screen up	Shift + Page Up
One screen down	Shift + Page Down
To end of document	Ctrl + Shift + End
To beginning of document	Ctrl + Shift + Home
Entire document	Ctrl + A or click Select button in Editing group and then Select All

Using the Undo and Redo Buttons

If you make a mistake and delete text that you did not intend to, or if you change your mind after deleting text and want to retrieve it, you can use the Undo or Redo buttons on the Quick Access toolbar. For example, if you type text and then click the Undo button, the text will be removed. You can undo text or commands. For example, if you add formatting such as bolding to text and then click the Undo button, the bolding is removed.

If you use the Undo button and then decide you do not want to reverse the original action, click the Redo button. For example, if you select and underline text and then decide to remove underlining, click the Undo button. If you then decide you want the underlining back on, click the Redo button. Many Word actions can be undone or redone. Some actions, however, such as printing and saving, cannot be undone or redone.

Word maintains actions in temporary memory. If you want to undo an action performed earlier, click the Undo button arrow. This causes a drop-down list to display. To make a selection from this drop-down list, click the desired action and the action, along with any actions listed above it in the drop-down list, is undone.

HINT You cannot undo a save.

Undo

Redo

1. With **WL1-C1-P4-CompKeyboards.docx** open, delete the last sentence in the last paragraph using the mouse by completing the following steps:
   a. Position the I-beam pointer anywhere in the sentence that begins *All keyboards have modifier keys . . . .*
   b. Hold down the Ctrl key and then click the left mouse button.

install software on a QWERTY keyboard that emulates a DVORAK keyboard. The ability to emulate other keyboards is convenient especially when working with foreign languages.

Keyboards have different physical appearances. Many keyboards have a separate numeric keypad, like that of a calculator, containing numbers and mathematical operators. Some keyboards are sloped and "broken" into two pieces to reduce strain. All keyboards have modifier keys that enable the user to change the symbol or character entered when a given key is pressed.

Steps 1a-1b

   c. Press the Delete key.
2. Delete the last paragraph by completing the following steps:
   a. Position the I-beam pointer anywhere in the last paragraph (the paragraph that begins *Keyboards have different physical appearances*).
   b. Triple-click the left mouse button.
   c. Press the Delete key.

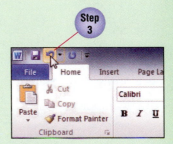

Step 3

3. Undo the deletion by clicking the Undo button on the Quick Access toolbar.
4. Redo the deletion by clicking the Redo button on the Quick Access toolbar.
5. Select the first sentence in the second paragraph and then delete it.
6. Select the first paragraph in the document and then delete it.
7. Undo the two deletions by completing the following steps:
   a. Click the Undo button arrow.
   b. Click the *second* Clear listed in the drop-down list. (This will redisplay the first sentence in the second paragraph as well as displaying the first paragraph. The sentence will be selected.)
8. Click outside the sentence to deselect it.
9. Save, print, and then close **WL1-C1-P4-CompKeyboards.docx**.

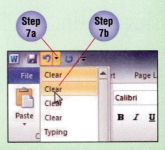

Step 7a   **Step 7b**

---

roject **5** **Complete a Spelling and Grammar Check**   **1 Part**

You will open a previously created document, save it with a new name, and then check the spelling and grammar in the document.

Checking the Spelling and Grammar in a Document ■■■

Two tools for creating thoughtful and well-written documents include a spelling checker and a grammar checker. The spelling checker finds misspelled words and offers replacement words. It also finds duplicate words and irregular capitalizations. When you spell check a document, the spelling checker compares the words in your document with the words in its dictionary. If the spelling checker finds a match, it passes over the word. If a match is not found for the word, the spelling checker will stop, select the word, and offer replacements.

The grammar checker will search a document for errors in grammar, punctuation, and word usage. The spelling checker and the grammar check can help you create a well-written document, but do not replace the need for proofreading. To complete a spelling and grammar check, click the Review tab and then click the Spelling & Grammar button in the Proofing group. You can also begin spelling and grammar checking by pressing the keyboard shortcut, F7. As the spelling and grammar checker selects text, make a choice from some of the options in the Spelling and Grammar dialog box as shown in Table 1.6.

By default, a spelling and grammar check are both completed on a document. If you want to check only the spelling in a document and not the grammar, remove the check mark from the *Check grammar* check box located in the lower left corner of the Spelling and Grammar dialog box. When spell checking a document, you can temporarily leave the Spelling and Grammar dialog box, make corrections in the document, and then resume spell checking by clicking the Resume button.

▼ **Quick Steps**

Check Spelling and Grammar
1. Click Review tab.
2. Click Spelling & Grammar button.
3. Change or ignore errors.
4. Click OK.

HINT

Complete a spelling and grammar check on a portion of a document by selecting the text first and then clicking the Spelling & Grammar button.

Spelling & Grammar

Table 1.6 Spelling and Grammar Dialog Box Buttons

Button	Function
Ignore Once	During spell checking, skips that occurrence of the word; in grammar checking, leaves currently selected text as written.
Ignore All	During spell checking, skips that occurrence of the word and all other occurrences of the word in the document.
Ignore Rule	During grammar checking, leaves currently selected text as written and ignores the current rule for remainder of the grammar check.
Add to Dictionary	Adds selected word to the spelling check dictionary.
Delete	Deletes the currently selected word(s).
Change	Replaces selected word in sentence with selected word in *Suggestions* list box.
Change All	Replaces selected word in sentence with selected word in *Suggestions* list box and all other occurrences of the word.
AutoCorrect	Inserts selected word and correct spelling of word in AutoCorrect dialog box.
Explain	During grammar checking, displays grammar rule information about the selected text.
Undo	Reverses most recent spelling and grammar action.
Next Sentence	Accepts manual changes made to sentence and then continues grammar checking.
Options	Displays a dialog box with options for customizing a spelling and grammar check.

1. Open **TechOccTrends.docx**.
2. Save the document with Save As and name it **WL1-C1-P5-TechOccTrends**.
3. Click the Review tab.
4. Click the Spelling & Grammar button in the Proofing group.

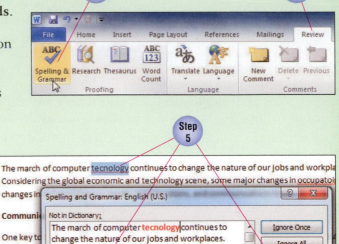

5. The spelling checker selects the word *tecnology*. The proper spelling is selected in the *Suggestions* list box, so click the Change button (or Change All button).
6. The spelling checker selects the word *occupatoins*. The proper spelling of the word is selected in the *Suggestions* list box, so click the Change button (or Change All button).
7. The grammar checker selects the sentence that begins *One key to being successful . . .* and displays *trends* and *a trend* in the *Suggestions* list box. Click *a trend* in the *Suggestions* list box and then click the Change button.

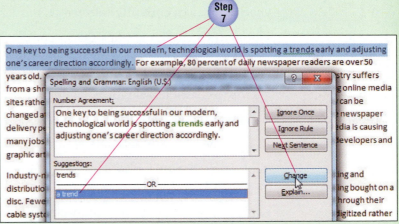

8. The grammar checker selects the sentence that begins *Young reader are not as interested . . .* and displays *reader is* and *readers are* in the *Suggestions* text box. Click the Explain button, read the information about subject-verb agreement that displays in the Word Help window, and then click the Close button located in the upper right corner of the Word Help window.
9. Click *readers are* in the *Suggestions* text box and then click the Change button.
10. The spelling checker selects *excelent*. The proper spelling is selected in the *Suggestions* list box, so click the Change button.
11. The grammar checker selects the sentence that begins *The number of printing and lithography job's is shrinking . . . .* Click the Explain button, read the information about plural or possessive that displays in the Word Help window, and then click the Close button located in the upper right corner of the Word Help window.
12. With *jobs* selected in the *Suggestions* list box, click the Change button.
13. The spelling checker selects the word *sucessful* and offers *successful* in the *Suggestions* text box. Since this word is misspelled in another location in the document, click the Change All button.

14. The spelling checker selects the word *are* that is used twice in a row. Click the Delete button to delete the word.
15. When the message displays telling you that the spelling and grammar check is complete, click the OK button.
16. Save, print, and then close **WL1-C1-P5-TechOccTrends .docx**.

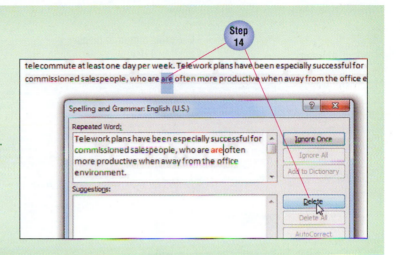

Project **6** **Use the Help Feature**   **2 Parts**

You need to learn more about selecting text and saving a document so you decide to use Help to research these features.

Using Help

Word's Help feature is an on-screen reference manual containing information about all Word features and commands. Word's Help feature is similar to Windows Help and the Help features in Excel, PowerPoint, and Access. Get help by clicking the Microsoft Word Help button located in the upper right corner of the screen (a question mark in a circle) or by pressing the keyboard shortcut, F1. This displays the Word Help window. In this window, type a topic, feature, or question in the Search text box and then press Enter. Topics related to the search text display in the Word Help window. Click a topic that interests you. If the topic window contains a <u>Show All</u> hyperlink in the upper right corner, click this hyperlink and the information expands to show all help information related to the topic. When you click the <u>Show All</u> hyperlink, it becomes the <u>Hide All</u> hyperlink.

The Help tab Backstage view, shown in Figure 1.9, contains an option for displaying the Word Help window as well as other options. To display the Help tab Backstage view, click the File tab and then click the Help tab. At the Help tab Backstage view, click the Microsoft Office Help button in the *Support* section to display the Word Help window and click the Getting Started button to access the Microsoft website that displays information about getting started with Word 2010. Click the Contact Us button in the *Support* section and the Microsoft Support website displays. Click the Options button in the *Tools for Working With Office* section and the Word Options dialog box displays. You will learn about this dialog box in a later chapter. Click the Check for Updates button and the Microsoft Update website displays with information on available updates. The right side of the Help tab Backstage view displays information about Office and Word.

▼ **Quick Steps**

Use Help Feature
1. Click Microsoft Word Help button.
2. Type topic, feature, or question.
3. Press Enter.
4. Click desired topic.

Figure 1.9 Help Tab Backstage View

Click this button to display the Word Help window.

Click this button to display the Microsoft website with information on getting started with Word.

Click this button to display the Microsoft Support website.

Click this button to display the Word Options dialog box.

Click this button to display the Microsoft Update website.

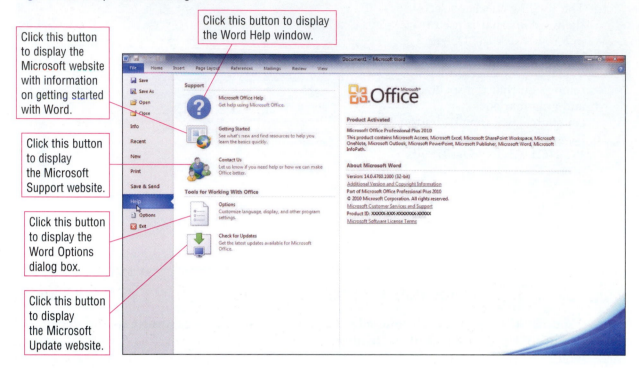

Project 6a **Using the Help Feature** **Part 1 of 2**

1. At a blank document, click the Microsoft Word Help button located in the upper right corner of the screen.
2. At the Word Help window, type **save a document** in the Search text box.
3. Press the Enter key.
4. When the list of topics displays, click the Save a document in Word hyperlink. (If your Word Help window does not display the online options, check the lower right corner of the window. If the word *Offline* displays, click *Offline* and then click the *Show content from Office.com* option at the drop-down list.)
5. Click the Show All hyperlink that displays in the upper right corner of the window.

Step 1

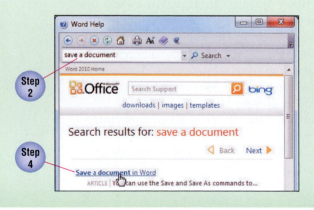

6. Read the information about saving a document.

7. Print the information by clicking the Print button located toward the top of the Word Help window.

8. At the Print dialog box, click the Print button.

9. Click the Close button to close the Word Help window.

10. Click the File tab and then click the Help tab.

11. Click the Getting Started button in the *Support* section. (You must be connected to the Internet to display the web page.)

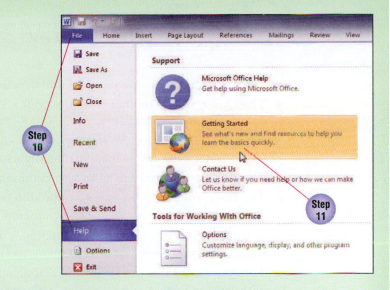

12. Look at the information that displays at the website and then click the Close button located in the upper right corner of the web page.

13. Click the File tab and then click the Help tab.

14. Click the Contact Us button, look at the information that displays at the website, and then close the web page.

Getting Help in a Dialog Box or Backstage View

Some dialog boxes, as well as the Backstage view, contain a Help button you can click to display a help window with specific information about the dialog box or Backstage view. After reading and/or printing the information, close a dialog box by clicking the Close button located in the upper right corner of the dialog box or close the Backstage view by clicking the File tab or clicking any other tab in the ribbon.

| Project 6b | Getting Help in a Dialog Box and Backstage View | Part 2 of 2 |

1. At a blank document, click the File tab and then click the Save As button.

2. At the Save As dialog box, click the Help button located in the upper right corner of the dialog box.

3. Read the information about saving files and then click the Close button located in the upper right corner of the dialog box.

4. Close the Save As dialog box.

5. Click the File tab.

6. At the Backstage view, click the Help button located in the upper right corner of the window.

7. Click the Introducing Backstage hyperlink.

8. Read the information about the Backstage view.

9. Close the Word Help window and then click the File tab to return to the document.

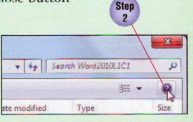

Chapter Summary

- Refer to Figure 1.1 and Table 1.1 for a listing of key word screen features.
- The Quick Access toolbar is located above the File tab and contains buttons for commonly used commands.
- Click the File tab and the Backstage view displays containing tabs and buttons for working with and managing documents
- The ribbon area contains tabs with commands and options divided into groups.
- The insertion point displays as a blinking vertical line and indicates the position of the next character to be entered in the document.
- Document names can contain a maximum of 255 characters, including the drive letter and folder names, and may include spaces.
- The insertion point can be moved throughout the document without interfering with text by using the mouse, the keyboard, or the mouse combined with the keyboard.
- The scroll box on the vertical scroll bar indicates the location of the text in the document in relation to the remainder of the document.
- Click the Select Browse Object button located at the bottom of the vertical scroll bar to display options for browsing through a document.
- You can move the insertion point by character, word, screen, or page, and from the first to the last character in a document. Refer to Table 1.2 for keyboard insertion point movement commands.
- You can delete text by character, word, line, several lines, or partial page using specific keys or by selecting text using the mouse or the keyboard.
- You can select a specific amount of text using the mouse or the keyboard. Refer to Table 1.4 for information on selecting with the mouse and refer to Table 1.5 for information on selecting with the keyboard.
- Use the Undo button on the Quick Access toolbar if you change your mind after typing, deleting, or formatting text and want to undo the action. Use the Redo button to redo something that had been undone with the Undo button.
- The spelling checker matches the words in your document with the words in its dictionary. If a match is not found, the word is selected and possible corrections are suggested. The grammar checker searches a document for errors in grammar, style, punctuation, and word usage. When a grammar error is detected, display information about the error by clicking the Explain button at the Spelling & Grammar dialog box.
- Word's Help feature is an on-screen reference manual containing information about all Word features and commands. Click the Microsoft Word Help button or press F1 to display the Word Help window.
- Click the File tab and then click the Help tab to display the Help tab Backstage view.
- Some dialog boxes, as well as the Backstage view, contain a Help button you can click to display information specific to the dialog box or Backstage view.

Commands Review

FEATURE	RIBBON TAB, GROUP	BUTTON, OPTION	FILE TAB	KEYBOARD SHORTCUT
Close document			Close	Ctrl + F4
Exit Word		❌	Exit	
Find and Replace dialog box with Go To tab selected	Home, Editing	🔍, Go To		Ctrl + G
Help tab Backstage view			Help	
New blank document			New, Create	Ctrl + N
Open dialog box			Open	Ctrl + O
Print tab Backstage view			Print	Ctrl + P
Save document		💾	Save	Ctrl + S
Select document	Home, Editing	▷, Select All		Ctrl + A
Spelling and Grammar dialog box	Review, Proofing	✓ ABC		F7
Word Help window		❓		F1

Concepts Check Test Your Knowledge

Completion: In the space provided at the right, indicate the correct term, symbol, or command.

1. This toolbar contains the Save button. _____

2. Click this tab to display the Backstage view. _____

3. This is the area located toward the top of the screen that contains tabs with commands and options divided into groups. _____

4. This bar, located toward the bottom of the screen, displays number of pages and words, View buttons, and the Zoom slider bar. _____

5. This tab is selected by default. _____

6. This feature automatically corrects certain words as you type them. _____

7. This feature inserts an entire item when you type a few identifying characters and then press Enter or F3.

    _____

8. This is the keyboard shortcut to display the Print tab Backstage view.

    _____

9. This is the keyboard shortcut to close a document.

    _____

10. This is the keyboard shortcut to display a new blank document.

    _____

11. Use this keyboard shortcut to move the insertion point to the beginning of the previous page.

    _____

12. Use this keyboard shortcut to move the insertion point to the end of the document.

    _____

13. Press this key on the keyboard to delete the character left of the insertion point.

    _____

14. Using the mouse, do this to select one word.

    _____

15. To select various amounts of text using the mouse, you can click in this bar.

    _____

16. Click this tab to display the Spelling & Grammar button in the Proofing group.

    _____

17. This is the keyboard shortcut to display the Word Help window. _____

Skills Check Assess Your Performance

Assessment

1 TYPE AND EDIT A DOCUMENT ON FUZZY LOGIC

1. Open Word and then type the text in Figure 1.10. Correct any errors highlighted by the spell checker and space once after end-of-sentence punctuation.
2. Make the following changes to the document:
   a. Delete *AI* in the first sentence of the first paragraph and then insert *artificial intelligence*.
   b. Insert the words *for approximations and* between the words *allowing* and *incomplete* located in the first sentence of the first paragraph.
   c. Insert the words *or numerical* between the words *yes/no* and *information* in the second sentence of the first paragraph.
   d. Delete the words *hard to come by* in the last sentence of the first paragraph and replace with the word *rare*.
   e. Insert the letters *SQL* between the words *logic* and *database* in the last sentence of the second paragraph.

f. Move the insertion point immediately left of the period at the end of the last sentence of the last paragraph, type a comma, and then insert the words *and trade shares on the Tokyo Stock Exchange*. Delete the word *and* before the words *automobile transmissions* in the last sentence.

g. Join the first and second paragraphs.

h. Delete the name *Marie Solberg* and then type your first and last names.

3. Save the document and name it **WL1-C1-A1-FuzzyLogic**.

4. Print and then close **WL1-C1-A1-FuzzyLogic.docx**.

Figure 1.10 Assessment 1

Fuzzy Logic

The fuzzy logic branch of AI attempts to model human reasoning by allowing incomplete input data. Instead of demanding precise yes/no information, fuzzy logic systems allow users to input "fuzzy" data. The terminology used by the system is deliberately vague and includes terms such as very probable, somewhat decreased, reasonable, or very slight. This is an attempt to simulate real-world conditions, where precise answers are hard to come by.

A fuzzy logic system attempts to work more naturally with the user by piecing together an answer in a manner similar to that used by a traditional expert system. Fuzzy logic database queries seem significantly more human than traditional queries.

Fuzzy logic systems are much more common in Japan than they are in the United States, where traditional expert systems and neural networks tend to be favored. In Japan, microprocessors specially designed by Toshiba and Hitachi to use fuzzy logic operate subways, consumer electronics, and automobile transmissions.

Created by Marie Solberg
Monday, October 1, 2012
Note: Please insert this information between 4th and 5th sections.

Assessment

2 CHECK THE SPELLING AND GRAMMAR OF A COMPUTER SOFTWARE DOCUMENT

1. Open **FutureSoftware.docx**.

2. Save the document with Save As and name it **WL1-C1-A2-FutureSoftware**.

3. Complete a spelling and grammar check on the document. You determine what to change and what to leave as written.

4. Insert the sentence *Wizards are small programs designed to assist users by automating tasks.* between the third and fourth sentences in the *User-Friendly System Software* section.

5. Move the insertion point to the end of the document, type your first and last names, press Shift + Enter, and then type the current date.

6. Save, print, and then close **WL1-C1-A2-FutureSoftware.docx**.

3 CREATE A DOCUMENT DESCRIBING KEYBOARD SHORTCUTS

1. Click the Microsoft Word Help button, type **keyboard shortcuts**, and then press Enter.
2. At the Word Help window, click the <u>Keyboard shortcuts for Microsoft Word</u> hyperlink.
3. At the keyboard shortcut window, click the <u>Show All</u> hyperlink.
4. Read through the information in the Word Help window.
5. Create a document describing four keyboard shortcuts.
6. Save the document and name it **WL1-C1-A3-KeyboardShortcuts**.
7. Print and then close **WL1-C1-A3-KeyboardShortcuts.docx**.

Visual Benchmark Demonstrate Your Proficiency

CREATE A COVER PAGE

1. At a blank document, press the Enter key three times and then type the personal business letter shown in Figure 1.11 on the next page by following the directions in red.
2. Save the completed letter and name it **WL1-C1-VB-CoverLtr**.
3. Print and then close the document.

Figure 1.11 Visual Benchmark

4520 South Park Street *(press Shift + Enter)*
Newark, NJ 07122 *(press Shift + Enter)*
(Current date) *(press Enter two times)*

Mrs. Sylvia Hammond *(press Shift + Enter)*
Sales Director, Eastern Division *(press Shift + Enter)*
Grand Style Products *(press Shift + Enter)*
1205 Sixth Street *(press Shift + Enter)*
Newark, NJ 07102 *(press Enter)*

Dear Mrs. Hammond: *(press Enter)*

Thank you for agreeing to meet with me next Wednesday. Based on our initial conversation, it seems that my ability to sell solutions rather than products is a good fit for your needs as you seek to expand your visibility in the region. *(press Enter)*

As noted in the enclosed resume, I have led an under-performing product division to generating 33 percent of total revenue (up from 5 percent) at our location, and delivering, from a single location, 25 percent of total sales for our 20-site company. Having completed this turnaround over the last 5 years, I'm eager for new challenges where my proven skills in sales, marketing, and program/event planning can contribute to a company's bottom line. *(press Enter)*

I have been thinking about the challenges you described in building your presence at the retail level, and I have some good ideas to share at our meeting. I am excited about the future of Grand Style Products and eager to contribute to your growth. *(press Enter)*

Sincerely, *(press Enter two times)*

(Student Name) *(press Enter)*

Enclosure

Case Study   Apply Your Skills

Part 1

You are the assistant to Paul Brewster, the training coordinator at a medium-sized service-oriented business. You have been asked by Mr. Brewster to prepare a document for Microsoft Word users within the company explaining how to use the Save As command when saving a document rather than the Save command. Save the document and name it **WL1-C1-CS-SaveAs**. Print and then close the document.

Part 2

Mr. Brewster would like a document containing a brief summary of some basic Word commands for use in Microsoft Word training classes. He has asked you to prepare a document containing the following information:

- A brief explanation on how to move the insertion point to a specific page
- Keyboard shortcuts to move the insertion point to the beginning and end of a text line and beginning and end of a document
- Commands to delete text from the insertion point to the beginning of the word and from the insertion point to the end of the word
- Steps to select a word, a sentence, a paragraph, and an entire document using the mouse.
- Keyboard shortcut to select the entire document

Save the document and name it **WL1-C1-CS-WordCommands**. Print and then close the document.

Part 3

According to Mr. Brewster, the company is considering updating the Resources Department computers to Microsoft Office 2010. He has asked you to use the Internet to go to the Microsoft home page at www.microsoft.com and then use the search feature to find information on the system requirements for Office Professional Plus 2010. When you find the information, type a document that contains the Office Professional Plus 2010 system requirements for the computer and processor, memory, hard disk space, and operating system. Save the document and name it **WL1-C1-CS-SystemReq**. Print and then close the document.

Formatting Characters and Paragraphs

PERFORMANCE OBJECTIVES

Upon successful completion of Chapter 2, you will be able to:

- Change the font and font effects
- Format selected text with buttons on the Mini toolbar
- Apply styles from Quick Styles sets
- Apply themes
- Change the alignment of text in paragraphs
- Indent text in paragraphs
- Increase and decrease spacing before and after paragraphs
- Repeat the last action
- Automate formatting with Format Painter
- Change line spacing in a document
- Reveal and compare formatting

A Word document is based on a template that applies default formatting. Some of the default formats include 11-point Calibri, line spacing of 1.15, 10 points of spacing after each paragraph, and left-aligned text. The appearance of a document in the document screen and how it looks when printed is called the *format*. In this chapter, you will learn about character formatting that can include such elements as changing the typeface, type size, and typestyle as well as applying font effects such as bolding and italicizing. The Paragraph group in the Home tab includes buttons for applying formatting to paragraphs of text. In Word, a paragraph is any amount of text followed by the press of the Enter key. In this chapter, you will learn to apply paragraph formatting to text such as changing text alignment, indenting text, applying formatting with Format Painter, and changing line spacing. Model answers for this chapter's projects appear on the following pages.

Word2010L1C2

Note: Before beginning the projects, copy to your storage medium the Word2010L1C2 subfolder from the Word2010L1 folder on the CD that accompanies this textbook and then make Word2010L1C2 the active folder.

GLOSSARY OF TERMS

A

Access time: The time a storage device spends locating a particular file.
Aggregation software: E-commerce software application that combines online activities to provide one-stop shopping for consumers.
Analog signals: Signals composed of continuous waves transmitted at a certain frequency range over a medium, such as a telephone line.

B

Backup: A second copy kept of valuable data.
Bandwidth: The number of bits that can be transferred per second over a given medium or network.
Beta-testing: One of the last steps in software development that involves allowing outside people to use the software to see if it works as designed.

C

Chinese abacus: Pebbles strung on a rod inside a frame. Pebbles in the upper part of an abacus correspond to 5×10^1, or 5, for the first column; 5×10^1, or 50, for the second column; 5×10^2, or 500, for the third column; and so on.
Chip: A thin wafer of *silicon* containing electronic circuitry that performs various functions, such as mathematical calculations, storage, or controlling computer devices.
Cluster: A group of two or more sectors on a disk, which is the smallest unit of storage space used to store data.
Coding: A term used by programmers to refer to the act of writing source code.
Crackers: A term coined by computer hackers for those who intentionally enter (or hack) computer systems to damage them.

CREATED BY SUSAN ASHBY
WEDNESDAY, FEBRUARY 22, 2012

Project 1 Apply Character Formatting

WL1-C2-P1-CompTerms.docx

COMMERCIAL LIFE CYCLE

The software life cycle is the term used to describe the phases involved in the process of creating, testing, and releasing new commercial software products. This cycle is similar to the process used in developing information systems, except that in this case the cycle focuses on the creation and release of a software program, not the development of a customized information system. The commercial software life cycle is repeated every time a new version of a program is needed. The phases in the software life cycle include the following: proposal and planning, design, implementation, testing, and public release.

PROPOSAL AND PLANNING

In the proposal and planning phase of a new software product, software developers will describe the proposed software program and what it is supposed to accomplish. In the case of existing software, the proposal and planning stage can be used to describe any new features and improvements. Older software programs are often revised to take advantage of new hardware or software developments and to add new functions or features.

DESIGN

Developers are ready to begin the design process once the decision has been made to create or upgrade a software program. This step produces specifications documenting the details of the software to be written by programmers. Developers use problem-solving steps to determine the appropriate specifications.

IMPLEMENTATION

The implementation phase of the software life cycle is usually the most difficult. Development teams often spend late nights and weekends writing code and making it work. If the planning and design efforts have been successful, this phase should go well, but unanticipated problems inevitably crop up and have to be solved. The end result of the implementation phase is the production of a prototype called an alpha product, which is used by the development team for testing purposes. The alpha product can be revised to incorporate any improvements suggested by team members.

TESTING

A quality assurance (QA) team usually develops a testing harness, which is a scripted set of tests that a program must undergo before being considered ready for public release. These tests might cover events such as very large input loads, maximum number of users, running on several different platforms, and simulated power outages. Once testing is finished, a beta version of the software program is created for testing outside of the development group, often by a select group of knowledgeable consumers. Any suggestions they make can be used to improve the product before it is released to the general public. Once the beta version is finalized, the user manual can be written or updated. At this point, the software developers would send the master CDs to duplicators for mass production.

PUBLIC RELEASE AND SUPPORT

When the product is deemed ready for widespread use, it is declared "gold" and released to the public. The software life cycle now goes back to the beginning phases as software developers think of new ways to improve the product.

Project 2 Apply Styles and Themes

WL1-C2-P2-SoftwareCycle.docx

PROPERTY PROTECTION ISSUES

The ability to link computers through the Internet offers many advantages. With linked computers, we can quickly and easily communicate with other users around the world, sharing files and other data with a few simple keystrokes. The convenience provided by linking computers through the Internet also has some drawbacks. Computer viruses can travel around the world in seconds, damaging programs and files. Hackers can enter into systems without authorization and steal or alter data. In addition, the wealth of information on the Web and the increased ease with which it can be copied have made plagiarizing easy. Plagiarism is using others' ideas and creations (their intellectual property) without permission.

All of these ethical issues revolve around property rights, the right of someone to protect and control the things he or she owns. A solid legal framework ensuring the protection of personal property exists, but computers have created many new issues that challenge conventional interpretations of these laws.

Intellectual Property

Intellectual property includes just about anything that can be created by the agency of the human mind. To encourage innovation and improvement and thus benefit society as a whole, our legal system grants patents to those who invent new and better ways of doing things. A patent awards ownership of an idea or invention to its creator for a fixed number of years. This allows the inventor the right to charge others for the use of the invention. To encourage and protect artistic and literary endeavors, authors and artists are awarded copyrights to the material they create, allowing them the right to control the use of their works and charge others for their use. Patent and copyright violation is punishable by law, and prosecutions and convictions are frequent. The legal framework protecting intellectual property has come under constant challenge as technology has moved forward.

With the Internet, accessing and copying written works that may be protected is easy. Today, authors are increasingly dismayed to find copies of their works appearing on the Internet without their permission. The same problem occurs with graphic and artistic images on the Internet, such as photographs and artwork. Once placed on the Web, they can be copied and reused numerous times. Unauthorized copying of items appearing on websites is difficult and sometimes even technically impossible to prevent.

Page 1

Project 3 Apply Paragraph Formatting and Use Format Painter

WL1-C2-P3-IntelProp.docx

Fair Use

Situations exist in which using work written by others is permissible. Using another person's material without permission is allowed as long as the use is acknowledged, is used for noncommercial purposes, and involves only the use of limited excerpts of protected material, such as no more than 300 words of prose and one line of poetry. Such a right is called fair use and is dealt with under the U.S. Copyright Act, Section 107. Here, in part, is what the Fair Use law states:

> [A] copyrighted work, including such use by reproduction in copies of phonorecords or by any other means specified by that section, for purposes such as criticism, comment, news reporting, teaching (including multiple copies for classroom use), scholarship, or research, is not an infringement of copyright.

Even under the Fair Use provision, describing the source of the material is important. Plagiarism may be punished by law, and in many educational institutions it can result in suspension or even expulsion.

Intellectual Property Protection

The problem faced by intellectual property owners in the digital age is twofold. First, new technology has presented new difficulties in interpreting previous understandings dealing with the protection of intellectual property, such as difficulties applying the Fair Use provision to Internet material. Second, the new technical capabilities brought about by digital technologies have greatly increased the ease with which intellectual property can be appropriated and used without authorization, making policing and protecting intellectual property very difficult. Intellectual property owners have formed new organizations to ensure the protection of their property.

REFERENCES

Fuller, Floyd and Brian Larson. (2010) *Computers: Understanding Technology* (pp. 659-661). St. Paul, MN: Paradigm Publishing.

Myerson, Jean A. (2008) *Intellectual Properties* (pp. 123-126). New Orleans, LA: Robicheaux Publishing House.

Patterson, Margaret and Montgomery Littleton. (2011) *Issues of Plagiarism*. Chicago, IL: Lansing and Edelman Publishers.

Page 2

Model Answers

Talbot, Lenora J. and Marcella S. Angleton. (2010) *Internet Considerations.* Portland, OR: Pacific Blue Publishing Group.

Prepared by Clarissa Markham
Edited by Joshua Streeter

Page 3

Solving Problems

In groups or individually, brainstorm possible solutions to the issues presented.

- Computers currently offer both *visual* and *audio* communications. Under development are devices and technologies that will allow users to smell various types of products while looking at them in the computer screen. What are some new applications of this technology for the food industry? Can you think of other industries that could use this capability?

- Picture yourself working in the Information Technology department of a mid-sized company. Your responsibilities include evaluating employees' computer system needs and recommending equipment purchases. Recently, the company president hired a new employee and you must evaluate her computer system needs. Considering that you have a budget of $5,500 for equipping the new employee with the computer system (or systems), research possible configurations and prepare a report outlining your recommendations, including costs. Assume that for her office she needs a complete system, including a system unit, monitor, printer, speakers, keyboard, and mouse.

Project 4 Format Computer Issues Document

WL1-C2-P4-CompIssues.docx

Project 1   Apply Character Formatting   4 Parts

You will open a document containing a glossary of terms, add additional text, and then format the document by applying character formatting.

Changing Fonts

The Font group shown in Figure 2.1 contains a number of buttons you can use to apply character formatting to text in a document. The top row contains buttons for changing the font and font size as well as buttons for increasing and decreasing the size of the font changing the text case, and clearing formatting. You can remove character formatting (as well as paragraph formatting) applied to text by clicking the Clear Formatting button in the Font group. Remove only character formatting from selected text by pressing the keyboard shortcut, Ctrl + spacebar. The bottom row contains buttons for applying typestyles such as bold, italic, and underline and for applying text effects, highlighting, and color.

A Word document is based on a template that formats text in 11-point Calibri. You may want to change this default to some other font for such reasons as changing the mood of the document, enhancing the visual appeal, and increasing the readability of the text. A font consists of three elements — typeface, type size, and typestyle.

A typeface is a set of characters with a common design and shape and can be decorative or plain and either monospaced or proportional. Word refers to typeface as *font*. A monospaced typeface allots the same amount of horizontal space for each

HINT
Change the default font by selecting the desired font at the Font dialog box and then clicking the Set As Default button.

HINT
Use a serif typeface for text-intensive documents.

Figure 2.1 Font Group Buttons

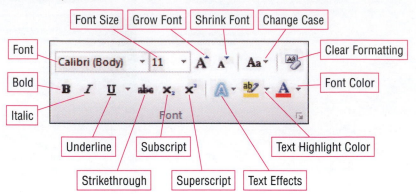

character while a proportional typeface allots a varying amount of space for each character. Proportional typefaces are divided into two main categories: *serif* and *sans serif*. A serif is a small line at the end of a character stroke. Consider using a serif typeface for text-intensive documents because the serifs help move the reader's eyes across the page. Use a sans serif typeface for headings, headlines, and advertisements.

Microsoft added six new fonts in Office 2007 that are available in Office 2010 including the default, Calibri, as well as Cambria, Candara, Consolas, Constantia, and Corbel. Calibri, Candara, and Corbel are sans serif typefaces; Cambria and Constantia are serif typefaces; and Consolas is monospaced. These six typefaces as well as some other popular typefaces are shown in Table 2.1.

Type size is generally set in proportional size. The size of proportional type is measured vertically in units called *points*. A point is approximately $1/72$ of an inch — the higher the point size, the larger the characters. Within a typeface, characters may have a varying style. Type styles are divided into four main categories: regular, bold, italic, and bold italic.

Use the Font button in the Font group to change the font and the Font Size button to change the size. When you select text and then click the Font button arrow, a drop-down gallery displays of font options. Hover your mouse pointer over a font option and the selected text in the document displays with the font applied. You can continue hovering your mouse pointer over different font options to see how the selected text displays in the specified font. The Font button drop-down gallery is an example of the *live preview* feature, which allows you to see how the font formatting affects your text without having to return to the document. The live preview feature is also available when you click the Font Size button arrow.

Table 2.1 Serif and Sans Serif Typefaces

Serif Typefaces	Sans Serif Typefaces	Monospaced Typefaces
Cambria	Calibri	Consolas
Constantia	Candara	Courier New
Times New Roman	Corbel	Lucida Console
Bookman Old Style	Arial	MS Gothic

1. Open **CompTerms.docx**.
2. Save the document with Save As and name it **WL1-C2-P1-CompTerms**.
3. Change the typeface to Cambria by completing the following steps:
   a. Select the entire document by pressing Ctrl + A. (You can also select all text in the document by clicking the Select button in the Editing group and then clicking *Select All* at the drop-down list.)
   b. Click the Font button arrow, scroll down the Font drop-down gallery until *Cambria* displays, and then hover the mouse pointer over *Cambria*. This displays a live preview of the text set in Cambria.
   c. Click the mouse button on *Cambria*.

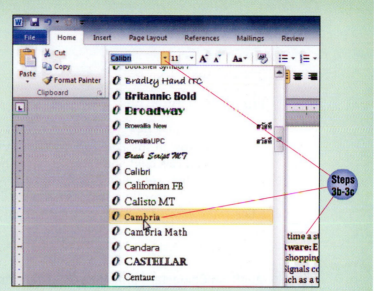

Steps 3b-3c

4. Change the type size to 14 by completing the following steps:
   a. With the text in the document still selected, click the Font Size button arrow.
   b. At the drop-down gallery that displays, hover the mouse pointer on *14* and look at the live preview of the text with 14 points applied.
   c. Click the left mouse button on *14*.

Step 4a

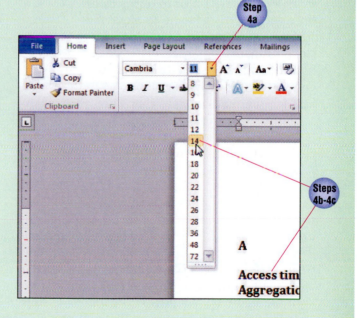

Steps 4b-4c

5. At the document screen, deselect the text by clicking anywhere in the document.
6. Change the type size and typeface by completing the following steps:
   a. Press Ctrl + A to select the entire document.
   b. Click three times on the Shrink Font button in the Font group. (This decreases the size to 10 points.)
   c. Click twice on the Grow Font button. (This increases the size of the font to 12 points.)

Step 6b

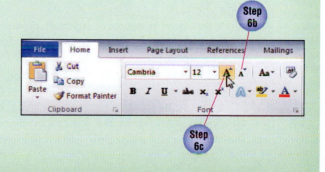

Step 6c

d. Click the Font button arrow, scroll down the drop-down gallery, and then click *Constantia*. (The most recently used fonts display at the beginning of the document, followed by a listing of all fonts.)
7. Save **WL1-C2-P1-CompTerms.docx**.

Choosing a Typestyle

Apply a particular typestyle to text with the Bold, Italic, or Underline buttons in the bottom row in the Font group. You can apply more than one style to text. For example, you can bold and italicize the same text or apply all three styles to the same text. Click the Underline button arrow and a drop-down gallery displays with underlining options such as a double line, dashed line, and thicker underline. Click the *Underline Color* option at the Underline button drop-down gallery and a side menu displays with color options.

| Project 1b | Applying Character Formatting to Text as You Type | Part 2 of 4 |

1. With **WL1-C2-P1-CompTerms.docx** open, press Ctrl + Home to move the insertion point to the beginning of the document.
2. Type a heading for the document by completing the following steps:
   a. Click the Bold button in the Font group. (This turns on bold.)
   b. Click the Underline button in the Font group. (This turns on underline.)
   c. Type Glossary of Terms.

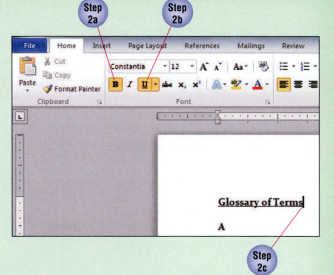

3. Press Ctrl + End to move the insertion point to the end of the document.
4. Type the text shown in Figure 2.2 with the following specifications:
   a. While typing the document, make the appropriate text bold as shown in the figure by completing the following steps:
      1) Click the Bold button in the Font group. (This turns on bold.)
      2) Type the text.
      3) Click the Bold button in the Font group. (This turns off bold.)
   b. While typing the document, italicize the appropriate text as shown in the figure by completing the following steps:
      1) Click the Italic button in the Font group.
      2) Type the text.
      3) Click the Italic button in the Font group.
5. After typing the text, press the Enter key twice and then press Ctrl + Home to move the insertion point to the beginning of the document.

6. Change the underlining below the title by completing the following steps:
   a. Select the title <u>Glossary of Terms</u>.
   b. Click the Underline button arrow and then click the third underline option from the top of the drop-down gallery.
   c. Click the Underline button arrow, point to the *Underline Color* option, and then click the Red color (second color option from the left) in the *Standard Colors* section.

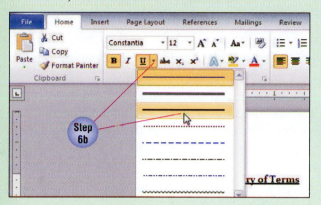

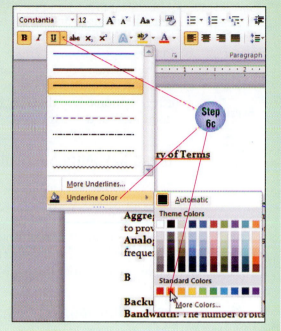

7. With the title still selected, change the font size to 14 points.
8. Save **WL1-C2-P1-CompTerms.docx**.

Figure 2.2 Project 1b

C

Chip: A thin wafer of *silicon* containing electronic circuitry that performs various functions, such as mathematical calculations, storage, or controlling computer devices.

Cluster: A group of two or more *sectors* on a disk, which is the smallest unit of storage space used to store data.

Coding: A term used by programmers to refer to the act of writing source code.

Crackers: A term coined by computer hackers for those who intentionally enter (or hack) computer systems to damage them.

Choosing a Font Effect

Apply font effects with some of the buttons in the top and bottom rows in the Font group or clear all formatting from selected text with the Clear Formatting button. Change the case of text with the Change Case button drop-down list. Click the Change Case button in the top row in the Font group and a drop-down list displays with the options *Sentence case*, *lowercase*, *UPPERCASE*, *Capitalize Each Word*, and *tOGGLE cASE*. You can also change the case of selected text with the keyboard shortcut, Shift + F3. Each time you press Shift + F3, selected text cycles through the case options.

Change Case

Clear Formatting

Strikethrough

Subscript

Superscript

Text Effects

Text Highlight
Color

Font Color

Press Ctrl +] to
increase font size by
one point and press
Ctrl + [to decrease
font size by one point.

The bottom row in the Font group contains buttons for applying font effects. Use the Strikethrough button to draw a line through selected text. This has a practical application in some legal documents in which deleted text must be retained in the document. Use the Subscript button to create text that is lowered slightly below the line such as the chemical formula H_2O. Use the Superscript button to create text that is raised slightly above the text line such as the mathematical equation four to the third power (written as 4^3). Click the Text Effects button in the bottom row and a drop-down gallery displays with effect options. Use the Text Highlight Color button to highlight specific text in a document and use the Font Color button to change the color of text.

Using Keyboard Shortcuts

Several of the buttons in the Font group have keyboard shortcuts. For example, you can press Ctrl + B to turn on bold or press Ctrl + I to turn on italics. Position the mouse pointer on a button and an enhanced ScreenTip displays with the name of the button; the keyboard shortcut, if any; a description of the action performed by the button; and sometimes access to the Word Help window. Table 2.2 identifies the keyboard shortcuts available for buttons in the Font group.

Formatting with the Mini Toolbar

When you select text, the Mini toolbar displays in a dimmed fashion above the selected text. Hover the mouse pointer over the Mini toolbar and it becomes active. Click a button on the Mini toolbar to apply formatting to selected text.

Table 2.2 Font Button Keyboard Shortcuts

Font Group Button	Keyboard Shortcut
Font	Ctrl + Shift + F
Font Size	Ctrl + Shift + P
Grow Font	Ctrl + Shift + >
Shrink Font	Ctrl + Shift + <
Bold	Ctrl + B
Italic	Ctrl + I
Underline	Ctrl + U
Subscript	Ctrl + =
Superscript	Ctrl + Shift + +
Change Case	Shift + F3

1. With **WL1-C2-P1-CompTerms.docx** open, move the insertion point to the beginning of the term *Chip*, press the Enter key, and then press the Up Arrow key. Type the text shown in Figure 2.3. Create the superscript numbers by clicking the Superscript button, typing the number, and then clicking the Superscript button.

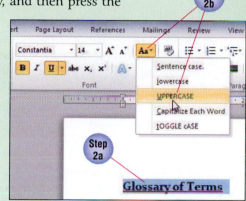

2. Change the case of text and remove underlining from the title by completing the following steps:
   a. Select the title *Glossary of Terms*.
   b. Click the Change Case button in the Font group and then click *UPPERCASE* at the drop-down list.
   c. Click the Underline button to remove underlining.
   d. Click the Text Effects button in the font group and then click the *Gradient Fill - Blue, Accent 1* option (fourth option from the left in the third row) at the drop-down gallery.

3. Strike through text by completing the following steps:
   a. Select the words and parentheses *(or hack)* in the *Crackers* definition.
   b. Click the Strikethrough button in the Font group.

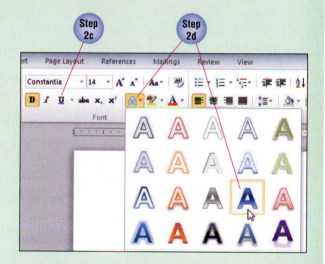

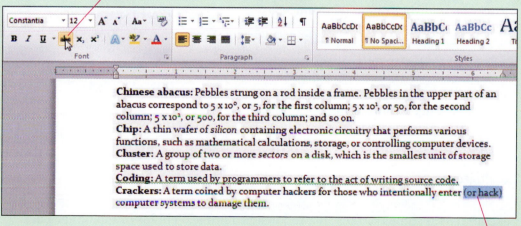

4. Change the font color by completing the following steps:
   a. Press Ctrl + A to select the entire document.

b. Click the Font Color button arrow.

c. Click the Dark Red color (first color option in the *Standard Colors* section) at the drop-down gallery.

d. Click in the document to deselect text.

5. Highlight text in the document by completing the following steps:

a. Click the Text Highlight Color button arrow in the Font group and then click the yellow color at the drop-down palette. (This causes the mouse pointer to display as an I-beam pointer with a highlighter pen attached.)

b. Select the term *Beta-testing* and the definition that follows.

c. Click the Text Highlight Color button arrow and then click the turquoise color (third color from the left in the top row).

d. Select the term *Cluster* and the definition that follows.

e. Click the Text Highlight Color button arrow and then click the yellow color at the drop-down gallery.

f. Click the Text Highlight Color button to turn off highlighting.

6. Apply italic formatting using the Mini toolbar by completing the following steps:

a. Select the text *one-stop shopping* located in the definition for the term *Aggregation software*. (When you select the text, the Mini toolbar displays.)

b. Click the Italic button on the Mini toolbar.

c. Select the word *bits* located in the definition for the term *Bandwidth* and then click the Italic button on the Mini toolbar.

7. Save **WL1-C2-P1-CompTerms.docx**.

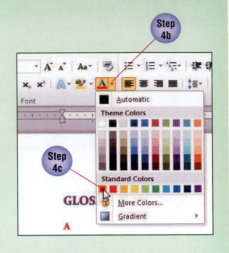

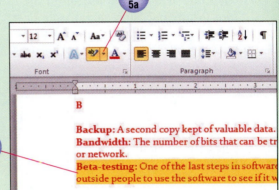

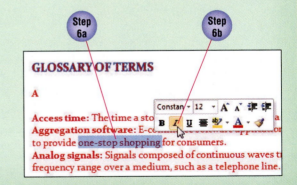

Figure 2.3 Project 1c

Chinese abacus: Pebbles strung on a rod inside a frame. Pebbles in the upper part of an abacus correspond to 5×10^0, or 5, for the first column; 5×10^1, or 50, for the second column; 5×10^2, or 500, for the third column; and so on.

Figure 2.4 Font Dialog Box

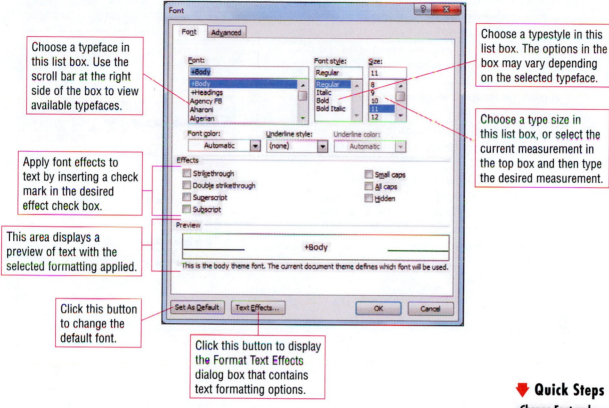

Choose a typeface in this list box. Use the scroll bar at the right side of the box to view available typefaces.

Choose a typestyle in this list box. The options in the box may vary depending on the selected typeface.

Choose a type size in this list box, or select the current measurement in the top box and then type the desired measurement.

Apply font effects to text by inserting a check mark in the desired effect check box.

This area displays a preview of text with the selected formatting applied.

Click this button to change the default font.

Click this button to display the Format Text Effects dialog box that contains text formatting options.

Changing Fonts at the Font Dialog Box

In addition to buttons in the Font group, you can use options at the Font dialog box shown in Figure 2.4 to change the typeface, type size, and typestyle of text as well as apply font effects. Display the Font dialog box by clicking the Font group dialog box launcher. The dialog box launcher is a small square containing a diagonal-pointing arrow that displays in the lower right corner of the Font group.

▼ **Quick Steps**

Change Font and Apply Effects
1. Select text if necessary.
2. Click Font group dialog box launcher.
3. Choose desired options at dialog box.
4. Click OK.

Project 1d **Changing the Font at the Font Dialog Box** Part 4 of 4

1. With **WL1-C2-P1-CompTerms.docx** open, press Ctrl + End to move the insertion point to the end of the document. (Make sure the insertion point is positioned a double space below the last line of text.)
2. Type **Created by Susan Ashby** and then press the Enter key.
3. Type **Wednesday, February 22, 2012**.
4. Change the font to 13-point Candara and the color to dark blue by completing the following steps:
   a. Press Ctrl + A to select the entire document.
   b. Click the Font group dialog box launcher.

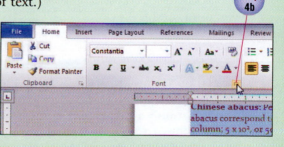

Step 4b

c. At the Font dialog box, click the up-pointing arrow at the right side of the *Font* list box to scroll up the list box and then click *Candara*.

d. Click in the *Size* text box and then type **13**.

e. Click the down-pointing arrow at the right side of the *Font color* list box and then click a dark blue color of your choosing at the drop-down color palette.

f. Click OK to close the dialog box.

5. Double underline text by completing the following steps:

a. Select *Wednesday, February 22, 2012*.

b. Click the Font group dialog box launcher.

c. At the Font dialog box, click the down-pointing arrow at the right side of the *Underline style* option box and then click the double-line option at the drop-down list.

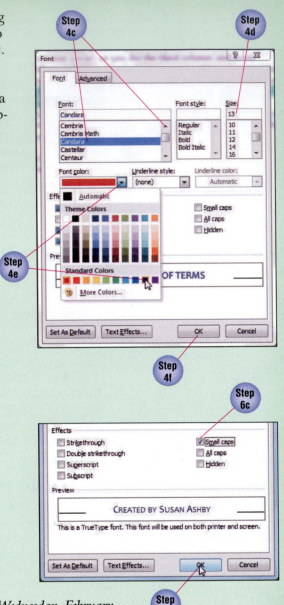

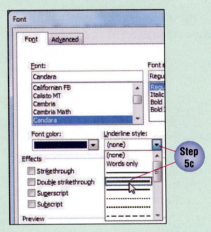

d. Click OK to close the dialog box.

6. Change text to small caps by completing the following steps:

a. Select the text *Created by Susan Ashby* and *Wednesday, February 22, 2012*.

b. Display the Font dialog box.

c. Click the *Small caps* option in the *Effects* section. (This inserts a check mark in the check box.)

d. Click OK to close the dialog box.

7. Save, print, and then close **WL1-C2-P1-CompTerms.docx**.

Project **2** **Apply Styles and Themes**   **3 Parts**

You will open a document containing information on the life cycle of software, apply styles to text, and then change the Quick Styles set. You will also apply a theme and then change the theme colors and fonts.

Applying Styles from a Quick Styles Set ■■■■■■■■■■

A Word document contains a number of predesigned formats grouped into style sets called Quick Styles. Several thumbnails of the styles in the default Quick Styles set display in the Styles group in the Home tab. Display additional styles by clicking the More button that displays at the right side of the style thumbnails. This displays a drop-down gallery of style choices. To apply a style, position the insertion point in the text or paragraph of text to which you want the style applied, click the More button at the right side of the style thumbnails in the Styles group, and then click the desired style at the drop-down gallery.

A Word document contains some default formatting including 10 points of spacing after paragraphs and a line spacing of 1.15. (You will learn more about these formatting options later in this chapter.) You can remove this default formatting as well as any character formatting applied to text in your document by applying the No Spacing style to your text. This style is located in the Styles group.

Changing the Quick Styles Set

Word contains a number of Quick Styles sets containing styles you can use to apply formatting to a document. To change to a different Quick Styles set, click the Change Styles button in the Styles group in the Home tab and then point to Style Set. This displays a side menu with Quick Styles sets. Click the desired set and the style formatting changes for the styles in the set.

▼ **Quick Steps**

Apply a Style
1. Position insertion point in desired text or paragraph of text.
2. Click More button in Styles group.
3. Click desired style.

Change Quick Styles Set
1. Click Change Styles button.
2. Point to *Style Set*.
3. Click desired set.

More

Change Styles

Project 2a **Applying Quick Styles**   **Part 1 of 3**

1. Open **SoftwareCycle.docx**.
2. Save the document with Save As and name it **WL1-C2-P2-SoftwareCycle**.
3. Remove the 10 points of spacing after paragraphs and change the line spacing to 1 by completing the following steps:
   a. Press Ctrl + A to select the entire document.
   b. Click the No Spacing style in the Styles group in the Home tab.

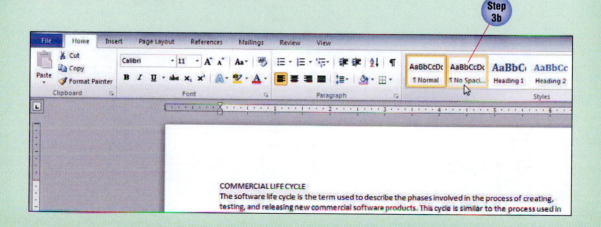

Step 3b

4. Position the insertion point on any character in the title *COMMERCIAL LIFE CYCLE* and then click the Heading 1 style that displays in the Styles group.

5. Position the insertion point on any character in the heading *Proposal and Planning* and then click the Heading 2 style that displays in the Styles group.

6. Position the insertion point on any character in the heading *Design* and then click the Heading 2 style in the Styles group.

7. Apply the Heading 2 style to the remaining headings (*Implementation*, *Testing*, and *Public Release and Support*).

8. Click the Change Styles button in the Styles group, point to *Style Set*, and then click *Modern*. (Notice how the Heading 1 and Heading 2 formatting changes.)

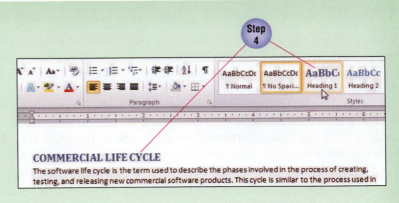

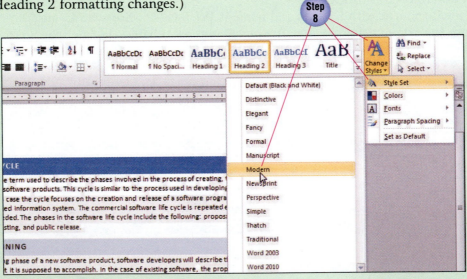

9. Save and then print **WL1-C2-P2-SoftwareCycle.docx**.

Applying a Theme ■■■■■■■■■■■■■■■■■■■■■■■

Word provides a number of themes you can use to format text in your document. A theme is a set of formatting choices that include a color theme (a set of colors), a font theme (a set of heading and body text fonts), and an effects theme (a set of lines and fill effects). To apply a theme, click the Page Layout tab and then click the Themes button in the Themes group. At the drop-down gallery that displays, click the desired theme. You can hover the mouse pointer over a theme and the live preview feature will display your document with the theme formatting applied. With the live preview feature you can see how the theme formatting affects your document before you make your final choice. Applying a theme is an easy way to give your document a professional look.

▼ **Quick Steps**

Apply a Theme
1. Click Page Layout tab.
2. Click Themes button.
3. Click desired theme.

Themes

Project 2b **Applying a Theme to Text in a Document** **Part 2 of 3**

1. With **WL1-C2-P2-SoftwareCycle.docx** open, click the Page Layout tab and then click the Themes button in the Themes group.
2. At the drop-down gallery, hover your mouse pointer over several different themes and notice how the text formatting changes in your document.
3. Scroll down the drop-down gallery and then click the *Module* theme.
4. Save and then print **WL1-C2-P2-SoftwareCycle.docx**.

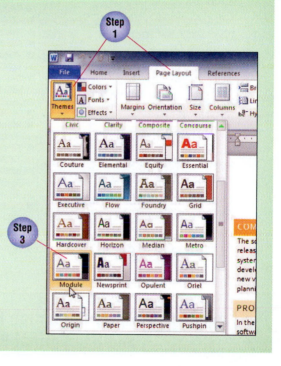

Changing Themes

You can change a theme with the three buttons that display at the right side of the Themes button. A theme contains specific color formatting, which you can change with options from the Theme Colors button in the Themes group. Click this button and a drop-down gallery displays with named color schemes. The names of the color schemes correspond to the names of the themes. Each theme applies specific fonts, which you can change with options from the Theme Fonts button in the Themes group. Click this button and a drop-down gallery displays with font choices. Each font group in the drop-down gallery contains two choices. The first choice in the group is the font that is applied to headings and the second choice is the font that is applied to body text in the document. If you are formatting a document containing graphics with lines and fills, you can apply a specific theme effect with options at the Theme Effects drop-down gallery.

▼ **Quick Steps**

Change Theme Color
1. Click Page Layout tab.
2. Click Theme Colors button.
3. Click desired theme color.

Change Theme Fonts
1. Click Page Layout tab.
2. Click Theme Fonts button.
3. Click desired theme fonts.

Theme Colors

Theme Fonts

Theme Effects

The buttons in the Themes group display a visual representation of the current theme. If you change the theme colors, the small color squares in the Themes button and the Theme Colors button reflect the change. Changing the theme fonts and the *As* on the Themes button as well as the uppercase *A* on the Theme Fonts button reflect the change. If you change the theme effects, the circle in the Theme Effects button reflects the change.

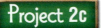 **Changing a Theme**   **Part 3 of 3**

1. With **WL1-C2-P2-SoftwareCycle.docx** open, click the Theme Colors button in the Themes group and then click *Foundry* at the drop-down gallery. (Notice how the colors in the title and headings change.)
2. Click the Theme Fonts button and then click the *Apex* option. (Notice how the document text font changes.)
3. Save, print, and then close **WL1-C2-P2-SoftwareCycle.docx**.

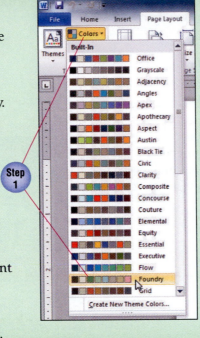

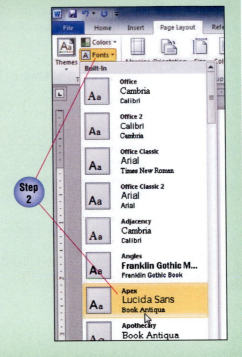

Project 3 Apply Paragraph Formatting and Use Format Painter   6 Parts

You will open a report on intellectual property and fair use issues and then format the report by changing the alignment of text in paragraphs, applying spacing before and after paragraphs of text, and repeating the last formatting action.

Changing Paragraph Alignment ■■■■■■■■■■■■■■■

By default, paragraphs in a Word document are aligned at the left margin and ragged at the right margin. Change this default alignment with buttons in the Paragraph group in the Home tab or with keyboard shortcuts as shown in Table 2.3.

You can change the alignment of text in paragraphs before you type the text or you can change the alignment of existing text. If you change the alignment before typing text, the alignment formatting is inserted in the paragraph mark.

Table 2.3 Paragraph Alignment Buttons and Keyboard Shortcuts

To align text	Paragraph Group Button	Keyboard Shortcut
At the left margin		Ctrl + L
Between margins		Ctrl + E
At the right margin		Ctrl + R
At the left and right margins		Ctrl + J

Center

Show/Hide ¶

Align Text Left

Align Text Right

As you type text and press Enter, the paragraph formatting is continued. For example, if you click the Center button in the Paragraph group, type text for the first paragraph, and then press the Enter key, the center alignment formatting is still active and the insertion point displays centered between the left and right margins. To display the paragraph symbols in a document, click the Show/Hide ¶ button in the Paragraph group. With the Show/Hide ¶ button active (displays with an orange background), nonprinting formatting symbols display such as the paragraph symbol ¶ indicating a press of the Enter key or a dot indicating a press of the spacebar.

To return paragraph alignment to the default (left-aligned), click the Align Text Left button in the Paragraph group. You can also return all paragraph formatting to the default with the keyboard shortcut, Ctrl + Q. This keyboard shortcut removes paragraph formatting from selected text. If you want to remove all formatting from selected text including character and paragraph formatting, click the Clear Formatting button in the Font group.

To change the alignment of existing text in a paragraph, position the insertion point anywhere within the paragraph. You do not need to select the entire paragraph. To change the alignment of several adjacent paragraphs in a document, select a portion of the first paragraph through a portion of the last paragraph. You do not need to select all of the text in the paragraphs.

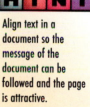

HINT

Align text in a document so the message of the document can be followed and the page is attractive.

Project 3a   Changing Paragraph Alignment   **Part 1 of 6**

1. Open **IntelProp.docx**. (Some of the default formatting in this document has been changed.)
2. Save the document with Save As and name it **WL1-C2-P3-IntelProp**.
3. Click the Show/Hide ¶ button in the Paragraph group in the Home tab to turn on the display of nonprinting characters.

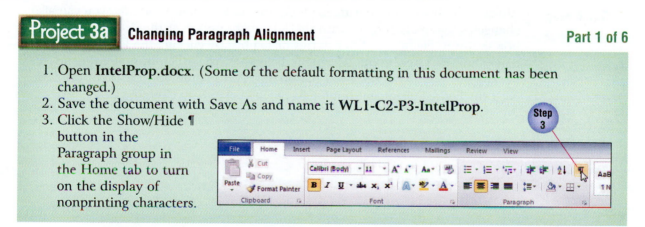

Step 3

4. Press Ctrl + A to select the entire document and then change the alignment to Justify by clicking the Justify button in the Paragraph group in the Home tab.
5. Press Ctrl + End to move the insertion point to the end of the document.
6. Press the Enter key once.
7. Press Ctrl + E to move the insertion point to the middle of the page.
8. Type **Prepared by Clarissa Markham**.
9. Press Shift + Enter and then type **Edited by Joshua Streeter**.

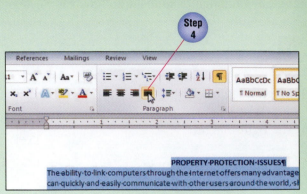

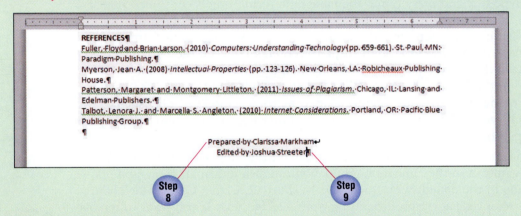

10. Click the Show/Hide ¶ button in the Paragraph group in the Home tab to turn off the display of nonprinting characters.
11. Save **WL1-C2-P3-IntelProp.docx**.

Changing Alignment at the Paragraph Dialog Box

▼ **Quick Steps**

Change Paragraph Alignment
Click desired alignment button in Paragraph group in Home tab.
OR
1. Click Paragraph group dialog box launcher.
2. Click *Alignment* option down-pointing arrow.
3. Click desired alignment.
4. Click OK.

Along with buttons in the Paragraph group and keyboard shortcuts, you can also change paragraph alignment with the Alignment option at the Paragraph dialog box shown in Figure 2.5. Display this dialog box by clicking the Paragraph group dialog box launcher. At the Paragraph dialog box, click the down-pointing arrow at the right side of the *Alignment* option box. At the drop-down list that displays, click the desired alignment option and then click OK to close the dialog box.

Figure 2.5 Paragraph Dialog Box with Alignment Options

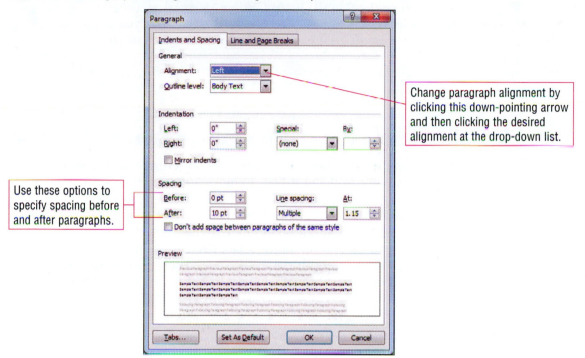

Change paragraph alignment by clicking this down-pointing arrow and then clicking the desired alignment at the drop-down list.

Use these options to specify spacing before and after paragraphs.

Project 3b **Changing Paragraph Alignment at the Paragraph Dialog Box** **Part 2 of 6**

1. With **WL1-C2-P3-IntelProp.docx** open, change paragraph alignment by completing the following steps:
   a. Select the entire document.
   b. Click the Paragraph group dialog box launcher.
   c. At the Paragraph dialog box with the Indents and Spacing tab selected, click the down-pointing arrow at the right of the *Alignment* list box and then click *Left*.
   d. Click OK to close the dialog box.
   e. Deselect the text.
2. Change paragraph alignment by completing the following steps:
   a. Press Ctrl + End to move the insertion point to the end of the document.
   b. Position the insertion point on any character in the text *Prepared by Clarissa Markham*.
   c. Click the Paragraph group dialog box launcher.
   d. At the Paragraph dialog box with the Indents and Spacing tab selected, click the down-pointing arrow at the right of the *Alignment* list box and then click *Right*.

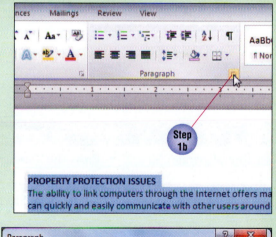

Step 1b

PROPERTY PROTECTION ISSUES
The ability to link computers through the Internet offers ma can quickly and easily communicate with other users around

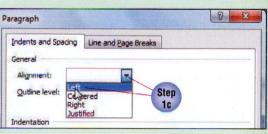

Step 1c

e. Click OK. (The line of text containing the name *Clarissa Markham* and the line of text containing the name *Joshua Streeter* are both aligned at the right since you used the New Line command, Shift + Enter, to separate the lines of text without creating a new paragraph.)

3. Save and then print **WL1-C2-P3-IntelProp.docx**.

▼ Quick Steps

Indent Text in Paragraph
Drag indent marker(s) on Ruler.
OR
Press keyboard shortcut keys.
OR
1. Click Paragraph group dialog box launcher.
2. Insert measurement in *Left, Right,* and/or *By* text box.
3. Click OK.

Indenting Text in Paragraphs ■■■■■■■■■■■■■■■■■

By now you are familiar with the word wrap feature of Word, which ends lines and wraps the insertion point to the next line. To indent text from the left margin, the right margin, or both, use the indent buttons in the Paragraph group, in the Page Layout tab, keyboard shortcuts, options from the Paragraph dialog box, markers on the Ruler, or use the Alignment button on the Ruler. Figure 2.6 identifies indent markers and the Alignment button on the Ruler. Refer to Table 2.4 for methods for indenting text in a document. If the Ruler is not visible, display the Ruler by clicking the View Ruler button located at the top of the vertical scroll bar.

Figure 2.6 Ruler and Indent Markers

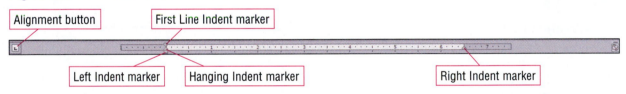

Alignment button   First Line Indent marker

Left Indent marker   Hanging Indent marker   Right Indent marker

Table 2.4 Methods for Indenting Text

Indent	Methods for Indenting
First line of paragraph	• Press the Tab key. • Display Paragraph dialog box, click the down-pointing arrow to the right of the *Special* list box, click *First line*, and then click OK. • Drag the First Line Indent marker on the Ruler. • Click the Alignment button located at the left side of the Ruler until the First Line Indent button displays and then click on the Ruler at the desired location.

continues

Table 2.4 Methods for Indenting Text, *continued*

Indent	Methods for Indenting
Text from left margin	• Click the Increase Indent button in the Paragraph group in the Home tab to increase the indent or click the Decrease Indent button to decrease the indent. • Insert a measurement in the *Indent Left* measurement button in the Paragraph group in the Page Layout tab. • Press Ctrl + M to increase the indent or press Ctrl + Shift + M to decrease the indent. • Display the Paragraph dialog box, type the desired indent measurement in the *Left* measurement box, and then click OK. • Drag the left indent marker on the Ruler.
Text from right margin	• Insert a measurement in the *Indent Right* measurement button in the Paragraph group in the Page Layout tab. • Display the Paragraph dialog box, type the desired indent measurement in the *Right* measurement box, and then click OK. • Drag the right indent marker on the Ruler.
All lines of text except the first (called a hanging indent)	• Press Ctrl + T. (Press Ctrl + Shift + T to remove hanging indent.) • Display the Paragraph dialog box, click the down-pointing arrow to the right of the *Special* list box, click *Hanging*, and then click OK. • Click the Alignment button located at the left side of the Ruler until the Hanging Indent button displays and then click on the Ruler at the desired location.
Text from both left and right margins	• Display the Paragraph dialog box, type the desired indent measurement in the *Left* measurement box, type the desired measurement in the *Right* measurement box, and then click OK. • Insert a measurement in the *Indent Right* and *Indent Left* measurement buttons in the Paragraph group in the Page Layout tab. • Drag the left indent marker on the Ruler; then drag the right indent marker on the Ruler.

Project 3c **Indenting Paragraphs**   Part 3 of 6

1. With **WL1-C2-P3-IntelProp.docx** open, indent the first line of text in paragraphs by completing the following steps:
   a. Select the first two paragraphs of text in the document (the text after the title *PROPERTY PROTECTION ISSUES* and before the heading *Intellectual Property*.
   b. Position the mouse pointer on the First Line Indent marker on the Ruler, hold down the left mouse button, drag the marker to the 0.5-inch mark, and then release the mouse button.

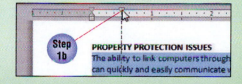

Step 1b

c. Select the paragraphs of text in the *Intellectual Property* section and then drag the First Line Indent marker on the Ruler to the 0.5-inch mark.

d. Select the paragraphs of text in the *Fair Use* section, click the Alignment button located at the left side of the Ruler until the First Line Indent button displays, and then click on the Ruler at the 0.5-inch mark.

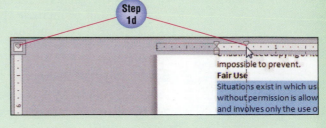

e. Position the insertion point on any character in the paragraph of text below the *Intellectual Property Protection* heading, make sure the First Line Indent button displays in the Alignment button, and then click at the 0.5-inch mark on the Ruler.

2. Since the text in the second paragraph in the *Fair Use* section is a quote, you need to indent the text from the left and right margins by completing the following steps:

   a. Position the insertion point anywhere within the second paragraph in the *Fair Use* section (the paragraph that begins *[A] copyrighted work, including such . . .*).

   b. Click the Paragraph group dialog box launcher.

   c. At the Paragraph dialog box, with the Indents and Spacing tab selected, select the current measurement in the *Left* measurement box and then type **0.5**.

   d. Select the current measurement in the *Right* measurement box and then type **0.5**.

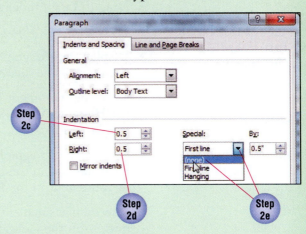

   e. Click the down-pointing arrow at the right side of the *Special* list box and then click *(none)* at the drop-down list.

   f. Click OK or press Enter.

3. Create a hanging indent for the first paragraph in the *REFERENCES* section by positioning the insertion point anywhere in the first paragraph below *REFERENCES* and then pressing Ctrl + T.

4. Create a hanging indent for the second paragraph in the *REFERENCES* section by completing the following steps:

   a. Position the insertion point anywhere in the second paragraph in the *REFERENCES* section.

   b. Make sure the Ruler is displayed. (If it is not, click the View Ruler button located at the top of the vertical scroll bar.)

   c. Click the Alignment button located at the left side of the Ruler until the Hanging Indent button displays.

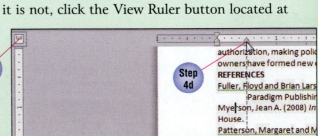

   d. Click on the 0.5-inch mark on the Ruler.

5. Create a hanging indent for the third and fourth paragraphs by completing the following steps:
   a. Select a portion of the third and fourth paragraphs.
   b. Click the Paragraph group dialog box launcher.
   c. At the Paragraph dialog box with the Indents and Spacing tab selected, click the down-pointing arrow at the right side of the *Special* list box and then click *Hanging* at the drop-down list.
   d. Click OK or press Enter.
6. Save **WL1-C2-P3-IntelProp.docx**.

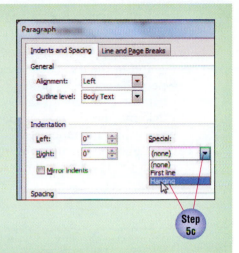

Step 5c

Spacing Before and After Paragraphs ■■■■■■■■■■■■■■

By default, Word applies 10 points of additional spacing after a paragraph. You can remove this spacing, increase or decrease the spacing, and insert spacing above the paragraph. To change spacing before or after a paragraph, use the *Spacing Before* and *Spacing After* measurement boxes located in the Paragraph group in the Page Layout tab, or the *Before* and/or *After* options at the Paragraph dialog box with the Indents and Spacing tab selected. You can also add spacing before and after paragraphs at the Line and Paragraph Spacing button drop-down list.

Spacing before or after a paragraph is part of the paragraph and will be moved, copied, or deleted with the paragraph. If a paragraph, such as a heading, contains spacing before it, and the paragraph falls at the top of a page, Word ignores the spacing.

Spacing before or after paragraphs is added in points and a vertical inch contains approximately 72 points. To add spacing before or after a paragraph you would click the Page Layout tab, select the current measurement in the *Spacing Before* or the *Spacing After* measurement box, and then type the desired number of points. You can also click the up- or down-pointing arrows at the right side of the *Spacing Before* and *Spacing After* measurement boxes to increase or decrease the amount of spacing.

HINT

Line spacing determines the amount of vertical space between lines while paragraph spacing determines the amount of space above or below paragraphs of text.

Repeating the Last Action ■■■■■■■■■■■■■■■■■■■■■■

If you apply formatting to text and then want to apply the same formatting to other text in the document, consider using the Repeat command. To use this command, apply the desired formatting, move the insertion point to the next location where you want the formatting applied, and then press the F4 function key or press Ctrl + Y.

▼ **Quick Steps**

Repeat Last Action
Press F4.
OR
Press Ctrl + Y.

1. With **WL1-C2-P3-IntelProp.docx** open, add 6 points of spacing before and after each paragraph in the document by completing the following steps:
   a. Select the entire document.
   b. Click the Page Layout tab.
   c. Click once on the up-pointing arrow at the right side of the *Spacing Before* measurement box in the Paragraph group (this inserts *6 pt* in the box).
   d. Click once on the up-pointing arrow at the right side of the *Spacing After* measurement box in the Paragraph group (this inserts *6 pt* in the text box).

2. Add an additional 6 points of spacing above the headings by completing the following steps:
   a. Position the insertion point on any character in the heading *Intellectual Property* and then click once on the up-pointing arrow at the right side of the *Spacing Before* measurement box (this changes the measurement to *12 pt*).

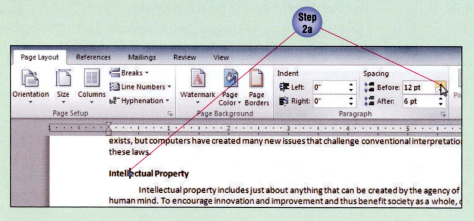

   b. Position the insertion point on any character in the heading *Fair Use* and then press F4. (F4 is the Repeat command.)
   c. Position the insertion point on any character in the heading *Intellectual Property Protection* and then press F4.
   d. Position the insertion point on any character in the heading *REFERENCES* and then press Ctrl + Y. (Ctrl + Y is also the Repeat command.)
3. Save **WL1-C2-P3-IntelProp.docx**.

Formatting with Format Painter ■■■■■■■■■■■■■■■■

The Clipboard group in the Home tab contains a button for copying formatting and displays in the Clipboard group as a paintbrush. To use the Format Painter button, position the insertion point on a character containing the desired formatting, click the Format Painter button, and then select text to which you want the formatting applied. When you click the Format Painter button, the mouse I-beam pointer displays with a paintbrush attached. If you want to apply formatting a single time, click the Format Painter button once. If you want to apply the formatting in more than one location in the document, double-click the Format Painter button and then select text to which you want formatting applied. When you are finished, click the Format Painter button to turn it off. You can also turn off Format Painter by pressing the Esc key.

▼ **Quick Steps**
Format with Format Painter
1. Format text.
2. Double-click Format Painter button.
3. Select text.
4. Click Format Painter button.

Format Painter

Project 3e | **Formatting Headings with the Format Painter** | **Part 5 of 6**

1. With **WL1-C2-P3-IntelProp.docx** open, click the Home tab.
2. Select the entire document and then change the font to 12-point Cambria.
3. Select the title *PROPERTY PROTECTION ISSUES*, click the Center button in the Paragraph group, and then change the font to 16-point Candara bold.
4. Apply 16-point Candara bold formatting to the *REFERENCES* heading by completing the following steps:
   a. Click on any character in the title *PROPERTY PROTECTION ISSUES*.
   b. Click once on the Format Painter button in the Clipboard group.
   c. Press Ctrl + End to move the insertion point to the end of the document and then click on any character in the heading

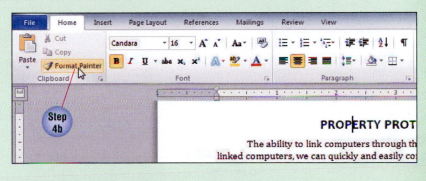

   REFERENCES. (This applies the 16-point Candara bold formatting and centers the text.)
5. With the insertion point positioned on any character in the heading *REFERENCES*, add an additional 6 points of spacing before the heading (for a total of 12 points before the heading).
6. Select the heading *Intellectual Property* and then change the font to 14-point Candara bold.
7. Use the Format Painter button and apply 14-point Candara bold formatting to the other headings by completing the following steps:
   a. Position the insertion point on any character in the heading *Intellectual Property*.
   b. Double-click the Format Painter button in the Clipboard group.
   c. Using the mouse, select the heading *Fair Use*.
   d. Using the mouse, select the heading *Intellectual Property Protection*.
   e. Click once on the Format Painter button in the Clipboard group. (This turns off the feature.)
   f. Deselect the heading.
8. Save **WL1-C2-P3-IntelProp.docx**.

Changing Line Spacing ■■■■■ ■■■ ■■■■ ■ ■■■ ■■■ ■ ■■

▼ Quick Steps

Change Line Spacing
1. Click Line and Paragraph Spacing button in Paragraph group.
2. Click desired option at drop-down list.
OR
Press shortcut command keys.
OR
1. Click Paragraph group dialog box launcher.
2. Click *Line Spacing* option down-pointing arrow.
3. Click desired line spacing option.
4. Click OK.
OR
1. Click Paragraph group dialog box launcher.
2. Type line measurement in *At* text box.
3. Click OK.

Line and Paragraph Spacing

The default line spacing for a document is 1.15. (The line spacing for the **IntelProp.docx** document, which you opened at the beginning of Project 3, had been changed to single.) In certain situations, Word automatically adjusts the line spacing. For example, if you insert a large character or object such as a graphic, Word increases the line spacing of that specific line. But you also may sometimes encounter a writing situation in which you decide to change the line spacing for a section or for the entire document.

Change line spacing using the Line and Paragraph Spacing button in the Paragraph group in the Home tab, with keyboard shortcuts, or with options from the Paragraph dialog box. Table 2.5 displays the keyboard shortcuts to change line spacing.

You can also change line spacing at the Paragraph dialog box with the *Line spacing* option or the *At* option. If you click the down-pointing arrow at the right side of the *Line spacing* option, a drop-down list displays with a variety of spacing options. For example, to change the line spacing to double you would click *Double* at the drop-down list. You can type a specific line spacing measurement in the *At* text box. For example, to change the line spacing to 1.75, type *1.75* in the *At* text box.

Table 2.5 Line Spacing Keyboard Shortcuts

Press	*To change line spacing to*
Ctrl + 1	single spacing
Ctrl + 2	double spacing
Ctrl + 5	1.5 line spacing

Project 3f Changing Line Spacing   Part 6 of 6

1. With **WL1-C2-P3-IntelProp.docx** open, change the line spacing for all paragraphs to double spacing by completing the following steps:
   a. Select the entire document.
   b. Click the Line and Paragraph Spacing button located in the Paragraph group in the Home tab.
   c. Click *2.0* at the drop-down list.
2. With the entire document still selected, press Ctrl + 5. (This changes the line spacing to 1.5 line spacing.)

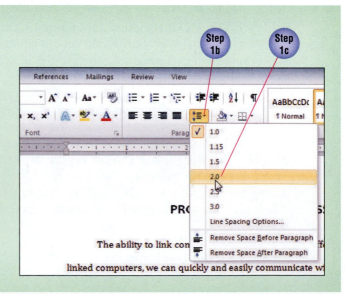

3. Change the line spacing to 1.3 using the Paragraph dialog box by completing the following steps:
   a. With the entire document still selected, click the Paragraph group dialog box launcher.
   b. At the Paragraph dialog box, make sure the Indents and Spacing tab is selected, click inside the *At* text box, and then type 1.3. (This text box is located to the right of the *Line spacing* list box.)
   c. Click OK or press Enter.
   d. Deselect the text.
4. Save, print, and then close **WL1-C2-P3-IntelProp.docx**.

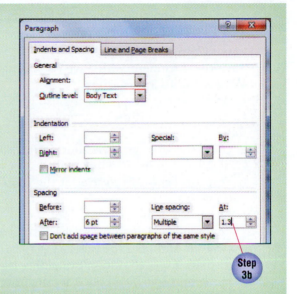

Step 3b

Project **4**   **Format Computer Issues Document**   **3 Parts**

You will open a document containing two computer-related problems to solve, apply predesigned paragraph spacing, reveal the formatting, compare the formatting, and make formatting changes.

Changing Paragraph Spacing with the Change Styles Button ■■■■■■■■■■■■■■■■■■■■■■■■

The Change Styles button in the Styles group in the Home tab contains a Paragraph Spacing option you can use to apply predesigned paragraph spacing to text in a document. Click the Change Styles button and then point to *Paragraph Spacing* and a side menu displays. Hover your mouse over an option at the side menu and, after a moment, a ScreenTip displays with information about the formatting applied by the option. For example, if you hover the mouse over the *Compact* option at the side menu, a ScreenTip displays telling you that the Compact option will change the spacing before paragraphs to zero points, the spacing after paragraphs to four points, and the line spacing to one. Use options at the *Paragraph Spacing* side menu to quickly apply paragraph spacing to text in your document.

1. Open **CompIssues.docx**.
2. Save the document with Save As and name it **WL1-C2-P4-CompIssues**.
3. Change the paragraph spacing using the Change Styles button by completing the following steps:
   a. Click the Change Styles button in the Styles group in the Home tab.
   b. Point to *Paragraph Spacing* at the drop-down list.
   c. Hover the mouse over each of the paragraph spacing options beginning with *Compact* and read the ScreenTip that displays for each option explaining the paragraph spacing applied by the option.
   d. Click the *Double* option at the side menu.
4. Scroll through the document and notice the paragraph spacing.
5. Change the paragraph spacing by clicking the Change Styles button, pointing to *Paragraph Spacing*, and then clicking *Relaxed* at the side menu.
6. Save **WL1-C2-P4-CompIssues.docx**.

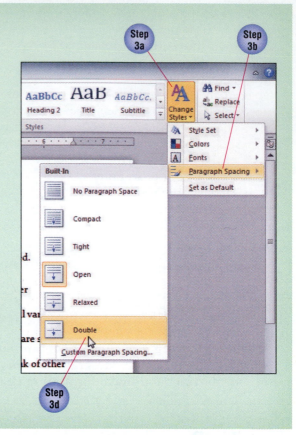

Revealing Formatting ■■■■■■■■■■■■■■■■■■■■■■

Display formatting applied to specific text in a document at the Reveal Formatting task pane as shown in Figure 2.7. The Reveal Formatting task pane displays font, paragraph, and section formatting applied to text where the insertion point is positioned or to selected text. Display the Reveal Formatting task pane with the keyboard shortcut Shift + F1. Generally, a minus symbol precedes *Font* and *Paragraph* and a plus symbol precedes *Section* in the *Formatting of selected text* section of the Reveal Formatting task pane. Click the minus symbol to hide any items below a heading and click the plus symbol to reveal items. Some of the items below headings in the *Formatting of selected text* section are hyperlinks. Click a hyperlink and a dialog box displays with the specific option.

1. With **WL1-C2-P4-CompIssues.docx** open, press Shift + F1 to display the Reveal Formatting task pane.
2. Click anywhere in the heading *Solving Problems* and then notice the formatting information that displays in the Reveal Formatting task pane.
3. Click in the bulleted paragraph and notice the formatting information that displays in the Reveal Formatting task pane.

Figure 2.7 Reveal Formatting Task Pane

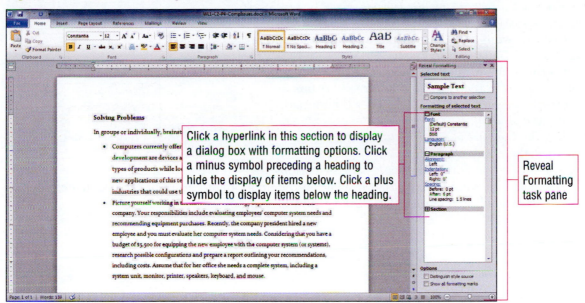

Click a hyperlink in this section to display a dialog box with formatting options. Click a minus symbol preceding a heading to hide the display of items below. Click a plus symbol to display items below the heading.

Reveal Formatting task pane

Comparing Formatting

Along with displaying formatting applied to text, you can use the Reveal Formatting task pane to compare formatting of two text selections to determine what formatting is different. To compare formatting, select the first instance of formatting to be compared, click the *Compare to another selection* check box, and then select the second instance of formatting to compare. Any differences between the two selections display in the *Formatting differences* list box.

▼ **Quick Steps**

Compare Formatting
1. Press Shift + F1 to display Reveal Formatting task pane.
2. Click or select text.
3. Click *Compare to another selection* check box.
4. Click or select text.

Project 4c **Comparing Formatting** **Part 3 of 3**

1. With **WL1-C2-P4-CompIssues.docx** open, make sure the Reveal Formatting task pane displays. If it does not, turn it on by pressing Shift + F1.
2. Select the first bulleted paragraph (the paragraph that begins *Computers currently offer both . . .*).
3. Click the *Compare to another selection* check box to insert a check mark.
4. Select the second bulleted paragraph (the paragraph that begins *Picture yourself working in the . . .*).
5. Determine the formatting differences by reading the information in the *Formatting differences* list box. (The list box displays *12 pt -> 11 pt* below the Font: hyperlink, indicating that the difference is point size.)
6. Format the second bulleted paragraph so it is set in 12-point size.
7. Click the *Compare to another selection* check box to remove the check mark.
8. Select the word *visual* that displays in the first sentence in the first bulleted paragraph.

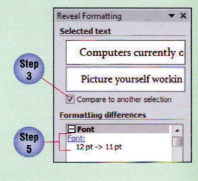

Step 3

Step 5

9. Click the *Compare to another selection* check box to insert a check mark.
10. Select the word *audio* that displays in the first sentence of the first bulleted paragraph.
11. Determine the formatting differences by reading the information in the *Formatting differences* list box.
12. Format the word *audio* so it matches the formatting of the word *visual*.
13. Click the *Compare to another selection* check box to remove the check mark.
14. Close the Reveal Formatting task pane by clicking the Close button (contains an X) that displays in the upper right corner of the task pane.
15. Save, print, and then close **WL1-C2-P4-CompIssues.docx**.

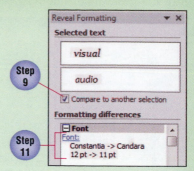

Step 9

Step 11

Chapter Summary

- A font consists of three parts: typeface, type size, and typestyle.

- A typeface (font) is a set of characters with a common design and shape. Typefaces are either monospaced, allotting the same amount of horizontal space to each character, or proportional, allotting a varying amount of space for each character. Proportional typefaces are divided into two main categories: serif and sans serif.

- Type size is measured in point size; the higher the point size, the larger the characters.

- A typestyle is a variation of style within a certain typeface. You can apply typestyle formatting with some of the buttons in the Font group.

- With some of the buttons in the Font group, you can apply font effects such as superscript, subscript, and strikethrough.

- The Mini toolbar automatically displays above selected text. Use buttons on this toolbar to apply formatting to selected text.

- With options at the Font dialog box, you can change the font, font size, and font style and apply specific effects. Display this dialog box by clicking the Font group dialog box launcher.

- A Word document contains a number of predesigned formats grouped into style sets called Quick Styles. Change to a different Quick Styles set by clicking the Change Styles button in the Styles group in the Home tab, pointing to Style Set, and then clicking the desired set.

- Apply a theme and change theme colors, fonts, and effects with buttons in the Themes group in the Page Layout tab.

- By default, paragraphs in a Word document are aligned at the left margin and ragged at the right margin. Change this default alignment with buttons in the Paragraph group, at the Paragraph dialog box, or with keyboard shortcuts.

- To turn on or off the display of nonprinting characters such as paragraph marks, click the Show/Hide ¶ button in the Paragraph group.
- Indent text in paragraphs with indent buttons in the Paragraph group in the Home tab, buttons in the Paragraph group in the Page Layout tab, keyboard shortcuts, options from the Paragraph dialog box, markers on the Ruler, or use the Alignment button on the Ruler.
- Increase and/or decrease spacing before and after paragraphs using the *Spacing Before* and *Spacing After* measurement boxes in the Paragraph group in the Page Layout tab, or using the *Before* and/or *After* options at the Paragraph dialog box.
- Use the Format Painter button in the Clipboard group in the Home tab to copy formatting already applied to text to different locations in the document.
- Change line spacing with the Line and Paragraph Spacing button in the Paragraph group in the Home tab, keyboard shortcuts, or options from the Paragraph dialog box.
- Display the Reveal Formatting task pane to display formatting applied to text. Use the *Compare to another selection* option in the task pane to compare formatting of two text selections to determine what formatting is different.

Commands Review

FEATURE	RIBBON TAB, GROUP	BUTTON	KEYBOARD SHORTCUT
Bold text	Home, Font	**B**	Ctrl + B
Center-align text	Home, Paragraph	≡	Ctrl + E
Change case of text	Home, Font	Aa ▾	Shift + F3
Change Quick Styles set	Home, Styles	A̲A̲	
Clear all formatting	Home, Font	A̲	
Clear character formatting			Ctrl + spacebar
Clear paragraph formatting			Ctrl + Q
Decrease font size	Home, Font	A̲ ▾	Ctrl + <
Display nonprinting characters	Home, Paragraph	¶	Ctrl + Shift + *
Font	Home, Font	Calibri (Body) ▾	
Font color	Home, Font	A̲ ▾	
Font dialog box	Home, Font	▣	Ctrl + Shift + F

FEATURE	RIBBON TAB, GROUP	BUTTON	KEYBOARD SHORTCUT
Format Painter	Home, Clipboard		Ctrl + Shift + C
Highlight text	Home, Font		
Increase font size	Home, Font		Ctrl + >
Italicize text	Home, Font		Ctrl + I
Justify-align text	Home, Paragraph		Ctrl + J
Left-align text	Home, Paragraph		Ctrl + L
Line spacing	Home, Paragraph		Ctrl + 1 (single) Ctrl + 2 (double) Ctrl + 5 (1.5)
Paragraph dialog box	Home, Paragraph		
Repeat last action			F4 or Ctrl + Y
Reveal Formatting task pane			Shift + F1
Right-align text	Home, Paragraph		Ctrl + R
Spacing after paragraph	Page Layout, Paragraph	After: 0 pt	
Spacing before paragraph	Page Layout, Paragraph	Before: 0 pt	
Strikethrough text	Home, Font		
Subscript text	Home, Font		Ctrl + =
Superscript text	Home, Font		Ctrl + Shift + +
Text Effects	Home, Font		
Theme Colors	Page Layout, Themes		
Theme Effects	Page Layout, Themes		
Theme Fonts	Page Layout, Themes		
Themes	Page Layout, Themes		
Underline text	Home, Font		Ctrl + U

Concepts Check Test Your Knowledge

Completion: In the space provided at the right, indicate the correct term, symbol, or command.

1. The Bold button is located in this group in the Home tab. _____

2. Click this button in the Font group to remove all formatting from selected text. _____

3. Proportional typefaces are divided into two main categories, serif and this. _____

4. This is the keyboard shortcut to italicize selected text. _____

5. This term refers to text that is raised slightly above the regular text line. _____

6. This automatically displays above selected text. _____

7. Click this to display the Font dialog box. _____

8. A Word document contains a number of predesigned formats grouped into style sets called this. _____

9. Apply a theme and change theme colors, fonts, and effects with buttons in the Themes group in this tab. _____

10. This is the default paragraph alignment. _____

11. Click this button in the Paragraph group to turn on the display of nonprinting characters. _____

12. Return all paragraph formatting to normal with this keyboard shortcut. _____

13. Click this button in the Paragraph group in the Home tab to align text at the right margin. _____

14. In this type of paragraph, the first line of text remains at the left margin and the remaining lines of text are indented to the first tab. _____

15. Repeat the last action by pressing F4 or with this keyboard shortcut. _____

16. Use this button in the Clipboard group in the Home tab to copy formatting already applied to text to different locations in the document. _____

17. Change line spacing to 1.5 with this keyboard shortcut. _____

18. Press these keys to display the Reveal Formatting task pane. _____

Skills Check Assess Your Performance

Assessment

1 APPLY CHARACTER FORMATTING TO A LEASE AGREEMENT DOCUMENT

1. Open **LeaseAgrmnt.docx**.
2. Save the document with Save As and name it **WL1-C2-A1-LeaseAgrmnt**.
3. Press Ctrl + End to move the insertion point to the end of the document and then type the text shown in Figure 2.8. Bold, italicize, and underline text as shown.
4. Select the entire document and then change the font to 12-point Candara.
5. Select and then bold *THIS LEASE AGREEMENT* located in the first paragraph.
6. Select and then bold *DOLLARS* located in the *Rent* section.
7. Select and then bold *DOLLARS* located in the *Damage Deposit* section.
8. Select and then italicize *12 o'clock midnight* in the *Term* section.
9. Select the title *LEASE AGREEMENT* and then change the font to 18-point Corbel and the font color to dark blue. (Make sure the title retains the bold formatting.)
10. Select the heading *Term*, change the font to 14-point Corbel, and apply small caps formatting. (Make sure the heading retains the bold formatting.)
11. Use Format Painter to change the formatting to small caps in 14-point Corbel for the remaining headings (*Rent*, *Damage Deposit*, *Use of Premises*, *Condition of Premises*, *Alterations and Improvements*, *Damage to Premises*, *Inspection of Premises*, *Default*, and *Late Charge*).
12. Save, print, and then close **WL1-C2-A1-LeaseAgrmnt.docx**.

Figure 2.8 Assessment 1

Inspection of Premises

Lessor shall have the right at all reasonable times during the term of this Agreement to exhibit the Premises and to display the usual *for sale, for rent,* or *vacancy* signs on the Premises at any time within <u>forty-five</u> days before the expiration of this Lease.

Default

If Lessee fails to pay rent when due and the default continues for <u>seven</u> days thereafter, Lessor may declare the entire balance immediately due and payable and may exercise any and all rights and remedies available to Lessor.

Late Charge

In the event that any payment required to be paid by Lessee is not made by the 10th day of the month, Lessee shall pay to Lessor a *late fee* in the amount of **$50**.

Assessment

2 APPLY STYLES, A QUICK STYLES SET, AND A THEME TO A HARDWARE TECHNOLOGY DOCUMENT

1. Open **FutureHardware.docx**.
2. Save the document with Save As and name it **WL1-C2-A2-FutureHardware**.
3. Apply the Heading 1 style to the title *ON THE HORIZON*.
4. Apply the Heading 2 style to the headings in the document (*Increased Optical Disc Storage Capacity, Improved Monitors, Holographic Storage,* and *Electronic Paper*).
5. Change the Quick Styles set to *Fancy*.
6. Apply the *Foundry* theme.
7. Change the theme colors to *Aspect*.
8. Change the theme fonts to *Flow*.
9. Change the paragraph spacing to Relaxed. ***Hint: Use the* Paragraph Spacing *option at the Change Styles button drop-down list.***
10. Highlight the second sentence in the *Increased Optical Disc Storage Capacity* section.
11. Highlight the second sentence in the *Holographic Storage* section.
12. Save, print, and then close **WL1-C2-A2-FutureHardware.docx**.

Assessment

3 APPLY CHARACTER AND PARAGRAPH FORMATTING TO AN EMPLOYEE PRIVACY DOCUMENT

1. Open **WorkplacePrivacy.docx**.
2. Save the document with Save As and name it **WL1-C2-A3-WorkplacePrivacy**.
3. Move the insertion point to the beginning of the document and then type **WORKPLACE PRIVACY** centered.
4. Select text from the beginning of the first paragraph to the end of the document (make sure you select the blank line at the end of the document) and then make the following changes:
   a. Change the line spacing to 1.5.
   b. Change the spacing after to 0 points.
   c. Indent the first line of each paragraph 0.5 inch.
   d. Change the alignment to Justify.
5. Move the insertion point to the end of the document and, if necessary, drag the First Line Indent marker on the Ruler back to 0″. Type the text shown in Figure 2.9. (Hang indent text as shown in Figure 2.9.)
6. Select the entire document and then change the font to Constantia.
7. Select the title *WORKPLACE PRIVACY* and then change the font to 14-point Calibri bold and apply the *Gradient Fill - Orange, Accent 6, Inner Shadow* text effect (second option from the left in the fourth row in the Text Effects button drop-down gallery).
8. Apply the same formatting to the title *BIBLIOGRAPHY* that you applied to the title *WORKPLACE PRIVACY*.
9. Save, print, and then close **WL1-C2-A3-WorkplacePrivacy.docx**.

Figure 2.9 Assessment 3

BIBLIOGRAPHY

Amaral, H. G. (2011). *Privacy in the workplace,* 2nd edition (pp. 103-112). Denver, CO:
    Goodwin Publishing Group.

Cuevas, R. A. (2010). *Employer and employee rights* (pp. 18-35). Los Angeles, CA:
    North Ridge Publishing Company.

Forsyth, S. M. (2011). *Protecting your privacy* (pp. 23-31). San Francisco, CA:
    Roosevelt & Carson Publishing.

Visual Benchmark Demonstrate Your Proficiency

CREATE AN ACTIVE LISTENING REPORT

1. At a blank document, press the Enter key twice, and then type the document shown in Figure 2.10. Set the body text in 12-point Cambria, the title in 16-point Candara bold, the headings in 14-point Candara bold, change the paragraph spacing after the headings to 6 points, and then apply additional formatting so the document appears as shown in the figure.
2. Save the document and name it **WL1-C2-VB-ActiveListen**.
3. Print and then close the document.

Figure 2.10 Visual Benchmark

ACTIVE LISTENING SKILLS

Speaking and listening is a two-way activity. When the audience pays attention, the speaker gains confidence, knowing that his or her message is being received and appreciated. At the same time, alert listeners obtain information, hear an amusing or interesting story, and otherwise benefit from the speaker's presentation.

Become an Active Listener

Active listeners pay attention to the speaker and to what is being said. They are respectful of the speaker and eager to be informed or entertained. In contrast, *passive listeners* "tune out" the presentation and may even display rudeness by not paying attention to the speaker. Here are ways in which you can become an active listener:

Listen with a purpose: Stay focused on what the speaker is saying and you will gain useful information or hear a suspenseful story narrated well. Try to avoid letting your attention wander.

Be courteous: Consider that the speaker spent time preparing for the presentation and thus deserves your respect.

Take brief notes: If the speaker is providing information, take brief notes on the main ideas. Doing so will help you understand and remember what is being said. If you have questions or would like to hear more about a particular point, ask the speaker for clarification after the presentation.

Practice Active Listening Skills in Conversation

Most people have had the experience of being in a one-way conversation in which one person does all the talking and the others just listen. In fact, this is not a conversation, which is by definition an exchange of information and ideas. In a true conversation, everyone has the chance to be heard. Do not monopolize the conversation. Give the other person or persons an opportunity to talk. Pay attention when others are speaking and show your interest in what is being said by making eye contact and asking questions. Avoid interrupting since this shows your disinterest and also suggests that what you have to say is more important.

Case Study   Apply Your Skills

Part 1

You work for your local chamber of commerce and are responsible for assisting the Office Manager, Teresa Alexander. Ms. Alexander would like to maintain consistency in articles submitted for publication in the monthly chamber newsletter. She wants you to explore various decorative and plain fonts. She would like you to choose two handwriting fonts, two decorative fonts, and two plain fonts and then prepare a document containing an illustration of each of these fonts. Save the document and name it **WL1-C2-CS-Fonts**. Print and then close the document.

Part 2

Ms. Alexander has asked you to write a short article for the upcoming chamber newsletter. In the article, she would like you to describe an upcoming event at your school, a local college or university, or your local community. Effectively use at least two of the fonts you wrote about in the document you prepared for Case Study Part 1. Save the document and name it **WL1-C2-CS-Article**. Print and then close the document.

Part 3

Help

When preparing the monthly newsletter, additional fonts may be necessary. Ms. Alexander has asked you to research the steps needed to install new fonts on your computer. Use the Help feature to research the steps and then prepare a document listing the steps. Format the document with appropriate headings and fonts. Save the document and name it **WL1-C2-CS-DownloadFonts**. Print and then close the document.

Customizing Paragraphs

PERFORMANCE OBJECTIVES

Upon successful completion of Chapter 3, you will be able to:

- Apply numbering and bulleting formatting to text
- Insert paragraph borders and shading
- Apply custom borders and shading
- Sort paragraph text
- Set, clear, and move tabs on the Ruler and at the Tabs dialog box
- Cut, copy, and paste text in a document
- Copy and paste text between documents

Tutorials

3.1 Creating Bulleted and Numbered Lists

3.2 Applying Custom Borders and Shading

3.3 Adding a Border and Shading to Selected Text

3.4 Sorting Text in Paragraphs

3.5 Setting Tabs Using the Ruler

3.6 Setting Tabs Using the Tabs Dialog Box

3.7 Cutting, Copying, and Pasting Text

3.8 Using the Office Clipboard

As you learned in Chapter 2, Word contains a variety of options for formatting text in paragraphs. In this chapter you will learn how to insert numbers and bullets in a document, how to apply borders and shading to paragraphs of text in a document, how to sort paragraphs of text, and how to manipulate tabs on the Ruler and at the Tabs dialog box. Editing some documents might include selecting and then deleting, moving, or copying text. You can perform this type of editing with buttons in the Clipboard group in the Home tab or with keyboard shortcuts. Model answers for this chapter's projects appear on the following pages.

Word2010L1C3

Note: Before beginning the projects, copy to your storage medium the Word2010L1C3 subfolder from the Word2010L1 folder on the CD that accompanies this textbook and then make Word2010L1C3 the active folder.

Project 1 Format a Document on Computer Technology

Technology Information Questions

1. Is programming just for professionals?
2. Could a bit of training as a programmer help your career?
3. Which elements in the procedure of creating a macro are similar to the steps in developing a program?
4. What kinds of networks are used in your local area?
5. How can networks improve efficiency?

Technology Timeline: Computers in the Workplace

➢ 1900 to 1930: Most Americans grow up on farms and live in rural communities.
➢ 1930 to 1940: Number of factory workers increases and cities swell in population; soon they outnumber rural communities.
➢ 1950s: Computers invade the business environment and the number of office "white-collar" workers increases.
➢ 1980: Personal computers enter the workplace and office workers become knowledge workers. Office workers outnumber factory workers in the job market.
➢ 1993: The Internet becomes publicly available and millions go online. Farmers number less than three percent of the population.
➢ 2002 to 2010: Seven of the ten fastest-growing occupations, according to the U.S. Department of Labor, are computer-specific jobs. The other three are desktop publishers, personal and home-care aides, and medical assistants.

Technology Career Questions

1. What is your ideal technical job?
2. Which job suits your personality?
3. Which is your first-choice certificate?
4. How does the technical job market look in your state right now? Is the job market wide open or are the information technology career positions limited?

Project 1 Format a Document on Computer Technology
WL1-C3-P1-TechInfo.docx

Project 2 Customize a Document on Online Shopping

Online Shopping

Online shopping, also called electronic shopping or e-shopping, is defined as using a computer, modem, browser, and the Internet to locate, examine, purchase, and pay for products.
Many businesses encourage consumers to shop online because it saves employee time, thus reducing staff needs and saving money for the company. For example, some major airlines offer special discounts to travelers who purchase their tickets over the Internet, and most are eliminating paper tickets altogether.

Advantages of Online Shopping

For the consumer, online shopping offers several distinct advantages over traditional shopping methods. Some of these conveniences include:

- Convenience. With e-shopping, you can browse merchandise and make purchases whenever you want from the privacy and comfort of your home or office.
- Ease of comparison shopping. E-shopping allows you to quickly find comparable items at similar stores and locate those venues with the best quality and lowest prices.
- Greater selection. Because they are not restricted by available shelf space, online stores can offer you an almost unlimited number of products.
- More product information. At many online stores, you can find detailed information about a wide variety of products, an advantage often unavailable in traditional stores.

Online Shopping Venues

Just as consumers can visit a variety of bricks-and-mortar retail outlets, such as stores and shopping malls, Internet shoppers can browse several types of online shopping venues, including online stores, superstores, and shopping malls.

Online Shopping Safety Tips

The number one concern about shopping online is security. The truth is, shopping online is safe and secure if you know what to look for. Following these guidelines can help you avoid trouble.

1. Only buy at secure sites.
2. Never provide your social security number.
3. Look for sites that follow privacy rules from a privacy watchdog such as TRUSTe.
4. Find out the privacy policy of shopping sites before you buy.
5. Keep current on the latest Internet scams.
6. Answer only the minimum questions when filling out forms.

REFERENCES

Claussen, Morgan. "Online Shopping Tips," *Technology Bytes*, October 2, 2012.
Fairmont, Gerald. "Securing Your Privacy," emcpnews.com, August 5, 2012.
Weyman, Jennifer. "Safe Online Shopping," *Computing Standards*, September 10, 2012.

Project 2 Customize a Document on Online Shopping
WL1-C3-P2-OnlineShop.docx

Project 3 Prepare a Document on Workshops and Training Dates

WORKSHOPS

Title	Price	Date
Quality Management	$240	Friday, February 3
Staff Development	229	Friday, February 17
Streamlining Production	175	Monday, March 5
Managing Records	150	Tuesday, March 27
Customer Service Training	150	Thursday, March 29
Sales Techniques	125	Tuesday, April 10

TRAINING DATES

January 3	February 7
January 12	February 15
January 24	February 21
January 26	February 23

TABLE OF CONTENTS

Project 3 Prepare a Document on Workshops and Training Dates
WL1-C3-P3-Tabs.docx

Project 4 Move and Copy Text in a Document on Online Shopping Tips

Online Shopping Safety Tips

The number one concern about shopping online is security. The truth is, shopping online is safe and secure if you know what to look for. Following these guidelines should help you avoid trouble.

Find out the privacy policy of shopping sites before you buy. Ask what information they gather, how that information will be used, and whether they share that information.

Only buy at secure sites. Secure sites use encryption to scramble your credit card information so that no one except the site can read it. When you enter a secure site, you'll get a pop-up notice in your browser, and then an icon of a closed lock will appear at the bottom of the browser.

Keep current with the latest Internet scams. The U.S. Consumer Gateway reports on Internet scams and tells you what actions the Federal Trade Commission has taken against Internet scammers. The Internet Fraud Watch, run by the National Consumers League, is a great source as well.

Never provide your social security number. A legitimate site will not ask you for your social security number.

Look for sites that follow privacy rules from a privacy watchdog such as TRUSTe. TRUSTe (www.truste.org) is a nonprofit group that serves as a watchdog for Internet privacy. It allows sites to post an online seal if the site adheres to TRUSTe's Internet privacy policies.

Answer only the minimum questions when filling out forms. Many sites put an asterisk next to the questions that must be answered, so only answer those.

Project 4 Move and Copy Text in a Document on Online Shopping Tips
WL1-C3-P4-ShoppingTips.docx

TECHNICAL SUPPORT TEAM
Staff Meeting
Wednesday, March 14, 2012
3:00 to 4:30 p.m., Room 20

TECHNICAL SUPPORT TEAM
Staff Meeting
Wednesday, March 14, 2012
3:00 to 4:30 p.m., Room 20

TECHNICAL SUPPORT TEAM
Staff Meeting
Wednesday, March 14, 2012
3:00 to 4:30 p.m., Room 20

TECHNICAL SUPPORT TEAM
Staff Meeting
Wednesday, March 14, 2012
3:00 to 4:30 p.m., Room 20

TECHNICAL SUPPORT TEAM
Staff Meeting
Wednesday, March 14, 2012
3:00 to 4:30 p.m., Room 20

TECHNICAL SUPPORT TEAM
Staff Meeting
Wednesday, March 14, 2012
3:00 to 4:30 p.m., Room 20

Project 5 Copy Text in a Staff Meeting Announcement
WL1-C3-P5-StaffMtg.docx

CONTRACT NEGOTIATION ITEMS

1. The Employer agrees that, during the term of this Agreement, it shall not cause or initiate any lockout of Employees.

2. During the term of this Agreement, the **LWU**, its members, and its representatives agree not to engage in, authorize, sanction, or support any strike, slowdown, or other acts of curtailment or work stoppage.

3. Employees transferring to another location at their own request due to bidding or exercise of seniority shall be provided with space-available transportation with no service charge for self and family.

4. Each employee requested by **RM** to be away from regular base on duty shall receive expenses.

5. An employee shall report to his/her **RM** supervisor that he/she is ill and unable to work at least two (2) hours prior to the start of his/her shift, if at all possible.

6. If **RM**, at any time, grants additional sick leave or assistance to any employee, the **LWU** will deem this a precedence requiring additional sick leave or assistance in any other case.

Project 6 Create a Contract Negotiations Document
WL1-C3-P6-NegotiateItems.docx

Project 1 Format a Document on Computer Technology   5 Parts

You will open a document containing information on computer technology, type numbered text in the document, and apply numbering and bullet formatting to paragraphs in the document.

Applying Numbering and Bullets ■■■■■■■■■■■■■■■■

Automatically number paragraphs or insert bullets before paragraphs using buttons in the Paragraph group. Use the Bullets button to insert bullets before specific paragraphs and use the Numbering button to insert numbers.

Numbering

Numbering Paragraphs

Bullets

If you type *1.*, press the spacebar, type a paragraph of text, and then press the Enter key, Word indents the number approximately 0.25 inch from the left margin and then hang indents the text in the paragraph approximately 0.5 inch from the left margin. Additionally, *2.* is inserted 0.25 inch from the left margin at the beginning of the next paragraph. Continue typing items and Word inserts the next number in the list. To turn off numbering, press the Enter key twice or click the Numbering button in the Paragraph group. (You can also remove paragraph formatting from a paragraph, including automatic numbering, with the keyboard shortcut, Ctrl + Q. Remove all formatting including character and paragraph formatting from selected text by clicking the Clear Formatting button in the Font group.)

▼ **Quick Steps**

Type Numbered Paragraphs
1. Type 1.
2. Press spacebar.
3. Type text.
4. Press Enter.

HINT

Define new numbering by clicking the Numbering button arrow and then clicking *Define New Number Format.*

If you press the Enter key twice between numbered paragraphs, the automatic number is removed. To turn it back on, type the next number in the list (and the period) followed by a space. Word will automatically indent the number and hang indent the text.

When the AutoFormat feature inserts numbering and indents text, the AutoCorrect Options button displays. Click this button and a drop-down list displays with options for undoing and/or stopping the automatic numbering. An AutoCorrect Options button also displays when AutoFormat inserts automatic bulleting in a document. If you want to insert a line break without inserting a bullet or number, you do not need to turn off the automatic numbering/bulleting and then turn it back on again. Instead, simply press Shift + Enter to insert the line break.

Project 1a **Typing Numbered Paragraphs** **Part 1 of 5**

1. Open **TechInfo.docx**.
2. Save the document with Save As and name it **WL1-C3-P1-TechInfo**.
3. Press Ctrl + End to move the insertion point to the end of the document and then type the text shown in Figure 3.1. Bold and center the title *Technology Career Questions*. When typing the numbered paragraphs, complete the following steps:
   a. Type **1.** and then press the spacebar.
   b. Type the paragraph of text and then press the Enter key. (This moves the insertion point down to the next line, inserts *2.* indented 0.25 inch from the left margin, and also indents the first paragraph of text approximately 0.5 inch from the left margin. Also, the AutoCorrect Options button displays. Use this button if you want to undo or stop automatic numbering.)
   c. Continue typing the remaining text. (Remember, you do not need to type the paragraph number and period — these are automatically inserted.)
   d. After typing the last question, press the Enter key twice. (This turns off paragraph numbering.)
4. Save **WL1-C3-P1-TechInfo.docx**.

Figure 3.1 Project 1a

Technology Career Questions

1. What is your ideal technical job?
2. Which job suits your personality?
3. Which is your first-choice certificate?
4. How does the technical job market look in your state right now? Is the job market wide open or are the information technology career positions limited?

If you do not want automatic numbering in a document, turn off the feature at the AutoCorrect dialog box with the AutoFormat As You Type tab selected as shown in Figure 3.2. To display this dialog box, click the File tab and then click the Options button located below the Help tab. At the Word Options dialog box, click the *Proofing* option located in the left panel and then click the AutoCorrect Options button that displays in the *AutoCorrect options* section of the dialog box. At the

Figure 3.2 AutoCorrect Dialog Box with AutoFormat As You Type Tab Selected

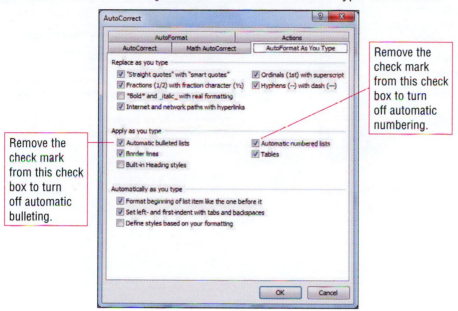

Remove the check mark from this check box to turn off automatic bulleting.

Remove the check mark from this check box to turn off automatic numbering.

AutoCorrect dialog box, click the AutoFormat As You Type tab and then click the *Automatic numbered lists* check box to remove the check mark. Click OK to close the AutoCorrect dialog box and then click OK to close the Word Options dialog box.

You can also automate the creation of numbered paragraphs with the Numbering button in the Paragraph group. To use this button, type the text (do not type the number) for each paragraph to be numbered, select the paragraphs to be numbered, and then click the Numbering button in the Paragraph group. You can insert or delete numbered paragraphs in a document.

▼ **Quick Steps**

Create Numbered Paragraph
1. Select text.
2. Click Numbering button.

Project 1b **Inserting Paragraph Numbering** **Part 2 of 5**

1. With **WL1-C3-P1-TechInfo.docx** open, apply numbers to paragraphs by completing the following steps:
   a. Select the five paragraphs of text in the *Technology Information Questions* section.
   b. Click the Numbering button in the Paragraph group.

Step 1b

Step 1a

2. Add text between paragraphs 4 and 5 in the *Technology Information Questions* section by completing the following steps:
   a. Position the insertion point immediately to the right of the question mark at the end of the fourth paragraph.
   b. Press Enter.
   c. Type **What kinds of networks are used in your local area?**
3. Delete the second question (paragraph) in the *Technology Information Questions* section by completing the following steps:
   a. Select the text of the second paragraph. (You will not be able to select the number.)
   b. Press the Delete key.
4. Save **WL1-C3-P1-TechInfo.docx**.

Technology Information Questions

1. Is programming just for professionals?
2. Does your school employ programmers?
3. Could a bit of training as a programmer help your career?
4. Which elements in the procedure of creating a macro are simila program?
5. What kinds of networks are used in your local area?
6. How can networks improve efficiency?

Step 2c

Bulleting Paragraphs

▼ **Quick Steps**

Type Bulleted Paragraphs
1. Type *, >, or - symbol.
2. Press spacebar.
3. Type text.
4. Press Enter.

Create Bulleted Paragraphs
1. Select text.
2. Click Bullets button.

In addition to automatically numbering paragraphs, Word's AutoFormat feature will create bulleted paragraphs. Bulleted lists with hanging indents are automatically created when a paragraph begins with the symbol *, >, or -. Type one of the symbols, press the spacebar, type text, and then press Enter. The AutoFormat feature inserts a bullet approximately 0.25 inch from the left margin and indents the text following the bullet another 0.25 inch. You can turn off the automatic bulleting feature at the AutoCorrect dialog box with the AutoFormat As You Type tab selected. You can demote or promote bulleted text by pressing the Tab key to demote text or pressing Shift + Tab to promote bulleted text. Word uses different bullets for demoted text.

You can also create bulleted paragraphs with the Bullets button in the Paragraph group. To create bulleted paragraphs using the Bullets button, type the text (do not type the bullet) of the paragraphs, select the paragraphs, and then click the Bullets button in the Paragraph group.

Project 1c **Typing and Inserting Bulleted Text** **Part 3 of 5**

1. With **WL1-C3-P1-TechInfo.docx** open, press Ctrl + End to move the insertion point to the end of the document and then press the Enter key once.
2. Type the heading *Technology Timeline: Computer Design* in bold as shown in Figure 3.3 and then press the Enter key.
3. Type a greater than symbol (**>**), press the spacebar, type the text of the first bulleted paragraph in Figure 3.3, and then press the Enter key.
4. Press the Tab key (this demotes the bullet to a hollow circle) and then type the bulleted text.
5. Press the Enter key (this displays another hollow circle bullet), type the bulleted text, and then press the Enter key.
6. Press Shift + Tab (this promotes the bullet to an arrow), type the bulleted text, and then press the Enter key twice (this turns off bullets).

7. Promote bulleted text by positioning the insertion point at the beginning of the text *1958: Jack Kilby, an engineer . . .* and then pressing Shift + Tab. Promote the other hollow circle bullet to an arrow. (The four paragraphs of text should be preceded by an arrow bullet.)

8. Format the paragraphs of text in the *Technology Timeline: Computers in the Workplace* section as a bulleted list by completing the following steps:

   a. Select the paragraphs of text in the *Technology Timeline: Computers in the Workplace* section.

   b. Click the Bullets button in the Paragraph group. (Word will insert the same arrow bullets that you inserted in Step 2. Word keeps the same bullet formatting until you choose a different bullet style.)

9. Save and then print **WL1-C3-P1-TechInfo.docx**. (This document will print on two pages.)

Figure 3.3 Project 1c

Technology Timeline: Computer Design

➤ 1937: Dr. John Atanasoff and Clifford Berry design and build the first electronic digital computer.

   o 1958: Jack Kilby, an engineer at Texas Instruments, invents the integrated circuit, thereby laying the foundation for fast computers and large-capacity memory.

   o 1981: IBM enters the personal computer field by introducing the IBM-PC.

➤ 2004: Wireless computer devices, including keyboards, mice, and wireless home networks, become widely accepted among users.

Inserting Paragraph Borders and Shading ▪▪▪▪▪▪▪▪▪▪

Every paragraph you create in Word contains an invisible frame. You can apply a border to the frame around the paragraph. You can apply a border to specific sides of the paragraph or to all sides, you can customize the type of border lines, and you can add shading and fill to the border. Add borders and shading to paragraphs in a document using the Borders and Shading buttons in the Paragraph group or options from the Borders and Shading dialog box.

Inserting Paragraph Borders

When a border is added to a paragraph of text, the border expands and contracts as text is inserted or deleted from the paragraph. You can create a border around a single paragraph or a border around selected paragraphs. One method for creating a border is to use options from the Borders button in the Paragraph group. Click the Borders button arrow and a drop-down list displays. At the drop-down list, click the option that will insert the desired border. For example, to insert a border at the bottom of the paragraph, click the *Bottom Border* option. Clicking an option

▼ Quick Steps

Apply Border
1. Select text.
2. Click Borders button.

Borders

will add the border to the paragraph where the insertion point is located. To add a border to more than one paragraph, select the paragraphs first and then click the desired option.

1. With **WL1-C3-P1-TechInfo.docx** open, select text from the beginning of the title *Technology Timeline: Computer Design* through the four bulleted paragraphs of text below and then press the Delete key.
2. Insert an outside border to specific text by completing the following steps:
   a. Select text from the title *Technology Information Questions* through the five numbered paragraphs of text.
   b. In the Paragraph group, click the Borders button arrow.
   c. At the Borders drop-down list, click the *Outside Borders* option.
3. Select text from the title *Technology Timeline: Computers in the Workplace* through the six bulleted paragraphs of text and then click the Borders button in the Paragraph group. (The button will apply the border option that was previously selected.)
4. Select text from the title *Technology Career Questions* through the four numbered paragraphs of text below and then click the Borders button in the Paragraph group.
5. Save and then print **WL1-C3-P1-TechInfo. docx**.

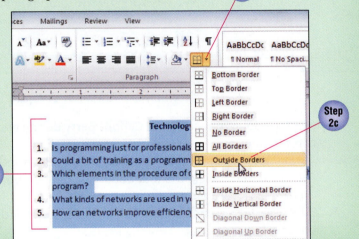

Adding Paragraph Shading

With the Shading button in the Paragraph group you can add shading to text in a document. Select text you want to shade and then click the Shading button. This applies a background color behind the text. Click the Shading button arrow and a Shading drop-down gallery displays.

Paragraph shading colors display in themes in the drop-down gallery. Use one of the theme colors or click one of the standard colors that displays at the bottom of the gallery. Click the *More Colors* option and the Colors dialog box displays. At the Colors dialog box with the Standard tab selected, click the desired color or click the Custom tab and then specify a custom color.

1. With **WL1-C3-P1-TechInfo.docx** open, apply paragraph shading and change border lines by completing the following steps:

   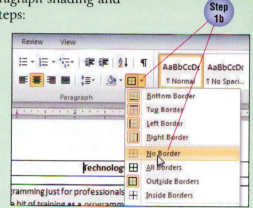
   Step 1b

   a. Position the insertion point on any character in the title *Technology Information Questions*.
   b. Click the Borders button arrow and then click *No Border* at the drop-down list.
   c. Click the Borders button arrow and then click *Bottom Border* at the drop-down list.
   d. Click the Shading button arrow and then click the *Purple, Accent 4, Lighter 60%* option.

2. Apply the same formatting to the other titles by completing the following steps:

   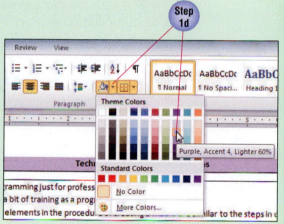
   Step 1d

   a. With the insertion point positioned on any character in the title *Technology Information Questions*, double-click the Format Painter button in the Clipboard group.
   b. Select the title *Technology Timeline: Computers in the Workplace*.
   c. Select the title *Technology Career Questions*.
   d. Click the Format Painter button in the Clipboard group.

3. Remove the paragraph border and apply shading to paragraphs by completing the following steps:

   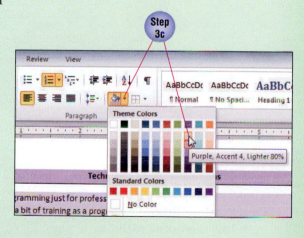
   Step 3c

   a. Select the numbered paragraphs of text below the *Technology Information Questions* title.
   b. Click the Borders button arrow and then click *No Border* at the drop-down list.
   c. Click the Shading button arrow and then click the *Purple, Accent 4, Lighter 80%* option.

4. Select the bulleted paragraphs of text below the *Technology Timeline: Computers in the Workplace* title, click the Borders button, and then click the Shading button. (Clicking the Borders button will apply the previous border option, which was *No Border*. Clicking the Shading button will apply the previous shading option, which was *Purple, Accent 4, Lighter 80%*.)

5. Select the numbered paragraphs of text below the *Technology Career Questions* title, click the Borders button, and then click the Shading button.

6. Save, print, and then close **WL1-C3-P1-TechInfo.docx**.

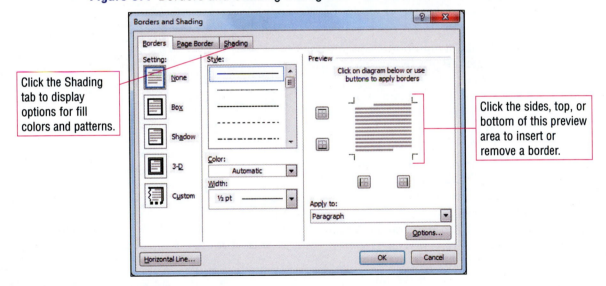

Project 2 Customize a Document on Online Shopping   2 Parts

You will open a document containing information on online shopping, apply and customize borders and shading, and then sort text in the document.

Customizing Borders and Shading

If you want to further customize paragraph borders and shading, use options at the Borders and Shading dialog box. Display this dialog box by clicking the Borders button arrow and then clicking *Borders and Shading* at the drop-down list. Click the Borders tab and options display for customizing the border; click the Shading tab and shading options display. As you learned in a previous section, you can add borders to a paragraph with the Borders button in the Paragraph group. If you want to further customize borders, use options at the Borders and Shading dialog box with the Borders tab selected as shown in Figure 3.4. At the Borders and Shading dialog box, specify the desired border, style, color, and width. Click the Shading tab and the dialog box displays with shading options.

Figure 3.4 Borders and Shading Dialog Box with the Borders Tab Selected

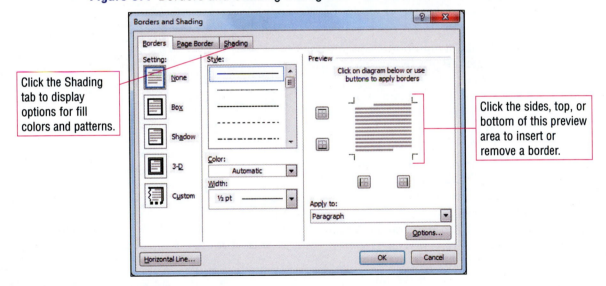

Click the Shading tab to display options for fill colors and patterns.

Click the sides, top, or bottom of this preview area to insert or remove a border.

Project 2a   Adding a Customized Border and Shading to a Document   Part 1 of 2

1. Open **OnlineShop.docx**.
2. Save the document with Save As and name it **WL1-C3-P2-OnlineShop**.
3. Make the following changes to the document:
   a. Insert 12 points of space before and 6 points of space after the headings *Online Shopping*, *Advantages of Online Shopping*, *Online Shopping Venues*, *Online Shopping Safety Tips*, and *REFERENCES*. (Do this with the *Spacing Before* and *Spacing After* measurement boxes in the Page Layout tab.)
   b. Center the *REFERENCES* title.

4. Insert a custom border and add shading to a heading by completing the following steps:
   a. Move the insertion point to any character in the heading *Online Shopping*.
   b. Click the Borders button arrow and then click *Borders and Shading* at the drop-down list.
   c. At the Borders and Shading dialog box with the Borders tab selected, click the down-pointing arrow at the right side of the *Color* option box and then click the *Dark Blue* color in the *Standard Colors* section.
   d. Click the down-pointing arrow at the right of the *Width* option box and then click *1 pt* at the drop-down list.

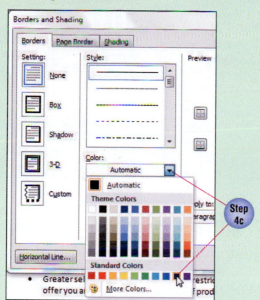

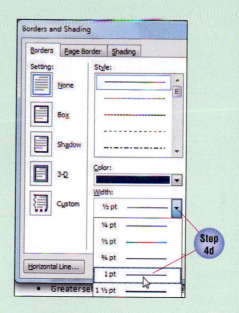

   e. Click the top border of the box in the *Preview* section of the dialog box.
   f. Click the down scroll arrow in the *Style* list box and then click the first thick/thin line.
   g. Click the down-pointing arrow at the right side of the *Color* option box and then click the *Dark Blue* color in the *Standard Colors* section.
   h. Click the bottom border of the box in the *Preview* section of the dialog box.

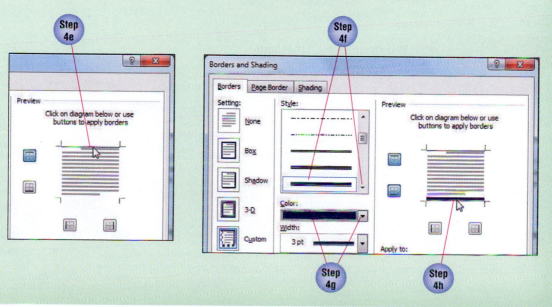

i. Click the Shading tab.
j. Click the down-pointing arrow at the right side of the *Fill* option box and then click *Olive Green, Accent 3, Lighter 60%*.
k. Click OK to close the dialog box.

5. Use Format Painter to apply the same border and shading formatting to the remaining headings by completing the following steps:
   a. Position the insertion point on any character in the heading *Online Shopping*.
   b. Double-click the Format Painter button in the Clipboard group in the Home tab.
   c. Select the heading *Advantages of Online Shopping*.
   d. Select the heading *Online Shopping Venues*.
   e. Select the heading *Online Shopping Safety Tips*.
   f. Click the Format Painter button once.
6. Move the insertion point to any character in the heading *Online Shopping* and then remove the 12 points of spacing above.
7. Save **WL1-C3-P2-OnlineShop.docx**.

Sorting Text in Paragraphs ■■■■■■■■■■■■ ■■

▼ **Quick Steps**

Sort Paragraphs of Text
1. Click Sort button.
2. Make any needed changes at Sort Text dialog box.
3. Click OK.

Sort

You can sort text arranged in paragraphs alphabetically by the first character. The first character can be a number, symbol (such as $ or #), or letter. Type paragraphs you want to sort at the left margin or indented to a tab stop. Unless you select specific paragraphs for sorting, Word sorts the entire document.

To sort text in paragraphs, open the document. If the document contains text you do not want sorted, select the specific paragraph you do want sorted. Click the Sort button in the Paragraph group and the Sort Text dialog box displays. At this dialog box, click OK. If you select text and then display the dialog box the *Sort by* option is set at *Paragraphs*. If the text you select is numbers, then *Numbers* displays in the Sort Text dialog box.

Project 2b   Sorting Paragraphs Alphabetically   Part 2 of 2

1. With **WL1-C3-P2-OnlineShop.docx** open, sort the bulleted text alphabetically by completing the following steps:
   a. Select the bulleted paragraphs in the *Advantages of Online Shopping* section.
   b. Click the Sort button in the Paragraph group.
   c. At the Sort Text dialog box, make sure *Paragraphs* displays in the *Sort by* option box and the *Ascending* option is selected.
   d. Click OK.
2. Sort the numbered paragraphs by completing the following steps:
   a. Select the numbered paragraphs in the *Online Shopping Safety Tips* section.

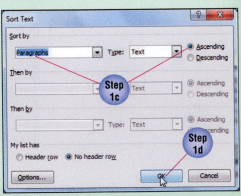

b. Click the Sort button in the Paragraph group.

c. Click OK at the Sort Text dialog box.

3. Sort alphabetically the three paragraphs of text below the *REFERENCES* title by completing the following steps:

a. Select the paragraphs of text below the *REFERENCES* title.

b. Click the Sort button in the Paragraph group.

c. Click the down-pointing arrow at the right side of the *Type* list box and then click *Text* at the drop-down list.

d. Click OK.

4. Save, print, and then close **WL1-C3-P2-OnlineShop.docx**.

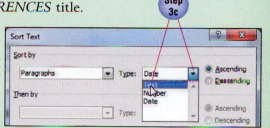

Project **3** **Prepare a Document on Workshops and Training Dates**   **4 Parts**

You will set and move tabs on the Ruler and at the Tabs dialog box and type tabbed text about workshops, training dates, and a table of contents.

Manipulating Tabs

When you work with a document, Word offers a variety of default settings such as margins and line spacing. One of these defaults is a left tab set every 0.5 inch. In some situations, these default tabs are appropriate; in others, you may want to create your own. Two methods exist for setting tabs. Tabs can be set on the Ruler or at the Tabs dialog box.

Manipulating Tabs on the Ruler

Use the Ruler to set, move, and delete tabs. If the Ruler is not visible, click the View Ruler button located at the top of the vertical scroll bar. The Ruler displays left tabs set every 0.5 inch. These default tabs are indicated by tiny vertical lines along the bottom of the Ruler. With a left tab, text aligns at the left edge of the tab. The other types of tabs that can be set on the Ruler are center, right, decimal, and bar. Use the Alignment button that displays at the left side of the Ruler to specify tabs. Each time you click the Alignment button, a different tab or paragraph alignment symbol displays. Table 3.1 shows the tab alignment buttons and what type of tab each will set.

Table 3.1 Tab Alignment Buttons

Tab Alignment Button	Type of Tab	Tab Alignment Button	Type of Tab
∟	Left tab	⊥	Decimal tab
⊥	Center tab	∣	Bar tab
⌐	Right tab		

Setting Tabs

▼ **Quick Steps**

Set Tabs on Ruler
1. Click Alignment button on Ruler.
2. Click desired location on Ruler.

When setting tabs on the Ruler, a dotted guideline displays to help align tabs.

Position the insertion point in any paragraph of text, and tabs for the paragraph appear on the Ruler.

To set a left tab on the Ruler, make sure the left alignment symbol (see Table 3.1) displays in the Alignment button. Position the arrow pointer just below the tick mark (the marks on the Ruler) where you want the tab symbol to appear and then click the left mouse button. When you set a tab on the Ruler, any default tabs to the left are automatically deleted by Word. Set a center, right, decimal, or bar tab on the Ruler in a similar manner.

Before setting a tab on the Ruler, click the Alignment button at the left side of the Ruler until the appropriate tab symbol displays and then set the tab. If you change the tab symbol in the Alignment button, the symbol remains until you change it again or you exit Word. If you exit and then reenter Word, the tab symbol returns to the default of left tab.

If you want to set a tab at a specific measurement on the Ruler, hold down the Alt key, position the arrow pointer at the desired position, and then hold down the left mouse button. This displays two measurements in the white portion in the Ruler. The first measurement displays the location of the arrow pointer on the Ruler in relation to the left margin. The second measurement is the distance from the location of the arrow pointer on the Ruler to the right margin. With the left mouse button held down, position the tab symbol at the desired location and then release the mouse button and the Alt key.

If you change tab settings and then create columns of text using the New Line command, Shift + Enter, the tab formatting is stored in the paragraph mark at the end of the columns. If you want to make changes to the tab settings for text in the columns, position the insertion point anywhere within the columns (all of the text in the columns does not have to be selected) and then make the changes.

Project 3a — Setting Left, Center, and Right Tabs on the Ruler   Part 1 of 4

1. At a new blank document, type **WORKSHOPS** centered and bolded as shown in Figure 3.5.
2. Press the Enter key and then return the paragraph alignment back to left and turn off bold for the new paragraph.
3. Set a left tab at the 0.5-inch mark, a center tab at the 3.25-inch mark, and a right tab at the 6-inch mark by completing the following steps:
   a. Click the Show/Hide ¶ button in the Paragraph group in the Home tab to turn on the display of nonprinting characters.
   b. Make sure the Ruler is displayed. (If not, click the View Ruler button located at the top of the vertical scroll bar.)
   c. Make sure the left tab symbol displays in the Alignment button at the left side of the Ruler.
   d. Position the arrow pointer on the 0.5-inch mark on the Ruler and then click the left mouse button.

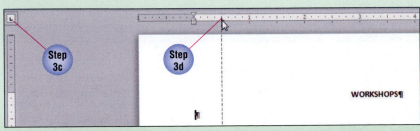

e. Position the arrow pointer on the Alignment button at the left side of the Ruler and then click the left mouse button until the center tab symbol displays (see Table 3.1).

f. Position the arrow pointer below the 3.25-inch mark on the Ruler. Hold down the Alt key and then the left mouse button. Make sure the first measurement on the Ruler displays as *3.25"* and then release the mouse button and the Alt key.

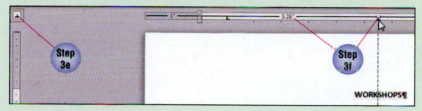

g. Position the arrow pointer on the Alignment button at the left side of the Ruler and then click the left mouse button until the right tab symbol displays (see Table 3.1).

h. Position the arrow pointer below the 6-inch mark on the Ruler. Hold down the Alt key and then the left mouse button. Make sure the first measurement on the Ruler displays as *6"* and then release the mouse button and the Alt key.

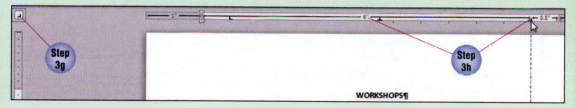

4. Type the text in columns as shown in Figure 3.5. Press the Tab key before typing each column entry and press Shift + Enter after typing the text in the third column.

5. After typing the last column entry, press the Enter key twice.

6. Press Ctrl + Q to remove paragraph formatting (tab settings).

7. Click the Show/Hide ¶ button to turn off the display of nonprinting characters.

8. Save the document and name it **WL1-C3-P3-Tabs**.

Figure 3.5 Project 3a

WORKSHOPS		
Title	Price	Date
Quality Management	$240	Friday, February 3
Staff Development	229	Friday, February 17
Streamlining Production	175	Monday, March 5
Managing Records	150	Tuesday, March 27
Customer Service Training	150	Thursday, March 29
Sales Techniques	125	Tuesday, April 10

Moving Tabs and Deleting Tabs

After a tab has been set on the Ruler, it can be moved to a new location. To move a tab, position the arrow pointer on the tab symbol on the Ruler, hold down the left mouse button, drag the symbol to the new location on the Ruler, and then release the mouse button. To delete a tab from the Ruler, position the arrow pointer on the tab symbol you want deleted, hold down the left mouse button, drag the symbol down into the document, and then release the mouse button.

Project 3b **Moving Tabs**   **Part 2 of 4**

1. With **WL1-C3-P3-Tabs.docx** open, position the insertion point on any character in the first entry in the tabbed text.
2. Position the arrow pointer on the left tab symbol at the 0.5-inch mark, hold down the left mouse button, drag the left tab symbol to the 1-inch mark on the Ruler, and then release the mouse button. *Hint: Use the Alt key to help you precisely position the tab symbol.*

3. Position the arrow pointer on the right tab symbol at the 6-inch mark, hold down the left mouse button, drag the right tab symbol to the 5.5-inch mark on the Ruler, and then release the mouse button. *Hint: Use the Alt key to help you precisely position the tab symbol.*
4. Save **WL1-C3-P3-Tabs.docx**.

Manipulating Tabs at the Tabs Dialog Box

▼ **Quick Steps**

Set Tabs at Tabs Dialog Box
1. Click Paragraph group dialog box launcher.
2. Click Tabs button.
3. Specify tab positions, alignments, and leader options.
4. Click OK.

Use the Tabs dialog box shown in Figure 3.6 to set tabs at a specific measurement. You can also use the Tabs dialog box to set tabs with preceding leaders and clear one tab or all tabs. To display the Tabs dialog box, click the Paragraph group dialog box launcher. At the Paragraph dialog box, click the Tabs button located in the bottom left corner of the dialog box.

Figure 3.6 Tabs Dialog Box

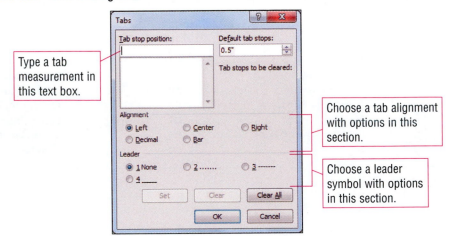

Clearing Tabs and Setting Tabs

At the Tabs dialog box, you can clear an individual tab or all tabs. To clear all tabs, click the Clear All button. To clear an individual tab, specify the tab position, and then click the Clear button.

At the Tabs dialog box, you can set a left, right, center, or decimal tab as well as a bar. (For an example of a bar tab, refer to Figure 3.7.) You can also set a left, right, center, or decimal tab with preceding leaders. To change the type of tab at the Tabs dialog box, display the dialog box and then click the desired tab in the Alignment section. Type the desired measurement for the tab in the *Tab stop position* text box.

Project 3c **Setting Left Tabs and a Bar Tab at the Tabs Dialog Box** Part 3 of 4

1. With **WL1-C3-P3-Tabs.docx** open, press Ctrl + End to move the insertion point to the end of the document.
2. Type the title **TRAINING DATES** bolded and centered as shown in Figure 3.7, press the Enter key, return the paragraph alignment back to left, and then turn off bold.
3. Display the Tabs dialog box and then set left tabs and a bar tab by completing the following steps:
   a. Click the Paragraph group dialog box launcher.
   b. At the Paragraph dialog box, click the Tabs button located in the lower left corner of the dialog box.
   c. Make sure *Left* is selected in the *Alignment* section of the dialog box.
   d. Type **1.75** in the *Tab stop position* text box.
   e. Click the Set button.
   f. Type **4** in the *Tab stop position* text box and then click the Set button.
   g. Type **3.25** in the *Tab stop position* text box, click *Bar* in the *Alignment* section, and then click the Set button.
   h. Click OK to close the Tabs dialog box.

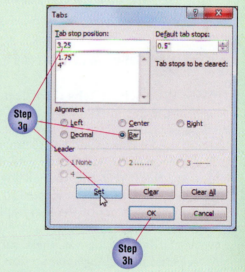

Step 3g

Step 3h

4. Type the text in columns as shown in Figure 3.7. Press the Tab key before typing each column entry and press Shift + Enter to end each line.
5. After typing *February 23*, complete the following steps:
   a. Press the Enter key.
   b. Clear tabs by displaying the Tabs dialog box, clicking the Clear All button, and then clicking OK.
   c. Press the Enter key.
6. Remove the 10 points of spacing after the last entry in the text by completing the following steps:
   a. Position the insertion point on any character in the *January 26* entry.
   b. Click the Page Layout tab.
   c. Click twice on the down-pointing arrow at the right side of the *Spacing After* measurement box. (This changes the measurement to *0 pt*.)
7. Save **WL1-C3-P3-Tabs.docx**.

Figure 3.7 Project 3c

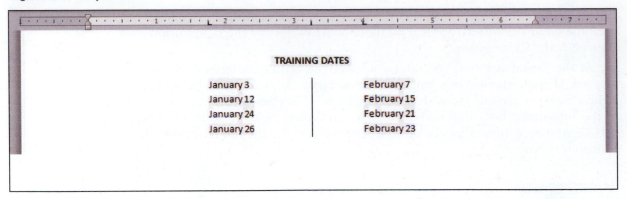

TRAINING DATES

January 3	February 7
January 12	February 15
January 24	February 21
January 26	February 23

Setting Leader Tabs

The four types of tabs can also be set with leaders. Leaders are useful in a table of contents or other material where you want to direct the reader's eyes across the page. Figure 3.8 shows an example of leaders. Leaders can be periods (.), hyphens (-), or underlines (_). To add leaders to a tab, click the type of leader desired in the *Leader* section of the Tabs dialog box.

Project 3d **Setting a Left Tab and a Right Tab with Dot Leaders**   **Part 4 of 4**

1. With **WL1-C3-P3-Tabs.docx** open, press Ctrl + End to move the insertion point to the end of the document.
2. Type the title **TABLE OF CONTENTS** bolded and centered as shown in Figure 3.8.
3. Press the Enter key and then return the paragraph alignment back to left and turn off bold.
4. Set a left tab and a right tab with dot leaders by completing the following steps:
   a. Click the Paragraph group dialog box launcher.
   b. Click the Tabs button located in the lower left corner of the Paragraph dialog box.
   c. At the Tabs dialog box, make sure *Left* is selected in the *Alignment* section of the dialog box.
   d. With the insertion point positioned in the *Tab stop position* text box, type **1** and then click the Set button.
   e. Type **5.5** in the *Tab stop position* text box.
   f. Click *Right* in the *Alignment* section of the dialog box.
   g. Click *2 ......* in the *Leader* section of the dialog box and then click the Set button.
   h. Click OK to close the dialog box.

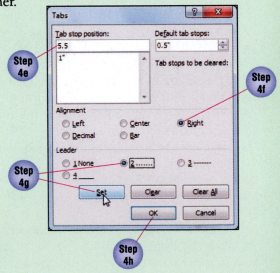

5. Type the text in columns as shown in Figure 3.8. Press the Tab key before typing each column entry and press Shift + Enter to end each line.
6. Save, print, and then close **WL1-C3-P3-Tabs.docx**.

Figure 3.8 Project 3d

Project **4** **Move and Copy Text in a Document on Online Shopping Tips**   **2 Parts**

You will open a document containing information on online shopping safety tips and then cut, copy, and paste text in the document.

Cutting, Copying, and Pasting Text

When editing a document, you may need to delete specific text, move text to a different location in the document, and/or copy text to various locations in the document. You can complete these activities using buttons in the Clipboard group in the Home tab.

Cut

Paste

Deleting Selected Text

Word offers different methods for deleting text from a document. To delete a single character, you can use either the Delete key or the Backspace key. To delete more than a single character, select the text, and then press the Delete key on the keyboard or click the Cut button in the Clipboard group. If you press the Delete key, the text is deleted permanently. (You can restore deleted text with the Undo button on the Quick Access toolbar.) The Cut button in the Clipboard group will remove the selected text from the document and insert it in the **Clipboard**. Word's Clipboard is a temporary area of memory. The Clipboard holds text while it is being moved or copied to a new location in the document or to a different document.

> **HINT**
>
> The Clipboard contents are deleted when the computer is turned off. Text you want to save permanently should be saved as a separate document.

Cutting and Pasting Text

To move text to a different location in the document, select the text, click the Cut button in the Clipboard group, position the insertion point at the location where you want the text inserted, and then click the Paste button in the Clipboard group.

You can also move selected text with a shortcut menu. To do this, select the text and then position the insertion point inside the selected text until it turns into an arrow pointer. Click the right mouse button and then click *Cut* at the shortcut menu. Position the insertion point where you want the text inserted, click the right mouse button, and then click *Paste* at the shortcut menu. Keyboard shortcuts are also available for cutting and pasting text. Use Ctrl + X to cut text and Ctrl + V to insert text.

▼ **Quick Steps**

Move Selected Text
1. Select text.
2. Click Cut button.
3. Move to desired location.
4. Click Paste button.

When selected text is cut from a document and inserted in the Clipboard, it stays in the Clipboard until other text is inserted in the Clipboard. For this reason, you can paste text from the Clipboard more than just once. For example, if you cut text to the Clipboard, you can paste this text in different locations within the document or other documents as many times as desired.

▼ Quick Steps

Move Text with Mouse
1. Select text.
2. Position mouse pointer in selected text.
3. Hold down left mouse button and drag to desired location.

Moving Text by Dragging with the Mouse

You can also use the mouse to move text. To do this, select text to be moved and then position the I-beam pointer inside the selected text until it turns into an arrow pointer. Hold down the left mouse button, drag the arrow pointer (displays with a gray box attached) to the location where you want the selected text inserted, and then release the button. If you drag and then drop selected text in the wrong location, immediately click the Undo button.

Project 4a **Moving and Dragging Selected Text** **Part 1 of 2**

1. Open **ShoppingTips.docx**.
2. Save the document with Save As and name it **WL1-C3-P4-ShoppingTips**.
3. Move a paragraph by completing the following steps:
   a. Select the paragraph that begins with *Only buy at secure sites.* including the blank line below the paragraph.
   b. Click the Cut button in the Clipboard group in the Home tab.
   c. Position the insertion point at the beginning of the paragraph that begins with *Look for sites that follow* . . . .
   d. Click the Paste button in the Clipboard group. (If the first and second paragraphs are not separated by a blank line, press the Enter key once.)

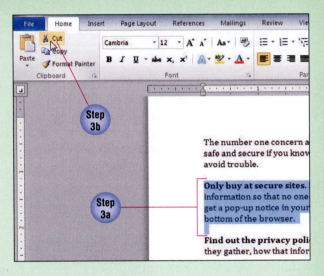

4. Following steps similar to those in Step 3, move the paragraph that begins with *Never provide your social* . . . so it is positioned before the paragraph that begins *Look for sites that follow privacy* . . . and after the paragraph that begins *Only buy at secure* . . . .
5. Use the mouse to select the paragraph that begins with *Keep current with the latest Internet* . . . including one blank line below the paragraph.
6. Move the I-beam pointer inside the selected text until it becomes an arrow pointer.
7. Hold down the left mouse button, drag the arrow pointer (displays with a small gray box attached) so that the insertion point, which displays as a grayed vertical bar, is positioned at the beginning of the paragraph that begins with *Never provide your social* . . . , and then release the mouse button.
8. Deselect the text.
9. Save **WL1-C3-P4-ShoppingTips.docx**.

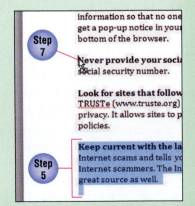

Using the Paste Options Button

When selected text is pasted, the Paste Options button displays in the lower right corner of the text. Click this button (or press the Ctrl key on the keyboard) and the *Paste Options* gallery displays as shown in Figure 3.9. Use options from this gallery to specify how you want information pasted in the document. Hover the mouse over a button in the gallery and the live preview displays the text in the document as it will appear when pasted. By default, pasted text retains the formatting of the selected text. You can choose to match the formatting of the pasted text with the formatting where the text is pasted or paste only the text without retaining formatting. To determine the function of a button in the *Paste Options* gallery, hover the mouse over a button and a ScreenTip displays with an explanation of the button function as well as the keyboard shortcut. For example, hover the mouse pointer over the first button from the left in the *Paste Options* gallery and the ScreenTip displays with the information *Keep Source Formatting (K)*. Click this button or press the letter *K* on the keyboard and the pasted text keeps its original formatting.

Paste Options

Figure 3.9 Paste Options Button Drop-down List

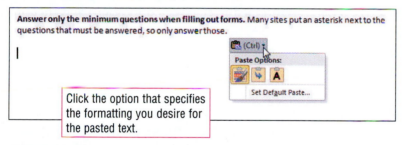

Click the option that specifies the formatting you desire for the pasted text.

Project 4b — Using the Paste Options Button — Part 2 of 2

1. With **L1-C3-P4-ShoppingTips.docx** open, open **Tip.docx**.
2. Select the paragraph of text in the document including the blank line below the paragraph and then click the Copy button in the Clipboard group.
3. Close **Tip.docx**.
4. Move the insertion point to the end of the document.
5. Click the Paste button in the Clipboard group.
6. Click the Paste Options button that displays at the end of the paragraph and then click the middle button in the Paste Options gallery (Merge Formatting (M) button). (This changes the font so it matches the formatting of the other paragraphs in the document.)

   Look for sites that follow privacy rules from a privacy watchdog such as TRUSTe. TRUSTe (www.truste.org) is a nonprofit group that serves as a watchdog for Internet privacy. It allows sites to post an online seal if the site adheres to TRUSTe's Internet privacy policies.

   Answer only the minimum questions when filling out forms. Many sites put an asterisk next to the questions that must be answered, so only answer those.

   Step 6

7. Save, print, and then close **WL1-C3-P4-ShoppingTips.docx**.

<table>
<tr><td>P</td><td colspan="2">roject 5</td><td>Copy Text in a Staff Meeting Announcement</td><td>1 Part</td></tr>
</table>

Project 5 — Copy Text in a Staff Meeting Announcement — 1 Part

You will copy and paste text in a document announcing a staff meeting for the Technical Support Team.

Copying and Pasting Text

▼ Quick Steps

Copy Selected Text
1. Select text.
2. Click Copy button.
3. Move to desired location.
4. Click Paste button.

Copy

Copying selected text can be useful in documents that contain repetitive portions of text. You can use this function to insert duplicate portions of text in a document instead of retyping the text. After you have selected text, copy the text to a different location with the Copy and Paste buttons in the Clipboard group in the Home tab or using the mouse. You can also use the keyboard shortcut, Ctrl + C, to copy text.

To use the mouse to copy text, select the text and then position the I-beam pointer inside the selected text until it becomes an arrow pointer. Hold down the left mouse button and hold down the Ctrl key. Drag the arrow pointer (displays with a small gray box and a box containing a plus symbol) to the location where you want the copied text inserted (make sure the insertion point, which displays as a grayed vertical bar, is positioned in the desired location) and then release the mouse button and then the Ctrl key.

Project 5 | **Copying Text** | Part 1 of 1

1. Open **StaffMtg.docx**.
2. Save the document with Save As and name it **WL1-C3-P5-StaffMtg**.
3. Copy the text in the document to the end of the document by completing the following steps:
   a. Select all of the text in the document and include one blank line below the text. *Hint: Click the Show/Hide ¶ button to turn on the display of nonprinting characters. When you select the text, select one of the paragraph markers below the text.*
   b. Click the Copy button in the Clipboard group.
   c. Move the insertion point to the end of the document.
   d. Click the Paste button in the Clipboard group.
4. Copy the text again at the end of the document. To do this, position the insertion point at the end of the document and then click the Paste button in the Clipboard group. (This inserts a copy of the text from the Clipboard.)
5. Select all of the text in the document using the mouse and include one blank line below the text. (Consider turning on the display of nonprinting characters.)
6. Move the I-beam pointer inside the selected text until it becomes an arrow pointer.
7. Hold down the Ctrl key and then the left mouse button. Drag the arrow pointer (displays with a box with a plus symbol inside) to the end of the document, release the mouse button, and then release the Ctrl key.
8. Deselect the text.

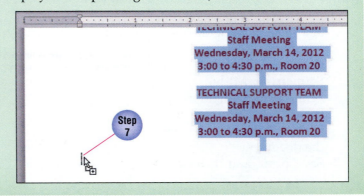

9. Make sure all text fits on one page. If not, consider deleting any extra blank lines.

10. Save, print, and then close **WL1-C3-P5-StaffMtg.docx**.

Project **6** **Create a Contract Negotiations Document** **1 Part**

You will use the Clipboard to copy and paste paragraphs to and from paragraphs in separate documents to create a contract negotiations document.

Using the Clipboard ▪▪▪▪▪▪▪▪▪▪▪▪▪▪▪▪▪▪▪▪▪▪▪▪▪▪▪▪▪

Use the Clipboard to collect and paste multiple items. You can collect up to 24 different items and then paste them in various locations. To display the Clipboard task pane, click the Clipboard group dialog box launcher located in the lower right corner of the Clipboard group. The Clipboard task pane displays at the left side of the screen in a manner similar to what you see in Figure 3.10.

Select text or an object you want to copy and then click the Copy button in the Clipboard group. Continue selecting text or items and clicking the Copy button. To insert an item, position the insertion point in the desired location and then click the option in the Clipboard task pane representing the item. Click the Paste All button to paste all of the items in the Clipboard into the document. If the copied item is text, the first 50 characters display beside the button on the Clipboard task pane. When all desired items are inserted, click the Clear All button to remove any remaining items.

▼ **Quick Steps**

Use Clipboard
1. Click Clipboard group dialog box launcher.
2. Select and copy desired text.
3. Move to desired location.
4. Click desired option in Clipboard task pane.

You can copy items to the Clipboard from various Office applications and then paste them into any Office file.

Figure 3.10 Clipboard Task Pane

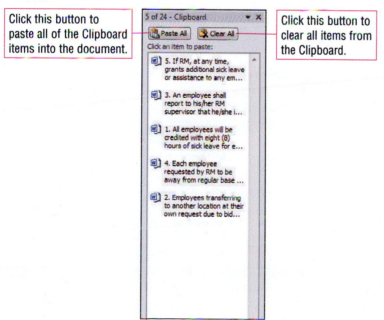

Click this button to paste all of the Clipboard items into the document.

Click this button to clear all items from the Clipboard.

Clear All

1. Open **ContractItems.docx**.
2. Turn on the display of the Clipboard task pane by clicking the Clipboard group dialog box launcher. (If the Clipboard task pane list box contains any text, click the Clear All button located toward the top of the task pane.)

Step 2

3. Select paragraph 1 in the document (the 1. is not selected) and then click the Copy button in the Clipboard group.
4. Select paragraph 3 in the document (the 3. is not selected) and then click the Copy button in the Clipboard group.
5. Close **ContractItems.docx**.
6. Paste the paragraphs by completing the following steps:
   a. Press Ctrl + N to display a new blank document. (If the Clipboard task pane does not display, click the Clipboard group dialog box launcher.)
   b. Type **CONTRACT NEGOTIATION ITEMS** centered and bolded.
   c. Press the Enter key, turn off bold, and return the paragraph alignment back to left.
   d. Click the Paste All button in the Clipboard task pane to paste both paragraphs in the document.
   e. Click the Clear All button in the Clipboard task pane.

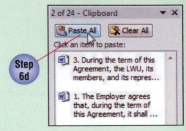

Step 6d

7. Open **UnionContract.docx**.
8. Select and then copy each of the following paragraphs:
   a. Paragraph 2 in the *Transfers and Moving Expenses* section.
   b. Paragraph 4 in the *Transfers and Moving Expenses* section.
   c. Paragraph 1 in the *Sick Leave* section.
   d. Paragraph 3 in the *Sick Leave* section.
   e. Paragraph 5 in the *Sick Leave* section.
9. Close **UnionContract.docx**.
10. Make sure the insertion point is positioned at the end of the document and then paste the paragraphs by completing the following steps:
    a. Click the button in the Clipboard task pane representing paragraph 2. (When the paragraph is inserted in the document, the paragraph number changes to 3.)
    b. Click the button in the Clipboard task pane representing paragraph 4.
    c. Click the button in the Clipboard task pane representing paragraph 3.
    d. Click the button in the Clipboard task pane representing paragraph 5.

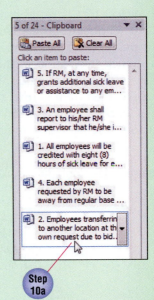

Step 10a

Step 11

11. Click the Clear All button located toward the top of the Clipboard task pane.
12. Close the Clipboard task pane.
13. Save the document and name it **WL1-C3-P6-NegotiateItems**.
14. Print and then close **WL1-C3-P6-NegotiateItems.docx**.

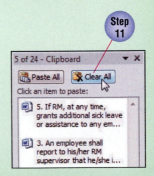

Chapter Summary

- Number paragraphs with the Numbering button in the Paragraph group in the Home tab and insert bullets before paragraphs with the Bullets button.

- Remove all paragraph formatting from a paragraph by pressing the keyboard shortcut, Ctrl + Q, and remove all character and paragraph formatting by clicking the Clear Formatting button in the Font group.

- The AutoCorrect Options button displays when the AutoFormat feature inserts numbers. Click this button to display options for undoing and/or stopping automatic numbering.

- Bulleted lists with hanging indents are automatically created when a paragraph begins with *, >, or -. The type of bullet inserted depends on the type of character entered.

- You can turn off automatic numbering and bullets at the AutoCorrect dialog box with the AutoFormat As You Type tab selected.

- A paragraph created in Word contains an invisible frame and you can insert a border around this frame. Click the Borders button arrow to display a drop-down list of border choices.

- Apply shading to text by clicking the Shading button arrow and then clicking the desired color at the drop-down gallery.

- Use options at the Borders and Shading dialog box with the Borders tab selected to add a customized border to a paragraph or selected paragraphs and use options with Shading tab selected to add shading or a pattern to a paragraph or selected paragraphs.

- With the Sort button in the Paragraph group in the Home tab, you can sort text arranged in paragraphs alphabetically by the first character, which includes numbers, symbols, or letters.

- By default, tabs are set every 0.5 inch. These settings can be changed on the Ruler or at the Tabs dialog box.

- Use the Alignment button at the left side of the Ruler to select a left, right, center, or decimal tab. When you set a tab on the Ruler, any default tabs to the left are automatically deleted.

- After a tab has been set on the Ruler, it can be moved or deleted using the mouse pointer.

- At the Tabs dialog box, you can set any of the four types of tabs as well as a bar tab at a specific measurement. You can also set tabs with preceding leaders and clear one tab or all tabs. Preceding leaders can be periods, hyphens, or underlines.

- Cut, copy, and paste text using buttons in the Clipboard group or with keyboard shortcuts.

- When selected text is pasted, the Paste Options button displays in the lower right corner of the text. Click the button and the *Paste Options* gallery displays with buttons for specifying how you want information pasted in the document.

- With the Office Clipboard, you can collect up to 24 items and then paste them in various locations in a document.

Commands Review

FEATURE	RIBBON TAB, GROUP	BUTTON, OPTION	KEYBOARD SHORTCUT
Borders	Home, Paragraph		
Borders and Shading dialog box	Home, Paragraph	, Borders and Shading	
Bullets	Home, Paragraph		
Clear character and paragraph formatting	Home, Font		
Clear paragraph formatting			Ctrl + Q
Clipboard task pane	Home, Clipboard		
Copy text	Home, Clipboard		Ctrl + C
Cut text	Home, Clipboard		Ctrl + X
New Line command			Shift + Enter
Numbering	Home, Paragraph		
Paragraph dialog box	Home, Paragraph		
Paste text	Home, Clipboard		Ctrl + V
Shading	Home, Paragraph		
Sort Text dialog box	Home, Paragraph		
Tabs dialog box	Home, Paragraph	, Tabs	

Concepts Check Test Your Knowledge

Completion: In the space provided at the right, indicate the correct term, symbol, or command.

1. The Numbering button is located in this group in the Home tab. _____

2. Automate the creation of bulleted paragraphs with this button in the Home tab. _____

3. This button displays when the AutoFormat feature inserts numbers. _____

4. You can turn off automatic numbering and bullets at the AutoCorrect dialog box with this tab selected. _____

5. Bulleted lists with hanging indents are automatically created when you begin a paragraph with the asterisk symbol (*), the hyphen (-), or this symbol.   _____

6. The Borders button is located in this group in the Home tab.   _____

7. Use options at this dialog box to add a customized border to a paragraph or selected paragraphs.   _____

8. Sort text arranged in paragraphs alphabetically by the first character, which includes numbers, symbols, or this.   _____

9. By default, each tab is set apart from the other by this measurement.   _____

10. This is the default tab type.   _____

11. When setting tabs on the Ruler, choose the tab type with this button.   _____

12. Tabs can be set on the Ruler or here.   _____

13. This group in the Home tab contains the Cut, Copy, and Paste buttons.   _____

14. To copy selected text with the mouse, hold down this key while dragging selected text.   _____

15. With this task pane, you can collect up to 24 items and then paste the items in various locations in the document.   _____

Skills Check   Assess Your Performance

Assessment

1   APPLY PARAGRAPH FORMATTING TO A COMPUTER ETHICS DOCUMENT

1. Open **CompEthics.docx**.
2. Save the document with Save As and name it **WL1-C3-A1-CompEthics**.
3. Move the insertion point to the end of the document and then type the text shown in Figure 3.11. Apply bullet formatting as shown in the figure.
4. Change the Quick Styles set to *Formal*.
5. Apply the Heading 1 style to the three headings in the document.
6. Apply the Paper theme.
7. Select the paragraphs of text in the *COMPUTER ETHICS* section and then apply numbering formatting.
8. Select the paragraphs of text in the *TECHNOLOGY TIMELINE* section and then apply bullet formatting.
9. Insert the following paragraph of text between paragraphs 2 and 3 in the *Computer Ethics* section: **Find sources relating to the latest federal and/or state legislation on privacy protection.**

10. Apply Blue-Gray, Accent 6, Lighter 60% paragraph shading to the three headings in the document.
11. Apply Gold, Accent 3, Lighter 80% paragraph shading to the numbered paragraphs in the *COMPUTER ETHICS* section and the bulleted paragraphs in the *TECHNOLOGY TIMELINE* and *ACLU FAIR ELECTRONIC MONITORING POLICY* sections.
12. Save, print, and then close **WL1-C3-A1-CompEthics.docx**.

Figure 3.11 Assessment 1

ACLU Fair Electronic Monitoring Policy

➢ Notice to employees of the company's electronic monitoring practices
➢ Use of a signal to let an employee know he or she is being monitored
➢ Employee access to all personal data collected through monitoring
➢ No monitoring of areas designed for the health or comfort of employees
➢ The right to dispute and delete inaccurate data
➢ A ban on the collection of data unrelated to work performance
➢ Restrictions on the disclosure of personal data to others without the employee's consent

---

Assessment

2 TYPE TABBED TEXT AND APPLY FORMATTING TO A COMPUTER SOFTWARE DOCUMENT

1. Open **ProdSoftware.docx**.
2. Save the document with Save As and name it **WL1-C3-A2-ProdSoftware**.
3. Move the insertion point to the end of the document and then type the tabbed text as shown in Figure 3.12. Before typing the text in columns, set left tabs at the 0.75-inch, 2.75-inch, and 4.5-inch marks on the Ruler.
4. Apply the Heading 1 style to the three headings in the document (*Productivity Software*, *Personal-Use Software*, and *Software Training Schedule*).
5. Change the Quick Styles set to *Distinctive*.
6. Apply the Elemental theme.
7. Select the productivity software categories in the *PRODUCTIVITY SOFTWARE* section (from *Word processing* through *Computer-aided design*) and then sort the text alphabetically.
8. With the text still selected, apply bullet formatting.
9. Select the personal-use software categories in the *PERSONAL-USE SOFTWARE* section (from *Personal finance software* through *Games and entertainment software*) and then sort the text alphabetically.
10. With the text still selected, apply bullet formatting.
11. Apply a single-line border to the top and a double-line border to the bottom of the three headings in the document and then apply paragraph shading of your choosing to each heading.
12. Position the insertion point on the first line of tabbed text below the *SOFTWARE TRAINING SCHEDULE* heading and then insert 12 points of spacing before the paragraph.
13. Select the text in columns and then move the tab symbols on the Ruler as follows:
    a. Move the tab at the 0.75-inch mark to the 1-inch mark.
    b. Move the tab at the 4.5-inch mark to the 4-inch mark.
14. Save, print, and then close **WL1-C3-A2-ProdSoftware.docx**.

Figure 3.12 Assessment 2

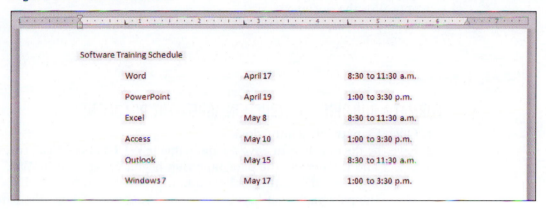

Assessment

3

TYPE AND FORMAT A TABLE OF CONTENTS DOCUMENT

1. At a new blank document, type the document shown in Figure 3.13 with the following specifications:
   a. Change the font to 11-point Cambria.
   b. Bold and center the title as shown.
   c. Before typing the text in columns, display the Tabs dialog box and then set left tabs at the 1-inch mark and the 1.5-inch mark, and a right tab with dot leaders at the 5.5-inch mark.
2. Save the document and name it **WL1-C3-A3-TofC**.
3. Print **WL1-C3-A3-TofC.docx**.
4. Select the text in columns and then move the tab symbols on the Ruler as follows:
   a. Delete the left tab symbol that displays at the 1.5-inch mark.
   b. Set a new left tab at the 0.5-inch mark.
   c. Move the right tab at the 5.5-inch mark to the 6-inch mark.

Figure 3.13 Assessment 3

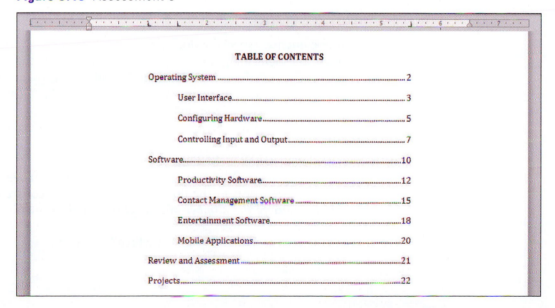

5. Apply paragraph borders and shading of your choosing to enhance the visual appeal of the document.

6. Save, print, and then close **WL1-C3-A3-TofC.docx**.

Assessment

4 FORMAT A BUILDING CONSTRUCTION AGREEMENT DOCUMENT

1. Open **ConstructAgrmnt.docx**.
2. Save the document with Save As and name it **WL1-C3-A4-ConstructAgrmnt**.
3. Select and then delete the paragraph that begins *Supervision of Work*.
4. Select and then delete the paragraph that begins *Exclusions*.
5. Move the paragraph that begins *Financing Arrangements* above the paragraph that begins *Start of Construction*.
6. Open **AgrmntItems.docx**.
7. Turn on the display of the Clipboard and then clear all the contents, if necessary.
8. Select and then copy the first paragraph.
9. Select and then copy the second paragraph.
10. Select and then copy the third paragraph.
11. Close **AgrmntItems.docx**.
12. With **WL1-C3-A4-ConstructAgrmnt.docx** open, turn on the display of the Clipboard and then paste the *Supervision* paragraph *above* the *Changes and Alterations* paragraph and merge the formatting. (Make sure you position the insertion point *above* the paragraph before you paste the text.)
13. Paste the *Pay Review* paragraph *above* the *Possession of Residence* paragraph and merge the formatting.
14. Clear all items from the Clipboard and then close the Clipboard.
15. Check the spacing between paragraphs. Insert or delete blank lines to maintain consistent spacing.
16. Save, print, and then close **L1-C3-A4-ConstructAgrmnt.docx**.

Assessment

5 HYPHENATE WORDS IN A REPORT

1. In some Word documents, especially documents with left and right margins wider than 1 inch, the right margin may appear quite ragged. If the paragraph alignment is changed to justified, the right margin will appear even, but there will be extra space added throughout the line. In these situations, hyphenating long words that fall at the end of the text line provides the document with a more balanced look. Use Word's Help feature to learn how to automatically hyphenate words in a document.
2. Open **InterfaceApps.docx**.
3. Save the document with Save As and name it **WL1-C3-A5-InterfaceApps**.
4. Automatically hyphenate words in the document, limiting the consecutive hyphens to 2. ***Hint: Specify the number of consecutive hyphens at the Hyphenation dialog box.***
5. Save, print, and then close **WL1-C3-A5-InterfaceApps.docx**.

Visual Benchmark Demonstrate Your Proficiency

CREATE A RESUME

1. At a blank document, click the No Spacing style and then type the resume document shown in Figure 3.14 on page 104. Apply character and paragraph formatting as shown in the figure. Insert six points of spacing after the heading *PROFESSIONAL EXPERIENCE* and after the heading *EDUCATION*. Change the font size of the name, DEVON CHAMBERS, to 16 points.
2. Save the document and name it **WL1-C3-VB-Resume**.
3. Print and then close the document.

Case Study Apply Your Skills

Part 1

You are the assistant to Gina Coletti, manager of La Dolce Vita, an Italian restaurant. She has been working on updating and formatting the lunch menu. She has asked you to complete the menu by opening the **Menu.docx** document (located in the Word2010L1C3 folder), determining how the appetizer section is formatted, and then applying the same formatting to the *Soups and Salads*; *Sandwiches, Calzones and Burgers*; and *Individual Pizzas* sections. Save the document and name it **WL1-C3-CS-Menu**. Print and then close the document.

Part 2

Ms. Coletti has reviewed the completed menu and is pleased with the menu but wants to add a page border around the entire page to increase visual interest. Open **WL1-C3-CS-Menu.docx** and then save the document and name it **WL1-C3-CS-MenuPgBorder**. Display the Borders and Shading dialog box with the Page Border tab selected and then experiment with the options available. Apply an appropriate page border to the menu (consider applying an art page border). Save, print, and then close **WL1-C3-CS-MenuPgBorder.docx**.

Part 3

Each week, the restaurant offers daily specials. Ms. Coletti has asked you to open and format the text in the **MenuSpecials.docx** document. She has asked you to format the specials menu in a similar manner as the main menu but to make some changes to make it unique from the main menu. Apply the same page border to the specials menu document that you applied to the main menu document. Save the document and name it **WL1-C3-CS-MenuSpecials**. Print and then close the document.

Part 4

You have been asked by the head chef to research a new recipe for an Italian dish. Using the Internet, find a recipe that interests you and then prepare a Word document containing the recipe and ingredients. Use bullets before each ingredient and use numbering for each step in the recipe preparation. Save the document and name it **WL1-C3-CS-Recipe**. Print and then close the document.

Figure 3.14 Visual Benchmark

DEVON CHAMBERS

344 North Anderson Road – Oklahoma City, OK 73177 – (404) 555-3228

PROFILE
Business manager with successful track record at entrepreneurial start-up and strong project management skills. Keen ability to motivate and supervise employees, strong hands-on experience with customer service, marketing, and operations. Highly organized and motivated professional looking to leverage strengths in leadership and organizational skills in a project coordinator role.

PROFESSIONAL EXPERIENCE

Midwest Deli, Oklahoma City, OK .... 02/10 to present
Assistant Manager
- Coordinated the opening of a new business, which included budgeting start-up costs, establishing relationships with vendors, ordering supplies, purchasing and installing equipment, and marketing the business to the community
- Manage business personnel, which includes recruitment, interviewing, hiring, training, motivating staff, and conflict resolution
- Manage daily business operations through customer satisfaction, quality control, employee scheduling, process improvement, and maintaining product inventory

Marin Associates, Shawnee, OK .... 06/08 to 06/09
Projects Coordinator
- Developed and maintained a secure office network and installed and repaired computers
- Provided support for hardware and software issues
- Directed agency projects such as equipment purchases, office reorganization, and building maintenance and repair

Moore Insurance Agency, Shawnee, OK .... 04/06 to 04/08
Administrative Assistant
- Prepared documents and forms for staff and clients
- Organized and maintained paper and electronic files and scheduled meetings and appointments
- Disseminated information using the telephone, mail services, websites, and email

EDUCATION

Associate of Arts, Business 2010
Oklahoma City Community College

TECHNOLOGY SKILLS
- Proficient in Microsoft Word, Excel, and PowerPoint
- Knowledgeable in current and previous versions of the Windows operating system
- Experience with networking, firewalls, and security systems

REFERENCES
Professional and personal references available upon request.

Microsoft® Word

CHAPTER 4

Formatting Pages

PERFORMANCE OBJECTIVES

Upon successful completion of Chapter 4, you will be able to:

- **Change document views**
- **Navigate in a document with the Navigation pane**
- **Change margins, page orientation, and paper size in a document**
- **Format pages at the Page Setup dialog box**
- **Insert a page break, blank page, and cover page**
- **Insert page numbering**
- **Insert and edit predesigned headers and footers**
- **Insert a watermark, page color, and page border**
- **Find and replace text and formatting**

Tutorials

4.1 Organizing the Document View
4.2 Navigating Using the Navigation Pane
4.3 Modifying Page Orientation and Changing Margins
4.4 Changing Page Setup
4.5 Inserting Page Numbers and Page Breaks
4.6 Creating Headers and Footers
4.7 Modifying Headers and Footers
4.8 Adding Borders, Shading, and Watermarks to Pages
4.9 Finding and Replacing Text
4.10 Finding and Replacing Formatting

A document generally displays in Print Layout view. You can change this default view with buttons in the View area on the Status bar or with options in the View tab. Use the Navigation pane to navigate in a document. A Word document, by default, contains 1-inch top, bottom, left, and right margins. You can change these default margins with the Margins button in the Page Setup group in the Page Layout tab or with options at the Page Setup dialog box. You can insert a variety of features in a Word document including a page break, blank page, and cover page as well as page numbers, headers, footers, a watermark, page color, and page border. Use options at the Find and Replace dialog box to search for specific text or formatting and replace with other text or formatting. Model answers for this chapter's projects appear on the following pages.

Note: Before beginning the projects, copy to your storage medium the Word2010L1C4 subfolder from the Word2010L1 folder on the CD that accompanies this textbook and then make Word2010L1C4 the active folder.

NETIQUETTE GUIDELINES

Distance conveys a degree of anonymity, and as a result, many people feel less inhibited in online situations than in their everyday lives. This lessening of inhibitions sometimes leads people to drop their normal standards of decorum when communicating online. In response, good cybercitizens have developed, over the years, an informal set of guidelines for online behavior called *netiquette*. Netiquette can be summarized by three simple precepts: Remember that there is a human being on the other end of your communication, treat that human being with respect, and do not transmit any message that you wouldn't be willing to communicate face to face. Some specific guidelines include:

- Be careful what you write about others. Assume that anyone about whom you are writing will read your comments or receive them by some circuitous route.
- Be truthful. Do not pretend to be someone or something that you are not.
- Be brief. Receiving and reading messages costs time and money.
- Use titles that accurately and concisely describe the contents of email and other postings.
- Consider your audience, and use language that is appropriate. Excessive use of jargon in a nontechnical chat room, for example, can be bad manners, and remember that children sometimes join chat rooms.
- Avoid offensive language, especially comments that might be construed as racist or sexist.
- Remember that the law still applies in cyberspace. Do not commit illegal acts online, such as libeling or slandering others, and do not joke about committing illegal acts.
- Be careful with humor and sarcasm. One person's humorous comment can be another person's boorish or degrading remark.
- Do not post a message more than once.
- Generally speaking, avoid putting words into full capitals. Online, all-caps is considered SHOUTING.
- If you are following up a previous message or posting, summarize that message or posting.
- Do not post irrelevant messages, referred to in hacker's jargon as spam.
- Do not post messages whose sole purpose is to sucker others into an irrelevant or unimportant discussion. Such messages are known as trolls.
- Read existing follow-up postings and don't repeat what has already been said.
- Respect other people's intellectual property. Don't post, display, or otherwise provide access to materials belonging to others, and cite references as appropriate.
- Temper online expressions of hostility; in hacker's jargon, avoid excessive flaming of others.
- Never send online chain letters.
- Some email programs allow one to place a signature containing text and graphics at the end of a mailing. Remember that elaborate materials take up valuable transmission time, and do not overdo these signatures.
- Limit the length of typed lines to less than 78 characters, and avoid unusual formatting.
- Identify any financial interests related to an email message or posting. If you are selling something, make that fact clear.
- Do not send email to people who might have no interest in it. In particular, avoid automatically copying email to large numbers of people.
- Online messages can be quite informal, but try, nevertheless, to express yourself using proper spelling, capitalization, grammar, usage, and punctuation.
- Avoid chastising others for their online typos. To err is human. To forgive is good cybercitizenship.

Project 2 Format a Document on Online Etiquette Guidelines

WL1-C4-P2-Netiquette.docx

2012

Computer Devices

Student Name
Drake Computing
1/1/2012

Cover Page

Project 3 Customize a Report on Computer Input and Output Devices

WL1-C4-P3-CompDevices.docx

COMPUTER INPUT DEVICES

Engineers have been especially creative in designing new ways to get information into computers. Some input methods are highly specialized and unusual, while common devices often undergo redesign to improve their capabilities or their ergonomics, the ways in which they affect people physically. Some common input devices include keyboards, mice, trackballs, and touchpads.

KEYBOARD

A keyboard can be an external device that is attached by means of a cable, or it can be attached to the CPU case itself as it is for laptop computers. Most keyboards today are QWERTY keyboards, which take their name from the first six keys at the left of the first row of letters. An alternative, the DVORAK keyboard, places the most commonly used keys close to the user's fingertips and speeds typing.

Many keyboards have a separate numeric keypad, like that of a calculator, containing numbers and mathematical operators. All keyboards have modifier keys that enable the user to change the symbol or character that is entered when a given key is pressed. The Shift key, for example, makes a letter uppercase. Keyboards also have special cursor keys that enable the user to change the position on the screen of the cursor, a symbol that appears on the monitor to show where in a document the next change will appear. Most keyboards also have function keys, labeled F1, F2, F3, and so on. These keys allow the user to issue commands by pressing a single key.

Page 1

MOUSE

Graphical operating systems contain many elements that a user can choose by pointing at them. Such elements include buttons, tools, pull-down menus, and icons for file folders, programs, and document files. Often pointing to and clicking on one of these elements is more convenient than using the cursor or arrow keys on the keyboard. This pointing and clicking can be done by using a mouse. The mouse is the second most common input device, after the keyboard. A mouse operates by moving the cursor on the computer screen to correspond to movements made with the mouse.

TRACKBALL

A trackball is like an upside-down mouse. A mouse is moved over a pad. A trackball remains stationary, and the user moves the ball with his or her fingers or palm. One or more buttons for choosing options are incorporated into the design of the trackball.

TOUCHPAD AND TOUCHSCREEN

A touchpad feels less mechanical than a mouse or trackball because the user simply moves a finger on the pad. A touchpad has two parts. One part acts as a button, while the other emulates a mouse pad on which the user traces the location of the cursor with a finger. People with carpal tunnel syndrome find touchpads and trackballs easier to use than mice. Many portable computers have built-in trackballs or touchpads as input devices.

A touchscreen allows the user to choose options by pressing the appropriate part of the screen. Touchscreens are widely used in bank ATMs and in kiosks at retail outlets and in tourist areas.

Page 2

COMPUTER OUTPUT DEVICES

To get information into a computer, a person uses an input device. To get information out, a person uses an output device. Some common output devices include monitors, printers, and speakers.

MONITOR

A monitor, or screen, is the most common output device used with a personal computer. A monitor creates a visual display and is either built into the CPU case or attached as an external device by means of a cable. Sometimes the cable is connected to a circuit board called a video card placed into an expansion slot in the CPU.

The most common monitors use either a thin film transistor (TFT) active matrix liquid crystal display (LCD) or a plasma display. Plasma displays have a very true level of color reproduction compared with LCDs. Emerging display technologies include surface-conduction electron-emitter displays (SED) and organic light emitting diodes (OLED).

PRINTER

After monitors, printers are the most important output devices. The print quality produced by these devices is measured in dpi, or dots per inch. As with screen resolution, the greater the number of dots per inch, the better the quality. The earliest printers for personal computers were dot matrix printers that used perforated computer paper. These impact printers worked something like typewriters, transferring the image of a character by using pins to strike a ribbon.

A laser printer uses a laser beam to create points of electrical charge on a cylindrical drum. Toner, composed of particles of ink with a negative electrical charge, sticks to the charged points on the

3 | P a g e

Page 3

---

4 | P a g e

Page 4

FUTURE OF THE INTERNET

The Internet is having trouble keeping up with the rapid increase in users and the increased workload created by the popularity of bandwidth-intensive applications such as music and video files. The broadband connections needed to enjoy these new applications are not evenly distributed. Several ongoing projects promise to provide solutions for these problems in the future. Once these connectivity problems are dealt with, people around the world will be able to enjoy the new web services that are only a few short years away.

SATELLITE INTERNET CONNECTIONS

Many people living in remote or sparsely populated areas are not served by broadband Internet connections. Cable or optical fiber networks are very expensive to install and maintain, and ISPs are not interested in providing service to areas or individuals unless they think it will be profitable. One hope for people without broadband connections is provided by satellite TV networks. Remote ISPs connect to the satellite network using antennae attached to their servers. Data is relayed to and from ISP servers to satellites, which are in turn connected to an Internet backbone access point. While the connection speeds might not be as fast as those offered by regular land-based broadband access, they are faster than the service twisted-pair cable can offer and much better than no access at all.

SECOND INTERNET

A remedy for the traffic clogging the information highway is **Internet2**, a revolutionary new type of Internet currently under development. When fully operational, Internet2 will enable large research universities in the United States to

Page 1

Project 4 Add Elements to a Report on the Future of the Internet

WL1-C4-P4-InternetFuture.docx

---

collaborate and share huge amounts of complex scientific information at amazing speeds. Led by over 170 universities working in partnership with industry and government, the Internet2 consortium is developing and deploying advanced network technologies and applications.

Internet2 is a testing ground for universities to work together and develop advanced Internet technologies such as telemedicine, digital libraries, and virtual laboratories. Internet2 universities will be connected to an ultrahigh-speed network called the Abilene backbone. Each university will use state-of-the-art equipment to take advantage of transfer speeds provided by the network.

INTERNET SERVICES FOR A FEE

Industry observers predict that large portals such as AOL, MSN, and Yahoo! will soon determine effective structures and marketing strategies to get consumers to pay for Internet services. This new market, called bring-your-own-access (BYOA), will combine essential *content*, for example, news and weather, with *services*, such as search, directory, email, IM, and online shopping, into a new product with monthly access charges. But to entice current and potential customers into the BYOA market, ISP and telecom companies must offer improvements in the area of security, privacy, and ease of use. Additionally, they are expected to develop new ways to personalize content and add value to the current range of Internet services.

Page 2

INTERNET IN 2030

Ray Kurzweil, a computer futurist, has looked ahead to the year 2030 and visualized a Web that offers no clear distinctions between real and simulated environments and people. Among the applications he sees as very possible are computerized displays in eyeglasses that could offer simultaneous translations of foreign language conversations, nanobots (microscopic robots) that would work with our brains to extend our mental capabilities, and sophisticated avatars (simulated on-screen persons) that people will interact with online. Technologies that allow people to project their feelings as well as their images and voices may usher in a period when people could "be" with another person even though they are physically hundreds or even thousands of miles apart.

Page 3

Project 5 Format a Report on Robots

Page 1

ROBOTS AS ANDROIDS

Robotic factories are increasingly commonplace, especially in heavy manufacturing, where tolerance of repetitive movements, great strength, and untiring precision are more important than flexibility. Robots are especially useful in hazardous work, such as defusing bombs or handling radioactive materials. They also excel in constructing tiny components like those found inside notebook computers, which are often too small for humans to assemble.

Most people think of robots in science fiction terms, which generally depict them as androids, or simulated humans. Real robots today do not look human at all and, judged by human standards, they are not very intelligent. The task of creating a humanlike body has proven incredibly difficult. Many technological advances in visual perception, audio perception, touch, dexterity, locomotion, and navigation need to occur before robots that look and act like human beings will live and work among us.

VISUAL PERCEPTION

Visual perception is an area of great complexity. A large percentage of the human brain is dedicated to processing data coming from the eyes. As our most powerful sense, sight is the primary means through which we understand the world around us. A single camera is not good enough to simulate the eye. Two cameras are needed to give stereoscopic vision, which allows depth and movement perception. Even with two cameras, visual perception is incomplete because the cameras cannot understand or translate what they see. Processing the image is the difficult part. In order for a robot to move through a room full of furniture it must build a mental map of that room, complete with obstacles. The robot must judge the distance and size of objects before it can figure out how to move around them.

AUDIO PERCEPTION

Audio perception is less complex than visual perception, but no less important. People respond to audible cues about their surroundings and the people they are with without even thinking about it. Listeners can determine someone's emotional state just by hearing the person's voice. A car starting up when someone crosses the street prompts the walker to glance in that direction to check for danger. Identifying a single voice and interpreting what is being said amid accompanying background noise is a task that is among the most important for human beings—and the most difficult.

Page 2

TACTILE PERCEPTION

Tactile perception, or touch, is another critical sense. Robots can be built with any level of strength, since they are made of steel and motors. How does a robot capable of lifting a car pick up an egg in the dark without dropping or crushing it? The answer is through a sense of touch. The robot must not only be able to feel an object, but also be able to sense how much pressure it is applying to that object. With this feedback it can properly judge how hard it should squeeze. This is a very difficult area, and it may prove that simulating the human hand is even more difficult than simulating the human mind.

Related to touch is the skill of dexterity, or hand-eye coordination. The challenge is to create a robot that can perform small actions, such as soldering tiny joints or placing a chip at a precise spot in a circuit board within half a millimeter.

LOCOMOTION

Locomotion includes broad movements such as walking. Getting a robot to move around is not easy. This area of robotics is challenging, as it requires balance within an endlessly changing set of variables. How does the program adjust for walking up a hill, or down a set of stairs? What if the wind is blowing hard or a foot slips? Currently most mobile robots work with wheels or treads, which limits their mobility in some circumstances but makes them much easier to control.

NAVIGATION

Related to perception, navigation deals with the science of moving a mobile robot through an environment. Navigation is not an isolated area of artificial intelligence, as it must work closely with a visual system or some other kind of perception system. Sonar, radar, mechanical "feelers," and other systems have been subjects of experimentation. A robot can plot a course to a location using an internal "map" built up by a navigational perception system. If the course is blocked or too difficult, the robot must be smart enough to backtrack so it can try another plan.

WL1-C4-P5-Robots.docx

Project 6 Format a Lease Agreement Document

Page 1

RENT AGREEMENT

THIS RENT AGREEMENT (hereinafter referred to as the "Agreement") is made and entered into this ___ day of _____, 2012, by and between Tracy Hartford and Michael Iwami.

Term

Tracy Hartford rents to Michael Iwami and Michael Iwami rents from Tracy Hartford the described premises together with any and all appurtenances thereto, for a term of ____ year(s), such term beginning on _____, and ending at 12 o'clock midnight on _____.

Rent

The total rent for the term hereof is the sum of _____ DOLLARS ($_____) payable on the ____ day of each month of the term. All such payments shall be made to Tracy Hartford at Tracy Hartford's address on or before the due date and without demand.

Damage Deposit

Upon the due execution of this Agreement, Michael Iwami shall deposit with Tracy Hartford the sum of _____ DOLLARS ($_____), receipt of which is hereby acknowledged by Tracy Hartford, as security for any damage caused to the Premises during the renting term hereof. Such deposit shall be returned to Michael Iwami, without interest, and minus any set off for damages to the Premises upon the termination of this renting Agreement.

Use of Premises

The Premises shall be used and occupied by Michael Iwami and Michael Iwami's immediately family, exclusively, as a private single family dwelling, and no part of the Premises shall be used at any time during the term of this Agreement by Michael Iwami for the purpose of carrying on any business, profession, or trade of any kind, or for any purpose other than as a private single family dwelling. Michael Iwami shall not allow any other person, other than Michael Iwami's immediate family or transient relatives and friends who are guests of Michael Iwami, to use or occupy the Premises without first obtaining Tracy Hartford's written consent to such use.

Condition of Premises

Michael Iwami stipulates, represents, and warrants that Michael Iwami has examined the Premises, and that they are at the time of this Agreement in good order, repair, and in a safe, clean, and tenantable condition.

Alterations and Improvements

Michael Iwami shall make no alterations to the buildings or improvements on the Premises without the prior written consent of Tracy Hartford. Any and all alterations, changes, and/or improvements

Page 2

built, constructed, or placed on the Premises by Michael Iwami shall, unminus otherwise provided by written agreement between Tracy Hartford and Michael Iwami, be and become the property of Tracy Hartford and remain on the Premises at the expiration or earlier termination of this Agreement.

Damage to Premises

In the event Premises are destroyed or rendered wholly unlivable, by fire, storm, earthquake, or other casualty not caused by the negligence of Michael Iwami, this Agreement shall terminate from such time except for the purpose of enforcing rights that may have then accrued hereunder.

WL1-C4-P6-LeaseAgrmnt.docx

Project **1** **Navigate in a Report on Computer Input and Output Devices** **2 Parts**

You will open a document containing information on computer input and output devices, change document views, navigate in the document using the Navigation pane, and show and hide white space at the top and bottom of pages.

Changing the View ■■■■■■■■■■■■■■■■■■■■■■■■■

By default a Word document displays in Print Layout view. This view displays the document on the screen as it will appear when printed. Other views are available such as Draft and Full Screen Reading. Change views with buttons in the View area on the Status bar or with options in the View tab. The buttons in the View area on the Status bar are identified in Figure 4.1. Along with the View buttons, the Status bar also contains a Zoom slider bar as shown in Figure 4.1. Drag the button on the Zoom slider bar to increase or decrease the size of display, or click the Zoom Out button to decrease size and click the Zoom In to increase size.

HINT

Click the 100% that displays at the left side of the Zoom slider bar to display the Zoom dialog box.

Displaying a Document in Draft View

Change to Draft view and the document displays in a format for efficient editing and formatting. At this view, margins and other features such as headers and footers do not display on the screen. Change to Draft view by clicking the Draft button in the View section on the Status bar or click the View tab and then click the Draft button in the Document Views group.

Zoom Out

Zoom In

Displaying a Document in Full Screen Reading View

The Full Screen Reading view displays a document in a format for easy viewing and reading. Change to Full Screen Reading view by clicking the Full Screen Reading button in the View section on the Status bar or by clicking the View tab and then clicking the Full Screen Reading button in the Document Views group.

Navigate in Full Screen Reading view using the keys on the keyboard as shown in Table 4.1. You can also navigate in Full Screen Reading view with options from the View Options button that displays toward the top right side of the screen or with the Next Screen and Previous Screen buttons located at the top of the window and also located at the bottom of each page.

You can customize the Full Screen Reading view with some of the options from the View Options drop-down list. Display this list by clicking the View Options button located in the upper right corner of the Full Screen Reading window.

Draft

Full Screen Reading

Figure 4.1 View Buttons and Zoom Slider Bar

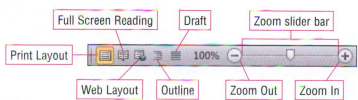

Table 4.1 Keyboard Commands in Full Screen Reading View

Press this key	To complete this action
Page Down key or spacebar	Move to the next page or section
Page Up key or Backspace key	Move to the previous page or section
Right Arrow key	Move to next page
Left Arrow key	Move to previous page
Home	Move to first page in document
End	Move to last page in document
Esc	Return to Print Layout

Navigating Using the Navigation Pane

▼ Quick Steps

Display Navigation Pane
1. Click View tab.
2. Click *Navigation Pane* check box.

Word includes a number of features you can use to navigate in a document. Along with the navigation features you have already learned, you can also navigate using the Navigation pane shown in Figure 4.2. When you click the *Navigation Pane* check box in the Show group in the View tab, the Navigation pane displays at the left side of the screen and includes a Search text box and a pane with three tabs. Click the first tab to display titles and headings with styles applied in the Navigation pane. Click a title or heading in the pane to move the insertion point to that title or heading. Click the second tab to display thumbnails of each page in the pane. Click a thumbnail to move the insertion point to the specific page. Click the third tab to browse the current search results in the document. Close the Navigation pane by clicking the *Navigation Pane* check box in the Show group in the View tab or by clicking the Close button located in the upper right corner of the pane.

Figure 4.2 Navigation Pane

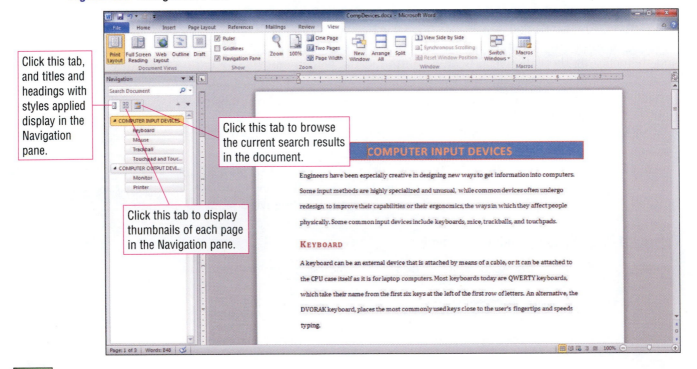

Click this tab, and titles and headings with styles applied display in the Navigation pane.

Click this tab to browse the current search results in the document.

Click this tab to display thumbnails of each page in the Navigation pane.

1. Open **CompDevices.docx**.
2. Click the Draft button located in the View section on the Status bar.

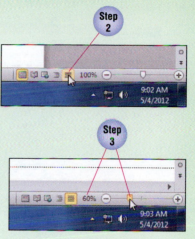

3. Using the mouse, drag the Zoom slider bar button to the left to decrease the size of the document display to approximately 60%. (The percentage displays at the left side of the Zoom Out button.)
4. Drag the Zoom slider bar button back to the middle until *100%* displays at the left side of the Zoom Out button.
5. Click the Print Layout button in the View section on the Status bar.
6. Click the Full Screen Reading button located in the View section on the Status bar.
7. Click the View Options button located toward the top of the viewing window and then click *Show Two Pages* at the drop-down list.
8. Click the Next Screen button to display the next two pages in the viewing window.
9. Click the Previous Screen button to display the previous two pages.

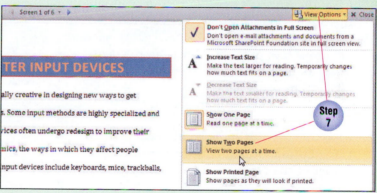

10. Click the View Options button located toward the top of the viewing window and then click *Show One Page* at the drop-down list.

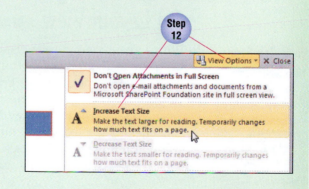

11. Practice navigating using the actions shown in Table 4.1. (Try all of the actions in Table 4.1 except pressing the Esc key since that action will close Full Screen Reading view.)
12. Increase the size of the text by clicking the View Options button and then clicking the *Increase Text Size* option.
13. Press the Home key to display the first viewing page.
14. Decrease the size of the text by clicking the View Options button and then clicking the *Decrease Text Size* option.
15. Click the Close button located in the upper right corner of the screen.

16. Click the View tab and then click the *Navigation Pane* check box.
17. Click the *COMPUTER OUTPUT DEVICES* title that displays in the Navigation pane.

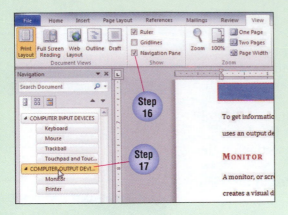

18. Click the *Keyboard* heading that displays in the Navigation pane.
19. Click the middle tab in the Navigation pane. (This displays page thumbnails in the pane.).
20. Click the number 3 thumbnail in the Navigation pane.
21. Click the number 1 thumbnail in the Navigation pane.
22. Close the Navigation pane by clicking the Close button located in the upper right corner of the Navigation pane.

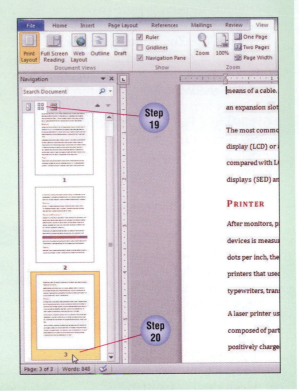

Hiding/Showing White Space in Print Layout View

▼ **Quick Steps**

Hide White Space
1. Position mouse pointer at top of page until pointer displays as *Hide White Space* icon.
2. Double-click left mouse button.

Show White Space
1. Position mouse pointer on thin line separating pages until pointer displays as *Show White Space* icon.
2. Double-click left mouse button.

In Print Layout view, a page displays as it will appear when printed including the white space at the top and bottom of the page representing the default margins. To save space on the screen in Print Layout view, you can remove the white space by positioning the mouse pointer at the top edge or bottom edge of a page or between pages until the pointer displays as the *Hide White Space* icon and then double-clicking the left mouse button. To redisplay the white space, position the mouse pointer on the thin, black line separating pages until the pointer turns into the *Show White Space* icon and then double-click the left mouse button.

Hide White Space

Show White Space

1. With **CompDevices.docx** open, make sure the document displays in Print Layout view.
2. Press Ctrl + Home to move the insertion point to the beginning of the document.
3. Hide the white spaces at the top and bottom of pages by positioning the mouse pointer at the top edge of the page until the pointer turns into the *Hide White Space* icon and then double-clicking the left mouse button.
4. Scroll through the document and notice the display of pages.
5. Redisplay the white spaces at the top and bottom of pages by positioning the mouse pointer on any thin, black, horizontal line separating pages until the pointer turns into the *Show White Space* icon and then double-clicking the left mouse button.
6. Close **CompDevices.docx**.

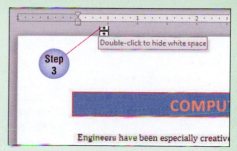

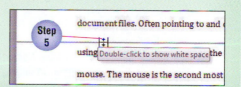

Project 2   Format a Document on Online Etiquette Guidelines   2 Parts

You will open a document containing information on guidelines for online etiquette and then change the margins, page orientation, and page size.

Changing Page Setup

The Page Setup group in the Page Layout tab contains a number of options for affecting pages in a document. With options in the group you can perform such actions as changing margins, orientation, and page size and inserting page breaks. The Pages group in the Insert tab contains three buttons for inserting a page break, blank page, and cover page.

Changing Margins

Change page margins with options at the Margins drop-down list as shown in Figure 4.3. To display this list, click the Page Layout tab and then click the Margins button in the Page Setup group. To change the margins, click one of the preset margins that display in the drop-down list. Be aware that most printers contain a required margin (between one-quarter and three-eighths inch) because printers cannot print to the edge of the page.

Changing Page Orientation

Click the Orientation button in the Page Setup group in the Page Layout tab and two options display — *Portrait* and *Landscape*. At the portrait orientation, which is the default, the page is 11 inches tall and 8.5 inches wide. At the landscape orientation, the page is 8.5 inches tall and 11 inches wide. Change the page orientation and the page margins automatically change.

Margins

▼ **Quick Steps**

Change Margins
1. Click Page Layout tab.
2. Click Margins button.
3. Click desired margin option.

Change Page Orientation
1. Click Page Layout tab.
2. Click Orientation button.
3. Click desired orientation.

Figure 4.3 Margins Drop-down List

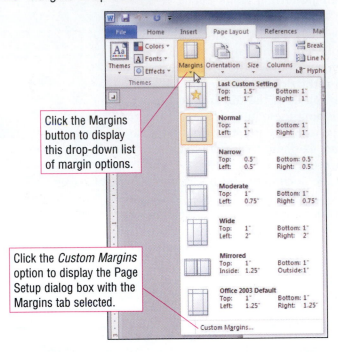

Click the Margins button to display this drop-down list of margin options.

Click the *Custom Margins* option to display the Page Setup dialog box with the Margins tab selected.

Quick Steps

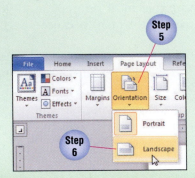

Size

Change Page Size
1. Click Page Layout tab.
2. Click Size button.
3. Click desired size option.

Changing Page Size

By default, Word uses a page size of 8.5 inches wide and 11 inches tall. You can change this default setting with options at the Size drop-down list. Display this drop-down list by clicking the Size button in the Page Setup group in the Page Layout tab.

Project 2a **Changing Margins, Page Orientation, and Size**   **Part 1 of 2**

1. Open **Netiquette.docx**.
2. Save the document with Save As and name it **WL1-C4-P2-Netiquette**.
3. Click the Page Layout tab.
4. Click the Margins button in the Page Setup group and then click the *Office 2003 Default* option.
5. Click the Orientation button in the Page Setup group.
6. Click *Landscape* at the drop-down list.

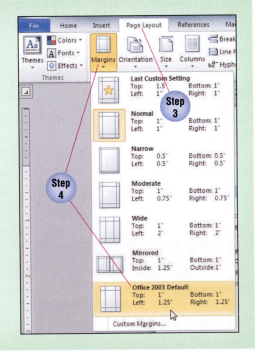

---

7. Scroll through the document and notice how the text displays on the page in landscape orientation.
8. Click the Orientation button in the Page Setup group and then click *Portrait* at the drop-down list. (This changes the orientation back to the default.)
9. Click the Size button in the Page Setup group.
10. Click the A5 option (displays with *5.83" × 8.27"* below *A5*). If this option is not available, choose an option with a similar size.
11. Scroll through the document and notice how the text displays on the page.
12. Click the Size button and then click *Legal* (displays with *8.5" × 14"* below *Legal*).
13. Scroll through the document and notice how the text displays on the page.
14. Click the Size button and then click *Letter* (displays with *8.5" × 11"* below *Letter*). (This returns the size back to the default.)
15. Save **WL1-C4-P2-Netiquette.docx**.

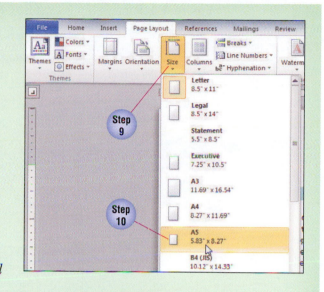

Changing Margins at the Page Setup Dialog Box

The Margins button in the Page Setup group provides you with a number of preset margins. If these margins do not fit your needs, you can set specific margins at the Page Setup dialog box with the Margins tab selected as shown in Figure 4.4. Display this dialog box by clicking the Page Setup group dialog box launcher or by clicking the Margins button and then clicking *Custom Margins* at the bottom of the drop-down list.

To change margins, select the current measurement in the *Top*, *Bottom*, *Left*, or *Right* text box, and then type the new measurement. You can also increase a measurement by clicking the up-pointing arrow at the right side of the text box. Decrease a measurement by clicking the down-pointing arrow. As you make changes to the margin measurements at the Page Setup dialog box, the sample page in the *Preview* section illustrates the effects of the margin changes.

Changing Paper Size at the Page Setup Dialog Box

The Size button drop-down list contains a number of preset page sizes. If these sizes do not fit your needs, you can specify page size at the Page Setup dialog box with the Paper tab selected. Display this dialog box by clicking the Size button in the Page Setup group and then clicking *More Paper Sizes* that displays at the bottom of the drop-down list.

▼ **Quick Steps**

Change Margins at Page Setup Dialog Box
1. Click Page Layout tab.
2. Click Page Setup group dialog box launcher.
3. Specify desired margins.
4. Click OK.

Change Page Size at Page Setup Dialog Box
1. Click Page Layout tab.
2. Click Size button.
3. Click *More Paper Sizes* at drop-down list.
4. Specify desired size.
5. Click OK.

Figure 4.4 Page Setup Dialog Box with Margins Tab Selected

Notice the default settings for the top, bottom, left, and right margins.

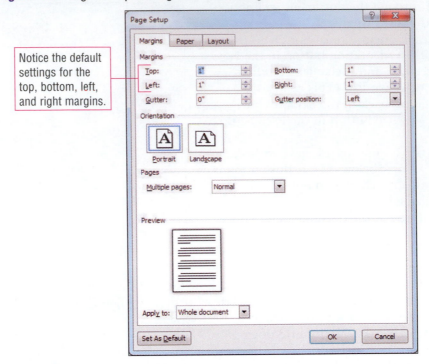

Changing Margins at the Page Setup Dialog Box   Part 2 of 2

1. With **WL1-C4-P2-Netiquette.docx** open, make sure the Page Layout tab is selected.
2. Click the Page Setup group dialog box launcher.
3. At the Page Setup dialog box with the Margins tab selected, click the down-pointing arrow at the right side of the *Top* text box until *0.5"* displays.
4. Click the down-pointing arrow at the right side of the *Bottom* text box until *0.5"* displays.
5. Select the current measurement in the *Left* text box and then type **0.75**.
6. Select the current measurement in the *Right* text box and then type **0.75**.
7. Click OK to close the dialog box.
8. Click the Size button in the Page Setup group and then click *More Paper Sizes* at the drop-down list.
9. At the Page Setup dialog box with the Paper tab selected, click the down-pointing arrow at the right side of the *Paper size* option, scroll down the list box, and then click *A4* at the drop-down list.
10. Click OK to close the dialog box.

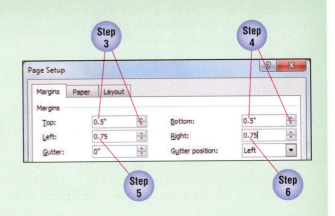

Step 3

Step 4

Step 5

Step 6

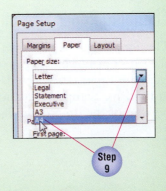

Step 9

11. Scroll through the document and notice how the text displays on the page.
12. Click the Size button in the Page Setup group and then click *Letter* at the drop-down list.
13. Save, print, and then close **WL1-C4-P2-Netiquette.docx**.

Project 3 Customize a Report on Computer Input and Output Devices

3 Parts

You will open a document containing information on computer input and output devices and then insert page breaks, a blank page, a cover page, and page numbering.

Inserting a Page Break

With the default top and bottom margins of one inch, approximately nine inches of text print on the page. At approximately the ten-inch mark, Word automatically inserts a page break. You can insert your own page break in a document with the keyboard shortcut, Ctrl + Enter, or with the Page Break button in the Pages group in the Insert tab.

A page break inserted by Word is considered a *soft* page break and a page break inserted by you is considered a *hard* page break. Soft page breaks automatically adjust if you add or delete text from a document. A hard page break does not adjust and is therefore less flexible than a soft page break. If you add or delete text from a document with a hard page break, check the break to determine whether it is still in a desirable location. In Draft view, a hard page break displays as a row of dots with the words *Page Break* in the center. To delete a page break, position the insertion point immediately below the page break and then press the Backspace key or change to Draft view, position the insertion point on the page break, and then press the Delete key.

▼ **Quick Steps**

Insert Page Break
1. Click Insert tab.
2. Click Page Break button.
OR
Press Ctrl + Enter.

Page Break

Project 3a   Inserting Page Breaks

Parts 1 of 3

1. Open **CompDevices.docx**.
2. Save the document with Save As and name it **WL1-C4-P3-CompDevices**.
3. Change the top margin by completing the following steps:
   a. Click the Page Layout tab.
   b. Click the Page Setup group dialog box launcher.
   c. At the Page Setup dialog box, click the Margins tab and then type **1.5** in the *Top* text box.
   d. Click OK to close the dialog box.
4. Insert a page break at the beginning of the heading *Mouse* by completing the following steps:
   a. Position the insertion point at the beginning of the heading *Mouse* (located toward the bottom of page 1).

Step 3c

b. Click the Insert tab and then click the Page Break button in the Pages group.

5. Move the insertion point to the beginning of the title *COMPUTER OUTPUT DEVICES* (located at the bottom of page 2) and then insert a page break by pressing Ctrl + Enter.

6. Move the insertion point to the beginning of the heading *Printer* and then press Ctrl + Enter to insert a page break.

7. Delete the page break by completing the following steps:
   a. Click the Draft button in the view area on the Status bar.
   b. With the insertion point positioned at the beginning of the heading *Printer*, press the Backspace key. (This displays the page break in the document.)
   c. Press the Backspace key again to delete the page break.
   d. Click the Print Layout button in the view area of the Status bar.

8. Pressing the Backspace key removed the formatting from the Printer heading. Apply formatting by completing the following steps;
   a. Move the insertion point to any character in the heading *Monitor*.
   b. Click the Home tab and then click once on the Format Painter button.
   c. Select the heading *Printer*.

9. Save **WL1-C4-P3-CompDevices.docx**.

Inserting a Blank Page

Blank Page

▼ **Quick Steps**

Insert Blank Page
1. Click Insert tab.
2. Click Blank Page button.

Insert Cover Page
1. Click Insert tab.
2. Click Cover Page button.
3. Click desired cover page at drop-down list.

Click the Blank Page button in the Pages group in the Insert tab to insert a blank page at the position of the insertion point. This might be useful in a document where you want to insert a blank page for an illustration, graphic, or figure.

Inserting a Cover Page

If you are preparing a document for distribution to others or you want to simply improve the visual appeal of your document, consider inserting a cover page. With the Cover Page button in the Pages group in the Insert tab, you can insert a predesigned and formatted cover page and then type personalized text in specific locations on the page. Click the Cover Page button and a drop-down list displays. The drop-down list provides a visual representation of the cover page. Scroll through the list and then click the desired cover page.

A predesigned cover page contains location placeholders where you can enter specific information. For example, a cover page might contain the placeholder *[Type the document title]*. Click anywhere in the placeholder text and the placeholder text is selected. With the placeholder text selected, type the desired text. You can delete a placeholder by clicking anywhere in the placeholder text, clicking the placeholder tab, and then pressing the Delete key.

Cover Page

A cover page provides a polished and professional look to a document.

1. With **WL1-C4-P3-CompDevices.docx** open, create a blank page by completing the following steps:
   a. Move the insertion point to the beginning of the heading *Touchpad and Touchscreen* located on the second page.
   b. Click the Insert tab.
   c. Click the Blank Page button in the Pages group.
2. Insert a cover page by completing the following steps:
   a. Press Ctrl + Home to move the insertion point to the beginning of the document.
   b. Click the Cover Page button in the Pages group.
   c. At the drop-down list, scroll down and then click the *Motion* cover page.
   d. Click anywhere in the placeholder text *[Type the document title]* and then type **Computer Devices**.

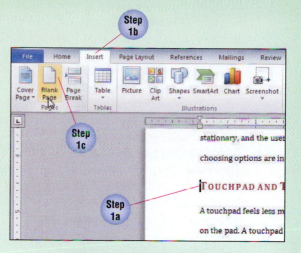

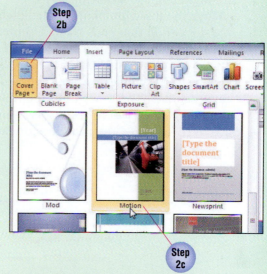

e. Click the placeholder text *[Year]*. Click the down-pointing arrow that displays at the right side of the placeholder and then click the Today button that displays at the bottom of the drop-down calendar.

f. Click anywhere in the placeholder text *[Type the company name]* and then type **Drake Computing**. (If a name displays in the placeholder, select the name and then type **Drake Computing**.)

g. Click anywhere in the placeholder text *[Type the author name]* and then type your first and last names. (If a name displays in the placeholder, select the name and then type your first and last names.)

3. Remove the blank page you inserted in Step 1 by completing the following steps:

a. Move the insertion point immediately right of the period that ends the last sentence in the paragraph of text in the *Trackball* heading (located toward the bottom of page 3).

b. Press the Delete key on the keyboard approximately six times until the heading *Touch Pad and Touch Screen* displays on page 3.

4. Save **WL1-C4-P3-CompDevices.docx**.

Step 2e

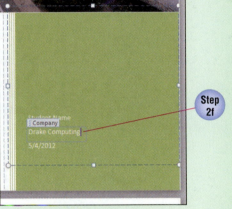

Step 2f

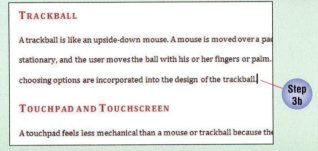

Step 3b

TRACKBALL

A trackball is like an upside-down mouse. A mouse is moved over a pa[d]

stationary, and the user moves the ball with his or her fingers or palm.

choosing options are incorporated into the design of the trackball.

TOUCHPAD AND TOUCHSCREEN

A touchpad feels less mechanical than a mouse or trackball because the

---

▼ **Quick Steps**

Insert Page Numbering
1. Click Insert tab.
2. Click Page Number button.
3. Click desired option at drop-down list.

Page Number

Inserting Predesigned Page Numbering ▪▪▪▪▪▪▪▪▪▪▪▪

Word, by default, does not print page numbers on a page. If you want to insert page numbering in a document, use the Page Number button in the Header & Footer group in the Insert tab. When you click the Page Number button, a drop-down list displays with options for specifying the page number location. Point to an option at this list and a drop-down list displays of predesigned page number formats. Scroll through the options in the drop-down list and then click the desired option. If you want to change the format of page numbering in a document, double-click the page number, select the page number text, and then apply the desired formatting. You can remove page numbering from a document by clicking the Page Number button and then clicking *Remove Page Numbers* at the drop-down list.

1. With **WL1-C4-P3-CompDevices.docx** open, insert page numbering by completing the following steps:
   a. Move the insertion point so it is positioned on any character in the title *COMPUTER INPUT DEVICES*.
   b. Click the Insert tab.
   c. Click the Page Number button in the Header & Footer group and then point to *Top of Page*.
   d. Scroll through the drop-down list and then click the *Brackets 2* option.

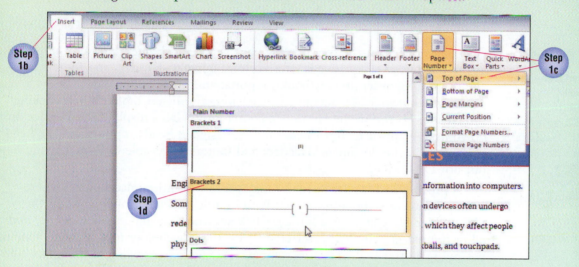

2. Double-click the document to make it active and then scroll through the document and notice the page numbering that displays at the top of each page except the cover page. (The cover page and text are divided by a section break, which you will learn more about in Chapter 5. Word considers the cover page as page 1 but does not include the numbering on the page.)

3. Remove the page numbering by clicking the Insert tab, clicking the Page Number button, and then clicking *Remove Page Numbers* at the drop-down list.

4. Click the Page Number button, point to *Bottom of Page*, scroll down the drop-down list and then click the *Accent Bar 2* option.

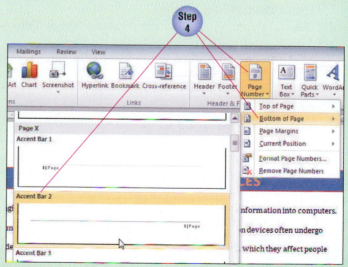

5. Double-click in the document to make it active.

6. Save, print, and then close **WL1-C4-P3-CompDevices.docx**.

You will open a document containing information on the future of the Internet, insert a predesigned header and footer in the document, remove a header, and format and delete header and footer elements.

Inserting Predesigned Headers and Footers ■■■■■■■■■

▼ Quick Steps

Insert Predesigned Header
1. Click Insert tab.
2. Click Header button.
3. Click desired option at drop-down list.
4. Type text in specific placeholders in header.

Header

Text that appears at the top of every page is called a *header* and text that appears at the bottom of every page is referred to as a *footer*. Headers and footers are common in manuscripts, textbooks, reports, and other publications. Insert a predesigned header in a document by clicking the Insert tab and then clicking the Header button in the Header & Footer group. This displays the Header drop-down list. At this list, click the desired predesigned header option and the header is inserted in the document. Headers and footers are visible in Print Layout view but not Draft view.

A predesigned header or footer may contain location placeholders where you can enter specific information. For example, a header might contain the placeholder *[Type the document title]*. Click anywhere in the placeholder text and all of the placeholder text is selected. With the placeholder text selected, type the desired text. You can delete a placeholder by clicking anywhere in the placeholder text, clicking the placeholder tab, and then pressing the Delete key.

Project **4a** **Inserting a Predesigned Header in a Document** **Part 1 of 3**

1. Open **InternetFuture.docx**.
2. Save the document with Save As and name it **WL1-C4-P4-InternetFuture**.
3. Make the following changes to the document:
   a. Select the entire document, change the line spacing to *2*, and then deselect the document.
   b. Apply the Heading 1 style to the title *FUTURE OF THE INTERNET*.
   c. Apply the Heading 2 style to the headings *Satellite Internet Connections*, *Second Internet*, *Internet Services for a Fee*, and *Internet in 2030*.
   d. Change the Quick Styles set to *Formal*. **Hint: Use the Change Styles button in the Styles group in the Home tab**.
   e. Apply the Origin theme by clicking the Page Layout tab, clicking the Themes button, and then clicking *Origin* at the drop-down gallery.
   f. Move the insertion point to the beginning of the heading *INTERNET IN 2030* (located toward the bottom of page 2) and then insert a page break by clicking the Insert tab and then clicking the Page Break button in the Pages group.

4. Press Ctrl + Home to move the insertion point to the beginning of the document and then insert a header by completing the following steps:

   a. If necessary, click the Insert tab.

   b. Click the Header button in the Header & Footer group.

   c. Scroll to the bottom of the drop-down list that displays and then click *Tiles*.

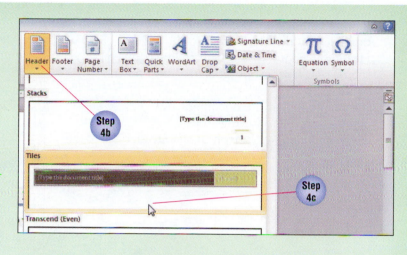

   d. Click anywhere in the placeholder text *[Type the document title]* and then type **Future of the Internet**.

   e. Click anywhere in the placeholder text *[Year]* and then type the current year.

   f. Double-click in the document text. (This makes the document text active and dims the header.)

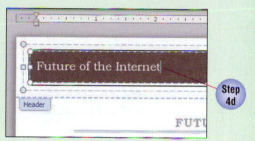

5. Scroll through the document to see how the header will print.

6. Save and then print **WL1-C4-P4-InternetFuture.docx**.

Insert a predesigned footer in the same manner as inserting a header. Click the Footer button in the Header & Footer group in the Insert tab and a drop-down list displays similar to the Header drop-down list. Click the desired footer and the predesigned footer formatting is applied to the document.

Removing a Header or Footer

Remove a header from a document by clicking the Insert tab and then clicking the Header button in the Header & Footer group. At the drop-down list that displays, click the *Remove Header* option. Complete similar steps to remove a footer.

▼ **Quick Steps**

Insert Predesigned Footer
1. Click Insert tab.
2. Click Footer button.
3. Click desired option at drop-down list.
4. Type text in specific placeholders in footer.

Footer

Project 4b   **Removing a Header and Inserting a Predesigned Footer**   **Part 2 of 3**

1. With **WL1-C4-P4-InternetFuture.docx** open, press Ctrl + Home to move the insertion point to the beginning of the document.

2. Remove the header by clicking the Insert tab, clicking the Header button in the Header & Footer group, and then clicking the *Remove Header* option at the drop-down menu.

3. Insert a footer in the document by completing the following steps:
   a. Click the Footer button in the Header & Footer group.
   b. Click *Alphabet* at the drop-down list.

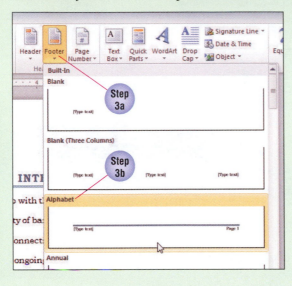

   c. Click anywhere in the placeholder text *[Type text]* and then type **Future of the Internet**.
   d. Double-click in the document text. (This makes the document text active and dims the footer.)

4. Scroll through the document to see how the footer will print.

5. Save and then print **WL1-C4-P4-InternetFuture.docx**.

You can double-click a header or footer in Print Layout view to display the header or footer pane for editing.

Editing a Predesigned Header or Footer

Predesigned headers and footers contain elements such as page numbers and a title. You can change the formatting of the element by clicking the desired element and then applying the desired formatting. You can also select and then delete an item.

Project 4c **Formatting and Deleting Header and Footer Elements** **Part 3 of 3**

1. With **WL1-C4-P4-InternetFuture.docx** open, remove the footer by clicking the Insert tab, clicking the Footer button, and then clicking *Remove Footer* at the drop-down list.

2. Insert and then format a header by completing the following steps:

   a. Click the Header button in the Header & Footer group in the Insert tab, scroll in the drop-down list, and then click *Motion (Odd Page)*. (This header inserts the document title as well as the page number.)

   b. Delete the document title from the header by clicking anywhere in the text *FUTURE OF THE INTERNET*, selecting the text, and then pressing the Delete key.

   c. Double-click in the document text.

3. Insert and then format a footer by completing the following steps:

   a. Click the Insert tab.

   b. Click the Footer button, scroll down the drop-down list, and then click *Motion (Odd Page)*.

   c. Click on any character in the date that displays in the footer, select the date, and then type the current date.

   d. Select the date, turn on bold, and then change the font size to 12.

   e. Double-click in the document text.

4. Scroll through the document to see how the header and footer will print.

5. Save, print, and then close **WL1-C4-P4-InternetFuture.docx**.

Project **5** **Format a Report on Robots** **2 Parts**

You will open a document containing information on the difficulties of creating a humanlike robot and then insert a watermark, change page background color, and insert a page border.

Formatting the Page Background ■■■■■■■ ■ ■ ■ ■ ■ ■

The Page Background group in the Page Layout tab contains three buttons for customizing a page background. Click the Watermark button and choose a predesigned watermark from a drop-down list. If a document is going to be viewed on-screen or on the Web, consider adding a page color. In Chapter 3, you learned how to apply borders and shading to text at the Borders and Shading dialog box. This dialog box also contains options for inserting a page border.

Inserting a Watermark

A **watermark** is a lightened image that displays behind text in a document. Using watermarks is an excellent way to add visual appeal to a document. Word provides a number of predesigned watermarks you can insert in a document. Display these watermarks by clicking the Watermark button in the Page Background group in the Page Layout tab. Scroll through the list of watermarks and then click the desired option.

▼ **Quick Steps**

Insert Watermark
1. Click Page Layout tab.
2. Click Watermark button.
3. Click desired option at drop-down list.

Change Page Color
1. Click Page Layout tab.
2. Click Page Color button.
3. Click desired option at color palette.

Watermark

Changing Page Color

Page Color

Use the Page Color button in the Page Background group to apply background color to a document. This background color is intended for viewing a document on-screen or on the Web. The color is visible on the screen but does not print. Insert a page color by clicking the Page Color button and then clicking the desired color at the color palette.

Project 5a   **Inserting a Watermark and Page Color**   Part 1 of 2

1. Open **Robots.docx** and then save the document with Save As and name it **WL1-C4-P5-Robots**.
2. Apply the Heading 1 style to the title *ROBOTS AS ANDROIDS* and the Heading 3 style to the five headings in the document. (You may need to click the Heading 2 style to display the Heading 3 style.)
3. Change the Quick Styles set to *Thatch* and then center the document title *ROBOTS AS ANDROIDS*.
4. Change the top margin to 1.5 inches.
5. Apply the Aspect theme.
6. Insert a page break at the beginning of the heading *Tactile Perception*.
7. Insert a watermark by completing the following steps:
   a. Move the insertion point to the beginning of the document.
   b. Click the Page Layout tab.
   c. Click the Watermark button in the Page Background group.
   d. At the drop-down list, click the *CONFIDENTIAL 1* option.

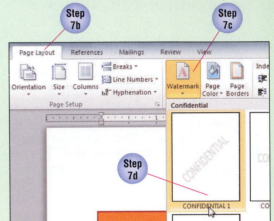

8. Scroll through the document and notice how the watermark displays behind the text.
9. Remove the watermark and insert a different one by completing the following steps:
   a. Click the Watermark button in the Page Background group and then click *Remove Watermark* at the drop-down list.
   b. Click the Watermark button and then click *DO NOT COPY 1* at the drop-down list.
10. Scroll through the document and notice how the watermark displays.
11. Move the insertion point to the beginning of the document.
12. Click the Page Color button in the Page Background group and then click *Dark Green, Accent 4, Lighter 80%* at the color palette.
13. Save **WL1-C4-P5-Robots.docx**.

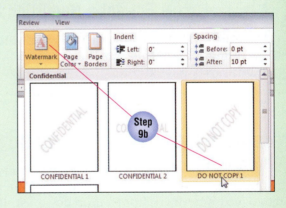

Inserting a Page Border

To improve the visual appeal of a document, consider inserting a page border. When you insert a page border in a multiple-page document, the border prints on each page. To insert a page border, click the Page Borders button in the Page Background group in the Page Layout tab. This displays the Borders and Shading dialog box with the Page Border tab selected as shown in Figure 4.5. At this dialog box, you can specify the border style, color, and width.

The dialog box contains an option for inserting a page border containing an image. To display the images available, click the down-pointing arrow at the right side of the *Art* list box. Scroll down the drop-down list and then click the desired image. (This feature may need to be installed the first time you use it.)

Changing Page Border Options

By default, a page border displays and prints 24 points from the top, left, right, and bottom edges of the page. Some printers, particularly inkjet printers, have a nonprinting area around the outside edges of the page that can interfere with the printing of a border. Before printing a document with a page border, click the File tab and then click the Print tab. Look at the preview of the page at the right side of the Print tab Backstage view and determine whether the entire border is visible. If a portion of the border is not visible in the preview page (generally at the bottom and right side of the page), consider changing measurements at the Border and Shading Options dialog box shown in Figure 4.6. You can also change measurements at the Border and Shading Options dialog box to control the location of the page border on the page.

Display the Border and Shading Options dialog box by clicking the Page Layout tab and then clicking the Page Borders button. At the Borders and Shading dialog box with the Page Border tab selected, click the Options button that displays in the lower right corner of the dialog box. The options at the Border and Shading Options dialog box change depending on whether you click the Options button at the Borders and Shading dialog box with the Borders tab selected or the Page Border tab selected.

▼ **Quick Steps**

Insert Page Border
1. Click Page Layout tab.
2. Click Page Borders button.
3. Specify desired options at dialog box.

Page Borders

Figure 4.5 Borders and Shading Dialog Box with Page Border Tab Selected

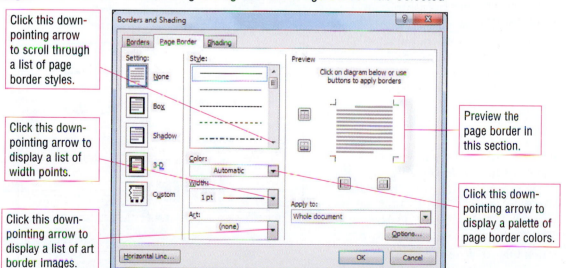

Click this down-pointing arrow to scroll through a list of page border styles.

Click this down-pointing arrow to display a list of width points.

Click this down-pointing arrow to display a list of art border images.

Preview the page border in this section.

Click this down-pointing arrow to display a palette of page border colors.

Figure 4.6 Border and Shading Options Dialog Box

Increase these measurements to move the page border away from the edge of the page or decrease the measurements to move the page border closer to the edge of the page.

Change this option to *Text* to specify the distance from the text to the page border.

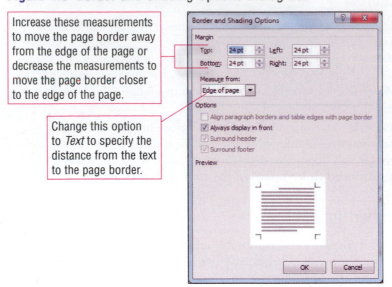

If your printer contains a nonprinting area and the entire page border will not print, consider increasing the spacing from the page border to the edge of the page. Do this with the *Top, Left, Bottom,* and/or *Right* measurement boxes. The *Measure from* option box has a default setting of *Edge of page*. You can change this option to *Text*, which changes the top and bottom measurements to *1 pt* and the left and right measurements to *4 pt* and moves the page border into the page. Use the measurement boxes to specify the distance you want the page border displayed and printed from the text in the document.

Project 5b   **Inserting a Page Border**   **Part 2 of 2**

1. With **WL1-C4-P5-Robots.docx** open, remove the page color by clicking the Page Color button in the Page Background group in the Page Layout tab and then clicking *No Color* at the color palette.
2. Insert a page border by completing the following steps:
   a. Click the Page Borders button in the Page Background group in the Page Layout tab.
   b. Click the *Box* option in the *Setting* section.
   c. Scroll down the list of line styles in the *Style* list box until the end of the list displays and then click the third line from the end.
   d. Click the down-pointing arrow at the right of the *Color* list box and then click *Red, Accent 2, Darker 25%* at the color palette.
   e. Click OK to close the dialog box.

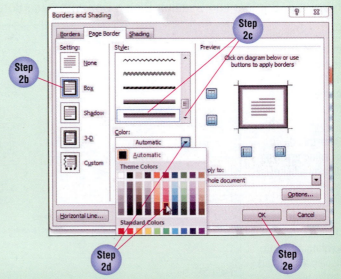

Step 2b

Step 2c

Step 2d

Step 2e

3. Increase the spacing from the page border to the edges of the page by completing the following steps:

a. Click the Page Borders button in the Page Background group in the Page Layout tab.

b. At the Borders and Shading dialog box with the Page Border tab selected, click the Options button located in the lower right corner.

c. At the Border and Shading Options dialog box, click the up-pointing arrow at the right side of the *Top* measurement box until *31 pt* displays. (This is the maximum measurement allowed.)

d. Increase the measurement for the *Left*, *Bottom*, and *Right* measurement boxes to *31 pt*.

e. Click OK to close the Border and Shading Options dialog box.

f. Click OK to close the Borders and Shading dialog box.

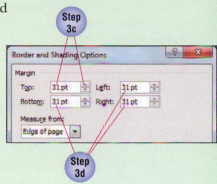

4. Save **WL1-C4-P5-Robots.docx** and then print only page 1.

5. Insert an image page border and change the page border spacing options by completing the following steps:

a. Click the Page Borders button in the Page Background group in the Page Layout tab.

b. Click the down-pointing arrow at the right side of the *Art* list box and then click the border image shown below (located approximately one-third of the way down the drop-down list).

c. Click the Options button located in the lower right corner of the Borders and Shading dialog box.

d. At the Border and Shading Options dialog box, click the down-pointing arrow at the right of the *Measure from* option box and then click *Text* at the drop-down list.

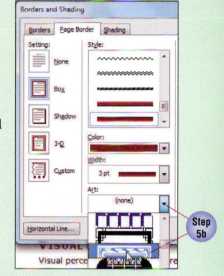

e. Click the up-pointing arrow at the right of the *Top* measurement box until *10 pt* displays.

f. Increase the measurement for the *Bottom* measurement to *10 pt* and the measurement in the *Left* and *Right* measurement boxes to *14 pt*.

g. Click the *Surround header* check box to remove the check mark.

h. Click the *Surround footer* check box to remove the check mark.

i. Click OK to close the Border and Shading Options dialog box.

j. Click OK to close the Borders and Shading dialog box.

6. Save, print, and then close **WL1-C4-P5-Robots.docx**.

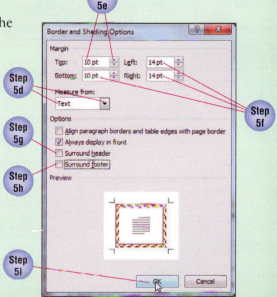

Project 6 Format a Lease Agreement Document

4 Parts

You will open a lease agreement document, search for specific text and replace it with other text, and then search for specific formatting and replace it with other formatting.

Finding and Replacing Text and Formatting ■■■■■■■ ■

▼ **Quick Steps**

Find Text
1. Click Find button in Home tab.
2. Type search text.
3. Click Next Search Result button.

Find

Replace

With Word's Find feature you can search for specific characters or formatting. With the Find and Replace feature, you can search for specific characters or formatting and replace them with other characters or formatting. The Find button and the Replace button are located in the Editing group in the Home tab.

Click the Find button in the Editing group in the Home tab (or press the keyboard shortcut, Ctrl + F) and the Navigation pane displays at the left side of the screen with the third tab selected. Hover the mouse over the third tab and a ScreenTip displays with the information *Browse the results from your current search*. With this tab selected, type search text in the Search text box and any occurrence of the text in the document is highlighted and a fragment of the text surrounding the search text displays in a thumbnail in the Navigation pane. For example, search for *Lessee* in the WL1-C4-P6-LeaseAgrmnt.docx document and the screen displays as shown in Figure 4.7. Notice that any occurrence of *Lessee* displays highlighted in yellow in the document and the Navigation pane displays thumbnails of text surrounding the occurrences of *Lessee*.

Figure 4.7 Navigation Pane Showing Search Results

Click this down-pointing arrow to display a drop-down list with options for displaying find and replace dialog boxes and options for specifying what you want to find in the document.

Type search text in this text box.

Click this button to move to the next occurrence of search text.

Click this button to move to the previous occurrence of search text.

Text thumbnails display search text in document and text surrounding the search text.

Occurrences of search text are highlighted in the document.

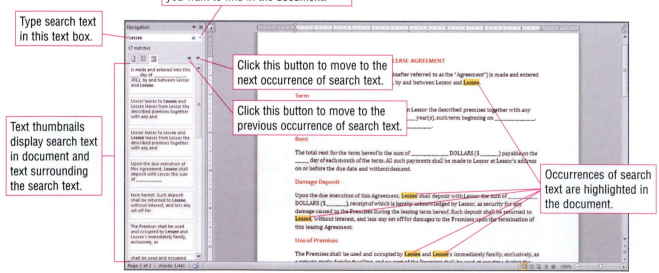

Click a text thumbnail in the Navigation pane and the occurrence of the search text is selected in the document. If you hover your mouse over a text thumbnail in the Navigation pane, the page number location displays in a small box near the mouse pointer. You can also move to the next occurrence of the search text by clicking the Next Search Result button located towards the upper right side of the Navigation pane. Click the Previous Search Result button to move to the previous occurrence of the search text.

Click the down-pointing arrow at the right side of the Search text box and a drop-down list displays with options for displaying dialog boxes such as the Find Options dialog box or the Find and Replace dialog box and also options for specifying what you want to find in the document such as figures, tables, and equations.

You can also highlight search text in a document with options at the Find and Replace dialog box with the Find tab selected. Display this dialog box by clicking the Find button arrow in the Editing group in the Home tab and then clicking *Advanced Find* at the drop-down list. You can also display the Find and Replace dialog box by clicking the down-pointing arrow at the right side of the Search text box in the Navigation pane with the Find tab selected and then clicking the *Advanced Find* option at the drop-down list. To highlight find text, type the search text in the *Find what* text box, click the Reading Highlight button, and then click *Highlight All* at the drop-down list. All occurrences of the text in the document are highlighted. To remove highlighting, click the Reading Highlight button and then click *Clear Highlighting* at the drop-down list.

Project 6a Finding and Highlighting Text   Part 1 of 4

1. Open **LeaseAgrmnt.docx** and then save the document with Save As and name it **WL1-C4-P6-LeaseAgrmnt**.
2. Find all occurrences of *lease* by completing the following steps:
   a. Click the Find button in the Editing group in the Home tab.
   b. Type lease in the search text box in the Navigation pane.
   c. After a moment, all occurrences of *lease* in the document are highlighted and text thumbnails display in the Navigation pane. Click a couple of the text thumbnails in the Navigation pane to select the text in the document.
   d. Click the Previous Search Result button to select the previous occurrence of *lease* in the document.
3. Use the Find and Replace dialog box with the Find tab selected to highlight all occurrences of *Premises* in the document by completing the following steps:
   a. Click in the document and press Ctrl + Home to move the insertion point to the beginning of the document.
   b. Click the down-pointing arrow at the right side of the search text box in the Navigation pane and then click *Advanced Find* at the drop-down list.

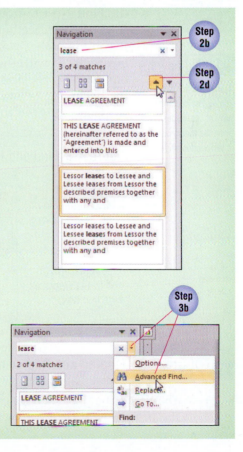

c. At the Find and Replace dialog box with the Find tab selected (and *lease* selected in the *Find what* text box), type **Premises**.

d. Click the Reading Highlight button and then click *Highlight All* at the drop-down list.

e. Click in the document to make it active and then scroll through the document and notice the occurrences of highlighted text.

f. Click in the dialog box to make it active.

g. Click the Reading Highlight button and then click *Clear Highlighting* at the drop-down list.

h. Click the Close button to close the Find and Replace dialog box.

4. Close the Navigation pane by clicking the Close button that displays in the upper right corner of the pane.

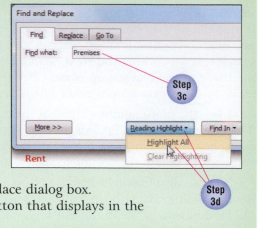

Finding and Replacing Text

Quick Steps

Find and Replace Text
1. Click Replace button in Home tab.
2. Type search text.
3. Press Tab key.
4. Type replace text.
5. Click Replace or Replace All button.

HINT

If the Find and Replace dialog box is in the way of specific text, drag the dialog box to a different location.

To find and replace text, click the Replace button in the Editing group in the Home tab or use the keyboard shortcut, Ctrl + H. This displays the Find and Replace dialog box with the Replace tab selected as shown in Figure 4.8. Type the text you want to find in the *Find what* text box, press the Tab key, and then type the replacement text.

The Find and Replace dialog box contains several command buttons. Click the Find Next button to tell Word to find the next occurrence of the characters. Click the Replace button to replace the characters and find the next occurrence. If you know that you want all occurrences of the characters in the *Find what* text box replaced with the characters in the *Replace with* text box, click the Replace All button. This replaces every occurrence from the location of the insertion point to the beginning or end of the document (depending on the search direction). Click the Cancel button to close the Find and Replace dialog box.

Figure 4.8 Find and Replace Dialog Box with the Replace Tab Selected

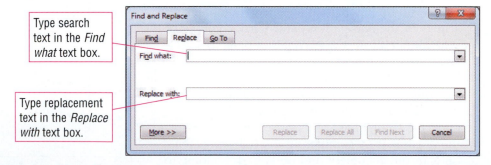

Type search text in the *Find what* text box.

Type replacement text in the *Replace with* text box.

Project 6b **Finding and Replacing Text** **Part 2 of 4**

1. With **WL1-C4-P6-LeaseAgrmnt.docx** open, make sure the insertion point is positioned at the beginning of the document.

2. Find all occurrences of *Lessor* and replace with *Tracy Hartford* by completing the following steps:

a. Click the Replace button in the Editing group in the Home tab.

b. At the Find and Replace dialog box with the Replace tab selected, type **Lessor** in the *Find what* text box.

c. Press the Tab key to move the insertion point to the *Replace with* text box.

d. Type **Tracy Hartford**.

e. Click the Replace All button.

f. At the message *Word has completed its search of the document and has made 11 replacements*, click OK. (Do not close the Find and Replace dialog box.)

3. With the Find and Replace dialog box still open, complete steps similar to those in Step 2 to find all occurrences of *Lessee* and replace with *Michael Iwami*.

4. Close the Find and Replace dialog box.

5. Save **WL1-C4-P6-LeaseAgrmnt.docx**.

Choosing Check Box Options

The Find and Replace dialog box contains a variety of check boxes with options you can choose for completing a search. To display these options, click the More button located at the bottom of the dialog box. This causes the Find and Replace dialog box to expand as shown in Figure 4.9. Each option and what will occur if

Figure 4.9 Expanded Find and Replace Dialog Box

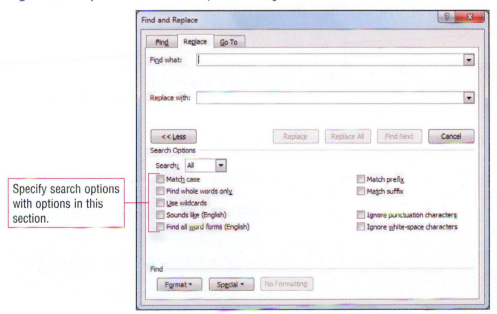

Specify search options with options in this section.

it is selected is described in Table 4.2. To remove the display of options, click the Less button. (The Less button was previously the More button.) Note that if you make a mistake when replacing text, you can close the Find and Replace dialog box and then click the Undo button on the Quick Access toolbar.

Table 4.2 Options at the Expanded Find and Replace Dialog Box

Choose this option	To
Match case	Exactly match the case of the search text. For example, if you search for *Book* and select the *Match case* option, Word will stop at *Book* but not *book* or *BOOK*.
Find whole words only	Find a whole word, not a part of a word. For example, if you search for *her* and did not select *Find whole words only*, Word would stop at *there*, *here*, *hers*, etc.
Use wildcards	Search for wildcards, special characters, or special search operators.
Sounds like	Match words that sound alike but are spelled differently such as *know* and *no*.
Find all word forms	Find all forms of the word entered in the *Find what* text box. For example, if you enter *hold*, Word will stop at *held* and *holding*.
Match prefix	Find only those words that begin with the letters in the *Find what* text box. For example, if you enter *per*, Word will stop at words such as *perform* and *perfect* but skip words such as *super* and *hyperlink*.
Match suffix	Find only those words that end with the letters in the *Find what* text box. For example, if you enter *ly*, Word will stop at words such as *accurately* and *quietly* but skip over words such as *catalyst* and *lyre*.
Ignore punctuation characters	Ignore punctuation within characters. For example, if you enter *US* in the *Find what* text box, Word will stop at *U.S.*
Ignore white space characters	Ignore spaces between letters. For example, if you enter *F B I* in the *Find what* text box, Word will stop at *FBI*.

Project 6c **Finding and Replacing Word Forms and Suffixes** **Part 3 of 4**

1. With **WL1-C4-P6-LeaseAgrmnt.docx** open, make sure the insertion point is positioned at the beginning of the document.
2. Find all word forms of the word *lease* and replace with *rent* by completing the following steps:
   a. Click the Replace button in the Editing group in the Home tab.
   b. At the Find and Replace dialog box with the Replace tab selected, type **lease** in the *Find what* text box.

c. Press the Tab key and then type rent in the *Replace with* text box.

d. Click the More button.

e. Click the *Find all word forms (English)* option. (This inserts a check mark in the check box.)

f. Click the Replace All button.

g. At the message telling you that Replace All is not recommended with Find All Word Forms, click OK.

h. At the message *Word has completed its search of the document and has made 6 replacements*, click OK.

i. Click the *Find all word forms* option to remove the check mark.

3. Find the word *less* and replace with the word *minus* and specify that you want Word to find only those words that end in *less* by completing the following steps:

a. At the expanded Find and Replace dialog box, select the text in the *Find what* text box and then type less.

b. Select the text in the *Replace with* text box and then type minus.

c. Click the *Match suffix* check box to insert a check mark and tell Word to find only words that end in *less*.

d. Click the Replace All button.

e. At the message telling you that 2 replacements were made, click OK.

f. Click the *Match suffix* check box to remove the check mark.

g. Click the Less button.

h. Close the Find and Replace dialog box.

4. Save **WL1-C4-P6-LeaseAgrmnt.docx**.

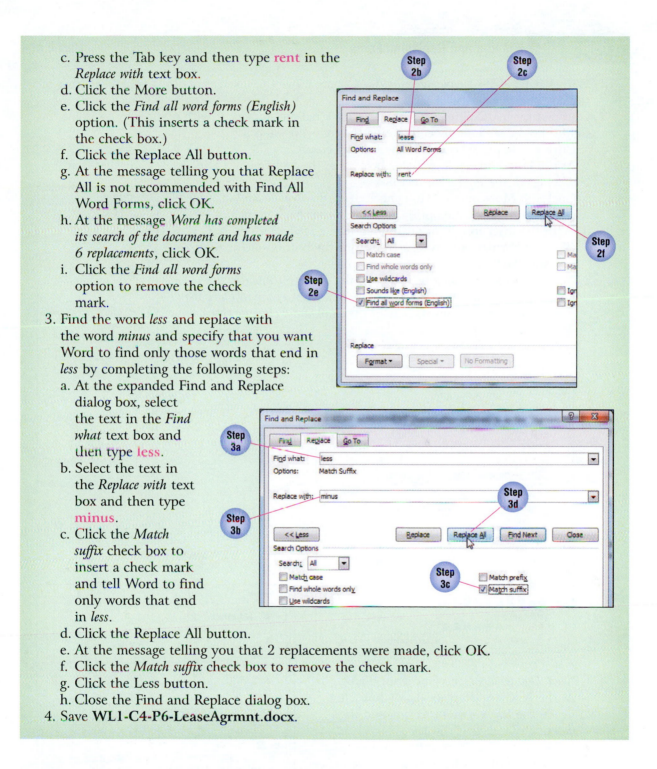

Finding and Replacing Formatting

With options at the Find and Replace dialog box with the Replace tab selected, you can search for characters containing specific formatting and replace them with other characters or formatting. To specify formatting in the Find and Replace dialog box, click the More button and then click the Format button that displays toward the bottom of the dialog box. At the pop-up list that displays, identify the type of formatting you want to find.

1. With **WL1-C4-P6-LeaseAgrmnt.docx** open, move the insertion point to the beginning of the document.
2. Find text set in 12-point Candara bold dark red and replace it with text set in 14-point Calibri bold dark blue by completing the following steps:
   a. Click the Replace button in the Editing group.
   b. At the Find and Replace dialog box, press the Delete key. (This deletes any text that displays in the *Find what* text box.)
   c. Click the More button. (If a check mark displays in any of the check boxes, click the option to remove the check mark.)
   d. With the insertion point positioned in the *Find what* text box, click the Format button located toward the bottom of the dialog box and then click *Font* at the pop-up list.
   e. At the Find Font dialog box, change the Font to *Candara*, the Font style to *Bold*, the Size to *12*, and the Font color to *Dark Red* (first color option from the left in the *Standard Colors* section).

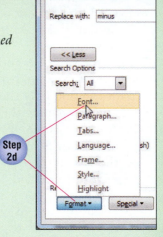

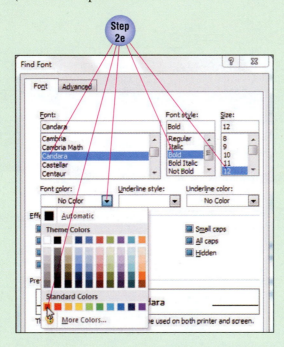

   f. Click OK to close the Find Font dialog box.
   g. At the Find and Replace dialog box, click inside the *Replace with* text box and then delete any text that displays.
   h. Click the Format button located toward the bottom of the dialog box and then click *Font* at the pop-up list.
   i. At the Replace Font dialog box, change the Font to *Calibri*, the Font style to *Bold*, the Size to *14*, and the Font color to *Dark Blue* (second color option from the right in the *Standard Colors* section).
   j. Click OK to close the Replace Font dialog box.

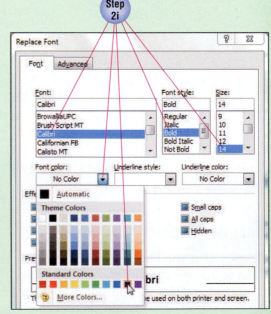

Chapter Summary

- You can change the document view with buttons in the View section on the Status bar or with options in the View tab.

- Print Layout is the default view, which can be changed to other views such as Draft view or Full Screen Reading view.

- The Draft view displays the document in a format for efficient editing and formatting.

- Use the Zoom slider bar to change the percentage of the display.

- Full Screen Reading view displays a document in a format for easy viewing and reading.

- Navigate in a document using the Navigation pane. Display the pane by clicking the *Navigation Pane* check box in the Show group in the View tab.

- By default, a Word document contains 1-inch top, bottom, left, and right margins. Change margins with preset margin settings at the Margins button drop-down list or with options at the Page Setup dialog box with the Margins tab selected.

- The default page orientation is portrait, which can be changed to landscape with the Orientation button in the Page Setup group in the Page Layout tab.

- The default page size is 8.5 by 11 inches, which can be changed with options at the Size drop-down list or options at the Page Setup dialog box with the Paper tab selected.

- The page break that Word inserts automatically is a soft page break. A page break that you insert is a hard page break. Insert a page break with the Page Break button in the Pages group in the Insert tab or by pressing Ctrl + Enter.

- Insert a predesigned and formatted cover page by clicking the Cover Page button in the Pages group in the Insert tab and then clicking the desired option at the drop-down list.

- Insert predesigned and formatted page numbering by clicking the Page Number button in the Header & Footer group in the Insert tab, specifying the desired location of page numbers, and then clicking the desired page numbering option.

- You can insert predesigned headers and footers in a document with the Header button and the Footer button in the Header & Footer group in the Insert tab.

- A watermark is a lightened image that displays behind text in a document. Use the Watermark button in the Page Background group in the Page Layout tab to insert a watermark.

- Insert page color in a document with the Page Color button in the Page Background group. Page color is designed for viewing a document on-screen and does not print.
- Click the Page Borders button in the Page Background group and the Borders and Shading dialog box with the Page Border tab selected displays. Use options at this dialog box to insert a page border or an image page border in a document.
- Use the Find feature to search for specific characters or formatting. Use the Find and Replace feature to search for specific characters or formatting and replace with other characters or formatting.
- At the Find and Replace dialog box, click the Find Next button to find the next occurrence of the characters and/or formatting. Click the Replace button to replace the characters or formatting and find the next occurrence, or click the Replace All button to replace all occurrences of the characters or formatting.
- Click the More button at the Find and Replace dialog box to display additional options for completing a search.

Commands Review

FEATURE	RIBBON TAB, GROUP	BUTTON, OPTION	KEYBOARD SHORTCUT
Blank page	Insert, Pages		
Borders and Shading dialog box with Page Border tab selected	Page Layout, Page Background		
Border and Shading Options dialog box	Page Layout, Page Background	, Options	
Cover page	Insert, Pages		
Draft view	View, Document Views		
Find and Replace dialog box with Find tab selected	Home, Editing	, Advanced Find	
Find and Replace dialog box with Replace tab selected	Home, Editing		Ctrl + H
Footer	Insert, Header & Footer		
Full Screen Reading view	View, Document Views		
Header	Insert, Header & Footer		
Margins	Page Layout, Page Setup		
Navigation Pane	View, Show		Ctrl + F
Orientation	Page Layout, Page Setup		
Page break	Insert, Pages		Ctrl + Enter

FEATURE	RIBBON TAB, GROUP	BUTTON, OPTION	KEYBOARD SHORTCUT
Page color	Page Layout, Page Background		
Page numbering	Insert, Header & Footer		
Page Setup dialog box with Margins tab selected	Page Layout, Page Setup	, Custom Margins OR	
Page Setup dialog box with Paper tab selected	Page Layout, Page Setup	, More Paper Sizes	
Page size	Page Layout, Page Setup		
Print Layout view	View, Document Views		
Watermark	Page Layout, Page Background		

Concepts Check Test Your Knowledge

Completion: In the space provided at the right, indicate the correct term, symbol, or command.

1. This is the default measurement for the top, bottom, left, and right margins.

2. This view displays a document in a format for efficient editing and formatting.

3. This view displays a document in a format for easy viewing and reading.

4. The Navigation pane check box is located in this group in the View tab.

5. To remove white space, double-click this icon.

6. This is the default page orientation.

7. Set specific margins at this dialog box with the Margins tab selected.

8. Press these keys on the keyboard to insert a page break.

9. The Cover Page button is located in the Pages group in this tab.

10. Text that appears at the top of every page is called this.

11. A footer displays in Print Layout view, but not this view.

12. A lightened image that displays behind text in a document is called this.

13. Change the position of the page border from the edge of the page with options at this dialog box.

14. The Page Borders button displays in this group in the Page Layout tab.

15. If you want to replace every occurrence of what you are searching for in a document, click this button at the Find and Replace dialog box.

16. Click this option at the Find and Replace dialog box if you are searching for a word and all of its forms.

Skills Check Assess Your Performance

Assessment

1 FORMAT A SOFTWARE LIFE CYCLE DOCUMENT AND CREATE A COVER PAGE

1. Open **SoftwareCycle.docx** and then save the document with Save As and name it **WL1-C4-A1-SoftwareCycle**.
2. Select the entire document, change the line spacing to *2*, and then deselect the document.
3. Apply the Heading 1 style to the title of the document and apply the Heading 2 style to the headings in the document.
4. Change the Quick Styles set to *Fancy*.
5. Select the entire document and then remove italic formatting.
6. Change the theme colors to *Elemental*. (Make sure you change the theme colors and not the theme.)
7. Insert a page break at the beginning of the heading *Testing*.
8. Move the insertion point to the beginning of the document and then insert the *Austere* cover page.
9. Insert the following text in the specified fields:
   a. Insert the current year in the *[Year]* placeholder.
   b. Insert your school's name in the *[Type the company name]* placeholder. (If a company displays, select the name and then type your school's name.)
   c. If a name displays below your school's name, select the name and then type your first and last names.
   d. Insert software life cycle in the *[TYPE THE DOCUMENT TITLE]* placeholder (the placeholder will convert the text you type to all uppercase letters).
   e. Click the text below the document title, click the Abstract tab, and then press the Delete key.
10. Move the insertion point to any character in the title *COMMERCIAL LIFE CYCLE* and then insert the *Thin Line* page numbering at the bottom of the pages (the page numbering will not appear on the cover page).
11. Save, print, and then close **WL1-C4-A1-SoftwareCycle.docx**.

Assessment

2 FORMAT AN INTELLECTUAL PROPERTY REPORT AND INSERT HEADERS AND FOOTERS

1. Open **IntelProp.docx** and then save the document with Save As and name it **WL1-C4-A2-IntelProp**.
2. Select text from the beginning of the first paragraph of text to just above the *REFERENCES* title located toward the end of the document and then indent the first line to 0.25 inch.
3. Apply the Heading 1 style to the titles *PROPERTY PROTECTION ISSUES* and *REFERENCES* (located toward the end of the document).
4. Apply the Heading 2 style to the headings in the document.
5. Change the Quick Styles set to *Distinctive* and change the paragraph spacing to *Relaxed*. (Use the Change Styles button to make these changes.)
6. Center the *PROPERTY PROTECTION ISSUES* and *REFERENCES* titles.
7. Select and then hang indent the paragraphs below the *REFERENCES* title.
8. Insert a page break at the beginning of the *REFERENCES* title.
9. Move the insertion point to the beginning of the document and then insert the *Exposure* header. Type **Property Protection Issues** in the *[Type the document title]* placeholder and, if necessary, insert the current date in the *[Pick the date]* placeholder.
10. Insert the *Pinstripes* footer and type your first and last names in the *[Type text]* placeholder.
11. Save and then print **WL1-C4-A2-IntelProp.docx**.
12. Remove the header and footer.
13. Insert the *Austere (Odd Page)* footer and then make the following changes:
    a. Delete the *[Type the company name]* placeholder.
    b. Select the text and page number in the footer and then change the font size to 12 and turn on bold.
14. Insert the *DRAFT 1* watermark in the document.
15. Insert a page border of your choosing to the document.
16. Display the Border and Shading Options dialog box and then change the top, left, bottom, and right measurements to *31 pt*. **Hint: Display the Border and Shading Options dialog box by clicking the Options button at the Borders and Shading dialog box with the Page Border tab selected.**
17. Save, print, and then close **WL1-C4-A2-IntelProp.docx**.

Assessment

3 FORMAT A REAL ESTATE AGREEMENT

1. Open **REAgrmnt.docx** and then save the document with Save As and name it **WL1-C4-A3-REAgrmnt**.
2. Find all occurrences of *BUYER* (matching the case) and replace with *James Berman*.
3. Find all occurrences of *SELLER* (matching the case) and replace with *Mona Trammell*.
4. Find all word forms of the word *buy* and replace with *purchase*.
5. Search for 14-point Tahoma bold formatting in dark red and replace with 12-point Constantia bold formatting in black.
6. Insert page numbers at the bottom center of each page.
7. Save, print, and then close **WL1-C4-A3-REAgrmnt.docx**.

Visual Benchmark Demonstrate Your Proficiency

FORMAT A RESUME STYLES REPORT

1. Open **ResumeStyles.docx** and then save it with Save As and name it **WL1-C4-VB-ResumeStyles**.
2. Format the document so it appears as shown in Figure 4.10 on page 143 with the following specifications:
   - Change the top margin to 1.5 inches.
   - Apply the Heading 1 style to the title and the Heading 2 style to the headings.
   - Change the Quick Styles set to *Formal*.
   - Apply the Aspect theme and then change the theme colors to *Origin*.
   - Insert the *Tiles* header and the *Tiles* footer. Insert the appropriate text in placeholders and/or delete placeholders so your headers and footers display similar to what you see in Figure 4.10 on page 143.
   - Apply other formatting so your document appears the same as the document shown in the figure.
   - Insert the *Tiles* cover page and insert the text in the placeholders and/or delete placeholders so your coverage page displays similar to what you see in Figure 4.10.
3. Save, print, and then close **WL1-C4-VB-ResumeStyles.docx**.

Case Study Apply Your Skills

Part

1

You work for Citizens for Consumer Safety, a nonprofit organization providing information on household safety. Your supervisor, Melinda Johansson, has asked you to attractively format a document on smoke detectors. She will be using the document as an informational handout during a presentation on smoke detectors. Open the document named **SmokeDetectors.docx** and then save the document with Save As and name it **WL1-C4-CS-SmokeDetectors**. Apply a theme to the document and apply appropriate styles to the title and headings. Ms. Johansson has asked you to change the page orientation and then change the left and right margins to 1.5 inches. She wants the extra space at the left and right margins so audience members can write notes in the margins. Use the Help feature or experiment with the options in the Header & Footer Tools Design tab and figure out how to number pages on every page but the first page. Insert page numbering in the document that prints at the top right side of every page except the first page. Save, print, and then close **WL1-C4-CS-SmokeDetectors.docx**.

Figure 4.10 Visual Benchmark

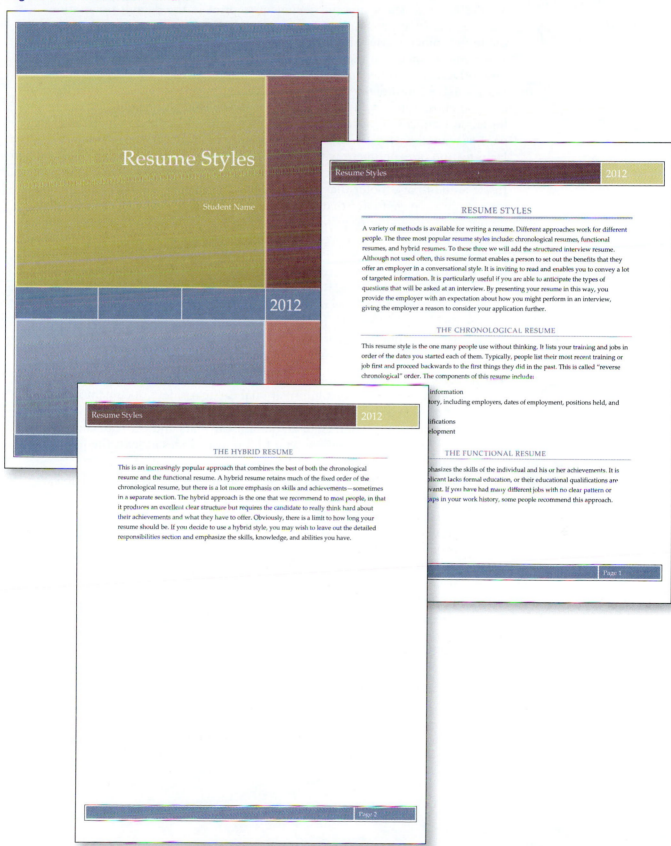

Part 2

After reviewing the formatted document on smoke detectors, Ms. Johansson has decided that she wants the document to print in the default orientation and she is not happy with the theme and style choices. She also noticed that the term "smoke alarm" should be replaced with "smoke detector." She has asked you to open and then format the original document. Open **SmokeDetectors.docx** and then save the document with Save As and name it **WL1-C4-CS-SmokeDetectors**. Apply a theme to the document (other than the one you chose for Part 1) and apply styles to the title and headings. Search for all occurrences of *smoke alarm* and replace with *smoke detector*. Insert a cover page of your choosing and insert the appropriate information in the page. Use the Help feature or experiment with the options in the Header & Footer Tools Design tab and figure out how to insert an odd-page and even-page footer in a document. Insert an odd-page footer that prints the page number at the right margin and insert an even-page footer that prints the page number at the left margin. You do not want the footer to print on the cover page so make sure you position the insertion point below the cover page before inserting the footers. After inserting the footers in the document, you decide that they need to be moved down the page to create more space between the last line of text on a page and the footer. Use the Help feature or experiment with the options in the Header & Footer Tools Design tab to figure out how to move the footers down and then edit each footer so they display 0.3" from the bottom of the page. Save, print, and then close **WL1-C4-CS-SmokeDetectors.docx**.

Part 3

Ms. Johansson has asked you to prepare a document on infant car seats and car seat safety. She wants this informational car seat safety document available for distribution at a local community center. Use the Internet to find websites that provide information on child and infant car seats and car seat safety. Write a report on the information you find that includes at least the following information:

- Description of the types of car seats (such as rear-facing, convertible, forward-facing, built-in, and booster)
- Safety rules and guidelines
- Installation information
- Specific child and infant seat models
- Sites on the Internet that sell car seats
- Price ranges
- Internet sites providing safety information

Format the report using a theme and styles and include a cover page and headers and/or footers. Save the completed document and name it **WL1-C4-CS-CarSeats**. Print and then close the document.

Performance Assessment

Word2010L1C1

Note: Before beginning unit assessments, copy to your storage medium the Word2010L1U1 subfolder from the Word2010L1 folder on the CD that accompanies this textbook and then make Word2010L1U1 the active folder.

Assessing Proficiency ▪▪▪▪▪▪▪▪▪▪▪▪▪

In this unit, you have learned to create, edit, save, and print Word documents. You also learned to format characters, paragraphs, and pages.

Assessment 1 Format *Designing an Effective Website* Document

1. Open **Website.docx** and then save the document with Save As and name it **WL1-U1-A1-Website**.
2. Complete a spelling and grammar check.
3. Select from the paragraph that begins *Make your home page work for you.* through the end of the document and then apply bullet formatting.
4. Select and then bold the first sentence of each bulleted paragraph.
5. Apply paragraph border and shading to the document title.
6. Save and then print **WL1-U1-A1-Website.docx**.
7. Change the top, left, and right margins to 1.5 inches.
8. Select the bulleted paragraphs, change the paragraph alignment to justified, and then insert numbering.
9. Select the entire document and then change the font to 12-point Cambria.
10. Insert the text shown in Figure U1.1 after paragraph number 2. (The number 3. should be inserted preceding the text you type.)
11. Save, print, and then close **WL1-U1-A1-Website.docx**.

Figure U1.1 Assessment 1

> **Avoid a cluttered look.** In design, less is more. Strive for a clean look to your pages, using ample margins and white space.

Assessment 2 Format *Accumulated Returns* Document

1. Open **ReturnChart.docx** and then save the document with Save As and name it **WL1-U1-A2-ReturnChart**.
2. Select the entire document and then make the following changes:
   a. Click the No Spacing style.
   b. Change the line spacing to 1.5.

  c. Change the font to 12-point Cambria.

  d. Apply 6 points of spacing after paragraphs.

3. Select the title *TOTAL RETURN CHARTS*, change the font to 14-point Corbel bold, change the alignment to center, and apply paragraph shading of your choosing.

4. Bold the following text that appears at the beginning of the second through the fifth paragraphs:

  Average annual total return: *Annual total return:*

  Accumulation units: *Accumulative rates:*

5. Select the paragraphs of text in the body of the document (all paragraphs except the title) and then change the paragraph alignment to justified.

6. Select the paragraphs that begin with the bolded words, sort the paragraphs in ascending order, and then indent the text 0.5 inch from the left margin.

7. Insert a watermark that prints *DRAFT* diagonally across the page.

8. Save, print, and then close **WL1-U1-A2-ReturnChart.docx**.

Assessment 3 Format Computer Ethics Report

1. Open **FutureEthics.docx** and then save the document with Save As and name it **WL1-U1-A3-FutureEthics.docx**.

2. Apply the Heading 1 style to the titles *FUTURE OF COMPUTER ETHICS* and *REFERENCES*.

3. Apply the Heading 2 style to the headings in the document.

4. Change the paragraph spacing to *Relaxed*. **Hint: Do this with the Change Styles button**.

5. Change the Quick Styles set to *Thatch*.

6. Apply the Hardcover theme and then change the theme colors to *Concourse*.

7. Center the two titles (*FUTURE OF COMPUTER ETHICS* and *REFERENCES*).

8. Hang indent the paragraphs of text below the *REFERENCES* title.

9. Insert page numbering that prints at the bottom center of each page.

10. Save, print, and then close **WL1-U1-A3-FutureEthics.docx**.

Assessment 4 Set Tabs and Type Division Income Text in Columns

1. At a new blank document, type the text shown in Figure U1.2 with the following specifications:

  a. Bold and center the title as shown.

  b. You determine the tab settings for the text in columns.

  c. Select the entire document and then change the font to 12-point Arial.

2. Save the document and name it **WL1-U1-A4-Income**.

3. Print and then close **WL1-U1-A4-Income.docx**.

Figure U1.2 Assessment 4

INCOME BY DIVISION			
	2009	**2010**	**2011**
Public Relations	$14,375	$16,340	$16,200
Database Services	9,205	15,055	13,725
Graphic Design	18,400	21,790	19,600
Technical Support	5,780	7,325	9,600

Assessment 5 Set Tabs and Type Table of Contents Text

1. At a blank document, type the text shown in Figure U1.3 with the following specifications:
   a. Bold and center the title as shown.
   b. You determine the tab settings for the text in columns.
   c. Select the entire document, change the font to 12-point Bookman Old Style (or a similar serif typeface), and then change the line spacing to 1.5.
2. Save the document and name it **WL1-U1-A5-TofC**.
3. Print and then close **WL1-U1-A5-TofC.docx**.

Figure U1.3 Assessment 5

TABLE OF CONTENTS

Online Shopping.................................... 2

Online Services.................................... 4

Peer-to-Peer Online Transactions..................... 5

Transaction Payment Methods....................... 8

Transaction Security and Encryption 11

Establishing a Website............................ 14

Assessment 6 Format Union Agreement Contract

1. Open **LaborContract.docx** and then save the document with Save As and name it **WL1-U1-A6-LaborContract**.
2. Find all occurrences of *REINBERG MANUFACTURING* and replace with *MILLWOOD ENTERPRISES*.
3. Find all occurrences of *RM* and replace with *ME*.
4. Find all occurrences of *LABOR WORKERS' UNION* and replace with *SERVICE EMPLOYEES' UNION*.
5. Find all occurrences of *LWU* and replace with *SEU*.
6. Select the entire document and then change the font to 12-point Cambria and the line spacing to double.
7. Select the numbered paragraphs in the *Transfers and Moving Expenses* section and change to bullets.
8. Select the numbered paragraphs in the *Sick Leave* section and change to bullets.
9. Change the page orientation to landscape and the top margin to 1.5".
10. Save and then print **WL1-U1-A6-LaborContract.docx**.
11. Change the page orientation to portrait and the left margin (previously the top margin) back to 1".
12. Insert the *Alphabet* footer and type **Union Agreement** in the *[Type text]* placeholder.
13. Insert the *Alphabet* cover page and insert *UNION AGREEMENT* as the document title and *Millwood Enterprises* as the document subtitle. Include any additional information required by the cover page.
14. Save, print, and then close **WL1-U1-A6-LaborContract.docx**.

Assessment 7 Copy and Paste Text in Health Plan Document

1. Open **KeyLifePlan.docx** and then save the document with Save As and name it **WL1-U1-A7-KeyLifePlan**.
2. Open **PlanOptions.docx** and then turn on the display of the Clipboard task pane. Make sure the Clipboard is empty.
3. Select the heading *Plan Highlights* and the six paragraphs of text below the heading and then copy the selected text to the clipboard.
4. Select the heading *Plan Options* and the two paragraphs of text below the heading and then copy the selected text to the clipboard.
5. Select the heading *Quality Assessment* and the six paragraphs of text below the heading and then copy the selected text to the clipboard.
6. Close **PlanOptions.docx**.
7. With **WL1-U1-A7-KeyLifePlan.docx** open, display the Clipboard task pane.
8. Move the insertion point to the beginning of the *Provider Network* heading, paste the *Plan Options* item from the Clipboard, and merge the formatting.
9. With the insertion point positioned at the beginning of the *Provider Network* heading, paste the *Plan Highlights* item from the Clipboard, and merge the formatting.
10. Move the insertion point to the beginning of the *Plan Options* heading, paste the *Quality Assessment* item from the Clipboard, and merge the formatting.
11. Clear the Clipboard and then close it.
12. Apply the Heading 1 style to the title, *KEY LIFE HEALTH PLAN*.
13. Apply the Heading 2 style to the headings in the document.
14. Change the top margin to 1.5 inches.
15. Change to the *Modern* Quick Styles set.
16. Apply the Grid theme.
17. Insert a double line, dark red page border.
18. Insert the *Sideline* header and type **Health Plans** in the *[Type the document title]* placeholder. Insert the *Sideline* footer.
19. Add the *Sideline* cover page. Delete the company name and document subtitle placeholders. Insert your first and last names in the Author placeholder and the current date in the Date placeholder.
20. Save, print, and then close **WL1-U1-A7-KeyLifePlan.docx**.

Writing Activities ▪▪▪▪▪▪▪▪▪▪▪▪▪▪▪▪

The following activities give you the opportunity to practice your writing skills along with demonstrating an understanding of some of the important Word features you have mastered in this unit. Use correct grammar, appropriate word choices, and clear sentence constructions. Follow the steps explained on the next page to improve your writing skills.

The Writing Process

Plan   Gather ideas, select which information to include, and choose the order in which to present the information.

Checkpoints
- What is the purpose?
- What information does the reader need in order to reach your intended conclusion?

Write   Following the information plan and keeping the reader in mind, draft the document using clear, direct sentences that say what you mean.

Checkpoints
- What are the subpoints for each main thought?
- How can you connect paragraphs so the reader moves smoothly from one idea to the next?

Revise Improve what is written by changing, deleting, rearranging, or adding words, sentences, and paragraphs.

Checkpoints
- Is the meaning clear?
- Do the ideas follow a logical order?
- Have you included any unnecessary information?
- Have you built your sentences around strong nouns and verbs?

Edit   Check spelling, sentence construction, word use, punctuation, and capitalization.

Checkpoints
- Can you spot any redundancies or clichés?
- Can you reduce any phrases to an effective word (for example, change *the fact that* to *because*)?
- Have you used commas only where there is a strong reason for doing so?
- Did you proofread the document for errors that your spell checker cannot identify?

Publish Prepare a final copy that could be reproduced and shared with others.

Checkpoints
- Which design elements, such as boldface or different fonts, would help highlight important ideas or sections?
- Would charts or other graphics help clarify meaning?

Activity 1   Write Hyphenation Steps and Hyphenate Text in Document

Use Word's Help feature to learn about hyphenating text in a document. Learn how to hyphenate text automatically as well as manually. Create a document following these instructions:

1. Include an appropriate title that is bolded and centered.
2. Write the steps required to automatically hyphenate text in a document.
3. Write the steps required to manually hyphenate text in a document.

Save the document and name it **WL1-U1-Act1-Hyphen**. Print and then close **WL1-U1-Act1-Hyphen.docx**. Open **WL1-U1-A3-FutureEthics.docx** and then save the document with Save As and name it **WL1-U1-Act1-FutureEthics**. Manually hyphenate text in the document. Save, print, and then close **WL1-U1-Act1-FutureEthics.docx**.

Activity 2 Write Information on Customizing Spelling and Grammar

Use Word's Help feature to learn about grammar and style options. Learn about grammar options and what they detect and style options and what they detect. Also, learn how to set rules for grammar and style. Once you have determined this information, create a document describing at least two grammar options and at least two style options. Also include in this document the steps required to change the writing style from grammar only to grammar and style. Save the completed document and name it **WL1-U1-Act2-CustomSpell**. Print and then close **WL1-U1-Act2-CustomSpell.docx**.

Internet Research ▪▪▪▪▪▪▪▪▪▪▪▪▪▪

Research Business Desktop Computer Systems

You hold a part-time job at a local newspaper, *The Daily Chronicle*, where you conduct Internet research for the staff writers. Mr. Woods, the editor, has decided to purchase new desktop computers for the staff. He has asked you to identify at least three PCs that can be purchased directly over the Internet, and he requests that you put your research and recommendations in writing. Mr. Woods is looking for solid, reliable, economical, and powerful desktop computers with good warranties and service plans. He has given you a budget of $1,300 per unit.

Search the Internet for three desktop PC computer systems from three different manufacturers. Consider price, specifications (processor speed, amount of RAM, hard drive space, and monitor type and size), performance, warranties, and service plans when making your choice of systems. Print your research findings and include them with your report. (For helpful information on shopping for a computer, read the articles "Buying and Installing a PC" and "Purchasing a Computer," posted in the Course Resources section of this book's Internet Resource Center, either at www.emcp.net/BenchmarkOffice10 or www.emcp.net/BenchmarkWord10.)

Using Word, write a brief report in which you summarize the capabilities and qualities of each of the three computer systems you recommend. Include a final paragraph detailing which system you suggest for purchase and why. If possible, incorporate user opinions and/or reviews about this system to support your decision. At the end of your report, include a table comparing the computer system. Format your report using the concepts and techniques you learned in Unit 1. Save the report and name it **WL1-U1-InternetResearch**. Print and then close the file.

Microsoft Word Level 1

Unit 2 ■ Enhancing and Customizing Documents

Microsoft® Word

CHAPTER 5

Applying Formatting and Inserting Objects

PERFORMANCE OBJECTIVES

Upon successful completion of Chapter 5, you will be able to:

- **Insert section breaks**
- **Create and format text in columns**
- **Hyphenate words automatically and manually**
- **Create a drop cap**
- **Insert symbols, special characters, and the date and time**
- **Use the Click and Type feature**
- **Vertically align text**
- **Insert, format, and customize pictures, clip art images, text boxes, shapes, and WordArt**

Tutorials

5.1 Inserting Section Breaks
5.2 Applying Columns
5.3 Hyphenating Words
5.4 Inserting Symbols and Special Characters
5.5 Creating a Drop Cap and Inserting the Date and Time
5.6 Using Click and Type
5.7 Using Vertical Alignment
5.8 Inserting, Sizing, and Moving Images
5.9 Inserting and Customizing a Pull Quote
5.10 Inserting and Formatting a Shape
5.11 Inserting and Modifying WordArt
5.12 Creating and Inserting a Screenshot

To apply page or document formatting to only a portion of the document, insert a section break. You can insert a continuous section break or a section break that begins a new page. A section break is useful when formatting text in columns. The hyphenation feature hyphenates words at the end of lines, creating a less ragged margin. Use buttons in the Text and Symbols groups in the Insert tab to insert symbols, special characters, and the date and time. With the Click and Type feature, you can position the insertion point at various locations in the document and change the paragraph alignment. Use the *Vertical alignment* option at the Page Setup dialog box with the Layout tab selected to align text vertically on the page. Along with these features, you will also learn how to increase the visual appeal of a document by inserting and customizing images such as pictures, clip art, text boxes, shapes, and WordArt. Model answers for this chapter's projects appear on the following pages.

Note: Before beginning the projects, copy to your storage medium the Word2010L1C5 subfolder from the Word2010L1 folder on the CD that accompanies this textbook and then make Word2010L1C5 the active folder.

153

COMPUTER INPUT DEVICES

Engineers have been especially creative in designing new ways to get information into computers. Some input methods are highly specialized and unusual, while common devices often undergo redesign to improve their capabilities or their ergonomics, the ways in which they affect people physically. Some common input devices include keyboards, mice, trackballs, and touchpads.

Keyboard

A keyboard can be an external device that is attached by means of a cable, or it can be attached to the CPU case itself as it is for laptop computers. Most keyboards today are QWERTY keyboards, which take their name from the first six keys at the left of the first row of letters. An alternative, the DVORAK keyboard, places the most commonly used keys close to the user's fingertips and speeds typing.

Many keyboards have a separate numeric keypad, like that of a calculator, containing numbers and mathematical operators. All keyboards have modifier keys that enable the user to change the symbol or character that is entered when a given key is pressed. The Shift key, for example, makes a letter uppercase. Keyboards also have special cursor keys that enable the user to change the position on the screen of the cursor, a symbol that appears on the monitor to show where in a document the next change will appear. Most keyboards also have function keys, labeled F_1, F_2, F_3, and so on. These keys allow the user to issue commands by pressing a single key.

Mouse

Graphical operating systems contain many elements that a user can choose by pointing at them. Such elements include buttons, tools, pull-down menus, and icons for file folders, programs, and document files. Often pointing to and clicking on one of these elements is more convenient than using the cursor or arrow keys on the keyboard. This pointing and clicking can be done by using a mouse. The mouse is the second most common input device, after the keyboard. A mouse operates by moving the cursor on the computer screen to correspond to movements made with the mouse.

Trackball

A trackball is like an upside-down mouse. A mouse is moved over a pad. A trackball remains stationary, and the user moves the ball with his or her fingers or palm. One or more buttons for choosing options are incorporated into the design of the trackball.

Touchpad and Touchscreen

A touchpad feels less mechanical than a mouse or trackball because the user simply moves a finger on the pad. A touchpad has two parts. One part acts as a button, while the other emulates a mouse pad on which the user traces the location of the cursor with a finger. People with carpal tunnel syndrome find touchpads and trackballs easier to use than mice. Many portable computers have built-in trackballs or touchpads as input devices.

A touchscreen allows the user to choose options by pressing the appropriate part of the screen. Touchscreens are widely used in bank ATMs and in kiosks at retail outlets and in tourist areas.

Prepared by: Matthew Viña

SoftCell Technologies®

June 11, 2012

11:40 AM

1

2

Project 1 Format a Document on Computer Input Devices

WL1-C5-P1-InputDevices.docx

SUPERVISORY TRAINING
Maximizing Employee Potential
Wednesday, February 15, 2012
Training Center
9:00 a.m. to 3:30 p.m.

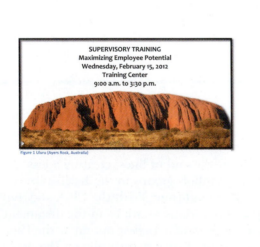

Figure 1 Uluru (Ayers Rock, Australia)

Project 2 Create an Announcement about Supervisory Training

WL1-C5-P2-Training.docx

ROBOTS AS ANDROIDS

Robotic factories are increasingly commonplace, especially in heavy manufacturing, where tolerance of repetitive movements, great strength, and untiring precision are more important than flexibility. Robots are especially useful in hazardous work, such as defusing bombs or handling radioactive materials. They also excel in constructing tiny components like those found inside notebook computers, which are often too small for humans to assemble.

Most people think of robots in science fiction terms, which generally depict them as androids, or simulated humans. Real robots today do not look human at all, and judged by human standards, they are not very intelligent. The task of creating a humanlike body has proven incredibly difficult. Many technological advances in visual perception, audio perception, touch, dexterity, locomotion, and navigation need to occur before robots that look and act like human beings will live and work among us.

VISUAL PERCEPTION

Visual perception is an area of great complexity. A large percentage of the human brain is dedicated to processing data coming from the eyes. As our most powerful sense, sight is the primary means through which we understand the world around us. A single camera is not good enough to simulate the eye. Two cameras are needed to give stereoscopic vision, which allows depth and movement perception. Even with two cameras, visual perception is incomplete because the cameras cannot understand or translate what they see.

"The task of creating a humanlike body has proven incredibly difficult."

Processing the image is the difficult part. In order for a robot to move through a room full of furniture it must build a mental map of that room, complete with obstacles. The robot must judge the distance and size of objects before it can figure out how to move around them.

AUDIO PERCEPTION

Audio perception is less complex than visual perception, but no less important. People respond to audible cues about their surroundings and the people they are with without even thinking about it. Listeners can determine someone's emotional state just by hearing the person's voice. A car starting up when someone crosses the street prompts the walker to glance in that direction to check for danger. Identifying a single voice and interpreting what is being said amid accompanying background noise is a task that is among the most important for human beings— and the most difficult.

TACTILE PERCEPTION

Tactile perception, or touch, is another critical sense. Robots can be built with any level of strength, since they are made of steel and motors. How does a robot capable of lifting a car pick up an egg in the dark without dropping or crushing it? The answer is through a sense of touch. The robot must not only be able to feel an object, but also be able to sense how much pressure it is applying to that object. With this feedback it can properly judge how hard it

Page 1

Project 3 Customize a Report on Robots

WL1-C5-P3-Robots.docx

should squeeze. This is a very difficult area, and it may prove that simulating the human hand is even more difficult than simulating the human mind.

Related to touch is the skill of dexterity, or hand-eye coordination. The challenge is to create a robot that can perform small actions, such as soldering tiny joints or placing a chip at a precise spot in a circuit board within half a millimeter.

LOCOMOTION

Locomotion includes broad movements such as walking. Getting a robot to move around is not easy. This area of robotics is challenging, as it requires balance within an endlessly changing set of variables. How does the program adjust for walking up a hill, or down a set of stairs? What if the wind is blowing hard or a foot slips? Currently most mobile robots work with wheels or treads, which limits their mobility in some circumstances but makes them much easier to control.

NAVIGATION

Related to perception, navigation deals with the science of moving a mobile robot through an environment. Navigation is not an isolated area of artificial intelligence, as it must work closely with a visual system or some other kind of perception system. Sonar, radar, mechanical "feelers," and other systems have been subjects of experimentation. A robot can plot a course to a location using an internal "map" built up by a navigational perception system. If the course is blocked or too difficult, the robot must be smart enough to backtrack so it can try another plan.

Page 2

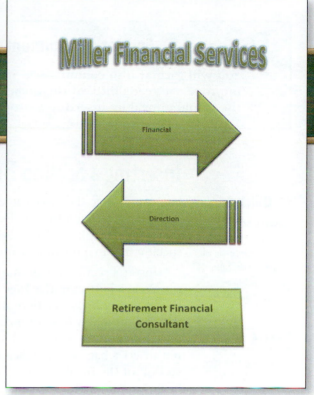

Project 4 Prepare a Company Flyer

WL1-C5-P4-FinConsult.docx

Project 5 Create and Format Screenshots

WL1-C5-P5-BackstageViews.docx

WL1-C5-P5-NSSCoverPages.docx

You will format into columns text in a document on computer input devices, improve the readability of the document by hyphenating long words, and improve the visual appeal by inserting a drop cap.

Inserting a Section Break ■■■■■■■■■ ■ ■ ■ ■ ■ ■ ■

▼ **Quick Steps**

Insert a Section Break
1. Click Page Layout tab.
2. Click Breaks button.
3. Click section break type in drop-down list.

If you delete a section break, the text that follows the section break takes on the formatting of the text preceding the break.

Breaks

You can change the layout and formatting of specific portions of a document by inserting section breaks. For example, you can insert section breaks and then change margins for the text between the section breaks. If you want to format specific text in a document into columns, insert a section break.

Insert a section break in a document by clicking the Page Layout tab, clicking the Breaks button in the Page Setup group, and then clicking the desired option in the *Section Breaks* section of the drop-down list. You can insert a section break that begins a new page or a continuous section break that does not begin a new page. A continuous section break separates the document into sections but does not insert a page break. Click one of the other three options in the *Section Breaks* section of the Breaks drop-down list if you want to insert a section break that begins a new page.

A section break inserted in a document is not visible in Print Layout view. Click the Draft button and a section break displays in the document as a double row of dots with the words *Section Break* in the middle. Depending on the type of section break you insert, text follows *Section Break*. For example, if you insert a continuous section break, the words *Section Break (Continuous)* display in the middle of the row of dots. To delete a section break, change to Draft view, position the insertion point on the section break, and then press the Delete key.

Project 1a **Inserting a Continuous Section Break** **Part 1 of 8**

1. Open **InputDevices.docx** and then save it with Save As and name it **WL1-C5-P1-InputDevices**.
2. Insert a continuous section break by completing the following steps:
   a. Move the insertion point to the beginning of the *Keyboard* heading.
   b. Click the Page Layout tab.
   c. Click the Breaks button in the Page Setup group and then click *Continuous* in the *Section Breaks* section of the drop-down list.
3. Click the Draft button in the view area on the Status bar and then notice the section break that displays across the screen.
4. Click the Print Layout button in the view area on the Status bar.

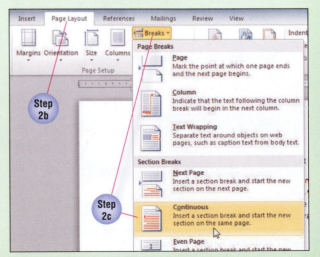

5. With the insertion point positioned at the beginning of the *Keyboard* heading, change the left and right margins to 1.5 inches. (The margin changes affect only the text after the continuous section break.)
6. Save and then print **WL1-C5-P1-InputDevices.docx**.

Creating Columns

▼ **Quick Steps**
Create Columns
1. Click Page Layout tab.
2. Click Columns button.
3. Click on desired number of columns.

When preparing a document containing text, an important point to consider is the readability of the document. Readability refers to the ease with which a person can read and understand groups of words. The line length of text in a document can enhance or detract from the readability of text. If the line length is too long, the reader may lose his or her place on the line and have a difficult time moving to the next line below. To improve the readability of some documents such as newsletters or reports, you may want to set the text in columns. One common type of column is newspaper, which is typically used for text in newspapers, newsletters, and magazines. Newspaper columns contain text that flows up and down in the document.

Columns

Create newspaper columns with the Columns button in the Page Setup group in the Page Layout tab or with options from the Columns dialog box. The Columns button creates columns of equal width. Use the Columns dialog box to create columns with varying widths. A document can include as many columns as room available on the page. Word determines how many columns can be included on the page based on the page width, the margin widths, and the size and spacing of the columns. Columns must be at least one-half inch in width. Changes in columns affect the entire document or the section of the document in which the insertion point is positioned.

Project 1b	Formatting Text into Columns	Part 2 of 8

1. With **WL1-C5-P1-InputDevices.docx** open, make sure the insertion point is positioned below the section break and then return the left and right margins to 1 inch.
2. Delete the section break by completing the following steps:
   a. Click the Draft button in the view area on the Status bar.
   b. Position the insertion point on the section break.

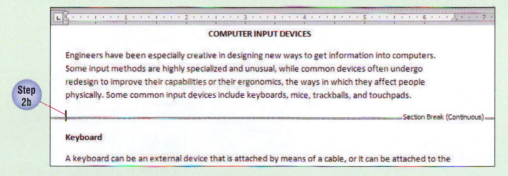

   c. Press the Delete key.
   d. Click the Print Layout button in the view area on the Status bar.

3. Move the insertion point to the beginning of the first paragraph of text in the document and then insert a continuous section break.
4. Format the text into columns by completing the following steps:
   a. Make sure the insertion point is positioned below the section break.
   b. Click the Page Layout tab.
   c. Click the Columns button in the Page Setup group.
   d. Click *Two* at the drop-down list.
5. Save **WL1-C5-P1-InputDevices.docx**.

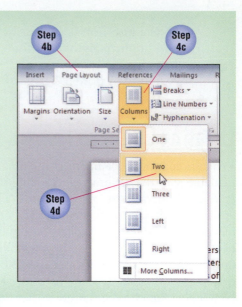

Creating Columns with the Columns Dialog Box

You can use the Columns dialog box to create newspaper columns that are equal or unequal in width. To display the Columns dialog box shown in Figure 5.1, click the Columns button in the Page Setup group of the Page Layout tab and then click *More Columns* at the drop-down list.

With options at the Columns dialog box you can specify the style and number of columns, enter your own column measurements, and create unequal columns. You can also insert a line between columns. By default, column formatting is applied to the whole document. With the *Apply to* option at the bottom of the Columns dialog box, you can change this from *Whole document* to *This point forward*. At the *This point forward* option, a section break is inserted and the column formatting is applied to text from the location of the insertion point to the end of the document or until other column formatting is encountered. The *Preview* section of the dialog box displays an example of how the columns will appear in your document.

Figure 5.1 Columns Dialog Box

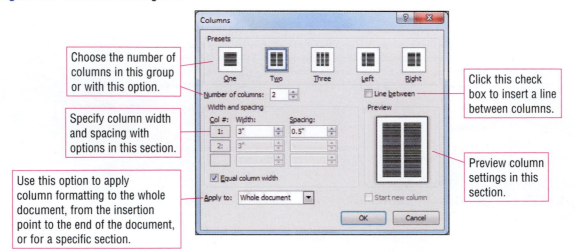

Choose the number of columns in this group or with this option.

Specify column width and spacing with options in this section.

Use this option to apply column formatting to the whole document, from the insertion point to the end of the document, or for a specific section.

Click this check box to insert a line between columns.

Preview column settings in this section.

Removing Column Formatting

To remove column formatting using the Columns button, position the insertion point in the section containing columns, click the Page Layout tab, click the Columns button, and then click *One* at the drop-down list. You can also remove column formatting at the Columns dialog box by selecting the *One* option in the *Presets* section.

Inserting a Column Break

When formatting text into columns, Word automatically breaks the columns to fit the page. At times, column breaks may appear in an undesirable location. You can insert a column break by positioning the insertion point where you want the column to end, clicking the Page Layout tab, clicking the Breaks button, and then clicking *Column* at the drop-down list.

HINT

You can also insert a column break with the keyboard shortcut, Ctrl + Shift + Enter.

Project 1c   **Formatting Columns at the Columns Dialog Box**   **Part 3 of 8**

1. With **WL1-C5-P1-InputDevices.docx** open, delete the section break by completing the following steps:
    a. Click the Draft button in the view area on the Status bar.
    b. Position the insertion point on the section break and then press the Delete key.
    c. Click the Print Layout button in the view area on the Status bar.
2. Remove column formatting by clicking the Columns button in the Page Setup group in the Page Layout tab and then clicking *One* at the drop-down list.
3. Format text in columns by completing the following steps:
    a. Position the insertion point at the beginning of the first paragraph of text in the document.
    b. Click the Columns button in the Page Setup group and then click *More Columns* at the drop-down list.
    c. At the Columns dialog box, click *Two* in the *Presets* section.
    d. Click the down-pointing arrow at the right of the *Spacing* option box until *0.3"* displays.
    e. Click the *Line between* check box to insert a check mark.
    f. Click the down-pointing arrow at the right side of the *Apply to* option box and then click *This point forward* at the drop-down list.
    g. Click OK to close the dialog box.

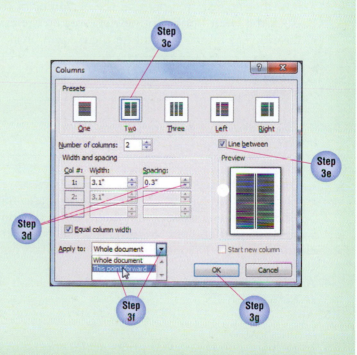

Step 3c

Step 3e

Step 3d

Step 3f

Step 3g

---

4. Insert a column break by completing the following steps:
   a. Position the insertion point at the beginning of the *Mouse* heading.
   b. Click the Breaks button in the Page Setup group and then click *Column* at the drop-down list.
5. Save and then print **WL1-C5-P1-InputDevices.docx**.

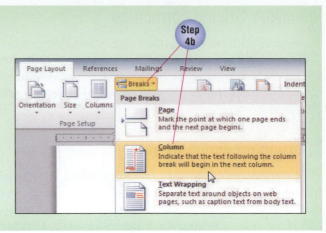

Balancing Columns on a Page

In a document containing text formatted into columns, Word automatically lines up (balances) the last line of text at the bottom of each column, except the last page. Text in the first column of the last page may flow to the end of the page, while the text in the second column may end far short of the end of the page. You can balance columns by inserting a continuous section break at the end of the text.

Project 1d Formatting and Balancing Columns of Text   Part 4 of 8

1. With **WL1-C5-P1-InputDevices.docx** open, delete the column break by completing the following steps:
   a. Position the insertion point at the beginning of the *Mouse* heading.
   b. Click the Draft button in the view area on the Status bar.
   c. Position the insertion point on the column break.

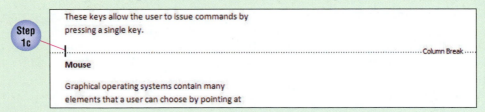

   d. Press the Delete key.
   e. Click the Print Layout button in the view area on the Status bar.
2. Select the entire document and then change the font to 12-point Constantia.
3. Move the insertion point to the end of the document and then balance the columns by clicking the Page Layout tab, clicking the Breaks button, and then clicking *Continuous* at the drop-down list.
4. Apply the Aqua, Accent 5, Lighter 60% paragraph shading to the title *COMPUTER INPUT DEVICES*.
5. Apply the Aqua, Accent 5, Lighter 80% paragraph shading to each of the headings in the document.
6. Insert page numbering that prints at the bottom of each page.
7. Save **WL1-C5-P1-InputDevices.docx**.

Hyphenating Words ■■■■■■ ■ ■ ■ ■ ■ ■ ■ ■ ■

In some Word documents, especially documents with left and right margins wider than 1 inch, or text set in columns, the right margin may appear quite ragged. To improve the display of text lines by making line lengths more uniform, consider hyphenating long words that fall at the end of a text line. When using the hyphenation feature, you can tell Word to hyphenate words automatically in a document or you can manually insert hyphens.

Automatically Hyphenating Words

To automatically hyphenate words in a document, click the Page Layout tab, click the Hyphenation button in the Page Setup group, and then click *Automatic* at the drop-down list. Scroll through the document and check to see if hyphens display in appropriate locations within the words. If, after hyphenating words in a document, you want to remove all hyphens, immediately click the Undo button on the Quick Access toolbar. This must be done immediately after hyphenating since the Undo feature undoes only the last function.

Manually Hyphenating Words

If you want to control where a hyphen appears in a word during hyphenation, choose manual hyphenation. To do this, click the Page Layout tab, click the Hyphenation button in the Page Setup group, and then click *Manual* at the drop-down list. This displays the Manual Hyphenation dialog box as shown in Figure 5.2. (The word in the *Hyphenate at* text box will vary.) At this dialog box, click Yes to hyphenate the word as indicated in the *Hyphenate at* text box, click No if you do not want the word hyphenated, or click Cancel to cancel hyphenation. You can also reposition the hyphen in the *Hyphenate at* text box. Word displays the word with syllable breaks indicated by a hyphen. The position where the word will be hyphenated displays as a blinking black bar. If you want to hyphenate at a different location in the word, position the blinking black bar where you want the hyphen and then click Yes. Continue clicking Yes or No at the Manual Hyphenation dialog box. Be careful with words ending in *-ed*. Several two-syllable words can be divided before that final syllable, for example, *noted*. However, one-syllable words ending in *-ed* should not be divided. An example is *served*. Watch for this type of occurrence and click No to cancel the hyphenation. At the hyphenation complete message, click OK.

▼ **Quick Steps**

Automatic Hyphenation
1. Click Page Layout tab.
2. Click Hyphenation button.
3. Click *Automatic* at drop-down list.

Manual Hyphenation
1. Click Page Layout tab.
2. Click Hyphenation button.
3. Click *Manual* at drop-down list.
4. Click Yes or No to hyphenate indicated words.
5. When complete, click OK.

Avoid dividing words at the ends of more than two consecutive lines.

Hyphenation

Figure 5.2 Manual Hyphenation Dialog Box

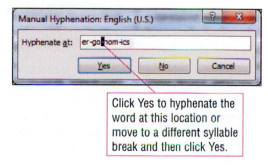

Click Yes to hyphenate the word at this location or move to a different syllable break and then click Yes.

If you want to remove all hyphens in a document, immediately click the Undo button on the Quick Access toolbar. To delete a few, but not all, of the optional hyphens inserted during hyphenation, use the Find and Replace dialog box. To do this, you would display the Find and Replace dialog box with the Replace tab selected, insert an optional hyphen symbol in the *Find what* text box (to do this, click the More button, click the Special button and then click *Optional Hyphen* at the pop-up list), and make sure the *Replace with* text box is empty. Complete the find and replace, clicking the Replace button to replace the hyphen with nothing or clicking the Find Next button to leave the hyphen in the document.

Project 1e **Automatically and Manually Hyphenating Words** Part 5 of 8

1. With **WL1-C5-P1-InputDevices.docx** open, hyphenate words automatically by completing the following steps:
   a. Press Ctrl + Home and then click the Page Layout tab.
   b. Click the Hyphenation button in the Page Setup group and then click *Automatic* at the drop-down list.

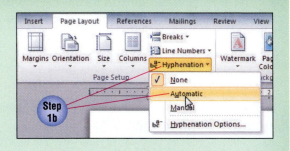

2. Scroll through the document and notice the automatic hyphenations.
3. Click the Undo button to remove the hyphens.
4. Manually hyphenate words by completing the following steps:
   a. Click the Hyphenation button in the Page Setup group and then click *Manual* at the drop-down list.
   b. At the Manual Hyphenation dialog box, make one of the following choices:
      • Click Yes to hyphenate the word as indicated in the *Hyphenate at* text box.
      • Move the hyphen in the word to a more desirable location, and then click Yes.
      • Click No if you do not want the word hyphenated.

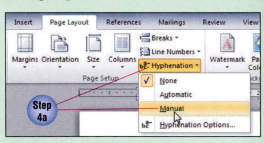

   c. Continue clicking Yes or No at the Manual Hyphenation dialog box.
   d. At the hyphenation complete message, click OK.
5. Save **WL1-C5-P1-InputDevices.docx**.

Creating a Drop Cap ■■■■■■ ■ ■ ■ ■ ■ ■ ■ ■ ■ ■ ■ ■

▼ Quick Steps

Create Drop Cap
1. Click Insert tab.
2. Click Drop Cap button.
3. Click desired type in drop-down list.

Drop Cap

Use a drop cap to enhance the appearance of text. A ***drop cap*** is the first letter of the first word of a paragraph that is set into a paragraph. Drop caps identify the beginning of major sections or parts of a document. Create a drop cap with the Drop Cap button in the Text group in the Insert tab. You can choose to set the drop cap in the paragraph or in the margin. At the Drop Cap dialog box, you can specify a font, the numbers of lines you want the letter to drop, and the distance you want the letter positioned from the text of the paragraph. You can drop cap the first word by selecting the word first and then clicking the Drop Cap button.

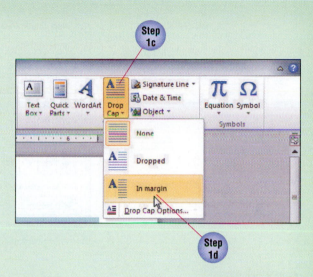

1. With **WL1-C5-P1-InputDevices.docx** open, create a drop cap by completing the following steps:
   a. Position the insertion point on the first word of the first paragraph of text (*Engineers*).
   b. Click the Insert tab.
   c. Click the Drop Cap button in the Text group.
   d. Click *In margin* at the drop-down gallery.
2. Looking at the drop cap, you decide that you do not like it in the margin and want it to be a little smaller. To change the drop cap, complete the following steps:
   a. With the E in the word *Engineers* selected, click the Drop Cap button in the Text group and then click *None* at the drop-down gallery.
   b. Click the Drop Cap button and then click *Drop Cap Options* at the drop-down gallery.
   c. At the Drop Cap dialog box, click *Dropped* in the *Position* section.
   d. Change the font to *Times New Roman*.
   e. Change the *Lines to drop* option to *2*.
   f. Click OK to close the dialog box.
   g. Click outside the drop cap to deselect it.
3. Save **WL1-C5-P1-InputDevices.docx**.

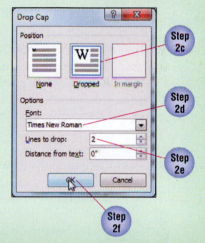

Inserting Symbols and Special Characters ■■■■■■■■

You can use the Symbol button in the Insert tab to insert special symbols in a document. Click the Symbol button in the Symbols group in the Insert tab and a drop-down list displays with the most recently inserted symbols along with a *More Symbols* option. Click one of the symbols that displays in the list to insert it in the document or click the *More Symbols* option to display the Symbol dialog box as shown in Figure 5.3. At the Symbol dialog box, double-click the desired symbol, and then click Close; or click the desired symbol, click the Insert button, and then click Close.

At the Symbol dialog box with the Symbols tab selected, you can change the font with the *Font* option. When you change the font, different symbols display in the dialog box. Click the Special Characters tab at the Symbol dialog box and a list of special characters displays along with keyboard shortcuts to create the special character.

▼ **Quick Steps**

Insert a Symbol
1. Click Insert tab.
2. Click Symbol button.
3. Click desired symbol in drop-down list.
OR
1. Click Insert tab.
2. Click Symbol button.
3. Click *More Symbols*.
4. Double-click desired symbol.
5. Click Close.

Symbol

Figure 5.3 Symbol Dialog Box with Symbols Tab Selected

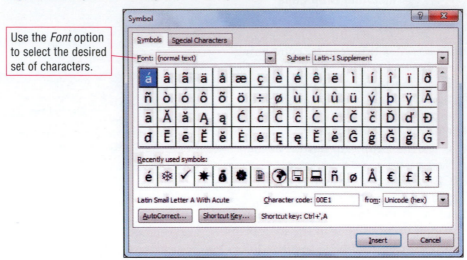

Use the *Font* option to select the desired set of characters.

Project 1g Inserting Symbols and Special Characters Part 7 of 8

1. With **WL1-C5-P1-InputDevices.docx** open, press Ctrl + End to move the insertion point to the end of the document.
2. Press the Enter key once, type **Prepared by:**, and then press the spacebar once.
3. Type the first name **Matthew**.
4. Insert the last name *Viña* by completing the following steps:
   a. Type **Vi**.
   b. Click the Symbol button in the Symbols group in the Insert tab.
   c. Click *More Symbols* at the drop-down list.
   d. At the Symbol dialog box, make sure the *Font* option displays as *(normal text)* and then double-click the ñ symbol (located in approximately the twelfth row).
   e. Click the Close button.
   f. Type **a**.
5. Press Shift + Enter.
6. Insert the keyboard symbol (⌨) by completing the following steps:
   a. Click the Symbol button and then click *More Symbols*.
   b. At the Symbol dialog box, click the down-pointing arrow at the right side of the *Font* option and then click *Wingdings* at the drop-down list. (You will need to scroll down the list to display this option.)
   c. Double-click ⌨ (located approximately in the second row).
   d. Click the Close button.
7. Type **SoftCell Technologies**.

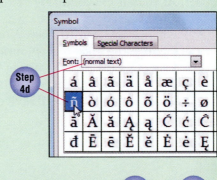

Step 4d

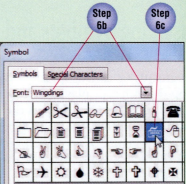

Step 6b   Step 6c

8. Insert the registered trademark symbol (®) by completing the following steps:
   a. Click the Symbol button and then click *More Symbols*.
   b. At the Symbol dialog box, click the Special Characters tab.
   c. Double-click the ® symbol (tenth option from the top).
   d. Click the Close button.
   e. Press Shift + Enter.
9. Select the keyboard symbol (⌨) and then change the font size to 18.
10. Save **WL1-C5-P1-InputDevices.docx**.

Step 8b

Step 8c

Symbol

Symbols | Special Characters

Character:		Shortcut key:
—	Em Dash	Alt+Ctrl+Num -
–	En Dash	Ctrl+Num -
-	Nonbreaking Hyphen	Ctrl+Shift+_
¬	Optional Hyphen	Ctrl+-
	Em Space	
	En Space	
	1/4 Em Space	
°	Nonbreaking Space	Ctrl+Shift+Space
©	Copyright	Alt+Ctrl+C
®	Registered	Alt+Ctrl+R
™	Trademark	Alt+Ctrl+T
§	Section	
¶	Paragraph	
...	Ellipsis	Alt+Ctrl+.
'	Single Opening Quote	Ctrl+`,`

Inserting the Date and Time ▪■■■■■■■■■■■■■■■■■■

Use the Date & Time button in the Text group in the Insert tab to insert the current date and time in a document. Click this button and the Date and Time dialog box displays as shown in Figure 5.4. (Your date will vary from what you see in the figure.) At the Date and Time dialog box, click the desired date and/or time format in the *Available formats* list box.

If the *Update automatically* check box does not contain a check mark, the date and/or time are inserted in the document as normal text that you can edit in the normal manner. You can also insert the date and/or time as a field. The advantage to inserting the date or time as a field is that the field can be updated with the Update Field keyboard shortcut, F9. Insert a check mark in the *Update automatically* check box to insert the data and/or time as a field. You can also insert the date as a field using the keyboard shortcut Alt + Shift + D, and insert the time as a field with the keyboard shortcut Alt + Shift + T.

▼ **Quick Steps**

Insert Date and Time
1. Click Insert tab.
2. Click Date and Time button.
3. Click option in list box.
4. Click OK.

Date & Time

Figure 5.4 Date and Time Dialog Box

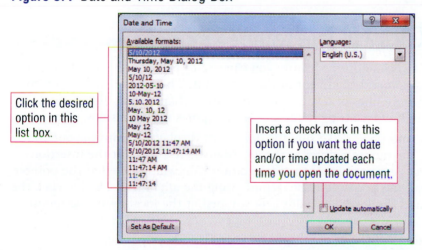

Click the desired option in this list box.

Insert a check mark in this option if you want the date and/or time updated each time you open the document.

1. With **WL1-C5-P1-InputDevices.docx** open, press Ctrl + End and make sure the insertion point is positioned below the company name.
2. Insert the current date by completing the following steps:
   a. Click the Date & Time button in the Text group in the Insert tab.
   b. At the Date and Time dialog box, click the third option from the top in the *Available formats* group.
   c. Click in the *Update automatically* check box to insert a check mark.
   d. Click OK to close the dialog box.
3. Press Shift + Enter.
4. Insert the current time by pressing Alt + Shift + T.
5. Save **WL1-C5-P1-InputDevices.docx**.
6. Update the time by clicking the time and then pressing F9.
7. Save, print, and then close **WL1-C5-P1-InputDevices.docx**.

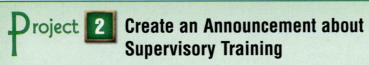

Project 2 Create an Announcement about Supervisory Training   3 Parts

You will create an announcement about upcoming supervisory training and use the click and type feature to center and right align text. You will vertically center the text on the page and insert and format a picture to add visual appeal to the announcement.

Using the Click and Type Feature ■■■■■■■■■ ■■■■■ ■ ■ ■

Word contains a click and type feature you can use to position the insertion point at a specific location and alignment in the document. This feature allows you to position one or more lines of text as you type, rather than typing the text and then selecting and reformatting the text, which requires multiple steps.

▼ **Quick Steps**

Use Click and Type
1. Hover mouse at left margin, between left and right margins, or at right margin.
2. Double-click left mouse button.

To use click and type, make sure the document displays in Print Layout view and then hover the mouse pointer at the location where you want the insertion point positioned. As you move the mouse pointer, you will notice that the pointer displays with varying horizontal lines representing the alignment. Double-click the mouse button and the insertion point is positioned at the location of the mouse pointer.

If the horizontal lines do not display next to the mouse pointer when you double-click the mouse button, a left tab is set at the position of the insertion point. If you want to change the alignment and not set a tab, make sure the horizontal lines display near the mouse pointer before double-clicking the mouse.

1. At a blank document, create the centered text shown in Figure 5.5 by completing the following steps:
   a. Position the I-beam pointer between the left and right margins at about the 3.25-inch mark on the horizontal ruler and the top of the vertical ruler.
   b. When the center alignment lines display below the I-beam pointer, double-click the left mouse button.

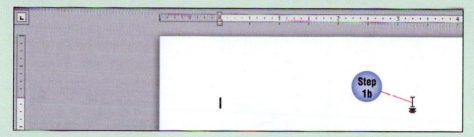

   c. Type the centered text shown in Figure 5.5. Press Shift + Enter to end each text line.
2. Change to right alignment by completing the following steps:
   a. Position the I-beam pointer near the right margin at approximately the 1.5-inch mark on the vertical ruler until the right alignment lines display at the left side of the I-beam pointer.
   b. Double-click the left mouse button.
   c. Type the right-aligned text shown in Figure 5.5. Press Shift + Enter to end the text line.
3. Select the centered text and then change the font to 14-point Candara bold and the line spacing to double.
4. Select the right-aligned text, change the font to 10-point Candara bold, and then deselect the text.
5. Save the document and name it **WL1-C5-P2-Training**.

Figure 5.5 Project 2a

> SUPERVISORY TRAINING
> Maximizing Employee Potential
> Wednesday, February 15, 2012
> Training Center
> 9:00 a.m. to 3:30 p.m.
>
>   Sponsored by
>   Cell Systems

Vertically Aligning Text

Text in a Word document is aligned at the top of the page by default. You can change this alignment with the *Vertical alignment* option at the Page Setup dialog box with the Layout tab selected as shown in Figure 5.6. Display this dialog box by clicking the Page Layout tab, clicking the Page Setup group dialog box launcher, and then clicking the Layout tab at the Page Setup dialog box.

Figure 5.6 Page Setup Dialog Box with Layout Tab Selected

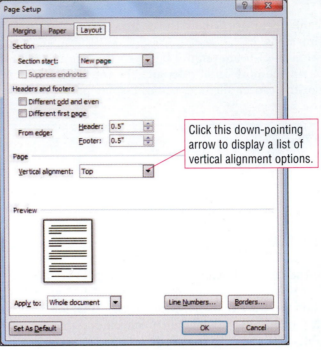

Click this down-pointing arrow to display a list of vertical alignment options.

▼ **Quick Steps**

Vertically Align Text
1. Click Page Layout tab.
2. Click Page Setup dialog box launcher.
3. Click Layout tab.
4. Click desired alignment.
5. Click OK.

The *Vertical alignment* option from the Page Setup dialog box contains four choices — *Top*, *Center*, *Justified*, and *Bottom*. The default setting is *Top*, which aligns text at the top of the page. Choose *Center* if you want text centered vertically on the page. The *Justified* option will align text between the top and the bottom margins. The *Center* option positions text in the middle of the page vertically, while the *Justified* option adds space between paragraphs of text (not within) to fill the page from the top to bottom margins. If you center or justify text, the text does not display centered or justified on the screen in the Draft view, but it does display centered or justified in the Print Layout view. Choose the *Bottom* option to align text in the document vertically along the bottom of the page.

Project 2b   Vertically Centering Text   Part 2 of 3

1. With **WL1-C5-P2-Training.docx** open, click the Page Layout tab and then click the Page Setup group dialog box launcher.
2. At the Page Setup dialog box, click the Layout tab.
3. Click the down-pointing arrow at the right side of the *Vertical alignment* option box and then click *Center* at the drop-down list.
4. Click OK to close the dialog box.
5. Save and then print **WL1-C5-P2-Training.docx**.

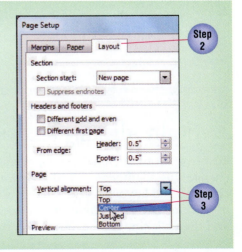

Inserting an Image ■■■■■■■■■■■■■■■■■■■■■■■■■■■■

You can insert an image such as a picture or clip art in a Word document with buttons in the Illustrations group in the Insert tab. Click the Picture button to display the Insert Picture dialog box where you can specify the desired picture file or click the Clip Art button and then choose from a variety of images available at the Clip Art task pane. When you insert a picture or a clip art image in a document, the Picture Tools Format tab displays. Use options on the Picture Tools Format tab to customize and format the image.

Customizing and Formatting an Image

With options in the Adjust group in the Picture Tools Format tab you can remove unwanted portions of the image, correct the brightness and contrast, change the image color, apply artistic effects, compress the size of the image file, change to a different image, and reset the image back to the original formatting. Use buttons in the Picture Styles group to apply a predesigned style to the image, change the image border, or apply other effects to the image. With options in the Arrange group, you can position the image on the page, specify how text will wrap around it, align the image with other elements in the document, and rotate the image. Use the Crop button in the Size group to remove any unnecessary parts of the image and specify the image size with the *Shape Height* and *Shape Width* measurement boxes.

Crop

In addition to the Picture Tools Format tab, you can customize and format an image with options at the shortcut menu. Display this menu by right-clicking the image. With options at the shortcut menu, you can change the picture, insert a caption, choose text wrapping, size and position the image, and display the Format Picture dialog box.

Sizing an Image

You can change the size of an image with the *Shape Height* and *Shape Width* measurement boxes in the Size group in the Picture Tools Format tab or with the sizing handles that display around the selected image. To change size with a sizing handle, position the mouse pointer on a sizing handle until the pointer turns into a double-headed arrow and then hold down the left mouse button. Drag the sizing handle in or out to decrease or increase the size of the image and then release the mouse button. Use the middle sizing handles at the left or right side of the image to make the image wider or thinner. Use the middle sizing handles at the top or bottom of the image to make the image taller or shorter. Use the sizing handles at the corners of the image to change both the width and height at the same time.

Resize a selected object horizontally, vertically, or diagonally from the center outward by holding down the Ctrl key and then dragging a sizing handle.

Moving an Image

Move an image to a specific location on the page with options from the Position button drop-down gallery. The Position button is located in the Arrange group in the Picture Tools Format tab. When you choose an option at the Position button drop-down gallery, the image is moved to the specified location on the page and square text wrapping is applied to the image.

Position

You can also move the image by dragging it to the desired location. Before dragging an image, you must first choose a text wrapping style by clicking the Wrap Text button in the Arrange group and then clicking the desired wrapping style at the drop-down list. After choosing a wrapping style, move the image by positioning the mouse pointer on the image border until the arrow pointer turns into a four-headed arrow. Hold down the left mouse button, drag the image to the desired position, and then release the mouse button. To help precisely position an image, consider turning on gridlines. Do this by clicking the Align button in the Arrange group in the Picture Tools Format tab and then clicking *View Gridlines*.

Rotate the image by positioning the mouse pointer on the green, round rotation handle until the pointer displays as a circular arrow. Hold down the left mouse button, drag in the desired direction, and then release the mouse button.

Inserting a Picture

To insert a picture in a document, click the Insert tab and then click the Picture button in the Illustrations group. At the Insert Picture dialog box, navigate to the folder containing the desired picture and then double-click the picture. Use buttons in the Picture Tools Format tab to format and customize the picture. You can insert a picture from a Web page by opening the Web page, opening a Word document, and then dragging the picture from the Web page to the document. If the picture is linked, the link (rather than the image) will display in your document.

Project 2c **Inserting and Customizing a Picture** **Part 3 of 3**

1. With **WL1-C5-P2-Training.docx** open, return the vertical alignment back to *Top* by completing the following steps:
   a. Click the Page Layout tab.
   b. Click the Page Setup group dialog box launcher.
   c. At the Page Setup dialog box, click the Layout tab.
   d. Click the down-pointing arrow at the right side of the *Vertical alignment* option box and then click *Top* at the drop-down list.
   e. Click OK to close the dialog box.
2. Select and then delete the text *Sponsored by* and the text *Cell Systems*.
3. Select the remaining text and change the line spacing to single.
4. Move the insertion point to the beginning of the document and then press the Enter key until the first line of text displays at approximately the 3-inch mark on the vertical ruler.
5. Insert a picture by completing the following steps:
   a. Click the Insert tab.
   b. Click the Picture button in the Illustrations group.
   c. At the Insert Picture dialog box, navigate to your Word2010L1C5 folder.
   d. Double-click *Uluru.jpg* in the list box.
6. Crop the picture by completing the following steps:
   a. Click the Crop button in the Size group.
   b. Position the mouse pointer on the bottom, middle crop handle (displays as a short black line) until the pointer turns into the crop tool (displays as a small, black T).

c. Hold down the left mouse button, drag up to just below the mountain as shown at the right, and then release the mouse button.

d. Click the Crop button in the Size group to turn off the feature.

7. Change the size of the picture by clicking in the *Shape Height* measurement box in the Size group, typing 3, and then pressing Enter.

8. Move the picture behind the text by clicking the Wrap Text button in the Arrange group and then clicking *Behind Text* at the drop-down list.

9. Rotate the image by clicking the Rotate button in the Arrange group and then clicking *Flip Horizontal* at the drop-down list.

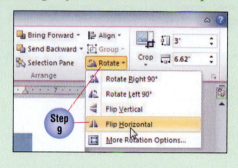

SUPERVISORY TRAINING

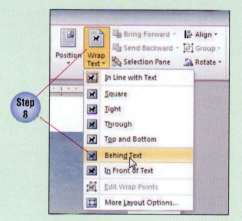

10. Change the picture color by clicking the Color button in the Adjust group and then clicking the second option from the right in the *Color Saturation* section (*Saturation: 300%*).

11. After looking at the coloring, you decide to return to the original color by clicking the Undo button on the Quick Access toolbar.

12. Sharpen the picture by clicking the Corrections button in the Adjust group and then clicking the second option from the right in the *Sharpen and Soften* section (*Sharpen: 25%*).

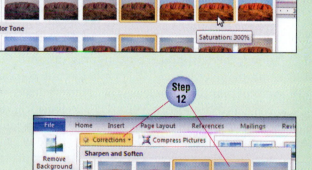

13. Change the contrast of the picture by clicking the Corrections button in the Adjust group and then clicking the third option from the left in the bottom row of the *Brightness and Contrast* section [*Brightness: 0% (Normal) Contrast: +40%*].

14. Apply a picture style by clicking the More button at the right side of the thumbnails in the Picture Styles section and then clicking the first option from the left in the second row (*Simple Frame, Black*).

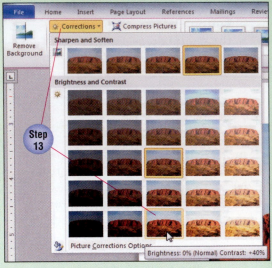

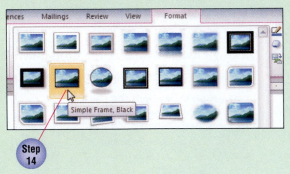

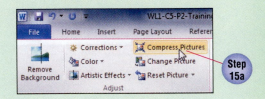

15. Compress the picture by completing the following steps:
    a. Click the Compress Pictures button in the Adjust group.
    b. At the Compress Pictures dialog box, make sure a check mark displays in both options in the *Compression options* section and then click OK.

16. Position the mouse pointer on the border of the selected picture until the pointer displays with a four-headed arrow attached and then drag the picture so the text is positioned in the sky above Ayres Rock.

17. If the text does not fit in the sky above the rock, increase the height of the picture. To do this, position the mouse pointer on the top border middle sizing handle until the pointer displays as a two-headed arrow pointing up and down. Hold down the left mouse button, drag up until the text displays approximately one-half inch below the top border of the picture, and then release the mouse button.

18. Save and then print **WL1-C5-P2-Training.docx**.

19. With the picture selected, remove the background by completing the following steps:
    a. Click the Remove Background button in the Adjust group in the Picture Tools Format tab.
    b. Using the left middle sizing handle, drag the left border to the left side of the image.

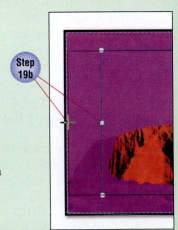

c. Drag the right middle sizing handle to the right side of the image.

d. Drag the bottom middle sizing handle to the bottom border of the image.

e. Click the Keep Changes button in the Close group in the Background Removal tab. (The picture should now display with the sky removed.)

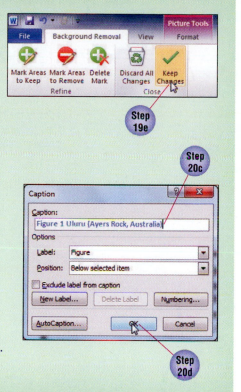

Step 19e

20. Insert a caption by completing the following steps:

a. Right-click the picture. (This displays the shortcut menu.)

b. Click the *Insert Caption* option at the shortcut menu.

c. At the Caption dialog box with the insertion point positioned in the *Caption* text box, press the spacebar and then type Uluru (Ayers Rock, Australia).

d. Click OK. (The caption displays below and at the left side of the picture.)

21. Save, print, and then close **WL1-C5-P2-Training.docx**.

Step 20c

Step 20d

Project 3 Customize a Report on Robots   2 Parts

You will open a report on robots and then add visual appeal to the report by inserting and formatting a clip art image and a built-in text box.

Inserting a Clip Art Image

Microsoft Office includes a gallery of media images you can insert in a document such as clip art, photographs, and movie images, as well as sound clips. To insert an image in a Word document, click the Insert tab and then click the Clip Art button in the Illustrations group. This displays the Clip Art task pane at the right side of the screen as shown in Figure 5.7.

To view all picture, sound, and motion files, make sure the *Search for* text box in the Clip Art task pane does not contain any text and then click the Go button. When the desired image is visible, click the image to insert it in the document. Use buttons in the Picture Tools Format tab to format and customize the clip art image.

Unless the Clip Art task pane default settings have been customized, the task pane displays all illustrations, photographs, videos, and audio files. The *Results should be* option has a default setting of *Selected media file types*. Click the down-pointing arrow at the right side of this option to display media types. To search for a specific media type, remove the check mark before all options at the drop-down list except for the desired type. For example, if you are searching only for photograph images, remove the check mark before *Illustrations*, *Videos*, and *Audio*.

▼ Quick Steps

Insert Clip Art Image
1. Click Insert tab.
2. Click Clip Art button.
3. Type search word or topic.
4. Press Enter.
5. Click desired image.

You can drag a clip art image from the Clip Art task pane to your document.

Clip Art

Figure 5.7 Clip Art Task Pane

Type the search word or topic in this text box.

Use this option to specify the type of files for which you are searching.

If you are searching for specific images, click in the *Search for* text box, type the desired topic, and then click the Go button. For example, if you want to find images related to business, click in the *Search for* text box, type **business**, and then click the Go button. Clip art images related to *business* display in the viewing area of the task pane. If you are connected to the Internet, Word will search for images at the Office Online website matching the topic.

Project 3a · Inserting an Image

Part 1 of 2

1. Open **Robots.docx** and then save the document with Save As and name it **WL1-C5-P3-Robots**.
2. Apply the Heading 1 style to the title *ROBOTS AS ANDROIDS* and apply the Heading 2 style to the headings in the document.
3. Change the Quick Styles set to *Modern*. **Hint: Do this with the Change Styles button in the Styles group in the Home tab.**
4. Insert a clip art image by completing the following steps:
   a. Move the insertion point so it is positioned at the beginning of the first paragraph of text (the sentence that begins *Robotic factories are increasingly . . .*).
   b. Click the Insert tab.
   c. Click the Clip Art button in the Illustrations group.
   d. At the Clip Art task pane, select any text that displays in the *Search for* text box, type **computer**, and then press Enter.
   e. Click the computer image in the list box as shown at the right.

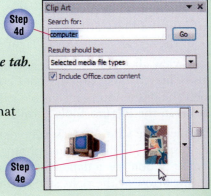

Step 4d

Step 4e

f. Close the Clip Art task pane by clicking the Close button (contains an X) located in the upper right corner of the task pane.

5. Format the clip art image by completing the following steps:

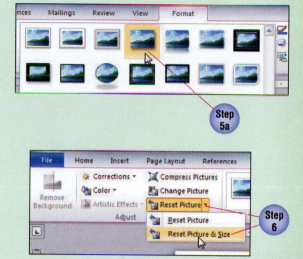
Step 5a

a. Click the More button at the right side of the thumbnails in the Picture Styles group and then click the *Drop Shadow Rectangle* option (fourth option from the left in the top row).

b. Click the Color button in the Adjust group and then click the *Blue, Accent color 1 Dark* option (second option from the left in the second row).

c. Click in the *Shape Height* measurement box in the Size group, type 3, and then press Enter.

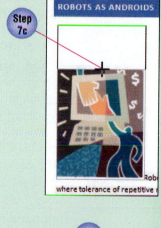
Step 6

6. Reset the image and the image size by clicking the Reset Picture button arrow in the Adjust group and then clicking the *Reset Picture & Size* option at the drop-down list.

7. Crop the clip art image by completing the following steps:

Step 7c
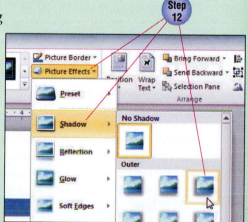

a. Click the Crop button in the Size group.

b. Position the mouse pointer on the top middle crop handle (displays as a short black line) until the pointer turns into the crop tool.

c. Hold down the left mouse button, drag down to just above the top of the computer as shown at the right, and then release the mouse button.

d. Click the Crop button in the Size group to turn off the feature.

8. Decrease the size of the picture by clicking in the *Shape Height* measurement box in the Size group, typing 1.3, and then pressing Enter.

9. Change the text wrapping by clicking the Wrap Text button in the Arrange group and then clicking *Square* at the drop-down list.

10. Rotate the image by clicking the Rotate button in the Arrange group and then clicking *Flip Horizontal* at the drop-down list.

11. Click the Corrections button in the Adjust group and then click the third option from the left in the bottom row [*Brightness: 0% (Normal) Contrast: +40%*].

12. Click the Picture Effects button in the Picture Styles group, point to *Shadow*, and then click the last option in the top row of the *Outer* section (*Offset Diagonal Bottom Left*).

13. Position the mouse pointer on the border of the selected picture until the pointer turns into a four-headed arrow and then drag the picture so it is positioned as shown at the right.
14. Click outside the clip art image to deselect it.
15. Save **WL1-C5-P3-Robots.docx**.

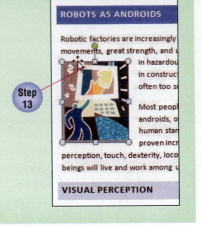

Step 13

Inserting and Customizing a Pull Quote ■■■■■■■■■ ■

▼ **Quick Steps**

Inserting Pull Quote
1. Click Insert tab.
2. Click Text Box button.
3. Click desired pull quote.

Text Box

Use a pull quote in a document such as an article to attract attention. A **pull quote** is a quote from an article that is "pulled out" and enlarged and positioned in an attractive location on the page. Some advantages of pull quotes are that they reinforce important concepts, summarize your message, and break up text blocks to make them easier to read. If you use multiple pull quotes in a document, keep them in order to ensure clear comprehension for readers.

You can insert a pull quote in a document with a predesigned built-in text box. Display the available pull quote built-in text boxes by clicking the Insert tab and then clicking the Text Box button in the Text group. Click the desired pull quote from the drop-down list that displays and the built-in text box is inserted in the document. Type the quote inside the text box and then format the text and/or customize the text box. Use buttons in the Drawing Tools Format tab to format and customize the built-in text box.

At the Drawing Tools Format tab, use options in the Insert Shapes group to insert a shape in the document. Click the Edit Shape button in the Insert Shapes group and a drop-down list displays. Click the *Change Shape* option if you want to change the shape of the selected text box. Click the *Edit Points* option and small black squares display at points around the text box. Use the mouse on these points to increase or decrease a point of the text box. Apply predesigned styles to a text box with options in the Shape Styles group. You can also change the shape fill, outline, and effects. Change the formatting of the text in the text box with options in the WordArt Styles group. Click the More button that displays at the right side of the WordArt style thumbnails and then click the desired style at the drop-down gallery. You can further customize text with the Text Fill, Text Outline, and Text Effects buttons in the Text group. Use options in the Arrange group to position the text box on the page, specify text wrapping in relation to the text box, align the text box with other objects in the document, and rotate the text box. Specify the text box size with the *Shape Height* and *Shape Width* measurement boxes in the Size group.

1. With **WL1-C5-P3-Robots.docx** open, click the Insert tab.
2. Click the Text Box button in the Text group.
3. Scroll down the drop-down list and then click the *Contrast Quote* option.
4. Type the following text in the text box: "The task of creating a humanlike body has proven incredibly difficult."
5. Make sure the Drawing Tools Format tab is active.
6. Click the More button at the right side of the style thumbnails in the Shape Styles group and then click the *Subtle Effect - Blue, Accent 1* option (second option from the left in the fourth row).

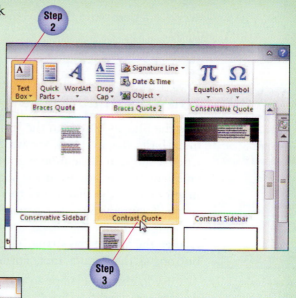

Step 2

Step 3

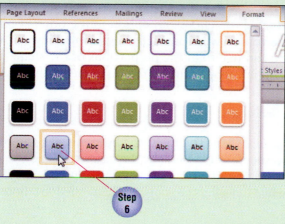

Step 6

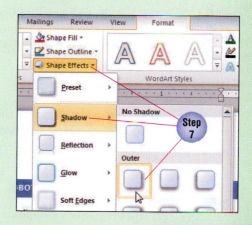

Step 7

7. Click the Shape Effects button in the Shape Styles group, point to *Shadow*, and then click the *Offset Diagonal Bottom Right* option (first option from the left in the first row in the *Outer Section*).
8. Position the mouse pointer on the border of the selected text box until the pointer turns into a four-headed arrow and then drag the text box so it is positioned as shown above.
9. Save, print, and then close **WL1-C5-P3-Robots.docx**.

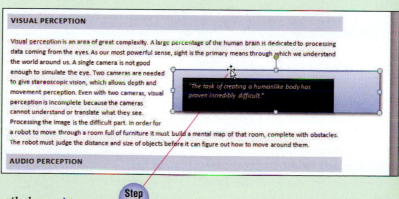

Step 8

You will prepare a company flyer by inserting and customizing shapes, text boxes, and WordArt.

Drawing Shapes ■■■■■■■■■■■■■■■■■■■■■■■

Use the Shapes button in the Insert tab to draw shapes in a document including lines, basic shapes, block arrows, flow chart shapes, stars and banners, and callouts. Click a shape and the mouse pointer displays as crosshairs (plus sign). Position the crosshairs where you want the shape to begin, hold down the left mouse button, drag to create the shape, and then release the mouse button. This inserts the shape in the document and also displays the Drawing Tools Format tab. Use buttons in this tab to change the shape, apply a style to the shape, arrange the shape, and change the size of the shape. This tab contains many of the same options and buttons as the Picture Tools Format tab and the Text Box Tools Format tab.

If you choose a shape in the *Lines* section of the drop-down list, the shape you draw is considered a **line drawing**. If you choose an option in the other sections of the drop-down list, the shape you draw is considered an **enclosed object**. When drawing an enclosed object, you can maintain the proportions of the shape by holding down the Shift key while dragging with the mouse to create the shape.

Copying Shapes

To copy a shape, select the shape and then click the Copy button in the Clipboard group in the Home tab. Position the insertion point at the location where you want the copied image and then click the Paste button. You can also copy a selected shape by holding down the Ctrl key while dragging the shape to the desired location.

P**roject 4a** **Drawing Arrow Shapes** **Part 1 of 3**

1. At a blank document, press the Enter key twice and then draw an arrow shape by completing the following steps:
   a. Click the Insert tab.
   b. Click the Shapes button in the Illustrations group and then click the *Striped Right Arrow* shape in the *Block Arrows* section.
   c. Position the mouse pointer (displays as crosshairs) in the document at approximately the 1-inch mark on the horizontal ruler and the 0.5-inch mark on the vertical ruler.
   d. Hold down the Shift key and the left mouse button, drag to the right until the tip of the arrow is positioned at approximately the 5.5-inch mark on the horizontal ruler, and then release the mouse button and the Shift key.

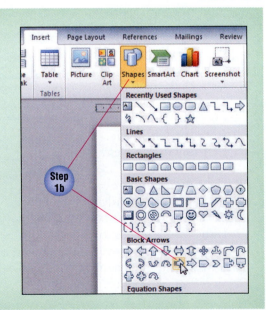

2. Format the arrow by completing the following steps:
   a. Click in the *Shape Height* measurement box in the Size group, type 2.4, and then press Enter.
   b. Click in the *Shape Width* measurement box in the Size group, type 4.5, and then press Enter.
   c. Click the More button at the right side of the thumbnails in the Shape Styles group and then click the *Intense Effect – Olive Green, Accent 3* option (fourth option from the left in the sixth row).

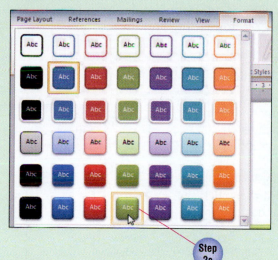

   d. Click the Shape Effects button in the Shape Styles group, point to *Bevel*, and then click the *Angle* option (first option from the left in the second row in the *Bevel* section).
   e. Click the Shape Outline button arrow in the Shape Styles group and then click the Dark Blue color (second color from the right in the *Standard Colors* section).
3. Copy the arrow by completing the following steps:
   a. With the mouse pointer positioned in the arrow (mouse pointer displays with a four-headed arrow attached), hold down the Ctrl key and the left mouse button.
   b. Drag down until the outline of the copied arrow displays just below the top arrow, release the mouse button, and then release the Ctrl key.
   c. Copy the arrow again by holding down the Ctrl key and the left mouse button and then dragging the outline of the copied arrow just below the second arrow.
4. Flip the middle arrow by completing the following steps:
   a. Click the middle arrow to select it.
   b. Click the Rotate button in the Arrange group in the Drawing Tools Format tab and then click *Flip Horizontal* at the drop-down gallery.
5. Insert the text *Financial* in the top arrow by completing the following steps:
   a. Click the top arrow to select it.
   b. Type Financial. (The text will appear in the middle of the arrow.)
   c. Select *Financial*.
   d. Click the Home tab.
   e. Change the font size to 16, turn on bold, and then change the font color to Olive Green, Accent 3, Darker 50%.
6. Complete steps similar to those in Step 5 to insert the word *Direction* in the middle arrow.
7. Complete steps similar to those in Step 5 to insert the word *Retirement* in the bottom arrow.
8. Save the document and name it **WL1-C5-P4-FinConsult**.
9. Print the document.

▼ **Quick Steps**

Draw a Text Box
1. Click Insert tab.
2. Click Text Box button in Text group.
3. Click *Draw Text Box*.
4. Drag in document screen to create box.

Drawing and Formatting a Text Box

You can use the built-in text boxes provided by Word or you can draw your own text box. To draw a text box, click the Insert tab, click the Text Box button in the Text group, and then click *Draw Text Box* at the drop-down list. The mouse pointer displays as crosshairs. Position the crosshairs in the document and then drag to create the text box. You can also just click in the document. When a text box is selected, the Text Box Tools Format tab displays. Use buttons in this tab to format text boxes in the same manner as formatting built-in text boxes.

Project 4b   **Inserting and Formatting a Text Box**   **Part 2 of 3**

1. With **WL1-C5-P4-FinConsult.docx** open, delete the bottom arrow by completing the following steps:
   a. Click the bottom arrow. (This displays a border around the arrow.)
   b. Position the mouse pointer on the border (displays with four-headed arrow attached) and then click the left mouse button. (This changes the dashed border to a solid border.)
   c. Press the Delete key.
2. Insert, size, and format a text box by completing the following steps:
   a. Click the Insert tab.
   b. Click the Text Box button in the Text group and then click *Draw Text Box* at the drop-down list.
   c. Click in the document at about the one-inch mark on the horizontal ruler and about one inch below the bottom arrow. (This inserts a text box in the document.)
   d. Click in the *Shape Height* measurement box in the Size group and then type 1.7.
   e. Click in the *Shape Width* measurement box, type 4.5, and then press Enter.
   f. Click the More button at the right side of the thumbnails in the Shape Styles group and then click the *Intense Effect – Olive Green, Accent 3* option at the drop-down gallery (fourth option from the left in the sixth row).
   g. Click the Shape Effects button in the Shape Styles group, point to *Bevel*, and then click the *Soft Round* option at the side menu (second option from the left in the second row in the *Bevel* section).

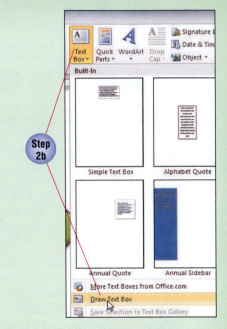

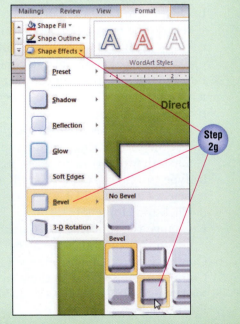

h. Click the Shape Effects button in the Shape Styles group, point to *3-D Rotation*, and then click the *Perspective Above* option (first option from the left in the second row in the *Perspective* section).

3. Insert and format text in the text box by completing the following steps:
   a. Press the Enter key twice. (The insertion point should be positioned in the text box.)
   b. Click the Home tab.
   c. Change the font size to 24 points, turn on bold, and change the font color to Olive Green, Accent 3, Darker 50%.
   d. Click the Center button in the Paragraph group.
   e. Type **Retirement Financial Consulting**. (Your text box should appear as shown below.)

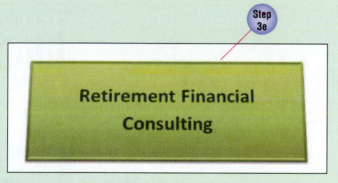

Step 3e

Retirement Financial Consulting

Step 2h

4. Save **WL1-C5-P4-FinConsult.docx**.

Creating and Modifying WordArt Text ■■■■■■■■■ ■■■

With the WordArt feature, you can distort or modify text to conform to a variety of shapes. This is useful for creating company logos, letterheads, flyer titles, or headings. To insert WordArt in a document, click the Insert tab and then click the WordArt button in the Text group. At the drop-down list that displays, click the desired option and a WordArt text box is inserted in the document containing the words *Your text here* and the Drawing Tools Format tab is active. Type the desired WordArt text and then format the WordArt with options in the Drawing Tools Format tab.

▼ **Quick Steps**
Create WordArt Text
1. Click Insert tab.
2. Click WordArt button.
3. Click desired WordArt option at drop-down list.
4. Type WordArt text.

WordArt

Project 4c **Inserting and Modifying WordArt**   **Part 3 of 3**

1. With **WL1-C5-P4-FinConsult.docx** open, press Ctrl + Home to move the insertion point to the beginning of the document.
2. Insert WordArt text by completing the following steps:
   a. Click the Insert tab.

b. Click the WordArt button in the Text group and then click the *Fill – Olive Green, Accent 3, Outline – Text 2* option.

c. Type **Miller Financial Services**.

3. Format the WordArt text by completing the following steps:

a. Click the outside border of the WordArt text so the border displays as a solid line instead of a dashed line.

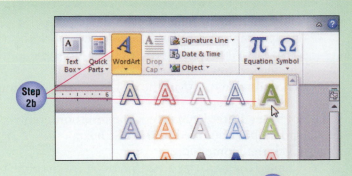

Step 2b

b. Click the Text Fill button arrow in the WordArt Styles group in the Drawing Tools Format tab and then click the *Olive Green, Accent 3, Darker 25%* option.

c. Click the Text Effects button in the WordArt Styles group, point to *Glow*, and then click the *Aqua, 5 pt glow, Accent color 5* option in the *Glow Variations* section.

Step 3b

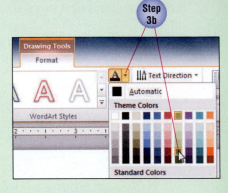

Step 3c

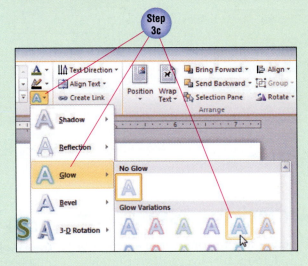

d. Click the Text Effects button in the WordArt Styles group, point to *3-D Rotation*, and then click the *Perspective Above* option in the *Perspective* section.

e. Click in the *Shape Height* measurement box in the Size group and then type **1**.

f. Click in the *Shape Width* measurement box in the Size group, type **6**, and then press Enter.

g. Click the Text Effects button in the WordArt Styles group, point to *Transform*, and then click the *Deflate* option in the *Warp* section (second option from the left in the sixth row).

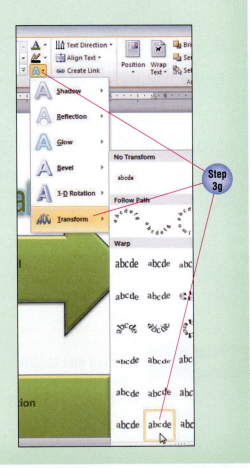

Step 3g

h. Click the Position button in the Arrange group and then click the second option from the left in the first row in the *With Text Wrapping* section (*Position in Top Center with Square Text Wrapping*).

4. Check to make sure that the WordArt, the two arrows, and the text box all fit on one page. If they do not, consider moving and/or sizing the arrows or text box to ensure that they fit on one page.

5. Save, print, and then close **WL1-C5-P4-FinConsult.docx**.

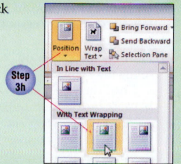

Step 3h

Project 5 Create and Format Screenshots

2 Parts

You will create screenshots of the Print tab and Save & Send tab Backstage views and then create screen clippings of cover pages and create a sample cover pages document.

Creating and Inserting a Screenshot ■■■■■■■■■■■■■■■

The Illustrations group in the Insert tab contains a Screenshot button, which you can use to capture the contents of a screen as an image or capture a portion of a screen. If you want to capture the entire screen, open a new document, click the Insert tab, click the Screenshot button in the Illustrations group, and then click the desired screen thumbnail at the drop-down list. The currently active document does not display as a thumbnail at the drop-down list, only any other documents or files that you have open. When you click the desired thumbnail, the screenshot is inserted as an image in the open document, the image is selected, and the Picture Tools Format tab is active. Use buttons in this tab to customize the screenshot image.

Screenshot

Project 5a Inserting and Formatting Screenshots

Part 1 of 2

1. Open a blank document.
2. Open a second blank document, type **Print Tab Backstage View** at the left margin, and then press the Enter key.
3. Save the document and name it **WL1-C5-P5-BackstageViews**.
4. Click the Word button on the Taskbar, click the thumbnail representing the blank document, and then display the Print tab Backstage view by clicking the File tab and then clicking the Print tab.

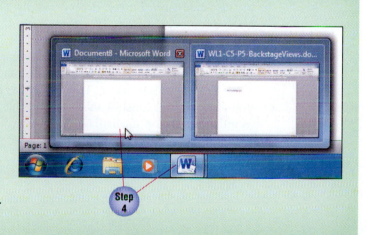

Step 4

5. Click the Word button on the Taskbar and then click the thumbnail representing **WL1-C5-P5-BackstageViews.docx**.

6. Insert and format a screenshot of the Print tab Backstage view by completing the following steps:

   a. Click the Insert tab.

   b. Click the Screenshot button in the Illustrations group and then click the thumbnail that displays in the drop-down list. (This inserts a screenshot of the Print tab Backstage view in the document.)

   c. With the screenshot image selected, click the More button that displays at the right side of the thumbnails in the Picture Styles group and then click the *Drop Shadow Rectangle* option.

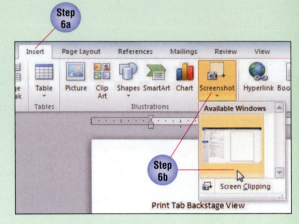

   d. Select the measurement in the *Shape Width* measurement box in the Size group, type 5.5, and then press Enter.

7. Press Ctrl + End and then press the Enter key twice. (This moves the insertion point below the screenshot image.)

8. Type **Save & Send Tab Backstage View** at the left margin and then press the Enter key.

9. Click the Word button on the Taskbar and then click the thumbnail representing the blank document.

10. At the Backstage view, click the Save & Send tab. (This displays the Save & Send tab Backstage view.)

11. Click the Word button on the Taskbar and then click the thumbnail representing **WL1-C5-P5-BackstageViews.docx**.

12. Insert and format a screenshot of the Save & Send tab Backstage view by completing Step 6.

13. Press Ctrl + Home to move the insertion point to the beginning of the document.

14. Save, print, and then close **WL1-C5-P5-BackstageViews.docx**.

15. At the Save & Send tab Backstage view, click the Close button to close the document without saving it.

In addition to making a screenshot of an entire screen, you can make a screenshot of a specific portion of the screen by clicking the *Screen Clipping* option at the Screenshot button drop-down list. When you click this option, the other open document, file, or Windows desktop displays in a dimmed manner and the mouse pointer displays as a crosshair. Using the mouse, draw a border around the specific area of the screen you want to capture. The specific area you identified is inserted in the other document as an image, the image is selected, and the Picture Tools Format tab is active. If you have only one document or file open when you click the Screenshot tab, clicking the *Screen Clipping* option will cause the Windows desktop to display.

1. Open **NSSLtrhd.docx** and save it with Save As and name it **WL1-C5-P5-NSSCoverPages**.
2. Type the text **Sample Cover Pages** and then press the Enter key twice.
3. Select the text you just typed, change the font to 18-point Copperplate Gothic Bold, and then center the text.
4. Press Ctrl + End to move the insertion point below the text.
5. Open the document named **NSSCoverPg01.docx**.
6. Click the Word button on the Taskbar and then click the thumbnail representing **WL1-C5-P5-NSSCoverPages.docx**.
7. Create and format a screenshot screen clipping by completing the following steps:

   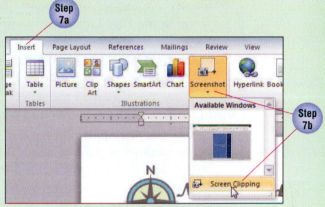

   a. Click the Insert tab.
   b. Click the Screenshot button in the Illustrations group and then click *Screen Clipping*.
   c. When the **NSSCoverPg01.docx** displays in a dimmed manner, position the mouse crosshairs in the upper left corner of the cover page, hold down the left mouse button, drag down to the lower right corner of the cover page, and then release the mouse button. (See image at the right.)

   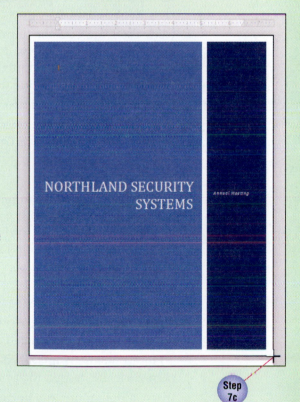

   d. With the cover page screenshot image inserted in **WL1-C5-P5-NSSCoverPages.docx**, make sure the image is selected (sizing handles display around the cover page image).
   e. Click the Wrap Text button in the Arrange group in the Picture Tools Format tab and then click *Square* at the drop-down gallery.
   f. Select the current measurement in the *Shape Width* measurement box in the Size group, type **3**, and then press Enter.
8. Click the Word button on the Taskbar and then click the thumbnail representing **NSSCoverPg01.docx** and then close the document.
9. Open **NSSCoverPg02.docx**.
10. Click the Word button on the Taskbar and then click the thumbnail representing **WL1-C5-P5-NSSCoverPages.docx**.
11. Create and format a screenshot by completing steps similar to those in Step 7.
12. Position the two cover page screenshot images so they are side by side in the document.
13. Save, print, and then close **WL1-C5-P5-NSSCoverPages.docx**.
14. Close **NSSCoverPg02.docx**.

Chapter Summary

- Insert a section break in a document to apply formatting to a portion of a document. You can insert a continuous section break or a section break that begins a new page. View a section break in Draft view since section breaks are not visible in Print Layout view.

- Set text in columns to improve readability of documents such as newsletters or reports. Format text in columns using the Columns button in the Page Setup group in the Page Layout tab or with options at the Columns dialog box.

- Remove column formatting with the Columns button in the Page Layout tab or at the Columns dialog box. Balance column text on the last page of a document by inserting a continuous section break at the end of the text.

- Improve the display of text lines by hyphenating long words that fall at the end of the line. You can automatically or manually hyphenate words in a document.

- To enhance the appearance of text, use drop caps to identify the beginning of major sections or parts of a paragraph. Create drop caps with the Drop Cap button in the Text group in the Insert tab.

- Insert symbols with options at the Symbol dialog box with the Symbols tab selected and insert special characters with options at the Symbol dialog box with the Special Characters tab selected.

- Click the Date & Time button in the Text group in the Insert tab to display the Date and Time dialog box. Insert the date or time with options at this dialog box or with keyboard shortcuts. If the date or time is inserted as a field, update the field with the Update Field key, F9.

- Use the click and type feature to center, right-align, and left-align text.

- Vertically align text in a document with the *Vertical alignment* option at the Page Setup dialog box with the Layout tab selected.

- Insert an image such as a picture or clip art with buttons in the Illustrations group in the Insert tab.

- Customize and format an image with options and buttons in the Picture Tools Format tab. Size an image with the *Shape Height* and *Shape Width* measurement boxes in the Size group in the Picture Tools Format tab or with the sizing handles that display around the selected image.

- Move an image with options from the Position button drop-down gallery located in the Picture Tools Format tab or by choosing a text wrapping style and then moving the image by dragging it with the mouse.

- To insert a picture, click the Insert tab, click the Picture button, navigate to the desired folder at the Insert Picture dialog box, and then double-click the picture.

- To insert a clip art image, click the Insert tab, click the Clip Art button, and then click the desired image in the Clip Art task pane.

- Insert a pull quote in a document with a built-in text box by clicking the Insert tab, clicking the Text Box button, and then clicking the desired built-in text box at the drop-down list.

- Draw shapes in a document by clicking the Shapes button in the Illustrations group in the Insert tab, clicking the desired shape at the drop-down list, and then dragging in the document to draw the shape. Customize a shape with options at the Drawing Tools Format tab. Copy a shape by holding down the Ctrl key while dragging the selected shape.

- Draw a text box by clicking the Text Box button in the Text group in the Insert tab, clicking *Draw Text Box* at the drop-down list, and then clicking in the document or dragging in the document. Customize a text box with buttons at the Drawing Tools Format tab.

- Use WordArt to distort or modify text to conform to a variety of shapes. Customize WordArt with options at the Drawing Tools Format tab.

- Use the Screenshot button in the Illustrations group in the Home tab to capture the contents of a screen or capture a portion of a screen.

- Use buttons in the Picture Tools Format tab to customize a screenshot image.

Commands Review

FEATURE	RIBBON TAB, GROUP	BUTTON, OPTION	KEYBOARD SHORTCUT
Continuous section break	Page Layout, Page Setup	, Continuous	
Columns dialog box	Page Layout, Page Setup	, More Columns	
Columns	Page Layout, Page Setup		
Hyphenate words automatically	Page Layout, Page Setup	, Automatic	
Manual Hyphenation dialog box	Page Layout, Page Setup	, Manual	
Drop cap	Insert, Text		
Symbol dialog box	Insert, Symbols		
Date and Time dialog box	Insert, Text		
Insert date			Alt + Shift + D
Insert time			Alt + Shift + T
Update field			F9
Page Setup dialog box	Page Layout, Page Setup		
Insert Picture dialog box	Insert, Illustrations		
Clip Art task pane	Insert, Illustrations		
Pull quote (Built-in text box)	Insert, Text		

FEATURE	RIBBON TAB, GROUP	BUTTON, OPTION	KEYBOARD SHORTCUT
Shapes	Insert, Illustrations		
Text box	Insert, Text		
WordArt	Insert, Text		
Screenshot	Insert, Illustrations		

Concepts Check Test Your Knowledge

Completion: In the space provided at the right, indicate the correct term, symbol, or command.

1. View a section break in this view.

2. Format text into columns with the Columns button located in this group in the Page Layout tab.

3. Balance column text on the last page of a document by inserting this type of break at the end of the text.

4. The first letter of the first word of a paragraph that is set into a paragraph is called this.

5. The Symbol button is located in this tab.

6. This is the keyboard shortcut to insert the current date.

7. Use this feature to position the insertion point at a specific location and alignment in a document.

8. Vertically align text with the *Vertical alignment* option at the Page Setup dialog box with this tab selected.

9. Insert an image in a document with buttons in this group in the Insert tab.

10. Customize and format an image with options and buttons in this tab.

11. Size an image with the sizing handles that display around the selected image or with these measurement boxes in the Picture Tools Format tab.

12. Click the Picture button in the Insert tab and this dialog box displays.

13. Click the Clip Art button in the Insert tab and this displays at the right side of the screen. _____

14. This is the term for a quote that is enlarged and positioned in an attractive location on the page. _____

15. Apply predesigned styles to a text box with options in this group. _____

16. The Shapes button is located in this tab. _____

17. To copy a selected shape, hold down this key while dragging the shape. _____

18. Use this feature to distort or modify text to conform to a variety of shapes. _____

19. To capture a portion of a screen, click the Screenshot button in the Illustrations group in the Insert tab and then click this option at the drop-down list. _____

Skills Check Assess Your Performance

Assessment

1 ADD VISUAL APPEAL TO A REPORT ON THE FUTURE OF THE INTERNET

1. Open **Internet2.docx** and then save the document with Save As and name it **WL1-C5-A1-Internet2**.
2. Apply the Heading 1 style to the title of the report and apply the Heading 3 style to the headings in the report. *Hint: You may need to click the Heading 2 style to display the Heading 3 style.*
3. Change the Quick Styles set to *Thatch* and then center the title.
4. Apply the Elemental theme and then change the theme colors to *Solstice*.
5. Format the text from the first paragraph to the end of the document into two columns with 0.4 inches between columns.
6. Balance the text on the second page.
7. Insert a clip art image related to *satellite*. (Choose the clip art image that is available with Word and does not require downloading. This clip art image is blue and black and contains a satellite and a person holding a telephone and a briefcase.)
8. Make the following customizations to the clip art image:
   a. Change the height to 1.2".
   b. Apply tight text wrapping.
   c. Change the color of the clip art image to *Aqua, Accent color 1 Light*.
   d. Correct the contrast to Brightness: *0% (Normal) Contrast: –20%*.
   e. Drag the image so it is positioned at the left margin in the *Satellite Internet Connections* section.

9. Insert the *Alphabet Quote* built-in text box and then make the following customizations:
   a. Type the following text in the text box: "A remedy for the traffic clogging the information highway is Internet2."
   b. Select the text and then change the font size to 12 and change the line spacing to 1.15.
   c. Apply the Subtle Effect - Aqua, Accent 1 style to the text box (second option from the left in the fourth row).
   d. Apply the Offset Bottom shadow effect to the text box.
   e. Drag the box so it is positioned above the SATELLITE INTERNET CONNECTIONS heading in the first column, below the SECOND INTERNET heading in the second column, and centered between the left and right margins.
10. Press Ctrl + End to move the insertion point to the end of the document. (The insertion point will be positioned below the continuous section break you inserted on the second page to balance the columns of text.)
11. Change back to one column.
12. Press the Enter key twice and then draw a shape using the *Plaque* shape (located in the second row in the *Basic Shapes* section) and make the following customizations:
    a. Recolor the shape to match the color formatting in the document or the built-in text box.
    b. Position the shape centered between the left and right margins.
    c. Make any other changes to enhance the visual appeal of the shape.
    d. Type the following text inside the shape: ❧ Felicité Compagnie ❧. Insert the ❧ and ❧ symbols at the Symbol dialog box with the Wingdings font selected. Insert the é symbol at the Symbol dialog box with the *(normal text)* font selected.
    e. Insert the current date below ❧ Felicité Compagnie ❧ and insert the current time below the date.
13. Manually hyphenate the document (do not hyphenate headings or proper names).
14. Create a drop cap with the first letter of the word *The* that begins the first paragraph of text.
15. Save, print, and then close **WL1-C5-A1-Internet2.docx**.

Assessment

2 CREATE A SALES MEETING ANNOUNCEMENT

1. Create an announcement about an upcoming sales meeting with the following specifications:
   a. Insert the company name *Inlet Corporation* as WordArt text.
   b. Insert the following text in the document:
      National Sales Meeting
      Northwest Division
      Ocean View Resort
      August 20 through August 22, 2012
   c. Insert the picture named **Ocean.jpg** and size and position the picture behind the text.
   d. Make any formatting changes to the WordArt, text, and picture to enhance the visual appeal of the document.
2. Save the announcement document and name it **WL1-C5-A2-SalesMtg**.
3. Print and then close **WL1-C5-A2-SalesMtg.docx**.

Assessment

3 CREATE AN ANNOUNCEMENT

1. At a blank document, create the announcement shown in Figure 5.8. Insert the caduceus clip art image as shown in the figure with the following specifications:
   a. Use the word *medicine* to locate the clip art image.
   b. Change the text wrapping to *Tight*.
   c. Change the clip art image color to *Blue, Accent color 1 Dark*.
   d. Correct the brightness and contrast to *Brightness: +20% Contrast: –20%*.
   e. Size and move the clip art image as shown in the figure.
2. Apply character (set the heading in 28-point Candara and the remaining text in 14-point Candara), paragraph, and page formatting so your document appears the same as the document in Figure 5.8.
3. Save the completed announcement and name it **WL1-C5-A3-FirstAidCourse**.
4. Print and then close **WL1-C5-A3-FirstAidCourse.docx**. (If some of the page border does not print, consider increasing the measurements at the Border and Shading Options dialog box.)

Figure 5.8 Assessment 3

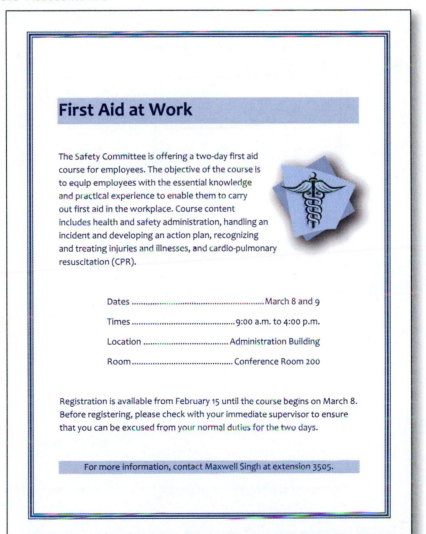

Assessment

4 INSERT SCREENSHOTS IN A MEMO

1. Open **FirstAidMemo.docx** and then save it with Save As and name it **WL1-C5-A4-FirstAidMemo**.
2. Insert screenshots so your document appears as shown in Figure 5.9. (Insert your initials in place of the XX located toward the end of the document.) Use the **FirstAidAnnounce.docx** document located in your Word2010L1C5 folder to create the first screenshot and use the document **WL1-C5-A3-FirstAidCourse.docx** you created in Assessment 3 for the second screenshot. *Hint: Decrease the size of the document so the entire document is visible on the screen*.
3. Save, print, and close **WL1-C5-A4-FirstAidMemo.docx**.

Figure 5.9 Assessment 4

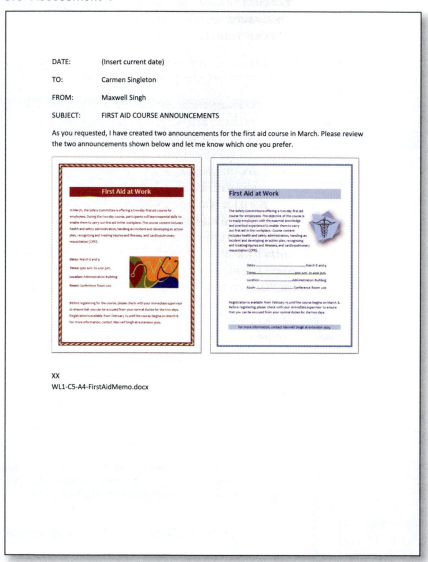

Visual Benchmark Demonstrate Your Proficiency

1 CREATE A SHAPE

1. At a blank document create the document shown in Figure 5.10 with the following specifications:
   a. Draw the shape using the *Quad Arrow Callout* located in the *Block Arrows* section.
   b. Apply the *Subtle Effect – Olive Green, Accent 3* shape style to the shape.
   c. Change the shape effect to *Soft Round* bevel.
   d. Change the height and width of the shape to 5 inches.
   e. Type the text in the shape as shown and set the text in 16-point Copperplate Gothic Bold and change the text color to dark green.
   f. Insert the truck clip art image and size and position it as shown in Figure 5.10. (If this truck clip art image is not available, choose another truck clip art image. Change the text wrap to *In Front of Text*.)
2. Center the shape on the page.
3. Save the document and name it **WL1-C5-VB1-FourCorners**.
4. Print and then close the document.

Figure 5.10 Visual Benchmark 1

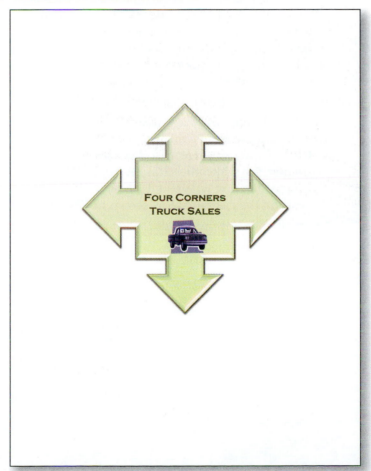

2 FORMAT A REPORT

1. Open **Resume.docx** and then save it with Save As and name it **WL1-C5-VB2-Resume**.

2. Format the report so it appears as shown in Figure 5.11 with the following specifications:

   a. Insert the WordArt text *Résumé Writing* with the following specifications:

   • Use the *Gradient Fill – Blue, Accent 1* option (fourth option from the left in the third row).
   • Type the text **Résumé Writing** and insert the é symbol using the Insert Symbol dialog box.
   • Change the position to *Position in Top Center with Square Text Wrapping* (middle option in the top row of the *With Text Wrapping* section).
   • Change the width of the WordArt to 5.5 inches and the height to 0.9 inch.
   • Apply the *Can Up* transform text effect. **Hint: Use the Transform option from the Text Effects button drop-down list**.

   b. Apply the Heading 3 style to the two headings in the report.
   c. Change the Quick Styles set to *Modern*.
   d. Change the theme to *Aspect* and change the theme colors to *Flow*.
   e. Format the report into two columns beginning with the first paragraph of text and balance the columns on the second page.
   f. Insert the pull quote with the following specifications:

   • Use the *Austere Quote*.
   • Type the text shown in the pull quote in Figure 5.11. (Use the Insert Symbol dialog box to insert the two é symbols in the word résumé.)
   • Change the pull quote text color to dark blue.
   • Select the text box (make sure the border displays as a solid line), make the Drawing Tools Format tab active, and then change the shape outline color to blue.

   g. Insert the cake clip art image with the following specifications:

   • Insert the clip art image shown in the figure. If this image is not available, choose a similar image of a cake.
   • Change the image color to *Blue, Accent color 1 Light*.
   • Change the width to 1.2 inches.
   • Change the text wrapping to *Tight*.
   • Position the cake image as shown in Figure 5.11.

   h. Insert the *Conservative* footer.
   i. Manually hyphenate text in the document.

3. Save, print, and then close **WL1-C5-VB2-Resume.docx**.

Figure 5.11 Visual Benchmark 2

winning résumé. It will be a useful list of tasks and achievements.

Writing a résumé is like baking a cake. You need all the right ingredients: flour, butter, eggs, and so on. It is what you do with the ingredients that makes the difference between a great résumé (or cake) and failure. Keeping your résumé up-to-date is like keeping a stock of ingredients in the pantry—it's potentially very useful, but do not imagine that is the end of it!

INFORMATION ABOUT THE JOB

You should tailor the information in your résumé to the main points in the job advertisement. Get as much information about the job and the company as you can. The main sources of information about a job are normally the following:

- A job advertisement
- A job description
- A friend in the company
- The media
- Gossip and rumor
- Someone already doing the job or something similar

There is no substitute for experience. Talking to someone who does a job similar to the one you wish to apply for in the same company may well provide you with a good picture of what the job is really like. Bear in mind, of course, that this source of information is not always reliable. You may react differently than the way that person does, and therefore their experience with a company may be very different from yours. However, someone with reliable information can provide a golden opportunity. Make sure you do not waste the chance to get some information.

Résumé Writing

To produce the best "fitting" résumé, you need to know about yourself and you need to know about the job you are applying for. Before you do anything else, ask yourself why you are preparing a résumé. The answer to this question is going to vary from one person to the next, and here are our top ten reasons for writing a résumé:

1. You have seen a job advertised in the paper that appeals to you.
2. You want to market yourself to win a contract or a proposal, or be elected to a committee or organization.
3. You have seen a job on an Internet job site that appeals to you.
4. Your friends or family told you of a job opening at a local company.
5. You want to work for the local company and thought that sending a résumé to them might get their attention.
6. You have seen a job advertised internally at work.
7. You are going for a promotion.
8. You are feeling fed up and writing down all your achievements will cheer you up and might motivate you to look for a better job.
9. You are thinking "Oh, so that's a résumé! I suppose I ought to try to remember what I've been doing with my life."
10. You are about to be downsized and want to update your résumé to be ready for any good opportunities.

> *"Updating your résumé from time to time is a good idea so you do not forget important details..."*

All of these certainly are good reasons to write a résumé, but the résumé serves many different purposes. One way of seeing the differences is to ask yourself who is going to read the résumé in each case.

Résumés 1 through 5 will be read by potential employers who probably do not know you. Résumés 6 and 7 are likely to be read by your boss or other people who know you. Résumés 8 through 10 are really for your own benefit and should not be considered as suitable for sending out to employers.

THE RIGHT MIX

Think about the list of reasons again. How else can you divide up these reasons? An important difference is that, in some cases, you will have a good idea of what the employer is looking for because you have a job advertisement in front of you and can tailor your résumé accordingly. For others, you have no idea what the reader might want to see. Updating your résumé from time to time is a good idea so you do not forget important details, but remember that the result of such a process will not be a

Case Study   Apply Your Skills

Part 1

You work for Honoré Financial Services and have been asked by the office manager, Jason Monroe, to prepare an information newsletter. Mr. Monroe has asked you to open the document named **Budget.docx** and then format it into columns. You determine the number of columns and any additional enhancements to the columns. He also wants you to proofread the document and correct any spelling and grammatical errors. Save the completed newsletter and name it **WL1-C5-CS-Budget** and then print the newsletter. When Mr. Monroe reviews the newsletter, he decides that it needs additional visual appeal. He wants you to insert visual elements in the newsletter such as WordArt, clip art, a built-in text box, and/or a drop cap. Save **WL1-C5-CS-Budget.docx** and then print and close the document.

Part 2

Honoré Financial Services will be offering a free workshop on Planning for Financial Success. Mr. Monroe has asked you to prepare an announcement containing information on the workshop. You determine what to include in the announcement such as the date, time, location, and so forth. Enhance the announcement by inserting a picture or clip art and by applying formatting such as font, paragraph alignment, and borders. Save the completed document and name it **WL1-C5-CS-Announce**. Print and then close the document.

Part 3

Honoré Financial Services has adopted a new slogan and Mr. Monroe has asked you to create a shape with the new slogan inside. Experiment with the shadow and 3-D shape effects available at the Drawing Tools Format tab and then create a shape and enhance the shape with shadow and/or 3-D effects. Insert the new Honoré Financial Services slogan "Retirement Planning Made Easy" in the shape. Include any additional enhancements to improve the visual appeal of the shape and slogan. Save the completed document and name it **WL1-C5-CS-Slogan**. Print and then close the document.

Part 4

Mr. Monroe has asked you to prepare a document containing information on teaching children how to budget. Use the Internet to find websites and articles that provide information on how to teach children to budget their money. Write a synopsis of the information you find and include at least four suggestions on how to teach children to manage their money. Format the text in the document into newspaper columns. Add additional enhancements to improve the appearance of the document. Save the completed document and name it **WL1-C5-CS-ChildBudget**. Print and then close the document.

Maintaining Documents

PERFORMANCE OBJECTIVES

Upon successful completion of Chapter 6, you will be able to:

- Create and rename a folder
- Select, delete, copy, move, rename, and print documents
- Save documents in different file formats
- Open, close, arrange, split, maximize, minimize, and restore documents
- Insert a file into an open document
- Print specific pages and sections in a document
- Print multiple copies of a document
- Print envelopes and labels
- Create a document using a Word template

Tutorials

6.1 Managing Documents
6.2 Managing Folders
6.3 Saving a Document as a Web Page
6.4 Sharing Documents
6.5 Working with Windows
6.6 Creating and Printing Envelopes
6.7 Creating and Printing Labels
6.8 Creating Documents Using a Word Template

Almost every company that conducts business maintains a filing system. The system may consist of documents, folders, and cabinets; or it may be a computerized filing system where information is stored on the computer's hard drive or other storage medium. Whatever type of filing system a business uses, daily maintenance of files is important to a company's operation. In this chapter, you will learn to maintain files (documents) in Word, including such activities as creating additional folders and copying, moving, and renaming documents. You will also learn how to create and print documents, envelopes, and labels and create a document using a Word template. Model answers for this chapter's projects appear on the following pages.

Note: Before beginning the projects, copy to your storage medium the Word2010L1C6 subfolder from the Word2010L1 folder on the CD that accompanies this textbook and then make Word2010L1C6 the active folder.

Project 1 Manage Documents

COMPUTER KEYBOARDS

To give commands to a computer or to enter data into it, a user needs an input device. An input device can be built into the computer, like the keyboard in a laptop, or it can be connected to the computer by a cable. Some input devices, like remote keyboards, send directions to the computer by means of an infrared signal and use no cabling at all.

QWERTY Keyboard

Keyboards can be external devices that are attached by means of a cable, or they can be attached to the CPU case itself as they are in laptops. Most keyboards today are QWERTY keyboards, which take their name from the first six keys at the left of the first row of letters. The QWERTY design was invented in the early days of mechanical typewriters to slow down typists and thus keep keys from jamming.

DVORAK Keyboard

The DVORAK keyboard is an alternative to the QWERTY keyboard. On the DVORAK keyboard, the most commonly used keys are placed close to the user's fingertips and this increases typing speed. You can install software on a QWERTY keyboard that emulates a DVORAK keyboard. The ability to emulate other keyboards is convenient especially when working with foreign languages. Keyboards have different physical appearances. Many keyboards have a separate numeric keypad, like that of a calculator, containing numbers and mathematical operators. Some keyboards are sloped and "broken" into two pieces to reduce strain. All keyboards have modifier keys that enable the user to change the symbol or characters entered when a given key is pressed.

WL1-C6-P1-CompKeyboards.docx

APARTMENT LEASE AGREEMENT

This Apartment Lease Agreement (hereinafter referred to as the "Agreement") is made and entered into this 30th day of September, 2012, by and between Monica Spellman, Lessor, and Jack Lowell, Lessee.

Term
Lessor leases to Lessee the described premises together with any and all appurtenances thereto, for a term of 1 year, such term beginning on October 1, 2012, and ending at 12 o'clock midnight on September 30, 2013.

Rent
The total rent for the term hereof is the sum of one thousand five hundred dollars ($1,500) payable on the 5th day of each month of the term. All such payments shall be made to Lessor on or before the due date and without demand.

Damage Deposit
Upon the due execution of this Agreement, Lessee shall deposit with Lessor the sum of seven hundred dollars ($700), receipt of which is hereby acknowledged by Lessor, as security for any damage caused to the Premises during the term hereof. Such deposit shall be returned to Lessee, without interest, and less any set off for damages to the Premises upon the termination of this Agreement.

Use of Premises
The Premises shall be used and occupied by Lessee and Lessee's immediate family, exclusively, as a private single family dwelling, and no part of the Premises shall be used at any time during the term of this Agreement by Lessee for the purpose of carrying on any business, profession, or trade of any kind, or for any purpose other than as a private single family dwelling. Lessee shall not allow any other person, other than Lessee's immediate family or transient relatives and friends who are guests, to use or occupy the Premises without first obtaining written consent to such use.

WL1-C6-P1-AptLease-PlainTxt.txt

APARTMENT LEASE AGREEMENT

This Apartment Lease Agreement (hereinafter referred to as the "Agreement") is made and entered into this 30th day of September, 2012, by and between Monica Spellman, Lessor, and Jack Lowell, Lessee.

Term
Lessor leases to Lessee the described premises together with any and all appurtenances thereto, for a term of 1 year, such term beginning on October 1, 2012, and ending at 12 o'clock midnight on September 30, 2013.

Rent
The total rent for the term hereof is the sum of one thousand five hundred dollars ($1,500) payable on the 5th day of each month of the term. All such payments shall be made to Lessor on or before the due date and without demand.

Damage Deposit
Upon the due execution of this Agreement, Lessee shall deposit with Lessor the sum of seven hundred dollars ($700), receipt of which is hereby acknowledged by Lessor, as security for any damage caused to the Premises during the term hereof. Such deposit shall be returned to Lessee, without interest, and less any set off for damages to the Premises upon the termination of this Agreement.

Use of Premises
The Premises shall be used and occupied by Lessee and Lessee's immediate family, exclusively, as a private single family dwelling, and no part of the Premises shall be used at any time during the term of this Agreement by Lessee for the purpose of carrying on any business, profession, or trade of any kind, or for any purpose other than as a private single family dwelling. Lessee shall not allow any other person, other than Lessee's immediate family or transient relatives and friends who are guests, to use or occupy the Premises without first obtaining written consent to such use.

WL1-C6-P1-AptLease-RichText.rtf

SECTION 1: COMPUTERS IN ENTERTAINMENT

Possibilities in the television and film industries have soared with computer technology, especially in production. Computer games have captured the public imagination and created an enormous growth in the computer game market.

TELEVISION AND FILM

Many of the spectacular graphics and special effects on television and in movies today are created with computers. The original *Star Wars* films, for example, relied heavily on hand-constructed models and hand-drawn graphics. Twenty years after the original release of the films, they were re-released with many new special effects, including futuristic cityscape backgrounds, new alien creatures, and new sounds that were created on computers and added to the films by means of computerized video editing.

The film *Jurassic Park* brought computer simulation to a new level by combining puppetry and computer animation to simulate realistic looking dinosaurs. *Toy Story*, released in 1996, was the first wholly computer-animated commercial movie. Software products that automatically format scripts of various kinds are commercially available.

HOME ENTERTAINMENT

In the 1970s, computer games such as Pong and Pac-Man captured the public imagination. Since then, there has been enormous growth in the computer game market. Manufacturers such as Sega and Nintendo produce large, complex video arcade games as well as small computer game systems for home use. Typical arcade-style computer games include simulations of boxing, warfare, racing, skiing, and flight.

The advent of powerful desktop personal computers has led to the production of home computer games that rival those of arcade machines in complexity. Other computer games make use of televisions or of small, independent, handheld devices. Games are now able to take advantage of three-dimensional graphics that create virtual environments.

Page 1

Project 2 Manage Multiple Documents

WL1-C6-P2-CommIndustry.docx

SECTION 2: COMPUTERS IN COMMUNICATION

Computers have become central to the communications industry. They play a vital role in telecommunications, publishing, and news services.

TELECOMMUNICATIONS

The industry that provides for communication across distances is called telecommunications. The telephone industry uses computers to switch and route calls automatically over telephone lines. Today, many kinds of information move over such lines, including the spoken word, faxes, and computer data. Data can be sent over telephone lines from computer to computer using a device known as a modem. One kind of data sent by modem is electronic mail, or email, which can be sent from person to person via the Internet or an online service. A recent innovation in telecommunications is teleconferencing, which allows people in various locations to see and hear one another and thus hold virtual meetings.

PUBLISHING

Just twenty years ago, a book manuscript had to be typeset mechanically or on a typesetting machine and then reproduced on a printing press. Now anyone who has access to a computer and either a modem or a printer can undertake what has come to be known as electronic publishing. Writers and editors use word processing applications to produce text. Illustrations and photographs are digitized, or turned into computer-readable files, by means of inexpensive scanners. Artists and designers use drawing and painting applications to create original graphics. Typesetters use personal computers to combine text, illustrations, and photographs. Publishers typically send computer-generated files to printers for production of the film and plates from which books and magazines are printed.

NEWS SERVICES

News providers rely on reporters located worldwide. Reporters use email to send, or upload, their stories to wire services. Increasingly, individuals get daily news reports from online services. News can also be accessed from specific providers, such as the *New York Times* or *U.S.A. Today*, via the Internet. One of the most popular Internet sites provides continuously updated weather reports.

Page 2

SECTION 3: COMPUTERS IN EDUCATION

The widespread use of home computers has brought about an increase in the availability of educational and reference software, making the computer a popular learning and reference tool. Examples of educational and reference software include encyclopedias, dictionaries, and learning tutorials.

ENCYCLOPEDIAS AND DICTIONARIES

Almost everyone has used an encyclopedia or dictionary at one time or another. An encyclopedia is a comprehensive reference work containing detailed articles on a broad range of subjects. Before computers, encyclopedias were only available in book form. They are now available electronically and many new PCs include a CD-based encyclopedia.

A standard dictionary is a reference work containing an alphabetical listing of words, with definitions that provide the word's meaning, pronunciation, and usage. Examples include *Webster's Dictionary* and *Webster's New World Dictionary of Computer Terms*. Other specialized dictionaries, such as multi-language dictionaries, contain words along with their equivalent in another language for use in translation. Many dictionaries are available on CD.

LEARNING TUTORIALS

Many people learn skills by using CD- or Internet-based tutorials. A tutorial is a form of instruction in which students are guided step-by-step through the learning process. Tutorials are available for almost any subject, including learning how to assemble a bicycle, use a word processor, or write a letter. Once an electronic tutorial is accessed, students need only follow the instructions displayed on the screen. Many tutorials include graphics to help guide students during the learning process.

Page 3

DAVID LOWRY 12033 S 152 ST HOUSTON TX 77340	MARCELLA SANTOS 394 APPLE BLOSSOM FRIENDSWOOD TX 77533	KEVIN DORSEY 26302 PRAIRIE DR HOUSTON TX 77316
AL AND DONNA SASAKI 1392 PIONEER DR BAYTOWN TX 77903	JACKIE RHYNER 29039 107 AVE E HOUSTON TX 77302	MARK AND TINA ELLIS 607 FORD AVE HOUSTON TX 77307

WENDY STEINBERG
4532 S 52 ST
BOSTON MA 21002-2334

GREGORY LINCOLN
4455 SIXTH AVE
BOSTON MA 21100-4409

Project 3 Create and Print Envelopes

WL1-C6-P3-Env.docx

Project 4 Create Mailing Labels

WL1-C6-P4-Labels.docx

WL1-C6-P4-LAProg.docx

Project 5 Use a Template to Create a Business Letter

WL1-C6-P5-SFunds.docx

Project 1 — Manage Documents — 8 Parts

You will perform a variety of file management tasks including creating and renaming a folder; selecting and then deleting, copying, cutting, pasting, and renaming documents; deleting a folder; and opening, printing, and closing a document.

Maintaining Documents

Many file (document) management tasks can be completed at the Open dialog box (and some at the Save As dialog box). These tasks can include copying, moving, printing, and renaming documents; opening multiple documents; and creating a new folder and renaming a folder.

Using Print Screen

Keyboards contain a Print Screen key that you can use to capture the contents of the screen into a file. That file can then be inserted in a Word document. The Print Screen feature is useful for file management in that you can print folder contents to help you keep track of documents and folders. To use the Print Screen key, display the desired information on the screen and then press the Print Screen key on your keyboard (generally located in the top row). When you press the Print Screen key, nothing seems to happen but, in fact, the screen image is captured in a file that is inserted in the Clipboard. To insert this file in a document, display a blank document and then click the Paste button in the Clipboard group in the Home tab. You can also paste the file by right-clicking in a blank location in a document screen and then clicking the *Paste* option at the shortcut menu.

Creating a Folder

Word documents, like paper documents, should be grouped logically and placed in *folders*. The main folder on a storage medium is called the **root folder** and you can create additional folders within the root folder. At the Open or Save As dialog box, documents display in the Content pane preceded by a document icon and folders are preceded by a folder icon. Create a new folder by clicking the New folder button located on the dialog box toolbar. This inserts a folder in the Content pane that contains the text *New folder*. Type a name for the folder (the name you type replaces *New folder*) and then press Enter. A folder name can contain a maximum of 255 characters. Numbers, spaces, and symbols can be used in the folder name, except those symbols explained in Chapter 1 in the "Naming a Document" section.

To make the new folder active, double-click the folder name in the Open dialog box Content pane. The current folder path displays in the Address bar in the Open dialog box. The path includes the current folder as well as any previous folders. If the folder is located in an external storage device, the drive letter and name may display in the path. For example, if you create a folder named *Correspondence* in the Word2010L1C6 folder on your storage medium, the Address bar will display *Word2010L1C6* followed by a right-pointing triangle and then *Correspondence*. Two left-pointing arrows display before *Word2010L1C6*. These arrows indicate that *Word2010L1C6* is a subfolder within a folder. Click the two left-pointing arrows and a drop-down list displays with the folder name or drive letter that is up one level from *Word2010L1C6*. The drop-down list also includes other common folders and locations.

▼ **Quick Steps**

Create a Folder
1. Display Open dialog box.
2. Click New folder button.
3. Type folder name.
4. Press Enter.

New Folder

Back

Project 1a   **Creating a Folder**   **Part 1 of 8**

1. Display the Open dialog box.
2. In the *Computer* list box in the Navigation pane, click the drive containing your storage medium. (You may need to scroll down the list to display the drive.)
3. Double-click the *Word2010L1C6* folder in the Content pane.
4. Click the New folder button on the dialog box toolbar.
5. Type **Correspondence** and then press Enter.
6. Print the screen contents and insert the file in a document by completing the following steps:
   a. With the Open dialog box displayed, press the Print Screen key on your keyboard (generally located in the top row of your keyboard).

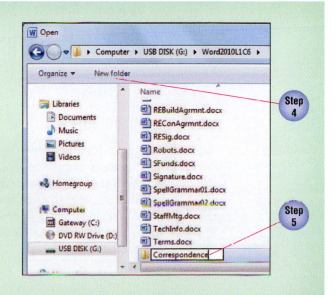

b. Close the Open dialog box.

c. At the blank document, click the Paste button in the Clipboard group in the Home tab. (If a blank document does not display on your screen, press Ctrl + N to open a blank document.)

d. With the print screen file inserted in the document, print the document by clicking the File tab, clicking the Print tab, and then clicking the Print button at the Print tab Backstage view.

7. Close the document without saving it.

8. Display the Open dialog box and make Word2010L1C6 the active folder.

▼ Quick Steps

Rename a Folder
1. Display Open dialog box.
2. Right-click folder.
3. Click *Rename*.
4. Type new name.
5. Press Enter.

Organize ▼

Organize

Renaming a Folder

As you organize your files and folders, you may decide to rename a folder. Rename a folder using the Organize button on the toolbar in the Open or Save As dialog box or using a shortcut menu. To rename a folder using the Organize button, display the Open or Save As dialog box, click the folder you want to rename, click the Organize button located on the toolbar in the dialog box, and then click *Rename* at the drop-down list. This selects the folder name and inserts a border around the name. Type the new name for the folder and then press Enter. To rename a folder using a shortcut menu, display the Open dialog box, right-click the folder name in the Content pane, and then click *Rename* at the shortcut menu. Type a new name for the folder and then press Enter.

Project 1b | **Renaming a Folder** | Part 2 of 8

1. With the Open dialog box open, right-click the *Correspondence* folder name in the Content pane.
2. Click *Rename* at the shortcut menu.
3. Type Documents and then press Enter.

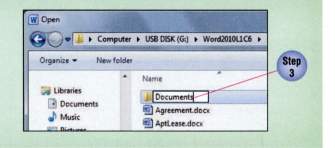

Selecting Documents

You can complete document management tasks on one document or selected documents. To select one document, display the Open dialog box, and then click the desired document. To select several adjacent documents (documents that display next to each other), click the first document, hold down the Shift key, and then click the last document. To select documents that are not adjacent, click the first document, hold down the Ctrl key, click any other desired documents, and then release the Ctrl key.

Deleting Documents

At some point, you may want to delete certain documents from your storage medium or any other drive or folder in which you may be working. To delete a document, display the Open or Save As dialog box, select the document, click the Organize button on the toolbar, and then click *Delete* at the drop-down list. At the dialog box asking you to confirm the deletion, click Yes. To delete a document using a shortcut menu, right-click the document name in the Content pane, click *Delete* at the shortcut menu, and then click Yes at the confirmation dialog box.

Documents deleted from the hard drive are automatically sent to the Recycle Bin. If you accidentally send a document to the Recycle Bin, it can be easily restored. To free space on the drive, empty the Recycle Bin on a periodic basis. Restoring a document from or emptying the contents of the Recycle Bin is completed at the Windows desktop (not in Word). To display the Recycle Bin, minimize the Word window, and then double-click the *Recycle Bin* icon located on the Windows desktop. At the Recycle Bin, you can restore file(s) and empty the Recycle Bin.

▼ **Quick Steps**

Delete Folder/ Document
1. Display Open dialog box.
2. Click folder or document name.
3. Click Organize button.
4. Click *Delete* at drop-down list.
5. Click Yes.

HINT

Remember to empty the Recycle Bin on a regular basis.

Project 1c ■ **Selecting and Deleting Documents**   **Part 3 of 8**

1. Open **FutureHardware.docx** and then save the document with Save As and name it **WL1-C6-P1-FutureHardware**.
2. Close **WL1-C6-P1-FutureHardware.docx**.
3. Delete **WL1-C6-P1-FutureHardware.docx** by completing the following steps:
   a. Display the Open dialog box.
   b. Click **WL1-C6-P1-FutureHardware.docx** to select it.
   c. Click the Organize button on the toolbar and then click *Delete* at the drop-down list.
   d. At the question asking if you want to delete **WL1-C6-P1-FutureHardware.docx**, click Yes.
4. Delete selected documents by completing the following steps:
   a. At the Open dialog box, click **CompCareers.docx**.
   b. Hold down the Shift key and then click **CompEthics.docx**.
   c. Position the mouse pointer on a selected document and then click the right mouse button.
   d. At the shortcut menu that displays, click *Delete*.
   e. At the question asking if you want to delete the items, click Yes.
5. Open **CompKeyboards.docx** and then save the document with Save As and name it **WL1-C6-P1-CompKeyboards**.
6. Save a copy of the **WL1-C6-P1-CompKeyboards.docx** document in the Documents folder by completing the following steps. (If your system does not contain this folder, check with your instructor to determine if another folder is available for you to use.)
   a. With **WL1-C6-P1-CompKeyboards.docx** open, click the File tab and then click the Save As button.

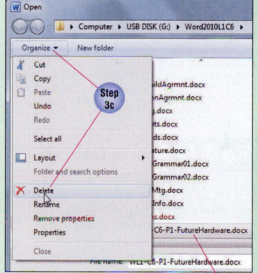

Step 3c

Step 3b

b. At the Save As dialog box, double-click the *Documents* folder located at the beginning of the Content. (Folders are listed before documents.)

c. Click the Save button located in the lower right corner of the dialog box.

7. Close **WL1-C6-P1-CompKeyboards. docx**.

8. Display the Open dialog box and then click *Word2010L1C6* in the Address bar.

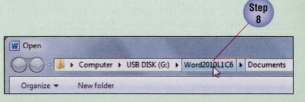

Step 8

Copying and Moving Documents

▼ **Quick Steps**

Copy Documents
1. Display Open dialog box.
2. Right-click document name.
3. Click *Copy.*
4. Navigate to desired folder.
5. Right-click blank area in Content pane.
6. Click *Paste.*

You can copy a document to another folder without opening the document first. To do this, use the *Copy* and *Paste* options from the Organize button drop-down list or the shortcut menu at the Open or Save As dialog box. You can copy a document or selected documents into the same folder. When you do this, Word inserts a hyphen followed by the word *Copy* to the document name. You can copy one document or selected documents into the same folder.

Remove a document from one folder and insert it in another folder using the *Cut* and *Paste* options from the Organize button drop-down list or the shortcut menu at the Open dialog box. To do this with the Organize button, display the Open dialog box, select the desired document, click the Organize button, and then click *Cut* at the drop-down list. Navigate to the desired folder, click the Organize button, and then click *Paste* at the drop-down list. To do this with the shortcut menu, display the Open dialog box, position the arrow pointer on the document to be removed (cut), click the right mouse button, and then click *Cut* at the shortcut menu. Navigate to the desired folder, position the arrow pointer in a blank area in the Content pane, click the right mouse button, and then click *Paste* at the shortcut menu.

Project 1d   Copying Documents   Part 4 of 8

1. At the Open dialog box with Word2010L1C6 the active folder, copy a document to another folder by completing the following steps:
   a. Click **CompTerms.docx** in the Content pane, click the Organize button, and then click *Copy* at the drop-down list.
   b. Navigate to the Documents folder by double-clicking *Documents* at the beginning of the Content pane.
   c. Click the Organize button and then click *Paste* at the drop-down list.
2. Change back to the Word2010L1C6 folder by clicking *Word2010L1C6* in the Address bar.
3. Copy several documents to the Documents folder by completing the following steps:
   a. Click once on ***IntelProp.docx***. (This selects the document.)
   b. Hold down the Ctrl key, click ***Robots.docx***, click ***TechInfo.docx***, and then release the Ctrl key. (You may need to scroll down the Content pane to display the three documents and then select the documents.)
   c. Position the arrow pointer on one of the selected documents, click the right mouse button, and then click *Copy* at the shortcut menu.
   d. Double-click the *Documents* folder.

e. Position the arrow pointer in any blank area in the Content pane, click the right mouse button, and then click *Paste* at the shortcut menu.

4. Click *Word2010L1C6* in the Address bar.

5. Move **CompIssues.docx** to the Documents folder by completing the following steps:
   a. Position the arrow pointer on **CompIssues.docx**, click the right mouse button, and then click *Cut* at the shortcut menu.
   b. Double-click *Documents* to make it the active folder.
   c. Position the arrow pointer in any blank area in the Content pane, click the right mouse button, and then click *Paste* at the shortcut menu.

6. Print the screen contents and insert the file in a document by completing the following steps:
   a. With the Open dialog box displayed, press the Print Screen key on your keyboard.
   b. Close the Open dialog box.
   c. At the blank document, click the Paste button in the Clipboard group in the Home tab. (If a blank document does not display on your screen, press Ctrl + N to open a blank document.)
   d. With the print screen file inserted in the document, print the document by clicking the File tab, clicking the Print tab, and then clicking the Print button at the Print tab Backstage view.

7. Close the document without saving it.

8. Display the Open dialog box and make Word2010L1C6 the active folder.

Renaming Documents

At the Open dialog box, use the *Rename* option from the Organize button drop-down list to give a document a different name. The *Rename* option changes the name of the document and keeps it in the same folder. To use Rename, display the Open dialog box, click once on the document to be renamed, click the Organize button, and then click *Rename* at the drop-down list. This causes a black border to surround the document name and the name to be selected. Type the desired name and then press Enter. You can also rename a document by right-clicking the document name at the Open dialog box and then clicking *Rename* at the shortcut menu. Type the desired name for the document and then press the Enter key.

▼ Quick Steps

Rename a Document
1. Display Open dialog box.
2. Click document name.
3. Click Organize button, *Rename*.
4. Type new name.
5. Press Enter.

Deleting a Folder

As you learned earlier in this chapter, you can delete a document or selected documents. Delete a folder and all its contents in the same manner as deleting a document.

Opening Multiple Documents

To open more than one document, select the documents in the Open dialog box, and then click the Open button. You can also open multiple documents by positioning the arrow pointer on one of the selected documents, clicking the right mouse button, and then clicking *Open* at the shortcut menu.

HINT

Open a recently opened document by clicking the File tab and then clicking the document in the *Recent Documents* list box.

1. Rename a document located in the Documents folder by completing the following steps:
   a. At the Open dialog box with the Word2010L1C6 folder open, double-click the *Documents* folder to make it active.
   b. Click once on **Robots.docx** to select it.
   c. Click the Organize button.
   d. Click *Rename* at the drop-down list.
   e. Type **Androids** and then press the Enter key.
2. Print the screen contents and insert the file in a document by completing the following steps:
   a. Press the Print Screen key on your keyboard.
   b. Close the Open dialog box.
   c. At the blank document, click the Paste button in the Clipboard group in the Home tab. (If a blank document does not display on your screen, press Ctrl + N to open a blank document.)
   d. With the print screen file inserted in the document, print the document.
3. Close the document without saving it.
4. Display the Open dialog box and make Word2010L1C6 the active folder.
5. At the Open dialog box, click the *Documents* folder to select it.
6. Click the Organize button and then click *Delete* at the drop-down list.
7. At the question asking if you want to remove the folder and its contents, click Yes.
8. Select **CompIndustry.docx**, **CompKeyboards.docx**, and **CompTerms.docx**.
9. Click the Open button located toward the lower right corner of the dialog box.
10. Close the open documents.

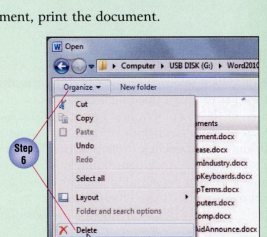

Sharing Documents ■■■■ ■ ■■ ■■■ ■ ■■ ■

Click the File tab and then click the Save & Send tab and the Save & Send tab Backstage view displays as shown in Figure 6.1. With options at this view, you can share a document by sending it as an email attachment or a fax, save your document as a different file type, and post your document to a special location such as a blog.

Figure 6.1 Save & Send Tab Backstage View

With the *Send Using E-mail* option selected, this section displays options for sending the document as an email attachment, as a PDF or XPS attachment, or as an Internet fax.

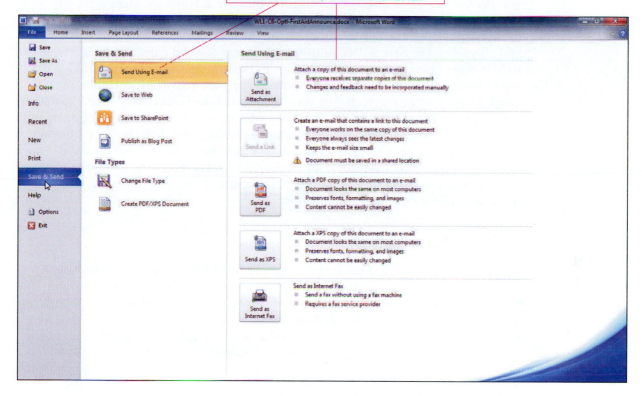

Sending a Document Using Email

When you click the *Send Using E-mail* option in the Save & Send category, options for sending a document display, such as sending a copy of the document as an attachment to an email, creating an email that contains a link to the document, attaching a PDF or XPS copy of the open document to an email, and sending an email as an Internet fax. To send the document as an attachment, you need to set up an Outlook email account. If you want to create an email that contains a link to the document, you need to save the document to a web server. Use the last button, Send as Internet Fax, to fax the current document without using a fax machine. To use this button, you must be signed up with a fax service provider. If you have not previously signed up for a service, you will be prompted to do so.

With the remaining two buttons in the Send Using E-mail category of the Save & Send tab Backstage view, you can send the document in PDF or XPS format. The letters *PDF* stand for *portable document format*, which is a document format developed by Adobe Systems® that captures all of the elements of a document as an electronic image. An XPS document is a Microsoft document format for publishing content in an easily viewable format. The letters *XPS* stand for *XML paper specification* and the letters *XML* stand for *Extensible Markup Language*, which is a set of rules for encoding documents electronically. The options below *Attach a PDF copy of this document to an e-mail* and below *Attach a XPS copy of this document to an e-mail* describe the format and the advantages of sending a document in the PDF or XPS format.

A file's format is indicated by a three- or four-letter extension after the file name.

Saving to SkyDrive

If you want to share documents with others, consider saving documents to SkyDrive, which is a file storage and sharing service that allows you to upload files that can be accessed from a web browser. To save a document to SkyDrive, you need a Windows Live ID account. If you have a Hotmail, Messenger, or Xbox LIVE account, you have a Windows Live ID account. To save a document to SkyDrive, open the document, click the File tab, click the Save & Send tab, and then click the *Save to Web* option in the Save & Send category. In the Save to Windows Live category, click the Sign In button. At the connecting dialog box, type your email address, press the Tab key, type your password, and then press Enter. Once you are connected to your Windows Live ID account, specify whether you want the file saved to your personal folder or saved to your shared folder, and then click the Save As button. At the Save As dialog box, click the Save button or type a new name in the *File name* text box and then click the Save button. One method for accessing your file from SkyDrive is to log into your Windows Live ID account and then look for the SkyDrive hyperlink. Click this hyperlink and your personal and shared folder contents display.

Saving to SharePoint

Microsoft SharePoint is a collection of products and software that includes a number of components. If your company or organization uses SharePoint, you can save a document in a library on your organization's SharePoint site so you and your colleagues have a central location for accessing documents. To save a document to a SharePoint library, open the document, click the File tab, click the Save & Send tab, and then click the *Save to SharePoint* option.

Saving a Document as a Blog Post

You can save a Word document as a blog post with the *Publish as Blog Post* option in the Save & Send tab Backstage view. To save a blog post, you must have a blog site established. Click the *Publish as Blog Post* option and information about supported blog sites displays at the right side of the Save & Send tab Backstage view. To publish a document as a blog post, open the document, click the File tab, click the Save & Send tab, click the *Publish as Blog Post* option in the Save & Send category, and then click the *Publish as Blog Post* option in the Publish as Blog Post category. If you do not have a blog site established, click the Register Now button and then complete the blog registration wizard steps. If you have a blog site established, the document will open in a new window. Type a title for the blog post and then click the Publish button that displays in the Blog group in the Blog Post tab.

Optional Project | **Sending a Document as an Email Attachment, Saving to SkyDrive, and Publishing as a Blog Post**

Before completing this optional exercise, check with your instructor to determine if you have Outlook set up as your email provider, if you have a Windows Live ID account, and if you have a blog site established for use in the course.

1. Open **FirstAidAnnounce.docx** and then save the document with Save As and name it **WL1-C6-Optl-FirstAidAnnounce**.
2. Send the document as an email attachment by completing the following steps:

a. Click the File tab, click the Save & Send tab, and then make sure the *Send Using E-mail* option is selected.

b. Click the Send as Attachment button in the Send Using E-mail category.

c. At the Outlook window, type your instructor's email address in the *To* text box.

d. Click the Send button.

3. With **WL1-C6-Optl-FirstAidAnnounce.docx** open, save the document to SkyDrive by completing the following steps:

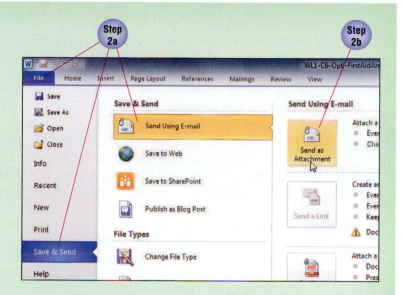

a. Click the File tab, click the Save & Send tab, and then click the *Save to Web* option in the Save & Send category.

b. In the Save to Windows Live category, click the Sign In button.

c. At the connecting dialog box, type your email address, press the Tab key, type your password, and then press Enter.

d. Once you are connected to your Windows Live ID account, specify whether you want the file saved to your personal folder or saved to your shared folder, and then click the Save As button.

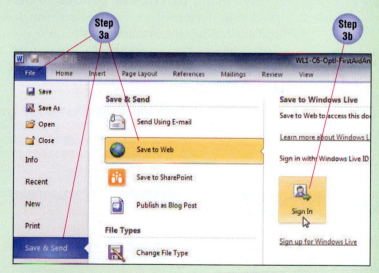

e. At the Save As dialog box, click the Save button.

f. Close **WL1-C6-Optl-FirstAidAnnounce.docx**.

4. If you have a blog site established, save the first aid announcement as a blog post by completing the following steps:

a. Open the **WL1-C6-Optl-FirstAidAnnounce.docx** document.

b. Click the File tab, click the Save & Send tab, and then click the *Publish as Blog Post* option in the Save & Send category.

c. Click the Publish as Blog Post button in the Publish as Blog Post category.

d. If you have a blog site established, the document will open in a new window. (If you do not have a blog site established, click the Register Now button and then complete the blog registration wizard steps.) Type a title for the blog post and then click the Publish button that displays in the Blog group in the Blog Post tab.

e. Close the blog post document.

5. Close **WL1-C6-Optl-FirstAidAnnounce.docx**.

Saving a Document in a Different Format

▼ **Quick Steps**

Save Document in Different Format
1. Click File tab.
2. Click Save & Send tab.
3. Click *Change File Type* option in File Types category.
4. Click desired format in Change File Type category.
5. Click Save As button.

When you save a document, the document is saved automatically as a Word document. If you need to share a document with someone who is using a different word processing program or a different version of Word, you may want to save the document in another format. At the Save & Send tab Backstage view, click the *Change File Type* option in the File Types category and the view displays as shown in Figure 6.2.

With options in the *Document File Types* section, you can choose to save a Word document with the default file format, save the document in a previous version of Word, save the document in the OpenDocument Text format, or save the document as a template. The OpenDocument Text format is an XML-based file format for displaying, storing, and editing files such as word processing, spreadsheet, or presentation files. OpenDocument Text format is free from any licensing, royalty payments, or other restrictions and, since technology changes at a rapid pace, saving a document in the OpenDocument Text format ensures that the information in the file can be accessed, retrieved, and used now and in the future.

Additional file types are available in the *Other File Types* section. If you need to send your document to another user who does not have access to Microsoft Word, consider saving the document in plain text or rich text file format. Use the *Plain Text (*.txt)* option to save the document with all formatting stripped, which is good for universal file exchange. Use the *Rich Text Format (*.rtf)* option to save the

Figure 6.2 Save & Send Tab Backstage View with *Change File Type* Option Selected

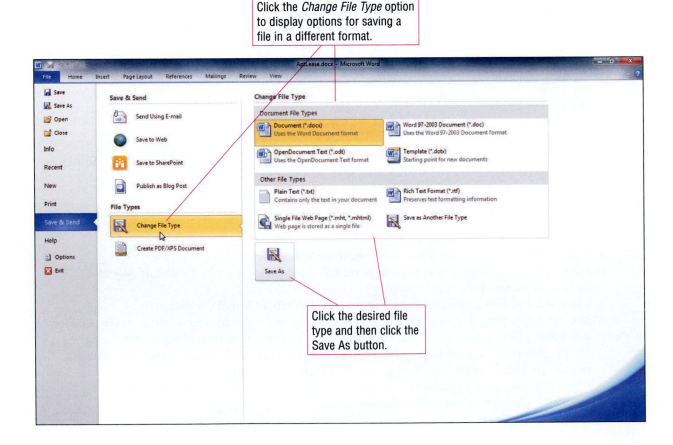

Click the *Change File Type* option to display options for saving a file in a different format.

Click the desired file type and then click the Save As button.

document with most of the character formatting applied to text in the document such as bold, italic, underline, bullets, and fonts as well as some paragraph formatting such as justification. Before the widespread use of Adobe's portable document format (PDF), rich text format was the most portable file format used to exchange files. With the *Single File Web Page (*.mht, *.mhtml)* option, you can save your document as a single page web document. Click the *Save as Another File Type* option and the Save As dialog box displays. Click the *Save as type* option box and a drop-down list displays with a variety of available file type options.

Project 1f Saving a Document in Different File Formats

Part 6 of 8

1. Open **AptLease.docx** and then save the document in Word 07-2003 format by completing the following steps:
   a. Click the File tab and then click the Save & Send tab.
   b. At the Save & Send tab Backstage view, click the *Change File Type* option in the File Types category.
   c. Click the *Word 97-2003 Document (*.doc)* option in the *Document File Types* section and then click the Save As button.

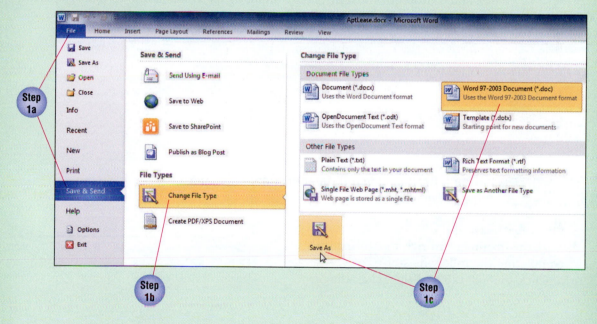

   d. At the Save As dialog box with the *Save as type* option changed to *Word 97-2003 Document (*.doc)*, type **WL1-C6-P1-AptLease-Word97-2003** and then press Enter.
2. At the document, notice the title bar displays the words *[Compatibility Mode]* after the document name.
3. Click the Page Layout tab and notice the buttons in the Themes group are dimmed. (This is because the themes features were not available in Word 97 through 2003.)
4. Close **WL1-C6-P1-AptLease-Word97-2003.doc**.
5. Open **AptLease.docx**
6. Save the document in plain text format by completing the following steps:
   a. Click the File tab and then click the Save & Send tab.
   b. At the Save & Send tab Backstage view, click the *Change File Type* option in the File Types category.

c. Click the *Plain Text (*.txt)* option in the *Other File Types* section and then click the Save As button.

d. At the Save As dialog box, type **WL1-C6-P1-AptLease-PlainTxt** and then press Enter.

e. At the File Conversion dialog box, click OK.

7. Close **WL1-C6-P1-AptLease-PlainTxt.txt**.

8. Display the Open dialog box and, if necessary, display all files. To do this, click the file type button at the right side of the *File name* text box and then click *All Files (*.*)* at the drop-down list.

9. Double-click **WL1-C6-P1-AptLease-PlainTxt.txt**. (If a File Conversion dialog box displays, click OK. Notice that the character and paragraph formatting has been removed from the document.)

10. Close **WL1-C6-P1-AptLease-PlainTxt.txt**.

▼ **Quick Steps**

Save Document in Different Format at Save As Dialog Box
1. Open document.
2. Click File tab, click Save As button.
3. Type document name.
4. Click *Save as type* option box.
5. Click desired format at drop-down list.
6. Click Save button.

In addition to options in the Save & Send tab Backstage view with the *Change File Type* option selected, you can save a document in a different format using the *Save as type* option box at the Save As dialog box. Click the *Save as type* option box and a drop-down list displays containing all available file formats for saving a document.

Project 1g | **Saving a Document in a Different Format Using the** *Save as type* **Option Box** | Part 7 of 8

1. Open **AptLease.docx**.
2. Save the document in rich text format by completing the following steps:
   a. Click the File tab and then click the Save As button.
   b. At the Save As dialog box, type **WL1-C6-P1-AptLease-RichTxt** in the *File name* text box.
   c. Click in the *Save as type* option box.
   d. Click *Rich Text Format (*.rtf)*.
   e. Click the Save button.
3. Close the document.
4. Display the Open dialog box and, if necessary, display all files.
5. Double-click **WL1-C6-P1-AptLease-RichText.rtf**. (Notice that the formatting was retained in the document.)
6. Close the document.

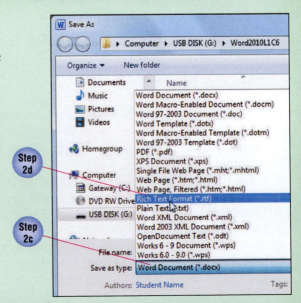

Saving in PDF/XPS Format

As you learned earlier, the portable document format (PDF) captures all of the elements of a document as an electronic image, and the XPS document format is a format for publishing content in an easily viewable format. To save a document in PDF or XPS format, click the File tab, click the Save & Send tab, click the *Create PDF/XPS Document* option in the File Types category, and then click the Create a PDF/XPS button in the *Create a PDF/XPS Document* section of the Backstage view. This displays the Publish as PDF or XPS dialog box with the *PDF (*.pdf)* option selected in the *Save as type* option box. If you want to save the document in XPS format, click in the *Save as type* option box and then click *XPS Document (*.xps)* at the drop-down list. At the Save As dialog box, type a name in the *File name* text box and then click the Publish button. If you save the document in PDF format, the document opens in Adobe Reader, and if you save the document in XPS format, the document opens in your browser window.

You can open a PDF file in Adobe Reader or in your web browser, and you can open an XPS file in your web browser. To open a PDF file or XPS file in your web browser, click File in the browser Menu bar and then click *Open* at the drop-down list. At the Open dialog box, click the Browse button. At the browser window Open dialog box, change the *Files of type* to *All Files (*.*)*, navigate to the desired folder, and then double-click the document.

Quick Steps

Save Document in PDF/XPS Format
1. Open document.
2. Click File tab.
3. Click Save & Send tab.
4. Click *Create PDF/XPS Document* option.
5. Click Create PDF/XPS button.
6. At Publish as PDF or XPS dialog box, specify if you want to save in PDF or XPS format.
7. Click Publish button.

Project 1h — **Saving a Document in PDF Format**   **Part 8 of 8**

1. Open **NSS.docx**
2. Save the document in PDF file format by completing the following steps:
   a. Click the File tab and then click the Save & Send tab.
   b. At the Save & Send tab Backstage view, click the *Create PDF/XPS Document* option in the File Types category.
   c. Click the Create PDF/XPS button.

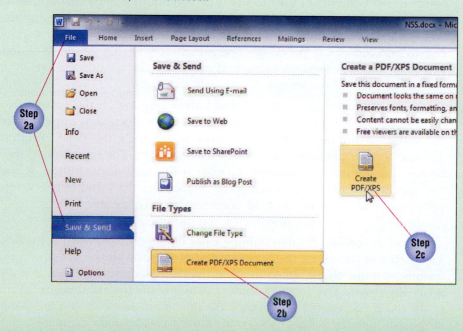

d. At the Publish as PDF or XPS dialog box, make sure *PDF (*.pdf)* is selected in the *Save as type* option box and then click the Publish button.

3. Scroll through the document in Adobe Reader.

4. Click the Close button located in the upper right corner of the window to close Adobe Reader.

5. Close **NSS.docx**.

6. Print the screen contents of the Word2010L1C6 folder by completing the following steps:

   a. Display the Open dialog box with the Word2010L1C6 folder active.

   b. Make sure the Files of type displays as *All Files (*.*)*. (If necessary, scroll down the content pane to display your completed project documents.)

   c. Press the Print Screen key.

   d. Close the Open dialog box.

   e. At a blank document, click the Paste button.

   f. Print the document and then close the document without saving it.

Project 2 Manage Multiple Documents   6 Parts

You will work with windows by arranging, maximizing, restoring, and minimizing windows; move selected text between split windows; compare formatting of documents side by side; print specific text, pages, and multiple copies; and create and modify document properties.

Working with Windows ■■■■■■■■ ■ ■■■■■ ■■■

Press Ctrl + F6 to switch between open documents.

In Word, you can open multiple documents and move the insertion point between the documents. You can also move and copy information between documents or compare the contents of documents. The maximum number of documents that you can have open at one time depends on the memory of your computer system and the amount of data in each document. When you open a new window, it displays on top of any previously opened window(s) that you have closed. Once you have multiple windows open, you can resize the windows to see all or a portion of each on the screen.

Press Ctrl + W or Ctrl + F4 to close the active document window.

When a document is open, a Word button displays on the Taskbar. Hover the mouse over this button and a thumbnail of the document displays above the button. If you have more than one document open, the Word button on the Taskbar displays another layer in a cascaded manner. The layer behind the Word button displays only a portion of the edge at the right of the button. If you have multiple documents open, hovering the mouse over the Word button on the Taskbar will cause thumbnails of all of the documents to display above the button. To change to the desired document, click the thumbnail that represents the document.

Switch Windows

Another method for determining what documents are open is to click the View tab and then click the Switch Windows button in the Window group. The document name that displays in the list with the check mark in front of it is the *active document*. The active document contains the insertion point. To make one of the other documents active, click the document name. If you are using the keyboard, type the number shown in front of the desired document.

Opening and Arranging Windows

If you open a document, click the View tab, and then click the New Window button in the Window group, Word opens a new window containing the same document. The document name in the Title bar displays followed by *:2*. Changes you make to one document are reflected in the other document.

If you have more than one document open, you can arrange them so a portion of each document displays. The portions that display are the titles (if present) and opening paragraphs of each document. To arrange a group of open documents, click the View tab and then click the Arrange All button in the Window group.

Maximizing, Restoring, and Minimizing Documents

Use the Maximize and Minimize buttons in the active document window to change the size of the window. The Maximize button is the button in the upper right corner of the active document immediately to the left of the Close button. (The Close button is the button containing the *X*.) The Minimize button is located immediately to the left of the Maximize button.

If you arrange all open documents and then click the Maximize button in the active document, the active document expands to fill the document screen. In addition, the Maximize button changes to the Restore button. To return the active document back to its size before it was maximized, click the Restore button. If you click the Minimize button in the active document, the document is reduced and a button displays on the Taskbar representing the document. To maximize a document that has been minimized, click the button on the Taskbar representing the document.

▼ **Quick Steps**

Open New Window
1. Open document.
2. Click View tab.
3. Click New Window button.

Arrange Windows
1. Open documents.
2. Click View tab.
3. Click Arrange All button.

Arrange All   Maximize

Minimize   Restore

Project 2a   **Arranging, Maximizing, Restoring, and Minimizing Windows**   Part 1 of 6

Note: If you are using Word on a network system that contains a virus checker, you may not be able to open multiple documents at once. Continue by opening each document individually.

1. Open the following documents: **AptLease.docx**, **IntelProp.docx**, **NSS.docx**, and **CommIndustry.docx**.
2. Arrange the windows by clicking the View tab and then clicking the Arrange All button in the Window group.
3. Make **IntelProp.docx** the active document by clicking the Switch Windows button in the Window group and then clicking **IntelProp.docx** at the drop-down list.
4. Close **IntelProp.docx**.
5. Make **NSS.docx** active and then close it.
6. Make **CommIndustry.docx** active and minimize it by clicking the Minimize button in the upper right corner of the active window.
7. Maximize **AptLease.docx** by clicking the Maximize button at the right side of the Title bar. (The Maximize button is the button at the right side of the Title bar, immediately left of the Close button.)
8. Close **AptLease.docx**.
9. Restore **CommIndustry.docx** by clicking the button on the Taskbar representing the document.
10. Maximize **CommIndustry.docx**.

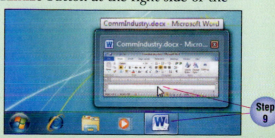

Splitting a Window

You can divide a window into two *panes*, which is helpful if you want to view different parts of the same document at one time. You may want to display an outline for a report in one pane, for example, and the portion of the report that you are editing in the other. The original window is split into two panes that extend horizontally across the screen.

Split a window by clicking the View tab and then clicking the Split button in the Window group. This causes a wide gray line to display in the middle of the screen and the mouse pointer to display as a double-headed arrow pointing up and down with a small double line between. Move this double-headed arrow pointer up or down, if desired, by dragging the mouse or by pressing the up- and/or down-pointing arrow keys on the keyboard. When the double-headed arrow is positioned at the desired location in the document, click the left mouse button or press the Enter key.

You can also split the window with the split bar. The split bar is the small black horizontal bar above the View Ruler button and up scroll arrow on the vertical scroll bar. To split the window with the split bar, position the arrow pointer on the split bar until it turns into a short double line with an up- and down-pointing arrow. Hold down the left mouse button, drag the double-headed arrow into the document screen to the location where you want the window split, and then release the mouse button. With the window split, you may decide you want to move certain objects or sections of text. Do this by selecting the desired object or text and then dragging and dropping it across the split bar.

When a window is split, the insertion point is positioned in the bottom pane. To move the insertion point to the other pane with the mouse, position the I-beam pointer in the other pane, and then click the left mouse button. To remove the split line from the document, click the View tab and then click the Remove Split button in the Window group. You can also double-click the split bar or drag the split bar to the top or bottom of the screen.

Project 2b **Moving Selected Text between Split Windows** Part 2 of 6

1. With **CommIndustry.docx** open, save the document with Save As and name it **WL1-C6-P2-CommIndustry**.
2. Click the View tab and then click the Split button in the Window group.
3. With the split line displayed in the middle of the document screen, click the left mouse button.
4. Move the first section below the second section by completing the following steps:
   a. Click the Home tab.
   b. Select the *SECTION 1: COMPUTERS IN COMMUNICATION* section from the title to right above *SECTION 2: COMPUTERS IN ENTERTAINMENT*.
   c. Click the Cut button in the Clipboard group in the Home tab.
   d. Position the arrow pointer at the end of the document in the bottom window pane and then click the left mouse button.
   e. Click the Paste button in the Clipboard group in the Home tab.

Viewing Documents Side by Side

If you want to compare the contents of two documents, open both documents, click the View tab, and then click the View Side by Side button in the Window group. Both documents are arranged in the screen side by side as shown in Figure 6.3. By default synchronous scrolling is active. With this feature active, scrolling in one document causes the same scrolling to occur in the other document. This feature is useful in situations where you want to compare text, formatting, or other features between documents. If you want to scroll in one document and not the other, click the Synchronous Scrolling button in the Window group in the View tab to turn it off.

▼ Quick Steps

View Side by Side
1. Open two documents.
2. Click View tab.
3. Click View Side by Side.

View Side
by Side

Figure 6.3 Viewing Documents Side by Side

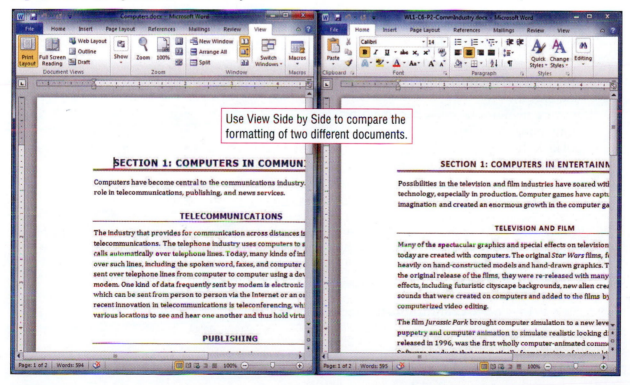

1. With **WL1-C6-P2-CommIndustry.docx** open, open **Computers.docx**.
2. Click the View tab and then click the View Side by Side button in the Window group.
3. Scroll through both documents simultaneously. Notice the difference between the two documents. (The title and headings are set in a different font and color.) Select and then format the title and headings in **WL1-C6-P2-CommIndustry.docx** so they match the formatting in **Computers.docx**.
4. Save **WL1-C6-P2-CommIndustry.docx**.
5. Make **Computers.docx** the active document and then close it.

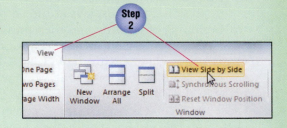

Step 2

▼ Quick Steps

Insert a File
1. Click Insert tab.
2. Click Object button arrow.
3. Click *Text from File*.
4. Navigate to desired folder.
5. Double-click document.

Inserting a File ■■■■■■■■■■■■■■■■■■■■■■■■■■■■

If you want to insert the contents of one document into another, use the Object button in the Text group in the Insert tab. Click the Object button arrow and then click *Text from File* and the Insert File dialog box displays. This dialog box contains similar features as the Open dialog box. Navigate to the desired folder and then double-click the document you want to insert in the open document.

Object

1. With **WL1-C6-P2-CommIndustry.docx** open, move the insertion point to the end of the document.
2. Insert a file into the open document by completing the following steps:
   a. Click the Insert tab.
   b. Click the Object button arrow in the Text group.
   c. Click *Text from File* at the drop-down list.
   d. At the Insert File dialog box, navigate to the Word2010L1C6 folder and then double-click *EduComp.docx*.

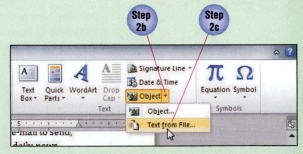

Step 2b

Step 2c

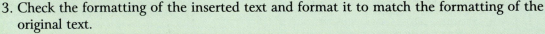

3. Check the formatting of the inserted text and format it to match the formatting of the original text.
4. Save **WL1-C6-P2-CommIndustry.docx**.

Printing and Previewing a Document ■■■■■■■■■■■

With options at the Print tab Backstage view shown in Figure 6.4, you can specify what you want to print and also preview the pages before printing. To display the Print tab Backstage view, click the File tab and then click the Print tab.

Previewing Pages in a Document

When you display the Print tab Backstage view, a preview of the page where the insertion point is positioned displays at the right side (see Figure 6.4). Click the Next Page button (right-pointing arrow), located below and to the left of the page, to view the next page in the document and click the Previous Page button (left-pointing arrow) to display the previous page in the document. Use the Zoom slider bar to increase/decrease the size of the page, and click the Zoom to Page button to fit the page in the viewing area in the Print tab Backstage view.

Zoom to
Page

Figure 6.4 Print Tab Backstage View

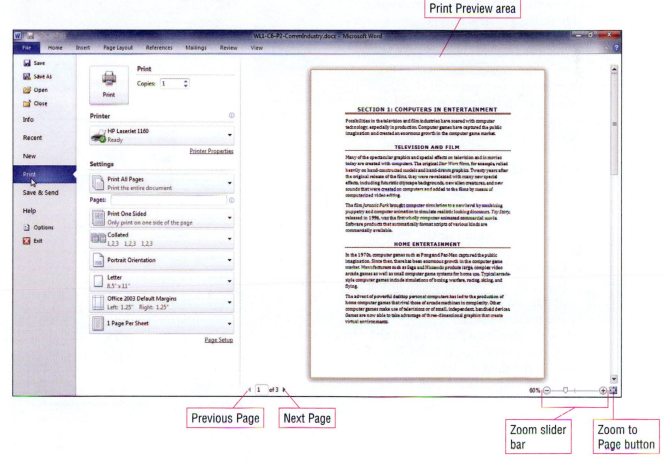

1. With **WL1-C6-P2-CommIndustry.docx** open, press Ctrl + Home to move the insertion point to the beginning of the document.
2. Preview the document by clicking the File tab and then clicking the Print tab.
3. At the Print tab Backstage view, click the Next Page button located below and to the left of the preview page. (This displays page 2 in the preview area.)
4. Click twice on the plus symbol that displays at the right side of the Zoom slider bar. (This increases the size of the preview page.)
5. Click four times on the minus symbol that displays at the left side of the Zoom slider bar. (This displays the two pages of the document in the preview area.)
6. Change the zoom at the Zoom dialog box by completing the following steps:
   a. Click the percentage number that displays at the left side of the Zoom slider bar.
   b. At the Zoom dialog box, click the *Many pages* option in the *Zoom to* section.
   c. Click OK to close the dialog box. (Notice that all pages in the document display as thumbnails in the preview area.)
7. Click the Zoom to Page button that displays at the right side of the Zoom slider bar. (This returns the page to the default size.)
8. Click the File tab to return to the document.

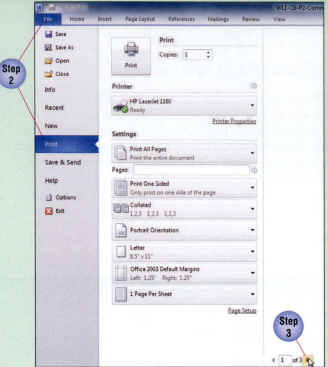

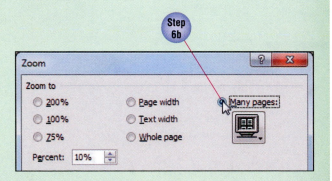

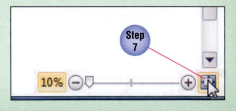

Printing Pages in a Document

Save a document before printing it.

If you want control over what prints in a document, use options at the Print tab Backstage view. Click the first gallery in the Settings category and a drop-down list displays with options for printing all pages in the document, selected text, the current page, or a custom range of pages in the document. If you want to select and then print a portion of the document, choose the *Print Selection* option.

With this option, only the text that you have selected in the current document prints. (This option is dimmed unless text is selected in the document.) Click the *Print Current Page* option to print only the page on which the insertion point is located. With the *Print Custom Range* option, you can identify a specific page, multiple pages, or a range of pages to print. If you want specific pages printed, use a comma (,) to indicate *and* and use a hyphen (-) to indicate *through*. For example, to print pages 2 and 5, you would type **2,5** in the *Pages* text box. To print pages 6 through 10, you would type **6-10**.

With the other galleries available in the Settings category of the Print tab Backstage view, you can specify on what sides of the pages you want to print, change the page orientation (portrait or landscape), specify how you want the pages collated, choose a page size, specify margins, and specify how many pages you want to print on a page.

If you want to print more than one copy of a document, use the *Copies* text box located to the right of the Print button. If you print several copies of a document that has multiple pages, Word collates the pages as they print. For example, if you print two copies of a three-page document, pages 1, 2, and 3 print, and then the pages print a second time. Printing collated pages is helpful for assembly but takes more printing time. To reduce printing time, you can tell Word *not* to print collated pages. To do this, click the Collated gallery in the Settings category and then click *Uncollated*.

If you want to send a document directly to the printer without displaying the Print tab Backstage view, consider adding the Quick Print button to the Quick Access toolbar. To do this click the Customize Quick Access Toolbar button located at the right side of the toolbar and then click *Quick Print* at the drop-down gallery. Click the Quick Print button and all pages of the active document print.

Project 2f **Printing Specific Text and Pages** **Part 6 of 6**

1. With **WL1-C6-P2-CommIndustry.docx** open, print selected text by completing the following steps:
   a. Select the heading *Television and Film* and the two paragraphs of text that follow it.
   b. Click the File tab and then click the Print tab.
   c. At the Print tab Backstage view, click the first gallery in the Settings category and then click *Print Selection* at the drop-down list.
   d. Click the Print button.
2. Change the margins and page orientation and then print only the first page by completing the following steps:
   a. Press Ctrl + Home to move the insertion point to the beginning of the document.

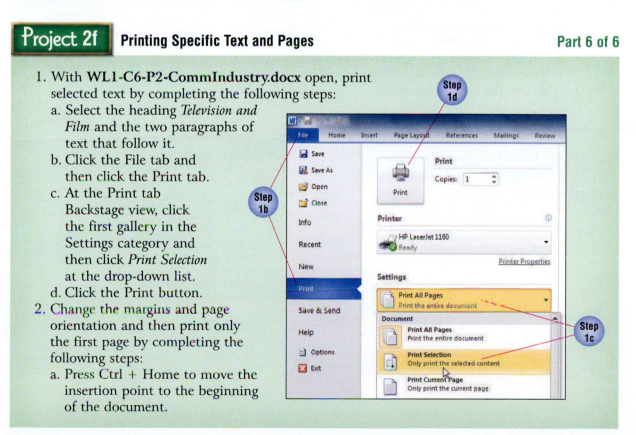

b. Click the File tab and then click the Print tab.

c. At the Print tab Backstage view, click the *Portrait Orientation* gallery in the Settings category and then click *Landscape Orientation* at the drop-down list.

d. Click the *Custom Margins* gallery in the Settings category and then click *Narrow* at the drop-down list.

e. Click the *Print All Pages* gallery in the Settings category and then click *Print Current Page* at the drop-down list.

f. Click the Print button. (The first page of the document prints in landscape orientation with 0.5-inch margins.)

3. Print all of the pages as thumbnails on one page by completing the following steps:

a. Click the File tab and then click the Print tab.

b. At the Print tab Backstage view, click the *1 Page Per Sheet* gallery in the Settings category and then click *4 Pages Per Sheet* at the drop-down list.

c. Click the *Print Current Page* gallery in the Settings category and then click *Print All Pages* at the drop-down list.

d. Click the Print button.

4. Select the entire document, change the line spacing to *1.5*, and then deselect the text.

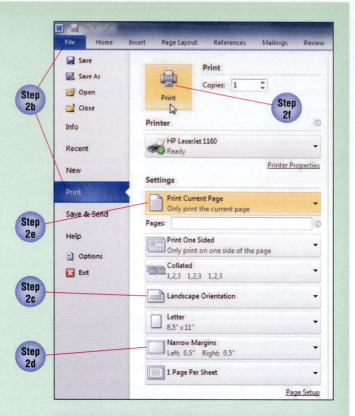

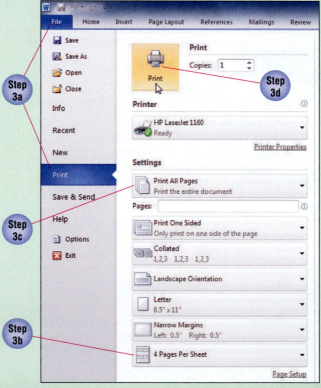

5. Print two copies of specific pages by completing the following steps:

   a. Click the File tab and then click the Print tab.

   b. Click the *Landscape Orientation* gallery in the Settings category and then click *Portrait Orientation* in the drop-down list.

   c. Click in the *Pages* text box (located below the *Print Custom Range* gallery in the Settings category and then type 1,3.

   d. Click the up-pointing arrow at the right side of the *Copies* text box (located to the right of the Print button) to display *2*.

   e. Click the *Collated* gallery in the Settings category and then click *Uncollated* at the drop-down list.

   f. Click the *4 Pages Per Sheet* gallery in the Settings category and then click *1 Page Per Sheet* at the drop-down list.

   g. Click the Print button. (The first page of the document will print twice and then the third page will print twice.)

6. Save and then close **WL1-C6-P2-CommIndustry.docx**.

Project **3** **Create and Print Envelopes**   **2 Parts**

You will create an envelope document and type the return address and delivery address using envelope addressing guidelines issued by the United States Postal Service. You will also open a letter document and then create an envelope using the inside address.

Creating and Printing Envelopes ▪▪▪▪▪▪▪▪▪▪▪▪

Word automates the creation of envelopes with options at the Envelopes and Labels dialog box with the Envelopes tab selected as shown in Figure 6.5. Display this dialog box by clicking the Mailings tab and then clicking the Envelopes button in the Create group. At the dialog box, type the delivery address in the *Delivery address* text box and the return address in the *Return address* text box. You can send the envelope directly to the printer by clicking the Print button or insert the envelope in the current document by clicking the Add to Document button.

Envelopes

Figure 6.5 Envelopes and Labels Dialog Box with Envelopes Tab Selected

Type the delivery name and address in this text box.

Type the return name and address in this text box.

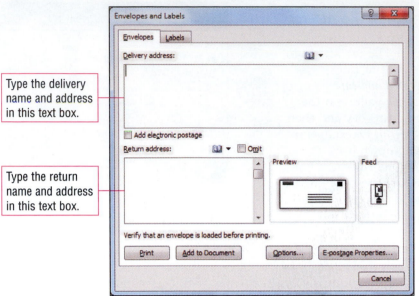

▼ **Quick Steps**

Create Envelope
1. Click Mailings tab.
2. Click Envelopes button.
3. Type delivery address.
4. Click in *Return address* text box.
5. Type return address.
6. Click Add to Document button or Print button.

If you enter a return address before printing the envelope, Word will display the question *Do you want to save the new return address as the default return address?* At this question, click Yes if you want the current return address available for future envelopes. Click No if you do not want the current return address used as the default. If a default return address displays in the *Return address* section of the dialog box, you can tell Word to omit the return address when printing the envelope. To do this, click the *Omit* check box to insert a check mark.

The Envelopes and Labels dialog box contains a *Preview* sample box and a *Feed* sample box. The *Preview* sample box shows how the envelope will appear when printed and the *Feed* sample box shows how the envelope should be inserted into the printer.

When addressing envelopes, consider following general guidelines issued by the United States Postal Service (USPS). The USPS guidelines suggest using all capital letters with no commas or periods for return and delivery addresses. Figure 6.6 shows envelope addresses following the USPS guidelines. Use abbreviations for street suffixes (such as *ST* for *Street* and *AVE* for *Avenue*). For a complete list of address abbreviations, visit the www.emcp.net/usps site and then search for *Official USPS Abbreviations*.

Project 3a   **Printing an Envelope**   **Part 1 of 2**

1. At a blank document, create an envelope that prints the delivery address and return address shown in Figure 6.6. Begin by clicking the Mailings tab.
2. Click the Envelopes button in the Create group.
3. At the Envelopes and Labels dialog box with the Envelopes tab selected, type the delivery address shown in Figure 6.6 (the one containing the name *GREGORY LINCOLN*). (Press the Enter key to end each line in the name and address.)
4. Click in the *Return address* text box. (If any text displays in the *Return address* text box, select and then delete it.)

5. Type the return address shown in Figure 6.6 (the one containing the name *WENDY STEINBERG*). (Press the Enter key to end each line in the name and address.)
6. Click the Add to Document button.
7. At the message *Do you want to save the new return address as the default return address?*, click No.
8. Save the document and name it **WL1-C6-P3-Env**.
9. Print and then close **WL1-C6-P3-Env.docx**. *Note: Manual feed of the envelope may be required. Please check with your instructor.*

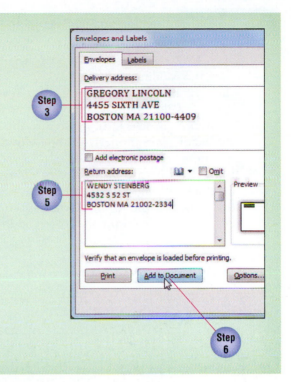

Figure 6.6 Project 3a

WENDY STEINBERG
4532 S 52 ST
BOSTON MA 21002-2334

GREGORY LINCOLN
4455 SIXTH AVE
BOSTON MA 21100-4409

If you open the Envelopes and Labels dialog box in a document containing a name and address (the name and address lines must end with a press of the Enter key and not Shift + Enter), the name and address are automatically inserted in the *Delivery address* section of the dialog box. To do this, open a document containing a name and address and then display the Envelopes and Labels dialog box. The name and address are inserted in the *Delivery address* section as they appear in the letter and may not conform to the USPS guidelines. The USPS guidelines for addressing envelopes are only suggestions, not requirements.

1. Open **LAProg.docx**.
2. Click the Mailings tab.
3. Click the Envelopes button in the Create group.
4. At the Envelopes and Labels dialog box (with the Envelopes tab selected), make sure the delivery address displays properly in the *Delivery address* section.
5. If any text displays in the *Return address* section, insert a check mark in the *Omit* check box (located to the right of the *Return address* option). (This tells Word not to print the return address on the envelope.)
6. Click the Print button.
7. Close **LAProg.docx** without saving changes.

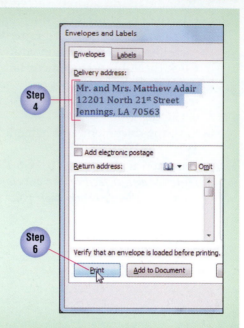

Step 4

Step 6

Project 4   Create Mailing Labels   2 Parts

You will create mailing labels containing names and addresses and then create mailing labels containing the inside address of a letter.

Creating and Printing Labels ▪▪▪▪▪▪▪▪▪▪▪▪▪▪▪▪▪▪▪▪

▼ **Quick Steps**

Create Labels
1. Click Mailings tab.
2. Click Labels button.
3. Type desired address(es).
4. Click New Document button or Print button.

Use Word's labels feature to print text on mailing labels, file labels, disc labels, or other types of labels. Word includes a variety of predefined formats for labels that can be purchased at an office supply store. To create a sheet of mailing labels with the same name and address using the default options, click the Labels button in the Create group in the Mailings tab. At the Envelopes and Labels dialog box with the Labels tab selected as shown in Figure 6.7, type the desired address in the *Address* text box. Click the New Document button to insert the mailing label in a new document or click the Print button to send the mailing label directly to the printer.

Labels

Changing Label Options

Click the Options button at the Envelopes and Labels dialog box with the Labels tab selected and the Label Options dialog box displays as shown in Figure 6.8. At the Label Options dialog box, choose the type of printer, the desired label product, and the product number. This dialog box also displays information about the selected label such as type, height, width, and paper size. When you select a label, Word automatically determines label margins. If, however, you want to customize these default settings, click the Details button at the Label Options dialog box.

Figure 6.7 Envelopes and Labels Dialog Box with Labels Tab Selected

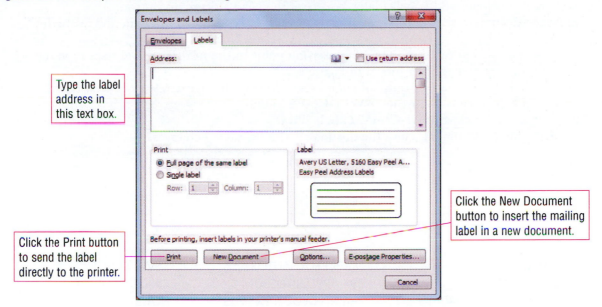

Type the label address in this text box.

Click the Print button to send the label directly to the printer.

Click the New Document button to insert the mailing label in a new document.

Figure 6.8 Label Options Dialog Box

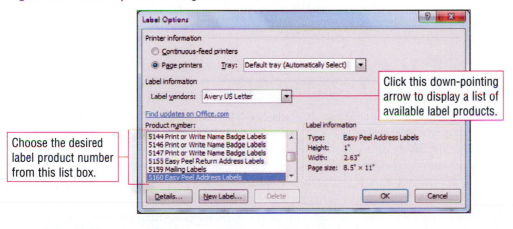

Click this down-pointing arrow to display a list of available label products.

Choose the desired label product number from this list box.

Project 4a   **Creating Customized Mailing Labels**   **Part 1 of 2**

1. At a blank document, click the Mailings tab.
2. Click the Labels button in the Create group.
3. At the Envelopes and Labels dialog box with the Labels tab selected, click the Options button.
4. At the Label Options dialog box, click the down-pointing arrow at the right side of the *Label vendors* option and then click *Avery US Letter* at the drop-down list.
5. Scroll down the *Product number* list box and then click *5160 Easy Peel Address Labels*.
6. Click OK or press Enter.

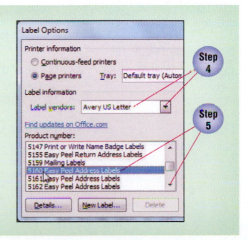

Step 4

Step 5

7. At the Envelopes and Labels dialog box, click the New Document button.
8. At the document screen, type the first name and address shown in Figure 6.9 in the first label.
9. Press the Tab key twice to move the insertion point to the next label and then type the second name and address shown in Figure 6.9.
10. Continue in this manner until all names and addresses in Figure 6.9 have been typed.
11. Save the document and name it **WL1-C6-P4-Labels**.
12. Print and then close **WL1-C6-P4-Labels.docx**.
13. At the blank document, close the document without saving changes.

Figure 6.9 Project 4a

DAVID LOWRY	MARCELLA SANTOS	KEVIN DORSEY
12033 S 152 ST	394 APPLE BLOSSOM	26302 PRAIRIE DR
HOUSTON TX 77340	FRIENDSWOOD TX 77533	HOUSTON TX 77316
AL AND DONNA SASAKI	JACKIE RHYNER	MARK AND TINA ELLIS
1392 PIONEER DR	29039 107 AVE E	607 FORD AVE
BAYTOWN TX 77903	HOUSTON TX 77302	HOUSTON TX 77307

If you open the Envelopes and Labels dialog box with the Labels tab selected in a document containing a name and address, the name and address are automatically inserted in the *Address* section of the dialog box. To enter different names in each of the mailing labels, start at a clear document screen, display the Envelopes and Labels dialog box with the Labels tab selected, and then click the New Document button. The Envelopes and Labels dialog box is removed from the screen and the document displays with label forms. The insertion point is positioned in the first label form. Type the name and address in this label and then press the Tab key once or twice (depending on the label) to move the insertion point to the next label. Pressing Shift + Tab will move the insertion point to the preceding label.

Project 4b   Creating Mailing Labels   Part 2 of 2

1. Open **LAProg.docx** and create mailing labels with the delivery address. Begin by clicking the Mailings tab.
2. Click the Labels button in the Create group.

3. At the Envelopes and Labels dialog box with the Labels tab selected, make sure the delivery address displays properly in the *Address* section.
4. Click the New Document button.
5. Save the mailing label document and name it **WL1-C6-P4-LAProg.docx**.
6. Print and then close **WL1-C6-P4-LAProg.docx**.
7. Close **LAProg.docx**.

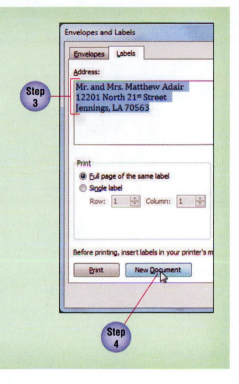

Step 3

Step 4

Project 5   Use a Template to Create a Business Letter   1 Part

You will use a letter template provided by Word to create a business letter.

Creating a Document Using a Template ■■■■■■■■■■■■

Word includes a number of template documents formatted for specific uses. Each Word document is based on a template document with the *Normal* template the default. With Word templates, you can easily create a variety of documents, such as letters, faxes, and awards, with specialized formatting. Display templates by clicking the File tab and then clicking the New tab. This displays the New tab Backstage view as shown in Figure 6.10.

Click the Sample templates button in the Available Templates category and installed templates display. Click the desired template in the *Sample templates* list box and a preview of the template displays at the right side of the screen. With options below the template preview, you can choose to open the template as a document or as a template. Click the Create button and the template opens and displays on the screen. Locations for personalized text display in placeholders in the template document. Select the placeholder text and then type the personalized text.

If you are connected to the Internet, you can download a number of predesigned templates that Microsoft offers. Templates are grouped into categories and the category names display in the *Office.com Templates* section of the New tab Backstage view. Click the desired template category and available templates display. Click the desired template and then click the Download button.

▼ **Quick Steps**

Create Document Using a Template
1. Click File tab.
2. Click New tab.
3. Click Sample templates button.
4. Double-click desired template.

Figure 6.10 New Tab Backstage View

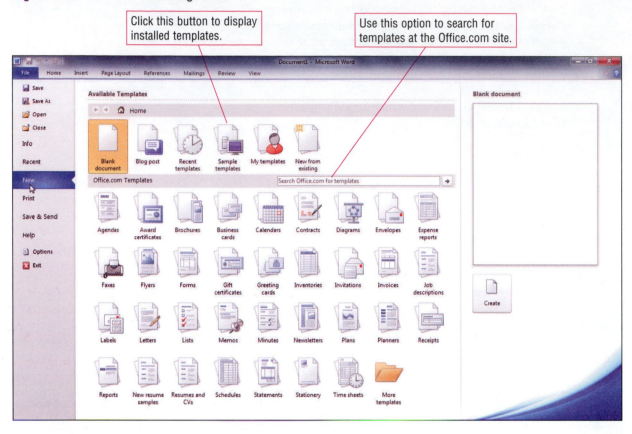

Click this button to display installed templates.

Use this option to search for templates at the Office.com site.

Project 5   **Creating a Letter Using a Template**   **Part 1 of 1**

1. Click the File tab and then click the New tab.
2. At the New tab Backstage view, click the Sample templates button in the Available Templates category.

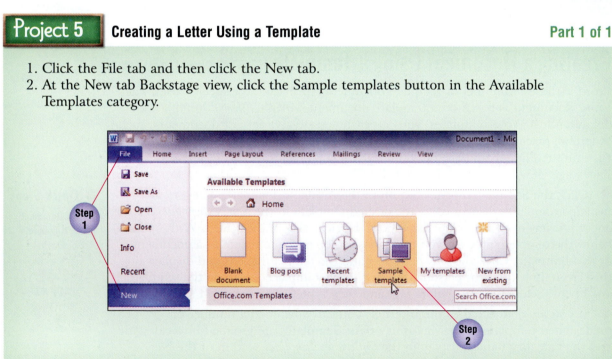

3. Double-click the *Equity Letter* template.

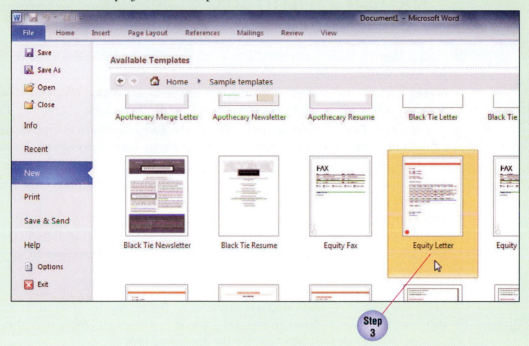

Step
3

4. At the letter document, click the placeholder text *[Pick the date]*, click the down-pointing arrow at the right side of the placeholder, and then click the Today button located at the bottom of the calendar.
5. Click in the name that displays below the date, select the name, and then type your first and last names.
6. Click the placeholder text *[Type the sender company name]* and then type **Sorenson Funds**.
7. Click the placeholder text *[Type the sender company address]*, type **6250 Aurora Boulevard**, press the Enter key, and then type **Baltimore, MD 20372**.
8. Click the placeholder text *[Type the recipient name]* and then type **Ms. Jennifer Gonzalez**.
9. Click the placeholder text *[Type the recipient address]*, type **12990 Boyd Street**, press the Enter key, and then type **Baltimore, MD 20375**.
10. Click the placeholder text *[Type the salutation]* and then type **Dear Ms. Gonzalez:**.
11. Insert a file in the document by completing the following steps:
    a. Click anywhere in the three paragraphs of text in the body of the letter and then click the Delete key.
    b. Click the Insert tab.
    c. Click the Object button arrow in the Text group and then click *Text from File* at the drop-down list.
    d. At the Insert File dialog box, navigate to the Word2010L1C6 folder on your storage medium and then double-click **SFunds.docx**.
12. Click the placeholder text *[Type the closing]* and then type **Sincerely,**.
13. Delete one blank line above Sincerely.
14. Click the placeholder text *[Type the sender title]* and then type **Financial Consultant**.
15. Save the document and name it **WL1-C6-P5-SFunds**.
16. Print and then close **WL1-C6-P5-SFunds.docx**.

Chapter Summary

- Group Word documents logically into folders. Create a new folder at the Open or Save As dialog box.

- You can select one or several documents at the Open dialog box. Copy, move, rename, delete, or open a document or selected documents.

- Use the *Cut*, *Copy*, and *Paste* options from the Organize button drop-down list or the Open dialog box shortcut menu to move or copy a document from one folder to another.

- Delete documents and/or folders with the *Delete* option from the Organize button drop-down list or shortcut menu.

- With options at the Save & Send tab Backstage view, you can send a document as an email attachment, save your document to SkyDrive and SharePoint, save your document in a different file format, and post your document to a special location such as a blog.

- Click the Change File Type button in the File Types category at the Save & Send tab Backstage view, and options display for saving the document in a different file format. You can also save documents in a different file format with the *Save as type* option box at the Save As dialog box.

- Move among the open documents by clicking the button on the Taskbar representing the desired document, or by clicking the View tab, clicking the Switch Windows button in the Window group, and then clicking the desired document name.

- View a portion of all open documents by clicking the View tab and then clicking the Arrange All button in the Window group.

- Use the Minimize, Restore, and Maximize buttons located in the upper right corner of the window to reduce or increase the size of the active window.

- Divide a window into two panes by clicking the View tab and then clicking the Split button in the Window group. This enables you to view different parts of the same document at one time.

- View the contents of two open documents side by side by clicking the View tab, and then clicking the View Side by Side button in the Window group.

- Insert a document into the open document by clicking the Insert tab, clicking the Object button arrow, and then clicking *Text from File* at the drop-down list. At the Insert File dialog box, double-click the desired document.

- Preview a document at the Print tab Backstage view. Scroll through the pages in the document with the Next Page and the Previous Page buttons that display below the preview page. Use the Zoom slider bar to increase/decrease the display size of the preview page.

- At the Print tab Backstage view you can customize the print job by changing the page orientation, size, and margins; specify how many pages you want to print on one page; the number of copies and whether or not to collate the pages; and specify the printer.

- With Word's envelope feature you can create and print an envelope at the Envelopes and Labels dialog box with the Envelopes tab selected.

- If you open the Envelopes and Labels dialog box in a document containing a name and address (with each line ending with a press of the Enter key), that information is automatically inserted in the *Delivery address* text box in the dialog box.

- Use Word's labels feature to print text on mailing labels, file labels, disc labels, or other types of labels.

- Word includes a number of template documents you can use to create a variety of documents. Display the list of template documents by clicking the File tab, clicking the New tab, and then clicking the Sample templates button.

Commands Review

FEATURE	RIBBON TAB, GROUP	BUTTON, OPTION	KEYBOARD SHORTCUT
Open dialog box	File	Open	Ctrl + O
Save As dialog box	File	Save As	
Print tab Backstage view	File	Print	Ctrl + P
Arrange all documents	View, Window		
Minimize document			
Maximize document			Ctrl + F10
Restore			
Split window	View, Window		Alt + Ctrl + S
View documents side by side	View, Window		
Insert file	Insert, Text	, Text from File	
Envelopes and Labels dialog box with Envelopes tab selected	Mailings, Create		
Envelopes and Labels dialog box with Labels tab selected	Maililngs, Create		
New tab Backstage view	File	New	

Concepts Check Test Your Knowledge

Completion: In the space provided at the right, indicate the correct term, command, or number.

1. Create a new folder with this button at the Open or Save As dialog box.

_____

2. At the Open dialog box, the current folder path displays in this.

_____

3. Using the mouse, select nonadjacent documents at the Open dialog box by holding down this key while clicking the desired documents.

_____

4. Documents deleted from the hard drive are automatically sent here.

_____

5. Copy a document to another folder without opening the document at the Open or Save As dialog box with the Organize button drop-down list or this menu

_____

6. The letters PDF stand for this.

_____

7. Saving a document in this format strips out all formatting.

_____

8. Click this button in the Window group in the View tab to arrange all open documents so a portion of each document displays.

_____

9. Click this button and the active document fills the editing window.

_____

10. Click this button to reduce the active document to a button on the Taskbar.

_____

11. To display documents side by side, click this button in the Window group in the View tab.

_____

12. Display the Insert File dialog box by clicking the Object button arrow in the Insert tab and then clicking this option.

_____

13. Type this in the *Pages* text box at the Print tab Backstage view to print pages 3 through 6 of the open document.

_____

14. Type this in the *Pages* text box at the Print tab Backstage view to print pages 4 and 9 of the open document.

_____

15. The Envelopes button is located in the Create group in this tab.

_____

16. Click the Sample templates button at this Backstage view to display a list of templates.

_____

Skills Check Assess Your Performance

Assessment

1 MANAGE DOCUMENTS

1. Display the Open dialog box with Word2010L1C6 the active folder and then create a new folder named *CheckingTools*.
2. Copy (be sure to copy and not cut) all documents that begin with *SpellGrammar* into the CheckingTools folder.
3. With the CheckingTools folder as the active folder, rename **SpellGrammar01.docx** to **Technology.docx**.
4. Rename **SpellGrammar02.docx** to **Software.docx**.
5. Print the screen contents by completing the following steps:
   a. With the Open dialog box displayed, press the Print Screen key on your keyboard.
   b. Close the Open dialog box.
   c. At a blank document, click the Paste button.
   d. Print the document.
   e. Close the document without saving it.
6. Display the Open dialog box and make Word2010L1C6 the active folder.
7. Delete the CheckingTools folder and all documents contained within it.
8. Open **StaffMtg.docx**, **Agreement.docx**, and **Robots.docx**.
9. Make **Agreement.docx** the active document.
10. Make **StaffMtg.docx** the active document.
11. Arrange all of the windows.
12. Make **Robots.docx** the active document and then minimize it.
13. Minimize the remaining documents.
14. Restore **StaffMtg.docx**.
15. Restore **Agreement.docx**.
16. Restore **Robots.docx**.
17. Maximize and then close **StaffMtg.docx** and then maximize and close **Robots.docx**.
18. Maximize **Agreement.docx** and then save the document and name it **WL1-C6-A1-Agreement**.
19. Open **AptLease.docx**.
20. View the **WL1-C6-A1-Agreement.docx** document and **AptLease.docx** document side by side.
21. Scroll through both documents simultaneously and notice the formatting differences between the title and headings in the two documents. Change the font and apply shading to the title and headings in **WL1-C6-A1-Agreement.docx** to match the font and shading of the title and headings in **AptLease.docx**.
22. Make **AptLease.docx** active and then close it.
23. Save **WL1-C6-A1-Agreement.docx**.
24. Move the insertion point to the end of the document and then insert the document named **Terms.docx**.
25. Apply formatting to the inserted text so it matches the formatting of the original text.

26. If the heading, *Damage to Premises*, displays at the bottom of page 1, insert a page break at the beginning of the heading.
27. Move the insertion point to the end of the document and then insert the document named **Signature.docx**.
28. Save, print, and then close **WL1-C6-A1-Agreement.docx**.

Assessment

2 CREATE AN ENVELOPE

1. At a blank document, create an envelope with the text shown in Figure 6.11.
2. Save the envelope document and name it **WL1-C6-A2-Env**.
3. Print and then close **WL1-C6-A2-Env.docx**.

Figure 6.11 Assessment 2

DR ROSEANNE HOLT
21330 CEDAR DR
LOGAN UT 84598

                    GENE MIETZNER
                    4559 CORRIN AVE
                    SMITHFIELD UT 84521

Assessment

3 CREATE MAILING LABELS

1. Create mailing labels with the names and addresses shown in Figure 6.12. Use a label option of your choosing. (You may need to check with your instructor before choosing an option.)
2. Save the document and name it **WL1-C6-A3-Labels**.
3. Print and then close **WL1-C6-A3-Labels.docx**.
4. At the clear document screen, close the document screen without saving changes.

Figure 6.12 Assessment 3

SUSAN LUTOVSKY	JIM AND PAT KEIL	IRENE HAGEN
1402 MELLINGER DR	413 JACKSON ST	12930 147TH AVE E
FAIRHOPE OH 43209	AVONDALE OH 43887	CANTON OH 43296
VINCE KILEY	LEONARD KRUEGER	HELGA GUNDSTROM
14005 288TH S	13290 N 120TH	PO BOX 3112
CANTON OH 43287	CANTON OH 43291	AVONDALE OH 43887

Assessment

4 PREPARE A FAX

1. Open the Equity fax template at the New tab Backstage view with sample templates selected and then insert the following information in the specified fields.

   To: Frank Gallagher
   From: (your first and last names)
   Fax: (206) 555-9010
   Pages: 3
   Phone: (206) 555-9005
   Date: (insert current date)
   Re: Consultation Agreement
   CC: Jolene Yin
   Insert an X in the *For Review* check box.
   Comments: Please review the Consultation Agreement and advise me of any legal issues.

2. Save the fax document and name it **WL1-C6-A4-Fax**.
3. Print and then close the document.

Assessment

5 SAVE A DOCUMENT AS A WEB PAGE

1. Experiment with the Save as type button at the Save As dialog box and figure out how to save a document as a single file web page.
2. Open **NSS.docx**, display the Save As dialog box, and then change Save as Type to a single file web page. Click the Change Title button that displays in the Save As dialog box. At the Enter Text dialog box, type Northland Security Systems in the *Page title* text box and then close the dialog box by clicking the OK button. Click the Save button in the Save As dialog box.
3. Close the **NSS.mht** file.
4. Open your web browser and then open the **NSS.mht** file.
5. Close your web browser.

Assessment

6 CREATE PERSONAL MAILING LABELS

1. At a blank document, type your name and address and then apply formatting to enhance the appeal of the text (you determine the font, font size, and font color).
2. Create labels with your name and address (you determine the label vendor and product number).
3. Save the label document and name it **WL1-C6-A6-PersonalLabels**.
4. Print and then close the document.

7 DOWNLOAD AND COMPLETE A STUDENT AWARD CERTIFICATE

1. Display the New tab Backstage view and then search for and download a student of the month award certificate template in the *Office.com Templates* section of the Available Templates category. (To find a student of the month award, click the *Award certificates* option in the *Office.com Templates* section, click the *Academic* folder, and then look for the *Basic certificate for student of the month* template.)
2. Insert the appropriate information in the award template placeholder identifying yourself as the recipient of the student of the month award.
3. Save the completed award and name the document **WL1-C6-A7-Award**.
4. Print and then close the document.

Visual Benchmark Demonstrate Your Proficiency

CREATE CUSTOM LABELS

1. You can create a sheet of labels with the same information in each label by typing the information in the Address text box at the Envelopes and Labels dialog box or you can type the desired information, select it, and then create the label. Using this technique, create the sheet of labels shown in Figure 6.13 with the following specifications:
   - Open **NSSLabels.docx**.
   - Set the text in 12-point Magneto.
   - Select the entire document and then create the labels by displaying the Envelopes and Labels dialog box with the Labels tab selected. Change to the Avery US Letter label, product number 5161, and then click the New Document button.

2. Save the label document and name it **WL1-C6-VB-NSSLabels**.
3. Print and then close the document.
4. Close **NSSLabels.docx** without saving it.

Figure 6.13 Visual Benchmark

Northland Security Systems
3200 North 22nd Street
Springfield, IL 62102

Case Study Apply Your Skills

Part 1

You are the office manager for the real estate company, Macadam Realty, and have been asked by the senior sales associate, Lucy Hendricks, to organize contract forms into a specific folder. Create a new folder named *RealEstate* and then copy into the folder documents that begin with the letters "RE." Ms. Hendricks has also asked you to prepare mailing labels for Macadam Realty. Include the name, Macadam Realty, and the address 100 Third Street, Suite 210, Denver, CO 80803, on the labels. Use a decorative font for the label and make the *M* in *Macadam* and the *R* in *Realty* larger and more pronounced than surrounding text. ***Hint: Format text in the label by selecting text, right-clicking in the selected text, and then choosing the desired option at the shortcut menu.*** Save the completed document and name it **WL1-C6-CS-RELabels**. Print and then close the document.

Part 2

One of your responsibilities is to format contract forms. Open the document named **REConAgrmnt.docx** and then save it and name it **WL1-C6-CS-REConAgrmnt**. The sales associate has asked you to insert signature information at the end of the document and so you decide to insert at the end of the document the file named **RESig.docx**. With **WL1-C6-CS-REConAgrmnt.docx** still open, open **REBuildAgrmnt.docx**. Format the **WL1-C6-CS-REConAgrmnt.docx** document so it is formatted in a manner similar to the **REBuildAgrmnt.docx** document. Consider the following when specifying formatting: margins, fonts, and paragraph shading. Save, print, and then close **WL1-C6-CS-REConAgrmnt.docx**. Close **REBuildAgrmnt.docx**.

Part 3

As part of the organization of contracts, Ms. Hendricks has asked you to insert document properties for the **REBuildAgrmnt.docx** and **WL1-C6-CS-REConAgrmnt.docx** documents. Use the Help feature to learn how to insert document properties. With the information you learn from the Help feature, open each of the two documents separately, display the Info tab Backstage view, click the <u>Show All Properties</u> hyperlink, and then insert document properties in the following fields (you determine the information to type): *Title*, *Subject*, *Categories*, and *Company*. Print the document properties for each document (change the first gallery in the Settings category in the Print tab Backstage view to *Document Properties*). Save each document with the original name and close the documents.

Part 4

A client of the real estate company, Anna Hurley, is considering purchasing several rental properties and has asked for information on how to locate real estate rental forms. Using the Internet, locate at least three websites that offer real estate rental forms. Write a letter to Anna Hurley at 2300 South 22nd Street, Denver, CO 80205. In the letter, list the websites you found and include information on which site you thought offered the most resources. Also include in the letter that Macadam Realty is very interested in helping her locate and purchase rental properties. Save the document and name it **WL1-C6-CS-RELtr**. Create an envelope for the letter and add it to the letter document. Save, print, and then close **WL1-C6-CS-RELtr.docx**. (You may need to manually feed the envelope in the printer.)

Word

_{Microsoft®}

Creating Tables and SmartArt

PERFORMANCE OBJECTIVES

Upon successful completion of Chapter 7, you will be able to:

- Create, edit, and format a table
- Change the table design and layout
- Sort text in a table
- Perform calculations on data in a table
- Create and format a SmartArt diagram
- Create and format a SmartArt organizational chart

Tutorials

7.1 Creating SmartArt
7.2 Creating a Table
7.3 Changing the Table Design
7.4 Modifying a Table
7.5 Inserting a Quick Table
7.6 Sorting Text in a Table and Performing Calculations

Some Word data can be organized in a table, which is a combination of columns and rows. With the Tables feature, you can insert data in columns and rows. This data can consist of text, values, and formulas. In this chapter you will learn how to create and format a table and insert and format data in the table. Word includes a SmartArt feature that provides a number of predesigned diagrams and organizational charts. Use this feature to create and then customize a diagram or organizational chart. Model answers for this chapter's projects appear on the following pages.

Word2010L1C7

Note: Before beginning the projects, copy to your storage medium the Word2010L1C7 subfolder from the Word2010L1 folder on the CD that accompanies this textbook and then make Word2010L1C7 the active folder.

Page 1

CONTACT INFORMATION, NORTH			
Name	Title	Company	Telephone
Maggie Rivera	Vice President	First Trust Bank	(203) 555-3440
Cecilia Nordyke	Loan Officer	American Financial	(509) 555-3995
Regina Stahl	Account Manager	United Fidelity	(301) 555-1221 x453

OPTIONAL PLAN PREMIUM RATES		
Waiting Period	Plan 2012 Employees	Basic Plan Employees
30 days	0.85%	0.81%
60 days	0.79%	0.67%
90 days	0.59%	0.49%
120 days	0.35%	0.30%
180 days	0.26%	0.23%

CONTACT INFORMATION, WEST			
Name	Title	Company	Telephone
Steven Adams	Vice President	Valley Bank	(213) 555-9002
Denise Bridgman	President	Freestone Mortgage	(323) 555-5300
Laura Coulter	Loan Officer	Pacific Savings	(310) 555-1048
Jack Gillespie	Vice President	Evergreen Trust	(323) 555-2102
Jessica Higgins	President	First Mortgage	(213) 555-4215
Eric Marquez	Vice President	Cascade Savings	(213) 555-0033
Cheryl Parente	President	Hillside Mortgage	(310) 555-1050

Page 1

Page 2

CONTACT INFORMATION, WEST			
Name	Title	Company	Telephone
Jane Scheibner	Loan Officer	Coastal Trust	(209) 555-3285
Charles Swayze	President	Skyline Bank	(310) 555-4892
Tracie Simmons	Loan Officer	Rosewood Mortgage	(323) 555-2330
Carole Wagner	President	Main Street Bank	(310) 555-5394
Dawn Wingstrand	Vice President	Lakeland Savings	(323) 555-2348
Cora Yates	Loan Officer	Douglas Mortgage	(213) 555-6588
Robert Ziebell	President	Central Trust	(310) 555-3444

December

Sun	Mon	Tue	Wed	Thu	Fri	Sat
						1
2	3	4	5	6	7	8
9	10	11	12	13	14	15
16	17	18	19	20	21	22
23	24	25	26	27	28	29
30	31					

Page 2

Project 1 Create and Format Tables with Company Information
WL1-C7-P1-Tables.docx

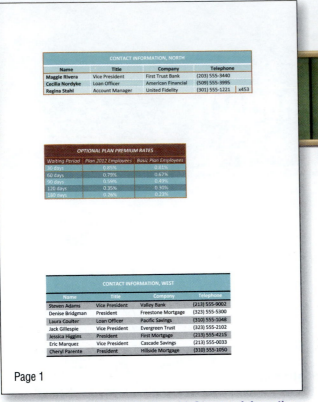

Tri-State Products	Name	Department
	Charles Hartman	Technical Support
	Erin Dodd-Trent	Public Relations
	Grace Murakami	Research and Development
	Elizabeth Gentry	Technical Support
	William Thatcher	Technical Support
	Stewart Zimmerman	Research and Development

TRI-STATE PRODUCTS		
Name	Employee #	Department
Whitaker, Christine	1432-323-09	Financial Services
Higgins, Dennis	1230-933-21	Public Relations
Coffey, Richard	1321-843-22	Research and Development
Porter, Robbie	1122-361-38	Public Relations
Buchanan, Lillian	1432-857-87	Research and Development
Kensington, Jacob	1112-473-31	Human Resources

TRI-STATE PRODUCTS	
Title	Name
President	Martin Sherwood
Vice President	Gina Lopez
Vice President	Sydney Fox
Manager	Stephen Powell
Manager	Linda Wu

Tri-State Products		
Washington Division	Oregon Division	California Division

Project 2 Create and Format Tables with Employee Information
WL1-C7-P2-TSPTables.docx

TRI-STATE PRODUCTS Sales Division		
Salesperson	Sales, 2010	Sales, 2011
Lagasa, Brianna	$294,653	$300,211
Sogura, Jeffrey	$375,630	$399,120
Whittier, Michelle	$395,630	$376,522
Kurkova, Martina	$490,310	$476,005
Byers, Darren	$490,655	$500,210
Novak, Diana	$543,241	$651,438
Guthrie, Jonathan	$623,214	$635,099
Total	$3,213,333	$3,338,605
Average	$459,048	$476,944
Top Sales	$623,214	$651,438

Region	First Qtr.	Second Qtr.	Third Qtr.	Fourth Qtr.	Total
Northwest	$125,430	$157,090	$139,239	$120,340	$542,099
Southwest	$133,450	$143,103	$153,780	$142,498	$572,831
Northeast	$275,340	$299,342	$278,098	$266,593	$1,119,373
Southeast	$211,349	$222,330	$201,849	$239,432	$874,960
Total	$745,569	$821,865	$772,966	$768,863	$3,109,263
Average	$186,392	$205,466	$193,242	$192,216	$777,316

Project 3 Sort and Calculate Sales Data
WL1-C7-P3-TSPSalesTables.docx

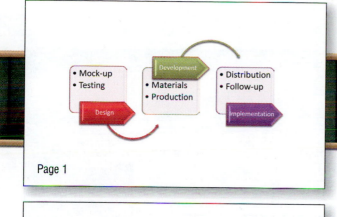

Page 1

Page 2

Project 4 Prepare and Format a Diagram
WL1-C7-P4-Diagrams.docx

Project 5 Prepare and Format a Company Organizational Chart
WL1-C7-P5-OrgChart.docx

roject **1** **Create and Format Tables with Company Information**   **9 Parts**

You will create a table containing contact information and another containing information on plans offered by the company. You will then change the design and layout of both tables.

Creating a Table ▪▪▪▪▪▪▪▪▪▪▪▪▪▪▪▪▪▪▪▪▪▪▪

Use the Tables feature to create boxes of information called *cells*. A cell is the intersection between a row and a column. A cell can contain text, characters, numbers, data, graphics, or formulas. Create a table by clicking the Insert tab, clicking the Table button, dragging down and to the right until the correct number of rows and columns displays, and then clicking the mouse button. You can also create a table with options at the Insert Table dialog box. Display this dialog box by clicking the Table button in the Tables group in the Insert tab and then clicking *Insert Table* at the drop-down list.

Figure 7.1 shows an example of a table with three columns and four rows. Various parts of the table are identified in Figure 7.1 such as the gridlines, move table column marker, end-of-cell marker, end-of-row marker, and the resize handle. In a table, nonprinting characters identify the end of a cell and the end of a row. To view these characters, click the Show/Hide ¶ button in the Paragraph group in the Home

▼ Quick Steps

Create a Table
1. Click Insert tab.
2. Click Table button.
3. Drag to create desired number of columns and rows.
4. Click mouse button.
OR
1. Click Insert tab.
2. Click Table button.
3. Click *Insert Table*.
4. Specify number of columns and rows.
5. Click OK.

Figure 7.1 Table

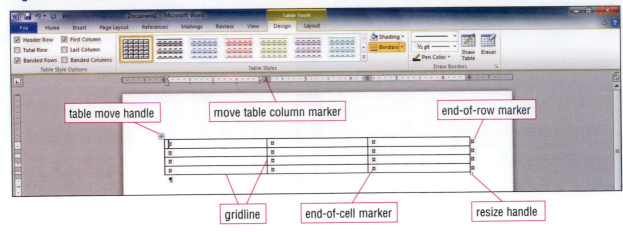

table move handle

move table column marker

end-of-row marker

gridline

end-of-cell marker

resize handle

Table

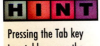

You can create a table within a table, creating a *nested* table.

Pressing the Tab key in a table moves the insertion point to the next cell. Pressing Ctrl + Tab moves the insertion point to the next tab within a cell.

tab. The end-of-cell marker displays inside each cell and the end-of-row marker displays at the end of a row of cells. These markers are identified in Figure 7.1.

When you create a table, the insertion point is located in the cell in the upper left corner of the table. Cells in a table contain a cell designation. Columns in a table are lettered from left to right, beginning with *A*. Rows in a table are numbered from top to bottom beginning with *1*. The cell in the upper left corner of the table is cell A1. The cell to the right of A1 is B1, the cell to the right of B1 is C1, and so on.

When the insertion point is positioned in a cell in the table, move table column markers display on the horizontal ruler. These markers represent the end of a column and are useful in changing the width of columns. Figure 7.1 identifies a move table column marker.

Entering Text in Cells

With the insertion point positioned in a cell, type or edit text. Move the insertion point to other cells with the mouse by clicking in the desired cell. If you are using the keyboard, press the Tab key to move the insertion point to the next cell or press Shift + Tab to move the insertion point to the previous cell.

If the text you type does not fit on one line, it wraps to the next line within the same cell. Or, if you press Enter within a cell, the insertion point is moved to the next line within the same cell. The cell vertically lengthens to accommodate the text, and all cells in that row also lengthen. Pressing the Tab key in a table causes the insertion point to move to the next cell in the table. If you want to move the insertion point to a tab stop within a cell, press Ctrl + Tab. If the insertion point is located in the last cell of the table and you press the Tab key, Word adds another row to the table. Insert a page break within a table by pressing Ctrl + Enter. The page break is inserted between rows, not within.

Moving the Insertion Point within a Table

To move the insertion point to a different cell within the table using the mouse, click in the desired cell. To move the insertion point to different cells within the table using the keyboard, refer to the information shown in Table 7.1.

Table 7.1 Insertion Point Movement within a Table Using the Keyboard

To move the insertion point	Press these keys
To next cell	Tab
To preceding cell	Shift + Tab
Forward one character	Right Arrow key
Backward one character	Left Arrow key
To previous row	Up Arrow key
To next row	Down Arrow key
To first cell in the row	Alt + Home
To last cell in the row	Alt + End
To top cell in the column	Alt + Page Up
To bottom cell in the column	Alt + Page Down

Project 1a Creating a Table   Part 1 of 9

1. At a blank document, turn on bold, and then type the title **CONTACT INFORMATION** shown in Figure 7.2.
2. Turn off bold and then press the Enter key.
3. Create the table shown in Figure 7.2. To do this, click the Insert tab, click the Table button in the Tables group, drag down and to the right until the number above the grid displays as *3x5*, and then click the mouse button. 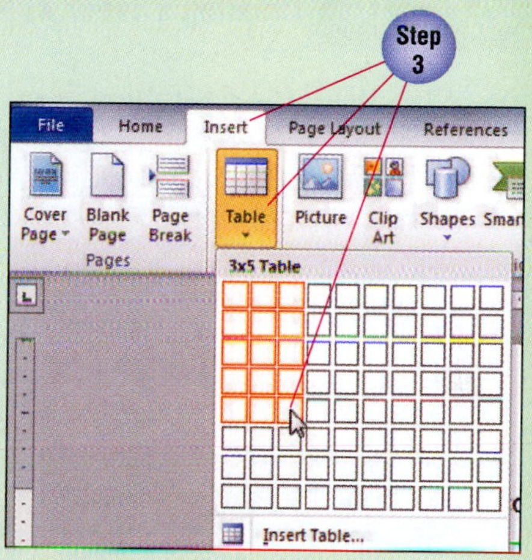
4. Type the text in the cells as indicated in Figure 7.2. Press the Tab key to move to the next cell or press Shift + Tab to move to the preceding cell. (If you accidentally press the Enter key within a cell, immediately press the Backspace key. Do not press Tab after typing the text in the last cell. If you do, another row is inserted in the table. If this happens, immediately click the Undo button on the Quick Access toolbar.)
5. Save the table and name it **WL1-C7-P1-Tables**.

Step 3

Figure 7.2 Project 1a

CONTACT INFORMATION

Maggie Rivera	First Trust Bank	(203) 555-3440
Les Cromwell	Madison Trust	(602) 555-4900
Cecilia Nordyke	American Financial	(509) 555-3995
Regina Stahl	United Fidelity	(301) 555-1221
Justin White	Key One Savings	(360) 555-8966

Using the Insert Table Dialog Box

You can also create a table with options at the Insert Table dialog box shown in Figure 7.3. To display this dialog box, click the Insert tab, click the Table button in the Tables group, and then click *Insert Table*. At the Insert Table dialog box, enter the desired number of columns and rows and then click OK.

Figure 7.3 Insert Table Dialog Box

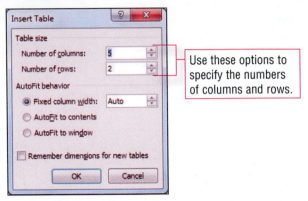

Use these options to specify the numbers of columns and rows.

Project 1b Creating a Table with the Insert Table Dialog Box

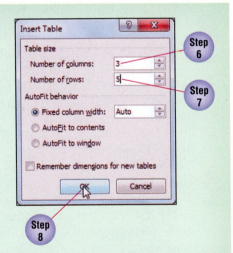

1. With **WL1-C7-P1-Tables.docx** open, press Ctrl + End to move the insertion point below the table.
2. Press the Enter key twice.
3. Turn on bold and then type the title **OPTIONAL PLAN PREMIUM RATES** shown in Figure 7.4.
4. Turn off bold and then press the Enter key.
5. Click the Insert tab, click the Table button in the Tables group, and then click *Insert Table* at the drop-down list.
6. At the Insert Table dialog box, type **3** in the *Number of columns* text box. (The insertion point is automatically positioned in this text box.)
7. Press the Tab key (this moves the insertion point to the *Number of rows* text box) and then type **5**.
8. Click OK.
9. Type the text in the cells as indicated in Figure 7.4.
   Press the Tab key to move to the next cell or press Shift + Tab to move to the preceding cell. To indent the text in cells B2 through B5 and cells C2 through C5, press Ctrl + Tab to move the insertion to a tab within cells and then type the text.
10. Save **WL1-C7-P1-Tables.docx**.

Figure 7.4 Project 1b

OPTIONAL PLAN PREMIUM RATES

Waiting Period	Basic Plan Employees	Plan 2012 Employees
60 days	0.67%	0.79%
90 days	0.49%	0.59%
120 days	0.30%	0.35%
180 days	0.23%	0.26%

Changing the Table Design

When you create a table, the Table Tools Design tab is selected and the tab contains a number of options for enhancing the appearance of the table as shown in Figure 7.5. With options in the Table Styles group, apply a predesigned style that applies color and border lines to a table. Maintain further control over the predesigned style formatting applied to columns and rows with options in the Table Style Options group. For example, if your table contains a total column, you would insert a check mark in the *Total Row* option. Apply additional design formatting to cells in a table with the Shading and Borders buttons in the Table Styles group. Draw a table or draw additional rows and/or columns in a table by clicking the Draw Table button in the Draw Borders group. Click this button and the mouse pointer turns into a pencil. Drag in the table to create the desired columns and rows. Click the Eraser button and the mouse pointer turns into an eraser. Drag through the column and/or row lines you want to erase in the table.

Draw a freeform table by clicking the Insert tab, clicking the Table button, and then clicking the *Draw Table* option. Drag in the document to create the table.

Shading

Draw Table

Figure 7.5 Table Tools Design Tab

1. With **WL1-C7-P1-Tables.docx** open, click in any cell in the top table.
2. Apply a table style by completing the following steps:
   a. Make sure the Table Tools Design tab is active.
   b. Click the More button at the right side of the table style thumbnails in the Table Styles group.
   c. Click the *Medium Grid 3 - Accent 5* style (second table style from the right in the tenth row in the *Built-in* section).

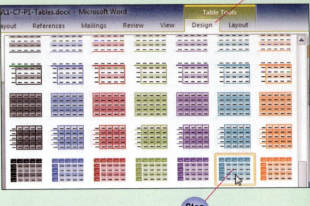

Step 2a

Step 2c

3. After looking at the table, you realize that the first row is not a header row and the first column should not be formatted differently than the other columns. To format the first row and first column in the same manner as the other rows and columns, click the *Header Row* check box and the *First Column* check box in the Table Style Options group to remove the check marks.

Step 3

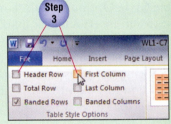

4. Click in any cell in the bottom table, apply the Dark List - Accent 5 table style (second option from the right in the eleventh row in the Built-in section), and then remove the check mark from the *First Column* check box.
5. Add color borders to the top table by completing the following steps:
   a. Click in any cell in the top table.
   b. Click the Pen Color button arrow in the Draw Borders group and then click the *Orange, Accent 6, Darker 50%* color.
   c. Click the Line Weight button arrow in the Draw Borders group and then click *1 ½ pt* at the drop-down list. (When you choose a line weight, the Draw Table button is automatically activated.)

Step 5b

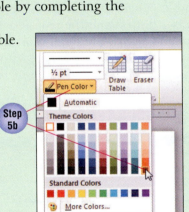

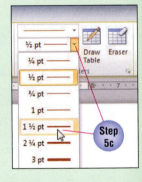

Step 5c

   d. Using the mouse (mouse pointer displays as a pen), drag along each side of the table. (As you drag with the mouse, a thick, brown border line is inserted. If you make a mistake or the line does not display as you intended, click the Undo button and then continue drawing along each side of the table.)
6. Drag along each side of the bottom table.
7. Click the Line Weight button in the Draw Borders group and then click *1 pt* at the drop-down list.
8. Drag along the row boundary separating the first row from the second row in the bottom table.
9. Click the Draw Table button to turn off the feature.
10. Save **WL1-C7-P1-Tables.docx**.

Selecting Cells ■■■■■■■■■■■■■■■■■■■■■■■■■■

You can format data within a table in several ways. For example, you can change the alignment of text within cells or rows, select and then move or copy rows or columns, or you can add character formatting such as bold, italic, or underlining. To format specific cells, rows, or columns, you must first select them.

Selecting in a Table with the Mouse

Use the mouse pointer to select a cell, row, column, or an entire table. Table 7.2 describes methods for selecting a table with the mouse. The left edge of each cell, between the left column border and the end-of-cell marker or first character in the cell, is called the *cell selection bar*. When you position the mouse pointer in the cell selection bar, it turns into a small, black arrow pointing up and to the right. Each row in a table contains a *row selection bar*, which is the space just to the left of the left edge of the table. When you position the mouse pointer in the row selection bar, the mouse pointer turns into a white arrow pointing up and to the right.

Table 7.2 Selecting in a Table with the Mouse

To select this	Do this
A cell	Position the mouse pointer in the cell selection bar at the left edge of the cell until it turns into a small, black arrow pointing up and to the right and then click the left mouse button.
A row	Position the mouse pointer in the row selection bar at the left edge of the table until it turns into an arrow pointing up and to the right and then click the left mouse button.
A column	Position the mouse pointer on the uppermost horizontal gridline of the table in the appropriate column until it turns into a short, black down-pointing arrow and then click the left mouse button.
Adjacent cells	Position the mouse pointer in the first cell to be selected, hold down the left mouse button, drag the mouse pointer to the last cell to be selected, and then release the mouse button.
All cells in a table	Click the table move handle or position the mouse pointer in the row selection bar for the first row at the left edge of the table until it turns into an arrow pointing up and to the right, hold down the left mouse button, drag down to select all rows in the table, and then release the left mouse button.
Text within a cell	Position the mouse pointer at the beginning of the text and then hold down the left mouse button as you drag the mouse across the text. (When a cell is selected, the cell background color changes to blue. When text within cells is selected, only those lines containing text are selected.)

Selecting in a Table with the Keyboard

In addition to the mouse, you can also use the keyboard to select specific cells within a table. Table 7.3 displays the commands for selecting specific amounts of a table.

If you want to select only text within cells, rather than the entire cell, press F8 to turn on the Extend mode and then move the insertion point with an arrow key. When a cell is selected, the cell background color changes to blue. When text within a cell is selected, only those lines containing text are selected.

Table 7.3 Selecting in a Table with the Keyboard

To select	Press
The next cell's contents	Tab
The preceding cell's contents	Shift + Tab
The entire table	Alt + 5 (on numeric keypad with Num Lock off)
Adjacent cells	Hold down Shift key and then press an arrow key repeatedly.
A column	Position insertion point in top cell of column, hold down Shift key, and then press down-pointing arrow key until column is selected.

Project 1d **Selecting, Moving and Formatting Cells in a Table** **Part 4 of 9**

1. With **WL1-C7-P1-Tables.docx** open, move two rows in the top table by completing the following steps:
   a. Position the mouse pointer in the row selection bar at the left side of the row containing the name *Cecilia Nordyke*, hold down the left mouse button, drag down to select two rows (the *Cecilia Nordyke* row and the *Regina Stahl* row).
   b. Click the Home tab and then click the Cut button in the Clipboard group.
   c. Move the insertion point so it is positioned at the beginning of the name *Les Cromwell* and then click the Paste button in the Clipboard group.

2. Move the third column in the bottom table by completing the following steps:
   a. Position the mouse pointer on the top border of the third column in the bottom table until the pointer turns into a short, black, down-pointing arrow and then click the left mouse button. (This selects the entire column.)
   b. Click the Cut button in the Clipboard group in the Home tab.
   c. With the insertion point positioned at the beginning of the text *Basic Plan Employees*, click the Paste button in the Clipboard group in the Home tab. (Moving the column removed the right border.)
   d. Insert the right border by clicking the Table Tools Design tab, clicking the Line Weight button arrow, and then clicking *1 ½ pt* at the drop-down list.

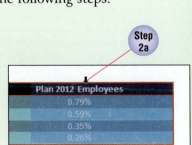

e. Hold down the left mouse button and then drag along the right border of the bottom table.

f. Click the Line Weight button arrow and then click *1 pt* at the drop-down list.

g. Click the Draw Table button to turn off the feature.

3. Apply shading to a row by completing the following steps:

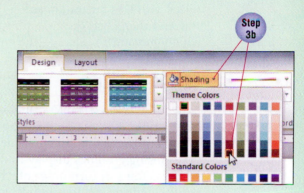

a. Position the mouse pointer in the row selection bar at the left edge of the first row in the bottom table until the pointer turns into an arrow pointing up and to the right and then click the left mouse button. (This selects the entire first row of the bottom table.)

b. Click the Shading button arrow in the Table Styles group and then click the *Red, Accent 2, Darker 50%* color.

4. Apply a border line to a column by completing the following steps:

a. Position the mouse pointer on the top border of the first column in the bottom table until the pointer turns into a short, black, down-pointing arrow and then click the left mouse button.

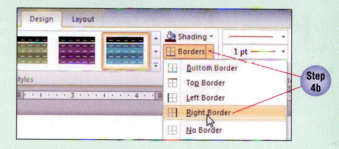

b. Click the Borders button arrow in the Table Styles group and then click *Right Border* at the drop-down list. (This inserts a 1 point dark orange border line at the right side of the column.)

5. Complete steps similar to those in Step 2 to insert a border line at the right side of the second column.

6. Apply italic formatting to a column by completing the following steps:

a. Position the insertion point in the first cell of the first row in the top table.

b. Hold down the Shift key and then press the Down Arrow key four times. (This should select all cells in the first column.)

c. Press Ctrl + I.

7. Save **WL1-C7-P1-Tables.docx**.

Changing Table Layout ■■■■■■■■■■■■■■■■■■■

To further customize a table, consider changing the table layout by inserting or deleting columns and rows and specifying cell alignments. Change table layout with options at the Table Tools Layout tab shown in Figure 7.6. Use options and buttons in the tab to select specific cells, delete and insert rows and columns, merge and split cells, specify cell height and width, sort data in cells, and insert a formula.

HINT

Some table layout options are available at a shortcut menu that can be viewed by right-clicking a table.

Figure 7.6 Table Tools Layout Tab

Select

View Gridlines

Insert Above

Insert Below

Insert Left

Insert Right

Delete

Selecting with the Select Button

Along with selecting cells with the keyboard and mouse, you can also select specific cells with the Select button in the Table group in the Table Tools Layout tab. To select with this button, position the insertion point in the desired cell, column, or row and then click the Select button. At the drop-down list that displays, specify what you want to select — the entire table or a column, row, or cell.

Viewing Gridlines

When you create a table, cell borders are identified by horizontal and vertical thin, black gridlines. You can remove a cell border gridline but maintain the cell border. If you remove cell border gridlines or apply a table style that removes gridlines, nonprinting gridlines display as dashed lines. This helps you visually determine cell borders. You can turn on or off the display of these nonprinting, dashed gridlines with the View Gridlines button in the Table group in the Table Tools Layout tab.

Inserting and Deleting Rows and Columns

With buttons in the Rows & Columns group in the Table Tools Layout tab, you can insert a row or column and delete a row or column. Click the button in the group that inserts the row or column in the desired location such as above, below, to the left, or to the right. Add a row to the bottom of a table by positioning the insertion point in the last cell and then pressing the Tab key. To delete a table, row, or column, click the Delete button and then click the option identifying what you want to delete. If you make a mistake while formatting a table, immediately click the Undo button on the Quick Access toolbar.

Project 1e Selecting, Inserting, and Deleting Columns and Rows **Part 5 of 9**

1. Make sure **WL1-C7-P1-Tables.docx** is open.
2. The table style applied to the bottom table removed row border gridlines. If you do not see dashed gridlines in the bottom table, turn on the display of these nonprinting gridlines by positioning your insertion point in the table, clicking the Table Tools Layout tab, and then clicking the View Gridlines button in the Table group. (The button should display with an orange background indicating it is active.)
3. Select a column and apply formatting by completing the following steps:
   a. Click in any cell in the first column in the top table.
   b. Click the Select button in the Table group and then click *Select Column* at the drop-down list.
   c. With the first column selected, press Ctrl + I to remove italics and then press Ctrl + B to apply bold formatting.
4. Select a row and apply formatting by completing the following steps:
   a. Click in any cell in the first row in the bottom table.
   b. Click the Select button in the Table group and then click *Select Row* at the drop-down list.
   c. With the first row selected in the bottom table, press Ctrl + I to apply italic formatting.

5. Insert a new row in the bottom table and type text in the new cells by completing the following steps:
   a. Click in the cell containing the text *60 days*.
   b. Click the Insert Above button in the Rows & Columns group.
   c. Type **30 days** in the first cell of the new row, type **0.85%** in the middle cell of the new row (make sure you press Ctrl + Tab before typing the text), and type **0.81%** in the third cell of the new row. (Make sure you press Ctrl + Tab before typing the text.)

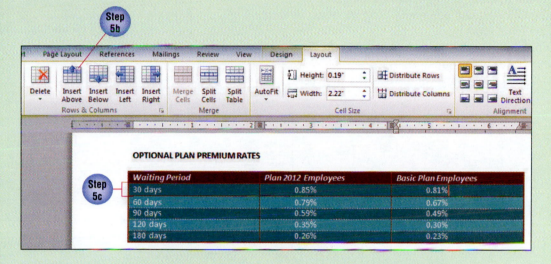

6. Insert three new rows in the top table and type text in the new cells by completing the following steps:
   a. Select the three rows of cells that begin with the names *Cecilia Nordyke*, *Regina Stahl*, and *Les Cromwell*.
   b. Click the Insert Below button in the Rows & Columns group.
   c. Type the following text in the new cells:

Teresa Getty	**Meridian Bank**	**(503) 555-9800**
Michael Vazquez	**New Horizon Bank**	**(702) 555-2435**
Samantha Roth	**Cascade Mutual**	**(206) 555-6788**

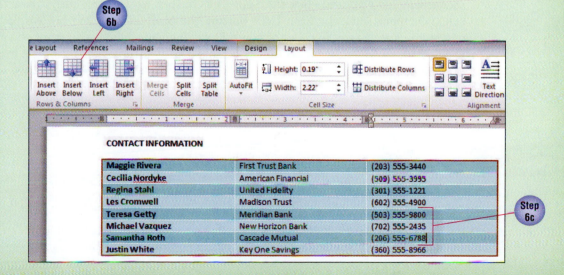

7. Delete a row by completing the following steps:
   a. Click in the cell containing the name *Les Cromwell*.
   b. Click the Delete button in the Rows & Columns group and then click *Delete Rows* at the drop-down list.
8. Insert a new column and type text in the new cells by completing the following steps:
   a. Click in the cell containing the text *First Trust Bank*.
   b. Click the Insert Left button in the Rows & Columns group.
   c. Type the following text in the new cells:
      - B1 = **Vice President**
      - B2 = **Loan Officer**
      - B3 = **Account Manager**
      - B4 = **Branch Manager**
      - B5 = **President**
      - B6 = **Vice President**
      - B7 = **Regional Manager**
9. Save **WL1-C7-P1-Tables.docx**.

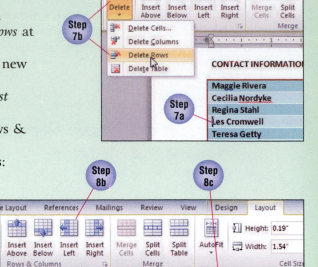

Merging and Splitting Cells and Tables

Merge Cells

Split Cells

Split Table

Click the Merge Cells button in the Merge group in the Table Tools Layout tab to merge selected cells and click the Split Cells button to split the currently active cell. When you click the Split Cells button, the Split Cells dialog box displays where you specify the number of columns or rows into which you want to split the active cell. If you want to split one table into two tables, position the insertion point in a cell in the row that you want to be the first row in the new table and then click the Split Table button.

Project 1f **Merging and Splitting Cells and Splitting a Table**

1. With **WL1-C7-P1-Tables.docx** open, insert a new row and merge cells in the row by completing the following steps:
   a. Click in the cell containing the text *Waiting Period* (located in the bottom table).
   b. Click the Insert Above button in the Rows & Columns group in the Table Tools Layout tab.

c. With all of the cells in the new row selected, click the Merge Cells button in the Merge group.

d. Type **OPTIONAL PLAN PREMIUM RATES** and then press Ctrl + E to center-align the text in the cell. (The text you type will be italicized.)

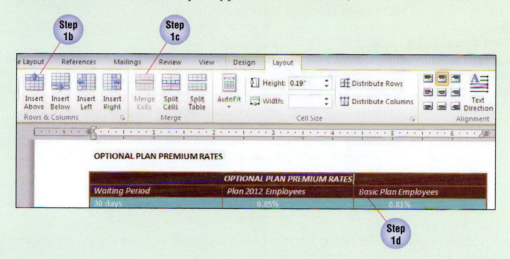

2. Select and then delete the text *OPTIONAL PLAN PREMIUM RATES* that displays above the bottom table.

3. Insert rows and text in the top table and merge cells by completing the following steps:

   a. Click in the cell containing the text *Maggie Rivera*.

   b. Click the Table Tools Layout tab.

   c. Click the Insert Above button twice. (This inserts two rows at the top of the table.)

   d. With the cells in the top row selected, click the Merge Cells button in the Merge group.

   e. Type **CONTACT INFORMATION, NORTH** and then press Ctrl + E to change the paragraph alignment to center.

   f. Type the following text in the four cells in the new second row.

   Name   **Title**   **Company**   **Telephone**

4. Apply heading formatting to the new top row by completing the following steps:

   a. Click the Table Tools Design tab.

   b. Click the *Header Row* check box in the Table Style Options dialog box.

5. Select and then delete the text *CONTACT INFORMATION* that displays above the top table.

6. Split a cell by completing the following steps:

   a. Click in the cell containing the telephone number *(301) 555-1221*.

   b. Click the Table Tools Layout tab.

   c. Click the Split Cells button in the Merge group.

   d. At the Split Cells dialog box, click OK. (The telephone number will wrap to a new line. You will change this in the next project.)

e. Click in the new cell.

f. Type x453 in the new cell. If AutoCorrect automatically capitalizes the *x*, hover the mouse pointer over the *X* until the AutoCorrect Options button displays. Click the AutoCorrect Options button and then click *Undo Automatic Capitalization* or click *Stop Auto-capitalizing First Letter of Table Cells*.

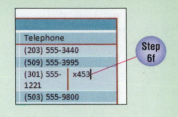

7. Split the cell containing the telephone number *(206) 555-6788* and then type x2310 in the new cell. (If necessary, make the *x* lowercase.)

8. Split the top table into two tables by completing the following steps:
   a. Click in the cell containing the name *Teresa Getty*.
   b. Click the Split Table button in the Merge group.
   c. Click in the cell containing the name *Teresa Getty* (in the first row of the new table).
   d. Click the Insert Above button in the Rows and Columns group in the Table Tools Layout tab.
   e. With the new row selected, click the Merge Cells button.
   f. Type CONTACT INFORMATION, SOUTH in the new row and then press Ctrl + E to center-align the text.

9. Draw a dark orange border at the bottom of the top table and the top of the middle table by completing the following steps:
   a. Click the Table Tools Design tab.
   b. Click the Line Weight button arrow in the Draw Borders group and then click *1 ½ pt* at the drop-down list. (This activates the Draw Table button.)
   c. Using the mouse (mouse pointer displays as a pen), drag along the bottom border of the top table.
   d. Click the top border of the middle table.
   e. Click the Draw Table button to turn it off.

10. Save and then print **WL1-C7-P1-Tables.docx**.

11. Delete the middle table by completing the following steps:
    a. Click in any cell in the middle table.
    b. Click the Table Tools Layout tab.
    c. Click the Delete button in the Rows & Columns group and then click *Delete Table* at the drop-down list.

12. Save **WL1-C7-P1-Tables.docx**.

Customizing Cell Size

When you create a table, column width and row height are equal. You can customize the width of columns or height of rows with buttons in the Cell Size group in the Table Tools Layout tab. Use the *Table Row Height* measurement box to increase or decrease the height of rows and use the *Table Column Width* measurement box to increase or decrease the width of columns. The Distribute Rows button will distribute equally the height of selected rows and the Distribute Columns button will distribute equally the width of selected columns.

Distribute Rows

Distribute Columns

You can also change column width using the move table column markers on the horizontal ruler or by using the table gridlines. To change column width using the horizontal ruler, position the mouse pointer on a move table column marker until it turns into a left and right arrow, and then drag the marker to the desired position. Hold down the Shift key while dragging a table column marker and the horizontal ruler remains stationary while the table column marker moves. Hold down the Alt key while dragging a table column marker and measurements display on the horizontal ruler. To change column width using gridlines, position the arrow pointer on the gridline separating columns until the insertion point turns into a left and right arrow with a vertical line between and then drag the gridline to the desired position. If you want to see the column measurements on the horizontal ruler as you drag a gridline, hold down the Alt key.

Adjust row height in a manner similar to adjusting column width. You can drag the adjust table row marker on the vertical ruler or drag the gridline separating rows. Hold down the Alt key while dragging the adjust table row marker or the row gridline and measurements display on the vertical ruler.

Use the AutoFit button in the Cell Size group to make the column widths in a table automatically fit the contents. To do this, position the insertion point in any cell in the table, click the AutoFit button in the Cell Size group, and then click *AutoFit Contents* at the drop-down list.

AutoFit

Project 1g   **Changing Column Width and Row Height**

1. With **WL1-C7-P1-Tables.docx** open, change the width of the first column in the top table by completing the following steps:
   a. Click in the cell containing the name *Maggie Rivera*.
   b. Position the mouse pointer on the move table column marker that displays just right of the 1.5-inch marker on the horizontal ruler until the pointer turns into an arrow pointing left and right.
   c. Hold down the Shift key and then the left mouse button.
   d. Drag the marker to the 1.25-inch mark, release the mouse button, and then release the Shift key.

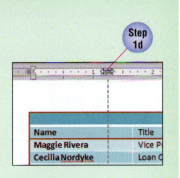

2. Complete steps similar to those in Step 1 to drag the move table column marker that displays just right of the 3-inch mark on the horizontal ruler to the 2.75-inch mark. (Make sure the text *Account Manager* in the second column does not wrap to the next line. If it does, slightly increase the width of the button.)

3. Change the width of the third column in the top table by completing the following steps:
   a. Position the mouse pointer on the gridline separating the third and fourth columns until the pointer turns into a left- and right-pointing arrow with a vertical double line between.
   b. Hold down the Alt key and then the left mouse button, drag the gridline to the left until the measurement for the third column on the horizontal ruler displays as *1.3"*, and then release the Alt key and then the mouse button.

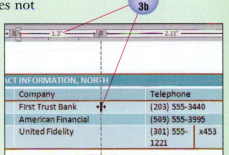

4. Position the mouse pointer on the gridline that separates the telephone number *(301) 555-1221* from the extension *x453* and then drag the gridline to the 5.25-inch mark on the horizontal ruler.

5. Drag the right border of the top table to the 5.75-inch marker on the horizontal ruler.

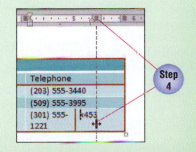

6. Automatically fit the columns in the bottom table by completing the following steps:
   a. Click in any cell in the bottom table.
   b. Click the AutoFit button in the Cell Size group in the Table Tools Layout tab and then click *AutoFit Contents* at the drop-down list.

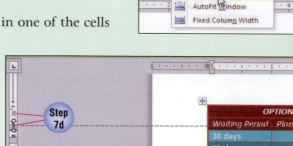

7. Increase the height of the first row in the bottom table by completing the following steps:
   a. Make sure the insertion point is located in one of the cells in the bottom table.
   b. Position the mouse pointer on the top adjust table row marker on the vertical ruler.
   c. Hold down the left mouse button and hold down the Alt key.
   d. Drag the adjust table row marker down until the first row measurement on the vertical ruler displays as *0.36"*, release the mouse button and then the Alt key.

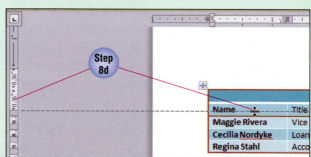

8. Increase the height of the first row in the top table by completing the following steps:
   a. Click in any cell in the top table.
   b. Position the arrow pointer on the gridline that displays at the bottom of the top row until the arrow pointer turns into an up- and down-pointing arrow with a vertical double line between.
   c. Hold down the left mouse button and then hold down the Alt key.
   d. Drag the gridline down until the first row measurement on the vertical ruler displays as *0.36"* and release the mouse button and then the Alt key.

9. Save **WL1-C7-P1-Tables.docx**.

Changing Cell Alignment

▼ **Quick Steps**

Repeat Header Row(s)
1. Click in header row or select rows.
2. Click Table Tools Layout tab.
3. Click Repeat Header Rows button.

Repeat
Header Rows

The Alignment group in the Table Tools Layout tab contains a number of buttons for specifying the horizontal and vertical alignment of text in cells. The buttons contain a visual representation of the alignment and you can also hover the mouse pointer over a button to determine the alignment.

Repeating a Header Row

If a table is divided between pages, consider adding the header row at the beginning of the table that extends to the next page. This helps the reader understand the data that displays in each column. To repeat a header row, click in the header row, and then click the Repeat Header Rows button in the Data group in the Table Tools Layout tab. If you want to repeat more than one header row, select the rows and then click the Repeat Header Rows button.

1. With **WL1-C7-P1-Tables.docx** open, click in the top cell in the top table (the cell containing the title *CONTACT INFORMATION, NORTH*).

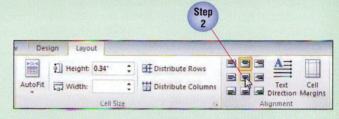

2. Click the Align Center button in the Alignment group in the Table Tools Layout tab.
3. Format and align text in the second row in the top table by completing the following steps:
   a. Select the second row.
   b. Press Ctrl + B (this turns off bold for the entry in the first cell) and then press Ctrl + B again (this turns on bold for all entries in the second row).
   c. Click the Align Top Center button in the Alignment group.
4. Click in the top cell in the bottom table and then click the Align Center button in the Alignment group.
5. Press Ctrl + End to move the insertion point to the end of the document, press the Enter key six times, and then insert a table into the current document by completing the following steps:
   a. Click the Insert tab.
   b. Click the Object button arrow in the Text group and then click *Text from File* at the drop-down list.
   c. At the Insert File dialog box, navigate to the Word2010L1C7 folder on your storage medium and then double-click *ContactsWest.docx*.
6. Repeat the header row by completing the following steps:
   a. Select the first two rows in the table you just inserted.
   b. Click the Table Tools Layout tab.
   c. Click the Repeat Header Rows button in the Data group.
7. Save **WL1-C7-P1-Tables.docx**.

Inserting a Quick Table

Word includes a Quick Tables feature you can use to insert predesigned tables in a document. To insert a quick table, click the Insert tab, click the Table button, point to *Quick Tables*, and then click the desired table at the side menu. A quick table has formatting applied but you can further format the table with options at the Table Tools Design tab and the Table Tools Layout tab.

▼ **Quick Steps**

Insert Quick Table
1. Click Insert tab.
2. Click Table button.
3. Point to *Quick Tables*.
4. Click desired table.

1. With **WL1-C7-P1-Tables.docx** open, press Ctrl + End to move the insertion point to the end of the document and then press the Enter key.
2. Insert a quick table by clicking the Insert tab, clicking the Table button, pointing to *Quick Tables*, and then clicking the *Calendar 3* option at the side menu.

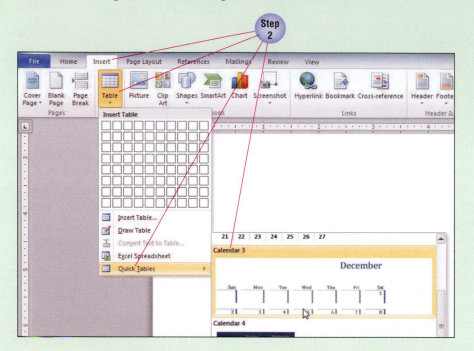

3. Edit text in each of the cells so the calendar reflects the current month.
4. Save, print, and then close **WL1-C7-P1-Tables.docx**.

Project 2 Create and Format Tables with Employee Information   5 Parts

You will create and format a table containing information on the names and departments of employees of Tri-State Products and also insert a table containing additional information on employees and then format the table.

Changing Cell Margin Measurements

Cell Margins

By default, cells in a table contain specific margin settings. Top and bottom margins in a cell have a default measurement of *0″* and left and right margins have a default setting of *0.08″*. Change these default settings with options at the Table Options dialog box shown in Figure 7.7. Display this dialog box by clicking the Cell Margins button in the Alignment group in the Table Tools Layout tab. Use the options in the *Default cell margins* section to change the top, bottom, left, and/ or right cell margin measurements.

Figure 7.7 Table Options Dialog Box

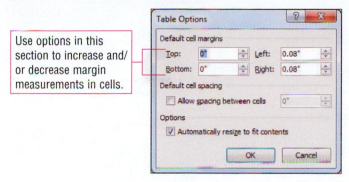

Use options in this section to increase and/or decrease margin measurements in cells.

Changes to cell margins will affect all cells in a table. If you want to change the cell margin measurements for one cell or for selected cells, position the insertion point in the cell or select the desired cells and then click the Properties button in the Table group in the Table Tools Layout tab. (You can also click the Cell Size group dialog box launcher.) At the Table Properties dialog box that displays, click the Cell tab and then the Options button that displays in the lower right corner of the dialog box. This displays the Cell Options dialog box shown in Figure 7.8.

Properties

Before setting the new cell margin measurements, remove the check mark from the *Same as the whole table* option. With the check mark removed from this option, the cell margin options become available. Specify the new cell margin measurements and then click OK to close the dialog box.

Figure 7.8 Cell Options Dialog Box

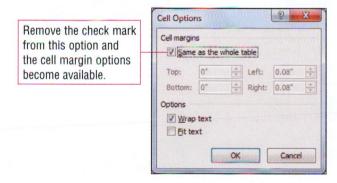

Remove the check mark from this option and the cell margin options become available.

Project 2a   **Changing Cell Margin Measurements**   **Part 1 of 5**

1. Open **TSPTables.docx** and then save the document with Save As and name it **WL1-C7-P2-TSPTables**.
2. Change the top and bottom margins for all cells in the table by completing the following steps:
   a. Position the insertion point in any cell in the table and then click the Table Tools Layout tab.

b. Click the Cell Margins button in the Alignment group.

c. At the Table Options dialog box, change the *Top* and *Bottom* measurements to *0.05"*.

d. Click OK to close the Table Options dialog box.

3. Change the top and bottom cell margin measurements for the first row of cells by completing the following steps:

a. Select the first row of cells (the cells containing *Name* and *Department*).

b. Click the Properties button in the Table group.

c. At the Table Properties dialog box, click the Cell tab.

d. Click the Options button.

e. At the Cell Options dialog box, remove the check mark from the *Same as the whole table* option.

f. Change the *Top* and *Bottom* measurements to *0.1"*.

g. Click OK to close the Cell Options dialog box.

h. Click OK to close the Table Properties dialog box.

4. Change the left cell margin measurement for specific cells by completing the following steps:

a. Select all rows in the table *except* the top row.

b. Click the Cell Size group dialog box launcher.

c. At the Table Properties dialog box, make sure the Cell tab is active.

d. Click the Options button.

e. At the Cell Options dialog box, remove the check mark from the *Same as the whole table* option.

f. Change the *Left* measurement to *0.3"*.

g. Click OK to close the Cell Options dialog box.

h. Click OK to close the Table Properties dialog box.

5. Save **WL1-C7-P2-TSPTables.docx**.

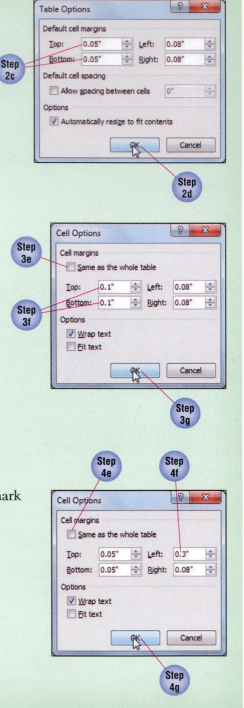

Step 2c

Step 2d

Step 3e

Step 3f

Step 3g

Step 4e

Step 4f

Step 4g

Changing Cell Direction

Text Direction

Change the direction of text in a cell using the Text Direction button in the Alignment group in the Table Tools Layout tab. Each time you click the Text Direction button, the text rotates in the cell 90 degrees.

Changing Table Alignment

By default, a table aligns at the left margin. Change this alignment with options at the Table Properties dialog box with the Table tab selected as shown in Figure 7.9. To change the alignment, click the desired alignment option in the *Alignment* section of the dialog box.

Figure 7.9 Table Properties Dialog Box with Table Tab Selected

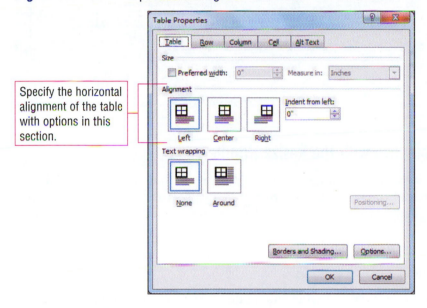

Specify the horizontal alignment of the table with options in this section.

---

1. With **WL1-C7-P2-TSPTables.docx** open, insert a new column and change text direction by completing the following steps:
   a. Click in any cell in the first column.
   b. Click the Insert Left button in the Rows & Columns group.
   c. With the cells in the new column selected, click the Merge Cells button in the Merge group.
   d. Type **Tri-State Products**.
   e. Click the Align Center button in the Alignment group.
   f. Click twice on the Text Direction button in the Alignment group.
   g. With *Tri-State Products* selected, click the Home tab, and then increase the font size to *16*.

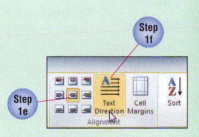

Step 1f

Step 1e

2. Automatically fit the contents by completing the following steps:
   a. Click in any cell in the table.
   b. Click the Table Tools Layout tab.
   c. Click the AutoFit button in the Cell Size group and then click the *AutoFit Contents* at the drop-down list.
3. Change the table alignment by completing the following steps:
   a. Click the Properties button in the Table group in the Table Tools Layout tab.

b. At the Table Properties dialog box, click the Table tab.
c. Click the *Center* option in the *Alignment* section.
d. Click OK.
4. Select the two cells containing the text *Name* and *Department* and then click the Align Center button in the Alignment group.
5. Save **WL1-C7-P2-TSPTables.docx**.

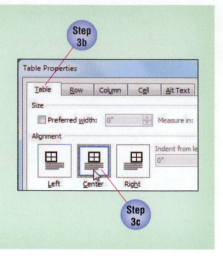

Step 3b

Step 3c

Changing Table Size with the Resize Handle

When you hover the mouse pointer over a table, a resize handle displays in the lower right corner of the table. The resize handle displays as a small, white square. Drag this resize handle to increase and/or decrease the size and proportion of the table.

Moving a Table

Position the mouse pointer in a table and a table move handle displays in the upper left corner. Use this handle to move the table in the document. To move a table, position the mouse pointer on the table move handle until the pointer turns into a four-headed arrow, hold down the left mouse button, drag the table to the desired position, and then release the mouse button.

Project 2c **Resizing and Moving Tables** **Part 3 of 5**

1. With **WL1-C7-P2-TSPTables.docx** open, insert a table into the current document by completing the following steps:
   a. Press Ctrl + End to move the insertion point to the end of the document and then press the Enter key.
   b. Click the Insert tab.
   c. Click the Object button arrow in the Text group and then click *Text from File* at the drop-down list.
   d. At the Insert File dialog box, navigate to the Word2010L1C7 folder and then double-click **TSPEmps.docx**.
2. Automatically fit the bottom table by completing the following steps:
   a. Click in any cell in the bottom table.
   b. Click the Table Tools Layout tab.
   c. Click the AutoFit button in the Cell Size group and then click *AutoFit Contents* at the drop-down list.
3. Format the bottom table by completing the following steps:
   a. Click the Table Tools Design tab.

b. Click the More button that displays at the right side of the styles thumbnails in the Table Styles group and then click the *Medium Shading 1 - Accent 2* style (third style from the left in the fourth row of the *Built-In* section).

c. Click the *First Column* check box in the Table Style Options group to remove the check mark.

d. Select the first and second rows, click the Table Tools Layout tab, and then click the Align Center button in the Alignment group.

e. Select the second row and then press Ctrl + B to turn on bold.

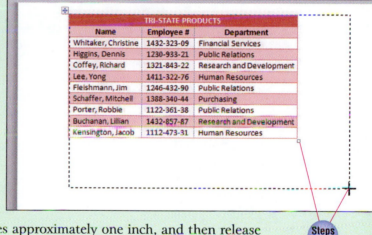

Step 3b

4. Resize the bottom table by completing the following steps:

a. Position the mouse pointer on the resize handle located in the lower right corner of the bottom table.

b. Hold down the left mouse button, drag down and to the right until the width and height of the table increases approximately one inch, and then release the mouse button.

Steps 4a-4b

5. Move the bottom table by completing the following steps:

a. Hover the mouse pointer over the bottom table.

b. Position the mouse pointer on the table move handle until the pointer displays with a four-headed arrow attached.

c. Hold down the left mouse button, drag the table so it is positioned equally between the left and right margins, and then release the mouse button.

Step 5c

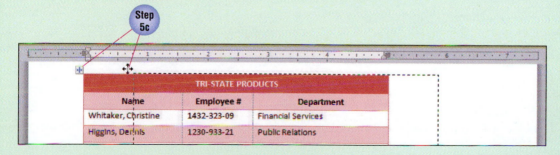

6. Select the cells in the column below the heading *Employee #* and then click the Align Top Center button in the Alignment group.

7. Save **WL1-C7-P2-TSPTables.docx**.

Quick Steps

Convert Text to Table
1. Select text.
2. Click Insert tab.
3. Click Table button.
4. Click *Convert Text to Table*.

Convert Table to Text
1. Click Table Tools Layout tab.
2. Click *Convert to Text*.
3. Specify desired separator.
4. Click OK.

Convert
to Text

Converting Text to a Table and a Table to Text

You can create a table and then enter data in the cells or you can create the data and then convert it to a table. To convert text to a table, type the text and separate it with a separator character such as a comma or tab. The separator character identifies where you want text divided into columns. To convert text, select the text, click the Insert tab, click the Table button in the Tables group, and then click *Convert Text to Table* at the drop-down list.

You can convert a table to text by positioning the insertion point in any cell of the table, clicking the Table Tools Layout tab, and then clicking the Convert to Text button in the Data group. At the Convert Table to Text dialog box, specify the desired separator and then click OK.

Project 2d **Converting Text to a Table** Part 4 of 5

1. With **WL1-C7-P2-TSPTables.docx** open, press Ctrl + End to move the insertion point to the end of the document and then press the Enter key until the insertion point is positioned approximately a double space below the bottom table.
2. Insert the document named **TSPExecs.docx** into the current document.
3. Convert the text to a table by completing the following steps:
   a. Select the text you just inserted.
   b. Make sure the Insert tab is active.
   c. Click the Table button in the Tables group and then click *Convert Text to Table* at the drop-down list.
   d. At the Convert Text to Table dialog box, type **2** in the *Number of columns* text box.
   e. Click the *AutoFit to contents* option in the *AutoFit behavior* section.
   f. Click the *Commas* option in the *Separate text at* section.
   g. Click OK.
4. Select and merge the cells in the top row (the row containing the title *TRI-STATE PRODUCTS*) and then change the alignment to Align Center.
5. Apply the Medium Shading 1 - Accent 2 style (third style from the left in the fourth row of the *Built-In* section) and remove the check mark from the *First Column* check box in the Table Style Options group in the Table Tools Design tab.
6. Drag the table so it is centered and positioned below the table above.
7. Apply the Medium Shading 1 - Accent 2 style to the top table. Increase the width of the columns so the text *TRI-STATE PRODUCTS* is visible and the text in the second and third columns displays on one line.
8. Drag the table so it is centered and positioned above the middle table. Make sure the three tables fit on one page.
9. Click in the middle table and then convert the table to text by completing the following steps:
   a. Click the Table Tools Layout tab and then click the Convert to Text button in the Data group.
   b. At the Convert Table to Text dialog box, click *Tabs* and then click OK.
10. Click the Undo button to return the text to a table.
11. Save **WL1-C7-P2-TSPTables.docx**.

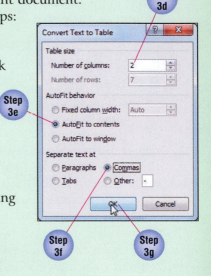

Step 3d

Step 3e

Step 3f

Step 3g

Drawing a Table ■■■■■■■■■■■■■■■■■■■■

In Project 1 you used options in the Draw Borders group in the Table Tools Design tab to draw borders around an existing table. You can also use these options to draw an entire table. To draw a table, click the Insert tab, click the Table button in the Tables group, and then click *Draw Table* at the drop-down list. This turns the mouse pointer into a pen. Drag the pen pointer in the document to create the table. The first time you release the mouse button when drawing a table, the Table Tools Design tab becomes active. Use buttons in this table to customize the table. If you make a mistake while drawing a table, click the Eraser button in the Draw Borders group (this changes the mouse pointer to an eraser) and then drag over any border lines you want to erase. You can also click the Undo button to undo your most recent action.

Eraser

Project 2e　　**Drawing and Formatting a Table**　　　　　　　Part 5 of 5

1. With **WL1-C7-P2-TSPTables.docx** open, select and then delete three rows in the middle table from the row that begins with the name *Lee, Yong* through the row that begins with the name *Schaffer, Mitchell*.
2. Move the insertion point to the end of the document (outside of any table) and then press the Enter key.
3. Click the Insert tab, click the Table button, and then click the *Draw Table* option at the drop-down list. (This turns the insertion point into a pen.)
4. Using the mouse, drag in the document (below the bottom table) to create the table shown at the right. If you make a mistake, click the Undo button. You can also click the Erase button and drag over a border line to erase it. Click the Draw Table button to turn it off.

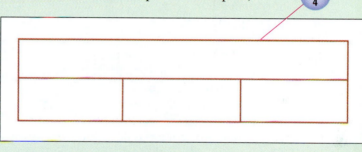

Step 4

5. After drawing the table, type Tri-State Products in the top cell, Washington Division in the cell at the left, Oregon Division in the middle bottom cell, and California Division in the cell at the right.
6. Apply the Light Grid - Accent 2 style to the table.
7. Select the table, change the font size to 12, turn on bold, and then center-align the text in the cells.
8. Make any adjustments needed to border lines so text displays on one line in each cell.
9. Drag the table so it is centered and positioned below the bottom table.
10. Save, print, and then close **WL1-C7-P2-TSPTables.docx**.

Project 3　　**Sort and Calculate Sales Data**　　　　　　　**2 Parts**

You will sort data in tables on Tri-State Products sales and then insert formulas to calculate total sales, average sales, and top sales.

Sorting Text in a Table ■■■■■■■■■■■■■■■

Sort Text in Tables
1. Select desired rows in table.
2. Click Sort button in Table Tools Layout tab.
3. Specify the column containing text to sort.
4. Click OK.

With the Sort button in the Data group in the Table Tools Layout tab, you can sort text in selected cells in a table in ascending alphabetic or numeric order. To sort text, select the desired rows in the table and then click the Sort button in the Data group. At the Sort dialog box, specify the column containing the text on which you want to sort, and then click OK.

Sort

Project 3a   **Sorting Text in a Table**   **Part 1 of 2**

1. Open **TSPSalesTables.docx** and then save the document with Save As and name it **WL1-C7-P3-TSPSalesTables**.
2. Sort text in the top table by completing the following steps:
   a. Select all of the rows containing names (from *Novak, Diana* through *Sogura, Jeffrey*).
   b. Click Table Tools Layout tab.
   c. Click the Sort button in the Data group.
   d. At the Sort dialog box, click OK. (This sorts the last names in the first column in alphabetical order.)

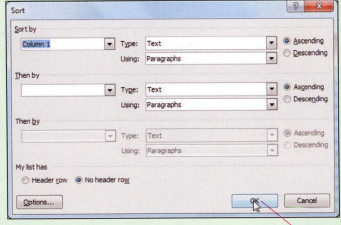

Step 2d

3. After looking at the table, you decide to sort by 2010 Sales. To do this, complete the following steps:
   a. With the rows still selected, click the Sort button in the Data group.
   b. At the Sort dialog box, click the down-pointing arrow at the right side of the *Sort by* option box and then click *Column 2* at the drop-down list.
   c. Click OK.
   d. Deselect the rows.
4. Save **WL1-C7-P3-TSPSalesTables.docx**.

Performing Calculations in a Table ■■■■■■■■■■■■■

Formula

You can use the Formula button in the Data group in the Table Tools Layout tab to insert formulas that calculate data in a table. Numbers in cells in a table can be added, subtracted, multiplied, and divided. In addition, you can calculate averages, percentages, and minimum and maximum values. You can calculate data in a Word table, but for complex calculations use an Excel worksheet.

To perform a calculation on data in a table, position the insertion point in the cell where you want the result of the calculation inserted and then click the Formula button in the Data group in the Table Tools Layout tab. This displays the Formula dialog box shown in Figure 7.10. At this dialog box, accept the default formula that displays in the *Formula* text box or type the desired calculation, and then click OK.

Figure 7.10 Formula Dialog Box

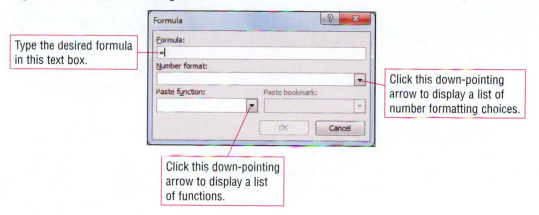

Type the desired formula in this text box.

Click this down-pointing arrow to display a list of number formatting choices.

Click this down-pointing arrow to display a list of functions.

You can use four basic operators when writing a formula including the plus sign (+) for addition, the minus sign (hyphen) for subtraction, the asterisk (*) for multiplication, and the forward slash (/) for division. If a calculation contains two or more operators, Word calculates from left to right. If you want to change the order of calculation, use parentheses around the part of the calculation to be performed first.

In the default formula, the **SUM** part of the formula is called a *function*. Word provides other functions you can use to write a formula. These functions are available with the *Paste function* option in the Formula dialog box. For example, you can use the AVERAGE function to average numbers in cells.

Specify the numbering format with the *Number format* option at the Formula dialog box. For example, if you are calculating money amounts, you can specify that the calculated numbers display with no numbers or two numbers following the decimal point.

Project 3b   **Inserting Formulas**   **Part 2 of 2**

1. With **WL1-C7-P3-TSPSalesTables.docx** open, insert a formula by completing the following steps:

   a. Click in cell B9 (the empty cell located immediately below the cell containing the amount *$623,214*).
   b. Click the Table Tools Layout tab.
   c. Click the Formula button in the Data group.
   d. At the Formula dialog box, make sure *=SUM(ABOVE)* displays in the *Formula* option box.
   e. Click the down-pointing arrow at the right side of the *Number format* option box and then click *#,##0* at the drop-down list (top option in the list).
   f. Click OK to close the Formula dialog box.
   g. At the table, type a dollar sign ($) before the number just inserted in cell B9.

   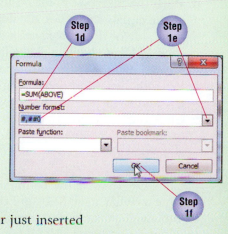

2. Complete steps similar to those in Steps 1c through 1g to insert a formula in cell C9 (the empty cell located immediately below the cell containing the amount *$635,099*).

3. Complete steps similar to those in Steps 1c through 1g to insert in the bottom table formulas that calculate totals. Insert formulas in the cells in the *Total* row and *Total* column. When inserting formulas in cells F3 through F6, you will need to change the formula to =*SUM(LEFT)*.

4. Insert a formula that calculates the average of amounts by completing the following steps:
   a. Click in cell B10 in the top table. (Cell B10 is the empty cell immediately right of the cell containing the word *Average*.)
   b. Click the Formula button in the Data group.
   c. At the Formula dialog box, delete the formula in the *Formula* text box *except* the equals sign.
   d. With the insertion point positioned immediately right of the equals sign, click the down-pointing arrow at the right side of the *Paste function* option box and then click *AVERAGE* at the drop-down list.
   e. With the insertion point positioned between the left and right parentheses, type **B2:B8**. (When typing cell designations in a formula, you can type either uppercase or lowercase letters.)

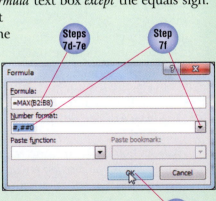

   f. Click the down-pointing arrow at the right side of the *Number format* option box and then click *#,##0* at the drop-down list (top option in the list).
   g. Click OK to close the Formula dialog box.
   h. Type a dollar sign (**$**) before the number just inserted in cell B10.

5. Complete steps similar to those in Steps 4b through 4h to insert a formula in cell C10 in the top table that calculates the average of cells C2 through C8.

6. Complete steps similar to those in Steps 4b through 4h to insert a formula in cell B7 in the bottom table that calculates the average of cells B2 through B5. Complete similar steps to insert in cell C7 the average of cells C2 through C5; insert in cell D7 the average of cells D2 through D5; insert in cell E7 the average of cells E2 through E5; and insert in cell F7 the average of cells F2 through F5.

7. Insert a formula that calculates the maximum number by completing the following steps:
   a. Click in cell B11 in the top table. (Cell B11 is the empty cell immediately right of the cell containing the words *Top Sales*.)
   b. Click the Formula button in the Data group.
   c. At the Formula dialog box, delete the formula in the *Formula* text box *except* the equals sign.
   d. With the insertion point positioned immediately right of the equals sign, click the down-pointing arrow at the right side of the *Paste function* option box and then click *MAX* at the drop-down list. (You will need to scroll down the list to display the *MAX* option.)
   e. With the insertion point positioned between the left and right parentheses, type **B2:B8**.
   f. Click the down-pointing arrow at the right side of the *Number format* option box and then click *#,##0* at the drop-down list (top option in the list).
   g. Click OK to close the Formula dialog box.
   h. Type a dollar sign (**$**) before the number just inserted in cell B11.

8. Complete steps similar to those in Steps 7b through 7h to insert the maximum number in cell C11.

9. Apply formatting to each table to enhance the visual appeal of the tables.

10. Save, print, and then close **WL1-C7-P3-TSPSalesTables.docx**.

Project 4 — Prepare and Format a Diagram

2 Parts

You will prepare a process diagram identifying steps in the production process and then apply formatting to enhance the diagram.

Creating SmartArt

With Word's SmartArt feature you can insert diagrams and organizational charts in a document. SmartArt offers a variety of predesigned diagrams and organizational charts that are available at the Choose a SmartArt Graphic dialog box shown in Figure 7.11. At this dialog box, *All* is selected in the left panel and all available predesigned diagrams display in the middle panel.

HINT
Use SmartArt to communicate your message and ideas in a visual manner.

SmartArt

Figure 7.11 Choose a SmartArt Graphic Dialog Box

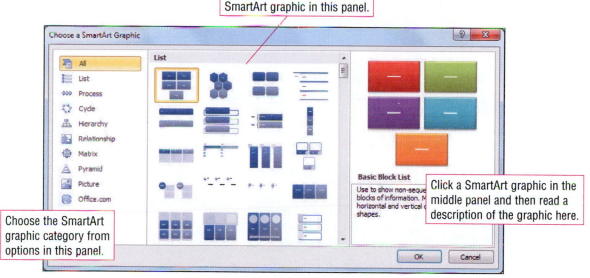

Double-click the desired SmartArt graphic in this panel.

Click a SmartArt graphic in the middle panel and then read a description of the graphic here.

Choose the SmartArt graphic category from options in this panel.

Inserting and Formatting a SmartArt Diagram

Predesigned diagrams display in the middle panel of the Choose a SmartArt Graphic dialog box. Use the scroll bar at the right side of the middle panel to scroll down the list of diagram choices. Click a diagram in the middle panel and the name of the diagram displays in the right panel along with a description of the diagram type. SmartArt includes diagrams for presenting a list of data; showing data processes, cycles, and relationships; and presenting data in a matrix or pyramid. Double-click a diagram in the middle panel of the dialog box and the diagram is inserted in the document.

When you double-click a diagram at the dialog box, the diagram is inserted in the document and a text pane displays at the left side of the diagram. You can type text in the diagram in the text pane or directly in the diagram. Apply design formatting to a diagram with options at the SmartArt Tools Design tab. This tab

▼ Quick Steps

Insert a SmartArt Diagram
1. Click Insert tab.
2. Click SmartArt button.
3. Double-click desired diagram.

HINT
Limit the number of shapes and the amount of text to key points.

is active when the diagram is inserted in the document. With options and buttons in this tab you add objects, change the diagram layout, apply a style to the diagram, and reset the diagram back to the original formatting.

Apply formatting to a diagram with options at the SmartArt Tools Format tab. With options and buttons in this tab you can change the size and shape of objects in the diagram; apply shape styles and WordArt styles; change the shape fill, outline, and effects; and arrange and size the diagram.

Project 4a **Inserting and Formatting a Diagram** **Part 1 of 2**

1. At a blank document, insert the diagram shown in Figure 7.12 by completing the following steps:
   a. Click the Insert tab.
   b. Click the SmartArt button in the Illustrations group.
   c. At the Choose a SmartArt Graphic dialog box, click *Process* in the left panel and then double-click the *Alternating Flow* diagram (see image at the right).

   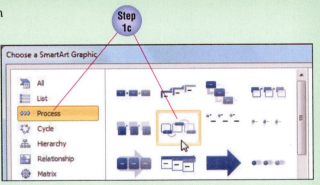

   d. If a *Type your text here* text pane does not display at the left side of the diagram, click the Text Pane button in the Create Graphic group to display the pane.
   e. With the insertion point positioned after the top bullet in the *Type your text here* text pane, type **Design**.
   f. Click *[Text]* that displays below *Design* and then type **Mock-up**.
   g. Continue clicking occurrences of *[Text]* and typing text so the text pane displays as shown at the right.
   h. Close the text pane by clicking the Close button (contains an X) that displays in the upper right corner of the pane. (You can also click the Text Pane button in the Create Graphic group.)

   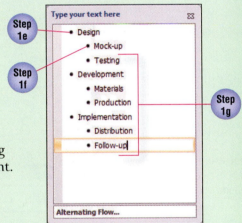

2. Change the diagram colors by clicking the Change Colors button in the SmartArt Styles group and then clicking the first option in the *Colorful* section (*Colorful - Accent Colors*).

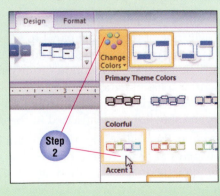

3. Apply a style by clicking the More button that displays at the right side of the thumbnails in the SmartArt Styles group and then clicking the second option from the left in the top row of the 3-D section (*Inset*).

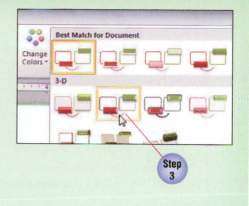

Step 3

4. Copy the diagram and then change the layout by completing the following steps:
   a. Click inside the diagram border but outside of any shapes.
   b. Click the Home tab and then click the Copy button in the Clipboard group.
   c. Press Ctrl + End, press the Enter key once, and then press Ctrl + Enter to insert a page break.
   d. Click the Paste button in the Clipboard group.
   e. Click the bottom diagram in the document.
   f. Click the SmartArt Tools Design tab.
   g. Click the More button that displays at the right side of the thumbnails in the Layouts group and then click the Continuous Block Process layout (see image at the right).
   h. Click outside the diagram to deselect it.

Step 4g **Step 4f**

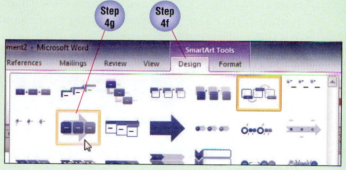

5. Save the document and name it **WL1-C7-P4-Diagrams**.

Figure 7.12 Project 4a

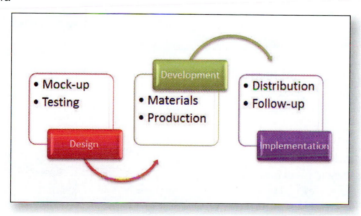

Arranging and Moving a SmartArt Diagram

Before moving a SmartArt diagram, you must select a text wrapping style. Select a text wrapping style with the Arrange button in the SmartArt Tools Format tab. Click the Position button, and then click the desired position at the drop-down gallery. You can also choose a text wrapping style by clicking the Wrap Text button

Position

Text Wrap

and then clicking the desired wrapping style at the drop-down list. Move the diagram by positioning the arrow pointer on the diagram border until the pointer turns into a four-headed arrow, holding down the left mouse button, and then dragging the diagram to the desired location. Nudge selected shape(s) with the up, down, left, or right arrow keys on the keyboard.

Project 4b   **Formatting Diagrams**   Part 2 of 2

1. With **WL1-C7-P4-Diagrams.docx** open, format shapes by completing the following steps:
   a. Click the diagram on the first page to select it (light gray border surrounds the diagram).
   b. Click the SmartArt Tools Format tab.
   c. In the diagram, click the rectangle shape containing the word *Design*.
   d. Hold down the Shift key and then click the shape containing the word *Development*.
   e. With the Shift key still down, click the shape containing the word *Implementation*. (All three shapes should now be selected.)
   f. Click the Change Shape button in the Shapes group.
   g. Click the seventh shape from the left in the second row of the *Block Arrows* section (the Pentagon shape).
   h. With the shapes still selected, click the Larger button in the Shapes group.
   i. With the shapes still selected, click the Shape Outline button arrow in the Shape Styles group and then click the red color *Red, Accent 2*.
   j. Click inside the diagram border but outside any shape. (This deselects the shapes but keeps the diagram selected.)

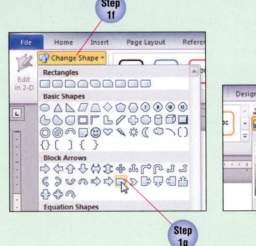

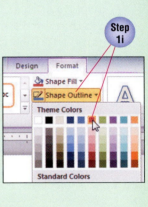

2. Change the size of the diagram by completing the following steps:
   a. Click the Size button located at the right side of the SmartArt Tools Format tab.
   b. Click in the *Height* measurement box, type **4**, and then press Enter.
3. Position the diagram by completing the following steps:
   a. Click the Position button in the Arrange group in the SmartArt Tools Format tab.
   b. Click the middle option in the second row of the *With Text Wrapping* section (the *Position in Middle Center with Square Text Wrapping* option).

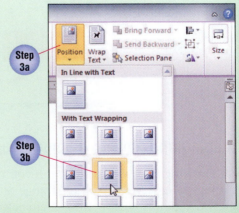

4. Format the bottom diagram by completing the following steps:
   a. Press Ctrl + End to move to the end of the document and then click in the bottom diagram to select it.
   b. Hold down the Shift key and then click each of the three shapes.
   c. Click the More button at the right side of the style thumbnail in the WordArt Styles group in the SmartArt Tools Format tab.
   d. Click the last WordArt style in the lower right corner of the drop-down gallery (*Fill - Blue, Accent 1, Metal Bevel, Reflection*).
   e. Click the Text Outline button arrow in the WordArt Styles group and then click the light blue color in the *Standard Colors* section (the seventh color from the left).
   f. Click the Text Effects button in the WordArt Styles group, point to *Glow* at the drop-down list, and then click the last option in the top row (*Orange, 5 pt glow, Accent color 6*).
   g. Click inside the diagram border but outside any shape.
5. Arrange the diagram by clicking the Position button in the Arrange group and then clicking the middle option in the second row of the *With Text Wrapping* section (the *Position in Middle Center with Square Text Wrapping* option).
6. Save, print, and then close **WL1-C7-P4-Diagrams.docx**.

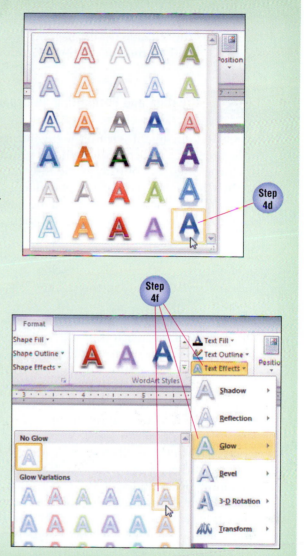

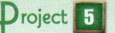 roject **5** **Prepare and Format a Company Organizational Chart** 1 Part

You will prepare an organizational chart for a company and then apply formatting to enhance the visual appeal of the organizational chart.

Creating an Organizational Chart with SmartArt

If you need to visually illustrate hierarchical data, consider creating an organizational chart with a SmartArt option. To display organizational chart SmartArt options, click the Insert tab and then click the SmartArt button in the Illustrations group. At the Choose a SmartArt Graphic dialog box, click *Hierarchy* in the left panel. Organizational chart options display in the middle panel of the dialog box. Double-click the desired organizational chart and the chart is inserted

▼ **Quick Steps**

Insert an Organizational Chart
1. Click Insert tab.
2. Click SmartArt button.
3. Click *Hierarchy*.
4. Double-click desired organizational chart.

in the document. Type text in a diagram by selecting the shape and then typing text in the shape or you can type text in the *Type your text here* window that displays at the left side of the diagram. Format a SmartArt organizational chart with options and buttons in the SmartArt Tools Design tab and the SmartArt Tools Format tab.

Project 5 Creating and Formatting an Organizational Chart   Part 1 of 1

1. At a blank document, create the organizational chart shown in Figure 7.13. To begin, click the Insert tab.
2. Click the SmartArt button in the Illustrations group.
3. At the Choose a SmartArt Graphic dialog box, click *Hierarchy* in the left panel of the dialog box and then double-click the first option in the middle panel, *Organization Chart*.

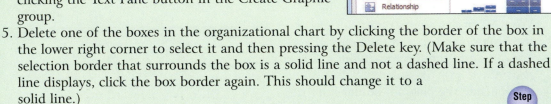

4. If a *Type your text here* window displays at the left side of the organizational chart, close the pane by clicking the Text Pane button in the Create Graphic group.
5. Delete one of the boxes in the organizational chart by clicking the border of the box in the lower right corner to select it and then pressing the Delete key. (Make sure that the selection border that surrounds the box is a solid line and not a dashed line. If a dashed line displays, click the box border again. This should change it to a solid line.)
6. With the bottom right box selected, click the Add Shape button arrow in the Create Graphic group and then click the *Add Shape Below* option.
7. Click *[Text]* in the top box, type **Blaine Willis**, press Shift + Enter, and then type **President**. Click in each of the remaining boxes and type the text as shown in Figure 7.13. (Press Shift + Enter after typing the name.)
8. Click the More button located at the right side of the style thumbnails in the SmartArt Styles group and then click the *Inset* style in the *3-D* section (second option from the left in the top row of the *3-D* section).
9. Click the Change Colors button in the SmartArt Styles group and then click the *Colorful Range - Accent Colors 4 to 5* in the *Colorful* section (fourth option from the left in the *Colorful* row).
10. Click the SmartArt Tools Format tab.
11. Click the tab (displays with a right-pointing and a left-pointing triangle) that displays at the left side of the diagram border. (This displays the *Type your text here* window.)
12. Using the mouse, select the text that displays in the *Type your text here* window.

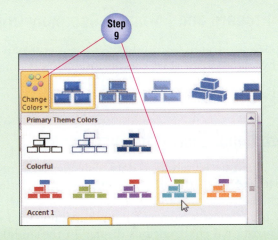

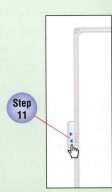

13. Click the Change Shape button in the Shapes group and then click the *Round Same Side Corner Rectangle* option (second option from the *right* in the top row).
14. Click the Shape Outline button arrow in the Shape Styles group and then click the dark blue color (second color from the *right* in the *Standard Colors* section).
15. Close the *Type your text here* window by clicking the Close button (marked with an X) located in the upper right corner of the window.
16. Click inside the organizational chart border but outside any shape.
17. Click the Size button located at the right side of the ribbon in the SmartArt Tools Format tab, click in the *Height* measurement box, and type 4. Click in the *Width* measurement box, type 6.5, and then press Enter.
18. Click outside the chart to deselect it.
19. Save the document and name it **WL1-C7-P5-OrgChart**.
20. Print and then close the document.

Figure 7.13 Project 5

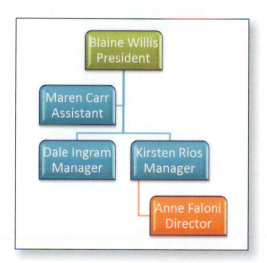

Chapter Summary

- Use the Tables feature to create columns and rows of information. Create a table with the Table button in the Tables group in the Insert tab or with options at the Insert Table dialog box.

- A cell is the intersection between a row and a column. The lines that form the cells of the table are called gridlines.

- Move the insertion point to cells in a document using the mouse by clicking in the desired cell or use the keyboard commands shown in Table 7.1.

- Change the table design with options and buttons in the Table Tools Design tab.

- Refer to Table 7.2 for a list of mouse commands for selecting specific cells in a table and Table 7.3 for a list of keyboard commands for selecting specific cells in a table.

- Change the layout of a table with options and buttons in the Table Tools Layout tab.

- You can select a table, column, row, or cell using the Select button in the Table group in the Table Tools Layout tab.

- Turn on and off the display of gridlines by clicking the Table Tools Layout tab and then clicking the View Gridlines button in the Table group.

- Insert and delete columns and rows with buttons in the Rows & Columns group in the Table Tools Layout tab.

- Merge selected cells with the Merge Cells button and split cells with the Split Cells button, both located in the Merge group in the Table Tools Layout tab.

- Change column width and row height using the height and width measurement boxes in the Cell Size group in the Table Tools Layout tab; by dragging move table column markers on the horizontal ruler, adjust table row markers on the vertical ruler, or gridlines in the table; or with the AutoFit button in the Cell Size group.

- Change alignment of text in cells with buttons in the Alignment group in the Table Tools Layout tab.

- If a table spans two pages, you can insert a header row at the beginning of the rows that extend to the next page. To do this, click in the header row, or select the desired header rows, and then click the Repeat Header Rows button in the Data group in the Table Tools Layout tab.

- Quick Tables are predesigned tables you can insert in a document by clicking the Insert tab, clicking the Table button, pointing to *Quick Tables*, and then clicking the desired table at the side menu.

- Change cell margins with options in the Table Options dialog box.

- Change text direction in a cell with the Text Direction button in the Alignment group.

- Change the table alignment at the Table Properties dialog box with the Table tab selected.

- You can use the resize handle to change the size of the table and the table move handle to move the table.

- Convert text to a table with the *Convert Text to Table* option at the Table button drop-down list. Convert a table to text with the Convert to Text button in the Data group in the Table Tools Layout tab.

- Draw a table in a document by clicking the Insert tab, clicking the Table button, and then clicking *Draw Table*. Using the mouse, drag in the document to create the table.

- Sort selected rows in a table with the Sort button in the Data group.

- Perform calculations on data in a table by clicking the Formula button in the Data group in the Table Tools Layout tab and then specifying the formula and number format at the Formula dialog box.

- Use the SmartArt feature to insert predesigned diagrams and organizational charts in a document. Click the SmartArt button in the Insert tab to display the Choose a SmartArt Graphic dialog box.

- Format a SmartArt diagram or organizational chart with options and buttons in the SmartArt Tools Design tab and the SmartArt Tools Format tab.

- To move a SmartArt diagram, first choose a position or a text wrapping style with the Arrange button in the SmartArt Tools Format tab.

Commands Review

FEATURE	RIBBON TAB, GROUP	BUTTON	OPTION
Table	Insert, Tables		
Insert Table dialog box	Insert, Tables		Insert Table
Draw table	Insert, Tables		Draw Table
View gridlines	Table Tools Layout, Table		
Insert column left	Table Tools Layout, Rows & Columns		
Insert column right	Table Tools Layout, Rows & Columns		
Insert row above	Table Tools Layout, Rows & Columns		
Insert row below	Table Tools Layout, Rows & Columns		
Delete table	Table Tools Layout, Rows & Columns		Delete Table
Delete row	Table Tools Layout, Rows & Columns		Delete Rows
Delete column	Table Tools Layout, Rows & Columns		Delete Columns
Merge cells	Table Tools Layout, Merge		
Split cells dialog box	Table Tools Layout, Merge		
AutoFit table contents	Table Tools Layout, Cell Size		
Cell alignment	Table Tools Layout, Alignment		
Repeat header row	Table Tools Layout, Data		
Insert Quick Table	Insert, Tables		Quick Tables
Table Options dialog box	Table Tools Layout, Alignment		
Text direction	Table Tools Layout, Alignment		
Convert text to table	Insert, Tables		Convert Text to Table
Convert table to text	Table Tools Layout, Data		
Sort text in table	Table Tools Layout, Data		
Formula dialog box	Table Tools Layout, Data		
Choose a SmartArt Graphic dialog box	Insert, Illustrations		

Concepts Check Test Your Knowledge

Completion: In the space provided at the right, indicate the correct term, command, or number.

1. The Table button is located in this tab. _____

2. This is another name for the lines that form the cells of the table. _____

3. Use this keyboard shortcut to move the insertion point to the previous cell. _____

4. Use this keyboard shortcut to move the insertion point to a tab within a cell. _____

5. This tab contains table styles you can apply to a table. _____

6. Click this button in the Table Tools Layout tab to insert a column at the left side of the column containing the insertion point. _____

7. Insert and delete columns and rows with buttons in this group in the Table Tools Layout tab. _____

8. One method for changing column width is dragging this on the horizontal ruler. _____

9. Use this button in the Cell Size group to make the column widths in a table automatically fit the contents. _____

10. Change the table alignment at this dialog box with the Table tab selected. _____

11. Hover the mouse pointer over a table and this displays in the lower right corner of the table. _____

12. Position the mouse pointer in a table and this displays in the upper left corner. _____

13. Display the Formula dialog box by clicking the Formula button in this group in the Table Tools Layout tab. _____

14. A variety of predesigned diagrams and organizational charts are available at this dialog box. _____

15. The SmartArt button is located in this tab. _____

16. If you need to visually illustrate hierarchical data, consider creating this with the SmartArt feature. _____

Skills Check   Assess Your Performance

Assessment

1   CREATE AND FORMAT A PROPERTY REPLACEMENT COSTS TABLE

1. At a blank document, create the table shown in Figure 7.14 with the following specifications:
   a. Create a table with two columns and eight rows.
   b. Merge the cells in the top row.
   c. Type the text in the cells as shown in Figure 7.14.
   d. Right-align the cells containing the money amounts as well as the blank line below the last amount (cells B2 through B8).
   e. Automatically fit the contents of the cells.
   f. Apply the *Light List - Accent 4* table style.
   g. Remove the check mark from the *First Column* check box.
   h. Draw a green (*Olive Green, Accent 3, Darker 25%*) 1½ pt border around the table.
   i. Change the font size to 14 for the text in cell A1 and change the alignment to Align Center.
   j. Use the resize handle located in the lower right corner of the table and increase the width and height of the table by approximately one inch.
2. Click in the *Accounts receivable* cell and insert a row below. Type **Equipment** in the new cell at the left and type **$83,560** in the new cell at the right.
3. Insert a formula in cell B9 that sums the amounts in cell B2 through B8. (Insert a dollar sign before the amount in cell B9.)
4. Save the document and name it **WL1-C7-A1-CostsTable**.
5. Print and then close **WL1-C7-A1-CostsTable.docx**.

Figure 7.14 Assessment 1

PROPERTY Replacement Costs	
Business personal property	$1,367,340
Earnings and expenses	$945,235
Domestic and foreign transit	$123,400
Accounts receivable	$95,460
Legal liability	$75,415
Computer coverage	$53,098
Total	

Assessment

2 FORMAT A TABLE CONTAINING TRANSPORTATION SERVICE INFORMATION

1. Open **ServicesTable.docx** and then save the document with Save As and name it **WL1-C7-A2-ServicesTable**.
2. Format the table so it appears as shown in Figure 7.15.
3. Position the table in the middle of the page.
4. Save, print, and then close **WL1-C7-A2-ServicesTable.docx**.

Figure 7.15 Assessment 2

Metro Area Transportation Services	Service	Telephone
	Langley City Transit	
	Subway and bus information	(507) 555-3049
	Service status hotline	(507) 555-4123
	Travel information	(507) 555-4993
	Valley Rail Road	
	Railway information	(202) 555-2300
	Status hotline	(202) 555-2343
	Travel information	(202) 555-2132
	Mainline Bus	
	Bus routes	(507) 555-6530
	Emergency hotline	(507) 555-6798
	Travel information	(507) 555-7542
	Village Travel Card	
	Village office	(507) 555-1232
	Card inquiries	(507) 555-1930

Assessment

3 CREATE AND FORMAT A COMPANY DIAGRAM

1. At a blank document, create the SmartArt diagram shown in Figure 7.16 with the following specifications:
   a. Use the Titled Matrix diagram.
   b. Apply the *Colorful - Accent Colors SmartArt* style.
   c. Type all of the text shown in Figure 7.16.
   d. Select all of the text and then apply the *Fill - Red, Accent 2, Matte Bevel WordArt* style.
2. Save the document and name it **WL1-C7-A3-SDCDiagram**.
3. Print and then close **WL1-C7-A3-SDCDiagram.docx**.

Figure 7.16 Assessment 3

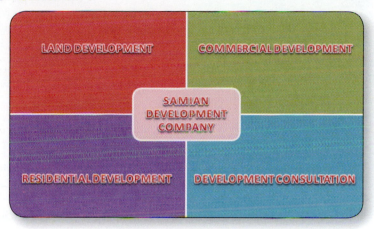

Assessment

4 CREATE AND FORMAT A COMPANY ORGANIZATIONAL CHART

1. At a blank document, create the organizational chart shown in Figure 7.17 with the following specifications:
   a. Use the Hierarchy chart.
   b. Select the top text box and insert a shape above.
   c. Select the top right text box and then add a shape below.
   d. Type the text shown in the organizational chart in Figure 7.17.
   e. Apply the *Colorful Range - Accent Colors 2 to 3* option.
   f. Increase the height to 4.5" and the width to 6.5".
   g. Position the organizational chart in the middle of the page.
2. Save the document and name it **WL1-C7-A4-OrgChart**.
3. Print and then close **WL1-C7-A4-OrgChart.docx**.

Figure 7.17 Assessment 4

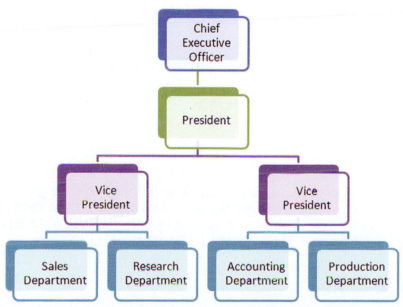

5 INSERT FORMULAS IN A TABLE

1. In this chapter, you learned how to insert formulas in a table. Experiment with writing formulas (consider using the Help feature or other reference) and then open **FinAnalysis.docx**. Save the document with Save As and name it **WL1-C7-A5-FinAnalysis**.
2. Format the table so it appears as shown in Figure 7.18.
3. Insert a formula in cell B13 that sums the amounts in cells B6 through B12. Complete similar steps to insert a formula in cell C13, D13, and E13.
4. Insert a formula in cell B14 that subtracts the amount in B13 from the amount in B4. *Hint: The formula should look like this: =(B4-B13)*. Complete similar steps to insert a formula in cells C14, D14, and E14.
5. Save, print, and then close **WL1-C7-A5-FinAnalysis.docx**.

Figure 7.18 Assessment 5

TRI-STATE PRODUCTS

Financial Analysis

	2009	2010	2011	2012
Revenue	$1,450,348	$1,538,239	$1,634,235	$1,523,455
Expenses				
Facilities	$250,220	$323,780	$312,485	$322,655
Materials	$93,235	$102,390	$87,340	$115,320
Payroll	$354,390	$374,280	$380,120	$365,120
Benefits	$32,340	$35,039	$37,345	$36,545
Marketing	$29,575	$28,350	$30,310	$31,800
Transportation	$4,492	$5,489	$5,129	$6,349
Miscellaneous	$4,075	$3,976	$4,788	$5,120
Total				
Net Revenue				

Visual Benchmark Demonstrate Your Proficiency

1 CREATE A COVER LETTER CONTAINING A TABLE

1. At a blank document, create the document shown in Figure 7.19. Create and format the table as shown in the figure. *Hint: Apply the* **Light Grid - Accent 5** *table style*.
2. Save the completed document and name it **WL1-C7-VB1-CoverLtr**.
3. Print and then close **WL1-C7-VB1-CoverLtr.docx**.

Figure 7.19 Visual Benchmark 1

10234 Larkspur Drive
Cheyenne, WY 82002
July 15, 2012

Dr. Theresa Solberg
Rocky Mountain News
100 Second Avenue
Cheyenne, WY 82001

Dear Dr. Solberg:

Your advertised opening for a corporate communications staff writer describes interesting challenges. As you can see from the table below, my skills and experience are excellent matches for the position.

QUALIFICATIONS AND SKILLS	
Your Requirements	**My Experience, Skills, and Value Offered**
Two years of business writing experience	Four years of experience creating diverse business messages, from corporate communications to feature articles and radio broadcast material.
Ability to complete projects on deadline	Proven project coordination skills and tight deadline focus. My current role as producer of a daily three-hour talk-radio program requires planning, coordination, and execution of many detailed tasks, always in the face of inflexible deadlines.
Oral presentation skills	Unusually broad experience, including high-profile roles as an on-air radio presence and "the voice" for an on-hold telephone message company.
Relevant education (BA or BS)	BA in Mass Communications; one year post-graduate study in Multimedia Communications.

As you will note from the enclosed résumé, my experience encompasses corporate, print media, and multimedia environments. I offer a diverse and proven skill set that can help your company create and deliver its message to various audiences to build image, market presence, and revenue. I look forward to meeting with you to discuss the value I can offer your company.

Sincerely,

Marcus Tolliver

Enclosure: Résumé

2 CREATE AND FORMAT A SMARTART DIAGRAM

1. At a blank document, create the document shown in Figure 7.20. Create and format the SmartArt diagram as shown in the figure. *Hint: Use the* **Step Up Process** *diagram*.
2. Save the completed document and name it **WL1-C7-VB2-SalesDiagram**.
3. Print and then close **WL1-C7-VB2-SalesDiagram.docx**.

Figure 7.20 Visual Benchmark 2

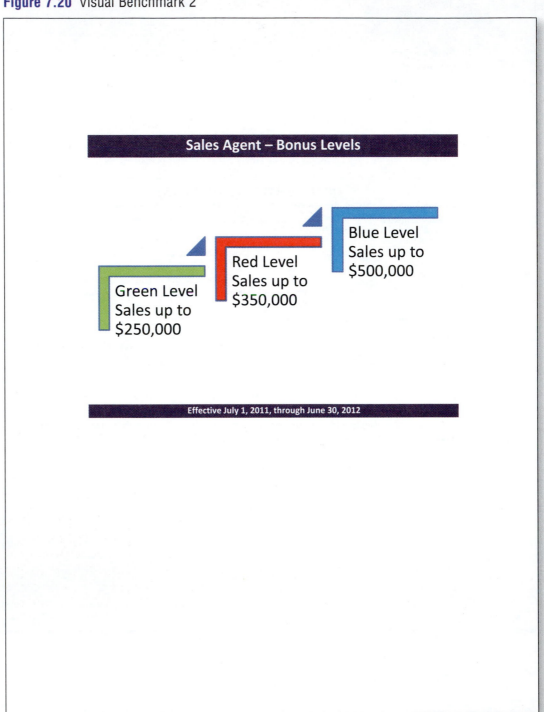

Case Study   Apply Your Skills

Part 1

You have recently been hired as an accounting clerk for a landscaping business, Landmark Landscaping, which has two small offices in your city. The accounting clerk prior to you kept track of monthly sales using Word, and the manager would prefer that you continue using that application. Open the file named **LLMoSales.docx** and then save the document with Save As and name it **WL1-C7-CS-LLMoSales**. After reviewing the information, you decide that a table would be a better way of maintaining and displaying the data. Convert the data to a table and modify its appearance so that it is easy to read and understand. Insert a total row at the bottom of the table and then insert formulas to sum the totals in the columns containing amounts. Apply formatting to the table to enhance the visual appeal. Determine a color theme for the table and then continue that same color theme when preparing other documents for Landmark Landscaping. Save, print, and then close the document.

Part 2

The president of Landmark Landscaping has asked you to prepare an organizational chart for the company that will become part of the company profile. Use a SmartArt organizational chart and create a chart with the following company titles (in the order shown below):

President		
Westside Manager		**Eastside Manager**
Landscape Architect	Landscape Director	Landscape Architect	Landscape Director
	Assistant		Assistant

Format the organizational chart to enhance the visual appeal and apply colors that match the color scheme you chose for the company in Part 1. Save the document and name it **WL1-C7-CS-LLOrgChart**. Print and then close the document.

Part 3

As part of the company profile, the president of the company would like to include a diagram that represents the services offered by the company and use the diagram as a company marketing tool. Use SmartArt to create a diagram that contains the following services: Maintenance Contracts, Planting Services, Landscape Design, and Landscape Consultation. Format the diagram to enhance the visual appeal and apply colors that match the color scheme you chose for the company in Part 1. Save the document and name it **WL1-C7-CS-LLServices**. Print and then close the document.

Part 4

The office manager has started a training document with information on using SmartArt. He has asked you to add information on keyboard shortcuts for working with shapes in a SmartArt graphic. Use the Help feature to learn about the keyboard shortcuts available for working with shapes and then create a table and insert the information in the table. Format the table to enhance the visual appeal and apply colors that match the color scheme you chose for the company in Part 1. Save the document and name it **WL1-C7-CS-SAShortcuts**. Print and then close the document.

Part 5

One of the landscape architects has asked you to prepare a table containing information on trees that need to be ordered next month. She would also like to have you include the Latin name for the trees since this is important when ordering. Create a table that contains the common name of the tree, the Latin name, the number required, and the price per tree as shown in Figure 7.21. Use the Internet (or any other resource available to you) to find the Latin name of each tree listed in Figure 7.21. Create a column in the table that multiplies the number of trees required by the price and include this formula for each tree. Format and enhance the table so it is attractive and easy to read. Save the document and name it **WL1-C7-CS-LLTrees**. Print and then close the document.

Figure 7.21 Case Study, Part 5

Douglas Fir, 15 required, $1.99 per tree
White Elm, 10 required, $2.49 per tree
Western Hemlock, 10 required, $1.89 per tree
Red Maple, 8 required, $6.99 per tree
Ponderosa Pine, 5 required, $2.69 per tree

Word

Microsoft®

CHAPTER 8

Merging Documents

PERFORMANCE OBJECTIVES

Upon successful completion of Chapter 8, you will be able to:

- **Create and merge letters, envelopes, labels, and a directory**
- **Create custom fields for a merge**
- **Edit main documents and data source files**
- **Input text during a merge**

Tutorials

8.1 Creating a Data Source File

8.2 Creating a Main Document

8.3 Creating Form Letters Using Mail Merge

8.4 Merging Envelopes

8.5 Editing a Data Source File

Word includes a Mail Merge feature you can use to create customized letters, envelopes, labels, directories, e-mail messages, and faxes. The Mail Merge feature is useful for situations where you need to send the same letter to a number of people and create an envelope for each letter. Use Mail Merge to create a main document that contains a letter, envelope, or other data and then merge the main document with a data source. In this chapter, you will use Mail Merge to create letters, envelopes, labels, and directories. Model answers for this chapter's projects appear on the following pages.

Word2010L1C8

Note: Before beginning the projects, copy to your storage medium the Word2010L1C8 subfolder from the Word2010L1 folder in the CD that accompanies this textbook and then make Word2010L1C8 the active folder.

February 23, 2012

«AddressBlock»

«GreetingLine»

McCormack Funds is lowering its expense charges beginning May 1, 2012. The reductions in expense charges mean that more of your account investment performance in the «Fund» is returned to you, «Title» «Last_Name». The reductions are worth your attention because most of our competitors' fees have gone up.

Lowering expense charges is noteworthy because before the reduction, McCormack expense deductions were already among the lowest, far below most mutual funds and variable annuity accounts with similar objectives. At the same time, services for you, our client, will continue to expand. If you would like to discuss this change, please call us at (212) 555-2277. Your financial future is our main concern at McCormack.

Sincerely,

Jodie Langstrom
Director, Financial Services

XX
WL1-C8-P1-MFMD.docx

February 23, 2012

Mr. Kenneth Porter
7645 Tenth Street
Apt. 314
New York, NY 10192

Dear Mr. Porter:

McCormack Funds is lowering its expense charges beginning May 1, 2012. The reductions in expense charges mean that more of your account investment performance in the Mutual Investment Fund is returned to you, Mr. Porter. The reductions are worth your attention because most of our competitors' fees have gone up.

Lowering expense charges is noteworthy because before the reduction, McCormack expense deductions were already among the lowest, far below most mutual funds and variable annuity accounts with similar objectives. At the same time, services for you, our client, will continue to expand. If you would like to discuss this change, please call us at (212) 555-2277. Your financial future is our main concern at McCormack.

Sincerely,

Jodie Langstrom
Director, Financial Services

XX
WL1-C8-P1-MFMD.docx

Page 1

Project 1 Merge Letters to Customers

WL1-C8-P1-MFMD.docx

February 23, 2012

Ms. Carolyn Renquist
13255 Meridian Street
New York, NY 10435

Dear Ms. Renquist:

McCormack Funds is lowering its expense charges beginning charges mean that more of your account investment perfo to you, Ms. Renquist. The reductions are worth your atter have gone up.

Lowering expense charges is noteworthy because before were already among the lowest, far below most mutual fu objectives. At the same time, services for you, our client, discuss this change, please call us at (212) 555-2277. Your McCormack.

Sincerely,

Jodie Langstrom
Director, Financial Services

XX
WL1-C8-P1-MFMD.docx

Page 2

February 23, 2012

Dr. Amil Ranna
433 South 17th
Apt. 17-D
New York, NY 10322

Dear Dr. Ranna:

McCormack Funds is lowering its expense charges beginni charges mean that more of your account investment perfe to you, Dr. Ranna. The reductions are worth your attentio gone up.

Lowering expense charges is noteworthy because before were already among the lowest, far below most mutual fu objectives. At the same time, services for you, our client, discuss this change, please call us at (212) 555-2277. Your McCormack.

Sincerely,

Jodie Langstrom
Director, Financial Services

XX
WL1-C8-P1-MFMD.docx

Page 3

February 23, 2012

Mrs. Wanda Houston
566 North 22nd Avenue
New York, NY 10634

Dear Mrs. Houston:

McCormack Funds is lowering its expense charges beginning May 1, 2012. The reductions in expense charges mean that more of your account investment performance in the Quality Care Fund is returned to you, Mrs. Houston. The reductions are worth your attention because most of our competitors' fees have gone up.

Lowering expense charges is noteworthy because before the reduction, McCormack expense deductions were already among the lowest, far below most mutual funds and variable annuity accounts with similar objectives. At the same time, services for you, our client, will continue to expand. If you would like to discuss this change, please call us at (212) 555-2277. Your financial future is our main concern at McCormack.

Sincerely,

Jodie Langstrom
Director, Financial Services

XX
WL1-C8-P1-MFMD.docx

Page 4

Project 2 Merge Envelopes

WL1-C8-P2-MFEnvs.docx

Project 3 Merge Mailing Labels

WL-C8-P3-LabelsMD.docx

Project 4 Merge a Directory

Last Name	First Name	Fund
Porter	Kenneth	Mutual Investment Fund
Renquist	Carolyn	Quality Care Fund
Ranna	Amil	Priority One Fund
Houston	Wanda	Quality Care Fund

WL1-C8-P4-Directory.docx

Project 5 Select Records and Merge Mailing Labels

Mr. Martin Saunders
231 South 41st Street
P.O. Box 3321
Baltimore, MD 20156

Ms. Amanda Perkins
9033 North Ridge Drive
Apt. #401
Baltimore, MD 20487

Ms. Anita Grenwald
580 Capital Lane
#1002-B
Baltimore, MD 20884

Mr. Steve Dutton
3490 East 145th
Apt. B
Baltimore, MD 20468

Mrs. Darlene Fernandez
12115 South 42nd
#20-G
Baltimore, MD 20376

Mrs. Kaycee Stahl
450 Washington Ave.
Baltimore, MD 20376

WL1-C8-P5-SFLabels.docx

Project 6 Edit Records in a Data Source File

Name	Home Phone	Cell Phone
Saunders, Martin	413-555-3492	410-555-1249
Delaney, Antonia	410-555-2009	413-555-3492
Perkins, Amanda	410-555-5743	410-555-0695
Hogan, Gregory	410-555-3448	410-555-9488
Grenwald, Anita	410-555-6784	413-555-1200
Childers, Jillian	410-555-3833	410-555-7522
Bellamy, Rebecca	410-555-4755	410-555-8833
Benoit, Victoria	410-555-3482	413-555-9378
Fernandez, Darlene	410-555-7833	410-555-4261
Kaszycki, Brian	410-555-3842	410-555-9944
Stahl, Kaycee	410-555-2331	413-555-2321
Davis, Jennae	410-555-5774	410-555-9435

WL1-C8-P6-Directory.docx

February 23, 2012

Mr. Kenneth Porter
7645 Tenth Street
Apt. 314
New York, NY 10192

Dear Mr. Porter:

McCormack Funds is lowering its expense charges beginning May 1, 2012. The reductions in expense charges mean that more of your account investment performance in the Mutual Investment Fund is returned to you, Mr. Porter. The reductions are worth your attention because most of our competitors' fees have gone up.

Lowering expense charges is noteworthy because before the reduction, McCormack expense deductions were already among the lowest, far below most mutual funds and variable annuity accounts with similar objectives. At the same time, services for you, our client, will continue to expand. If you would like to discuss this change, please call our service representative, Marilyn Smythe, at (646) 555-8944.

Sincerely,

Jodie Langstrom
Director, Financial Services

XX
WL1-C8-P1-MFMD.docx

Page 1

February 23, 2012

Ms. Carolyn Renquist
13255 Meridian Street
New York, NY 10435

Dear Ms. Renquist:

McCormack Funds is lowering its expense charges mean that more of your account to you, Ms. Renquist. The reductions are have gone up.

Lowering expense charges is noteworthy were already among the lowest, far below objectives. At the same time, services discuss this change, please call our se

Sincerely,

Jodie Langstrom
Director, Financial Services

XX
WL1-C8-P1-MFMD.docx

Page 2

February 23, 2012

Dr. Amil Ranna
433 South 17th
Apt. 17-D
New York, NY 10322

Dear Dr. Ranna:

McCormack Funds is lowering its expense charges mean that more of your account to you, Dr. Ranna. The reductions are gone up.

Lowering expense charges is noteworthy were already among the lowest, far below objectives. At the same time, services discuss this change, please call our se

Sincerely,

Jodie Langstrom
Director, Financial Services

XX
WL1-C8-P1-MFMD.docx

Page 3

February 23, 2012

Mrs. Wanda Houston
566 North 22nd Avenue
New York, NY 10634

Dear Mrs. Houston:

McCormack Funds is lowering its expense charges beginning May 1, 2012. The reductions in expense charges mean that more of your account investment performance in the Quality Care Fund is returned to you, Mrs. Houston. The reductions are worth your attention because most of our competitors' fees have gone up.

Lowering expense charges is noteworthy because before the reduction, McCormack expense deductions were already among the lowest, far below most mutual funds and variable annuity accounts with similar objectives. At the same time, services for you, our client, will continue to expand. If you would like to discuss this change, please call our service representative, Thomas Rivers, at (646) 555-0793.

Sincerely,

Jodie Langstrom
Director, Financial Services

XX
WL1-C8-P1-MFMD.docx

Page 4

Project 7 Add Fill-in Fields to a Main Document
WL1-C8-P7-MFMD.docx

January 22, 2013

Mr. Martin Saunders
231 South 41st Street
P.O. Box 3321
Baltimore, MD 20156

Dear Mr. Saunders:

Last year, a law went into effect that changes the maximum amounts that may be contributed to defined contribution pension and tax-deferred annuity plans, such as those using Sorenson Funds annuities. Generally, the changes slow down the rate at which the maximums will increase in the future. A likely result is that more people will reach the maximum and, if they wish to save more for their retirement, they will have to use after-tax savings instruments.

The amount of money you can voluntarily contribute to your fund was expected to rise above the current maximum. The amendments will delay any cost-of-living adjustments, and the limit will probably not go up for several years. The changes in the law will have an effect on your next annuity statement. If you want to increase or decrease the amount you contribute to your fund, please let us know.

Sincerely,

Jennifer Tann
Director of Financial Services

XX
SFLtrMD.docx

6250 Aurora Boulevard ✦ Baltimore, MD 20372 ✦ 1-888-555-0344

Page 1

January 22, 2013

Mrs. Antonia Delaney
11220 East Madison
Rosedale, MD 21237

Dear Mrs. Delaney:

Last year, a law went into effect that changes the maximum amounts that may be contributed to defined contribution pension and tax-deferred annuity plans, such as those using Sorenson Funds annuities. Generally, the changes slow down the rate at which the maximums will increase in the future. A likely result is that more people will reach the maximum and, if they wish to save more for their retirement, they will have to use after-tax savings instruments.

The amount of money you can voluntarily contribute to your fund was expected to rise above the current maximum. The amendments will delay any cost-of-living adjustments, and the limit will probably not go up for several years. The changes in the law will have an effect on your next annuity statement. If you want to increase or decrease the amount you contribute to your fund, please let us know.

Sincerely,

Jennifer Tann
Director of Financial Services

XX
SFLtrMD.docx

6250 Aurora Boulevard ✦ Baltimore, MD 20372 ✦ 1-888-555-0344

Page 2

Project 8 Use Mail Merge Wizard
WL1-C8-P8-SFLtrs.docx

Completing a Merge ■■■■■■■■■■■■■■■■■■■■■■■■

Use buttons and options in the Mailings tab to complete a merge. A merge generally takes two files — the ***data source*** file and the ***main document***. The main document contains the standard text along with fields identifying where variable information is inserted during the merge. The data source file contains the variable information that will be inserted in the main document.

Start Mail Merge

Use the Start Mail Merge button in the Mailings tab to identify the type of main document you want to create and use the Select Recipients button to create a data source file or to specify an existing data source file. You can also use the Mail Merge Wizard to guide you through the merge process. Start the wizard by clicking the Mailings tab, clicking the Start Mail Merge button, and then clicking *Step by Step Mail Merge Wizard*.

Select Recipients

Creating a Data Source File

Before creating a data source file, determine what type of correspondence you will be creating and the type of information you will need to insert in the correspondence. Word provides predetermined field names you can use when creating the data source file. Use these field names if they represent the data you are creating. Variable information in a data source file is saved as a ***record***. A record contains all of the information for one unit (for example, a person, family, customer, client, or business). A series of fields makes one record, and a series of records makes a data source file.

> **▼ Quick Steps**
>
> **Create Data Source File**
> 1. Click Mailings tab.
> 2. Click Select Recipients button.
> 3. Click *Type New List* at drop-down list.
> 4. Type data in predesigned or custom fields.
> 5. Click OK.

Create a data source file by clicking the Select Recipients button in the Start Mail Merge group in the Mailings tab and then clicking *Type New List* at the drop-down list. At the New Address List dialog box shown in Figure 8.1, use the predesigned fields offered by Word or edit the fields by clicking the Customize

Figure 8.1 New Address List Dialog Box

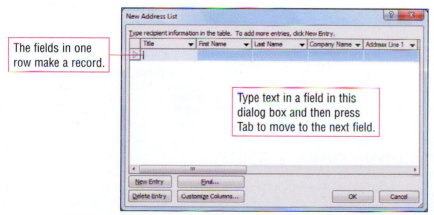

The fields in one row make a record.

Type text in a field in this dialog box and then press Tab to move to the next field.

Columns button. At the Customize Address List dialog box that displays, insert new fields or delete existing fields and then click OK. With the desired fields established, type the required data. Note that fields in the main document correspond to the column headings in the data source file. When all records have been entered, click OK. At the Save Address List dialog box, navigate to the desired folder, type a name for the data source file, and then click OK. Word saves a data source file as an Access database. You do not need Access on your computer to complete a merge with a data source file.

Project 1a Creating a Data Source File

Part 1 of 3

1. At a blank document, click the Mailings tab.
2. Click the Start Mail Merge button in the Start Mail Merge group and then click *Letters* at the drop-down list.
3. Click the Select Recipients button in the Start Mail Merge group and then click *Type New List* at the drop-down list.

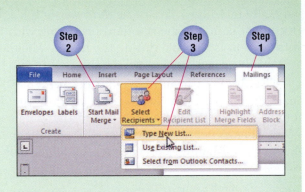

4. At the New Address List dialog box, Word provides a number of predesigned fields. Delete the fields you do not need by completing the following steps:
   a. Click the Customize Columns button.
   b. At the Customize Address List dialog box, click *Company Name* to select it and then click the Delete button.
   c. At the message asking if you are sure you want to delete the field, click the Yes button.
   d. Complete steps similar to those in 4b and 4c to delete the following fields:
      Country or Region
      Home Phone
      Work Phone
      E-mail Address

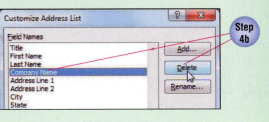

5. Insert a custom field by completing the following steps:
   a. At the Customize Address List dialog box, click the Add button.
   b. At the Add Field dialog box, type **Fund** and then click OK.
   c. Click the OK button to close the Customize Address List dialog box.

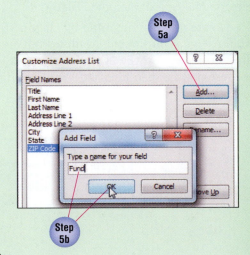

6. At the New Address List dialog box, enter the information for the first client shown in Figure 8.2 by completing the following steps:
   a. Type **Mr.** in the Title field and then press the Tab key. (This moves the insertion point to the *First Name* field. You can also press Shift + Tab to move to the previous field.)
   b. Type **Kenneth** and then press the Tab key.
   c. Type **Porter** and then press the Tab key.
   d. Type **7645 Tenth Street** and then press the Tab key.

e. Type **Apt. 314** and then press the Tab key.
f. Type **New York** and then press the Tab key.
g. Type **NY** and then press the Tab key.
h. Type **10192** and then press the Tab key.
i. Type **Mutual Investment Fund** and then press the Tab key. (This makes the Title field active in the next row.)
j. With the insertion point positioned in the *Title* field, complete steps similar to those in 6a through 6i to enter the information for the three other clients shown in Figure 8.2.

7. After entering all of the information for the last client in Figure 8.2 (Mrs. Wanda Houston), click the OK button located in the bottom right corner of the New Address List dialog box.

8. At the Save Address List dialog box, navigate to the Word2010L1C8 folder on your storage medium, type **WL1-C8-P1-MFDS** in the *File name* text box, and then click the Save button.

Figure 8.2 Project 1a

Title	= Mr.		Title	= Ms.
First Name	= Kenneth		First Name	= Carolyn
Last Name	= Porter		Last Name	= Renquist
Address Line 1	= 7645 Tenth Street		Address Line 1	= 13255 Meridian Street
Address Line 2	= Apt. 314		Address Line 2	= (leave this blank)
City	= New York		City	= New York
State	= NY		State	= NY
Zip Code	= 10192		Zip Code	= 10435
Fund	= Mutual Investment Fund		Fund	= Quality Care Fund
Title	= Dr.		Title	= Mrs.
First Name	= Amil		First Name	= Wanda
Last Name	= Ranna		Last Name	= Houston
Address Line 1	= 433 South 17th		Address Line 1	= 566 North 22nd Avenue
Address Line 2	= Apt. 17-D		Address Line 2	= (leave this blank)
City	= New York		City	= New York
State	= NY		State	= NY
Zip Code	= 10322		Zip Code	= 10634
Fund	= Priority One Fund		Fund	= Quality Care Fund

Creating a Main Document

When you begin a mail merge, you specify the type of main document you are creating. After creating and typing the records in the data source file, type the main document. Insert in the main document fields identifying where you want the variable information inserted when the document is merged with the data source file. Use buttons in the Write & Insert Fields group to insert fields and field blocks in the main document.

Insert all of the fields required for the inside address of a letter with the Address Block button in the Write & Insert Fields group. Click this button and the Insert Address Block dialog box displays with a preview of how the fields will be inserted in the document to create the inside address; the dialog box also contains buttons and options for customizing the fields. Click OK and the «AddressBlock» field is inserted in the document. The «AddressBlock» field is an example of a composite field that groups a number of fields together.

Click the Greeting Line button and the Insert Greeting Line dialog box displays with options for customizing how the fields are inserted in the document to create the greeting line. When you click OK at the dialog box, the «GreetingLine» composite field is inserted in the document.

If you want to insert an individual field from the data source file, click the Insert Merge Field button. This displays the Insert Merge Field dialog box with a list of fields from the data source file. Click the Insert Merge Field button arrow and a drop-down list displays containing the fields in the data source file. If you want merged data formatted, you can format the merge fields at the main document.

Address Block   Greeting Line   Insert Merge Field

Project 1b Creating a Main Document   Part 2 of 3

1. At the blank document, create the letter shown in Figure 8.3. Begin by clicking the No Spacing style in the Styles group in the Home tab.
2. Press the Enter key six times and then type February 23, 2012.
3. Press the Enter key four times and then insert the address fields by completing the following steps:
   a. Click the Mailings tab and then click the Address Block button in the Write & Insert Fields group.
   b. At the Insert Address Block dialog box, click the OK button.
   c. Press the Enter key twice.
4. Insert the greeting line fields by completing the following steps:
   a. Click the Greeting Line button in the Write & Insert Fields group.
   b. At the Insert Greeting Line dialog box, click the down-pointing arrow at the right of the option box containing the comma (the box to the right of the box containing *Mr. Randall*).
   c. At the drop-down list that displays, click the colon.
   d. Click OK to close the Insert Greeting Line dialog box.
   e. Press the Enter key twice.

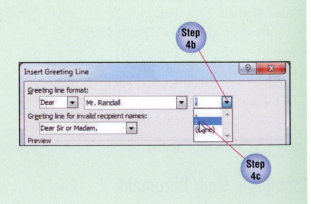

5. Type the letter to the point where «Fund» displays and then insert the «Fund» field by clicking the Insert Merge Field button arrow and then clicking *Fund* at the drop-down list.

6. Type the letter to the point where the «Title» field displays and then insert the «Title» field by clicking the Insert Merge Field button arrow and then clicking *Title* at the drop-down list.

7. Press the spacebar and then insert the «Last_Name» field by clicking the Insert Merge Field button arrow and then clicking *Last_Name* at the drop-down list.

8. Type the remainder of the letter shown in Figure 8.3. (Insert your initials instead of the *XX* at the end of the letter.)

9. Save the document and name it **WL1-C8-P1-MFMD**.

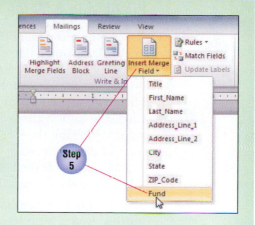

Figure 8.3 Project 1b

February 23, 2012

«AddressBlock»

«GreetingLine»

McCormack Funds is lowering its expense charges beginning May 1, 2012. The reductions in expense charges mean that more of your account investment performance in the «Fund» is returned to you, «Title» «Last_Name». The reductions are worth your attention because most of our competitors' fees have gone up.

Lowering expense charges is noteworthy because before the reduction, McCormack expense deductions were already among the lowest, far below most mutual funds and variable annuity accounts with similar objectives. At the same time, services for you, our client, will continue to expand. If you would like to discuss this change, please call us at (212) 555-2277. Your financial future is our main concern at McCormack.

Sincerely,

Jodie Langstrom
Director, Financial Services

XX
WL1-C8-P1-MFMD.docx

Previewing a Merge

Preview Results

First Record   **Last Record**

Previous Record   **Next Record**

To view how the main document will appear when merged with the first record in the data source file, click the Preview Results button in the Mailings tab. You can view the main document merged with other records by using the navigation buttons in the Preview Results group. This group contains the First Record buttons, Previous Record, Go to Record, Next Record, and Last Record buttons. Click the button that will display the main document merged with the desired record. Viewing the merged document before printing is helpful to ensure that the merged data is correct. To use the Go to Record button, click the button, type the number of the desired record, and then press Enter. Turn off the preview feature by clicking the Preview Results button.

The Preview Results group in the Mailings tab also includes a Find Recipient button. If you want to search for and preview merged documents with specific entries, click the Preview Results button and then click the Find Recipient button. At the Find Entry dialog box that displays, type the specific field entry for which you are searching in the *Find* text box and then click the Find Next button. Continue clicking the Find Next button until Word displays a message telling you that there are no more entries that contain the text you typed.

Checking for Errors

Auto Check for Errors

Before merging documents, you can check for errors using the Auto Check for Errors button in the Preview Results group in the Mailings tab. Click this button and the Checking and Reporting Errors dialog box shown in Figure 8.4 displays containing three options. Click the first option, *Simulate the merge and report errors in a new document,* to tell Word to test the merge, not make any changes, and report errors in a new document. Choose the second option, *Complete the merge, pausing to report each error as it occurs,* and Word will merge the documents and display errors as they occur during the merge. Choose the third option, *Complete the merge without pausing. Report errors in a document,* and Word will complete the merge without pausing and insert any errors in a new document.

Merging Documents

Finish & Merge

To complete the merge, click the Finish & Merge button in the Finish group in the Mailings tab. At the drop-down list that displays, you can choose to merge the records and create a new document, send the merged documents directly to the printer, or send the merged documents by email.

Figure 8.4 Checking and Reporting Errors Dialog Box

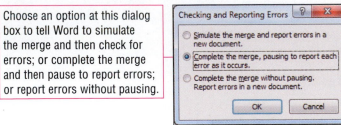

Choose an option at this dialog box to tell Word to simulate the merge and then check for errors; or complete the merge and then pause to report errors; or report errors without pausing.

To merge the documents and create a new document with the merged records, click the Finish & Merge button and then click *Edit Individual Documents* at the drop-down list. At the Merge to New Document dialog box, make sure *All* is selected in the *Merge records* section and then click OK. This merges the records in the data source file with the main document and inserts the merged documents in a new document. You can also display the Merge to New Document dialog box by pressing Alt + Shift + N. Press Alt + Shift + M to display the Merge to Printer dialog box.

You can identify specific records you want merged with options at the Merge to New Document dialog box. Display this dialog box by clicking the Finish & Merge button in the Mailings tab and then clicking the *Edit Individual Documents* option at the drop-down list. Click the *All* option in the Merge to New Document dialog box to merge all records in the data source and click the *Current record* option if you want to merge only the current record. If you want to merge specific adjacent records, click in the *From* text box, type the beginning record number, press the Tab key, and then type the ending record number in the *To* text box.

▼ **Quick Steps**
Merge Documents
1. Click Finish & Merge button.
2. Click *Edit Individual Documents* at drop-down list.
3. Make sure *All* is selected in Merge to New Document dialog box.
4. Click OK.

Project 1c — Merging the Main Document with the Data Source File — Part 3 of 3

1. With **WL1-C8-P1-MFMD.docx** open, preview the main document merged with the first record in the data source file by clicking the Preview Results button in the Mailings tab.
2. Click the Next Record button to view the main document merged with the second record in the data source file.
3. Click the Preview Results button to turn it off.
4. Automatically check for errors by completing the following steps:
   a. Click the Auto Check for Errors button in the Preview Results group in the Mailings tab.
   b. At the Checking and Reporting Errors dialog box, click the first option, *Simulate the merge and report errors in a new document*.
   c. Click OK.
   d. If a new document displays with any errors, print the document and then close it without saving it. If a message displays telling you that no errors were found, click OK.
5. Click the Finish & Merge button in the Finish group and then click *Edit Individual Documents* at the drop-down list.
6. At the Merge to New Document dialog box, make sure *All* is selected and then click OK.
7. Save the merged letters and name the document **WL1-C8-P1-MFLtrs**.
8. Print **WL1-C8-P1-MFLtrs.docx**. (This document will print four letters.)
9. Close **WL1-C8-P1-MFLtrs.docx**.
10. Save and then close **WL1-C8-P1-MFMD.docx**.

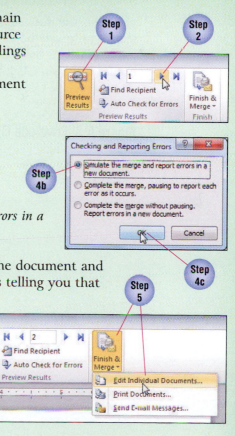

You will use Mail Merge to prepare envelopes with customer names and addresses.

Merging Envelopes ▪▪▪▪▪▪▪▪▪▪▪▪▪▪▪▪▪▪▪▪▪▪

If you create a letter as a main document and then merge it with a data source file, more than likely you will need properly addressed envelopes in which to send the letters. To prepare an envelope main document that is merged with a data source file, click the Mailings tab, click the Start Mail Merge button, and then click *Envelopes* at the drop-down list. This displays the Envelope Options dialog box as shown in Figure 8.5. At this dialog box, specify the desired envelope size, make any other changes, and then click OK.

The next step in the envelope merge process is to create the data source file or identify an existing data source file. To identify an existing data source file, click the Select Recipients button in the Start Mail Merge group and then click *Use Existing List* at the drop-down list. At the Select Data Source dialog box, navigate to the folder containing the desired data source file and then double-click the file.

With the data source file attached to the envelope main document, the next step is to insert the appropriate fields. Click in the envelope in the approximate location where the recipient's address will appear and a box with a dashed blue border displays. Click the Address Block button in the Write & Insert Fields group and then click OK at the Insert Address Block dialog box.

Figure 8.5 Envelope Options Dialog Box

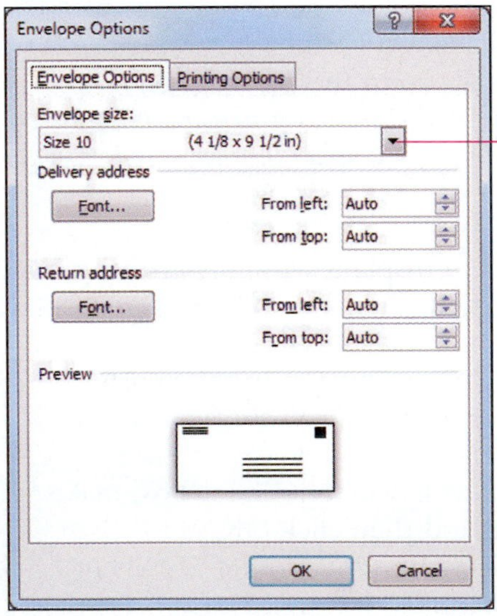

Click this down-pointing arrow to display a list of available envelope options.

1. At a blank document, click the Mailings tab.
2. Click the Start Mail Merge button in the Start Mail Merge group and then click *Envelopes* at the drop-down list.
3. At the Envelope Options dialog box, make sure the envelope size is 10 and then click OK.
4. Click the Select Recipients button in the Start Mail Merge group and then click *Use Existing List* at the drop-down list.
5. At the Select Data Source dialog box, navigate to the Word2010L1C8 folder on your storage medium and then double-click the data source file named **WL1-C8-P1-MFDS.mdb**.
6. Click in the approximate location in the envelope document where the recipient's address will appear. (This causes a box with a dashed blue border to display. If you do not see this box, try clicking in a different location on the envelope.)

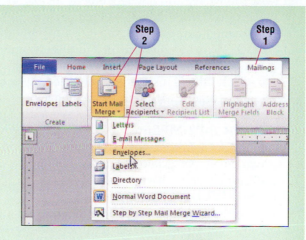

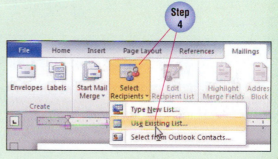

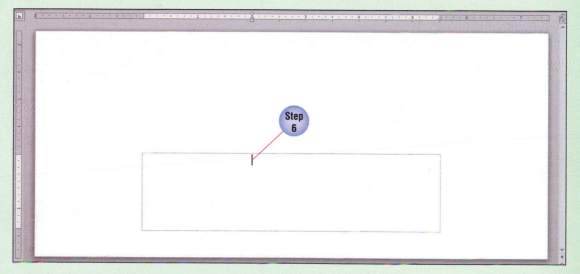

7. Click the Address Block button in the Write & Insert Fields group.
8. At the Insert Address Block dialog box, click the OK button.
9. Click the Preview Results button to see how the envelope appears merged with the first record in the data source file.
10. Click the Preview Results button to turn it off.
11. Click the Finish & Merge button in the Finish group and then click *Edit Individual Documents* at the drop-down list.

12. At the Merge to New Document dialog box, specify that you want only the first two records to merge by completing the following steps:

a. Click in the *From* text box and then type 1.

b. Click in the *To* text box and then type 2.

c. Click OK. (This merges only the first two records and opens a document with two merged envelopes.)

13. Save the merged envelopes and name the document **WL1-C8-P2-MFEnvs**.

14. Print **WL1-C8-P2-MFEnvs.docx**. (This document will print two envelopes. Manual feed of the envelopes may be required. Please check with your instructor.)

15. Close **WL1-C8-P2-MFEnvs.docx**.

16. Save the envelope main document and name it **WL1-C8-P2-EnvMD**.

17. Close **WL1-C8-P2-EnvMD.docx**.

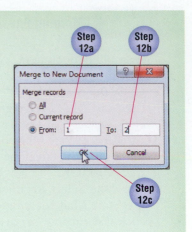

Step 12a

Step 12b

Step 12c

Project **3** Merge Mailing Labels

1 Part

You will use Mail Merge to prepare mailing labels with customer names and addresses.

Merging Labels

Create mailing labels for records in a data source file in much the same way that you create envelopes. Click the Start Mail Merge button and then click *Labels* at the drop-down list. This displays the Label Options dialog box as shown in Figure 8.6. Make sure the desired label is selected and then click OK to close the dialog box. The next step is to create the data source file or identify an existing data source file. With the data source file attached to the label main document, insert the appropriate fields and then complete the merge.

Figure 8.6 Label Options Dialog Box

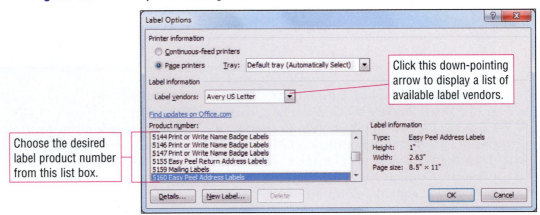

Choose the desired label product number from this list box.

Click this down-pointing arrow to display a list of available label vendors.

1. At a blank document, click the Mailings tab.
2. Click the Start Mail Merge button in the Start Mail Merge group and then click *Labels* at the drop-down list.
3. At the Label Options dialog box, complete the following steps:

   a. If necessary, click the down-pointing arrow at the right side of the *Label vendors* option and then click *Avery US Letter* at the drop-down list. (If this product vendor is not available, choose a vendor name that offers labels that print on a full page.)

   b. Scroll in the *Product number* list box and then click *5160 Easy Peel Address Labels*. (If this option is not available, choose a label number that prints labels in two or three columns down a full page.)

   c. Click OK to close the dialog box.

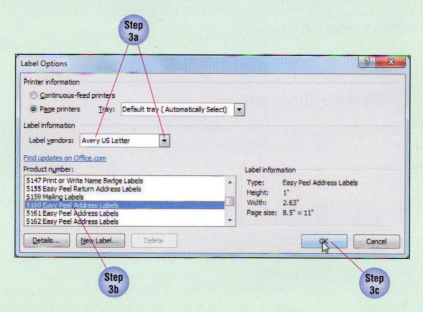

4. Click the Select Recipients button in the Start Mail Merge group and then click *Use Existing List* at the drop-down list.
5. At the Select Data Source dialog box, navigate to the Word2010L1C8 folder on your storage medium and then double-click the data source file named **WL1-C8-P1-MFDS.mdb**.
6. At the labels document, click the Address Block button in the Write & Insert Fields group.
7. At the Insert Address Block dialog box, click the OK button. (This inserts «AddressBlock» in the first label. The other labels contain the «Next Record» field.)
8. Click the Update Labels button in the Write & Insert Fields group. (This adds the «AddressBlock» field after each «Next Record» field in the second and subsequent labels.)
9. Click the Preview Results button to see how the labels appear merged with the records in the data source file.
10. Click the Preview Results button to turn it off.

11. Click the Finish & Merge button in the Finish group and then click *Edit Individual Documents* at the drop-down list.
12. At the Merge to New Document dialog box, make sure *All* is selected, and then click OK.
13. Format the labels by completing the following steps:
    a. Click the Table Tools Layout tab.
    b. Click the Select button in the Table group and then click *Select Table*.
    c. Click the Align Center Left button in the Alignment group.
    d. Click the Home tab and then click the Paragraph group dialog box launcher.
    e. At the Paragraph dialog box, click the up-pointing arrow at the right of *Before* and also at the right of *After* to change the measurement to 0 pt. Click the up-pointing arrow at the right of the *Inside* option to change the measurement to 0.3" and then click OK.
14. Save the merged labels and name the document **WL1-C8-P3-MFLabels**.
15. Print and then close **WL1-C8-P3-MFLabels.docx**.
16. Save the label main document and name it **WL1-C8-P3-LabelsMD**.
17. Close **WL1-C8-P3-LabelsMD.docx**.

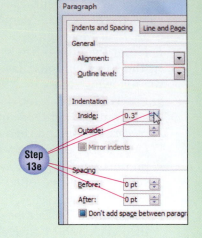

Step 13e

Project **4** **Merge a Directory**   **1 Part**

You will use Mail Merge to prepare a directory list containing customer names and type of financial investment funds.

Merging a Directory

When merging letters, envelopes, or mailing labels, a new form is created for each record. For example, if the data source file merged with the letter contains eight records, eight letters are created. If the data source file merged with a mailing label contains twenty records, twenty labels are created. In some situations, you may want merged information to remain on the same page. This is useful, for example, when creating a list such as a directory or address list.

Begin creating a merged directory by clicking the Start Mail Merge button and then clicking *Directory* at the drop-down list. Create or identify an existing data source file and then insert the desired fields in the directory document. You may want to set tabs to insert text in columns.

1. At a blank document, click the Mailings tab.
2. Click the Start Mail Merge button in the Start Mail Merge group and then click *Directory* at the drop-down list.
3. Click the Select Recipients button in the Start Mail Merge group and then click *Use Existing List* at the drop-down list.
4. At the Select Data Source dialog box, navigate to the Word2010L1C8 folder on your storage medium and then double-click the data source file named **WL1-C8-P1-MFDS.mdb**.
5. At the document screen, set left tabs at the 1-inch mark, the 2.5-inch mark, and the 4-inch mark on the Ruler and then press the Tab key. (This moves the insertion point to the tab set at the 1-inch mark.)
6. Click the Insert Merge Field button arrow and then click *Last_Name* at the drop-down list.
7. Press the Tab key to move the insertion point to the 2.5-inch mark.
8. Click the Insert Merge Field button arrow and then click *First_Name* at the drop-down list.
9. Press the Tab key to move the insertion point to the 4-inch mark.
10. Click the Insert Merge Field button arrow and then click *Fund* at the drop-down list.
11. Press the Enter key once.
12. Click the Finish & Merge button in the Finish group and then click *Edit Individual Documents* at the drop-down list.
13. At the Merge to New Document dialog box, make sure *All* is selected and then click OK. (This merges the fields in the document.)
14. Press Ctrl + Home, press the Enter key once, and then press the Up Arrow key once.
15. Press the Tab key, turn on bold, and then type **Last Name**.
16. Press the Tab key and then type **First Name**.
17. Press the Tab key and then type **Fund**.

18. Save the directory document and name it **WL1-C8-P4-Directory**.
19. Print and then close the document.
20. Close the directory main document without saving it.

You will use Mail Merge to prepare mailing labels with names and addresses of customers living in Baltimore.

Editing a Data Source File ■■■■■■■■■■■■■■■■■■■■

▼ Quick Steps

Edit Data Source File
1. Open main document.
2. Click Mailings tab.
3. Click Edit Recipient List button.
4. Make desired changes at Mail Merge Recipients dialog box.
5. Click OK.

Edit a main document in the normal manner. Open the document, make the required changes, and then save the document. Since a data source is actually an Access database file, you cannot open it in the normal manner. Open a data source file for editing using the Edit Recipient List button in the Start Mail Merge group in the Mailings tab. When you click the Edit Recipient List button, the Mail Merge Recipients dialog box displays as shown in Figure 8.7. Select or edit records at this dialog box.

Selecting Specific Records

All of the records in the Mail Merge Recipients dialog box contain a check mark before the first field. If you want to select specific records, remove the check mark from those records you do not want included in a merge. In this way you can select and then merge specific records in the data source file with the main document.

Figure 8.7 Mail Merge Recipients Dialog Box

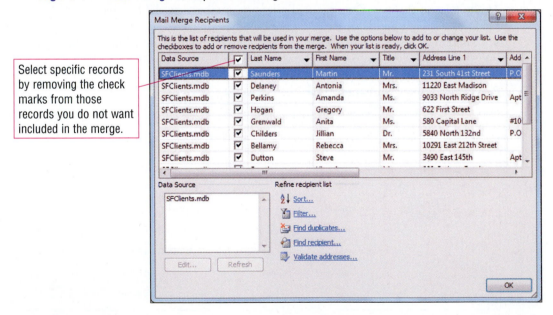

Select specific records by removing the check marks from those records you do not want included in the merge.

1. At a blank document, create mailing labels for customers living in Baltimore. Begin by clicking the Mailings tab.
2. Click the Start Mail Merge button in the Start Mail Merge group and then click *Labels* at the drop-down list.
3. At the Label Options dialog box, make sure *Avery US Letter* displays in the *Label products* option box, and *5160 Easy Peel Address Labels* displays in the *Product number* list box, and then click OK.
4. Click the Select Recipients button in the Start Mail Merge group and then click *Use Existing List* at the drop-down list.
5. At the Select Data Source dialog box, navigate to the Word2010L1C8 folder on your storage medium and then double-click the data source file named **SFClients.mdb**.
6. Click the Edit Recipient List button in the Start Mail Merge group.
7. At the Mail Merge Recipients dialog box, complete the following steps:
   a. Click the check box located immediately left of the *Last Name* field column heading to remove the check mark. (This removes all of the check marks from the check boxes.)

   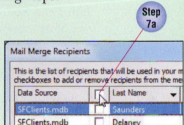
   Step 7a

   b. Click the check box immediately left of each of the following last names: *Saunders, Perkins, Grenwald, Dutton, Fernandez,* and *Stahl*. (These are the customers who live in Baltimore.)
   c. Click OK to close the dialog box.
8. At the labels document, click the Address Block button in the Write & Insert Fields group.
9. At the Insert Address Block dialog box, click the OK button.
10. Click the Update Labels button in Write & Insert Fields group.
11. Click the Preview Results button and then click the Previous Record button to display each of the labels and make sure only those customers living in Baltimore display.
12. Click the Preview Results button to turn it off.
13. Click the Finish & Merge button in the Finish group and then click *Edit Individual Documents* at the drop-down list.
14. At the Merge to New Document dialog box, make sure *All* is selected, and then click OK.
15. Format the labels by completing the following steps:
   a. Click the Table Tools Layout tab.
   b. Click the Select button in the Table group and then click *Select Table*.
   c. Click the Align Center Left button in the Alignment group.
   d. Click the Home tab and then click the Paragraph group dialog box launcher.
   e. At the Paragraph dialog box, click the up-pointing arrow at the right of *Before* and also at the right of *After* to change the measurement to 0 pt. Click the up-pointing arrow at the right of the *Inside* option to change the measurement to 0.3" and then click OK.
16. Save the merged labels and name the document **WL1-C8-P5-SFLabels**.
17. Print and then close **WL1-C8-P5-SFLabels.docx**.
18. Close the main labels document without saving it.

Project 6 Edit Records in a Data Source File — 1 Part

You will edit records in a data source file and then use Mail Merge to prepare a directory with the edited records that contains customer names, telephone numbers, and cell phone numbers.

Editing Records

A data source file may need editing on a periodic basis to add or delete customer names, update fields, insert new fields, or delete existing fields. To edit a data source file, click the Edit Recipient List button in the Start Mail Merge group. At the Mail Merge Recipients dialog box, click the data source file name in the *Data Source* list box and then click the Edit button that displays below the list box. This displays the Edit Data Source dialog box shown in Figure 8.8. At this dialog box you can add a new entry, delete an entry, find a particular entry, and customize columns.

Figure 8.8 Edit Data Source Dialog Box

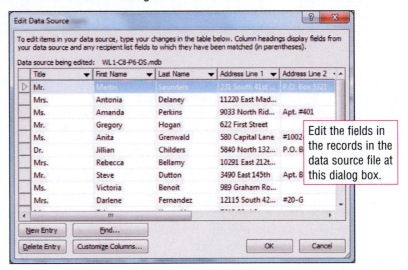

Edit the fields in the records in the data source file at this dialog box.

Project 6 Editing Records in a Data Source File — Part 1 of 1

1. Make a copy of the **SFClients.mdb** file by completing the following steps:
   a. Display the Open dialog box and make Word2010L1C8 the active folder.
   b. If necessary, change the file type button to *All Files (*.*)*.
   c. Right-click on the **SFClients.mdb** file and then click *Copy* at the shortcut menu.
   d. Position the mouse pointer in a white portion of the Open dialog box Content pane (outside of any file name), click the right mouse button, and then click *Paste* at the shortcut menu. (This inserts a copy of the file in the dialog box Content pane and names the file **SFClients-Copy.mdb**.)
   e. Right-click on the file name **SFClients-Copy.mdb** and then click *Rename* at the shortcut menu.

f. Type **WL1-C8-P6-DS** and then press Enter.

g. Close the Open dialog box.

2. At a blank document, click the Mailings tab.

3. Click the Select Recipients button and then click *Use Existing List* from the drop-down list.

4. At the Select Data Source dialog box, navigate to the Word2010L1C8 folder on your storage medium and then double-click the data source file named **WL1-C8-P6-DS.mdb**.

5. Click the Edit Recipient List button in the Start Mail Merge group.

6. At the Mail Merge Recipients dialog box, click **WL1-C8-P6-DS.mdb** that displays in the *Data Source* list box and then click the Edit button.

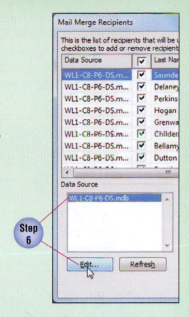

7. Delete the record for Steve Dutton by completing the following steps:

a. Click the square that displays at the beginning of the row for *Mr. Steve Dutton*.

b. Click the Delete Entry button.

c. At the message asking if you want to delete the entry, click the Yes button.

8. Insert a new record by completing the following steps:

a. Click the New Entry button in the dialog box.

b. Type the following text in the new record in the specified fields:

    Title = **Ms.**

    First Name = **Jennae**

    Last Name = **Davis**

    Address Line 1 = **3120 South 21st**

    Address Line 2 = (none)

    City = **Rosedale**

    State = **MD**

    ZIP Code = **20389**

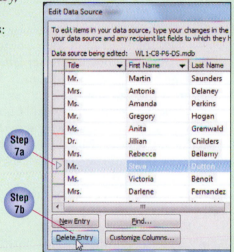

9. Insert a new field and type text in the field by completing the following steps:

a. At the Edit Data Source dialog box, click the Customize Columns button.

b. At the message asking if you want to save the changes made to the data source file, click Yes.

c. At the Customize Address List dialog box, click *ZIP Code* in the *Field Names* list box. (A new field is inserted below the selected field.)

d. Click the Add button.

e. At the Add Field dialog box, type **Cell Phone** and then click OK.

f. You decide that you want the *Cell Phone* field to display after the *Home Phone* field. To move the *Cell Phone* field, make sure it is selected and then click the Move Down button.

g. Click OK to close the Customize Address List dialog box.

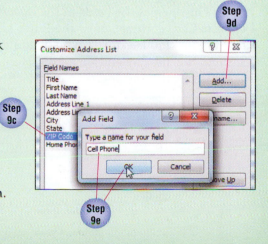

h. At the Edit Data Source dialog box, scroll to the right to display the *Cell Phone* field (last field in the file) and then type the following cell phone numbers (after typing each cell phone number, except the last number, press the Down Arrow key to make the next cell below active):

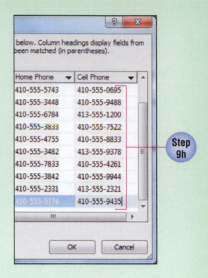

Record 1 = 410-555-1249
Record 2 = 413-555-3492
Record 3 = 410-555-0695
Record 4 = 410-555-9488
Record 5 = 413-555-1200
Record 6 = 410-555-7522
Record 7 = 410-555-8833
Record 8 = 413-555-9378
Record 9 = 410-555-4261
Record 10 = 410-555-9944
Record 11 = 413-555-2321
Record 12 = 410-555-9435

i. Click OK to close the Edit Data Source dialog box.

j. At the message asking if you want to update the recipient list and save changes, click Yes.

k. At the Mail Merge Recipients dialog box, click OK.

10. Create a directory by completing the following steps:

a. Click the Start Mail Merge button and then click *Directory* at the drop-down list.

b. At the blank document, set left tabs on the horizontal ruler at the 1-inch mark, the 3-inch mark, and the 4.5-inch mark.

c. Press the Tab key. (This moves the insertion point to the first tab set at the 1-inch mark.)

d. Click the Insert Merge Field button arrow and then click *Last_Name* at the drop-down list.

e. Type a comma and then press the spacebar.

f. Click the Insert Merge Field button arrow and then click *First_Name* at the drop-down list.

g. Press the Tab key, click the Insert Merge Field button arrow, and then click *Home_Phone* at the drop-down list.

h. Press the Tab key, click the Insert Merge Field button arrow, and then click *Cell_Phone* at the drop-down list.

i. Press the Enter key once.

j. Click the Finish & Merge button in the Finish group and then click *Edit Individual Documents* at the drop-down list.

k. At the Merge to New Document dialog box, make sure *All* is selected and then click OK. (This merges the fields in the document.)

11. Press Ctrl + Home, press the Enter key once, and then press the Up Arrow key once.

12. Press the Tab key, turn on bold, and then type **Name**.

13. Press the Tab key and then type **Home Phone**.

14. Press the Tab key and then type **Cell Phone**.

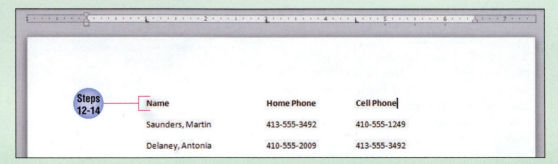

15. Save the directory document and name it **WL1-C8-P6-Directory**.
16. Print and then close the document.
17. Close the directory main document without saving it.

roject **7** **Add Fill-in Fields to a Main Document** 1 Part

You will edit a form letter and insert sales representative contact information during a merge.

Inputting Text during a Merge ■■■■■■■■■■■■■■■

Word's Merge feature contains a large number of Word fields you can insert in a main document. In this chapter, you will learn about the *Fill-in* field that is used for information input at the keyboard during a merge. For more information on the other Word fields, please refer to the on-screen help.

Situations may arise in which you do not need to keep all variable information in a data source file. For example, variable information that changes on a regular basis might include a customer's monthly balance, a product price, and so on. Word lets you input variable information into a document during the merge using the keyboard. A Fill-in field is inserted in a main document by clicking the Rules button in the Write & Insert Fields group in the Mailings tab and then clicking *Fill-in* at the drop-down list. This displays the Insert Word Field: Fill-in dialog box shown in Figure 8.9. At this dialog box, type a short message indicating what should be entered at the keyboard and then click OK. At the Microsoft Word dialog box with the message you entered displayed in the upper left corner, type text you want to display in the document and then click OK. When the Fill-in field or fields are added, save the main document in the normal manner. A document can contain any number of Fill-in fields.

When you merge the main document with the data source file, the first record is merged with the main document and the Microsoft Word dialog box displays with the message you entered displayed in the upper left corner. Type the required information for the first record in the data source file and then click the OK

▼ **Quick Steps**

Insert *Fill-in* Field in Main Document
1. Click Mailings tab.
2. Click Rules button.
3. Click *Fill-in* at drop-down list.
4. Type prompt text.
5. Click OK.
6. Type text to be inserted in document.
7. Click OK.

Rules

Figure 8.9 Insert Word Field: Fill-in Dialog Box

In this text box, type a short message indicating what should be entered at the keyboard.

button. Word displays the dialog box again. Type the required information for the second record in the data source file and then click OK. Continue in this manner until the required information has been entered for each record in the data source file. Word then completes the merge.

Project 7   Adding Fill-in Fields to a Main Document   Part 1 of 1

1. Open the document named **WL1-C8-P1-MFMD.docx** (at the message asking if you want to continue, click Yes) and then save the document with Save As and name it **WL1-C8-P7-MFMD**.

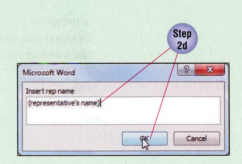

2. Change the second paragraph in the body of the letter to the paragraph shown in Figure 8.10. Insert the first Fill-in field (representative's name) by completing the following steps:
   a. Click the Mailings tab.
   b. Click the Rules button in the Write & Insert Fields group and then click *Fill-in* at the drop-down list.
   c. At the Insert Word Field: Fill-in dialog box, type **Insert rep name** in the *Prompt* text box and then click OK.
   d. At the Microsoft Word dialog box with *Insert rep name* displayed in the upper left corner, type **(representative's name)** and then click OK.

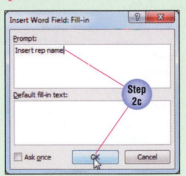

3. Complete steps similar to those in Step 2 to insert the second Fill-in field (phone number), except type **Insert phone number** in the *Prompt* text box at the Insert Word Field: Fill-in dialog box and type **(phone number)** at the Microsoft Word dialog box.

4. Save **WL1-C8-P7-MFMD.docx**.

5. Merge the main document with the data source file by completing the following steps:
   a. Click the Finish & Merge button and then click *Edit Individual Documents* at the drop-down list.
   b. At the Merge to New Document dialog box, make sure *All* is selected, and then click OK.
   c. When Word merges the main document with the first record, a dialog box displays with the message *Insert rep name* and the text *(representative's name)* selected. At this dialog box, type **Marilyn Smythe** and then click OK.
   d. At the dialog box with the message *Insert phone number* and *(phone number)* selected, type **(646) 555-8944** and then click OK.

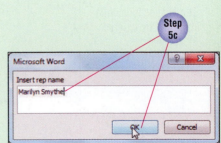

e. At the dialog box with the message *Insert rep name*, type **Anthony Mason** (over *Marilyn Smythe*) and then click OK.

f. At the dialog box with the message *Insert phone number*, type **(646) 555-8901** (over the previous number) and then click OK.

g. At the dialog box with the message *Insert rep name*, type **Faith Ostrom** (over *Anthony Mason*) and then click OK.

h. At the dialog box with the message *Insert phone number*, type **(646) 555-8967** (over the previous number) and then click OK.

i. At the dialog box with the message *Insert rep name*, type **Thomas Rivers** (over *Faith Ostrom*) and then click OK.

j. At the dialog box with the message *Insert phone number*, type **(646) 555-0793** (over the previous number) and then click OK.

6. Save the merged document and name it **WL1-C8-P7-MFLtrs**.

7. Print and then close **WL1-C8-P7-MFLtrs.docx**.

8. Save and then close **WL1-C8-P7-MFMD.docx**.

Figure 8.10 Project 7

Lowering expense charges is noteworthy because before the reduction, McCormack expense deductions were already among the lowest, far below most mutual funds and variable annuity accounts with similar objectives. At the same time, services for you, our client, will continue to expand. If you would like to discuss this change, please call our service representative, **(representative's name)**, at **(phone number)**.

Project **8** **Use Mail Merge Wizard** **1 Part**

You will use the Mail Merge wizard to merge a main document with a data source file and create letters to clients of Sorenson Funds.

Merging Using the Mail Merge Wizard ■■■■■■■■■■■■■■

The Mail Merge feature includes a Mail Merge wizard that guides you through the merge process. To access the Wizard, click the Mailings tab, click the Start Mail Merge button, and then click the *Step By Step Mail Merge Wizard* option at the drop-down list. The first of six Mail Merge task panes displays at the right side of the screen. Completing the tasks at one task pane displays the next task pane. The options in each task pane may vary depending on the type of merge you are performing. Generally, you complete one of the following steps at each task pane:

- Step 1: Select the type of document you want to create such as a letter, email message, envelope, label, or directory.

- Step 2: Specify whether you want to use the current document to create the main document, start from a template, or start from an existing document.

- Step 3: Specify whether you are typing a new list, using an existing list, or selecting from an Outlook contacts list.

- Step 4: Use the items in this task pane to help you prepare the main document such as inserting fields in the main document.
- Step 5: Preview the merged documents.
- Step 6: Complete the merge.

Project 8   **Preparing Form Letters Using the Mail Merge Wizard**   **Part 1 of 1**

1. At a blank document, click the Mailings tab, click the Start Mail Merge button in the Start Mail Merge group, and then click *Step by Step Mail Merge Wizard* at the drop-down list.
2. At the first Mail Merge task pane, make sure *Letters* is selected in the *Select document type* section and then click the <u>Next: Starting document</u> hyperlink located toward the bottom of the task pane.
3. At the second Mail Merge task pane, click the *Start from existing document* option in the *Select starting document* section.
4. Click the Open button in the *Start from existing* section of the task pane.
5. At the Open dialog box, navigate to the Word2010L1C8 folder on your storage medium and then double-click *SFLtrMD.docx*.
6. Click the <u>Next: Select recipients</u> hyperlink located toward the bottom of the task pane.
7. At the third Mail Merge task pane, click the <u>Browse</u> hyperlink that displays in the *Use an existing list* section of the task pane.
8. At the Select Data Source dialog box, navigate to the Word2010L1C8 folder on your storage medium and then double-click *SFClients.mdb*.
9. At the Mail Merge Recipients dialog box, click OK.
10. Click the <u>Next: Write your letter</u> hyperlink that displays toward the bottom of the task pane.
11. At the fourth Mail Merge task pane, enter fields in the form letter by completing the following steps:
    a. Position the insertion point a double space above the first paragraph of text in the letter.
    b. Click the <u>Address block</u> hyperlink located in the *Write your letter* section of the task pane.
    c. At the Insert Address Block dialog box, click the OK button.
    d. Press the Enter key twice and then click the <u>Greeting line</u> hyperlink located in the *Write your letter* section of the task pane.
    e. At the Insert Greeting Line dialog box, click the down-pointing arrow at the right of the option box containing the comma (the box to the right of the box containing *Mr. Randall*).
    f. At the drop-down list that displays, click the colon.
    g. Click OK to close the Insert Greeting Line dialog box.

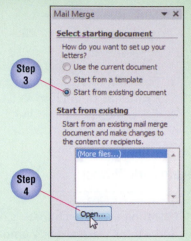

Step 3

Step 4

Step 7

Step 11b

Step 11d

12. Click the <u>Next: Preview your letters</u> hyperlink located toward the bottom of the task pane.
13. At the fifth Mail Merge task pane, look over the letter that displays in the document window and make sure the information merged properly. If you want to see the letters for the other recipients, click the button in the Mail Merge task pane containing the right-pointing arrow.
14. Click the Preview Results button in the Preview Results group to turn off the preview feature.
15. Click the <u>Next: Complete the merge</u> hyperlink that displays toward the bottom of the task pane.
16. At the sixth Mail Merge task pane, click the <u>Edit individual letters</u> hyperlink that displays in the *Merge* section of the task pane.
17. At the Merge to New Document dialog box, make sure *All* is selected and then click the OK button.
18. Save the merged letters documents with the name **WL1-C8-P8-SFLtrs**.
19. Print only the first two pages of **WL1-C8-P8-SFLtrs.docx**.
20. Close the document.
21. At the sixth Mail Merge task pane, close the letter main document without saving it.

Chapter Summary

- Use the Mail Merge feature to create letters, envelopes, labels, directories, email messages, and faxes, all with personalized information.

- Generally, a merge takes two documents — the data source file containing the variable information and the main document containing standard text along with fields identifying where variable information is inserted during the merge process.

- Variable information in a data source file is saved as a record. A record contains all of the information for one unit. A series of fields makes one record, and a series of records makes a data source file.

- A data source file is saved as an Access database but you do not need Access on your computer to complete a merge with a data source.

- You can use predesigned fields when creating a data source file or you can create your own custom field at the Customize Address List dialog box.

- Use the Address Block button in the Write & Insert Fields group in the Mailings tab to insert all of the fields required for the inside address of a letter. This inserts the «AddressBlock» field, which is considered a composite field because it groups a number of fields together.

- Click the Greeting Line button in the Write & Insert Fields group in the Mailings tab to insert the «GreetingLine» composite field in the document.

- Click the Insert Merge Field button arrow in the Write & Insert Fields group in the Mailings tab to display a drop-down list of fields contained in the data source file.

- Click the Preview Results button in the Mailings tab to view the main document merged with the first record in the data source. Use the navigation buttons in the Preview Results group in the Mailings tab to display the main document merged with the desired record.
- Before merging documents, check for errors by clicking the Auto Check for Errors button in the Preview Results group in the Mailings tab. This displays the Checking and Reporting Errors dialog box with three options for checking errors.
- Click the Finish & Merge button in the Mailings tab to complete the merge.
- Select specific records for merging by inserting or removing check marks from the desired records in the Mail Merge Recipients dialog box. Display this dialog box by clicking the Edit Recipient List button in the Mailings tab.
- Edit specific records in a data source file at the Edit Data Source dialog box. Display this dialog box by clicking the Edit Recipient List button in the Mailings tab, clicking the desired data source file name in the *Data Source* list box, and then clicking the Edit button.
- Use the Fill-in field in a main document to insert variable information at the keyboard during a merge.
- Word includes a Mail Merge wizard you can use to guide you through the process of creating letters, envelopes, labels, directories, and email messages with personalized information.

Commands Review

FEATURE	RIBBON TAB, GROUP	BUTTON	OPTION
New Address List dialog box	Mailings, Start Mail Merge		Type New List
Letter main document	Mailings, Start Mail Merge		Letters
Checking and Reporting Errors dialog box	Mailings, Preview Results		
Envelopes main document	Mailings, Start Mail Merge		Envelopes
Labels main document	Mailings, Start Mail Merge		Labels
Directory main document	Mailings, Start Mail Merge		Directory
Preview merge results	Mailings, Preview Results		
Mail Merge Recipients dialog box	Mailings, Start Mail Merge		
Address Block field	Mailings, Write & Insert Fields		
Greeting Line field	Mailings, Write & Insert Fields		
Insert merge fields	Mailings, Write & Insert Fields		

FEATURE	RIBBON TAB, GROUP	BUTTON	OPTION
Fill-in merge field	Mailings, Write & Insert Fields		Fill-in
Mail Merge wizard	Mailings, Start Mail Merge		Step by Step Mail Merge Wizard

Concepts Check Test Your Knowledge

Completion: In the space provided at the right, indicate the correct term, command, or number.

1. A merge generally takes two files — a data source file and this. _____

2. This term refers to all of the information for one unit in a data source file. _____

3. Create a data source file by clicking this button in the Mailings tab and then clicking *Type New List* at the drop-down list. _____

4. A data source file is saved as this type of file. _____

5. Create your own custom fields in a data source file with options at this dialog box. _____

6. Use this button in the Mailings tab to insert all of the required fields for the inside address in a letter. _____

7. The «GreetingLine» field is considered this type of field because it includes all of the fields required for the greeting line. _____

8. Click this button in the Mailings tab to display the first record merged with the main document. _____

9. Before merging a document, check for errors using this button in the Preview Results group in the Mailings tab. _____

10. To complete a merge, click this button in the Finish group in the Mailings tab. _____

11. When creating the envelope main document, click in the approximate location where the recipient's address will appear and then click this button in the Write & Insert Fields group. _____

12. Select specific records in a data source file by inserting or removing check marks from the records in this dialog box. _____

13. Use this field to insert variable information at the keyboard during a merge. _____

14. Click this option at the Start Mail Merge button drop-down list to begin the Mail Merge wizard. _____

Skills Check Assess Your Performance

Assessment

1 PREPARE AND MERGE LETTERS, ENVELOPES, AND LABELS

1. Open **CCLtrhd.docx** and then save the document with Save As and name it **WL1-C8-A1-CCMD**.
2. Look at the information in Figure 8.11 and Figure 8.12 and then use the Mail Merge feature to prepare four letters. Create the data source file with the information in Figure 8.11 and then save the file and name it **WL1-C8-A1-CCDS**.
3. Merge the **WL1-C8-A1-CCMD** main document with the **WL1-C8-A1-CCDS.mdb** data source file and then save the merged letters document and name it **WL1-C8-A1-CCLtrs**.
4. Print and then close **WL1-C8-A1-CCLtrs.docx** and then save and close **WL1-C8-A1-CCMD.docx**.
5. Create an envelope main document and then merge it with the **WL1-C8-A1-CCDS.mdb** data source file.
6. Save the merged envelopes document and name it **WL1-C8-A1-CCEnvs**. Print and then close the envelopes document. (Check with your instructor before printing the envelopes.) Close the envelope main document without saving it.
7. Create a labels main document (use the Avery US Letter product number 5160 label) and then merge it with the **WL1-C8-A1-CCDS.mdb** data source file. When the labels are merged, press Ctrl + A to select the entire document, click the Home tab, and then click the No Spacing style in the Styles group.
8. Save the merged labels document and name it **WL1-C8-A1-CCLabels**. Print and then close the labels document and then close the labels main document without saving it.

Figure 8.11 Assessment 1

Mr. Tony Benedetti 1315 Cordova Road Apt. 402 Santa Fe, NM 87505 Home Phone: 505-555-0489	Ms. Theresa Dusek 12044 Ridgway Drive (leave this blank) Santa Fe, NM 87505 Home Phone: 505-555-1120
Mrs. Mary Arguello 2554 Country Drive #105 Santa Fe, NM 87504 Home Phone: 505-555-7663	Mr. Preston Miller 120 Second Street (leave this blank) Santa Fe, NM 87505 Home Phone: 505-555-3551

Figure 8.12 Assessment 1

May 8, 2012

«AddressBlock»

«GreetingLine»

The Cordova Children's Community Center is a nonprofit agency providing educational and recreational activities to children in the Cordova community. We are funded by donations from the community and rely on you and all of our volunteers to provide quality care and services to our children. As a member of our outstanding volunteer team, we are inviting you to attend our summer volunteer open house on Saturday, May 26, at the community center from 1:00 to 4:30 p.m. We want to honor you and our other volunteers for your commitment to children so please plan to attend so we can thank you in person.

The Center's summer volunteer session begins Friday, June 1, and continues through August 31. According to our volunteer roster, you have signed up to volunteer during the summer session. Throughout the summer we will be offering a variety of services to our children including tutoring, creative art classes, recreational activities, and a science camp. At the open house, you can sign up for the specific area or areas in which you want to volunteer. We look forward to seeing you at the open house and during the upcoming summer session.

Sincerely,

Andy Amura
Volunteer Coordinator

XX
WL1-C8-A1-CCMD.docx

Assessment

2 EDIT AND MERGE LETTERS

1. Open **WL1-C8-A1-CCMD.docx** (at the message asking if you want to continue, click Yes) and then save the main document with Save As and name it **WL1-C8-A2-CCMD**.
2. Edit the **WL1-C8-A1-CCDS.mdb** data source file by making the following changes:
   a. Display the record for Ms. Theresa Dusek and then change the address from *12044 Ridgway Drive* to *1390 Fourth Avenue*.
   b. Display the record for Mr. Preston Miller and change the home phone number from *505-555-3551* to *505-555-1289*.
   c. Delete the record for Mrs. Mary Arguello.
   d. Insert a new record with the following information:
      Mr. Cesar Rivera
      3201 East Third Street
      Santa Fe, NM 87505
      505-555-6675
3. At the main document, edit the second sentence of the second paragraph so it reads as follows (insert a *Fill-in* field for the *(number of hours)* shown in the sentence below):
      According to our volunteer roster, you have signed up to volunteer for *(number of hours)* during the summer session.
4. Merge the main document with the data source file and type the following text for each of the records:
      Record 1 = four hours a week
      Record 2 = six hours a week
      Record 3 = twelve hours a week
      Record 4 = four hours a week
5. Save the merged document and name it **WL1-C8-A2-CCLtrs**.
6. Print and then close **WL1-C8-A2-CCLtrs.docx**.
7. Save and then close **WL1-C8-A2-CCMD.docx**.

Assessment

3 CREATE A DIRECTORY

1. At a blank document, create a directory main document and specify **WL1-C8-A1-CCDS.mdb** as the data source file. Insert a left tab at the 1.5-inch mark and the 4-inch mark on the Ruler. Press the Tab key and then insert the «First_Name» field at the 1.5-inch tab. Press the spacebar and then insert the «Last_Name» field. Press the Tab key, insert the «Home_Phone» field at the second tab, and then press the Enter key.
2. Merge the directory main document with the data source.
3. Insert the heading *Volunteer* in bold above the first column and insert the heading *Telephone* in bold above the second column.
4. Save the directory document and name it **WL1-C8-A3-CCDir**.
5. Print and then close the document.
6. Close the directory main document without saving it.

4 MERGE LETTERS AND ENVELOPES USING THE MAIL MERGE WIZARD

1. Open **TTSLtrMD.docx** from the Word2010L1C8 folder on your storage medium. Insert your initials in place of the *XX* that display toward the bottom of the letter.
2. Use the Mail Merge wizard to prepare letters using the **TTSLtrMD.docx** document as the main document and specify **TTSClients.mdb** as the data source file.
3. When the merge is complete save the merged letters document and name it **WL1-C8-A4-TTSLtrs**.
4. Print only the first two pages (letters) in the document.
5. Close **WL1-C8-A4-TTSLtrs.docx**.
6. Close **TTSLtrMD.docx** without saving the changes.

Visual Benchmark Demonstrate Your Proficiency

PREPARE AND MERGE LETTERS

1. Open **FPLtrhd.docx** and then save the document with Save As and name it **WL1-C8-VB-FPMD**.
2. Look at the information in Figure 8.13 and Figure 8.14 and then use Mail Merge to prepare four letters. (When creating the main document as shown in Figure 8.14, insert the appropriate fields where you see the text Title; First Name; Last Name; Street Address; and City, State ZIP. Insert the appropriate field where you see the text Title and Last Name in the first paragraph of text.) Create the data source file with the information in Figure 8.13 and then save the file and name it **WL1-C8-VB-FPDS**.
3. Merge the **WL1-C8-VB-FPMD.docx** main document with the **WL1-C8-VB-FPDS.mdb** data source file and then save the merged letters document and name it **WL1-C8-VB-FPLtrs**.
4. Print and then close **WL1-C8-VB-FPLtrs.docx**.
5. Save and then close **WL1-C8-VB-FPMD.docx**.

Figure 8.13 Visual Benchmark Data Source Records

Mr. and Mrs. Chris Gallagher
17034 234th Avenue
Newport, VT 05855

Ms. Heather Segarra
4103 Thompson Drive
Newport, VT 05855

Mr. Gene Goodrich
831 Cromwell Lane
Newport, VT 05855

Mrs. Sonya Kraus
15933 Ninth Street
Newport, VT 05855

Figure 8.14 Visual Benchmark Main Document

Frontline Photography Equipment and Supplies

(Current Date)

Title First Name Last Name
Street Address
City, State ZIP

Dear Title Last Name:

We have enjoyed being a part of the Newport community for the past two years. Our success in the community is directly related to you, Title Last Name, and all of our other loyal customers. Thank you for shopping at our store for all of your photography equipment and supply needs.

To show our appreciation for your loyalty and your business, we are enclosing a coupon for 20 percent off any item in our store, even our incredibly low-priced clearance items. Through the end of the month, all of our camera accessories are on sale. So, use your coupon and take advantage of additional savings on items such as camera lenses, tripods, cleaning supplies, and camera bags.

To accommodate our customers' schedules, we have increased our weekend hours. Our store will be open Saturdays until 7:00 p.m. and Sundays until 5:00 p.m. Come by and let our sales associates find just the right camera and camera accessories for you.

Sincerely,

(Student Name)

XX
WL1-C8-VB-FPMD.docx
Enclosure

559 Tenth Street, Suite A ◈ Newport, VT 05855 ◈ (802) 555-4411

Case Study Apply Your Skills

Part 1

You are the office manager for Freestyle Extreme, a sporting goods store that specializes in snowboarding and snow skiing equipment and supplies. The store has two branches, one on the east side of town and the other on the west side. One of your job responsibilities is to send letters to customers letting them know about sales, new equipment, and upcoming events. Next month, both stores are having a sale and all snowboard and snow skiing supplies will be 15% off the regular price. Create a data source file that contains the following customer information: first name, last name, address, city, state, ZIP code, and branch. Add six customers to the data source file and indicate that three usually shop at the East branch and the other three usually shop at the West branch. Create a letter as a main document that includes information about the upcoming sale. The letter should contain at least two paragraphs and, in addition to the information on the sale, might include information about the store, snowboarding, and/or snow skiing. Save the data source file with the name **WL1-C8-CS-FEDS**, save the main document with the name **WL1-C8-CS-FEMD**, and save the merged document with the name **WL1-C8-CS-FELtrs**. Create envelopes for the six merged letters and name the merged envelope document **WL1-C8-CS-FEEnvs**. Do not save the envelope main document. Print the merged letters document and the merged envelopes document.

Part 2

A well-known extreme snowboarder will be visiting both branches of the store to meet with customers and sign autographs. Use the Help feature to learn how to insert an If . . . Then . . . Else merge field in a document and then create a letter that includes the name of the extreme snowboarder (you determine the name), the time, which is 1:00 p.m. to 4:30 p.m., and any additional information that might interest the customer. Also include in the letter an If . . . Then . . . Else merge field that will insert *Wednesday, September 26* if the customer's Branch is *East* and will insert *Thursday, September 27* if the Branch is *West*. Add visual appeal to the letter by inserting a picture, clip art image, WordArt, or any other feature that will attract the reader's attention. Save the letter main document and name it **WL1-C8-CS-MD**. Merge the letter main document with the **WL1-C8-CS-FEDS.mdb** data source. Save the merged letters document and name it **WL1-C8-CS-AnnLtrs**. Print the merged letters document.

Part 3

The store owner wants to try selling shorter skis known as "snow blades" or "skiboards." He has asked you to research the shorter skis and identify one type and model to sell only at the West branch of the store. If the model sells well, he will consider selling it at the East branch at a future time. Prepare a main document letter that describes the new snow blade or skiboard that the West branch is selling. Include information about pricing and tell customers that the new item is being offered at a 40% discount if purchased within the next week. Merge the letter main document with the **WL1-C8-CS-FEDS.mdb** data source file and include only those customers that shop at the West branch. Save the merged letters document and name it **WL1-C8-CS-SBLtrs**. Print the merged letters document. Save the letter main document and name it **WL1-C8-CS-SBMD**. Print and then close the main document.

Performance Assessment

Note: Before beginning unit assessments, copy to your storage medium the Word2010L1U2 subfolder from the Word2010L1 folder on the CD that accompanies this textbook and then make Word2010L1U2 the active folder.

Assessing Proficiency

In this unit, you have learned to format text into columns; insert, format, and customize objects to enhance the visual appeal of a document; manage files, print envelopes and labels, and create documents using templates; create and edit tables; visually represent data in SmartArt diagrams and organizational charts; and use Mail Merge to create letters, envelopes, labels, and directions.

Assessment 1 Format a Technology Occupations Document

1. Open **TechOccs.docx** and then save the document with Save As and name it **WL1-U2-A01-TechOccs**.
2. Move the insertion point to the beginning of the heading *Telecommuting* and then insert the file named **CommMedia.docx**.
3. Apply the Heading 1 style to the title and the Heading 2 style to the headings in the document.
4. Change the Quick Styles set to *Formal* and change the paragraph spacing to *Open*.
5. Insert a continuous section break at the beginning of the first paragraph of text (the paragraph that begins *The march of computer technology . . .*).
6. Format the text below the section break into two columns.
7. Balance the columns on the second page.
8. Insert a pull quote of your choosing on the first page of the document that includes the text *"As the future of wireless unfolds, many new jobs will emerge as well."*
9. Create a drop cap with the first letter of the first word *The* that begins the first paragraph of text and make the drop cap two lines in height.
10. Manually hyphenate words in the document.
11. Insert page numbering that prints at the bottom of each page (you determine the page number formatting).
12. Save, print, and then close **WL1-U2-A01-TechOccs.docx**.

Assessment 2 Create a Workshop Flyer

1. Create the flyer shown in Figure U2.1 with the following specifications:
   a. Create the WordArt with the following specifications:
      - Use the *Fill - Tan, Text 2, Outline - Background 2* option (first option from the left in the top row) at the WordArt button drop-down gallery.
      - Increase the width to 6.5 inches and the height to 1 inch.
      - Apply the *Deflate* text effect transform shape.
      - Change the text fill color to *Olive Green, Accent 3, Lighter 40%*.
   b. Type the text shown in the figure set in 22-point Calibri bold and center the text.
   c. Insert the clip art image shown in the figure (use the keyword *buildings* to find the clip art) and then change the wrapping style to *Square*. Position and size the image as shown in the figure.
2. Save the document and name it **WL1-U2-A02-TravelFlyer**.
3. Print and then close **WL1-U2-A02-TravelFlyer.docx**.

Figure U2.1 Assessment 2

Assessment 3 Create a Staff Meeting Announcement

1. Create the announcement shown in Figure U2.2 with the following specifications:
   a. Use the *Hexagon* shape in the *Basic Shapes* section of the Shapes drop-down list to create the shape.
   b. Apply the *Subtle Effect - Aqua, Accent 5* shape style.
   c. Apply the *Art Deco* bevel shape effect.
   d. Type the letter **A** (this makes active many of the tab options), click the Home tab, and then click the No Spacing style in the Styles group.
   e. Type the remaining text in the shape as shown in the figure. Insert the ñ as a symbol (in the *(normal text)* font and insert the clock as a symbol (in the *Wingdings* font). Set the text and clock symbol in larger font sizes.
2. Save the completed document and name it **WL1-U2-A03-MeetNotice**.
3. Print and then close **WL1-U2-A03-MeetNotice.docx**.

Figure U2.2 Assessment 3

Assessment 4 Create a River Rafting Flyer

1. At a blank document, insert the picture named **River.jpg**. (Insert the picture using the Picture button.)
2. Crop out a portion of the trees at the left and right and a portion of the hill at the top.
3. Correct the brightness and contrast to *Brightness: +20% Contrast: +40%*.
4. Specify that the picture should wrap behind text.
5. Insert the text *River Rafting Adventures* on one line, *Salmon River, Idaho* on the next line, and *1-888-555-3322* on the third line.
6. Increase the size of the picture so it is easier to see and the size of the text so it is easier to read. Center the text and position it on the picture on top of the river so the text is readable.
7. Save the document and name it **WL1-U2-A04-RaftingFlyer**.
8. Print and then close **WL1-U2-A04-RaftingFlyer.docx**.

Assessment 5 Create an Envelope

1. At a blank document, create an envelope with the text shown in Figure U2.3.
2. Save the envelope document and name it **WL1-U2-A05-Env**.
3. Print and then close **WL1-U2-A05-Env.docx**.

Figure U2.3 Assessment 5

Mrs. Eileen Hebert
15205 East 42nd Street
Lake Charles, LA 71098

Mr. Earl Robicheaux
1436 North Sheldon Street
Jennings, LA 70542

Assessment 6 Create Mailing Labels

1. Create mailing labels with the name and address for Mrs. Eileen Hebert shown in Figure U2.3 using a label vendor and product of your choosing.
2. Save the document and name it **WL1-U2-A06-Labels**.
3. Print and then close **WL1-U2-A06-Labels.docx**.

Assessment 7 Create and Format a Table with Software Training Information

1. At a blank document, create the table shown in Figure U2.4. Format the table and the text in a manner similar to what is shown in Figure U2.4.
2. Insert a formula in B8 that totals the numbers in cells B4 through B7.
3. Insert a formula in C8 that totals the numbers in cells C4 through C7.
4. Save the document and name it **WL1-U2-A07-TechTraining**.
5. Print and then close **WL1-U2-A07-TechTraining.docx**.

Figure U2.4 Assessment 7

TRI-STATE PRODUCTS		
Computer Technology Department **Microsoft® Office 2010 Training**		
Application	**# Enrolled**	**# Completed**
Access 2010	20	15
Excel 2010	62	56
PowerPoint 2010	40	33
Word 2010	80	72
Total		

Assessment 8 Create and Format a Table Containing Training Scores

1. Open **TrainingScores.docx** and then save the document with Save As and name it **WL1-U2-A08-TrainingScores**.
2. Insert formulas that calculate the averages in the appropriate row and column. (When writing the formulas, change the *Number format* option to *0*.)
3. Autofit the contents of the table.
4. Apply a table style of your choosing to the table.
5. Appy any other formatting to improve the visual appeal of the table.
6. Save, print, and then close **WL1-U2-A08-TrainingScores.docx**.

Assessment 9 Create an Organizational Chart

1. Use SmartArt to create an organizational chart for the following text (in the order displayed). Change the colors to *Colorfuttl Range - Accent Colors 2 to 3* and apply the *Metallic Scene* SmartArt style.
2. Save the completed document and name it **WL1-U2-A09-OrgChart**.
3. Print and then close **WL1-U2-A09-OrgChart.docx**.

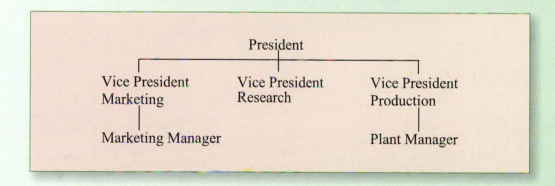

Assessment 10 Create a SmartArt Diagram

1. At a blank document, create the WordArt and diagram shown in Figure U2.5 with the following specifications:
   a. Insert the WordArt text with the *Gradient Fill - Blue, Accent 1, Outline - White* option. Change the shape height to 1 inch and the shape width to 6 inches and then apply the *Square* transform text effect.
   b. Create the diagram using the Vertical Picture Accent List diagram. Click the picture icon that displays in the top circle and then insert the picture named **Seagull.jpg** located in the Word2010L1U2 folder. Insert the same picture in the other two circles. Type the text in each rectangle shape as shown in Figure U2.5. Change the colors to *Colorful Range - Accent Colors 4 to 5* and apply the *Cartoon* SmartArt style.
2. Save the document and name it **WL1-U2-A10-SPDiagram**.
3. Print and then close **WL1-U2-A10-SPDiagram.docx**.

Figure U2.5 Assessment 10

Assessment 11 Merge and Print Letters

1. Look at the information shown in Figure U2.6 and Figure U2.7. Use the Mail Merge feature to prepare six letters using the information shown in the figures. When creating the letter main document, open **SMLtrhd.docx** and then save the document with Save As and name it **WL1-U2-A11-MD**. Insert Fill-in fields in the main document in place of the *(coordinator name)* and *(telephone number)* text. Create the data source file with the text shown in Figure U2.6 and name the file **WL1-U2-A11-DS**.

2. Type the text in the main document as shown in Figure U2.7 and then merge the document with the **WL1-U2-A11-DS.mdb** data source file. When merging, enter the first name and telephone number shown below for the first three records and enter the second name and telephone number shown below for the last three records.

   Jeff Greenswald   (813) 555-9886
   Grace Ramirez   (813) 555-9807

3. Save the merged letters document and name it **WL1-U2-A11-Ltrs**. Print and then close the document.

4. Save and then close the main document.

Figure U2.6 Assessment 11

Mrs. Antonio Mercado
3241 Court G
Tampa, FL 33623

Ms. Alexandria Remick
909 Wheeler South
Tampa, FL 33620

Mr. Curtis Iverson
10139 93rd Court South
Tampa, FL 33654

Ms. Kristina Vukovich
1120 South Monroe
Tampa, FL 33655

Mr. Minh Vu
9302 Lawndale Southwest
Tampa, FL 33623

Mrs. Holly Bernard
8904 Emerson Road
Tampa, FL 33620

December 12, 2012

«AddressBlock»

«GreetingLine»

Sound Medical is switching hospital care in Tampa to St. Jude's Hospital beginning January 1, 2013. As mentioned in last month's letter, St. Jude's Hospital was selected because it meets our requirements for high-quality, customer-pleasing care that is also affordable and accessible. Our physicians look forward to caring for you in this new environment.

Over the past month, staff members at Sound Medical have been working to make this transition as smooth as possible. Surgeries planned after January 1 are being scheduled at St. Jude's Hospital. Mothers delivering babies any time after January 1 are receiving information about delivery room tours and prenatal classes available at St. Jude's. Your Sound Medical doctor will have privileges at St. Jude's and will continue to care for you if you need to be hospitalized.

You are a very important part of our patient family, «Title» «Last_Name», and we hope this information is helpful. If you have any additional questions or concerns, please call your Sound Medical health coordinator, (coordinator name), at (telephone number), between 8:00 a.m. and 4:30 p.m.

Sincerely,

Jody Tiemann
District Administrator

XX
WL1-U2-A11-MD.docx

Assessment 12 Merge and Print Envelopes

1. Use the Mail Merge feature to prepare envelopes for the letters created in Assessment 11.
2. Specify **WL1-U2-A11-DS.mdb** as the data source document.
3. Save the merged envelopes document and name the document **WL1-U2-A12-Envs**.
4. Print and then close **WL1-U2-A12-Envs.docx**.
5. Do not save the envelope main document.

Writing Activities ■■■■■■■■■■■■■■■■

The following activities give you the opportunity to practice your writing skills along with demonstrating an understanding of some of the important Word features you have mastered in this unit. Use correct grammar, appropriate word choices, and clear sentence constructions.

Activity 1 Compose a Letter to Volunteers

You are an employee for the City of Greenwater and are responsible for coordinating volunteers for the city's Safe Night program. Compose a letter to the volunteers listed below and include the following information in the letter:

- Safe Night event scheduled for Saturday, June 16, 2012.
- Volunteer orientation scheduled for Thursday, May 17, 2012, at 7:30 p.m. At the orientation, participants will learn about the types of volunteer positions available and the work schedule.

Include any additional information in the letter, including a thank you to the volunteers. Use the Mail Merge feature to create a data source with the names and addresses shown below that is attached to the main document, which is the letter to the volunteers. Save the merged letters as **WL1-U2-Act01-Ltrs** and then print the letters.

Mrs. Laura Reston
376 Thompson Avenue
Greenwater, OR 99034

Ms. Cecilia Sykes
1430 Canyon Road
Greenwater, OR 99034

Mr. Ralph Emerson
1103 Highlands Avenue
Greenwater, OR 99034

Mr. Matthew Klein
7408 Ryan Road
Greenwater, OR 99034

Mr. Brian McDonald
8980 Union Street
Greenwater, OR 99034

Mrs. Nola Alverez
598 McBride Street
Greenwater, OR 99034

Activity 2 Create a Business Letterhead

You have just opened a new mailing and shipping business and need letterhead stationery. Create a letterhead for your company in a header and/or footer. Use Word's Help feature to learn about creating a header that only displays and prints on the first page. Create the letterhead in a header that displays and prints only on the first page and include *at least* one of the following: a clip art image, a picture, a shape, a text box, and/or WordArt. Include the following information in the header:

Global Mailing
4300 Jackson Avenue
Toronto, ON M4C 3X4
(416) 555-0095
www.emcp.net/globalmailing

Save the completed letterhead and name it **WL1-U2-Act02-Ltrhd**. Print and then close the document.

Internet Research ▪▪▪▪▪▪▪▪▪▪▪▪▪▪▪▪▪▪▪▪▪

Create a Flyer on an Incentive Program

The owner of Terra Travel Services is offering an incentive to motivate travel consultants to increase travel bookings. The incentive is a sales contest with a grand prize of a one-week paid vacation to Cancun, Mexico. The owner has asked you to create a flyer that will be posted on the office bulletin board that includes information about the incentive program and some information about Cancun. Create this flyer using information about Cancun that you find on the Internet. Include a photo you find on a website (make sure it is not copyrighted) or include a clip art image representing travel. Include any other information or object to add visual appeal to the flyer. Save the completed flyer and name it **WL1-U2-InternetResearch**. Print and then close the document.

Job Study ▪▪▪▪▪▪▪▪▪▪▪▪▪▪▪▪▪▪▪▪▪▪

Develop Recycling Program Communications

The Chief Operating Officer of Harrington Engineering has just approved your draft of the company's new recycling policy (see the file named **RecyclingPolicy.docx** located in the Word2010L1U2 folder). Edit the draft and prepare a final copy of the policy along with a memo to all employees describing the new guidelines. To support the company's energy resources conservation effort, you will send hard copies of the new policy to the Somerset Recycling Program president and to directors of Somerset Chamber of Commerce.

Using the concepts and techniques you learned in this unit, prepare the following documents:

- Format the recycling policy manual, including a cover page, appropriate headers and footers, and page numbers. Add at least one graphic and one diagram where appropriate. Format the document using a Quick Styles set and styles. Save the manual and name it **WL1-U2-JobStudyManual**. Print the manual.

- Download a memo template from Office.com Templates (at the New tab Backstage view) and then create a memo from Susan Gerhardt, Chief Operating Officer of Harrington Engineering to all employees introducing the new recycling program. Copy the *Procedure* section of the recycling policy manual into the memo where appropriate. Include a table listing five employees who will act as Recycling Coordinators at Harrington Engineering (make up the names). Add columns for the employees' department names and their telephone extensions. Save the memo and name it **WL1-U2-JobStudyMemo**. Print the memo.
- Write a letter to the President of the Somerset Recycling Program, William Elizondo, enclosing a copy of the recycling policy manual. Add a notation indicating copies with enclosures were sent to all members of the Somerset Chamber of Commerce. Save the letter and name it **WL1-U2-JobStudyLetter**. Print the letter.
- Create mailing labels (see Figure U2.8). Save the labels and name the file **WL1-U2-JobStudyLabels**. Print the file.

Figure U2.8 Mailing Labels

William Elizondo, President Somerset Recycling Program 700 West Brighton Road Somerset, NJ 55123	Paul Schwartz Somerset Chamber of Commerce 45 Wallace Road Somerset, NJ 55123
Ashley Crighton Somerset Chamber of Commerce 45 Wallace Road Somerset, NJ 55123	Carol Davis Somerset Chamber of Commerce 45 Wallace Road Somerset, NJ 55123
Robert Knight Somerset Chamber of Commerce 45 Wallace Road Somerset, NJ 55123	

Index

Text Box Tools Format tab,
    178, 179
Text Effects button, 42
Text Highlight Color button, 42
Theme Colors button, 49, 50
Theme Effects button, 49, 50
Theme Fonts button, 49, 50
themes
    applying, 49–50
    changing, 49–50
    defined, 49
this point forward option, 158
time, inserting, 165–166
Title bar, 6
typeface
    defined, 37
    monospaced, 37–38
    proportional, 5, 7, 38
    sans serif, 38
    serif, 38
type size, 38
type styles, 38
    choosing, 40–41

U

Undo button, 21–22, 92
United States Postal Service
    (USPS) guidelines for
    addresses, 224, 225
unpinning of document, 13

V

vertical alignment option, 153
vertically aligning text, 167–168
vertically centering text, 168
vertical ruler, 6
vertical scroll bar, 6, 15
view, changing, 109–110
View buttons, 109
viewing, documents side by side,
    217–218
View Options button, 109
View Ruler button, 85
View Side by Side button, 217

W

watermark, 125
    inserting, 125
web browser, opening XPS files
    in, 213
white space
    at end of sentence, 7
    hiding/showing in Print
        Layout view, 112–113
windows
    arranging, 215
    opening, 215
    splitting, 216–218
    working with, 214–217
Windows Live ID account, 208

Word, exiting, 14
WordArt, creating and
    modifying, 181–183
word forms, finding and
    replacing, 134–135
Word Options dialog box, 76
words
    automatically hyphenating,
        161
    manually hyphenating,
        161–162
word wrap, 5
Write & Insert Fields group,
    295–296

X

XML (Extensible Markup
    Language), 207
XPS (XML paper specification)
    format, 207
    saving document as,
        213–214

Z

Zoom In button, 109
Zoom Out button, 109
Zoom slider bar, 109, 219
Zoom to Page button, 219

Microsoft Word

Level 2

Unit 1 ■ Formatting and Customizing Documents

Word

Microsoft®

CHAPTER 1

Customizing Paragraphs and Pages

PERFORMANCE OBJECTIVES

Upon successful completion of Chapter 1, you will be able to:

- **Apply custom numbering and bulleting formatting to text**
- **Define new bullets**
- **Insert and define multilevel list numbering**
- **Insert, format, and customize images and text boxes**
- **Insert headers and footers in documents**
- **Format, edit, and remove a header or footer**
- **Control widow/orphans and keep text together on a page**
- **Print sections**
- **Insert and format charts**

Tutorials

1.1 Inserting Custom Numbers and Bullets
1.2 Inserting Multilevel Lists
1.3 Customizing and Formatting an Image
1.4 Applying Advanced Formatting to Images
1.5 Inserting and Formatting Text Boxes
1.6 Customizing Headers and Footers
1.7 Printing Sections of a Document
1.8 Keeping Text Together
1.9 Creating Charts
1.10 Changing Chart Design, Layout, and Formatting

Word contains a variety of options for formatting text in paragraphs and applying page formatting. In this chapter you will learn how to insert custom numbers and bullets, define new numbering formats, define new picture and symbol bullets, apply multilevel numbering to text, and define a new multilevel list. You will also learn about inserting and editing headers and footers, printing specific sections of a document, controlling text flow on pages, and presenting text visually in a chart. Model answers for this chapter's projects appear on the following pages.

Word2010L2C1

Note: Before beginning the projects, copy to your storage medium the Word2010L2C1 subfolder from the Word2010L2 folder on the CD that accompanies this textbook. Steps on how to copy a folder are presented on the inside of the back cover of this textbook. Do this every time you start a chapter's projects.

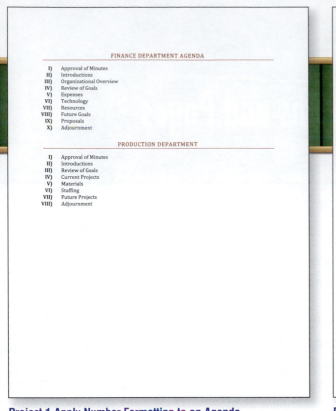

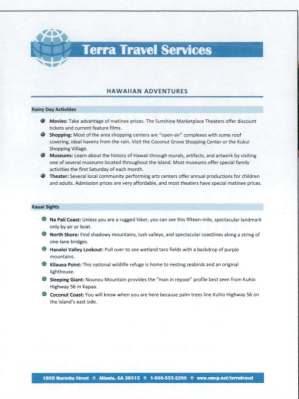

Project 1 Apply Number Formatting to an Agenda

WL2-C1-P1-FDAgenda.docx

Project 2 Apply Custom Bullets to a Technology Document

WL2-C1-P2-TTSHawaii.docx

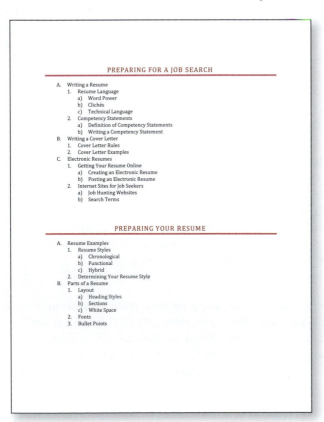

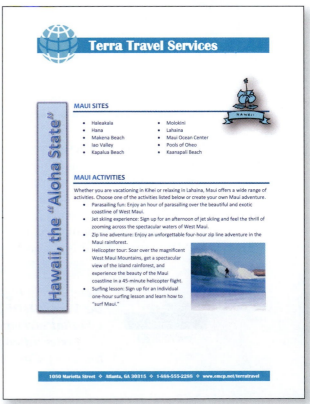

Project 3 Apply Multilevel List Numbering to a Computer Devices Document

WL2-C1-P3-JSList.docx

Project 4 Insert Images and a Text Box in a Travel Document

WL2-C1-P4-TTSMaui.docx

PRODUCTIVITY SOFTWARE

Productivity software includes software that people typically use to complete work, such as a word processor (working with words), spreadsheet (working with data, numbers, and calculations), database (organizing and retrieving data records), and presentation (creating slideshows with text and graphics) programs. Productivity software is often compiled into suites of applications, such as Microsoft Office, because many people use two or more of these products to get their work completed. Office suites often include a word processor, a spreadsheet application, presentation software, and database management software. Suites also allow users to integrate content from one program into another, such as including a spreadsheet chart in a report created with a word processor.

WORD PROCESSING SOFTWARE

Word processor software certainly does "process" words, but today it does a great deal more. With a word processor you can create documents that include sophisticated formatting; change text fonts (styles applied to text); add special effects such as bold, italics, and underlining; add shadows, background colors, and other effects to text and objects; and include tables, photos, drawings, and links to online content. You can also use templates (predesigned documents with formatting and graphics already in place for you to fill in) to design web pages, newsletters, and more. A mail merge feature makes it easy to take a list of names and addresses and print personalized letters and envelopes or labels.

SPREADSHEET SOFTWARE

Spreadsheet software, such as Microsoft Excel, is an application where numbers rule. Using spreadsheet software you can perform calculations that range from simple (adding, averaging, and multiplying) to complex (estimating standard deviations based on a range of numbers, for example). In addition, spreadsheet software offers sophisticated charting and graphing capabilities. Formatting tools help you create polished looking documents such as budgets, invoices, schedules, attendance records, and purchase orders. With spreadsheet software, you can also keep track of data such as your holiday card list and sort that list or search for specific names or other data.

DATABASE SOFTWARE

Database software can manage large quantities of data. The software provides functions for organizing the data into related lists and retrieving useful information from these lists. For example, imagine that you are a salesperson who wants to create a list of customers. Of course you want to include the name, address, and company name for each person. However, you might also want each customer record to include the customer's birthday, spouse's name, and favorite hobby as well as a record of purchases in the past year. You can also set up fields to look up data such as city names based on a ZIP code, saving you time reentering data. Once that data is entered into a table you can view information in a spreadsheet-like list or as individual customer record forms. You can create queries that let you find specific data sets. For example, say you want to find every customer with a birthday in June who is interested in sports and has purchased at least $2,000 of products in the last year so you can invite them to a company sponsored sports event. With a database, you can generate a list of those records easily.

PRESENTATION SOFTWARE

Presentation software, such as Microsoft PowerPoint, uses the concept of individual slides that form a slideshow. Slides may contain bulleted lists of key concepts, graphics, tables, animations, hyperlinks to web pages, diagrams, and charts. A slideshow can support a presenter's comments during a talk, can run continuously on its own, or can be browsed by an individual online or on a computer. A presentation program can help users create attractive slides by allowing them to use background art from a template, placeholders for titles and bulleted lists, and graphics.

GRAPHICS AND MULTIMEDIA SOFTWARE

With graphics software, you can create, edit, and format images such as pictures and photos. Use multimedia software to work with media such as animations, audio, and video.

GRAPHICS SOFTWARE

If you like working with drawings, photos, or other kinds of images, you may have used graphics software, which is software that allows you to create, edit, or manipulate images such as drawings and photos. Though most productivity software such as word processors and presentation software include graphics features, design professionals work with products that are much more feature-rich such as desktop publishing software, photo editing software, and screen capture software.

Desktop publishing software is used by design professionals to lay out pages for books, magazines, brochures, product packaging, and other print materials. Photo editing software is used by design professionals to enhance photo quality or apply special effects such as blurring elements or feathering the edges of a photo. With screen capture software you can capture an entire computer screen or only a portion of it, which is helpful for showing people how to use software features.

MULTIMEDIA SOFTWARE

Use multimedia software to work with media such as animations, audio, and video. Animation software enables you to animate objects and create interactive content. Animations are sometimes combined with music or narration. Use audio software to work with music files and record and edit audio used for podcasts or as audio files to be shared with others. Create and edit video programs with video software. Videos might include an audio track with voice or music, or a variety of specific effects.

Project 5 Insert Headers and Footers in a Computer Report

WL2-C1-P5-CompSoftware.docx

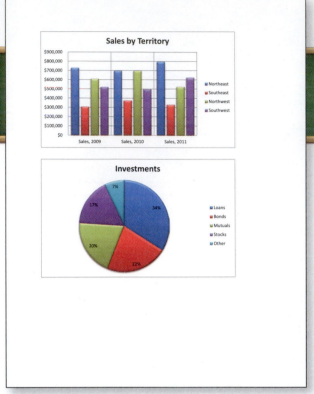

Project 6 Create and Format a Column Chart and Pie Chart

WL2-C1-P6-SalesChart.docx

Project 1 — Apply Number Formatting to an Agenda

2 Parts

You will open an agenda document, apply formatting including number formatting, and then define and apply custom numbering.

Inserting Custom Numbers and Bullets

Numbering

Bullets

Automatically number paragraphs or insert bullets before paragraphs using buttons in the Paragraph group in the Home tab. Use the Bullets button to insert bullets before specific paragraphs and use the Numbering button to insert numbers. If you want to insert custom numbering of bullets, click the button arrow and then choose from the drop-down list that displays.

Inserting Custom Numbers

HINT

If the automatic numbering or bullets feature is on, press Shift + Enter to insert a line break without inserting a bullet or number.

You can insert numbers as you type text or select text and then apply numbering formatting. If you type *1.*, press the spacebar, type a paragraph of text, and then press the Enter key, Word indents the number approximately 0.25 inch and then hang indents the text in the paragraph approximately 0.5 inch from the left margin. Additionally, *2.* is inserted 0.25 inch from the left margin at the beginning of the next paragraph. Continue typing items and Word inserts the next number in the list. To number existing paragraphs of text, select the paragraphs and then click the Numbering button in the Paragraph group in the Home tab.

When you click the Numbering button in the Paragraph group, Arabic numbers (1., 2., 3., etc.) are inserted in the document. You can change this default numbering by clicking the Numbering button arrow and then clicking the desired option at the Numbering drop-down gallery.

To change list levels, click the Numbering button arrow, point to the *Change List Level* option located toward the bottom of the drop-down gallery, and then click the desired list level at the side menu. You can set the numbering value with options at the Set Numbering Value dialog box. Display this dialog box by clicking the Numbering button arrow and then clicking the *Set Numbering Value* option located at the bottom of the drop-down gallery.

Project 1a   **Inserting Custom Numbers**   **Part 1 of 2**

1. Open **FDAgenda.docx** and then save the document and name it **WL2-C1-P1-FDAgenda**.
2. Restart the numbering for the list to begin at 1 by completing the following steps:
   a. Select the numbered paragraphs.
   b. Click the Numbering button arrow in the Paragraph group in the Home tab and then click *Set Numbering Value* at the drop-down menu.
   c. At the Set Numbering Value dialog box, select the number in the *Set value to* option box, type 1, and then press the Enter key.

Step 2c

3. Change the numbering of the paragraphs to letters by completing the following steps:
   a. With the numbered paragraphs selected, click the Numbering button arrow.
   b. At the Numbering drop-down gallery, click the option that uses capital letters as shown below (the location of the option may vary).

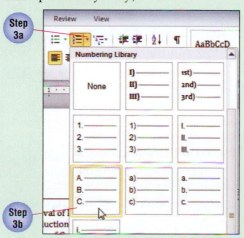

Step 3a

Step 3b

4. Add text to the agenda by positioning the insertion point immediately to the right of the text *Introductions*, pressing the Enter key, and then typing **Organizational Overview**.

5. Demote the lettered list by completing the following steps:
   a. Select the lettered paragraphs.
   b. Click the Numbering button arrow, point to the *Change List Level* option and then click the *a.* option at the side menu.
6. With the paragraphs still selected, promote the list by clicking the Decrease Indent button in the Paragraph group in the Home tab. (The list changes back to capital letters.)
7. Move the insertion point to the end of the document and then type **The meeting will stop for lunch, which is catered and will be held in the main conference center from 12:15 to 1:30.**
8. Press the Enter key twice and then click the Numbering button.
9. Click the AutoCorrect Options button that displays next to the *A.* inserted in the document and then click the *Continue Numbering* option at the drop-down list. (This changes the letter from *A.* to *H.*)

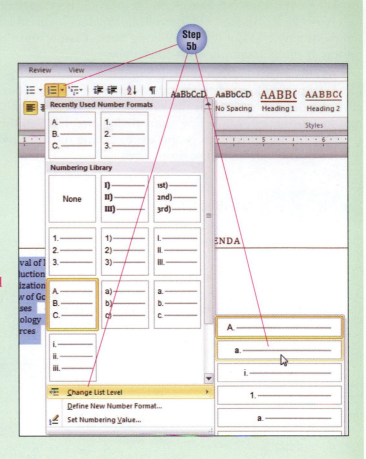

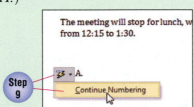

10. Type **Future Goals**, press the Enter key, type **Proposals**, press the Enter key, and then type **Adjournment**.
11. Press the Enter key and the letter *K.* is inserted in the document. Turn off the list creation by clicking the Numbering button arrow and then click the *None* option at the drop-down gallery.
12. Save and then print **WL2-C1-P1-FDAgenda.docx**.
13. Select and then delete the paragraph of text in the middle of the list, including the blank lines above and below the text. (All of the lettered items should be listed consecutively with the same spacing between.)
14. Select the lettered paragraphs, click the Numbering button arrow, and then click the option that uses numbers followed by a right parenthesis *1), 2), 3),* and so on.
15. Save **WL2-C1-P1-FDAgenda.docx**.

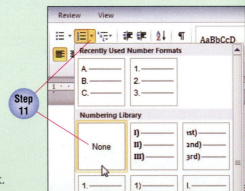

Defining Numbering Formatting

Along with the default numbers and the custom numbers, you can also define your own numbering formatting with options at the Define New Number Format dialog box shown in Figure 1.1. Display this dialog box by clicking the Numbering button arrow and then clicking *Define New Number Format* at the drop-down gallery. With options at the dialog box, you can specify the number style, font, and alignment and preview the formatting in the *Preview* section.

A numbering format you create at the Define New Number Format dialog box is automatically included in the *Numbering Library* section in the Numbering button drop-down list. You can remove a number formatting from the drop-down list by right-clicking the number format and then clicking *Remove* at the shortcut menu.

▼ **Quick Steps**

Define Numbering Formatting
1. Click Numbering button arrow.
2. Click *Define New Number Format*.
3. Specify desired format.
4. Click OK.

Figure 1.1 Define New Number Format Dialog Box

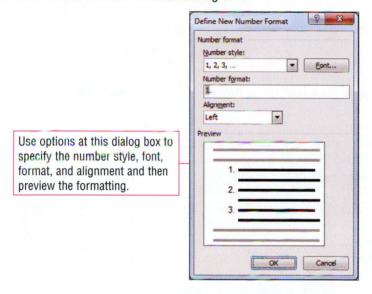

Use options at this dialog box to specify the number style, font, format, and alignment and then preview the formatting.

Project 1b **Defining a Numbering Format**   **Part 2 of 2**

1. With **WL2-C1-P1-FDAgenda.docx** open, define a new number format by completing the following steps:
   a. With the insertion point positioned on any character in the numbered paragraphs, click the Numbering button arrow in the Paragraph group in the Home tab.
   b. Click *Define New Number Format* at the drop-down list.
   c. At the Define New Number Format dialog box, click the down-pointing arrow at the right of the *Number style* option and then click the *1st, 2nd, 3rd ...* option.
   d. Click the Font button that displays at the right side of the *Number style* list box.

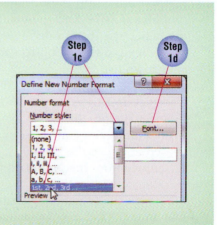

e. At the Font dialog box, scroll down the *Font* list box and then click *Candara*.
f. Click *Bold* in the *Font style* list box.

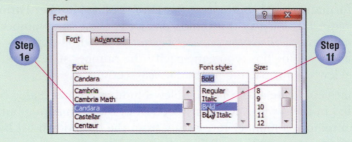

g. Click OK to close the Font dialog box.
h. Click the down-pointing arrow at the right of the *Alignment* option box and then click *Right* at the drop-down list.

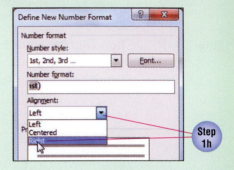

i. Click OK to close the Define New Number Format dialog box. (This applies the new formatting to the numbered paragraphs in the document.)

2. After looking at the numbering, you decide to define another number format by completing the following steps:
   a. Click the Numbering button arrow.
   b. Click *Define New Number Format* at the drop-down list.
   c. At the Define New Number Format dialog box, click the down-pointing arrow at the right of the *Number style* option and then click the *I, II, III, …* option.
   d. Click the Font button that displays at the right side of the *Number style* list box.

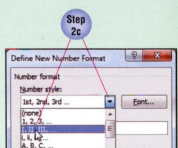

   e. At the Font dialog box, click *Cambria* in the list box.
   f. Check to make sure *Bold* is selected in the *Font style* list box, and then click OK to close the Font dialog box.
   g. At the Define New Number Format dialog box, make sure *Right* is selected in the *Alignment* option box and then click OK. (This applies the new formatting to the numbered paragraphs in the document.)

3. Insert a file into the current document by completing the following steps:
   a. Press Ctrl + End to move the insertion point to end of the document.
   b. Click the Insert tab.
   c. Click the Object button arrow in the Text group and then click *Text from File* at the drop-down list.
   d. At the Insert File dialog box, navigate to the Word2010L2C1 folder and then double-click **PDAgenda.docx**.

4. Select the text below the title *PRODUCTION DEPARTMENT*, click the Home tab, click the Numbering button arrow, and then click the Roman numeral style that you created in Step 2.

5. Remove from the Numbering Library the number format you created by completing the following steps:
   a. Click the Numbering button arrow.
   b. In the *Numbering Library* section, right-click the Roman numeral numbering format you created.
   c. Click *Remove* at the shortcut menu.

6. Save, print, and then close **WL2-C1-P1-FDAgenda.docx**.

Project **2**   **Apply Custom Bullets to a Technology Document**   **1 Part**

You will open a technology document and then define and insert custom picture and symbol bullets.

Defining and Inserting Custom Bullets

When you click the Bullets button in the Paragraph group, a round bullet is inserted in the document. You can insert custom bullets by clicking the Bullets button arrow and then clicking the desired bullet at the drop-down gallery. This drop-down gallery displays the most recently used bullets along with an option for defining new bullets. Click the *Define New Bullet* option and the Define New Bullet dialog box displays as shown in Figure 1.2. With options at the dialog box, you can choose a symbol or picture bullet, change the font size of the bullet, and specify the alignment of the bullet. When you choose a custom bullet, consider matching the theme or mood of the document to maintain a consistent look, or create a picture bullet to add visual interest

A bullet you create at the Define New Bullet dialog box is automatically included in the *Bullet Library* section in the Bullets button drop-down list. You can remove a bullet from the drop-down list by right-clicking the bullet and then clicking *Remove* at the shortcut menu.

As with a numbered list, you can change the level of a bulleted list. To do this, click the item or select the items you want to change, click the Bullets button arrow, and then point to *Change List Level*. At the side menu of bullet options that displays, click the desired bullet. If you want to insert a line break in the list while the automatic bullets feature is on without inserting a bullet, press Shift + Enter. (You can also insert a line break in a numbered list without inserting a number by pressing Shift + Enter.)

▼ Quick Steps

Define Custom Bullet
1. Click Bullets button arrow.
2. Click *Define New Bullet* at drop-down gallery.
3. Click Symbol button or Picture button.
4. Click desired symbol or picture.
5. Click OK.
6. Click OK.

HINT

Create a picture bullet to add visual interest in a document.

Figure 1.2 Define New Bullet Dialog Box

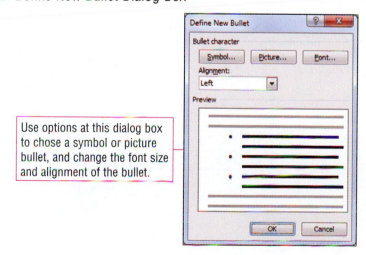

Use options at this dialog box to chose a symbol or picture bullet, and change the font size and alignment of the bullet.

1. Open **TTSHawaii.docx** and then save the document with Save As and name it **WL2-C1-P2-TTSHawaii**.

2. Define and insert a picture bullet by completing the following steps:

    a. Select the four paragraphs of text below the heading *Rainy Day Activities*.

    b. Click the Bullets button arrow in the Paragraph group in the Home tab and then click *Define New Bullet* at the drop-down gallery.

    c. At the Define New Bullet dialog box, click the Picture button.

    d. At the Picture Bullet dialog box, click the round, green bullet shown at the right.

    e. Click OK to close the Picture Bullet dialog box.

    f. Click OK to close the Define New Bullet dialog box. (The new bullet is applied to the selected paragraphs.)

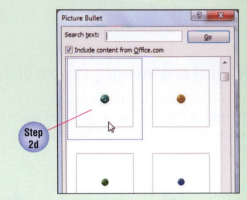

3. Define and insert a symbol bullet by completing the following steps:

    a. Select the six paragraphs below the heading *Kauai Sights*.

    b. Click the Bullets button arrow and then click *Define New Bullet* at the drop-down gallery.

    c. At the Define New Bullet dialog box, click the Symbol button.

    d. At the Symbol dialog box, click the down-pointing arrow at the right of the *Font* option, scroll down the drop-down list, and then click *Wingdings*.

    e. Click the flower symbol shown at the right below.

    f. Click OK to close the Symbol dialog box.

    g. At the Define New Bullet dialog box, click the Font button.

    h. At the Font dialog box, click *14* in the *Size* list box.

    i. Click the down-pointing arrow at the right of the Font color option and then click the color *Bright Green, Accent 4, Darker 25%*.

    j. Click OK to close the Font dialog box and then click OK to close the Define New Bullet dialog box.

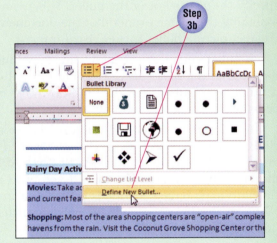

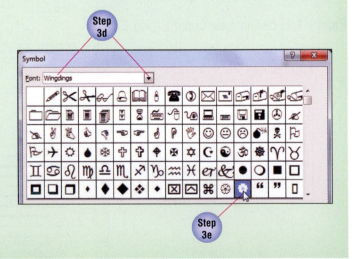

4. Remove the two bullets from the Bullet Library by completing the following steps:
   a. Click the Bullets button arrow.
   b. Right-click the round, green picture bullet in the *Bullet Library* section and then click *Remove* at the shortcut menu.
   c. Click the Bullets button arrow.
   d. Right-click the flower symbol bullet in the *Bullet Library* section and then click *Remove* at the shortcut menu.
5. Save, print, and then close **WL2-C1-P2-TTSHawaii.docx**.

 Project **3** **Apply Multilevel List Numbering to a Computer Devices Document** 2 Parts

You will open a document containing a list of job search terms, apply multilevel list numbering to the text, and then define and apply a new multilevel list numbering style. You will also type text in a multilevel list.

Inserting Multilevel List Numbering ■■■■■■■■■■■

Use the Multilevel List button in the Paragraph group in the Home tab to specify the type of numbering for paragraphs of text at the left margin, first tab, second tab, and so on. Apply predesigned multilevel numbering to text in a document by clicking the Multilevel List button and then clicking the desired numbering style at the drop-down gallery. Some options at the Multilevel List drop-down gallery display with *Heading 1*, *Heading 2*, and so on, after the number. Click one of these options and Word inserts the numbering and applies the heading styles to the text.

▼ **Quick Steps**

Insert Multilevel List Numbering
1. Click Multilevel List button.
2. Click desired style at drop-down gallery.

Multilevel List

Project **3a** **Inserting Multilevel List Numbering** Part 1 of 2

1. Open **JSList.docx** and then save the document with Save As and name it **WL2-C1-P3-JSList**.
2. Select the paragraphs of text below the title and then apply multilevel numbers by completing the following steps:
   a. Click the Multilevel List button in the Paragraph group in the Home tab.
   b. At the drop-down gallery, click the middle option in the top row of the *List Library* section.
   c. Deselect the text.
3. Save and then print **WL2-C1-P3-JSList.docx**.

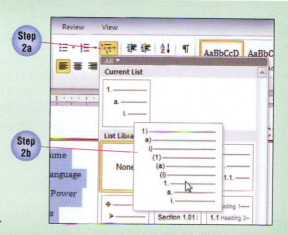

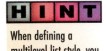

▼ Quick Steps

Define Multilevel List
1. Click Multilevel List button.
2. Click *Define New Multilevel List* at drop-down gallery.
3. Choose desired level, number format, and/or position.
4. Click OK.

HINT

When defining a multilevel list style, you can mix numbers and bullets in the same list.

Defining a Multilevel List

The Multilevel List button drop-down gallery contains predesigned level numbering options. If the gallery does not contain the type of numbering you desire, you can create your own. To do this, click the Multilevel List button and then click *Define New Multilevel List*. This displays the Define new Multilevel list dialog box shown in Figure 1.3. At this dialog box, click a level in the *Click level to modify* option box and then specify the number format, style, position, and alignment.

Typing a Multilevel List

You can select and apply a multilevel list or you can apply the list and then type the text. As you type text, press the Tab key to move to the next level or press Shift + Tab to move to the previous level.

Figure 1.3 Define New Multilevel List Dialog Box

Click a level in this option box and then specify the number format, style, position, and alignment.

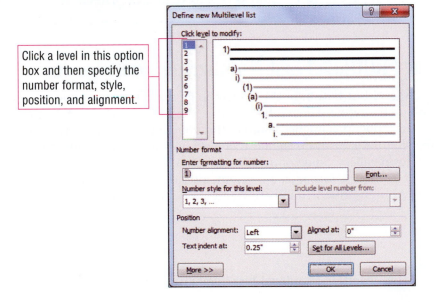

Project 3b   **Defining and Typing a New Multilevel List**   **Part 2 of 2**

1. Make sure **WL2-C1-P3-JSList.docx** is open.
2. Select the paragraphs of text below the title.
3. Click the Multilevel List button in the Paragraph group in the Home tab.
4. Click the *Define New Multilevel List* option at the drop-down gallery.

5. At the Define new Multilevel list dialog box, make sure *1* is selected in the *Click level to modify* list box.

6. Click the down-pointing arrow at the right side of the *Number style for this level* option and then click *A, B, C, …* at the drop-down list.

7. Click in the *Enter formatting for number* text box, delete any text that displays after *A*, and then type a period (.). (The entry in the text box should now display as *A.*)

8. Click the up-pointing arrow at the right side of the *Aligned at* measurement box until *0.3"* displays in the measurement box.

9. Click the up-pointing arrow at the right side of the *Text indent at* measurement box until *0.6"* displays in the measurement box.

10. Click *2* in the *Click level to modify* list box.

11. Click the down-pointing arrow at the right side of the *Number style for this level* option and then click *1, 2, 3, …* at the drop-down list.

12. Click in the *Enter formatting for number* text box, delete any text that displays after the *1*, and then type a period (.).

13. Click the up-pointing arrow at the right side of the *Aligned at* measurement box until *0.6"* displays in the measurement box.

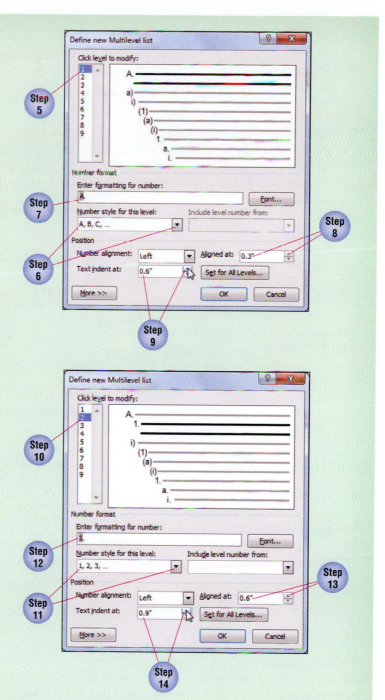

14. Click the up-pointing arrow at the right side of the *Text indent at* measurement box until *0.9"* displays in the measurement box.

15. Click *3* in the *Click level to modify* list box.
16. Click the down-pointing arrow at the right side of the *Number style for this level* option and then click *a, b, c, ...* at the drop-down list.
17. Make sure *a)* displays in the *Enter formatting for number* text box. (If not, delete any text that displays after the *a* and then type a right parenthesis.)
18. Click the up-pointing arrow at the right side of the *Aligned at* measurement box until *0.9"* displays in the measurement box.
19. Click the up-pointing arrow at the right side of the *Text indent at* measurement box until *1.2"* displays in the measurement box.
20. Click OK to close the dialog box. (This applies the new multilevel numbering to the selected text.)
21. Deselect the text.

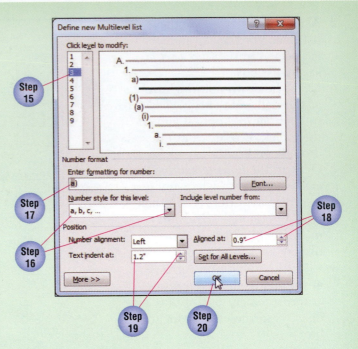

22. With the document still open, make the following changes:
    a. Select and then delete *Competency Statements on a Resume* in the *Competency Statements* section.
    b. Move the insertion point immediately right of *Clichés*, press the Enter key, and then type **Technical Language**.
23. Press Ctrl + End to move the insertion point to the end of the document and then press the Enter key five times.
24. Type **PREPARING YOUR RESUME** and then press the Enter key.
25. Turn on the multilevel list you created by clicking the Multilevel List button and then clicking the list you created (displays in the *Lists in Current Documents* section of the drop-down gallery).
26. Type **Resume Examples** as shown in Figure 1.4.
27. Press the Enter key, press the Tab key, and then type **Resume Styles** as shown in Figure 1.4.
28. Continue typing the text shown in Figure 1.4. Press the Tab key to indent text to the next level or press Shift + Tab to decrease the indent to the previous level. (The multilevel list will apply letter and number formatting.)
29. Apply the Heading 1 style to the title *PREPARING YOUR RESUME*.
30. Save, print, and then close **WL2-C1-P3-JSList.docx**.

Figure 1.4 Project 3b

Resume Examples
    Resume Styles
        Chronological
        Functional
        Hybrid
    Determining Your Resume Style
Parts of a Resume
    Layout
        Heading Styles
        Sections
        White Space
    Fonts
    Bullet Points

Project 4 Insert Images and a Text Box in a Travel Document 3 Parts

You will open a travel document on Maui, insert and customize a clip art image and photograph, and then insert and customize a text box.

Customizing Images and Text Boxes ▪▪▪▪▪▪▪▪▪▪▪▪▪

Word provides a number of methods for formatting and customizing graphic images such as pictures, clip art images, and text boxes. You can format pictures and clip art images with options at the Picture Tools Format tab and further customize images with options at the Format Picture dialog box and the Layout dialog box. Use options at the Drawing Tools Format tab to format and customize text boxes and further customize text boxes with options at the Format Shape dialog box and the Layout dialog box.

Customizing Layout

Customize the layout of images with options at the Layout dialog box. Display the Layout dialog box by clicking the Size group dialog box launcher in the Picture Tools Format tab. The Layout dialog box has three tabs. Click the Position tab and the dialog box displays as shown in Figure 1.5.

Figure 1.5 Layout Dialog Box with Position Tab Selected

Use options in this section to specify the horizontal position of the image.

Use options in this section to specify the vertical position of the image.

Use options in this section to specify how you want the image positioned.

Use options at the Layout dialog box with the Position tab selected to specify horizontal and vertical layout options. In the *Horizontal* section, choose the *Alignment* option to specify whether you want the image horizontally left-, center-, or right-aligned relative to the margin, page, column, or character. Choose the *Book layout* option if you want to align the image with inside or outside margins on the page. Use the *Absolute position* option to align the image horizontally with the specified amount of space between the left edge of the image and the left edge of the page, column, left margin, or character. In the *Vertical* section of the dialog box, use the *Alignment* option to align the image at the top, bottom, center, inside, or outside relative to the page, margin, or line. In the *Options* section, you can attach (anchor) the image to a paragraph so that the image and paragraph move together. Choose the *Move object with text* option if you want the image to move up or down on the page with the paragraph to which it is anchored. Keep the image anchored in the same place on the page by choosing the *Lock anchor* option. Choose the *Allow overlap* option if you want images with the same wrapping style to overlap.

Use options at the Layout dialog box with the Text Wrapping tab selected to specify the wrapping style for the image. You can also specify which sides you want text to wrap around, and you can specify the amount of space you want between the text and the top, bottom, left, and right edges of the image. Click the Size tab at the Layout dialog box to display options for specifying the height and width measurements of the image relative to the margin, page, top margin, bottom margin, inside margin, or outside margin. Use the *Rotation* option to rotate the image by degrees and use options in the *Scale* section to change the percentage of height and width scale. Click the Reset button located in the lower right corner of the dialog box to reset the image size.

1. Open **TTSMaui.docx** and then save the document with Save As and name it
   WL2-C1-P4-TTSMaui.
2. Insert a clip art image by completing the following steps:
   a. Click the Insert tab and then click the Clip Art button in the Illustrations group.
   b. At the Clip Art task pane, select any text that displays in the *Search for* text box, type
      Hawaii, and then press the Enter key.
   c. Click the clip art image in the list box as shown below.

   d. Close the Clip Art task pane.
3. Select the current measurement in the *Shape Height* measurement box in the Picture Tools
   Format tab, type 1.5, and then press Enter.
4. Click the *Beveled Matte, White* style thumbnail in the Picture Styles group (second
   thumbnail from the left).

5. Click the Corrections button in the Adjust group and then click the second option from
   the left in the fourth row (*Brightness: –20% Contrast: +20%*).
6. After looking at the image, you decide to
   reset the image. Do this by clicking the
   Reset Picture button arrow in the Adjust
   group and then clicking *Reset Picture & Size*
   at the drop-down list.

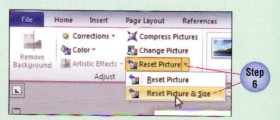

7. Select the current measurement in the
   Shape Height measurement box, type 1.3,
   and then press Enter.
8. Click the Wrap Text button in the Arrange
   group and then click *In Front of Text* at the drop-down list.

9. Position the clip art image precisely on the page by completing the following steps:
   a. With the image selected, click the Size group dialog box launcher.
   b. At the Layout dialog box, click the Position tab.
   c. Make sure the *Absolute position* option in the *Horizontal* section is selected.
   d. Press the Tab key and then type **6.2** in the *Absolute position* measurement box.
   e. Click the down-pointing arrow at the right of the *to the right of* option box and then click *Page* at the drop-down list.
   f. Make sure the *Absolute position* option in the *Vertical* section is selected.

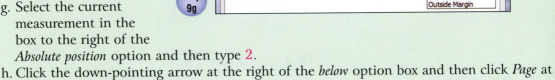

   g. Select the current measurement in the box to the right of the *Absolute position* option and then type **2**.
   h. Click the down-pointing arrow at the right of the *below* option box and then click *Page* at the drop-down list.
   i. Click OK to close the Layout dialog box.
10. Click the *Drop Shadow Rectangle* style thumbnail in the Picture Styles group (fourth thumbnail from the left).
11. Click the Color button in the Adjust group and then click the third option from the left in the second row (*Turquoise, Accent color 2 Dark*).
12. Compress the clip art image by clicking the Compress Pictures button in the Adjust group and then clicking OK at the Compress Pictures dialog box.
13. Click outside the clip art image to deselect it.
14. Save **WL2-C1-P4-TSSMaui.docx**.

Applying Advanced Formatting to Images

You can format an image with options at the Format Picture dialog box shown in Figure 1.6. Display this dialog box by clicking the Picture Styles group dialog box launcher in the Picture Tools Format tab. Formatting categories display at the left side of the dialog box. Click a formatting category and the options at the right side of the dialog box change to reflect formatting options related to the category. Many of the options available at the Format Picture dialog box are also available in the Picture Tools Format tab. The dialog box is a central location for formatting options and also includes some additional advanced formatting options.

Figure 1.6 Format Picture Dialog Box

Click a category in the left panel and the options at the right change to reflect the selected category.

Format Picture

Fill
Line Color
Line Style
Shadow
Reflection
Glow and Soft Edges
3-D Format
3-D Rotation
Picture Corrections
Picture Color
Artistic Effects
Crop
Text Box
Alt Text

Picture Corrections

Sharpen and Soften

Presets:
Soften   Sharpen   0%

Brightness and Contrast

Presets:
Brightness: 0%
Contrast: 0%

Reset

Close

Customizing the Clip Art Task Pane

Unless the Clip Art task pane default setting has been customized, the task pane displays all illustrations, photographs, videos, and audio files. The *Results should be* option has a default setting of *Selected media file types*. Click the down-pointing arrow at the right of this option to display media types. To search for a specific media type, remove the check mark before all options at the drop-down list except for the desired type. For example, if you are searching only for photograph images, remove the check mark before *Illustrations*, *Videos*, and *Audio*.

Applying Artistic Effects

If you insert a picture or photograph, the Artistic Effects button in the Adjust group in the Picture Tools Format tab is active. Click this button and a drop-down gallery displays with effect options. Hover the mouse over an option at the drop-down gallery to see the effect applied to the selected picture or photograph. This button is not active when a clip art image is selected. You can also apply artistic effects at the Format Picture dialog box.

Project 4b   **Inserting and Customizing a Photograph**   **Part 2 of 3**

1. With **WL2-C1-P4-TTSMaui.docx** open, press Ctrl + End to move the insertion point to the end of the document and then insert a photograph by completing the following steps:
   a. Click the Insert tab and then click the Clip Art button in the Illustrations group.
   b. At the Clip Art task pane, click the down-pointing arrow at the right of the *Results should be* option box and then click in the *Illustrations*, *Videos*, and *Audio* check boxes to remove the check marks. (The *Photographs* check box should be the only one with a check mark.)

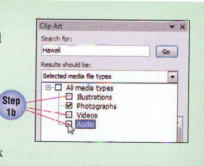

Step 1b

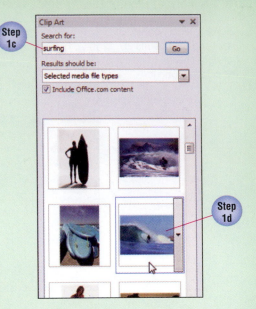

c. Select any text that displays in the *Search for* text box, type **surfing**, and then press the Enter key.

d. Click the image in the list box as shown at the right.

e. Close the Clip Art task pane.

2. With the surfing photograph selected, click the Picture Effects button in the Picture Styles group, point to *Bevel*, and then click the first option in the *Bevel* section (*Circle*).

3. Click the Artistic Effects button in the Adjust group and then click the *Cutout* option (first option in the bottom row).

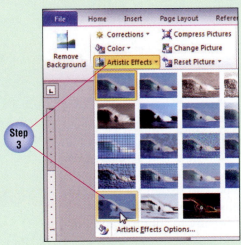

4. After looking at the formatting, you decide to remove the formatting by clicking the Reset Picture button in the Adjust group.

5. Select the current measurement in the *Shape Height* measurement box, type **1.4**, and then press Enter.

6. Format the photograph by completing the following steps:

a. Click the Picture Styles group dialog box launcher.

b. At the Format Picture dialog box, click the *Reflection* option at the left side of the dialog box.

c. Click the Presets button in the *Reflection* section and then click the first option in the *Reflection Variations* section (*Tight Reflection, touching*).

d. Click the *Artistic Effects* option at the left side of the dialog box.

e. Click the Artistic Effect button and then click the third option from the left in the second row at the drop-down list (the *Paint Brush* option).

f. Click the Close button to close the Format Picture dialog box.

7. Click the Wrap Text button in the Arrange group and then click *Tight* at the drop-down list.
8. Position the photograph precisely on the page by completing the following steps:
   a. With the photograph selected, click the Size group dialog box launcher.
   b. At the Layout dialog box, click the Position tab.
   c. Select the current measurement in the *Absolute position* measurement box in the *Horizontal* section and then type 5.3.
   d. Click the down-pointing arrow to the right of the *to the right of* option box and then click *Page* at the drop-down list.
   e. Select the current measurement in the *Absolute position* measurement box in the *Vertical* section and then type 6.6.
   f. Click the down-pointing arrow at the right of the *below* option box and then click *Page* at the drop-down list.
   g. Click OK to close the Layout dialog box.
9. Click outside the photograph to deselect it.
10. Save **WL2-C1-P4-TTSMaui.docx**.

Customizing Text Boxes

When you insert a text box in a document, the Drawing Tools Format tab is active. Use options at this tab to format and customize a text box. You can also format and customize a text box with options at the Format Shape dialog box that contains options similar to those in the Format Picture dialog box. Display the Format Shape dialog box by clicking the Shape Styles group dialog box launcher. Click the WordArt Styles group dialog box launcher to display the Format Text Effects dialog box with options for formatting the text in a text box. Display the Layout dialog box by clicking the Size group dialog box launcher.

Project 4c   **Inserting and Customizing a Text Box**   **Part 3 of 3**

1. With **WL2-C1-P4-TTSMaui.docx** open, insert a text box by completing the following steps:
   a. Click the Insert tab, click the Text Box button in the Text group, and then click the *Draw Text Box* option at the drop-down list.
   b. Click above the heading *MAUI SITES* and then type Hawaii, the "Aloha State".
2. Select the text box by clicking the border of the text box. (This changes the text box border from a dashed line to a solid line.)
3. Press Ctrl + E to center the text in the text box.
4. Click the Text Direction button in the Text group and then click *Rotate all text 270°* at the drop-down list.
5. Select the current measurement in the *Shape Height* measurement box, type 5.8, and then press Enter.
6. Select the current measurement in the *Shape Width* measurement box, type 0.8, and then press Enter.

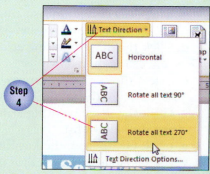

Step 4

7. Format the text box by completing the following steps:
   a. Click the Shape Styles group dialog box launcher.
   b. At the Format Shape dialog box with *Fill* selected at the left side of the dialog box, click the Color button and then click the *Blue, Accent 1, Lighter 80%* option (located in the fifth column).

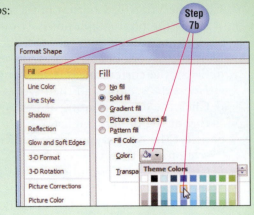

Step 7b

   c. Click the *Shadow* option at the left side of the dialog box.
   d. Click the Presets button and then click the *Offset Bottom* option at the drop-down list (second option in the top row of the *Outer* section).
   e. Click the *Glow and Soft Edges* option at the left side of the dialog box.

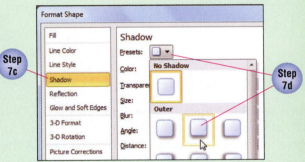

Step 7c

Step 7d

   f. Click the Presets button in the *Glow* section and then click the *Blue, 5 pt glow, Accent color 1* option (first option in the *Glow Variations* section).
   g. Click the Close button to close the Format Shape dialog box.
8. Click the More button at the right side of the WordArt Styles thumbnails and then click the fourth option from the left in the fourth row (*Gradient Fill - Blue, Accent 1, Outline - White*).
9. Position the text box precisely on the page by completing the following steps:
   a. With the text box selected, click the Size group dialog box launcher.
   b. At the Layout dialog box, click the Position tab.

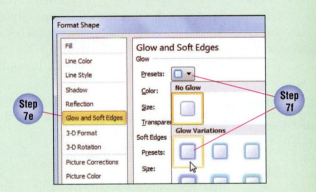

Step 7e

Step 7f

   c. Select the current measurement in the *Absolute position* measurement box in the *Horizontal* section and then type 1.
   d. Click the down-pointing arrow at the right of the *to the right of* option box and then click *Page* at the drop-down list.
   e. Select the current measurement in the *Absolute position* measurement box in the *Vertical* section and then type 2.7.
   f. Click the down-pointing arrow at the right of the *below* option box and then click *Page* at the drop-down list.
   g. Click OK to close the Layout dialog box.
10. Click the Home tab, click the Font Size button arrow, and then click *36* at the drop-down list.
11. Click outside the text box to deselect it.
12. Save, print, and then close **WL2-C1-P4-TTSMaui.docx**.

Project 5 — Insert Headers and Footers in a Computer Report — 7 Parts

You will open a report on computers in communication and entertainment and then create and position headers and footers. You will also create headers and footers for different pages in a document, divide a document into sections, and then create footers for specific sections.

Inserting Headers and Footers ■■■■■■■■■■■■

Text that appears at the top of every page is called a **header** and text that appears at the bottom of every page is referred to as a **footer**. Headers and footers are commonly used in manuscripts, textbooks, reports, and other publications to display the page number and section or chapter title. For example, see the footer at the bottom of this page. You can insert a predesigned header by clicking the Insert tab and then clicking the Header button. This displays a drop-down list of header choices. Click the predesigned header and the formatted header is inserted in the document. Complete similar steps to insert a predesigned footer.

If the predesigned headers and footers do not meet your needs, you can create your own. For example, to create a header you would click the Insert tab, click the Header button in the Header & Footer group, and then click *Edit Header* at the drop-down list. This displays a Header pane in the document and also displays the Header & Footer Tools Design tab as shown in Figure 1.7. With options in this tab you can insert elements such as page numbers, pictures, and clip art; navigate to other headers or footers in the document; and position headers and footers on different pages in a document.

Inserting Elements in Headers and Footers

Use buttons in the Insert group in the Header & Footer Tools Design tab to insert elements into the header or footer such as the date and time, quick parts, pictures, and clip art images. Click the Date & Time button and the Date and Time dialog box displays with options for inserting the current date as well as the current time. Click the Picture button and the Insert Picture dialog box displays. At this dialog box, navigate to the desired folder and double-click the picture file. Click the Clip Art button and the Clip Art task pane displays where you can search for and then insert an image into the header or footer.

HINT

One method for formatting a header or footer is to select the header or footer text and then use options on the Mini toolbar.

Header

Footer

▼ **Quick Steps**

Insert Element in Header
1. Click Insert tab.
2. Click Header button.
3. Click *Edit Header* at drop-down gallery.
4. Click desired elements.

Insert Element in Footer
1. Click Insert tab.
2. Click Footer button.
3. Click *Edit Footer* at drop-down gallery.
4. Click desired elements.

Date & Time

Picture

Clip Art

Figure 1.7 Header & Footer Tools Design tab

1. Open **CompSoftware.docx** and then save the document with Save As and name it **WL2-C1-P5-CompSoftware**.
2. Insert a header by completing the following steps:
   a. Click the Insert tab.
   b. Click the Header button in the Header & Footer group.
   c. Click *Edit Header* at the drop-down list.
   d. With the insertion point positioned in the Header pane, click the Picture button in the Insert group in the Header & Footer Tools Design tab.

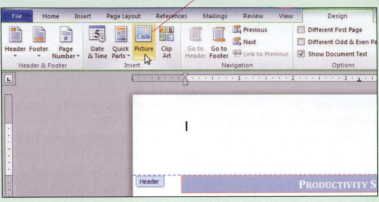

   e. At the Insert Picture dialog box, navigate to the Word2010L2C1 folder on your storage medium and then double-click **Worldwide.jpg**.
   f. With the image selected, click in the *Shape Height* measurement box, type **0.6**, and then press Enter.
   g. Click the Wrap Text button in the Arrange group and then click *Square* at the drop-down list.

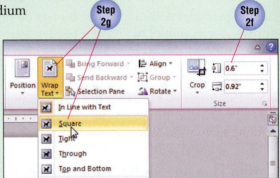

   h. Drag the image up approximately one-third of an inch.
   i. Click to the right of the picture to deselect it.
   j. Press the Tab key twice. (This moves the insertion point to the right margin.)
   k. Click the Header & Footer Tools Design tab and then click the Date & Time button in the Insert group.
   l. At the Date and Time dialog box, click the twelfth option from the top (the option that displays the date in numbers and the time) and then click OK to close the dialog box.
   m. Select the date and time text and then click the Home tab. Click the Bold button in the Font group, click the Font Size button arrow, and then click *9* at the drop-down gallery.
   n. Double-click in the document to make the document active and dim the header.
3. Save **WL2-C1-P5-CompSoftware.docx**.

Positioning a Header or Footer

Word inserts a header 0.5 inch from the top of the page and a footer 0.5 inch from the bottom of the page. You can change these default positions with buttons in the Position group in the Header & Footer Tools Design tab. Use the *Header from Top* and *Footer from Bottom* measurement boxes to adjust the position of the header or footer on the page.

By default a header and footer contain two tab settings. A center tab is set at 3.25 inches and a right tab is set at 6.5 inches. If the document contains default left and right margin settings of 1 inch, the center tab set at 3.25 inches is the center of the document and the right tab set at 6.5 inches is at the right margin. If you make changes to the default margins, you may need to move the default tabs before inserting header or footer text at the center or right tabs. You can also set and position tabs with the Insert Alignment Tab button in the Position group. Click this button and the Alignment Tab dialog box displays. Use options at this dialog box to change tab alignment and set tabs with leaders.

Project 5b   Positioning Headers and Footers   Part 2 of 7

1. With **WL2-C1-P5-CompSoftware.docx** open, change the margins by completing the following steps:
   a. Click the Page Layout tab, click the Margins button in the Page Setup group, and then click the *Custom Margins* option that displays at the bottom of the drop-down list.
   b. At the Page Setup dialog box with the Margins tab selected, select the measurement in the *Left* measurement box and then type **1.25**.
   c. Select the measurement in the *Right* measurement box and then type **1.25**.
   d. Click OK to close the dialog box.
2. Create a footer by completing the following steps:
   a. Click the Insert tab.
   b. Click the Footer button in the Header & Footer group and then click *Edit Footer* at the drop-down list.
   c. With the insertion point positioned in the Footer pane, type your first and last names at the left margin.
   d. Press the Tab key. (This moves the insertion point to the center tab position.)
   e. Click the Page Number button in the Header & Footer group, point to *Current Position*, and then click *Accent Bar 2* at the drop-down list.

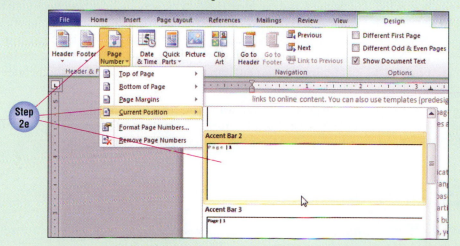

   f. Press the Tab key and then type **WL2-C1-P5-CompSoftware**.
   g. You notice that the center tab and the right tab are off slightly since the left and right margins in the document are set at 1.25" instead of 1". To correctly align the text, drag the center tab marker to the 3-inch mark on the Ruler and drag the right tab marker to the 6-inch mark on the Ruler.

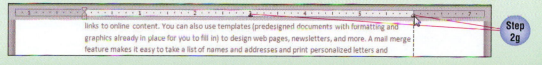

h. Select all of the footer text and then change the font to 9-point Calibri bold.
3. Edit the header by completing the following steps:
   a. Click the Header & Footer Tools Design tab.
   b. Click the Go to Header button in the Navigation group.
   c. Drag the right tab marker to the 6-inch mark on the ruler.
4. Change the position of the header and footer by completing the following steps:
   a. With the Header & Footer Tools Design tab active, click the up-pointing arrow at the right side of the *Header from Top* measurement box until *0.8"* displays.
   b. Click in the *Footer from Bottom* measurement box, type **0.6**, and then press Enter.
   c. Click the Close Header and Footer button.
5. Save and then print the first two pages of the document.

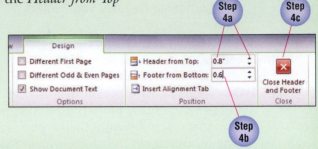

Step 4a

Step 4c

Step 4b

▼ **Quick Steps**

Create Different First Page Header or Footer
1. Click Insert tab.
2. Click Header or Footer button.
3. Click *Edit Header* or *Edit Footer* at drop-down gallery.
4. Click *Different First Page* check box.
5. Insert desired elements and/or text.
6. Click Next button.
7. Insert desired elements and/or text.

Creating a Different First Page Header or Footer

By default, Word will insert a header or footer on every page in the document. You can create different headers or footers within one document. For example, you can create a unique header or footer on the first page and then insert a different header or footer on subsequent pages. To create a different first page header, click the Insert tab, click the Header button, and then click *Edit Header* at the drop-down list. Click the *Different First Page* check box to insert a check mark and the First Page Header pane displays with the insertion point inside. Insert elements or type text to create the first page header and then click the Next button in the Navigation group. This displays the Header pane with the insertion point positioned inside. Insert elements and/or type text to create the header. Complete similar steps to create a different first page footer.

In some situations you may want the first page header or footer to be blank. This is particularly useful if a document contains a title page and you do not want the header or footer to print at the top or bottom of the first page.

Project 5c — Creating a Header That Prints on All Pages Except the First Page — Part 3 of 7

1. With **WL2-C1-P5-CompSoftware.docx** open, press Ctrl + A to select the entire document and then press Ctrl + 2 to change the line spacing to 2.
2. Remove the header and footer by completing the following steps:
   a. Click the Insert tab.
   b. Click the Header button in the Header & Footer group and then click *Remove Header* at the drop-down list.
   c. Click the Footer button in the Header & Footer group and then click *Remove Footer* at the drop-down list.

3. Press Ctrl + Home and then create a header that prints on all pages except the first page by completing the following steps:
   a. With the Insert tab active, click the Header button in the Header & Footer group.
   b. Click *Edit Header* at the drop-down list.
   c. Click the *Different First Page* check box located in the Options group in the Header & Footer Tools Design tab.
   d. With the insertion point positioned in the First Page Header pane, click the Next button in the Navigation group. (This tells Word that you want the first page header to be blank.)
   e. With the insertion point positioned in the Header pane, click the Page Number button in the Header & Footer group, point to *Top of Page*, and then click *Accent Bar 2* at the drop-down gallery.
   f. Click the Close Header and Footer button.
4. Scroll through the document and notice that the header appears on the second through fourth pages.
5. Save and then print the first two pages of the document.

Creating Odd and Even Page Headers or Footers

If your document will be read in book form with facing pages, consider inserting odd and even page headers or footers. When presenting pages in a document in book form with facing pages, the outside margin is the left side of the left page and the right side of the right page. Also, when a document has facing pages, the page at the right side is generally numbered with odd page numbers and the page at the left side is generally numbered with even page numbers. You can create even and odd headers or footers to insert this type of page numbering. Use the *Different Odd & Even Pages* check box in the Options group in the Header & Footer Tools Design tab to create odd and even headers and/or footers.

▼ **Quick Steps**

Create Odd and Even Page Headers or Footers
1. Click Insert tab.
2. Click Header or Footer button.
3. Click *Edit Header* or *Edit Footer* at drop-down gallery.
4. Click *Different Odd & Even Pages* check box.
5. Insert desired elements and/or text.

Project 5d   **Creating Odd and Even Page Footers**   **Part 4 of 7**

1. With **WL2-C1-P5-CompSoftware.docx** open, remove the header from the document by completing the following steps:
   a. Click the Insert tab.
   b. Click the Header button in the Header & Footer group and then click *Edit Header* at the drop-down list.
   c. Click the *Different First Page* check box in the Options group in the Header & Footer Tools Design tab to remove the check mark.
   d. Click the Header button in the Header & Footer group and then click *Remove Header* at the drop-down list. (This displays the insertion point in an empty Header pane.)

2. Create a footer that prints on odd pages and another that prints on even pages by completing the following steps:

a. Click the Go to Footer button in the Navigation group in the Header & Footer Tools Design tab.

b. Click the *Different Odd & Even Pages* check box in the Options group. (This displays the Odd Page Footer pane with the insertion point inside.)

c. Click the Footer button in the Header & Footer group.

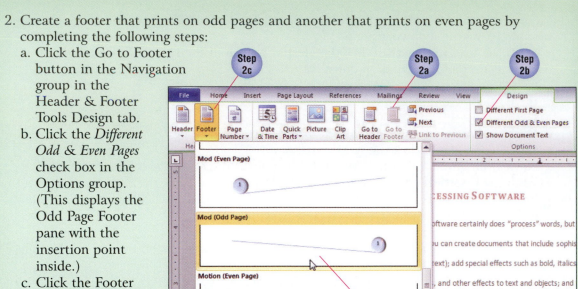

d. Scroll down the list of predesigned footers and then click the *Mod (Odd Page)* option.

e. Click the Next button in the Navigation group. (This displays the Even Page Footer pane with the insertion point inside.)

f. Click the Footer button in the Header & Footer group.

g. Scroll down the list of predesigned footers and then click the *Mod (Even Page)* option.

h. Click the Close Header and Footer button.

3. Scroll through the document and notice the odd and even page footers.

4. Save and then print the first two pages of the document.

▼ **Quick Steps**

Create Header/Footer for Different Sections

1. Insert section break in desired location.
2. Click Insert tab.
3. Click Header or Footer button.
4. Click *Edit Header* or *Edit Footer* at drop-down gallery.
5. Click Link to Previous button to deactivate.
6. Insert desired elements and/or text.
7. Click Next button.
8. Insert desired elements and/or text.

Link to Previous

Creating a Header or Footer for Different Sections

You can divide a document into sections and then apply different formatting in each section. You can insert a section break that begins a new page or insert a continuous section break. You can also insert a section break that starts the new section on the next even-numbered page or a section break that starts the new section on the next odd-numbered page. If you want different headers and/or footers for pages in a document, divide the document into sections.

For example, if a document contains several chapters, you can create a section for each chapter, and then create a different header or footer for each section. When dividing a document into sections by chapter, insert a section break that also begins a new page.

When a header or footer is created for a specific section in a document, the header or footer can be created for all previous and next sections or just for next sections. If you want a header or footer to print on only those pages in a section and not the previous or next sections, you must deactivate the Link to Previous button. This tells Word not to print the header or footer on previous sections. Word will, however, print the header or footer on following sections. If you do not want the header or footer to print on following sections, create a blank header or footer at the next section. When creating a header or footer for a specific section in a document, preview the document to determine if the header or footer appears on the correct pages.

1. With **WL2-C1-P5-CompSoftware.docx** open, remove the odd and even page footers by completing the following steps:
   a. Click the Insert tab.
   b. Click the Footer button in the Header & Footer group and then click *Edit Footer* at drop-down list.
   c. Click the *Different Odd & Even Pages* check box in the Options group in the Header & Footer Tools Design tab to remove the check mark.
   d. Click the Footer button in the Header & Footer group and then click *Remove Footer* at the drop-down list.
   e. Click the Close Header and Footer button.
2. Remove the page break before the second title in the document by completing the following steps:
   a. Move the insertion point immediately right of the period that ends the last paragraph in the *Presentation Software* section (located toward the top of page 3).
   b. Press the Delete key twice. (The title GRAPHICS AND MULTIMEDIA SOFTWARE should now display below the paragraph on the third page.)
3. Insert an odd page section break by completing the following steps:
   a. Position the insertion point at the beginning of the title GRAPHICS AND MULTIMEDIA SOFTWARE.
   b. Click the Page Layout tab, click the Breaks button in the Page Setup group, and then click *Odd Page* at the drop-down list. (The section break takes the place of the hard page break.)

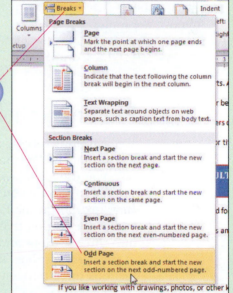

Step 3b

4. Create section and page numbering footers for the two sections by completing the following steps:
   a. Position the insertion point at the beginning of the document.
   b. Click the Insert tab.
   c. Click the Footer button in the Header & Footer group and then click *Edit Footer* at the drop-down list.
   d. At the Footer -Section 1- pane, make sure bold is on, type **Section 1**, and then press the Tab key twice. (This moves the insertion point to the right margin.)
   e. Type **Page** and then press the spacebar.
   f. Click the Header & Footer Tools Design tab.
   g. Click the Page Number button in the Header & Footer group, point to *Current Position*, and then click *Plain Number* at the side menu.
   h. Click the Next button in the Navigation group.
   i. Click the Link to Previous button to deactivate it. (This removes the message *Same as Previous* from the top right side of the footer pane.)
   j. Change the text *Section 1* to *Section 2* in the footer.
   k. Click the Close Header and Footer button.

Step 4i   Step 4h

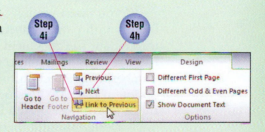

5. Position the insertion point at the beginning of the heading DATABASE SOFTWARE, click the Page Layout tab, click the Breaks button in the Page Setup group, and then click *Even Page* at the drop-down list.

6. Scroll through the document and notice the page numbering in the sections.

7. Position the insertion point at the beginning of the heading DATABASE SOFTWARE and then remove the even page section break by completing the following steps:
   a. Click the Draft button in the view section located toward the right side of the Status bar.
   b. Scroll up the document, position the insertion point on the section break (displays as a double row of dots with the words *Section Break (Even Page)* in the center, and then press the Delete key.

8. Change the odd page section break to a next page section break by completing the following steps:
   a. Position the insertion point on the section break that displays above the title GRAPHICS AND MULTIMEDIA SOFTWARE (blue fill displays behind the section break) and then press the Delete key.
   b. Click the Breaks button in the Page Setup group and then click *Next Page* at the drop-down list.
   c. Click the Print Layout button in the view section located toward the right side of the Status bar.

9. Remove the footer.

10. Insert section footers by completing Step 4 on the previous page.

11. Save **WL2-C1-P5-CompSoftware.docx**.

Printing Sections ■■■■■■■■■■■■■■■■■■■■■■■■

You can print specific pages in a document by inserting page numbers in the *Pages* text box at the Print tab Backstage view. When entering page numbers in this text box, you use a hyphen to indicate a range of consecutive pages for printing or a comma to specify nonconsecutive pages. If a document contains sections, use the *Pages* text box at the Print tab Backstage view to specify the section and pages within the section that you want printed. For example, if a document is divided into three sections and you want to print only section two, you would type *s2* in the *Pages* text box. If a document contains six sections and you want to print sections three through five, you would type *s3-s5* in the *Pages* text box.

You can also identify specific pages within or between sections for printing. For example, to print pages two through five of section four, you would type *p2s4-p5s4*; to print from page three of section one through page five of section four, you would type *p3s1-p5s4*; to print page one of section three, page four of section five, and page six of section eight, you would type *p1s3,p4s5,p6s8*.

If you insert section breaks in a document and then insert headers or footers with page numbering for each section, the page numbering is sequential throughout the document. The **WL2-C1-P5-CompSoftware.docx** document has a section break but the pages are numbered sequentially. If you want page numbering in a section to start with a new number such as 1, use the *Start at* option at the page Number Format dialog box. Display this dialog box by clicking the Page Number button in the Header & Footer group in the Header & Footer Tools Design tab and then clicking the *Format Page Numbers* option at the drop-down list. At the Page Number Format dialog box, click the *Start at* option. This inserts *1* in the text box. You can leave this number or type a different page number in the text box.

1. With **WL2-C1-P5-CompSoftware.docx** open, change the starting page number to *1* for section 2 by completing the following steps:
   a. Click the Insert tab, click the Footer button in the Header & Footer group, and then click *Edit Footer* at the drop-down list.
   b. At the *Footer -Section 1-* footer pane, click the Next button in the Navigation group in the Header & Footer Tools Design tab.
   c. At the *Footer -Section 2-* footer pane, click the Page Number button in the Header & Footer group and then click the *Format Page Numbers* option at the drop-down list.
   d. At the Page Number Format dialog box, click the *Start at* option (this insert *1* in the text box).
   e. Click OK to close the dialog box.
   f. Click the Close Header and Footer button.
2. Print only page 1 of section 1 and page 1 of section 2 by completing the following steps:
   a. Click the File tab and then click the Print tab.
   b. At the Print tab Backstage view, specify that you want to print only page one of section one and page one of section 2. To do this, click in the *Pages* text box in the Settings category and then type **p1s1,p1s2**.
   c. Click the Print button.
3. Save the document.

Step 2a   Step 2c   Step 2b

Keeping Text Together ▪▪▪▪▪▪▪▪▪▪▪▪▪▪▪▪▪▪▪▪▪▪

In a multiple-page document, the soft page breaks inserted by Word may occur in undesirable locations. For example, a soft page break may cause a heading to display at the bottom of a page while the text connected to the heading displays at the beginning of the next page. A soft page break may also create a *widow* or *orphan*. A widow is the last line of text in a paragraph that appears at the top of a page and an orphan is the first line of text in a paragraph that appears at the bottom of a page. Use options at the Paragraph dialog box with the Line and Page Breaks tab selected, as shown in Figure 1.8, to control widows and orphans as well as keep a paragraph, a group of paragraphs, or a group of lines together.

By default, the *Widow/Orphan control* option is active and Word tries to avoid creating a widow or orphan when inserting a soft page break. The other three options in the *Pagination* section of the dialog box are not active by default. Use the *Keep with next* option if you want to keep a line together with the next line. This is useful for keeping a heading together with the first line below the heading. If you want to keep a group of selected lines together, use the *Keep lines together* option. Use the *Page break before* option to tell Word to insert a page break before selected text.

▼ **Quick Steps**

Keep Text Together
1. Click Paragraph group dialog box launcher.
2. Click Line and Page Breaks tab.
3. Click *Keep with next*, *Keep lines together*, and/or *Page break before*.
4. Click OK.

Figure 1.8 Paragraph Dialog Box with Line and Page Breaks Tab Selected

Use options in this section to control the location of page breaks in a document.

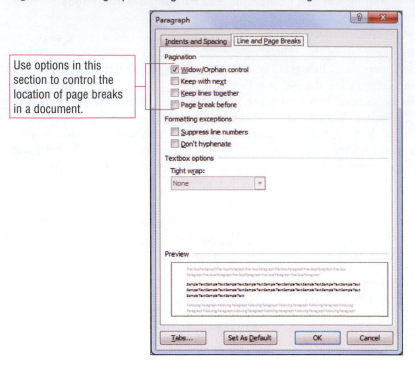

Project 5g **Keeping Text Together**

1. With **WL2-C1-P5-CompSoftware.docx** open, scroll through the document and notice that the *SPREADSHEET SOFTWARE* heading displays at the bottom of page 1 and the paragraph that follows it displays at the top of page 1. Keep the heading with the paragraph of text by completing the following steps:
   a. Position the insertion point on any character in the heading *SPREADSHEET SOFTWARE*.
   b. Click the Paragraph group dialog box launcher.
   c. At the Paragraph dialog box, click the Line and Page Breaks tab.
   d. Click the *Keep with next* check box to insert a check mark.
   e. Click OK to close the dialog box.

2. Scroll through the document and notice that the heading *PRESENTATION SOFTWARE* displays at the bottom of page 2. Insert a soft page break at the beginning of the heading by completing the following steps:
   a. Move the insertion point to the beginning of the *PRESENTATION SOFTWARE* heading.
   b. Click the Paragraph group dialog box launcher.
   c. At the Paragraph dialog box with the Line and Page Breaks tab selected, click the *Page break before* check box to insert a check mark.
   d. Click OK to close the dialog box.

3. Save the document, print pages 1 and 2, and then close the document.

Project 6 **Create and Format a Column Chart and a Pie Chart**   **4 Parts**

You will use the Chart feature to create and format a column chart and then create and format a pie chart.

Creating a Chart ▪▪▪▪▪▪▪▪▪▪▪▪▪▪▪▪▪▪▪▪▪▪▪▪▪▪

A chart, sometimes referred to as a graph, is a visual presentation of data. In Word, you can create a variety of charts including bar and column charts, pie charts, area charts, and much more. To create a chart, click the Insert tab and then click the Chart button in the Illustrations group. This displays the Insert Chart dialog box shown in Figure 1.9. At this dialog box, choose the desired chart type in the list at the left side, click the chart style, and then click OK.

When you click OK, a sample chart is inserted in your Word document and Excel opens with sample data as shown in Figure 1.10. Type the desired data in the Excel worksheet cells over the existing data. As you type data, the chart in the Word document reflects the typed data. To type data in the Excel worksheet, click in the desired cell, type the data, and then press the Tab key to make the next cell active, press Shift + Tab to make the previous cell active, or press Enter to make the cell below active.

Cells used by Excel to create the chart are surrounded by a blue border and below the border is displayed the message "To resize chart data range, drag lower right corner of range." If you need to change the data range, position the mouse pointer on the bottom right corner of the border until the mouse pointer displays as a double-headed arrow pointing diagonally. Hold down the left mouse button and then drag up, down, left, and/or right until the border is in the desired location. You can also click in a cell immediately outside the border and, when you insert data, the border will expand.

▼ **Quick Steps**

Insert a Chart
1. Click Insert tab.
2. Click Chart button.
3. Enter data in Excel spreadsheet.
4. Close Excel.

H I N T

You can copy a chart from Excel to Word and embed it as static data or link it to the worksheet.

Chart

Figure 1.9 Insert Chart Dialog Box

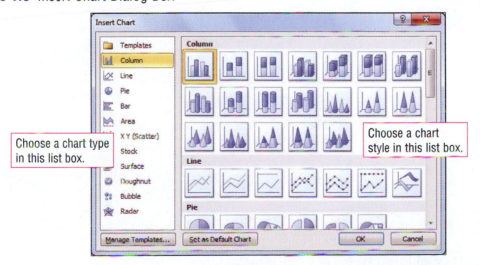

Choose a chart type in this list box.

Choose a chart style in this list box.

Figure 1.10 Sample Chart

Enter data in the cells in the Excel worksheet. The data entered is reflected in the Word document chart.

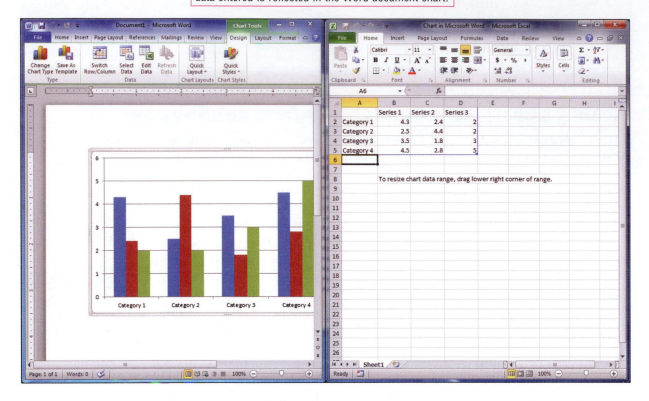

When you have entered all data in the worksheet, click the Close Window button that displays in the upper right corner of the screen. This closes the Excel window, expands the Word document window, and displays the chart in the document.

Project 6a　**Creating a Column Chart**　　　　　　　　　　　　　　**Part 1 of 4**

1. At a blank document, click the Insert tab and then click the Chart button in the Illustrations group.
2. At the Insert Chart dialog box, click OK.
3. Click in cell B1 in the Excel worksheet and then type **Sales, 2009**.

4. Press the Tab key and then type **Sales, 2010** in cell C1.

5. Press the Tab key and then type Sales, 2011 in cell D1.
6. Press the Tab key. (This makes cell A2 active.)
7. Continue typing the remaining data in cells as indicated in Figure 1.11.
8. When all data is entered, click the Close button that displays in the upper right corner of the Excel window (first Close button from the top).
9. Save the document and name it **WL2-C1-P6-SalesChart**.

Figure 1.11 Project 6a

⊿	A	B	C	D	E	F	G
1		Sales, 2009	Sales, 2010	Sales, 2011			
2	Northeast	$729,300	$698,453	$798,340			
3	Southeast	$310,455	$278,250	$333,230			
4	Northwest	$610,340	$700,100	$525,425			
5	Southwest	$522,340	$500,278	$625,900			
6							
7							
8		To resize chart data range, drag lower right corner of range.					

Formatting Chart Design

When the chart is first inserted in the document, the Chart Tools Design tab is active. Use options in this tab to change the chart type, edit chart data, change the chart layout, and apply a chart style. If you need to edit data in a chart, click the Edit Data button and the Excel worksheet opens on the screen. Make the desired change and then click the Close Window button.

Project 6b **Changing the Chart Design**   **Part 2 of 4**

1. With **WL2-C1-P6-SalesChart.docx** open, make sure the chart is selected. (If it is not selected, click in the chart to select it. Make sure you click on an empty location in the chart. The chart should display with a light gray border and no element should be selected.)
2. Make sure the Chart Tools Design tab is active.
3. Click the Edit Data button in the Data group.
4. In the Excel worksheet, double-click cell C3.
5. Edit the data in cell C3 so it displays as *$378,250* rather than *$278,250* and then press the Enter key.
6. You decide that the chart might be easier to read if the columns and rows are reversed so click in a blank area in the Word document and then click the Switch Row/Column button in the Data group in the Chart Tools Design tab. (This button is located in the Word document.)
7. Click the Close button to close Excel.

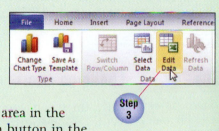

8. Click the third option in the Chart Layouts group (*Layout 3*).
9. Click the More button at the right side of the Chart Styles options and then click *Style 26* (second option from the left in the fourth row).
10. Save **WL2-C1-P6-SalesChart.docx**.

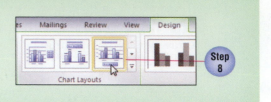

Formatting Chart Layout

Click the Chart Tools Layout tab and options display for changing and customizing chart elements. With options in this tab you can specify chart elements, insert objects, add labels to the chart, customize the chart background, and add analysis items to the chart.

Project 6c   Formatting Chart Layout   Part 3 of 4

1. With **WL2-C1-P6-SalesChart.docx** open, make sure the chart is selected and then click the Chart Tools Layout tab.
2. Click the Chart Elements button arrow in the Current Selection group and then click *Chart Title* at the drop-down list. (This selects the chart title.)
3. With the chart title selected, type **Sales by Territory**.
4. Move the legend by clicking the Legend button in the Labels group and then clicking *Show Legend at Right*.
5. Add data labels by clicking the Data Labels button in the Labels group and then clicking *Outside End*.
6. After looking at the data labels, you decide to turn them off. To do this, click the Data Labels button and then click *None*.
7. Click the Gridlines button in the Axes group, point to *Primary Vertical Gridlines*, and then click *Major Gridlines*.
8. Save **WL2-C1-P6-SalesChart.docx**.

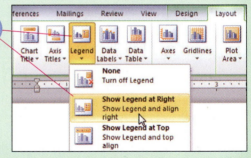

HINT

Use a pie chart if you have one data series that you want to plot and you have seven categories or less and the categories represent parts of the whole pie.

Changing Chart Format

Click the Chart Tools Layout tab and options display for formatting the chart. With options in this tab you can change shape style, fill, outline, and effects; apply WordArt style, fill, outline, and effects to text; and arrange, position, and size the chart in the document.

1. With **WL2-C1-P6-SalesChart.docx** open, click in the chart outside of the title, press Ctrl + End (this deselects the chart), and then press the Enter key twice.
2. Click the Insert tab and then click the Chart button in the Illustrations group.
3. At the Insert Chart dialog box, click *Pie* in the left panel and then click OK.
4. In Excel, drag the bottom right corner of the data range border down one row.
5. Type data in the Excel worksheet cells as shown in Figure 1.12.
6. When all data is entered, click the Close button in Excel.
7. Click the More button located at the right side of the Chart Styles group and then click *Style 26* (second option from the left in the fourth row) at the drop-down list.
8. Click the chart title *Percentage* and then type **Investments**.
9. Click the Chart Tools Layout tab.
10. Click the Data Labels button in the Labels group and then click *Inside End* at the drop-down list.
11. Click in the chart outside of the title and any other chart element.
12. Click the Chart Tools Format tab.
13. Click the Wrap Text button in the Arrange group and then click *Square* at the drop-down list.
14. Click in the chart outside any chart elements.
15. Click the down-pointing arrow at the right side of the *Shape Height* measurement box until *3.3"* displays in the box.
16. Click the down-pointing arrow at the right side of the *Shape Width* measurement box until *5.5"* displays in the box.
17. Click the column chart to select it.
18. Click the Wrap Text button in the Arrange group and then click *Square* at the drop-down list. (The charts may overlap.)
19. Click the down-pointing arrow at the right side of the *Shape Height* measurement box until *3.3"* displays in the box.
20. Click the down-pointing arrow at the right side of the *Shape Width* measurement box until *5.5"* displays in the box.
21. Change the zoom to *Whole Page* and then drag each chart so they are positioned attractively on the page.
22. Change the zoom back to *100%*.
23. Save, print, and then close **WL2-C1-P6-SalesChart.docx**.

Figure 1.12 Project 6d

	A	B	C
1	Assets	Percentage	
2	Loans	34%	
3	Bonds	22%	
4	Mutuals	20%	
5	Stocks	17%	
6	Other	7%	
7			
8		To resize chart data ra	

Chapter Summary

- Use the Bullets button to insert bullets before specific paragraphs of text and use the Numbering button to insert numbers.

- Insert custom numbers by clicking the Numbering button arrow and then clicking the desired option at the drop-down gallery.

- Define your own numbering formatting with options at the Define New Number Format dialog box. Display this dialog box by clicking the Numbering button arrow and then clicking *Define New Number Format* at the drop-down gallery.

- Insert custom bullets by clicking the Bullets button arrow and then clicking the desired option at the drop-down list.

- Define your own custom bullet with options at the Define New Bullet dialog box. Display this dialog box by clicking the Bullets button arrow and then clicking *Define New Bullet* at the drop-down gallery.

- Apply numbering to multilevel paragraphs of text by clicking the Multilevel List button in the Paragraph group in the Home tab.

- Define your own multilevel list numbering with options at the Define New Multilevel List dialog box. Display this dialog box by clicking the Multilevel List button and then clicking *Define New Multilevel List* at the drop-down gallery.

- When typing a multilevel list, press the Tab key to move to the next level and press the Shift + Tab key to move to the previous level.

- By default, the Clip Art task pane displays all available media images. Narrow the search to specific locations by clicking the down-pointing arrow at the right of the *Results should be* option and then removing the check mark from any option you do not want searched.

- Use options at the Format Picture dialog box to format an image such as a picture or clip art image. Display this dialog box by clicking the Picture Styles group dialog box launcher in the Picture Tools Format tab.

- At the Format Picture dialog box, click the desired category at the left side of the dialog box and the options at the right side of the dialog box change to reflect the category.

- Customize the layout of images with options at the Layout dialog box. Display this dialog box by clicking the Size group dialog box launcher in the Picture Tools Format tab.

- The Layout dialog box contains three tabs. Click the Position tab to specify the position of the image in the document, click the Text Wrapping tab to specify a wrapping style for the image, and click the Size tab to display options for specifying the height and width of the image.

- Text that appears at the top of every page is called a header; text that appears at the bottom of every page is called a footer.

- You can insert predesigned headers and footers in a document and also create your own.

- To create a header, click the Header button and then click *Edit Header*. At the Header pane, insert the desired elements or text. Complete similar steps to create a footer.

- Use buttons in the Insert group in the Header & Footer Tools Design tab to insert elements such as the date and time, quick parts, pictures, and clip art images into a header or footer.

- Word inserts a header or footer 0.5 inch from the edge of the page. Reposition a header or footer with buttons in the Position group in the Header & Footer Tools Design tab.

- You can create a unique header or footer on the first page; omit a header or footer on the first page; create different headers or footers for odd and even pages; or create different headers or footers for sections in a document. Use options in the Options group in the Header & Footer Tools Design tab to specify the type of header or footer you want to create.

- Word attempts to avoid creating a widow or orphan when inserting soft page breaks. Turn on or off the widow/orphan control feature at the Paragraph dialog box with the Line and Page Breaks tab selected. This dialog box also contains options for keeping a paragraph, a group of paragraphs, or a group of lines together.

- Insert page numbering in a document in a header or footer or with options from the Page Number button, which is located in the Header & Footer group in the Insert tab.

- Remove page numbering with the *Remove Page Numbers* option from the Page Number button drop-down menu.

- If you want to remove page numbering from the first page, edit the page number as a header or footer.

- Format page numbers with options at the Page Number Format dialog box.

- To print sections or specific pages within a section, use the *Pages* text box at the Print dialog box. When specifying sections and pages, use the letter *s* before the section number and the letter *p* before the page number.

- A chart is a visual presentation of data. Create a chart with the Chart button in the Insert tab. Choose the desired chart type at the Insert Chart dialog box. Enter chart data in an Excel worksheet.

- Format and customize a chart with options in the Chart Tools Design tab, the Chart Tools Layout tab, and the Chart Tools Format tab.

Commands Review

FEATURE	RIBBON TAB, GROUP	BUTTON, OPTION
Numbering	Home, Paragraph	
Bullets	Home, Paragraph	
Multilevel List	Home, Paragraph	
Define New Number Format dialog box	Home, Paragraph	, Define New Number Format
Define New Bullet dialog box	Home, Paragraph	, Define New Bullet
Define New Multilevel List dialog box	Home, Paragraph	, Define New Multilevel List
Clip Art task pane	Insert, Illustrations	
Text box	Insert, Text	
Header	Insert, Header & Footer	, Edit Header
Footer	Insert, Header & Footer	, Edit Footer
Create header	Insert, Header & Footer	
Create footer	Insert, Header & Footer	
Paragraph dialog box	Home, Paragraph	
Insert Chart dialog box	Insert, Illustrations	

Concepts Check Test Your Knowledge

Completion: In the space provided at the right, indicate the correct term, symbol, or command.

1. Define your own numbering format with options at this dialog box. _____

2. A bullet you create at the Define New Bullet dialog box is automatically included in this section in the Bullets button drop-down list. _____

3. Click this button to number paragraphs of text at the left margin, first tab, second tab, and so on. _____

4. When typing a multilevel list, press these keys to move to the previous level.

_____

5. With options in the Layout dialog box with this tab selected, you can specify horizontal and vertical layout options.

_____

6. Click this dialog box launcher at the Picture Tools Format tab to display the Format Picture dialog box.

_____

7. To create your own header, click the Insert tab, click the Header button in the Header & Footer group, and then click this option at the drop-down list.

_____

8. By default, a header is positioned this distance from the top of the page.

_____

9. By default a header and footer contain two tab settings— a center tab and this type of tab.

_____

10. When creating a header, clicking the *Different First Page* check box causes this pane to display.

_____

11. Type this in the *Pages* text box at the Print dialog box to print section 5.

_____

12. Type this in the *Pages* text box at the Print dialog box to print page 2 of section 4 and page 5 of section 8.

_____

13. The *Keep lines together* option is available at the Paragraph dialog box with this tab selected.

_____

14. When creating a chart, enter data in this.

_____

15. The Edit Data button is located in this tab.

_____

Skills Check Assess Your Performance

Assessment

1 DEFINE AND APPLY CUSTOM BULLETS AND MULTILEVEL LISTS TO A TECHNOLOGY DOCUMENT

1. Open **TechTimeline.docx** and then save the document with Save As and name it **WL2-C1-A1-TechTimeline**.
2. Select the questions below the *TECHNOLOGY INFORMATION QUESTIONS* heading and then insert check mark (✔) bullets.
3. Define a cell phone symbol bullet in 14-point font size and then apply the symbol bullet to the seven paragraphs of text below the *TECHNOLOGY*

TIMELINE: PERSONAL COMMUNICATIONS TECHNOLOGY heading. (You can find the cell phone symbol in the Webdings font [ninth image from the left in the eleventh row].)

4. Select the paragraphs of text below the heading *INFORMATION SYSTEMS AND COMMERCE*, click the Multilevel List button, and then click the middle option in the top row of the *List Library* section.

5. Select the paragraphs of text below the heading *INTERNET* and then apply the same multilevel list numbering.

6. Save and then print page 3 of **WL2-C1-A1-TechTimeline.docx**.

7. Select the paragraphs of text below the heading *INFORMATION SYSTEMS AND COMMERCE* and then define a new multilevel list with the following specifications:
   a. Level 1 that inserts Arabic numbers (1, 2, 3) followed by a period and is aligned at 0" and indented at 0.25".
   b. Level 2 that inserts capital letters (A, B, C) followed by a period and is aligned at 0.25" and indented at 0.5".
   c. Level 3 that inserts Arabic numbers (1, 2, 3) followed by a right parenthesis and is aligned at 0.5" and indented at 0.75".
   d. Make sure the new multilevel list numbering is applied to the selected paragraphs.

8. Select the paragraphs of text below the heading *INTERNET* and then apply the new multilevel list numbering.

9. Insert a header that prints the page number at the right margin on all pages *except* the first page.

10. Insert the text *Cell phones* and *YouTube* in text boxes as shown in Figure 1.13 with the following specifications:
    a. Insert a text box below the arrow line located toward the bottom of page 1 and then type **Cell phones** in the text box.
    b. Rotate the text in the text box 270 degrees.
    c. Remove the outline from the text box. **Hint: Do this with the Shape Outline button in the Shape Styles group**.
    d. Change the text wrapping to *Behind Text*.
    e. Drag the text box so it is positioned as shown in Figure 1.13.
    f. Complete similar steps to create the text box with the text *YouTube* and position the text box as shown in Figure 1.13.

11. Move the insertion point to the right of the text *Electronic Commerce* (item 2) located on page 2 and then insert a clip art photograph as shown in Figure 1.14 with the following specifications:
    a. Display the Clip Art task pane, change the *Results should be* option to *Photographs* only, and then search for photographs related to *credit card*.
    b. Insert the photograph shown in Figure 1.14. (If this photograph is not available, choose another photograph that shows a credit card.)
    c. Change the height of the photograph to 2 inches.
    d. Apply a shadow and glow effect of your choosing to the photograph.
    e. Apply the *Paint Strokes* artistic effect.
    f. Change the text wrapping to *Tight*.
    g. Precisely position the photograph on the second page with an absolute horizontal measurement of 4.5 inches to the right of the page and an absolute vertical measurement of 4 inches below the page.
    h. Compress the photograph. (Use the Compress Pictures button in the Adjust group in the Picture Tools Format tab.)

12. Save, print, and then close **WL2-C1-A1-TechTimeline.docx**.

Figure 1.13 Assessment 1, Step 10

Figure 1.14 Assessment 1, Step 11

Assessment

2 INSERT SPECIALIZED HEADERS AND FOOTERS IN A REPORT

1. Open **Robots.docx** and then save the document with Save As and name it **WL2-C1-A2-Robots**.
2. Make the following changes to the document:
   a. Apply the Heading 2 style to the title *ROBOTS AS ANDROIDS*.
   b. Apply the Heading 3 style to the headings *Visual Perception*, *Audio Perception*, *Tactile Perception*, *Locomotion*, and *Navigation*.
   c. Change the style set to *Manuscript*.
   d. Center the title *ROBOTS AS ANDROIDS*.
   e. Keep the heading *Audio Perception* together with the following paragraph of text.
3. Create an odd page footer that includes the following:
   a. Insert the current date at the left margin. (Choose the date option that displays the month spelled out such as *January 1, 2013*.)
   b. Insert a clip art image related to *robot* in the middle of the footer. Change the size of the robot image to approximately 0.7 inches and apply *Tight* text wrapping. Drag the robot image down so it is positioned below the footer pane border. (If you do not have robot images available, choose another clip art image related to computers or technology.)

c. At the right margin, type **Page**, press the spacebar and then insert a page number at the current position.

4. Create an even page footer that includes the following:
   a. At the left margin, type **Page**, press the spacebar and then insert a page number at the current position.
   b. Insert in the middle of the footer the same clip art image you inserted in the odd page footer.
   c. Insert the current date at the right margin in the same format you choose for the odd page footer.

5. Save, print, and then close **WL2-C1-A2-Robots.docx**.

Assessment

3 FORMAT A REPORT INTO SECTIONS AND THEN FORMAT AND PRINT SECTIONS

1. Open **CompViruses.docx** and then save the document with Save As and name it **WL2-C1-A3-CompViruses**.
2. Make the following changes to the document:
   a. Change the theme to Origin.
   b. Change the top margin to 1.5".
   c. Insert at the beginning of the title *CHAPTER 2: SECURITY RISKS* a section break that begins a new page.
   d. Keep the heading *CRACKING SOFTWARE FOR COPYING* together with the following paragraph.
3. Create a footer for the first section in the document that prints *Chapter 1* at the left margin, the page number in the middle, and your first and last names at the right margin.
4. Edit the footer for the second section so it prints *Chapter 2* instead of *Chapter 1*.
5. Print only section 2 pages.
6. Save and then close **WL2-C1-A3-CompViruses.docx**.

Assessment

4 CREATE AND FORMAT A COLUMN CHART AND PIE CHART

1. At a blank document, use the data in Figure 1.15 to create a column chart with the following specifications:
   a. Apply a chart style of your choosing.
   b. Position the legend at the bottom of the chart.
   c. Insert the chart title *Sales Figures*.
   d. Change the chart height to 4 inches.
2. Move the insertion point to the end of the document, press the Enter key twice, and then create a pie chart with the data shown in Figure 1.16 with the following specifications:
   a. Apply the same chart style to the pie chart that you applied to the column chart.
   b. Position the legend at the bottom of the chart.
   c. Insert the chart title *Expense Distribution*.
   d. Insert the percentages inside the pie.
   e. Change the chart height to 3 inches and the width to 5.5 inches.
3. Apply *Square* text wrapping to both charts and then position the pie chart centered below the column chart.
4. Save the document and name it **WL2-C1-A4-Charts**.
5. Print and then close **WL2-C1-A4-Charts.docx**.

Figure 1.15 Assessment 4, Data for Column Chart

Salesperson	Sales, 1st Half	Sales, 2nd Half
Barnett	$543,241	$651,438
Carson	$612,348	$684,245
Fanning	$397,908	$412,724
Han	$412,209	$468,908
Mahoney	$563,205	$600,345

Figure 1.16 Assessment 4, Data for Pie Chart

Category	Percentage
Salaries	67%
Travel	15%
Equipment	11%
Supplies	7%

Assessment

5 INSERT A HORIZONTAL LINE IN A FOOTER

1. Word includes a horizontal line feature you can use to insert a graphic line in a document or header or footer. Look at the horizontal line options that are available at the Horizontal Line dialog box. At a blank document, display this dialog box by clicking the Borders button arrow in the Paragraph group in the Home tab and then clicking *Borders and Shading* at the drop-down list. At the Borders and Shading dialog box, click the Horizontal Line button that displays at the bottom left side of the dialog box. Experiment inserting horizontal lines in a document and then close the document.
2. Open **ShopOnline.docx** and then save the document with Save As and name it **WL2-C1-A5-ShopOnline**.
3. Keep the heading *ONLINE SHOPPING MALLS* together with the following paragraph.
4. Create a footer that prints the leaf horizontal line (left option in the twenty-first row from the top at the Horizontal Line dialog box) on each page.
5. Save, print, and then close **WL2-C1-A5-ShopOnline.docx**.

Visual Benchmark Demonstrate Your Proficiency

CREATE AND FORMAT AN INTERNATIONAL CORRESPONDENCE DOCUMENT

1. At a blank document, create the document shown in Figure 1.17 on page 49 with the following specifications:
   - Change the top margin to 1.5 inches and the left and right margins to 1.25 inches.
   - Use symbol bullets as shown in the figure. (Find the globe bullet in the *Webdings* font at the Symbol dialog box.)
   - Apply automatic numbering as shown in the figure and start the number with 11 after the *Canadian Codes and Territories* heading.
   - Apply the Heading 1 style to the title and the Heading 2 style to the three headings. Change the style set to *Modern*, apply the *Paper* theme, and change the theme colors to *Foundry*.
   - Apply any other formatting required to make your document look like the document in the figure.
2. Save the document and name it **WL2-C1-VB-IntlCorres**.
3. Save, print, and then close **WL2-C1-VB-IntlCorres.docx**.

Case Study Apply Your Skills

Part 1

You work in the Human Resources Department at Oceanside Medical Services. Your supervisor, Michael Jennison, has given you a Word document containing employee handbook information and has asked you to format the book. Open the **OMSHandbook.docx** document, save it and name it **WL2-C1-CS-OMSHandbook**, and then apply the following formatting:

- Apply heading styles to the titles and headings.
- Change to a style set of your choosing.
- Apply a theme that makes the handbook easy to read.
- Define a new symbol bullet and then apply it to all of the currently bulleted paragraphs.
- Insert a section break that begins a new page at the beginning of each section heading (beginning with *Section 1: General Information*).
- Insert a footer that prints the section name at the left margin and the page number at the right margin. Insert the correct section name for each section footer.

Figure 1.17 Visual Benchmark

INTERNATIONAL CORRESPONDENCE

With the increased number of firms conducting business worldwide, international written communication has assumed new importance. Follow these guidelines when corresponding internationally, especially with people for whom English is not the primary language:

- ✓ Use a direct writing style and clear, precise words.
- ✓ Avoid slang, jargon, and idioms.
- ✓ Develop an awareness of cultural differences that may interfere with the communication process.

INTERNATIONAL ADDRESSES

Use the company's letterhead or a business card as a guide for spelling and other information. Include the following when addressing international correspondences:

- Line 1: Addressee's Name, Title
- Line 2: Company Name
- Line 3: Street Address
- Line 4: City and Codes
- Line 5: COUNTRY NAME (capitalized)

CANADIAN CODES AND PROVINCES

1) ON – Ontario
2) QC – Quebec
3) NS – Nova Scotia
4) NB – New Brunswick
5) MB – Manitoba
6) BC – British Columbia
7) PE – Prince Edward Island
8) SK – Saskatchewan
9) AB – Alberta
10) NL – Newfoundland and Labrador

CANADIAN CODES AND TERRITORIES

11) NT – Northwest Territories
12) YT – Yukon
13) NU – Nunavut

Part 2

After reviewing the formatted handbook, you decide to apply additional formatting to improve the readability and visual appeal of the handbook. With **WL2-C1-CS-OMSHandbook.docx** open, apply the following formatting:

- Select the lines of text on the first page beginning with *Section 1: General Information* through *Compensation Procedures* and then define and apply a new multilevel list number format that applies capital letters followed by a period to the first level and Arabic numbers (1, 2, 3) followed by a period to the second level. You determine the indents.

- Insert a cover page of your choosing and insert the appropriate information in the placeholders.

Save, print, and then close **WL2-C1-CS-OMSHandbook.docx**.

Part 3

A new employee orientation is scheduled for Friday, October 5, 2012, from 9:00 a.m. until 3:30 p.m. Michael Jennison will be conducting the orientation and has asked you to prepare a flyer regarding the orientation that can be placed on all bulletin boards in the clinic. Include in the flyer the date and times as well as the location, which is Conference Room 100. Include as bullets additional information about what will be covered during the orientation. Use the information in the multilevel list in the **WL2-C1-CS-OMSHandbook.docx** document to come up with approximately six to eight bulleted points. Using the Help feature, learn how to insert a picture watermark and then insert the **Ocean.jpg** file as a watermark. Make sure the text is readable on the flyer. Include any other additional features to improve the visual appeal of the flyer. Save the completed flyer document and name it **WL2-C1-CS-Flyer**. Print and then close **WL2-C1-CS-Flyer.docx**.

Part 4

During the orientation, Mr. Jennison discusses vacation allowances with the new employees and he wants to present the information in a readable format. He has asked you to look at the information in **OMSVacAllowances.docx** and then insert the information in an Excel worksheet. After inserting the information in an Excel worksheet, apply formatting to improve the visual appeal of the worksheet. (If Excel is not available to you, create tables in Word for the data.) Save the completed workbook and name it **WL2-C1-CS-OMSVacAllowances**. Save, print, and then close **WL2-C1-CS-OMSVacAllowances.xlsx**.

CHAPTER 2

Proofing Documents

PERFORMANCE OBJECTIVES

Upon successful completion of Chapter 2, you will be able to:

- Complete a spelling and grammar check on text in a document
- Create a custom dictionary and change the default dictionary
- Display synonyms and antonyms for specific words using the Thesaurus
- Display document word, paragraph, and character counts
- Use the translation feature to translate words from English to other languages
- Search for information online

Tutorials

2.1 Changing Spelling and Grammar Checking Options

2.2 Displaying Readability Statistics

2.3 Creating a Custom Dictionary

2.4 Displaying Word, Paragraph, and Character Counts

2.5 Using the Thesaurus

2.6 Searching for Specific Information from Online Sources

2.7 Using Translation Features

Microsoft Word includes proofing tools to help create a thoughtful and well-written document. These tools include a spelling checker, grammar checker, and thesaurus. With options at the Research task pane you can translate words from English to other languages and search for and request specific information from online sources. In this chapter you will learn how to use these proofing tools as well as how to create a custom dictionary. Model answers for this chapter's projects appear on the following page.

Word2010L2C2

Note: Before beginning the projects, copy to your storage medium the Word2010L2C2 subfolder from the Word2010L2 folder on the CD that accompanies this textbook and then make Word2010L2C2 the active folder.

EARLY DISTRIBUTIONS

If you want to withdraw funds or begin income from any PLAN20, PLAN30, or PLAN40 before you reach age 59, you may have to pay an extra 10 percent "early distributions" tax on the taxable amount. However, you will not have to pay an early distribution tax on any part of a withdrawal if:

- the distribution is because you are disabled;
- you separated from your job at or after age 55 and take your withdrawal after that (not applicable for PLAN20);
- you begin annuity income withdrawal after you leave your job (termination is not required for PLAN40), as long as your annuity income consists of a series of regular substantially equal payments (at least annually) over your lifetime or life expectancy;
- you have medical expenses in excess of 8 percent of your adjusted gross income and the withdrawal is less than or equal to your expenses (not applicable for PLAN20); or
- you are required to make a payment to someone besides yourself under a MIRA plan.

Project 1 Check Spelling and Grammar in an Investment Plan Document
WL2-C2-P1-PlanDists.docx

Nationwide Medical Databases

The medical community looks forward to the day when medical records change from manila folders full of dusty documents to a nationwide registry off electronic medical records available to medical personnel anywhere. With these new medical database systems, doctors located anywhere in the world could pull up charts immediately, with a few clicks of the mouse. Full color 3-D X-rays could be included in electronic patient records. People receiving care away from home would no longer have to worry that their doctor did not have all of their medical records.

At this point, some obstacles may obstruct the widespread use of this new technology. Medical systems tend to cost much more than other systems do to legalities and the need for complicated approval processes. Everyone involved must have medical training, raising costs even further. Data validation is critical, as lives may be lost if data is faulty. Privacy issues are another roadblock. Medical records are as private and closely guarded as financial ones. Should any doctor be able to see a record? Can patients access their own records? How would incapacitated patience grant permission?

Some medical providers are embracing such databases with a more limited scope, only sharing information about patients in the same HBO, for example. So far, no nationwide system exists, but such systems may appear within the next few years.

Project 2 Check the Grammar in a Medical Database Document
WL2-C2-P2-MedData.docx

ONLINE BANKING IN BRAZIL

Brazilian Rodrigo Abreu has not been inside a bank for several years, nor has he written a paper check for any regular expense. For about a decade, Mr. Abreu, a thirtyish technology executive, has made every kind of scheduled payment through the Internet arm of his Brazilian bank, Banco Itau. He pays his car insurance, buys stocks, and conducts e-commerce transactions through the bank's website. His mother, other family members, and all of his friends also do most of their business transactions online. Advanced Internet technology may not be normally associated with Brazil, where a vast majority of the population of 171.2 million has no online access. But when it comes to Internet banking, Brazil is the leader.

Brazil's economic problems in the early 1990s helped pressure major banks—Bradesco, Unibanco, and Banco Itau—to build advanced electronic payment systems that formed the backbone of the Internet services they offer today. At the time, the economy faces an almost daily inflationary rate of 3 percent. To battle the hyperinflation, banks built communications systems to clear checks and allow their customers to pay bills as soon as possible. That helped the customers avoid losing money during processing. "We were able to cash checks within 24 hours when the U.S. banks were still taking nearly a week," said Milton Monteiro, who is vice president and is in charge of Internet banking at Banco Itau. "We had to be very efficient."

By 1993, each major Brazilian bank had built a complex private network so that when a customer's paycheck came in it was cleared overnight and moved into an account that was hedged against inflation. Home banking was coming into fashion and people were already dialing directly into the banks' networks to move money and pay bills instantly. In the United States, meanwhile, manual check processing and human bank tellers were still the norm.

While many United States banks are catching up with the range of their online offerings, Bradesco, Banco Itau, and Unibanco still have a wider array of Internet services. Brazilians can complete nearly any type of financial transaction through the banks' websites. Banks offer e-commerce portals, advanced business-to-business services, brokerage services, direct deposit, and bill-paying, all integrated into their websites. In fact, under a bill-paying standard now used in Brazil, bank customers can simply type in the bar code number of any bill; the bank immediately knows its amount and pays it upon request.

Source: Lipschultz, David. The New York Times.

Project 3 Check the Spelling in an Online Banking Document
WL2-C2-P3-BankBrazil.dox

Résumé Styles

The traditional chronological résumé lists your work experience in reverse-chronological order (starting with your current or most recent position). The functional style deemphasizes the "where" and "when" of your career and instead groups similar experience, talents, and qualifications, regardless of when they occurred. Today, however, most résumés follow neither a strictly chronological nor strictly functional format; rather, they are an effective mixture of the two styles usually known as a "combination" or "hybrid" format.

Estilos de curriculum vitae

El currículum cronológico tradicional muestra su experiencia de trabajo en orden cronológico inverso (comenzando con su posición actual o más reciente). El estilo funcional deemphasizes el "dónde" y "cuándo" de su carrera y en su lugar grupos experiencia similar, talentos y calificaciones, independientemente de cuando se produjeron. Hoy, sin embargo, currículos mayoría siguen un formato ni estrictamente cronológico ni estrictamente funcional; más bien, son una mezcla efectiva de los dos estilos, conocido habitualmente como un formato de "híbrido" o "combinación".

Project 4 Research Information and Translate Text
WL2-C2-P4-ResumeStyles.docx

TRANSLATION		
English to Spanish		
English to French		
Term	**Spanish**	**French**
Central	centrico	central
Data	datos	donnees
Directory	directorio	repertoire
External	externo	exterieur

WL2-C2-P4-TranslateTerms.docx

Model Answers

You will open an investment plan document and then complete a spelling and grammar check on the document.

Checking the Spelling and Grammar in a Document ▪■▪

Word provides proofing tools to help you create professional and polished-looking documents. Two of these proofing tools include the spelling checker and the grammar checker. The spelling checker finds misspelled words and offers replacement words. It also finds duplicate words and irregular capitalizations. When you spell check a document, the spelling checker compares the words in your document with the words in its dictionary. If the spelling checker finds a match, it passes over the word. If the spelling checker does not find a match, it will stop and select:

- a misspelled word when the misspelling does not match another word that exists in the dictionary
- typographical errors such as transposed letters
- double word occurrences (such as *the the*)
- irregular capitalization
- some proper names
- jargon and some technical terms

The grammar checker will search a document for errors in grammar, punctuation, and word usage. The spelling checker and the grammar checker can help you create a well-written document, but do not replace the need for proofreading.

Before checking the spelling or grammar of a document, save the document currently displayed or open a document and then complete these basic steps:

1. Click the Review tab.
2. Click the Spelling and Grammar button. (You can also press the keyboard shortcut F7.)
3. If the spelling checker detects an error, it selects the misspelled word and displays a Spelling and Grammar dialog box, similar to the one shown in Figure 2.1. The sentence containing the misspelled word displays in the *Not in Dictionary* text box. If the spelling checker detects a grammatical error, it selects the sentence containing the error and displays the Spelling and Grammar dialog box, similar to the one shown in Figure 2.2.
4. If the spelling checker selects a misspelled word, replace the word with the correct spelling, tell Word to ignore it and continue checking the document, or add the word to a custom dictionary. If the grammar checker selects a sentence containing a grammatical error, it displays the sentence in the top text box in the Spelling and Grammar dialog box. Choose to ignore or change errors found by the grammar checker.
5. When the spelling and grammar check is completed, the message *The spelling and grammar check is complete* displays. Click OK to close the message box.

▼ Quick Steps

Check Spelling and Grammar
1. Click Review tab.
2. Click Spelling & Grammar button.
3. Change or ignore error.
4. Click OK.

H I N T

Complete a spelling and grammar check on a portion of a document by selecting the text first and then clicking the Spelling & Grammar button.

Spelling &
Grammar

Figure 2.1 Spelling and Grammar Dialog Box with Spelling Error Selected

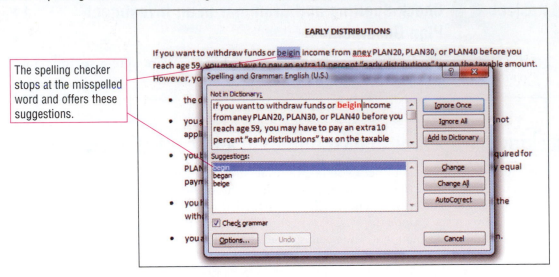

The spelling checker stops at the misspelled word and offers these suggestions.

Figure 2.2 Spelling and Grammar Dialog Box with Grammar Error Selected

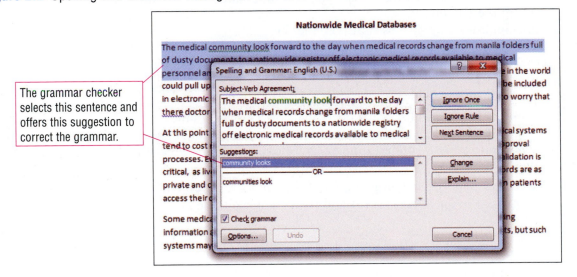

The grammar checker selects this sentence and offers this suggestion to correct the grammar.

When a word is selected during a spelling and grammar check, you need to determine if the word should be corrected or if it should be ignored. Word provides buttons at the right side and bottom of the Spelling and Grammar dialog box to make decisions. The buttons in the Spelling and Grammar dialog box change depending on the type of error selected. Table 2.1 lists the buttons and their functions.

Spell Checking a Document

By default, a spelling and grammar check are both completed on a document. If you want to check only the spelling in a document and not the grammar, remove the check mark from the *Check grammar* check box located in the lower left corner of the Spelling and Grammar dialog box.

Table 2.1 Spelling and Grammar Dialog Box Buttons

Button	Function
Ignore Once	During spell checking, skips that occurrence of the word; in grammar checking, leaves currently selected text as written.
Ignore All	During spell checking, skips that occurrence of the word and all other occurrences of the word in the document.
Ignore Rule	During grammar checking, leaves currently selected text as written and ignores the current rule for remainder of the grammar check.
Add to Dictionary	Adds selected word to the main spelling check dictionary.
Delete	Deletes the currently selected word(s).
Change	Replaces selected word in sentence with selected word in Suggestions list box.
Change All	Replaces selected word in sentence with selected word in Suggestions list box and all other occurrences of the word.
AutoCorrect	Inserts selected word and correct spelling of word in AutoCorrect dialog box.
Explain	During grammar checking, displays grammar rule information about the selected text.
Undo	Reverses most recent spelling and grammar action.
Next Sentence	Accepts manual changes made to sentence and then continues grammar checking.
Options	Displays a dialog box with options for customizing a spelling and grammar check.

Editing While Spell Checking

When spell checking a document, you can temporarily leave the Spelling and Grammar dialog box, make corrections in the document, and then resume spell checking. For example, suppose while spell checking you notice a sentence that you want to change. To correct the sentence, move the mouse pointer to the location in the sentence where the change is to occur, click the left mouse button, and then make changes to the sentence. To resume spell checking, click the Resume button, which was formerly the Ignore Once button.

Changing Spelling Options

Click the Options button at the Spelling and Grammar dialog box and the Word Options dialog box displays with the *Proofing* option selected as shown in Figure 2.3. You can also display the Word Options dialog box by clicking the File tab, clicking the Options button located below the Help tab, and then clicking *Proofing* in the left panel of the dialog box. Use options at this dialog box to customize spell checking by identifying what you want the spell checker to check or ignore. You can also create or edit a custom dictionary.

▼ **Quick Steps**

Change Spelling Options
1. Click File tab.
2. Click Options button.
3. Click *Proofing*.
4. Specify options.
5. Click OK.

Figure 2.3 Word Options Dialog Box with Proofing Selected

Click *Proofing* to display spelling and grammar checking options.

Click this button to create a custom dictionary.

Insert a check mark in this check box to tell Word to display words that sound similar to other words.

You can change this option from *Grammar Only* to *Grammar & Style*.

Project 1 Spell Checking a Document with Words in Uppercase and with Numbers   **Part 1 of 1**

1. Open **PlanDists.docx** and then save the document with Save As and name it **WL2-C2-P1-PlanDists**.
2. Check spell checking options by completing the following steps:
   a. Click the File tab.
   b. Click the Options button located below the Help tab.
   c. At the Word Options dialog box, click the *Proofing* option in the left panel.
   d. Make sure the *Ignore words in UPPERCASE* check box and the *Ignore words that contain numbers* check box each contain a check mark.
   e. Click OK to close the dialog box.

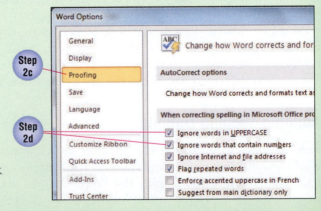

3. Complete a spelling check on the document by completing the following steps:
   a. Click the Review tab.
   b. Click the Spelling & Grammar button in the Proofing group.
   c. The spelling checker selects the word *beigin*. The proper spelling is selected in the *Suggestions* list box, so click the Change button (or Change All button).

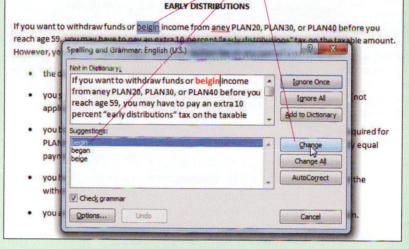

Step 3c

   d. The spelling checker selects the word *aney*. The proper spelling of the word is selected in the *Suggestions* list box, so click the Change button.
   e. The spelling checker selects *seperated*. The proper spelling is selected in the *Suggestions* list box, so click the Change button.
   f. The spelling checker selects *fater*. The proper spelling *after* is not selected in the *Suggestions* list box but it is one of the words suggested. Click *after* in the *Suggestions* list box and then click the Change button.

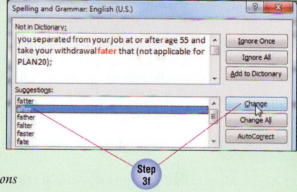

Step 3f

   g. The spelling checker selects *annuty*. The proper spelling is selected in the *Suggestions* list box, so click the Change button.
   h. The spelling checker selects *searies*. The proper spelling is selected in the *Suggestions* list box, so click the Change button.
   i. The spelling checker selects *gros*. The proper spelling is selected in the *Suggestions* list box, so click the Change button.
   j. When the message displays telling you that the spelling and grammar check is complete, click the OK button.
4. Save, print, and then close **WL2-C2-P1-PlanDists.docx**.

---

roject **2**   **Check the Grammar in a Medical Database Document**   **3 Parts**

You will check the grammar in a document, change grammar settings, and then check the grammar again. You will also display a word count for the document.

Checking the Grammar in a Document

Word includes a grammar checking feature that you can use to search a document for grammar, style, punctuation, and word usage. Like the spelling checker, the grammar checker does not find every error in a document and may stop at correct phrases. The grammar checker can help you create a well-written document, but does not replace the need for proofreading.

To complete a grammar check (as well as a spelling check) on a document, click the Review tab, and then click the Spelling & Grammar button in the Proofing group. The grammar checker selects the first sentence with a grammatical error and displays the sentence in the top text box in the dialog box with a suggested correction in the *Suggestions* text box. Choose to ignore or change errors found by the grammar checker. When the grammar checker is finished, the open document displays on the screen. The changes made during the check are inserted in the document. By default, a spelling check is completed on a document during a grammar check.

The grammar checker checks a document for a variety of grammar and style errors. In some situations, you may want the grammar checker to ignore a particular grammar or style rule. To do this, click the Ignore Rule button the first time the grammar checker displays text breaking the particular grammar or style rule you want ignored. If the grammar checker selects a sentence in a document containing a grammar or style error and you want the sentence left as written, click the Next Sentence button. This tells the grammar checker to leave the current sentence unchanged and move to the next sentence.

When a grammar error displays in the Spelling and Grammar dialog box, click the Explain button and the Word Help window displays with information about the specific grammar rule. After reading the information in the Word Help window, click the Close button located in the upper right corner of the window.

Project 2a **Checking Grammar in a Document**   **Part 1 of 3**

1. Open **MedData.docx** and then save it with Save As and name it **WL2-C2-P2-MedData**.
2. Check the grammar in the document by completing the following steps:
   a. Click the Review tab.
   b. Click the Spelling & Grammar button in the Proofing group.
   c. The grammar checker selects the sentence that begins *The medical community look forward . . .* and displays *community looks* in the *Suggestions* text box.
   d. Click the Explain button.
   e. Read the information about subject-verb agreement that displays in the Word Help window and then click the Close button located in the upper right corner of the window.
   f. Click the Change button in the Spelling and Grammar dialog box.

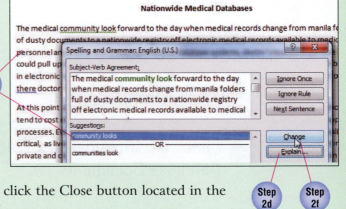

g. The grammar checker selects the sentence that begins *With these new medical database systems . . .* and displays *doctors* in the *Suggestions* list box.

h. Click the Explain button, read the information on plural or possessives that displays in the Word Help window and then close the window.

i. Click the Change button to change *doctor's* to *doctors*.

j. When the grammar checker selects the sentence that begins *People receiving care away from home . . .* and inserts *their* in the *Suggestions* list box, click the Change button.

k. When the grammar checker selects the sentence that begins *Privacy issues is . . .* , click the Change button.

l. At the message telling you that the spelling and grammar check is complete, click OK.

3. Save **WL2-C2-P2-MedData.docx**.

Changing Grammar Checking Options

You can customize the type of grammar checking you complete on a document with options in the *When correcting spelling and grammar in Word* section of the Word Options dialog box with *Proofing* selected. Insert a check mark in those options you want active in a document and remove the check mark from those you want inactive.

Consider making active the *Use contextual spelling* option when correcting a document that contains words that sound similar but have different meanings such as *to* and *too* and *there* and *their*. When you make this feature active, Word inserts a wavy blue line below words that sound similar to other words.

By default, the grammar checker checks only the grammar in a document. The *Writing Style* option at the Word Options dialog box with *Proofing* selected has a default setting of *Grammar Only*. You can change this default setting to *Grammar & Style*. To determine what style issues the grammar checker will select, click the Settings button and the Grammar Settings dialog box displays with grammar options. Insert a check mark for those options you want active and remove the check mark from those options you want inactive during a grammar check.

▼ **Quick Steps**

Change Grammar Checking Options
1. Click File tab.
2. Click Options button.
3. Click *Proofing*.
4. Specify options.
5. Click OK.

Project 2b **Changing Grammar Settings**   Part 2 of 3

1. With **WL2-C2-P2-MedData.docx** open, change grammar settings by completing the following steps:
   a. Click the File tab.
   b. Click the Options button located below the Help tab.
   c. At the Word Options dialog box, click the *Proofing* option in the left panel.
   d. Click the down-pointing arrow at the right side of the *Writing Style* option box and then click *Grammar & Style* at the drop-down list.
   e. Click the Recheck Document button.
   f. At the message that displays, click Yes.
   g. Click OK to close the Word Options dialog box.
2. Complete a grammar and style check on the document by completing the following steps:
   a. Press Ctrl + Home to move the insertion point to the beginning of the document.
   b. Make sure the Review tab is selected.
   c. Click the Spelling & Grammar button in the Proofing group.

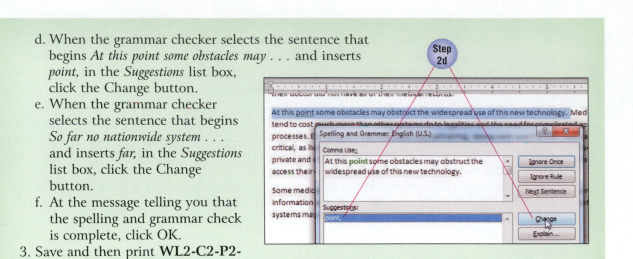

d. When the grammar checker selects the sentence that begins *At this point some obstacles may . . .* and inserts *point,* in the *Suggestions* list box, click the Change button.

e. When the grammar checker selects the sentence that begins *So far no nationwide system . . .* and inserts *far,* in the *Suggestions* list box, click the Change button.

f. At the message telling you that the spelling and grammar check is complete, click OK.

3. Save and then print **WL2-C2-P2-MedData.docx**.

Displaying Readability Statistics

▼ **Quick Steps**

Show Readability Statistics
1. Click File tab.
2. Click Options.
3. Click *Proofing.*
4. Click *Show readability statistics* check box.
5. Click OK.
6. Complete spelling and grammar check.

When completing a spelling and grammar check, you can display readability statistics about the document. Figure 2.4 displays the readability statistics for **WL2-C2-P2-MedData.docx**. Statistics include word, character, paragraph, and sentence count; average number of sentences per paragraph, words per sentence, and characters per word; and readability information such as the percentage of passive sentences in the document, the Flesch Reading Ease, and the Flesch-Kincaid Grade Level. Control the display of readability statistics with the *Show readability statistics* check box in the Word Options dialog box with *Proofing* selected.

The Flesch Reading Ease score is based on the average number of syllables per word and average number of words per sentence. The higher the score, the greater the number of people who will be able to understand the text in the document. Standard writing generally scores in the 60 to 70 range. The Flesch-Kincaid Grade Level score is based on the average number of syllables per word and the average number of words per sentence. The score indicates a grade level. Standard writing is generally written at the seventh or eighth grade level.

Figure 2.4 Readability Statistics Dialog Box

Readability Statistics	
Counts	
Words	227
Characters	1198
Paragraphs	4
Sentences	15
Averages	
Sentences per Paragraph	5.0
Words per Sentence	14.9
Characters per Word	5.1
Readability	
Passive Sentences	0%
Flesch Reading Ease	45.8
Flesch-Kincaid Grade Level	10.5

1. With **WL2-C2-P2-MedData.docx** open, display readability statistics about the document by completing the following steps:
   a. Click the File tab and then click the Options button.
   b. At the Word Options dialog box, click *Proofing* in the left panel.
   c. Click the *Show readability statistics* check box to insert a check mark.
   d. Click OK to close the Word Options dialog box.
   e. At the document, make sure the Review tab is selected, and then click the Spelling & Grammar button.
   f. Look at the readability statistics that display in the Readability Statistics dialog box and then click OK to close the dialog box.
2. Change the grammar options back to the default by completing the following steps:
   a. Click the File tab and then click the Options button.
   b. At the Word Options dialog box, click *Proofing* in the left panel.
   c. Click the *Show readability statistics* check box to remove the check mark.
   d. Click the down-pointing arrow at the right side of the *Writing Style* option box and then click *Grammar Only* at the drop-down list.
   e. Click OK to close the Word Options dialog box.
3. Save and then close **WL2-C2-P2-MedData.docx**.

Project 3   Check the Spelling in an Online Banking Document   3 Parts

You will open a document, create a custom dictionary, and then add specific terms to the custom dictionary. You will then complete a spelling check on the document.

Creating a Custom Dictionary

When completing a spelling check on a document, by default Word uses the CUSTOM.DIC custom dictionary. You can add or remove words from this default dictionary. In a multiple-user environment, you might also consider adding your own custom dictionary and then selecting that dictionary as the default. In this way, multiple users can create their own dictionary to use when spell checking a document.

To create a custom dictionary, display the Word Options dialog box with *Proofing* selected and then click the Custom Dictionaries button. This displays the Custom Dictionaries dialog box shown in Figure 2.5. To create a new dictionary, click the New button. At the Create Custom Dictionary dialog box, type a name for the dictionary in the *File name* text box and then press Enter. The new dictionary name will display in the *Dictionary List* box in the Custom Dictionaries dialog box. You can use more than one dictionary when spell checking a document. Insert a check mark in the check box next to any dictionary you want to use.

▼ **Quick Steps**

Create Custom Dictionary
1. Click File tab.
2. Click Options button.
3. Click *Proofing*.
4. Click Custom Dictionaries button.
5. Click New button.
6. Type name for dictionary, press Enter.

H I N T

When you change custom dictionary settings in one Microsoft Office program, the change affects all other programs in the suite.

Figure 2.5 Custom Dictionaries Dialog Box

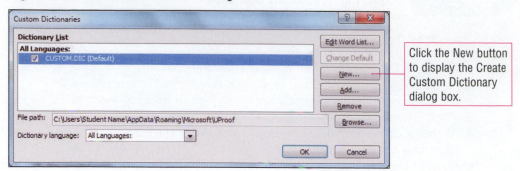

Click the New button to display the Create Custom Dictionary dialog box.

Changing the Default Dictionary

At the Custom Dictionaries dialog box, the default dictionary displays in the *Dictionaries List* box followed by *(Default)*. You can change this default by clicking the desired dictionary name in the list box and then clicking the Change Default button.

Removing a Dictionary

Remove a custom dictionary with the Remove button at the Custom Dictionaries dialog box. To do this, display the Custom Dictionaries dialog box, click the dictionary name in the *Dictionary List* box, and then click the Remove button. You are not prompted to confirm the removal so make sure you select the correct dictionary name before clicking the Remove button.

Project 3a   **Creating a Custom Dictionary and Changing the Default Dictionary**   **Part 1 of 3**

1. Open **BankBrazil.docx**, notice the wavy red lines indicating words not recognized by the spelling checker (words not in the custom dictionary), and then close the document.
2. At a blank document, create a custom dictionary, add words to the dictionary, and then change the default dictionary by completing the following steps:
   a. Click the File tab and then click the Options button.
   b. At the Word Options dialog box, click *Proofing* in the left panel.
   c. Click the Custom Dictionaries button.
   d. At the Custom Dictionaries dialog box, click the New button.
   e. At the Create Custom Dictionary dialog box, type your first and last names (without a space between) in the *File name* text box, and then press Enter.

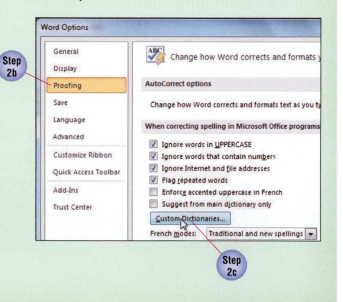

f. At the Custom Dictionaries dialog box, add a word to your dictionary by completing the following steps:

1) Click your dictionary name in the *Dictionary List* box.
2) Click the Edit Word List button.

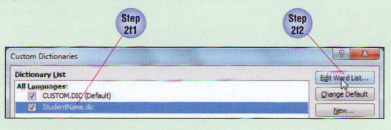

3) At your custom dictionary dialog box, type **Abreu** in the *Word(s)* text box.
4) Click the Add button.

g. Complete steps similar to those in 2f3 and 2f4 to add the following words:

> *Banco*
> *Itau*
> *Bradesco*
> *Unibanco*
> *Monteiro*
> *Lipschultz*

h. When all the words have been added, click the OK button to close the dialog box.

i. At the Custom Dictionaries dialog box with your dictionary name selected in the *Dictionary List* box, click the Change Default button. (Notice that the word *(Default)* displays after your custom dictionary.)

j. Click OK to close the Custom Dictionaries dialog box.

k. Click OK to close the Word Options dialog box.

3. Open **BankBrazil.docx** and then save the document with Save As and name it **WL2-C2-P3-BankBrazil**.

4. Complete a spelling and grammar check on your document. (The spelling checker will not stop at the words you added to your custom dictionary.)

5. Save and then print **WL2-C2-P3-BankBrazil.docx**.

6. Change the default dictionary and then remove your custom dictionary by completing the following steps:

a. Click the File tab and then click the Options button.

b. At the Word Options dialog box, click *Proofing* in the left panel.

c. Click the Custom Dictionaries button.

d. At the Custom Dictionaries dialog box, click *CUSTOM.DIC* in the *Dictionary List* box.

e. Click the Change Default button. (This changes the default back to the CUSTOM.DIC dictionary.)

f. Click your dictionary name in the *Dictionary List* box.

g. Click the Remove button.

h. Click OK to close the Custom Dictionaries dialog box.

i. Click OK to close the Word Options dialog box.

Displaying Word Count ■■■■■■■■■■■■■■■■■■

Quick Steps

Display Word Count
Click word count section
of Status bar.
OR
1. Click Review tab.
2. Click Word Count
   button.

Word Count

The Status bar displays the total number of words in your document. Word 2010 counts your words as you type. If you want to display more information such as the number of pages, paragraphs, and lines, display the Word Count dialog box. Display the Word Count dialog box by clicking the word count section of the Status bar or by clicking the Review tab and then clicking the Word Count button in the Proofing group.

You can count words in a portion of the document rather than the entire document by selecting the portion of text and then accessing the Word Count dialog box. If you want to get a word count on several sections throughout a document, select the first section, hold down the Ctrl key, and then select the other sections.

Using the Thesaurus ■■■■■■■■■■■■■■■■■■

Quick Steps

Use Thesaurus
1. Click Review tab.
2. Click Thesaurus
   button.
3. Type word in *Search
   for* text box.
4. Press Enter.

HINT

Hold down the Alt key and then click anywhere in the document and the Research task pane displays.

Thesaurus

Word offers a Thesaurus feature for finding synonyms, antonyms, and related words for a particular word. Synonyms are words that have the same or nearly the same meaning. When you are using the Thesaurus, Word may display antonyms for some words, which are words with opposite meanings. With the Thesaurus, you can improve the clarity of business documents.

To use the Thesaurus, click the Review tab and then click the Thesaurus button in the Proofing group. (You can also use the keyboard shortcut Shift + F7.) This displays the Research task pane. Click in the *Search for* text box located toward the top of the Research task pane, type the word for which you want to find synonyms and antonyms, and then press Enter or click the Start searching button (button containing a white arrow on a green background). This causes a list of synonyms and antonyms to display in the task pane list box. Figure 2.6 shows the Research task pane displaying synonyms and antonyms for the word *generally*.

Depending on the word you are looking up, the words in the Research task pane list box may display followed by *(n.)* for *noun*, *(adj.)* for *adjective*, or *(adv.)* for *adverb*. Antonyms may display at the end of the list of related synonyms and are followed by the word *(Antonym)*. Figure 2.6 shows the Research task pane with synonyms for the word generally.

The Thesaurus provides synonyms for the selected word as well as a list of related synonyms. For example, in the task pane list box shown in Figure 2.6, the main synonym *usually* displays for *generally* and is preceded by a minus symbol in a square. The minus symbol indicates that the list of related synonyms is displayed. Click the minus symbol and the list of related synonyms is removed from the task pane list box and the minus symbol changes to a plus symbol. If a synonym displays preceded by a plus symbol, click this symbol to show the list of related synonyms.

As you look up synonyms and antonyms for various words, you can display the list of synonyms and antonyms for the previous word by clicking the Previous search button (contains a left arrow and the word *Back*) located above the Research task pane list box. Click the Next search button to display the next search in the sequence. You can also click the down-pointing arrow at the right side of the Next search button to display a list of words for which you have looked up synonyms and antonyms.

Figure 2.6 Research Task Pane

Type a word in this text box, press Enter, and synonyms and antonyms for the word display in the list box below.

> Research
>
> Search for:
> generally
>
> Thesaurus: English (U.S.)
>
> Back
>
> ◢ Thesaurus: English (U.S.)
> ◢ **usually (adv.)**
>   usually
>   normally
>   commonly
>   mostly
>   largely
>   in general (Dictionary F...
>   by and large (Dictionar...
>   in the main (Dictionary ...
>   as a rule (Dictionary Fo...
>   all in all (Dictionary Form)
>   rarely (Antonym)
> ◢ Can't find it?
>   Try one of these alternatives or see Help for hints on refining your search.
>   **Other places to search**
>   Search for 'generally' in:
>   All Reference Books
>   All Research Sites
> Get services on Office Marketplace
> Research options...

Project 3b — Displaying Word Count and Using Thesaurus

Part 2 of 3

1. With **WL2-C2-P3-BankBrazil.docx** open, click the word count section of the Status bar.
2. After reading the statistics in the Word Count dialog box, click the Close button.
3. Display the Word Count dialog box by clicking the Review tab and then clicking the Word Count button in the Proofing group.
4. Click the Close button to close the Word Count dialog box.
5. Change the word *generally* in the first paragraph to *normally* using Thesaurus by completing the following steps:
   a. Select the word *generally* located in the first paragraph.
   b. Click the Review tab if necessary.
   c. Click the Thesaurus button in the Proofing group.
   d. At the Research task pane, hover the mouse pointer over the synonym *normally*, click the down-pointing arrow that displays at the right of the word, and then click *Insert* at the drop-down list.
6. Follow similar steps to make the following changes using Thesaurus:
   a. Change *acquaintances* in the first paragraph to *friends*.
   b. Change *combat* in the second paragraph to *battle*.
7. Close the Research task pane by clicking the Close button located in the upper right corner of the task pane.
8. Save **WL2-C2-P3-BankBrazil.docx**.

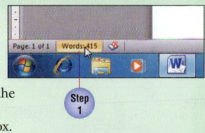

Step 1

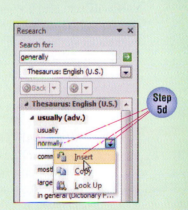

Step 5d

Another method for displaying synonyms for a word is to use a shortcut menu. To do this, position the mouse pointer on the word and then click the *right* mouse button. At the shortcut menu that displays, point to *Synonyms* and then click the desired synonym at the side menu. Click the Thesaurus option at the bottom of the side menu to display synonyms and antonyms for the word in the Research task pane.

Project 3c   **Replacing Synonyms Using a Shortcut Menu**   **Part 3 of 3**

1. With **WL2-C2-P3-BankBrazil.docx** open, position the mouse pointer on the word *vogue* located in the second sentence of the third paragraph.
2. Click the *right* mouse button.
3. At the shortcut menu that displays, point to *Synonyms*, and then click *fashion* at the side menu.
4. Save, print, and then close **WL2-C2-P3-BankBrazil.docx**.

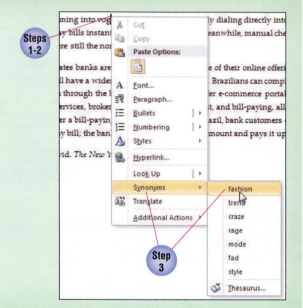

Project 4   Research Information and Translate Text   3 Parts

You will use the Research task pane to search for information online and use the translation feature to translate text from English to Spanish and English to French.

Researching Information ■■■■■■■■■■■■■■■■■■■■■■■■

Research

Along with Thesaurus, the Research task pane offers options that you can use to research information from online sources. The online resources available to you depend on the locale to which your system is set, authorization information indicating that you are allowed to download the information, and your Internet service provider.

Display the Research task pane by clicking the Review tab and then clicking the Research button in the Proofing group. You can also display the Research task pane by holding down the Alt key and then clicking anywhere in the open document. Determine which resources are available by clicking the down-pointing arrow at the right of the resources option box (the option box located below the *Search for* text box). The drop-down list includes reference books, research sites, business and financial sites, and other services. If you want to use a specific reference in your search, click it at the drop-down list, type the desired word or topic in the *Search for* text box, and then press the Enter key. Items matching your word or topic display in the task pane list box. Depending on the item, the list box may contain hyperlinks you can click to access additional information on the Internet.

You can control the available research options by clicking the <u>Research options</u> hyperlink located at the bottom of the Research task pane. Clicking this link displays the Research Options dialog box where you can insert a check mark before those items you want available and remove the check mark from those items you do not want available.

Project 4a	Researching Information	Part 1 of 3

Note: Your computer must be connected to the Internet to complete this exercise.

1. At a blank document, display the Research task pane by clicking the Review tab and then clicking the Research button in the Proofing group.
2. Search for information in a dictionary on the term *avatar* by completing the following steps:
   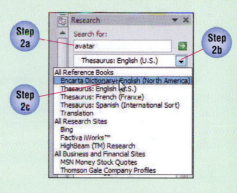
   a. Click in the *Search for* text box or select any text that displays in the text box and then type **avatar**.
   b. Click the down-pointing arrow to the right of the resources option box (the down-pointing arrow located immediately below the Start searching button).
   c. At the drop-down list of resources, click *Encarta Dictionary: English (North America)*. If this reference is not available, click any other dictionary available to you.
   d. Read the dictionary definitions for *avatar*.
3. Search for information on the term *avatar* in an encyclopedia by completing the following steps:
   a. Make sure *avatar* displays in the *Search for* text box.
   b. Click the down-pointing arrow at the right of the resources option box and then click *Bing* in the *All Research Sites* section of the list box.
   c. Look at the information that displays in the task pane list box and then click the Wikipedia hyperlink.
   d. After reading the information that displays in your Web browser, close the browser window.
   e. Close the Research task pane by clicking the close button located in the upper right corner of the task pane.

Translating Text

▼ Quick Steps

Translate Text
1. Click Review tab.
2. Click Research button.
3. Type word in *Search for* text box.
4. Click down-pointing arrow at right of resources option box.
5. Click *Translation*.
6. If necessary, specify *From* language and *To* language.

Word provides features you can use to translate text from one language into another. You can translate words at the Research task pane or with options from the Translate button in the language group in the Review tab.

Translating Text at the Research Task Pane

To translate a word using the Research task pane, type the word in the *Search for* text box, click the down-pointing arrow at the right of the resources option box, and then click *Translation* at the drop-down list. In the *Translation* list box, specify the languages you are translating to and from.

Project 4b   **Translating Words**   **Part 2 of 3**

1. At a blank document, click the Review tab and then click the Research button in the Proofing group.
2. Click in the *Search for* text box (or select any text that appears in the text box) and then type **keyboard**.
3. Click the down-pointing arrow at the right of the resources option box and then click *Translation* at the drop-down list.
4. Make sure that *English (U.S.)* displays in the *From* option box. (If it does not, click the down-pointing arrow at the right of the *From* option and then click *English (U.S.)* at the drop-down list.)
5. Click the down-pointing arrow at the right of the *To* option and then click *Spanish (International Sort)* at the drop-down list.
6. Read the Spanish translation of *keyboard* in the Research task pane.
7. Click the down-pointing arrow at the right of the *To* option and then click *French (France)* at the drop-down list.
8. Read the French translation of *keyboard* in the Research task pane and then close the Research task pane.

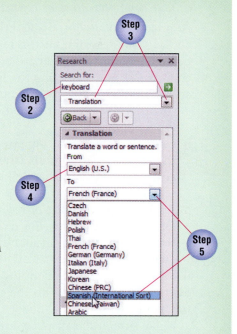

Translating Text with the Translate Button

Translate

In addition to the Research task pane, you can use the Translate button in the Language group in the Review tab to translate text. The Translate button contains options for translating with a mini translator as well as accessing online the Microsoft® Translator. Click the Translate button and a drop-down list displays with four options. Click the top option, *Translate Document*, and Word will send your document for translation by Microsoft® Translator. When you click the option, a message displays telling you that Word is about to send your document for translation in unencrypted HTML format and asking if you want to continue.

Figure 2.7 Translation Language Options Dialog Box

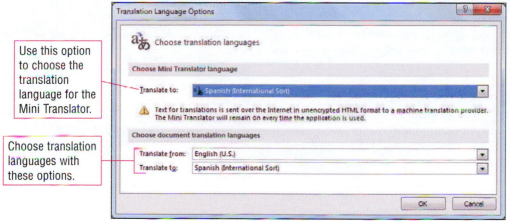

Use this option to choose the translation language for the Mini Translator.

Choose translation languages with these options.

To continue to the translator, click the Send button. With the second option, *Translate Selected Text*, Microsoft® Translator will translate the selected text in a document and insert the translation in the Research task pane.

Click the third option, *Mini Translator*, to turn this feature on. With the mini translator turned on, point to a word or select a phrase in your document and the translation of the text displays in a box above the text. To turn off the mini translator, click the Translate button in the Language group in the Review tab and then click the *Mini Translator* option. If the mini translator is turned on, the icon that displays to the left of the *Mini Translator* option displays with an orange background.

Use the fourth option from the Translate button, *Choose Translation Language*, to specify the language from which you want to translate and the language to which you want to translate. When you click the option, the Translation Language Options dialog box displays as shown in Figure 2.7. At this dialog box, specify the translation language and whether you want to translate the entire document or turn on the mini translator.

▼ **Quick Steps**

Translate Entire Document
1. Open document.
2. Click Review tab.
3. Click Translate button.
4. Click *Translate Document* at drop-down list.
5. At message, click Send button.

Translate Selected Text
1. Select text.
2. Click Review tab.
3. Click Translate button.
4. Click *Translate Selected Text*.

Turn on Mini Translator
1. Click Review tab.
2. Click Translate button.
3. Click *Mini Translator*.

Project 4c   **Using the Translate Button**   **Part 3 of 3**

Note: Check with your instructor before completing this exercise.

1. Open **ResumeStyles.docx** and then save the document with Save As and name it **WL2-C2-P4-ResumeStyles**.
2. Change the translation language to Spanish by completing the following steps:
   a. Click the Review tab.
   b. Click the Translate button in the Language group and then click the *Choose Translation Language* option at the drop-down list.
   c. At the Translation Language Options dialog box, make sure that *English (U.S.)* displays in the *Translate from* option box.

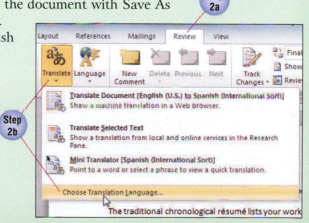

Step 2a

Step 2b

d. Click the down-pointing arrow at the right of the *Translate to* option box in the *Choose document translation languages* section and then click *Spanish (International Sort)* at the drop-down list. (Skip this step if *Spanish (International Sort)* is already selected.)

e. Click OK to close the dialog box.

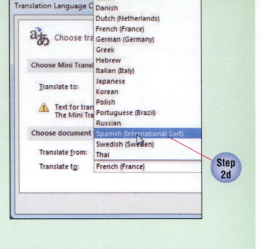

3. Translate the entire document to Spanish by completing the following steps:

a. Click the Translate button and then click the *Translate Document [English (U.S.) to Spanish (International Sort)]* option.

b. At the message telling you that Word is about to send the document for translation over the Internet in unencrypted HTML format, click the Send button.

c. In a few moments the Microsoft® Translator window will open. (If the window does not display, check the Status bar and click the button on the bar representing the translator.)

d. Select the translated text.

e. Press Ctrl + C to copy the text.

f. Close the Microsoft® Translator window.

g. At the **WL2-C2-P4-ResumeStyles.docx** document, press Ctrl + End to move the insertion point to the end of the document and then press Ctrl + V to insert the copied text.

4. Save, print, and then close **WL2-C2-P4-ResumeStyles.docx**.

5. Open **TranslateTerms.docx** and then save the document with Save As and name it **WL2-C2-P4-TranslateTerms**.

6. Translate the word *Central* into Spanish by completing the following steps:

a. Click the Review tab.

b. Click the Translate button and then click the *Choose Translation Language* option at the drop-down list.

c. At the Translation Language Options dialog box, click the down-pointing arrow at the right of the *Translate to* option box

in the *Choose Mini Translator language* section and then click *Spanish (International Sort)* at the drop-down list. (Skip this step if *Spanish (International Sort)* is already selected.)

d. Click OK to close the dialog box.

e. Click the Translate button and then click *Mini Translator [Spanish (International Sort)]* at the drop-down list. (This turns on the mini translator.)

f. Hover the mouse over the word *Central* in the table. Look at the translation that displays in the box above the word. Type one of the Spanish terms in the Spanish column.

g. Complete steps similar to those in Step 6f to display Spanish translations for the remaining terms. For each term, type one of the Spanish terms in the appropriate location in the table. Type the terms without any accents or special symbols.

7. Use the mini translator to translate terms into French by completing the following steps:
   a. Click the Translate button and then click the *Choose Translation Language* option at the drop-down list.
   b. At the Translation Language Options dialog box, click the down-pointing arrow at the right of the *Translate to* option box and then click *French (France)* at the drop-down list.
   c. Click OK to close the dialog box.
   d. With the mini translator turned on, hover the mouse over the word *Central* in the table (the mini translator displays dimmed above the word).
   e. Move the mouse pointer to the mini translator and then choose one of the French terms and type it in the French column.
   f. Complete steps similar to those in Steps 7d and 7e to display French translations for the remaining terms. Type one of the French terms in the appropriate locations in the table and type the terms without any accents or special symbols.
8. Turn off the mini translator by clicking the Translate button and then clicking *Mini Translator [French (France)]* at the drop-down list.
9. Save, print, and then close **WL2-C2-P4-TranslateTerms.docx**.

Chapter Summary

- The spelling checker matches the words in your document with the words in its dictionary. If a match is not found, the word is selected and possible corrections are suggested.

- When checking the spelling and/or grammar in a document, you can temporarily leave the Spelling and Grammar dialog box, make corrections in the document, and then resume checking.

- Customize spell checking options at the Word Options dialog box with *Proofing* selected in the left panel.

- With the grammar checker, you can search a document for correct grammar, style, punctuation, and word usage.

- When a grammar error is detected, display information about the error by clicking the Explain button at the Spelling and Grammar dialog box.

- Customize grammar checking with options in the *When correcting spelling and grammar in Word* section of the Word Options dialog box with *Proofing* selected.

- To display readability statistics on a document, insert a check mark in the *Show readability statistics* check box in the Word Options dialog box with *Proofing* selected and then complete a spelling and grammar check.

- Word uses the CUSTOM.DIC custom dictionary when spell checking a document. Add your own custom dictionary at the Custom Dictionaries dialog box. Display this dialog box by clicking the Custom Dictionaries button at the Word Options dialog box with *Proofing* selected.

- The Word Count dialog box displays the number of pages, words, characters, paragraphs, and lines in a document. Display this dialog box by clicking the word count section of the Status bar or clicking the Word Count button in the Proofing group in the Review tab.

- Use the Thesaurus to find synonyms and antonyms for words in your document. Display synonyms and antonyms at the Research task pane or by right-clicking a word and then pointing to *Synonyms* at the shortcut menu.
- Use options at the Research task pane to research information from online sources and to translate words from a variety of languages.
- Use the Translate button in the Language group in the Review tab to translate a document, selected text, or a word from one language to another.

Commands Review

FEATURE	RIBBON TAB, GROUP	BUTTON, OPTION	KEYBOARD SHORTCUT
Spelling and Grammar dialog box	Review, Proofing	ABC✓	F7
Word Options dialog box	File	Options	
Word Count dialog box	Review, Proofing	ABC 123	
Research task pane	Review, Proofing	🔍	
Research task pane for synonyms and antonyms	Review, Proofing	📖	Shift + F7
Translate text in document	Review, Language	aあ, Translate Document	
Translate selected text	Review, Language	aあ, Translate Selected Text	
Translation Language Option dialog box	Review, Language	aあ, Choose Translation Language	
Mini Translator	Review, Language	aあ, Mini Translator	

Concepts Check Test Your Knowledge

Completion: In the space provided at the right, indicate the correct term, symbol, or command.

1. Click this tab to display the Proofing group. _____

2. This is the keyboard shortcut to display the Spelling and Grammar dialog box. _____

3. Click this button in the Spelling and Grammar dialog box to replace the selected word with the word in the *Suggestions* list box. _____

4. During spell checking, click this button to skip the occurrence of the word and all other occurrences of the word in the document. _____

5. To display the Word Options dialog box with spelling and grammar options, click the File tab, click the Options button, and then click this option in the left panel. _____

6. Click this button in the Spelling and Grammar dialog box to display the Word Help window with information about the selected text. _____

7. This is the default setting for the *Writing Style* option at the Word Options dialog box with *Proofing* selected. _____

8. This reading ease is based on the average number of syllables per word and average number of words per sentence. _____

9. When completing a spelling check on a document, Word uses this custom dictionary by default. _____

10. Click the Translate button and then click the *Translate Document* option and the text in the document is translated by this. _____

11. Turn on this feature to point to a word or selected text and view a quick translation. _____

Skills Check   Assess Your Performance

Assessment

1   CHECK SPELLING IN A PUNCTUATION DOCUMENT

1. Open **QuoteMarks.docx** and then save the document with Save As and name it **WL2-C2-A1-QuoteMarks**.
2. Complete a spelling and grammar check on the document.
3. Apply heading styles of your choosing to the title and headings (display in bold) in the document.
4. Change the style set to *Formal*.
5. Save, print, and then close **WL2-C2-A1-QuoteMarks.docx**.

Assessment

2   CHECK SPELLING AND GRAMMAR AND PROOFREAD A LETTER

1. Open **AirMiles.docx** and then save the document with Save As and name it **WL2-C2-A2-AirMiles**.
2. Complete a spelling and grammar check on the document. (Proper names are spelled correctly.)

3. After completing the spelling and grammar check, proofread the letter and make necessary changes. (The letter contains mistakes that the spelling and grammar checker will not select.) Replace the XX located toward the end of the document with your initials.
4. Select the entire document and then change the font to 12-point Candara.
5. Save, print, and then close **WL2-C2-A2-AirMiles.docx**.

Assessment

3 CUSTOMIZE OPTIONS AND CHECK SPELLING AND GRAMMAR IN A DOCUMENT

1. Open **CyberScenario.docx** and then save the document with Save As and name it **WL2-C2-A3-CyberScenario**.
2. Display the Word Options dialog box with *Proofing* selected, make sure a check mark displays in the *Use contextual spelling* check box, change the *Writing Style* option to *Grammar & Style*, and then close the dialog box.
3. Complete a spelling and grammar check on the document.
4. Apply formatting to enhance the visual appeal of the document.
5. Display the Word Options dialog box with *Proofing* selected, change the *Writing Style* option to *Grammar Only*, and then close the dialog box.
6. Save, print, and then close **WL2-C2-A3-CyberScenario.docx**.

Assessment

4 TRANSLATE AND INSERT WORDS IN A TABLE

1. At a blank document, use the translation feature to find the Spanish and French translations for the following terms:
   Abbreviation
   Adjective
   Adverb
   Punctuation
   Grammar
   Hyphen
   Paragraph
2. Type the English words followed by the Spanish and French translations. (You do not need to include accents or special symbols.) Set the text in a table and then apply formatting to enhance the visual appearance of the table.
3. Save the document and name it **WL2-C2-A4-Translations**.
4. Print and then close **WL2-C2-A4-Translations.docx**.

Visual Benchmark Demonstrate Your Proficiency

USE THE TRANSLATOR FEATURE

1. Open **CCLtrhd.docx** and then save it and name it **WL2-C2-VB-CCDonations**.
2. Type the title *Support Your Local Community Center* shown in Figure 2.8 and the English paragraph of text below the title and then complete a spelling and grammar check.

Figure 2.8 Visual Benchmark

Cordova Children's Community Center

Support Your Local Community Center

English:
As you consider your donation contributions for the new year, we ask that you consider supporting your community by supporting the Cordova Children's Community Center. The center is a nonprofit agency providing educational and recreational activities for children. Please stop by for a visit. Our dedicated staff will be available to discuss with you the services offered by the center, how your donation dollars are spent, and provide information on current and future activities and services.

Spanish:
Considere la posibilidad de sus contribuciones caritativas para el nuevo año, pedimos que fortalecer su comunidad mediante el apoyo a Community Center la infancia Córdoba. El centro es una agencia sin fines de lucro que proporciona actividades educativas y recreativas para los niños. Por favor, para detener una visita. Nuestro personal dedicado estará disponible para discutir con usted los servicios ofrecidos por el centro, cómo se gastan sus dólares de la donación y proporcionar información sobre las actividades actuales y futuras y servicios.

French:
Que vous considérez vos contributions charitables pour la nouvelle année, nous demandons que vous renforcer votre communauté en prenant en charge le centre communautaire de l'enfance de Cordoue. Le centre est un organisme sans but lucratif offrant des activités éducatives et récréatives pour les enfants. Veuillez arrêter visite. Notre personnel dédié sera disponible pour discuter avec vous les services offerts par le Centre, comment votre dollars de don sont dépensés et fournissent des informations sur les services et les activités actuelles et futures.

"Children are our most valuable natural resource." ~ Herbert Hoover

770 Sunrise Terrace ♦ Santa Fe, NM 87509 ♦ 505-555-7700

3. Select the paragraph of text below the heading *English:* and then translate the paragraph into Spanish and then into French. Copy the translated text into the document as shown in Figure 2.8.
4. Use the Curlz MT font for the title, the quote, and the headings at the beginning of each paragraph. Apply paragraph shading as shown in the figure. Apply any other formatting to make your document appear similar to the document shown in Figure 2.8.
5. Save, print, and then close **WL2-C2-VB-CCDonations.docx**.

Case Study   Apply Your Skills

Part 1

You work in the executive offices at Nickell Industries and have been asked to develop a writing manual for employees. The company has not used a consistent theme when formatting documents, so you decide to choose a theme and use that when formatting all documents. Open **NIManual.docx** and then save the document with Save As and name it **WL2-C2-CS-NIManual**. Check the spelling and grammar in the document and have Word check for contextual spelling. Make the following changes to the document:

- Insert a section break at the beginning of the title *Editing and Proofreading*.
- Apply styles of your choosing to the titles and headings in the document.
- Apply the theme you have chosen for company documents.
- Insert headers and/or footers.
- Create a cover page.

Save the document.

Part 2

As you review the writing manual document, you decide to highlight the points for developing document sections. You decide that a process SmartArt diagram would present the ideas in an easy-to-read format and provide some visual interest to the manual. Insert a page break at the end of the **WL2-C2-CS-NIManual. docx** document, type the title *Developing a Document*, and insert the following in the appropriate shapes:

Beginning
- Introduce main idea
- Get reader's attention
- Establish positive tone

Middle
- Provide detail for main idea
- Lead reader to intended conclusion

End
- State conclusion
- State action you want reader to take

Apply theme colors that follow the theme you chose for company documents. Save the document.

Part 3

You decide to purchase some reference books on grammar and punctuation. Using the Internet, search bookstores for books providing information on grammar and punctuation and then choose three books. You know that the books will be purchased soon, so you decide to add the information in the writing manual document telling the readers what reference books are available. Include this information on a separate page at the end of the **WL2-C2-CS-NIManual.docx** document. Save, print, and then close the document.

Part 4

Nickell Industries does business in other countries, including Mexico. One of the executives in the finance department has asked you to translate some terms into Spanish that will be used to develop an invoice. Create a document that translates the following terms from English to Spanish and also include in the document the steps to translate text. You figure that if the executive knows the steps, she can translate at her computer.

- City
- Telephone
- Invoice
- Product
- Description
- Total

Format the document with the theme you chose for company documents and add any other enhancements to improve the visual appeal of the document. Save the completed document and name it **WL2-C2-CS-Translations**. Print and then close **WL2-C2-CS-Translations.docx**.

Microsoft® Word

CHAPTER 3

Automating and Customizing Formatting

PERFORMANCE OBJECTIVES

Upon successful completion of Chapter 3, you will be able to:

- **Insert exceptions and add words to and delete words from the AutoCorrect dialog box**
- **Use the AutoCorrect Options button**
- **Sort and insert building blocks**
- **Create, edit, modify, and delete building blocks**
- **Insert and update fields from Quick Parts**
- **Customize the Quick Access toolbar**

Tutorials

3.1 Customizing AutoCorrect and AutoFormatting

3.2 Inserting and Sorting Building Blocks

3.3 Saving Building Block Content

3.4 Editing Building Block Properties

3.5 Inserting Custom Building Blocks

3.6 Inserting Document Properties

3.7 Inserting and Updating Fields from Quick Parts

3.8 Customizing the Quick Access Toolbar

3.9 Customizing the Ribbon

Microsoft Word offers a number of features to help you customize documents and to streamline the formatting of documents. In this chapter you will learn how to customize the AutoCorrect feature and use the AutoCorrect Options button. You will also learn how to build a document using building blocks; create, save, and edit your own building blocks; and customize the Quick Access toolbar. Model answers for this chapter's projects appear on the following pages.

Word2010L2C3

Note: Before beginning computer projects, copy to your storage medium the Word2010L2C3 subfolder from the Word2010L2 folder on the CD that accompanies this textbook and then make Word2010L2C3 the active folder.

Family Adventure Vacations

Namibia and Victoria Falls Adventure

Terra Travel Services is partnering with Family Adventure Vacations® to provide adventurous and thrilling family vacations. Our first joint adventure is a holiday trip to Namibia. Namibia is one of the most fascinating holiday destinations in Africa and offers comfortable facilities, great food, cultural interaction, abundant wildlife, and a wide variety of activities to interest people of all ages.

During the 12-day trip, you and your family will travel across Namibia through national parks, enjoying the beautiful and exotic scenery and watching wildlife in natural habitats. You will cruise along the Kwando and Chobe rivers and spend time at the Okapuka Lodge located near Windhoek, the capital of Namibia.

If you or your family member is a college student, contact one of our college travel adventure consultants to learn more about the newest Student Travel package titled "STudent STyle" that offers a variety of student discounts, rebates, and free travel accessories for qualifying participants.

Through the sponsorship of Ameria Resorts, we are able to offer you a 15 percent discount for groups of twelve or more people.

For additional information on the Namibia adventure, as well as other exciting vacation specials, please visit our website at www.emcp.net/terratravel or visit www.emcp.net/famadv.

1050 Marietta Street ◇ Atlanta, GA 30315 ◇ 1-888-555-2288 ◇ www.emcp.net/terratravel

Project 1 Create a Travel Document Using AutoCorrect

WL2-C3-P1-TTSAfrica.docx

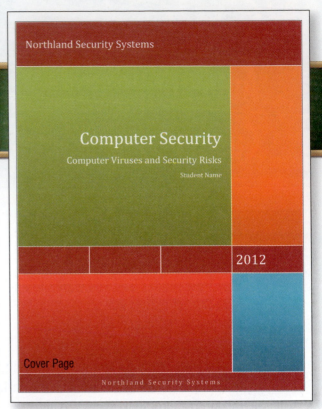

Project 2 Build a Document with Predesigned and Custom Building Blocks

WL2-C3-P2-CompViruses.docx

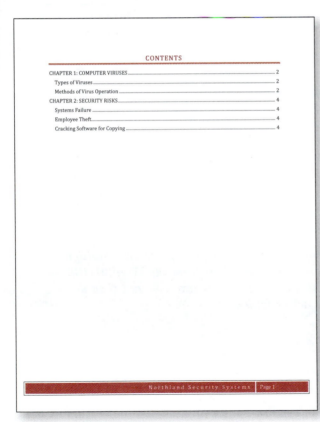

CONTENTS

Northland Security Systems   Page I

"Although accurate estimates are difficult to pinpoint, businesses certainly lose millions of dollars a year in stolen computer hardware and software."

CHAPTER 1: COMPUTER VIRUSES

One of the most familiar forms of risk to computer security is the computer virus. A computer virus is a program written by a hacker or cracker designed to perform some kind of trick upon an unsuspecting victim. The trick performed in some cases is mild, such as drawing an offensive image on the screen, or changing all of the characters in a document to another language. Sometimes the trick is much more severe, such as reformatting the hard drive and erasing all the data, or damaging the motherboard so that it cannot operate properly.

TYPES OF VIRUSES

Viruses can be categorized by their effect, which include nuisance, data-destructive, espionage, and hardware-destructive. A nuisance virus usually does no real damage, but is rather just an inconvenience. The most difficult part of a computer to replace is the data on the hard drive. The installed programs, the documents, databases, and saved emails form the heart of a personal computer. A data-destructive virus is designed to destroy this data. Some viruses are designed to create a backdoor into a system to bypass security. Called espionage viruses, they do no damage, but rather allow a hacker or cracker to enter the system later for the purpose of stealing data or spying on the work of the competitor. Very rarely, a virus is created that attempts to damage the hardware of the computer system itself. Called hardware-destructive viruses, these

bits of programming can weaken or destroy chips, drives, and other components.

METHODS OF VIRUS OPERATION

Viruses can create effects that range from minor and annoying to highly destructive, and are operated and transmitted by a variety of methods. An email virus is normally transmitted as an attachment to a message sent over the Internet. Email viruses require the victim to click on the attachment and cause it to execute. Another common form of virus transmission is by a macro, a small subprogram that allows users to customize and automate certain functions. A macro virus is written specifically for one program, which then becomes infected when it opens a file with the virus stored in its macros. The boot sector of a compact disc or hard drive contains a variety of information, including how the disc is organized and whether it is capable of loading an operating system. When a disc is left in a drive and the computer reboots, the operating system automatically reads the boot sector to learn about that disc and to attempt to start any operating system on that disc. A boot sector virus is designed to alter the boot sector of a disc, so that whenever the operating system reads the boot sector, the computer will automatically become infected.

Other methods of virus infection include the Trojan horse virus, which hides inside another legitimate program or data file, and a stealth virus, which is designed to hide itself from detection software. Polymorphic viruses

Northland Security Systems   Page 2

Model Answers

alter themselves to prevent antivirus software from detecting them by examining familiar patterns. Polymorphic viruses alter themselves randomly as they move from computer to computer, making detection more difficult. Multipartite viruses alter their form of attack. Their name derives from their ability to attack in several different ways. They may first infect the boot sector, and then later move on to become a Trojan horse type by infecting a disc file. These viruses are more sophisticated, and therefore more difficult to guard against. Another type of virus is the logic bomb, which generally sits quietly dormant waiting for a specific event or set of conditions to occur. A famous logic bomb was the widely publicized Michelangelo virus, which infected personal computers and caused them to display a message on the artist's birthday.

CHAPTER 2: SECURITY RISKS

Although hackers, crackers, and viruses garner the most attention as security risks, companies face a variety of other dangers to their hardware and software systems. Principally, these risks involve types of system failure, employee theft, and the cracking of software for copying.

SYSTEMS FAILURE

A fundamental element in making sure that computer systems operate properly is protecting the electrical power that runs them. Power interruptions such as blackouts and brownouts have very adverse effects on computers. An inexpensive type of power strip called a surge protector can guard against power fluctuations and can also serve as an extension cord and splitter. A much more vigorous power protection system is an uninterruptible power supply (UPS), which provides a battery backup. Similar in nature to a power strip but much more bulky and a bit more expensive, a UPS provides not only steady spike-free power, but also keeps computers running during a blackout.

EMPLOYEE THEFT

Although accurate estimates are difficult to pinpoint, businesses certainly lose millions of dollars a year in stolen computer hardware and software. Often, in large organizations, such theft goes unnoticed or unreported. Someone takes a hard drive or a scanner home for legitimate use, then leaves the job some time later, and keeps the machine. Sometimes, employees take components to add to their home PC systems or a thief breaks into a business and hauls away computers. Such thefts cost far more than the price of the stolen computers because they also involve the cost of replacing the lost data, the cost of the time lost while the machines are gone, and the cost of installing new machines and training people to use them.

CRACKING SOFTWARE FOR COPYING

A common goal of hackers is to crack a software protection scheme. A crack is a method of circumventing a security scheme that prevents a user from copying a program. A common protection scheme for software is to require that the installation CD be resident in the drive whenever the program runs. Making copies of the CD with a burner, however, easily fools this protection scheme. Some game companies are taking the extra step of making duplication difficult by scrambling some of the data on the original CDs, which CD burners will automatically correct when copying. When the copied and corrected CD is used, the software checks for the scrambled track information. If the error is not found, the software will not run.

FAMILY ADVENTURE VACATIONS

6553 Copper Avenue ◆ Albuquerque, NM 87107 ◆ 505-555-4910

Current Date

Mrs. Jody Lancaster
Pacific Sky Cruise Lines
120 Montgomery Boulevard
Los Angeles, CA 97032

Dear Jody:

Your colorful brochures have made quite an impression on our clients, and consequently, we have given away our entire stock. Please send us an additional box of brochures as well as information and fact sheets about the various specialized cruises coming up.

Are you planning to offer the "Northern Lights" cruise next year? The cruise has been very popular with our clients, and I have had three inquiries in the past three weeks regarding the cruise. As soon as you know the dates of the cruise and stateroom prices, please let me know.

Sincerely,

Student Name
Travel Consultant

XX
WL2-C3-P3-PSLtr.docx

Visit our website at www.emcp.net/worldwide to learn about our weekly vacation specials!

"Making your vacation dreams a reality"

FAMILY ADVENTURE VACATIONS

6553 Copper Avenue ◆ Albuquerque, NM 87107 ◆ 505-555-4910

Current Date

Mrs. Jody Lancaster
Pacific Sky Cruise Lines
120 Montgomery Boulevard
Los Angeles, CA 97032

Dear Jody:

I imagine you are extremely busy finalizing the preparations for the Pacific Sky Cruise Line's inaugural trip to the Alaska Inside Passage. The promotional literature you provided our company has been very effective in enticing our clients to sign up. This letter is a confirmation of the thirty staterooms that we have reserved for our clients for the inaugural cruise. We have reserved ten each of the following staterooms:

- Category H: Inside stateroom with two lower beds
- Category D: Deluxe ocean-view stateroom with window, sitting area, and two lower beds
- Category B: Superior deluxe ocean-view stateroom with window, sitting area, and two lower beds
- Category S: Superior deluxe suite with ocean view, private balcony, sitting area, and two lower beds

With only a few weeks to go before the cruise, I want to make sure our clients' bookings are finalized so they can enjoy the eight-day, seven-night cruise to the Alaska Inside Passage. Please confirm the stateroom reservations and send me a fax or email with the confirmation numbers.

Sincerely,

Student Name
Senior Travel Consultant

XX
WL2-C3-P4-PSLtr.docx

"Making your vacation dreams a reality"

Project 3 Create a Letter Document Using Custom Building Blocks
WL2-C3-P3-PSLtr.docx

Project 4 Create a Letter Document with Modified Building Blocks
WL2-C3-P4-PSLtr.docx

TESTING AGREEMENT

THIS AGREEMENT is made by and between Frontier Video Productions and _____ ("Licensee") having a principal place of business located at _____.

In consideration of the mutual covenants and premises herein contained, the parties hereto agree as follows:

Frontier Video Productions grants to Licensee a non-exclusive, non-transferable license to use the Software on a single computer at Licensee's business location solely for beta testing and internal use until _____, 20___, at which time the Software and all copies shall be returned to Frontier Video Productions.

In consideration for receiving a copy of the Software for testing, Licensee agrees to serve as a beta testing site for the Software and will notify Frontier Video Productions of all problems and ideas for enhancements which come to Licensee's attention during the period of this Agreement, and hereby assigns to Frontier Video Productions all rights, title and interest to such enhancements and all property rights therein including without limitation all patent, copyright, trade secret, mask work, trademark, moral right, or other intellectual property rights.

This Agreement shall be governed, construed, and enforced in accordance with the laws of the United States of America and of the State of California. Any notice required by this Agreement shall be given by prepaid, first class, certified mail, return receipt requested.

Frontier Video Productions: Licensee:

_____   _____
Name   Name

First Draft
WL2-C3-P5-TestAgrmnt.docx
5/23/2012 9:31:00 AM

TESTING AGREEMENT

THIS AGREEMENT is made by and between Frontier Video Productions and _____ ("Licensee") having a principal place of business located at _____.

In consideration of the mutual covenants and premises herein contained, the parties hereto agree as follows:

Frontier Video Productions grants to Licensee a non-exclusive, non-transferable license to use the Software on a single computer at Licensee's business location solely for beta testing and internal use until _____, 20___, at which time the Software and all copies shall be returned to Frontier Video Productions.

In consideration for receiving a copy of the Software for testing, Licensee agrees to serve as a beta testing site for the Software and will notify Frontier Video Productions of all problems and ideas for enhancements which come to Licensee's attention during the period of this Agreement, and hereby assigns to Frontier Video Productions all rights, title and interest to such enhancements and all property rights therein including without limitation all patent, copyright, trade secret, mask work, trademark, moral right, or other intellectual property rights.

This Agreement shall be governed, construed, and enforced in accordance with the laws of the United States of America and of the State of California. Any notice required by this Agreement shall be given by prepaid, first class, certified mail, return receipt requested.

Frontier Video Productions: Licensee:

_____   _____
Name   Name

First Draft
WL2-C3-P5-FVPAgrmnt.docx
5/23/2012 9:46:00 AM

Project 5 Insert Document Properties and Fields in an Agreement Document

WL2-C3-P5-TestAgrmnt.docx

WL2-C3-P5-FVPAgrmnt.docx

NATURAL INTERFACE APPLICATIONS

A major area of artificial intelligence has the goal of creating a more natural interface between human and machine. Currently, computer users are restricted in most instances to using a mouse and keyboard for input. For output, they must gaze at a fairly static, two-dimensional screen. Speakers are used for sound, and a printer for hard copy. The user interface consists of typing, pointing, and clicking. New speech recognition and natural-language technologies promise to change that soon.

SPEECH RECOGNITION

One of the most immediately applicable improvements comes in the area of speech recognition. Rather than typing information into the computer, users can direct it with voice commands. A computer that can take dictation and perform requested actions is a real step forward in convenience and potential. Speech recognition has developed rather slowly, mainly because the typical PC did not have the necessary speed and capacity until very recently.

NATURAL-LANGUAGE INTERFACE

Computers that are able to communicate using spoken English, Japanese, or any of the hundreds of other languages currently in use around the world, would certainly be helpful. In the not-so-distant future, computers will most likely be able to read, write, speak, and understand many human languages. Language translators already exist, and they are getting better all the time.

Programmers can look forward to a human-language computer interface. With better interfaces, programmers may be able to describe what they want using natural (human) languages, rather than writing programs in the highly restrictive and rather alien programming languages in use today. Natural-language interfaces are an area of artificial intelligence that is broader in scope than simple speech recognition. The goal is to have a machine that can read a set of news articles on any topic and understand what it has read. Ideally, it could then write its own report summarizing what it has learned.

VIRTUAL REALITY

Virtual reality (VR) describes the concept of creating a realistic world within the computer. Online games with thousands of interacting players already exist. In these games people can take on a persona and move about a virtual landscape, adventuring and chatting with other players. The quality of a virtual reality system is typically characterized in terms of its immersiveness, which measures how real the simulated world feels and how well it can make users accept the simulated world as their own and forget about reality. With each passing year, systems are able to

---

provide increasing levels of immersion. Called by some the "ultimate in escapism," VR is becoming increasingly common—and increasingly realistic.

MENTAL INTERFACE

Although still in the experimental phase, a number of interfaces take things a bit further than VR, and they don't require users to click a mouse, speak a word, or even lift a finger. Mental interfaces use sensors mounted around the skull to read the alpha waves given off by our brains. Thinking of the color blue could be used to move the mouse cursor to the right, or thinking of the number seven could move it to the left. The computer measures brain activity and interprets it as a command, eliminating the need to physically manipulate a mouse to move the screen cursor. While this technology has obvious applications for assisting people with disabilities, military researchers are also using it to produce a superior form of interface for pilots.

Project 6 Minimize the Ribbon and Customize the Quick Access Toolbar and Ribbon

WL2-C3-P6-InterfaceApps.docx

Project 1   **Create a Travel Document Using AutoCorrect**   **3 Parts**

You will create several AutoCorrect entries, open a letterhead document, and then use the AutoCorrect entries to type text in the document.

Customizing AutoCorrect ▪▪▪▪▪▪▪▪▪▪▪▪▪▪▪▪▪▪▪▪▪

The AutoCorrect feature in Word corrects certain text automatically as you type. You can control what types of corrections are made with options at the AutoCorrect dialog box with the AutoCorrect tab selected as shown in Figure 3.1. At this dialog box, you can turn an AutoCorrect feature on or off by inserting or removing check marks from the check boxes, specify AutoCorrect exceptions, replace frequently misspelled words with the correct spelling, and add frequently used words and specify keys to quickly insert the words in a document.

Specifying AutoCorrect Exceptions

The check box options at the AutoCorrect dialog box with the AutoCorrect tab selected identify the types of corrections made by AutoCorrect. You can make exceptions to the corrections with options at the AutoCorrect Exceptions dialog box shown in Figure 3.2. Display this dialog box by clicking the Exceptions button at the AutoCorrect dialog box with the AutoCorrect tab selected.

AutoCorrect will usually capitalize words that come after an abbreviation ending in a period since a period usually ends a sentence. Exceptions to this display in the AutoCorrect Exceptions dialog box with the First Letter tab selected. Many exceptions already display in the dialog box but you can add

▼ **Quick Steps**

Display the AutoCorrect Exceptions Dialog Box
1. Click File tab, Options button.
2. Click *Proofing*.
3. Click AutoCorrect Options button.
4. Click AutoCorrect tab.
5. Click Exceptions button.

Figure 3.1 AutoCorrect Dialog Box with AutoCorrect Tab Selected

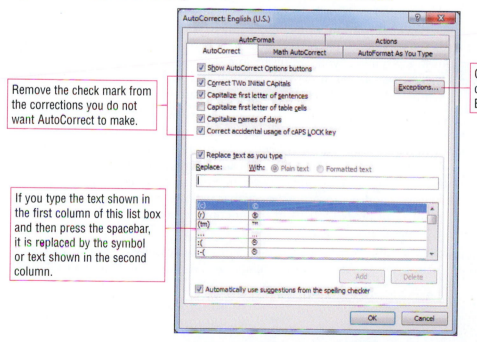

Remove the check mark from the corrections you do not want AutoCorrect to make.

Click this button to display the AutoCorrect Exceptions dialog box.

If you type the text shown in the first column of this list box and then press the spacebar, it is replaced by the symbol or text shown in the second column.

Figure 3.2 AutoCorrect Exceptions Dialog Box

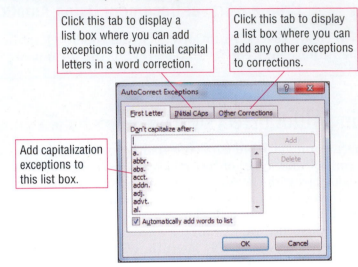

Click this tab to display a list box where you can add exceptions to two initial capital letters in a word correction.

Click this tab to display a list box where you can add any other exceptions to corrections.

Add capitalization exceptions to this list box.

additional exceptions by typing the desired exception in the *Don't capitalize after* text box and then clicking the Add button. By default, AutoCorrect will correct two initial capital letters in a word. If you do not want AutoCorrect to correct the capitalizing of two initial capitals in a word, display the AutoCorrect Exceptions dialog box with the INitial CAps tab selected and then type the exception text in the *Don't correct* text box. At the AutoCorrect Exceptions dialog box with the Other Corrections tab selected, type text that you do not want corrected in the *Don't correct* text box. You can delete exceptions from the dialog box with any of the tabs selected by clicking the desired text in the list box and then clicking the Delete button.

Adding Words to AutoCorrect

Quick Steps

Insert Word(s) to AutoCorrect
1. Click File tab.
2. Click Options button.
3. Click *Proofing*.
4. Click AutoCorrect Options button.
5. Click AutoCorrect tab.
6. Type misspelled or abbreviated word.
7. Press Tab.
8. Type correctly spelled word or complete word(s).
9. Click Add button.
10. Click OK.

You can add commonly misspelled words or typographical errors to AutoCorrect. For example, if you consistently type *relavent* instead of *relevant*, you can add *relavent* to AutoCorrect and tell it to correct it as *relevant*. The AutoCorrect dialog box contains a few symbols you can insert in a document. For example, type *(c)* and AutoCorrect changes the text to ©. Type *(r)* and AutoCorrect changes the text to ®. The symbols display at the beginning of the AutoCorrect dialog box list box.

You can also add an abbreviation to AutoCorrect that, when typed, will insert the entire word (or words). For example, in Project 1a, you will add *fav* to AutoCorrect that will insert *Family Adventure Vacations* when you type *fav* and then press the spacebar. You can also control the capitalization of the word (or words) inserted by controlling the capitalization of the abbreviation. For example, in Project 1a, you will add *Na* to AutoCorrect that will insert *Namibia* when you type *Na*. If you want to insert *NAMIBIA* in the document, you would type *NA* and then press the spacebar.

Note that the AutoCorrect feature does not automatically correct text in hyperlinks. Also, AutoCorrect is only available in Word, Outlook, and Visio.

1. At a blank document, click the File tab and then click the Options button.
2. At the Word Options dialog box, click *Proofing* in the left panel.
3. Click the AutoCorrect Options button in the *AutoCorrect options* section.
4. At the AutoCorrect dialog box with the AutoCorrect tab selected, add an exception to AutoCorrect by completing the following steps:
    a. Click the Exceptions button.
    b. At the AutoCorrect Exceptions dialog box, click the INitial CAps tab.
    c. Click in the *Don't correct* text box, type **STudent**, and then click the Add button.
    d. Click in the *Don't correct* text box, type **STyle**, and then click the Add button.
    e. Click the OK button.

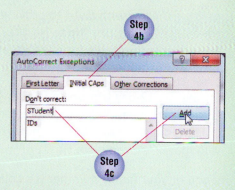

5. At the AutoCorrect dialog box with the AutoCorrect tab selected, click in the *Replace* text box and then type **fav**.
6. Press the Tab key (this moves the insertion point to the *With* text box) and then type **Family Adventure Vacations**.
7. Click the Add button. (This adds *fav* and *Family Adventure Vacations* to the AutoCorrect and also selects *fav* in the *Replace* text box.)
8. Type **Na** in the *Replace text* box. (The text *fav* is automatically deleted when you begin typing *Na*.)
9. Press the Tab key and then type **Namibia**.
10. Click the Add button.
11. With the insertion point positioned in the *Replace* text box, type **vf**.
12. Press the Tab key and then type **Victoria Falls**.
13. Click the Add button.
14. With the insertion point positioned in the *Replace* text box, type **tts**.

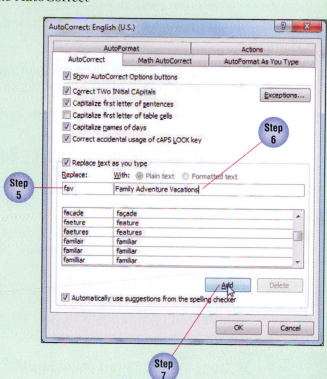

15. Press the Tab key and then type **Terra Travel Services**.
16. Click the Add button.
17. Click OK to close the AutoCorrect dialog box and then click OK to close the Word Options dialog box.
18. Open **TTSLtrhd.docx** and then save the document with Save As and name it **WL2-C3-P1-TTSAfrica**.
19. Type the text shown in Figure 3.3. Type the text exactly as shown. AutoCorrect will correct words as you type.
20. Save **WL2-C3-P1-TTSAfrica.docx**.

Figure 3.3 Project 1a

fav

Na and vf Adventure

tts is partnering with fav(r) to provide adventurous and thrilling family vacations. Our first joint adventure is a holiday trip to Na. Na is one of the most fascinating holiday destinations in Africa and offers comfortable facilities, great food, cultural interaction, abundant wildlife, and a wide variety of activities to interest people of all ages.

During the 12-day trip, you and your family will travel across Na through national parks, enjoying the beautiful and exotic scenery and watching wildlife in natural habitats. You will cruise along the Kwando and Chobe rivers and spend time at the Okapuka Lodge located near Windhoek, the capital of Na.

If you or your family member is a college student, contact one of our college travel adventure consultants to learn more about the newest Student Travel package titled "STudent STyle" that offers a variety of student discounts, rebates, and free travel accessories for qualifying participants.

tts and fav are offering a 15 percent discount if you sign up for this once-in-a-lifetime trip to Na. This exciting adventure is limited to twenty people, so don't wait to sign up.

Using the AutoCorrect Options Button

AutoCorrect
Options

When AutoCorrect corrects text, rest the mouse pointer near the text and a small blue box displays below the corrected text. Move the mouse pointer to this blue box and the AutoCorrect Options button displays. Click this button and a drop-down list displays with options to change back to the original spelling, stop automatically correcting the specific text, and display the AutoCorrect dialog box. If the AutoCorrect Options button does not display, you will need to turn the feature on. To do this, display the AutoCorrect dialog box with the AutoCorrect tab selected, click the *Show AutoCorrect Options buttons* check box to insert a check mark, and then click OK to close the dialog box.

Project 1b Using the AutoCorrect Options Button   Part 2 of 3

1. With **WL2-C3-P1-TTSAfrica.docx** open, select and then delete the last paragraph.
2. With the insertion point positioned on the blank line below the last paragraph of text (you may need to press the Enter key), type the following (AutoCorrect will automatically change *Ameria* to *America*, which you will change in the next step): Through the sponsorship of Ameria Resorts, we are able to offer you a 15 percent discount for groups of twelve or more people.
3. Change the spelling of *America* back to *Ameria* by completing the following steps:
   a. Position the mouse pointer over *America* until a blue box displays below the word.
   b. Position the mouse pointer on the blue box until the AutoCorrect Options button displays.

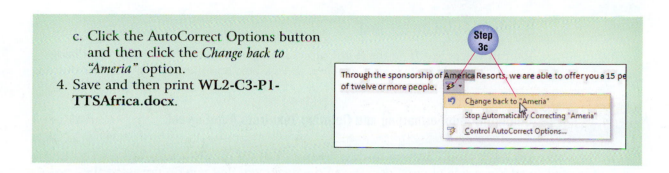
Customizing AutoFormatting

When you type text, Word provides options to automatically apply some formatting such as changing a fraction to a fraction character (such as changing 1/2 to ½), changing numbers to ordinals (such as changing 1st to 1st), changing an Internet or network path to a hyperlink (such as changing www.emcp.net to www.emcp.net), and applying bullets or numbers to text. The autoformatting options display in the AutoCorrect dialog box with the AutoFormat As You Type tab selected as shown in Figure 3.4. Display this dialog box by clicking the File tab and then clicking the Options button. At the Word Options dialog box, click *Proofing* in the left panel and then click the AutoCorrect Options button. At the AutoCorrect dialog box, click the AutoFormat As You Type tab. At the dialog box, remove the check mark from those options you want to turn off and insert a check mark for those options you want Word to automatically format.

Figure 3.4 AutoCorrect Dialog Box with AutoFormat As You Type Tab Selected

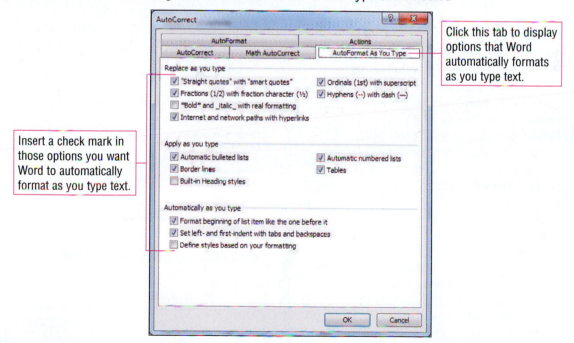

Deleting AutoCorrect Text

You can delete text from the AutoCorrect dialog box. To do this, display the dialog box, click the desired word or words in the list box, and then click the Delete button.

Project 1c Changing AutoFormatting and Deleting Text from AutoCorrect Part 3 of 3

1. Make sure **WL2-C3-P1-TTSAfrica.docx** is open.
2. You need to add a couple of web addresses to the document and you do not want the addresses automatically formatted as hyperlinks (since you are sending the document as hard copy rather than electronically). Turn off the autoformatting of web addresses by completing the following steps:
   a. Click the File tab and then click the Options button.
   b. At the Word Options dialog box, click *Proofing* in the left panel.
   c. Click the AutoCorrect Options button.
   d. At the AutoCorrect dialog box, click the AutoFormat As You Type tab.
   e. Click the *Internet and network paths with hyperlinks* check box to remove the check mark.
   f. Click OK to close the AutoCorrect dialog box.
   g. Click OK to close the Word Options dialog box.
3. Press Ctrl + End to move the insertion point to the end of the document, press the Enter key, and then type the text shown in Figure 3.5.
4. Turn on the autoformat feature you turned off in Step 2 by completing Steps 2a through 2g (except in Step 2e you are inserting the check mark rather than removing it).
5. Delete *fav* from AutoCorrect by completing the following steps:
   a. Click the File tab and then click the Options button.
   b. At the Word Options dialog box, click *Proofing* in the left panel.
   c. Click the AutoCorrect Options button.
   d. At the AutoCorrect dialog box, click the AutoCorrect tab.
   e. At the AutoCorrect dialog box, click in the *Replace* text box and then type **fav**. (This selects the entry in the list box.)
   f. Click the Delete button.

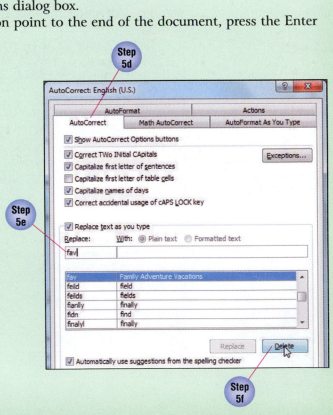

Step 2d

Step 2e

Step 5d

Step 5e

Step 5f

6. Complete steps similar to those in Step 5 to delete the *Na*, *tts*, and *vf* AutoCorrect entries.
7. Delete the exceptions you added to the AutoCorrect Exceptions dialog box by completing the following steps:

   a. At the AutoCorrect dialog box with the AutoCorrect tab selected, click the Exceptions button.
   b. At the AutoCorrect Exceptions dialog box, click the INitial CAps tab.
   c. Click *STudent* in the list box and then click the Delete button.
   d. Click *STyle* in the list box and then click the Delete button.
   e. Click OK to close the AutoCorrect Exceptions dialog box.

8. Click OK to close the AutoCorrect dialog box.
9. Click OK to close the Word Options dialog box.
10. Save, print, and then close **WL2-C3-P1-TTSAfrica.docx**.

Figure 3.5 Project 1c

For additional information on the Na adventure, as well as other exciting vacation specials, please visit our website at www.emcp.net/terratravel or visit www.emcp.net/famadv.

 **roject 2 Build a Document with Predesigned and Custom Building Blocks**   **1 Part**

You will open a report document and then add elements to the document by inserting predesigned building blocks.

Inserting Quick Parts

Word includes a variety of tools you can use to insert data such as text, fields, objects, and other items to help build a document. To view some of the tools available, click the Quick Parts button in the Text group in the Insert tab. This displays a drop-down list of choices for inserting document properties, fields, and building blocks, and options for saving selected data to the AutoText gallery and the Quick Part gallery.

Inserting Building Blocks

Building blocks are tools you can use to develop or "build" a document. Word provides a number of building blocks you can insert in a document or you can create your own. To insert a building block into a document, click the Insert tab, click the Quick Parts button in the Text group, and then click *Building Blocks*

Quick Parts

▼ **Quick Steps**

Insert Building Block
1. Click Insert tab.
2. Click Quick Parts button.
3. Click *Building Blocks Organizer* at drop-down list.
4. Click desired building block.
5. Click Insert button.
6. Click Close.

Organizer at the drop-down list. This displays the Building Blocks Organizer dialog box shown in Figure 3.6. The dialog box displays columns of information about the building blocks. The columns in the dialog box display the building block name, the gallery that contains the building block, the template in which the building block is stored, the behavior of the building block, as well as a brief description.

The Building Blocks Organizer dialog box is a central location where you can view all of the predesigned building blocks available in Word. You have been using some of the building blocks in previous chapters when you inserted a predesigned header or footer, cover page, page number, or watermark. Other galleries in the Building Blocks Organizer dialog box containing predesigned building blocks include bibliographies, equations, table of contents, tables, and text boxes. The Building Blocks Organizer dialog box provides a convenient location for viewing and inserting building blocks.

▼ **Quick Steps**

Sort Building Blocks
1. Click Insert tab.
2. Click Quick Parts button.
3. Click *Building Blocks Organizer* at drop-down list.
4. Click desired column heading.

Sorting Building Blocks

When you open the Building Blocks Organizer dialog box, the building blocks display in the list box sorted by the Gallery column. You can sort the building blocks by other columns by clicking the column heading. For example, to sort building blocks alphabetically by name click the *Name* column heading.

Figure 3.6 Building Blocks Organizer Dialog Box

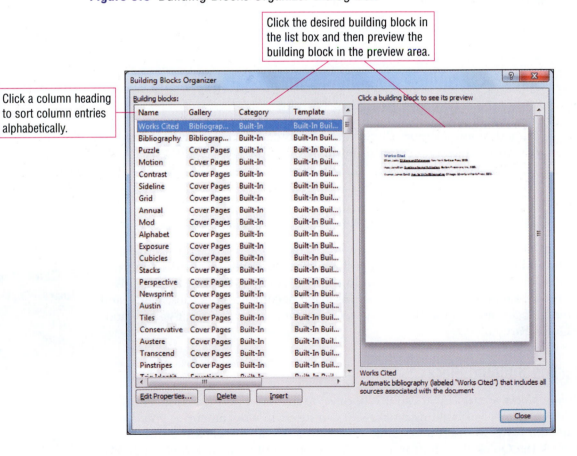

Click the desired building block in the list box and then preview the building block in the preview area.

Click a column heading to sort column entries alphabetically.

1. Open **CompViruses.docx** and then save the document with Save As and name it **WL2-C3-P2-CompViruses**.
2. Make the following changes to the document:
   a. Insert a continuous section break at the beginning of the first paragraph below the title *CHAPTER 1: COMPUTER VIRUSES*.
   b. Insert a section break that begins a new page at the beginning of the title *CHAPTER 2: SECURITY RISKS* located in the middle of the second page.
   c. Insert a continuous section break at the beginning of the first paragraph below the title *CHAPTER 2: SECURITY RISKS*.
   d. Change the line spacing to 1.15 for the entire document.
   e. Format the section below the first title *CHAPTER 1: COMPUTER VIRUSES* into two columns of equal width.
   f. Balance the columns of text on the second page.
   g. Format the section below the second title *CHAPTER 2: SECURITY RISKS* into two equally spaced columns.
   h. Balance the columns of text on the page.
3. Sort the building blocks and then insert a table of contents building block by completing the following steps:
   a. Press Ctrl + Home, press Ctrl + Enter to insert a page break, and then press Ctrl + Home to move the insertion point back to the beginning of the document.
   b. Click the Insert tab, click the Quick Parts button in the Text group, and then click *Building Blocks Organizer* at the drop-down list.
   c. At the Building Blocks Organizer dialog box, notice the arrangement of building blocks in the list box. (More than likely, the building blocks are organized alphabetically by Gallery.)
   d. Click the *Name* column heading. (This sorts the building blocks alphabetically by name. However, some blank building blocks may display at the beginning of the list box.)

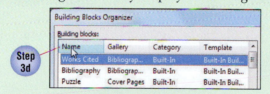

   e. Scroll down the list box and then click *Automatic Table 1*. (You may see only a portion of the name. Click the name and the full name as well as a description display in the dialog box below the preview of the table of contents building block.)
   f. Click the Insert button that displays toward the bottom of the dialog box. (This inserts a Contents page at the beginning of the page and uses the heading styles applied to the titles and headings in the document to create the table of contents.)
4. Insert a sidebar building block by completing the following steps:
   a. Position the insertion point at the beginning of the title *CHAPTER 1: COMPUTER VIRUSES*.
   b. With the Insert tab selected, click the Quick Parts button in the Text group and then click *Building Blocks Organizer* at the drop-down list.

c. At the Building Blocks Organizer dialog box, scroll down the list box and then click *Tiles Sidebar* in the *Name* column. (This displays the sidebar in the preview section of the dialog box.)

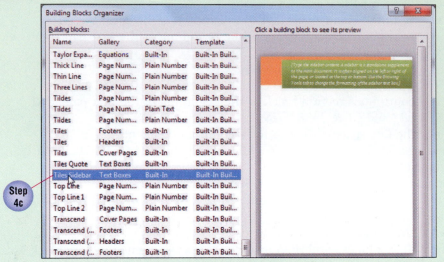

d. Click the Insert button that displays toward the bottom of the dialog box.

e. With the pull quote placeholder text selected, type "**Although accurate estimates are difficult to pinpoint, businesses certainly lose millions of dollars a year in stolen computer hardware and software.**"

f. Select the text you just typed, change the font size to 14 points, and then click in the document outside the pull quote text box.

5. Insert a footer building block by completing the following steps:

a. Click the Insert tab, click the Quick Parts button, and then click *Building Blocks Organizer*.

b. Scroll down the Building Blocks Organizer list box, click the *Tiles* footer, and then click the Insert button.

c. Click the placeholder text *[Type the company address]* and then type **Northland Security Systems**.

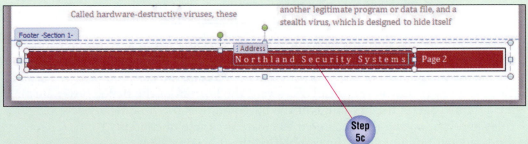

d. Double-click in the document.

6. Insert a cover page building block by completing the following steps:

a. Press Ctrl + Home to move the insertion point to the beginning of the document.

b. Click the Insert tab, click the Quick Parts button, and then click *Building Blocks Organizer*.

c. Scroll down the Building Blocks Organizer list box, click the *Tiles* cover page, and then click the Insert button.

d. Click the placeholder text *[TYPE THE COMPANY NAME]* and then type **Northland Security Systems**.

e. Click the placeholder text *[Type the document title]* and then type **Computer Security**.

f. Click the placeholder text *[Type the document subtitle]* and then type **Computer Viruses and Security Risks**.

g. Click the placeholder text *[Type the author name]* and then type your first and last names. (If a name displays instead of the placeholder *[Type the author name]*, select the name and then type your first and last names.)

h. Click the placeholder text *[Year]* and then type the current year.

7. Scroll through the document and look at each page in the document. The sidebar, footer, and cover page building blocks you inserted have similar formatting and are part of the *Tiles* group. Using building blocks from the same group provides consistency in the document and gives the document a polished and professional appearance.

8. Save, print, and then close **WL2-C3-P2-CompViruses.docx**.

 **roject 3 Create a Letter Document Using Custom Building Blocks** 　　　　　　　　**3 Parts**

You will create custom building blocks and then use those building blocks to prepare a business letter.

Saving Content as a Building Block

If you find yourself typing and formatting the same data on a regular basis, consider saving the data as a ***building block***. Saving commonly created data as a building block saves you time and reduces errors that might occur each time you type data or apply formatting. You can save content as a building block in a specific gallery. For example, you can save a text box in the Text Box gallery, save content in the Header gallery, save content in the Footer gallery, and so on. To save content in a specific gallery, use the button for the desired gallery. For example, to save a text box in the Text Box gallery, use the Text Box button. To do this, select the text box, click the Insert tab, click the Text Box button, and then click the *Save Selection to Text Box Gallery* option at the drop-down gallery. At the Create New Building Block dialog box that displays, as shown in Figure 3.7, type a name for the text box building block, type a description if desired, and then click OK.

To save content in the Header gallery, select the content, click the Insert tab, click the Header button, and then click the *Save Selection to Header Gallery* option at the drop-down gallery. This displays the Create New Building Block dialog box as shown in Figure 3.7 (except *Headers* displays with the *Gallery* option box). Complete similar steps to save content to the Footer gallery or the Cover Page gallery.

▼ **Quick Steps**

Save Content to Text Box Gallery
1. Select content.
2. Click Insert tab.
3. Click Text Box button.
4. Click *Save Selection to Text Box Gallery*.

Save Content to Header Gallery
1. Select content.
2. Click Insert tab.
3. Click Header button.
4. Click *Save Selection to Header Gallery*.

Save Content to Footer Gallery
1. Select content.
2. Click Insert tab.
3. Click Footer button.
4. Click *Save Selection to Footer Gallery*.

Figure 3.7 Create New Building Block Dialog Box

At this dialog box, type the building block name, specify the gallery and category, and enter a description of the building block.

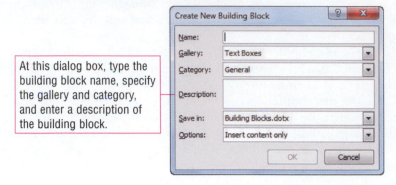

When you save data as a building block it becomes available in the Building Blocks Organizer dialog box. If you save content as a building block in a specific gallery, the building block is available at the Building Blocks Organizer dialog box as well as the gallery. For example, if you save a building block in the Footer gallery, the building block is available when you click the Footer button in the Insert tab.

Content you save as a building block is saved in either the Building Blocks.dotx template or the Normal.dotm template. Saving a building block in either of these templates makes it available each time you open Word. In a public environment such as a school, you may not be able to save data to a template. Before completing Project 3, check with your instructor to determine if you can save your building blocks. At the completion of Project 3, you will be instructed to delete the building blocks you create.

Saving Content to the AutoText Gallery

You can save content as a building block in the AutoText gallery and the building block can be easily inserted in a document by clicking the Insert tab, clicking the Quick Parts button, pointing to *AutoText*, and then clicking the desired AutoText building block at the side menu. To save content in the AutoText gallery, type and format the desired content and then select the content. Click the Insert tab, click the Quick Parts button, point to *AutoText*, and then click the *Save Selection to AutoText Gallery* option at the side menu. You can also press Alt + F3 to display the dialog box. At the Create New Building Block dialog box, type a name for the building block, type a description if desired, and then click OK.

Saving Content to the Quick Part Gallery

In addition to saving content in the AutoText gallery, you can save selected content in the Quick Part gallery. To do this, select the desired content, click the Insert tab, click the Quick Parts button, and then click the *Save Selection to Quick Part Gallery* option at the drop-down gallery. This displays the Create New Building Block dialog box with *Quick Parts* specified in the *Gallery* option box and *Building Blocks.dotx* specified in the *Save in* option box. Type a name for the building block, type a description if desired, and then click OK.

When selecting content to save as a building block, you may want to turn on the display of nonprinting characters by clicking the Show/Hide ¶ button in the Home tab.

▼ **Quick Steps**

Save Content to AutoText Gallery
1. Select content.
2. Click Insert tab.
3. Click Quick Parts button.
4. Point to *AutoText*.
5. Click *Save Selection to AutoText Gallery*.

Save Content to Quick Part Gallery
1. Select content.
2. Click Insert tab.
3. Click Quick Parts button.
4. Click *Save Selection to Quick Part Gallery*.

1. Open **FAVContent.docx**.
2. Save the text box as a building block in the Text Box gallery by completing the following steps:
   a. Select the text box by clicking in the text box and then clicking the text box border.
   b. Click the Insert tab, click the Text Box button, and then click the *Save Selection to Text Box Gallery* at the drop-down gallery.
   c. At the Create New Building Block dialog box, type your last name followed by **FAVTextBox** and then click OK.

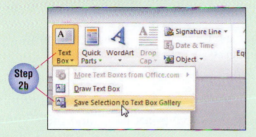
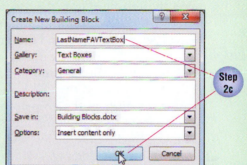

3. Save content as a building block in the Footer gallery by completing the following steps:
   a. Select the text *"Making your vacation dreams a reality"* located below the text box. (Make sure you select the paragraph mark at the end of the text. If necessary, click the Show/Hide ¶ button in the Paragraph group in the Home tab to display the paragraph mark.)
   b. Click the Footer button in the Header & Footer group in the Insert tab and then click *Save Selection to Footer Gallery* at the drop-down gallery.
   c. At the Create New Building Block dialog box, type your last name followed by **FAVFooter** and then click OK.

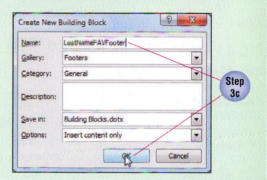

4. Save the company name *Pacific Sky Cruise Lines* and the address below it as a building block in the AutoText gallery by completing the following steps:
   a. Select the company name and the address (the two lines below the company name). (Make sure you include the paragraph mark at the end of the last line of the address.)
   b. Click the Quick Parts button in the Text group in the Insert tab, point to *AutoText*, and then click *Save Selection to AutoText Gallery* at the side menu.

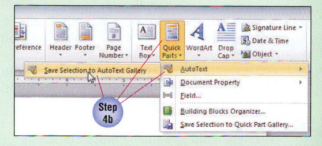

   c. At the Create New Building Block dialog box, type your last name and then type **PacificSky**.
   d. Click OK to close the dialog box.
5. Type your name and company title and then save the text as a building block in the AutoText gallery by completing the following steps:
   a. Move the insertion point to a blank line a double space below the Pacific Sky Cruise Lines address.
   b. Type your first and last names and then press the spacebar.

c. Press the Down Arrow key to move the insertion point to the next line and then type **Travel Consultant**. (Do not press the Enter key.)

d. Select your first and last names and the title *Travel Consultant*. (Include the paragraph mark at the end of the title.)

e. Press Alt + F3.

f. At the Create New Building Block dialog box, type your last name and then type **Title**.

g. Click OK to close the dialog box.

6. Save the letterhead as a building block in the Quick Part gallery by completing the following steps:

a. Select the letterhead text (the company name *FAMILY ADVENTURE VACATIONS*, the address below the name, and the paragraph mark at the end of the address and telephone number).

b. Click the Quick Parts button in the Text group in the Insert tab and then click *Save Selection to Quick Part Gallery* at the drop-down list.

c. At the Create New Building Block dialog box, type your last name and then type **FAV**.

d. Click OK to close the dialog box.

7. Close **FAVContent.docx** without saving it.

Editing Building Block Properties

▼ **Quick Steps**

Edit Building Block
1. Click Insert tab.
2. Click Quick Parts button.
3. Click *Building Blocks Organizer.*
4. Click desired building block.
5. Click Edit Properties button.
6. Make desired changes.
7. Click OK.
OR
1. Click desired button.
2. Right-click custom building block.
3. Click *Edit Properties.*
4. Make desired changes.
5. Click OK.

You can make changes to the properties of a building block with options at the Modify Building Block dialog box. This dialog box contains the same options as the Create New Building Block dialog box. Display the Modify Building Block dialog box by opening the Building Blocks Organizer dialog box, clicking the desired building block in the list box, and then clicking the Edit Properties button. You can also display this dialog box for a building block that displays in the drop-down gallery. To do this, click the Quick Parts button, right-click on the building block that displays in the drop-down gallery, and then click *Edit Properties* at the shortcut menu. Make desired changes to the Modify Building Block dialog box and then click OK. At the message asking if you want to redefine the building block entry, click Yes.

You can also display this dialog box for a custom building block in a button drop-down gallery by clicking the button, right-clicking the custom building block, and then clicking the *Edit Properties* option at the shortcut menu. For example, to modify a custom text box building block, click the Insert tab, click the Text Box button, and then scroll down the drop-down gallery to display the custom text box building block. Right-click the custom text box and then click *Edit Properties* at the shortcut menu.

Project 3b **Editing Building Block Properties** **Part 2 of 3**

1. At a blank document, click the Insert tab, click the Quick Parts button in the Text group, and then click *Building Blocks Organizer* at the drop-down list.

2. At the Building Blocks Organizer dialog box, click the Gallery heading to sort the building blocks by gallery. (This displays the AutoText galleries at the beginning of the list.)

3. Scroll to the right in the list box, and notice that the building block that displays with your last name followed by *PacificSky* does not contain a description. Edit the building block properties by completing the following steps:

a. Click the building block in the AutoText gallery that begins with your last name followed by *PacificSky*. (The entire building block name does not display in the list box. To view the entire name, click the building block name in the *Building Blocks* list box and then look at the name that displays below the preview page at the right side of the dialog box.)

b. Click the Edit Properties button located at the bottom of the dialog box.

c. At the Modify Building Block dialog box, click in the *Name* text box and then add *Address* to the end of the name.

d. Click in the *Description* text box and then type **Inserts the Pacific Sky name and address.**

e. Click OK to close the dialog box.

f. At the message asking if you want to redefine the building block entry, click Yes.

g. Close the Building Blocks Organizer dialog box.

4. Edit the letterhead building block by completing the following steps:

a. Click the Quick Parts button in the Text group in the Insert tab, right-click the Family Adventure Vacations letterhead building block that begins with your last name, and then click *Edit Properties* at the shortcut menu.

b. At the Modify Building Block dialog box, click in the *Name* text box and then add *Letterhead* to the end of the name.

c. Click in the *Description* text box and then type **Inserts the Family Adventure Vacations letterhead including the company name and address.**

d. Click OK to close the dialog box.

e. At the message asking if you want to redefine the building block entry, click Yes.

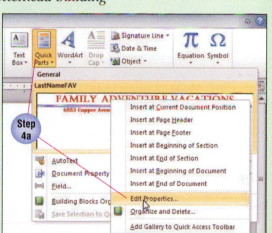

Inserting Custom Building Blocks

Any content you save as a building block can be inserted in a document at the Building Blocks Organizer dialog box. Some content also can be inserted at specific drop-down galleries. For example, insert a custom text box building block by clicking the Text Box button in the Insert tab and then clicking the desired text box at the drop-down gallery. Insert a custom header at the Header button drop-down gallery, a custom footer at the Footer button drop-down gallery, a custom cover page at the Cover Page button drop-down gallery, and so on.

You can specify where you want custom building block content inserted in a document at the button drop-down gallery. To do this, display the button drop-down gallery, right-click the custom building block, and then click the desired location at the shortcut menu. For example, if you click the Insert tab, click the Quick Parts button, and then right-click the *FAVLetterhead* building block (that is preceded by your last name), a shortcut menu displays as shown in Figure 3.8.

Figure 3.8 Quick Parts Button Drop-down List Shortcut Menu

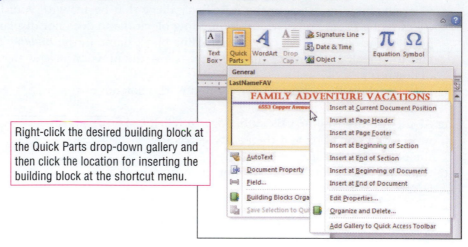

Right-click the desired building block at the Quick Parts drop-down gallery and then click the location for inserting the building block at the shortcut menu.

Project 3c · Inserting Custom Building Blocks

Part 3 of 3

1. At the blank document, click the No Spacing style and then change the font to 11-point Candara.
2. Insert the letterhead building block as a header by completing the following steps:
   a. Click the Insert tab.
   b. Click the Quick Parts button, right-click the Family Adventure Vacations letterhead (that is preceded by your last name), and then click the *Insert at Page Header* option at the shortcut menu.

   Step 2b

3. Press the Enter key twice, type the current date, and then press the Enter key four times.
4. Type **Mrs. Jody Lancaster** and then press the Enter key.
5. Insert the Pacific Sky Cruise Lines name and address building block by clicking the Quick Parts button, pointing to *AutoText*, and then clicking the Pacific Sky Cruise Lines building block (that is preceded by your last name) at the side menu.

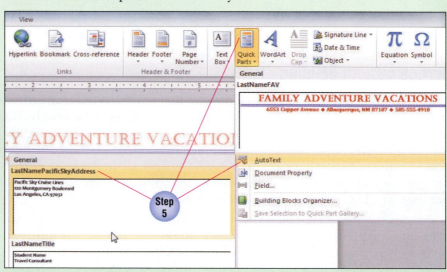

Step 5

6. Press the Enter key once and then insert a letter document by completing the following steps:
   a. Click the Object button arrow in the Text group in the Insert tab and then click *Text from File* at the drop-down list.
   b. At the Insert File dialog box, navigate to the Word2010L2C3 folder on your storage medium and then double-click **PacificSkyLetter01.docx**.
7. With the Insertion point positioned a double space below the last paragraph of text in the body of the letter, type Sincerely, and then press the Enter key four times.
8. Insert your name and title building block by clicking the Quick Parts button, pointing to *AutoText,* and then clicking your name and title at the side menu.
9. Press the Enter key, type your initials, press the Enter key, and then type **WL2-C3-P3-PSLtr.docx**.
10. Press the Enter key five times and then insert the custom text box you saved as a building block by completing the following steps:
    a. Click the Text Box button in the Text group in the Insert tab.
    b. Scroll to the end of the drop-down gallery and then click your custom text box. (Your custom text box will display in the *General* section of the drop-down gallery.)
    c. Click in the document to deselect the text box.
11. Insert the custom footer you created by completing the following steps:
    a. Click the Insert tab.
    b. Click the Footer button in the Header & Footer group.
    c. Scroll to the end of the drop-down gallery and then click your custom footer. (Your custom footer will display in the *General* section of the drop-down gallery.)
    d. Close the footer pane by double-clicking in the document.
12. Save the completed letter and name it **WL2-C3-P3-PSLtr**.
13. Print and then close **WL2-C3-P3-PSLtr.docx**.

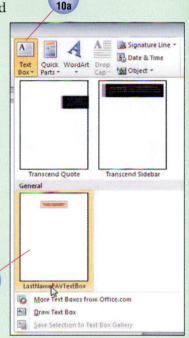

Step 10a

Step 10b

LastNameFAVTextBox

roject **4** **Create a Letter Document with Modified Building Blocks**

2 Parts

You will modify your custom building blocks and then use the building blocks to prepare a business letter. You will then delete your custom building blocks.

Modifying a Building Block

You can insert a building block in a document, make corrections or changes, and then save the building block with the same name or a different name. Save a building block with the same name when you want to update the building block to reflect any changes. Save the building block with a new name if you want to use an existing building block as a beginning to creating a new building block.

To save a modified building block with the same name, insert the building block in the document and then make the desired modifications. Select the building block data and then specify the gallery. At the Create New Building Block dialog box, type the original name and description and then click OK. At the message asking if you want to redefine the building block entry, click Yes.

Project 4a **Modifying Building Blocks** Part 1 of 2

1. As a travel consultant at Family Adventure Vacations, you have been given a promotion and are now a senior travel consultant. You decide to modify your name and title building block by completing the following steps:

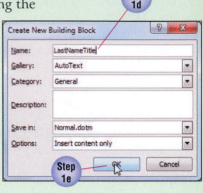

   a. At a blank document, click the Insert tab, click the Quick Parts button in the Text group, point to *AutoText*, and then click your name and title building block at the side menu.
   b. Edit your title so it displays as *Senior Travel Consultant*.
   c. Select your name and title, click the Quick Parts button, point to *AutoText*, and then click the *Save Selection to AutoText Gallery* option.
   d. At the Create New Building Block dialog box, type the original name (your last name followed by *Title*).
   e. Click OK.
   f. At the message asking if you want to redefine the building block entry, click Yes.
2. Since most of the correspondence you send to Pacific Sky Cruise Lines is addressed to Jody Lancaster, you decide to include her name at the beginning of the company name and address by completing the following steps:
   a. Click the Insert tab, click the Quick Parts button, point to *AutoText*, and then click the Pacific Sky Cruise Lines name and address building block at the side menu.
   b. Insert the name *Mrs. Jody Lancaster* above the name of the cruise line.
   c. Select the name, company name, and address.
   d. Click the Quick Parts button, point to *AutoText*, and then click the *Save Selection to AutoText Gallery* option.
   e. At the Create New Building Block dialog box, type the original name (your last name followed by *PacificSkyAddress*).
   f. Click OK.
   g. At the message asking if you want to redefine the building block entry, click Yes.
3. Close the document without saving it.
4. Create a business letter by completing the following steps:
   a. Press Ctrl + N to display a blank document and then click the No Spacing style in the Styles group in the Home tab.
   b. At the blank document, insert the Family Adventure Vacations letterhead building block as a page header.
   c. Press the Enter key twice, type today's date, and then press the Enter key four times.
   d. Insert the building block that includes Jody Lancaster's name as well as the cruise line name and address.

e. Press the Enter key and then insert the file named **PacificSkyLetter02.docx** located in the Word2010L2C3 folder on your storage medium. *Hint: Do this with the Object button in the Text group in the Insert tab.*

f. Type Sincerely, and then press the Enter key four times.

g. Insert the building block that contains your name and title.

h. Press the Enter key, type your initials, press the Enter key, and then type WL2-C3-P4-PSLtr.

i. Insert the footer building block you created.

5. Select the text in the document and then change the font to 11-point Candara.

6. Save the completed letter and name it **WL2-C3-P4-PSLtr**.

7. Print and then close **WL2-C3-P4-PSLtr.docx**.

Deleting Building Blocks

If you no longer use a building block you created, consider deleting it. To do this, display the Building Blocks Organizer dialog box, click the building block you want to delete, and then click the Delete button. At the message asking if you are sure you want to delete the selected building block, click Yes.

You can also delete a custom building block by right-clicking the building block at the drop-down gallery and then clicking the *Organize and Delete* option at the shortcut menu. This displays the Building Blocks Organizer dialog box with the building block selected. Click the Delete button that displays at the bottom of the dialog box and then click Yes at the confirmation question.

▼ **Quick Steps**

Delete Building Block
1. Display Building Blocks Organizer dialog box.
2. Click desired building block.
3. Click Delete button.
4. Click Yes.
5. Close dialog box.
OR
1. Display desired button drop-down gallery.
2. Right-click desired building block.
3. Click *Organize and Delete* option.
4. Click Delete button.
5. Click Yes.
6. Close dialog box.

Project 4b   **Deleting Building Blocks**   **Part 2 of 2**

1. At a blank document, delete the FAVLetterhead building block (that is preceded by your last name) by completing the following steps:

a. Click the Insert tab and then click the Quick Parts button in the Text group.

b. Right-click the FAVLetterhead building block (preceded by your last name) and then click *Organize and Delete* at the shortcut menu.

c. At the Building Blocks Organizer dialog box with the building block selected, click the Delete button.

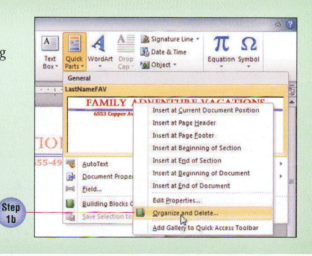

Step 1b

   d. At the message that displays asking if you are sure you want to delete the selected building block, click Yes.

   e. Close the Building Blocks Organizer dialog box.

2. Delete the PacificSkyAddress building block (preceded by your last name) by completing the following steps:

   a. Click the Quick Parts button, point to *AutoText*, and then right-click the PacificSkyAddress building block (preceded by your last name).

   b. Click *Organize and Delete* at the shortcut menu.

   c. At the Building Blocks Organizer dialog box with the building block selected, click the Delete button.

   d. At the message asking if you are sure you want to delete the selected building block, click Yes.

   e. Close the Building Blocks Organizer dialog box.

3. Complete steps similar to those in Step 2 to delete the Title building block (preceded by your last name).

4. Delete the custom footer (located in the Footer gallery) building block by completing the following steps:

   a. Click the Footer button in the Insert tab.

   b. Scroll down the drop-down gallery to display your custom footer.

   c. Right-click your footer and then click *Organize and Delete* at the shortcut menu.

   d. At the Building Blocks Organizer dialog box with the building block selected, click the Delete button.

   e. At the message asking if you are sure you want to delete the selected building block, click Yes.

   f. Close the Building Blocks Organizer dialog box.

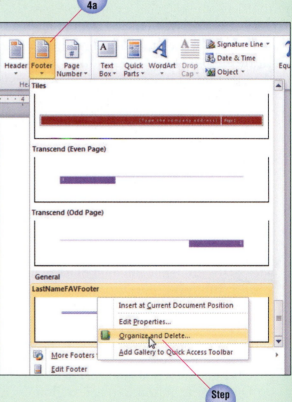

Step 4a

Step 4c

5. Delete the custom text box (located in the Text Box gallery) by completing the following steps:

   a. Click the Text Box button in the Text group in the Insert tab.

   b. Scroll down the drop-down gallery to display your custom text box.

   c. Right-click your text box and then click *Organize and Delete* at the shortcut menu.

   d. At the Building Blocks Organizer dialog box with the building block selected, click the Delete button.

   e. At the message asking if you are sure you want to delete the selected building block, click Yes.

   f. Close the Building Blocks Organizer dialog box.

6. Close the document without saving it.

You will open a testing agreement document and then insert and update document properties and fields.

Inserting Document Properties

If you click the Quick Parts button in the Insert tab and then point to *Document Property* at the drop-down list, a side menu displays with document property options. Click an option at this side menu and a document property placeholder is inserted in the document. Type the desired text in the placeholder.

If you insert a document property placeholder in multiple locations in a document, updating one of the placeholders will automatically update all occurrences of that placeholder in the document. For example, in Project 5a you will insert a Company document property placeholder in six locations in a document. You will then update the first occurrence of the placeholder and the remaining placeholders will update to reflect the change.

When you click the File tab, the Info tab Backstage view displays containing information about the document. At the right side of the Info tab Backstage view, a thumbnail of your document displays along with document properties such as the document size, number of pages, title, and comments. Some document properties that you insert with the Quick Parts button will display at the Info tab Backstage view.

Project 5a **Inserting Document Properties Placeholders** **Part 1 of 3**

1. Open **TestAgrmnt.docx** and save the document with Save As and name it **WL2-C3-P5-TestAgrmnt**.
2. Select the first occurrence of *FP* in the document (located in the first line of text after the title) and then insert a document property placeholder by completing the following steps:
   a. Click the Insert tab, click the Quick Parts button in the Text group, point to *Document Property*, and then click *Company* at the side menu.
   b. Click the Company placeholder tab and then type Frontier Productions.
   c. Press the Right Arrow key to move the insertion point outside the Company placeholder.
3. Select each of the remaining occurrences of *FP* in the document (FP appears five more times in the document) and insert the Company document property placeholder.

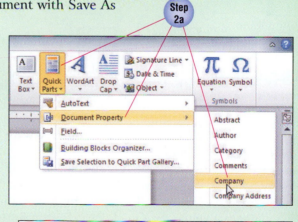

Step 2a

Step 2b

4. Press Ctrl + End to move the insertion point to the end of the document and then insert a Comments document property placeholder by completing the following steps:
    a. Click the Quick Parts button, point to *Document Property*, and then click *Comments* at the side menu.
    b. Click the Comments placeholder tab and then type **First Draft**.
    c. Press the Right Arrow key.
    d. Press Shift + Enter.
5. Click the File tab, make sure the Info tab is selected, and then notice that the comment you typed in the Comments document property placeholder displays at the right below the document thumbnail. Click the File tab again to display the document.
6. Save and then print **WL2-C3-P5-TestAgrmnt.docx**.
7. Click in the first occurrence of the company name *Frontier Productions*. (This selects the Company document property placeholder.)
8. Click the Company placeholder tab and then type **Frontier Video Productions**.
9. Press the Right Arrow key. (Notice that the other occurrences of the Company document property placeholder are automatically updated to reflect the new name.)
10. Save **WL2-C3-P5-TestAgrmnt.docx**.

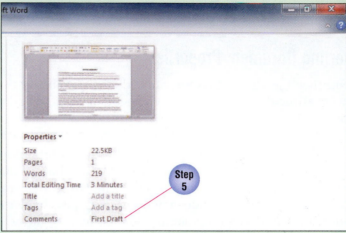

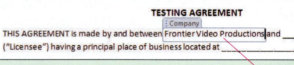

Inserting Fields ■■■■■■■■■■■■■■■■■■■■■■■■■

Fields are placeholders for data that changes and for merging main documents with data source files. You have inserted fields in documents when you inserted fields in a main document, inserted the date and time in a document, inserted page numbering in a document, and so on. Word provides buttons for many of the types of fields you may want to enter into a document. You can also insert a field in a document with options at the Field dialog box shown in Figure 3.9. This dialog box contains a list of all available fields. Just as the Building Blocks Organizer dialog box is a central location for building blocks, the Field dialog box is a central location for fields. To display the Field dialog box, click the Insert tab, click the Quick Parts button in the Text group, and then click *Field* at the drop-down list. At the Field dialog box, click the desired field in the *Field names* list box and then click OK.

Figure 3.9 Field Dialog Box

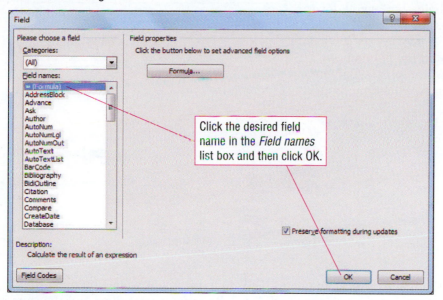

Click the desired field name in the *Field names* list box and then click OK.

Project 5b **Inserting Fields** **Part 2 of 3**

1. With **WL2-C3-P5-TestAgrmnt.docx** open, press Ctrl + End and then insert a field that inserts the current file name by completing the following steps:
   a. Click the Insert tab, click the Quick Parts button in the Text group, and then click *Field* at the drop-down list.
   b. At the Field dialog box, scroll down the *Field names* list box and then double-click *FileName*. (This inserts the current file name in the document and closes the Field dialog box.)
2. Insert a field that inserts the date the file is printed by completing the following steps:
   a. Press Shift + Enter.
   b. Click the Quick Parts button and then click *Field* at the drop-down list.
   c. At the Field dialog box, scroll down the *Field names* list box and then double-click *PrintDate*. (The date and time will display with zeros. The correct date and time will display when you send the document to the printer.)
3. Insert a header and then insert a field in the header by completing the following steps:
   a. Click the Header button in the Header & Footer group and then click *Edit Header* at the drop-down list.
   b. At the header pane, press the Tab key twice. (This moves the insertion point to the right tab at the right margin.)
   c. Click the Insert tab, click the Quick Parts button in the Text group, and then click *Field* at the drop-down list.

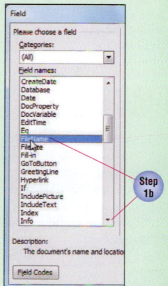

Step 1b

d. At the Field dialog box, scroll down the *Field names* list box and then click once on *Date*.

e. Click the date in the *Date formats* list box that will insert the date in figures followed by the time (hours and minutes).

f. Click OK to close the dialog box.

g. Double-click in the document.

4. Save and then print **WL2-C3-P5-TestAgrmnt.docx**.

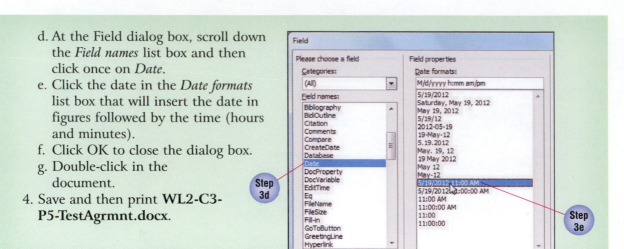

Step 3d

Step 3e

▼ **Quick Steps**

Update a Field
1. Click field.
2. Click Update tab.
OR
1. Click field.
2. Press F9.
OR
1. Right-click field.
2. Click *Update Field* at shortcut menu.

Word automatically updates fields in a document when you open the document. For example, open **WL2-C3-P5-TestAgrmnt.docx** and the time in the header is automatically updated. You can manually update a field by clicking the field and then clicking the Update tab, by clicking the field and then pressing F9, or by right-clicking the field and then clicking *Update Field* at the shortcut menu. You can also update all fields in a document except headers, footers, and text boxes by pressing Ctrl + A to select the document and then pressing F9.

Project 5c **Updating Fields** **Part 3 of 3**

1. With **WL2-C3-P5-TestAgrmnt.docx** open, update the time in the header by completing the following steps:
   a. Double-click the header.
   b. Click the date and time and then click the Update tab.
   c. Double-click in the document.
2. Save the document with Save As and name it **WL2-C3-P5-FVPAgrmnt**.
3. Press Ctrl + A to select the entire document and then press F9.
4. Save, print, and then close **WL2-C3-P5-FVPAgrmnt.docx**.

Project 6 **Minimize the Ribbon and Customize the Quick Access Toolbar and Ribbon** **3 Parts**

You will open a document and then minimize the ribbon, customize the Quick Access toolbar by adding and removing buttons, and customize the ribbon by inserting a new tab.

Minimizing the Ribbon ■■■■■■■■■■■■■■■■■■

The Word ribbon displays toward the top of the screen and displays tabs and commands divided into groups. If you want to free up some room on the screen, you can minimize the ribbon by clicking the Minimize the Ribbon button that displays immediately left of the Microsoft Word Help button that displays in the upper right corner of the screen. You can also minimize the ribbon with the keyboard shortcut Ctrl + F1. Click the Minimize the Ribbon button or press Ctrl + F1 and the ribbon is reduced to tabs. To redisplay the ribbon, click the Expand the Ribbon button (previously the Minimize the Ribbon button), press Ctrl + F1, or double-click one of the tabs.

Customizing the Quick Access Toolbar ■■■■■■■■■■■

The Quick Access toolbar contains buttons for some of the most commonly performed tasks. By default, the toolbar contains the Save, Undo, and Redo buttons. You can easily add or remove some basic buttons to and from the Quick Access toolbar with options at the Customize Quick Access Toolbar drop-down list. Display this list by clicking the Customize Quick Access Toolbar button that displays at the right side of the toolbar. Insert a check mark before those buttons you want displayed on the toolbar and remove the check mark from those you do not want to appear.

The Customize Quick Access Toolbar button drop-down list includes an option for moving the location of the Quick Access toolbar. By default, the Quick Access toolbar is positioned above the ribbon. You can move the toolbar below the ribbon by clicking the *Show Below the Ribbon* option at the drop-down list.

You can add buttons or commands from a tab to the Quick Access toolbar. To do this, click the tab, right-click on the desired button or command, and then click *Add to Quick Access Toolbar* at the shortcut menu.

▼ **Quick Steps**

Customize Quick Access Toolbar
1. Click Customize Quick Access Toolbar button.
2. Insert check mark before desired button(s).
3. Remove check mark before undesired button(s).

Customize Quick Access Toolbar

Project 6a **Minimizing the Ribbon and Customizing the Quick Access Toolbar**   **Part 1 of 3**

1. Open **InterfaceApps.docx** and then save the document with Save As and name it **WL2-C3-P6-InterfaceApps**.
2. Minimize the ribbon by clicking the Minimize the Ribbon button that displays immediately left of the Microsoft Word Help button located in the upper right corner of the screen.
3. Add a New button to the Quick Access toolbar by clicking the Customize Quick Access Toolbar button that displays at the right of the toolbar and then clicking *New* at the drop-down list.
4. Add an Open button to the Quick Access toolbar by clicking the Customize Quick Access Toolbar button that displays at the right of the toolbar and then clicking *Open* at the drop-down list.
5. Click the New button on the Quick Access toolbar. (This displays a new blank document.)
6. Close the document.
7. Click the Open button on the Quick Access toolbar to display the Open dialog box.

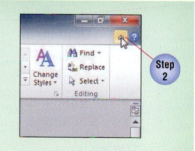

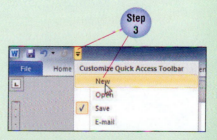

8. Close the Open dialog box.

9. Redisplay the ribbon by double-clicking one of the tabs. (You can also redisplay the ribbon by clicking the Expand the Ribbon button or by pressing Ctrl + F1.)

10. Move the Quick Access toolbar by clicking the Customize Quick Access Toolbar button and then clicking *Show Below the Ribbon* at the drop-down list.

11. Move the Quick Access toolbar back to the default position by clicking the Customize Quick Access Toolbar button and then clicking *Show Above the Ribbon* at the drop-down list.

12. Add the Margins and Themes buttons to the Quick Access toolbar by completing the following steps:

   a. Click the Page Layout tab.

   b. Right-click the Margins button in the Page Setup group and then click *Add to Quick Access Toolbar* at the shortcut menu.

   c. Right-click the Themes button in the Themes group and then click *Add to Quick Access Toolbar* at the shortcut menu.

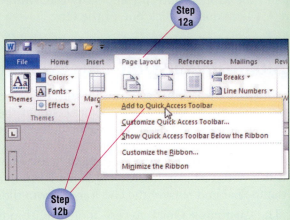

13. Change the top margin by completing the following steps:

   a. Click the Margins button on the Quick Access toolbar and then click *Custom Margins* at the drop-down list.

   b. At the Page Setup dialog box, change the top margin measurement to 1.5 inches and then click OK.

14. Change the theme by clicking the Themes button on the Quick Access toolbar and then clicking *Paper* at the drop-down list. (You will need to scroll down the list to display this theme.)

15. Create a screenshot of the Quick Access toolbar by completing the following steps:

   a. Click the New button on the Quick Access toolbar. (This displays a new blank document.)

   b. Click the Insert tab, click the Screenshot button in the Illustrations group, and then click *Screen Clipping* at the drop-down list.

   c. In a few moments, the **WL2-C3-P6-InterfaceApps .docx** document displays in a dimmed manner. Using the mouse, drag from the upper left corner of the screen down

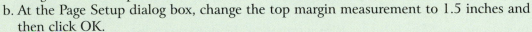

   and to the right to capture the Quick Access toolbar, and then release the mouse.

   d. With the screenshot image inserted in the document, print the document and then close it without saving it.

16. Save **WL2-C3-P6-InterfaceApps.docx**.

The Customize Quick Access Toolbar button drop-down list contains eleven of the most commonly used buttons. You can, however, insert many other buttons on the toolbar. To display the buttons available, click the Customize Quick Access Toolbar button and then click *More Commands* at the drop-down list. This displays the Word Options dialog box with *Quick Access Toolbar* selected in the left panel as shown in Figure 3.10. You can also display this dialog box by clicking the File tab, clicking the Options button, and then clicking *Quick Access Toolbar* in the left panel of the Word Options dialog box.

To reset the Quick Access toolbar to the default (Save, Undo, and Redo buttons), click the Reset button that displays toward the bottom of the dialog box. At the message asking if you are sure you want to restore the Quick Access toolbar shared between all documents to its default contents, click Yes.

You can customize the Quick Access toolbar for all documents or for a specific document. To customize the toolbar for the currently open document, display the Word Options dialog box with *Quick Access Toolbar* selected, click the down-pointing arrow at the right side of the *Customize Quick Access Toolbar* option, and then click the *For (document name)* option where the name of the currently open document displays.

▼ **Quick Steps**

Add Buttons to Quick Access Toolbar from Word Options Dialog Box
1. Click Customize Quick Access Toolbar button.
2. Click *More Commands* at drop-down list.
3. Click desired command at left list box.
4. Click Add button.
5. Click OK.

Figure 3.10 Word Options Dialog Box with Quick Access Toolbar Selected

Click the desired command in the list box at the left, click the Add button, and the command displays in the list box at the right.

Click the Reset button to reset the Quick Access toolbar to the default buttons.

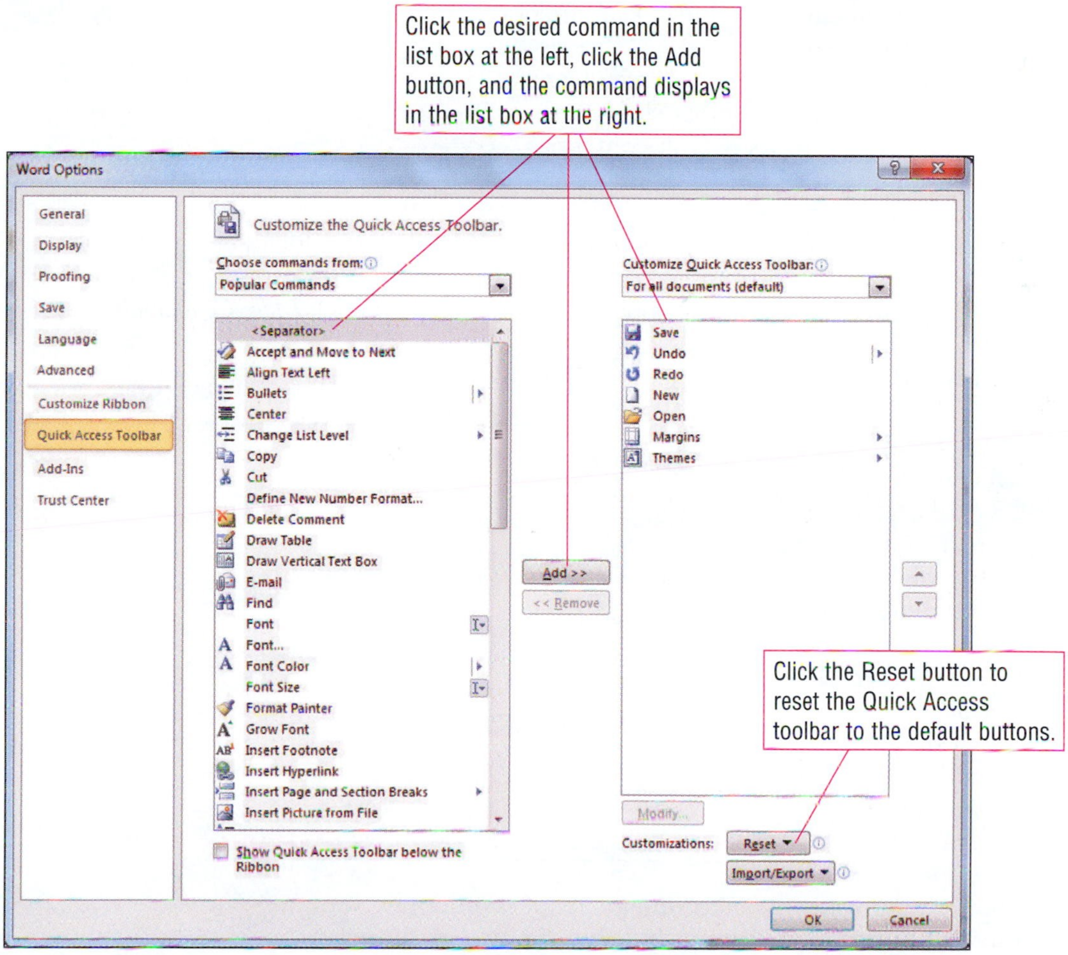

The *Choose commands from* option has a default setting of *Popular Commands*. At this setting, the list box below the option displays only a portion of all of the commands available to insert as a button on the Quick Access toolbar. To display all of the commands available, click the down-pointing arrow at the right side of the *Choose commands from* option box and then click *All Commands*. The drop-down list also contains options for specifying commands that are not currently available in the ribbon, as well as commands in the File tab and various other tabs.

To add a button, click the desired command in the list box at the left side of the commands list box and then click the Add button that displays between the two list boxes. Continue adding all desired buttons and then click OK to close the dialog box.

Project 6b   Inserting and Removing Buttons from the Quick Access Toolbar   Part 2 of 3

1. With **WL2-C3-P6-InterfaceApps.docx** open, reset the Quick Access toolbar by completing the following steps:
   a. Click the Customize Quick Access Toolbar button that displays at the right of the Quick Access toolbar and then click *More Commands* at the drop-down list.
   b. At the Word Options dialog box, click the Reset button that displays toward the bottom of the dialog box, and then click *Reset only Quick Access Toolbar* at the drop-down list.

   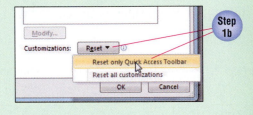

   c. At the message asking if you are sure you want to restore the Quick Access toolbar shared between all documents to its default contents, click Yes.
   d. Click OK to close the dialog box.
2. Insert buttons on the Quick Access toolbar for the currently open document by completing the following steps:
   a. Click the Customize Quick Access Toolbar button and then click *More Commands*.
   b. At the Word Options dialog box, click the down-pointing arrow at the right of the *Customize Quick Access Toolbar* option and then click *For WL2-C3-P6-InterfaceApps. docx* at the drop-down list.
   c. Click the down-pointing arrow at the right of the *Choose commands from* option box and then click *All Commands*.

   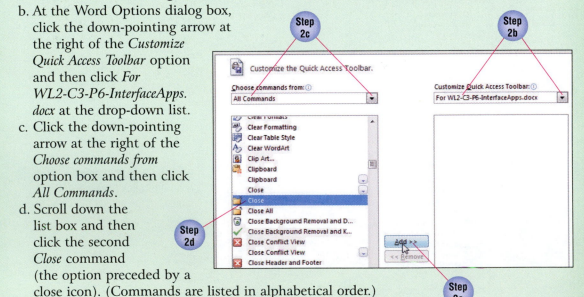

   d. Scroll down the list box and then click the second *Close* command (the option preceded by a close icon). (Commands are listed in alphabetical order.)
   e. Click the Add button that displays between the two list boxes.
   f. Scroll down the list box and then click *Footer*.
   g. Click the Add button.

Customizing the Ribbon ▪▪▪▪▪▪▪▪▪▪▪▪▪▪▪▪▪▪▪▪▪▪▪

In addition to customizing the Quick Access toolbar, you can also customize the ribbon by creating a new tab and inserting groups with buttons in the new tab. To customize the ribbon, click the File tab and then click the Options button. At the Word Options dialog box, click *Customize Ribbon* in the left panel and the dialog box displays as shown in Figure 3.11.

At the *Choose commands from* drop-down list, you can choose to display only popular commands, which is the default, or choose to display all commands, commands not on the ribbon, and all tabs or commands in the File tab, main tabs, and tool tabs. The commands in the list box vary depending on the option you select at the *Choose commands from* option drop-down list. Click the down-pointing arrow at the right of the Customize the Ribbon option and a drop-down list displays with options for customizing all tabs, only the main tabs, or only tool tabs. By default, *Main Tabs* is selected.

Creating a New Tab

You can choose to add a command to an existing tab or create a new tab and then add commands in groups in the new tab. To create a new tab, click the tab name in the list box at the right side of the dialog box that you want to precede the new tab and then click the New Tab button that displays at the bottom of the list box. This inserts a new tab in the list box along with a new group below the new tab (see Figure 3.11). You can move the new tab up or down the list box by clicking the new tab and then clicking the Move Up or the Move Down buttons that display at the right of the list box.

Renaming a Tab and Group

You can rename a tab by clicking the tab in the list box and then clicking the Rename button that displays below the list box at the right. At the Rename dialog box, type the desired name for the tab and then click OK. You can also display the Rename dialog box by right-clicking the tab name and then clicking *Rename* at the shortcut menu. Complete similar steps to rename the group name. When you click the group name and then click the Rename button (or right-click the group name and then click *Rename* at the shortcut menu), a Rename dialog box displays that contains a variety of symbols. Use the symbols to identify new buttons in the group rather than the group name.

Figure 3.11 Word Options Dialog Box with Customize Ribbon Selected

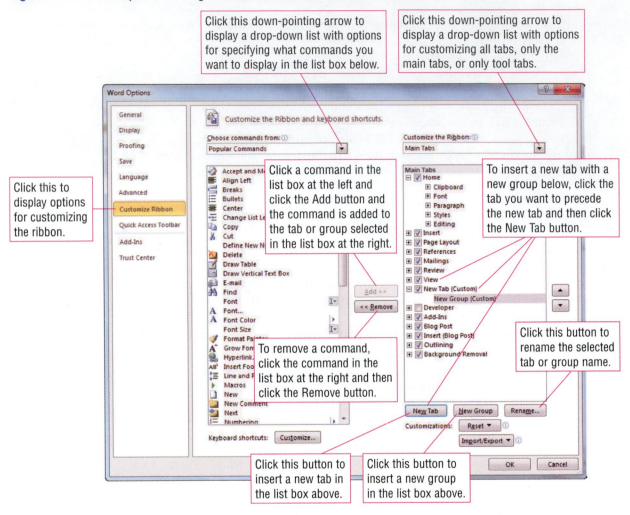

Click this down-pointing arrow to display a drop-down list with options for specifying what commands you want to display in the list box below.

Click this down-pointing arrow to display a drop-down list with options for customizing all tabs, only the main tabs, or only tool tabs.

Click this to display options for customizing the ribbon.

Click a command in the list box at the left and click the Add button and the command is added to the tab or group selected in the list box at the right.

To insert a new tab with a new group below, click the tab you want to precede the new tab and then click the New Tab button.

To remove a command, click the command in the list box at the right and then click the Remove button.

Click this button to rename the selected tab or group name.

Click this button to insert a new tab in the list box above.

Click this button to insert a new group in the list box above.

Adding Commands to a Tab Group

Add commands to a tab by clicking the group name within the tab, clicking the desired command in the list box at the left, and then clicking the Add button that displays between the two list boxes. Remove commands in a similar manner. Click the command you want to remove from the tab group and then click the Remove button that displays between the two list boxes.

Resetting the Ribbon

If you customize the ribbon by adding tabs and groups, you can remove all customizations and return to the original ribbon by clicking the Reset button that displays below the list box at the right side of the dialog box. When you click the Reset button, a drop-down list displays with two options—*Reset only selected Ribbon tab* and *Reset all customizations*. If you click the *Reset all customizations* option, a message displays asking if you want to delete all ribbon and Quick Access toolbar customizations for this program. At this message, click Yes to reset all customizations to the ribbon.

1. Open **WL2-C3-P6-InterfaceApps.docx** and then add a new tab and group by completing the following steps:
   a. Click the File tab and then click the Options button.
   b. At the Word Options dialog box, click *Customize Ribbon* in the left panel.
   c. Click the View tab that displays in the list box at the right side of the dialog box.
   d. Click the New Tab button located below the list box. (This inserts a new tab below the View tab.)

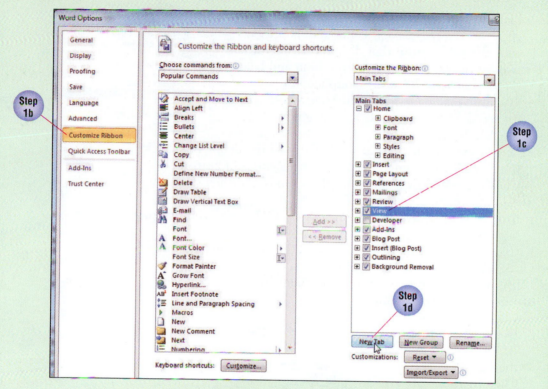

2. Rename the tab and the groups by completing the following steps:
   a. Click the *New Tab (Custom)* tab.
   b. Click the Rename button that displays below the list box.
   c. At the Rename dialog box, type your initials and then click OK.
   d. Click the *New Group (Custom)* group name that displays below your initials tab.
   e. Click the Rename button.
   f. At the Rename dialog box, type **IP Movement** (use IP to indicate insertion point) and then click OK.

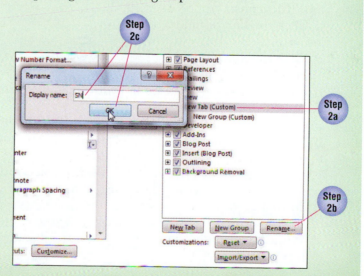

3. Add buttons to the *IP Movement (Custom)* group by completing the following steps:

   a. Click the *IP Movement (Custom)* group in the list box at the right side.

   b. Click the down-pointing arrow at the right of the *Choose commands from* option box and then click *Commands Not in the Ribbon* at the drop-down list.

   c. Scroll down the list box at the left side of the dialog box (the list displays alphabetically), click the *End of Document* command, and then click the Add button that displays between the two list boxes. (This inserts the command below the *IP Movement (Custom)* group name.)

   d. With the *End of Line* command selected in the list box at the left side of the dialog box, click the Add button.

   e. Scroll down the list box at the left side of the dialog box, click the *Page Down* command, and then click the Add button.

   f. Click the *Page Up* command in the list box and then click the Add button.

   g. Scroll down the list box, click the *Start of Document* command, and then click the Add button.

   h. Click the *Start of Line* command and then click the Add button.

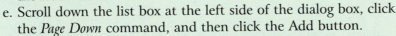

4. Click OK to close the Word Options dialog box.

5. Move the insertion point in the document by completing the following steps:

   a. Click the tab containing your initials.

   b. Click the End of Document button in the IP Movement group in the tab.

   c. Click the Start of Document button in the IP Movement group.

   d. Click the End of Line button.

   e. Click the Start of Line button.

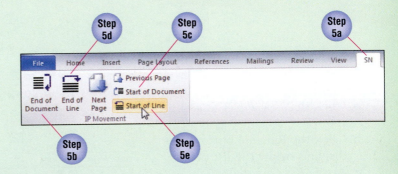

6. Create a screenshot of the ribbon with the tab containing your initials the active tab by completing the following steps:

   a. Make sure your tab is active and then press Ctrl + N to display a new blank document.

   b. Click the Insert tab, click the Screenshot button in the Illustrations group, and then click *Screen Clipping* at the drop-down list.

   c. In a few moments, the **WL2-C3-P6-InterfaceApps.docx** document displays in a dimmed manner. Using the mouse, drag from the upper left corner of the screen down and to the right to capture the Quick Access toolbar and the buttons in the tab containing your initials, and then release the mouse.

   d. With the screenshot image inserted in the document, print the document and then close it without saving it.

7. Reset the Quick Access toolbar and the ribbon by completing the following steps:
   a. Click the File tab and then click the Options button.
   b. At the Word Options dialog box, click *Customize Ribbon* in the left panel.
   c. Click the Reset button that displays below
      the list box at the right side of the dialog box
      and then click *Reset all customizations* at the
      drop-down list.

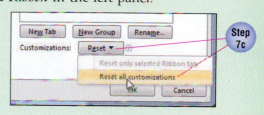

Step 7c

   d. At the message asking if you want to
      delete all ribbon and Quick Access toolbar
      customizations, click Yes.
   e. Click OK to close the Word Options dialog box. (The buttons you added to the Quick
      Access toolbar will display while this document is open.)
8. Save and then close **WL2-C3-P6-InterfaceApps.docx**.

Chapter Summary

- You can add words to AutoCorrect during a spelling check as well as at the
  AutoCorrect dialog box. Display the AutoCorrect dialog box by clicking the
  File tab, clicking the Options button, clicking *Proofing*, and then clicking the
  AutoCorrect Options button.

- Display the AutoCorrect Exceptions dialog box by clicking the Exceptions
  button at the AutoCorrect dialog box with the AutoCorrect tab selected.
  Specify AutoCorrect exceptions at this dialog box.

- Use the AutoCorrect Options button that displays when you hover the mouse
  over corrected text to change corrected text back to the original spelling, stop
  automatically correcting specific text, or display the AutoCorrect dialog box.

- When typing text, control what Word automatically formats with options at
  the AutoCorrect dialog box with the AutoFormat As You Type tab selected.

- Word provides a number of predesigned building blocks you can use to help
  build a document.

- Insert building blocks at the Building Blocks Organizer dialog box. Display the
  dialog box by clicking the Quick Parts button in the Insert tab and then clicking
  Building Blocks Organizer at the drop-down list. Sort building blocks in the dialog
  box by clicking the desired column heading.

- You can save content as a building block to specific galleries such as the Text
  Box, Header, Footer and Cover Page galleries.

- Save content to the AutoText gallery by selecting the content, clicking the
  Insert tab, clicking the Quick Parts button, pointing to *AutoText*, and then
  clicking the *Save Selection to AutoText Gallery* option.

- Save content to the Quick Part gallery by selecting the content, clicking the
  Insert tab, clicking the Quick Parts button, and then clicking *Save Selection to
  Quick Part Gallery* at the drop-down gallery.

- Insert a building block at the Building Blocks Organizer dialog box by displaying the dialog box, clicking the desired building block in the *Building blocks* list box, and then clicking the Insert button.

- Insert a custom building block from a gallery using a button by clicking the specific button (such as the Text Box, Header, Footer, or Cover Page button), scrolling down the drop-down gallery, and then clicking the custom building block that displays toward the end of the gallery.

- Insert a custom building block saved to the AutoText gallery by clicking the Insert tab, clicking the Quick Parts button, pointing to *AutoText*, and then clicking the desired building block at the side menu.

- Insert a custom building block saved to the Quick Part gallery by clicking the Insert tab, clicking the Quick Parts button, and then clicking the desired building block at the drop-down list.

- Edit a building block with options at the Modify Building Block dialog box. Display this dialog box by displaying the Building Blocks Organizer dialog box, clicking the desired building block, and then clicking the Edit Properties button.

- Delete a building block at the Building Blocks Organizer dialog box by clicking the building block, clicking the Delete button, and then clicking Yes at the confirmation question.

- Insert a document property placeholder by clicking the Insert tab, clicking the Quick Parts button, pointing to *Document Property*, and then clicking the desired option at the side menu.

- Fields are placeholders for data and can be inserted with options at the Field dialog box, which is a central location for all fields provided by Word. Display the Field dialog box by clicking the Quick Parts button and then clicking *Field*.

- Fields in a document are automatically updated when you open the document or you can manually update a field by clicking the field and then clicking the Update tab, pressing F9, or right-clicking the field and then clicking *Update*.

- Minimize the ribbon by clicking the Minimize the Ribbon button or with the keyboard shortcut Ctrl + F1. Maximize the ribbon by clicking the Expand the Ribbon button (previously the Minimize the Ribbon button), with the keyboard shortcut Ctrl + F1, or by double-clicking one of the tabs.

- Customize the Quick Access toolbar with options from the Customize Quick Access Toolbar button drop-down list and with options at the Word Options dialog box with the *Quick Access Toolbar* selected.

- Add a button or command to the Quick Access toolbar by right-clicking the desired button or command and then clicking *Add to Quick Access Toolbar* at the shortcut menu.

- With options at the Word Options dialog box with *Quick Access Toolbar* selected, you can reset the Quick Access toolbar and display all options and buttons available for adding to the Quick Access toolbar. You can customize the Quick Access toolbar for all documents or for a specific document.

- With options at the Word Options dialog box with *Customize Ribbon* selected, you can rename a tab or group, add a command tab to a new group, remove a command from a tab group, and reset the ribbon.

Commands Review

FEATURE	RIBBON TAB, GROUP	BUTTON, OPTION	KEYBOARD SHORTCUT
AutoCorrect dialog box	File	Word Options, Proofing, AutoCorrect Options	
Building Blocks Organizer dialog box	Insert, Text	, Building Blocks Organizer	
Create New Building Block dialog box	Insert, Text	Select text, , Save Selection to Quick Part Gallery	Alt + F3
Document Property side menu	Insert, Text	, Document Property	
Field dialog box	Insert, Text	, Field	
Word Options dialog box	File	Options	
Minimize/Maximize ribbon		⌃	Ctrl + F1

Concepts Check   Test Your Knowledge

Completion: In the space provided at the right, indicate the correct term, symbol, or command.

1. This feature corrects certain words automatically as you type them.

2. Use this button, which displays when you hover the mouse over corrected text, to change corrected text back to the original spelling.

3. The Quick Parts button is located in this tab.

4. This dialog box is a central location where you can view all of the predesigned building blocks.

5. With the Quick Parts button, you can save a custom building block in the Quick Part gallery or this gallery.

6. To save a text box as a building block, select the text box, click the Insert tab, click the Text Box button, and then click this option at the drop-down gallery.

7. Delete a building block at this dialog box.

8. Complete these steps to display the Field dialog box.

9. You can manually update a field by pressing this key on the keyboard. _____

10. Add or remove some basic buttons to and from the Quick Access toolbar with options at this drop-down list. _____

11. Minimize the Ribbon by clicking the Minimize the Ribbon button or with this keyboard shortcut. _____

12. This is the default setting for the *Choose commands from* option at the Word Options dialog box with *Quick Access Toolbar* selected in the left panel. _____

13. Add a new tab at the Word Options dialog box with this option selected in the left panel. _____

Skills Check Assess Your Performance

Assessment

1 FORMAT A HEALTH PLAN DOCUMENT WITH AUTOCORRECT AND BUILDING BLOCKS

1. Open **KLHPlan.docx** and then save the document with Save As and name it **WL2-C3-A1-KLHPlan**.
2. Add the following text to AutoCorrect:
   a. Insert *kl* in the *Replace* text box and insert *Key Life Health Plan* in the *With* text box.
   b. Insert *m* in the *Replace* text box and insert *medical* in the *With* text box.
3. With the insertion point positioned at the beginning of the document, type the text shown in Figure 3.12.
4. Make the following changes to the document:
   a. Apply the Heading 1 style to the title *Key Life Health Plan*.
   b. Apply the Heading 2 style to the four headings in the document.
   c. Change the style set to *Formal*.
   d. Change the theme to *Black Tie*.
   e. Apply the Relaxed paragraph spacing style. **Hint: Do this with the Change Styles button in the Home tab**.
5. Insert the Puzzle (Odd Page) header building block, click the *[Type the document title]* placeholder, and then type **Key Life Health Plan**.
6. Insert the Puzzle (Odd Page) footer building block, click the *[Type the company name]* placeholder, and then type your first and last names.
7. Delete the text *Confidential* that displays in the footer.
8. Double-click in the document.
9. Press Ctrl + End to move the insertion point to the end of the document, press the Enter key, and then insert the *FileName* field.
10. Press Shift + Enter and then insert the *PrintDate* field.
11. Save and then print **WL2-C3-A1-KLHPlan.docx**.
12. Delete the two entries you made at the AutoCorrect dialog box.
13. Close **WL2-C3-A1-KLHPlan.docx**.

Figure 3.12 Assessment 1

kl

How the Plan Works

When you enroll in the kl, you and each eligible family member select a plan option. A kl option includes a main m clinic, any affiliated satellite clinics, and designated hospitals. Family members may choose different m plan options and can easily change options.

Some m plan options do not require you to choose a primary care physician. This means a member may self-refer for specialty care within that m plan option. However, members are encouraged to establish an ongoing relationship with a primary care physician and develop a valuable partnership in the management of their m care.

kl provides coverage for emergency m services outside the service area. If the m emergency is not life threatening, call your primary care physician to arrange for care before going to an emergency facility. If you have a life-threatening emergency, go directly to the nearest appropriate facility. Any follow-up care to emergency m services must be coordinated within your plan option.

Assessment

2 FORMAT A PROPERTY PROTECTION ISSUES REPORT

1. Open **PropProIssues.docx** and then save the document with Save As and name it **WL2-C3-A2-PropProIssues**.
2. Make the following changes to the document:
   a. Select the entire document and then change the spacing after paragraphs to 6 points.
   b. Press Ctrl + Home and then press Ctrl + Enter to insert a hard page break.
   c. Apply the Heading 1 style to the two titles (*PROPERTY PROTECTION ISSUES* and *REFERENCES*).
   d. Apply the Heading 2 style to the three headings in the document.
   e. Change the style set to *Formal*.
   f. Change the theme to *Flow*.
   g. Change the theme colors to *Foundry*.
   h. Hang indent the paragraphs of text below the title *REFERENCES*.
   i. Indent the second paragraph in the *Fair Use* section 0.5 inch from the left and right margins.
3. Press Ctrl + Home to move the insertion point to the beginning of the document and then insert the Automatic Table 2 table of contents building block.
4. Make sure the Heading 1 style is applied to the title *TABLE OF CONTENTS*.
5. Insert the Pinstripes header building block, make sure the *Title* placeholder is selected, and then type **Woodland Legal Services**.
6. Double-click in the document.
7. Insert the Pinstripes footer building block, click the *[Type text]* placeholder, and then type **Property Protection Issues**.
8. Double-click in the document.

9. Press Ctrl + Home and then insert the *Pinstripes* cover page with the following specifications:
    a. At the cover page, click the *[Type the document subtitle]* placeholder and then type **Property Protection Issues**.
    b. Click the *[Pick the date]* placeholder and then insert today's date.
    c. Click the *[Type the company name]* placeholder and then type the name of your school.
    d. Click the *[Type the author name]* placeholder and then type your first and last names. (If a name displays below the company name, select the name and then type your first and last names.)
10. Press Ctrl + End to move the insertion point to the end of the document, press the Enter key, and then insert a field that will insert the file name.
11. Press Shift + Enter and then insert a field that will insert the current date and time.
12. Press Shift + Enter, insert the *Status* document property, and then type **Final Draft** in the property placeholder. Click in the document outside the document property placeholder.
13. Save, print, and then close **WL2-C3-A2-PropProIssues.docx**.

Assessment

3 CREATE BUILDING BLOCKS AND PREPARE AN AGREEMENT

1. Open **WLSCSFooter.docx**.
2. Select the entire document, save the selected text in a custom building block in the Footer gallery, and name the building block with your initials followed by *WLSCSFooter*. **Hint: Use the Footer button to save the content to the Footer gallery.**
3. Close **WLSCSFooter.docx**.
4. Open **WLSCSHeading.docx**.
5. Select the entire document, save the selected text in a custom building block in the Quick Part gallery, and name the building block with your initials followed by *WLSCSHeading*.
6. Close **WLSCSHeading.docx**.
7. At a blank document type the text shown in Figure 3.13.
8. Select the entire document, save the selected text in a custom building block in the AutoText gallery, and name the building block with your initials followed by *WLSCSFeesPara*.
9. Close the document without saving it.

Figure 3.13 Assessment 3

Fees: My hourly rate is $350, billed in one-sixth (1/6th) of an hour increments. All time spent on work performed, including meetings, telephone calls, correspondences, and emails, will be billed at the hourly rate set forth in this paragraph. Additional expenses such as out-of-pocket expenses for postage, courier fees, photocopying charges, long distance telephone charges, and search fees, will be charged at the hourly rate set forth in this paragraph.

10. At a blank document, create an agreement with the following specifications:
   a. Insert the custom building block in the Quick Part gallery that is named with your initials followed by *WLSCSHeading*.
   b. Insert the custom building block in the AutoText gallery that is named with your initials followed by *WLSCSFeesPara*.
   c. Insert the file named **WLSRepAgrmnt.docx** located in Word2010L2C3 folder on your storage medium. ***Hint: Use the* Text from File *option from the Object button arrow drop-down list.***
   d. Insert the footer custom building block that is named with your initials followed by *WLSCSFooter*. ***Hint: Do this with the Footer button.***
11. Save the completed agreement and name it **WL2-C3-A3-WLSRepAgrmnt**.
12. Print and then close **WL2-C3-A3-WLSRepAgrmnt.docx**.
13. Press Ctrl + N to open a blank document.
14. Click the Insert tab, click the Quick Parts button, and then point to *AutoText*.
15. Press the Print Screen button on your keyboard and then click in the document.
16. At the blank document, click the Paste button.
17. Print the document and then close it without saving it.

Assessment

4 CREATE A CUSTOM TAB AND GROUP

1. At the blank screen, create a new tab with the following specifications:
   a. Insert the new tab after the View tab in the list box at the Word Options dialog box with *Customize Ribbon* selected.
   b. Rename the tab *C3* followed by your initials.
   c. Rename the custom group below your new tab to *File Management*.
   d. Change the *Choose commands from* option to *File Tab*.
   e. From the list box at the left side of the dialog box, add the following commands to the *File Management* group in the new tab: *Close, Open, Open Recent File, Quick Print, Save As*, and *Save As Other Format*.
   f. Change the *Choose commands from* option to *Popular Commands*.
   g. From the list box at the left side of the dialog box, add the New command.
   h. Click OK to close the Word Options dialog box.
2. At the blank screen, click your new tab (the one that begins with *C3* and is followed by your initials).
3. Click the Open Recent File button in the File Management group in your new tab.
4. At the Recent tab Backstage view, click *WL2-C3-A3-WLSRepAgrmnt.docx* that displays at the beginning of the Recent Documents list.
5. Save the document with Save As and name it **WL2-C3-A4-WLSRepAgrmnt**.
6. Save the document in the Word 97-2003 format by completing the following steps:
   a. Click the new tab that begins with *C3* and is followed by your initials.
   b. Click the Save As button arrow (this is the second Save As button in the File Management group in your new tab).
   c. Click *Word 97-2003 Document* at the drop-down list.
   d. At the Save As dialog box with *Word 97-2003 Document (*.doc)* selected in the *Save as type* option box, type **WL2-C3-A4-WLSRA-Word97-2003Format** and then press the Enter key.
   e. Close the document by clicking the Close button in the File Management group in the new tab.

7. Click the Open Recent File button in the new tab and then click **WL2-C3-A4-WLSRepAgrmnt.docx** in the Recent Documents list.

8. Send the document to the printer by clicking your new tab (the tab that begins with *C3* and is followed by your initials) and then clicking the Quick Print button in the File Management group.

9. Close the document by clicking the Close button in the File Management group in the new tab.

10. Click the New Blank Document button in the File Management group in the new tab.

11. At the blank document, click your new tab (the tab that begins with *C3* and is followed by your initials) and then click the New Blank Document button. (You now have two blank documents open.)

12. Click the Insert tab, click the Screenshot button, and then click *Screen Clipping* at the drop-down list.

13. When the first blank document displays in a dimmed manner, use the mouse to select the Quick Access toolbar and the ribbon including the new tab you created with the File Management group buttons.

14. Print the document containing the screen clipping and then close the document without saving it.

15. Display the Word Options dialog box with *Customize Ribbon* selected and then reset the ribbon back to the default.

Assessment

5 INSERT AN EQUATION BUILDING BLOCK

1. The Building Blocks Organizer dialog box contains a number of predesigned equations you can insert in a document. Display the Building Blocks Organizer dialog box and then insert one of the predesigned equations.

2. Select the equation and then click the Equation Tools Design tab. Notice the groups of commands available for editing an equation.

3. Delete the equation and then type the steps you followed to insert the equation and type a list of the groups available in the Equation Tools Design tab.

4. Save the document and name it **WL2-C3-A5-Equations**. Print and then close the document.

Visual Benchmark Demonstrate Your Proficiency

CREATE AN AGREEMENT WITH BUILDING BLOCKS AND AUTOCORRECT TEXT

1. At a blank document, create the document shown in Figure 3.14 with the following specifications:
   a. Create AutoCorrect entries for *Woodland Legal Services* (use wls) and *Till-Harris Management* (use thm). Use these AutoCorrect entries when typing the text in Figure 3.14.
   b. Insert the WLSCSHeading building block (the one preceded by your initials) at the beginning of the document and insert the WLSCSFooter as a footer (the one preceded by your initials).
   c. Change the paragraph alignment to *Justify* for the six paragraphs of text in the document and center align the signature lines.
2. Save the completed document and name it **WL2-C3-VB-THMAgrmnt**.
3. Print and then close **WL2-C3-VB-THMAgrmnt.docx**.
4. Open a blank document, display the AutoCorrect dialog box, and then display the *thm* entry. Press the Alt + Print Screen button, close the dialog box, close the Word Options dialog box, and then click the Paste button at the blank document. (This inserts an image of the AutoCorrect dialog box. Alt + Print Screen makes a capture of the active dialog box.)
5. Press Ctrl + End and then press the Enter key.
6. Complete steps similar to those in Step 4 to make a screen capture of the AutoCorrect dialog box with the *wls* entry displayed and insert the screen capture image in the document (below the first screen capture image).
7. Make sure both images display on one page. Print and then close the document without saving it.
8. At a blank document delete the *wls* and *thm* AutoCorrect entries and the custom building blocks you created.

Figure 3.14 Visual Benchmark

REPRESENTATION AGREEMENT

Carlos Sawyer, Attorney at Law

This agreement is made between Carlos Sawyer of Woodland Legal Services, hereafter referred to as "Woodland Legal Services" and Till-Harris Management for legal services to be provided by Woodland Legal Services.

Legal Representation: Woodland Legal Services will perform the legal services required by Till-Harris Management, keep Till-Harris Management informed of progress and developments, and respond promptly to Till-Harris Management's inquiries and communications.

Attorney's Fees and Costs: Till-Harris Management will pay Woodland Legal Services for attorney's fees for legal services provided under this agreement at the hourly rate of the individuals providing the services. Under this agreement, Till-Harris Management will pay all costs in incurred by Woodland Legal Services for representation of Till-Harris Management. Costs will be advanced by Woodland Legal Services and then billed to Till-Harris Management unless the costs can be met from deposits.

Deposit for Fees: Till-Harris Management will pay to Woodland Legal Services an initial deposit of $5,000, to be received by Woodland Legal Services on or before November 1, 2012. Twenty percent of the deposit is nonrefundable and will be applied against attorney's fees. The refundable portion will be deposited by Woodland Legal Services in an interest-bearing trust account. Till-Harris Management authorizes Woodland Legal Services to withdraw the principal from the trust account to pay attorney's fees in excess of the nonrefundable portion.

Statement and Payments: Woodland Legal Services will send Till-Harris Management monthly statements indicating attorney's fees and costs incurred, amounts applied from deposits, and current balance owed. If no attorney's fees or costs are incurred for a particular month, the statement may be held and combined with that for the following month. Any balance will be paid in full within 30 days after the statement is mailed.

Effective Date of Agreement: The effective date of this agreement will be the date when it is executed by both parties.

Client: _____ Date: _____

Attorney: _____ Date: _____

7110 FIFTH STREET ◆ SUITE 200 ◆ OMAHA, NE 68207 ◆ 402-555-7110

Case Study   Apply Your Skills

Part 1

You have been hired as the office manager for Highland Construction Company. The address of the company is 9025 Palmer Park Boulevard, Colorado Springs, CO 80904, and the telephone number is (719) 555-4575. You are responsible for designing business documents that maintain a common appearance and formatting. You decide your first task is to create a letterhead document. Create a letterhead for Highland Construction Company and consider including the company name, the address, telephone number, a clip art image, and/or any other elements to add visual interest to the letterhead. Save the completed letterhead document and name it **HCCLetterhead**. Using the text and elements in the letterhead document, create a building block and name it with your initials followed by *HCCLetterhead*. Save, print, and then close **HCCLetterhead.docx**. Create the following additional building blocks for your company (use your initials in the name of the building blocks [you decide on the names]):

- Create a building block footer that contains a border line (in a color matching the colors in the letterhead) and the company slogan:
  Building Dreams Since 1985

- Create the following complimentary close building block:
  Sincerely,

  Your Name
  Office Manager

- Create the following company name and address building block:
  Mr. Eric Rashad
  Roswell Industries
  1020 Wasatch Street
  Colorado Springs, CO 80902

- Create the following company name and address building block:
  Ms. Claudia Sanborn
  S & S Supplies
  537 Constitution Avenue
  Colorado Springs, CO 80911

Part 2

At a blank document, create a letter to Eric Rashad by inserting the company letterhead (the building block that begins with your initials followed by *HCCLetterhead*). Type today's date, press the Enter key twice, and then insert the Eric Rashad building block. Insert the file named **HCCLetter.docx** and then insert your complimentary close building block. Finally, insert the footer building block you created for the company. Save the letter and name it **WL2-C3-CS-RashadLtr**. Print and then close the letter. Complete similar steps to create a letter to Claudia Sanborn. Save the completed letter and name it **WL2-C3-CS-SanbornLtr**. Print and then close the letter.

Part 3

At a blank document, insert the company letterhead building block you created in Part 1, type the title *Company Services*, and then insert a SmartArt of your choosing that contains the following text:

> Residential Construction
> Commercial Construction
> Design Consultation
> Site Preparation

Apply a heading style to the *Company Services* title, insert the company footer building block, and then save the document and name it **WL2-C3-CS-CoServices**. Print and then close the document.

Part 4

Create an AutoCorrect entry that will replace *hcc* with *Highland Construction Company* and *bca* with *Building Construction Agreement*. Open **HCCAgrmnt.docx** and then type the text shown in Figure 3.15 at the beginning of the document. Apply or insert the following to the document:

- Insert at the end of the document a date printed field and a file name field.
- Insert your footer building block as a footer.
- Insert a cover page of your choosing.

Add or apply any other enhancements to improve the visual appeal of the document and then save the document and name it **WL2-C3-CS-HCCAgrmnt**. Print and then close the document.

Part 5

Make sure you are connected to the Internet and then display the New tab Backstage view. Choose a business card template, download the template, and then create business cards for Highland Construction Company. Include your name and title (Office Manager) on the cards. Save the completed business cards document and name it **WL2-C3-CS-HCCBusCards**. Print and then close the document. Download an Expense report form and then customize the form with Highland Construction Company information. Save the completed expense report form and name it **WL2-C3-CS-HCCExpRep**. Print and then close the document.

Delete the building blocks you created and then delete the AutoCorrect entries *hcc* and *bca*.

Figure 3.15 Case Study, Part 4

---

bca

THIS bca made this _____ day of _____, 2013 by and between hcc and _____, hereinafter referred to as "owner," for the considerations hereinafter named, hcc and owner agree as follows:

Financing Arrangements: The owner will obtain a construction loan to finance construction under this bca. If adequate financing has not been arranged within 30 days of the date of this bca, or the owner cannot provide evidence to hcc of other financial ability to pay the full amount, then hcc may treat this bca as null and void, and retain the down payment made on the execution of this bca.

Microsoft Word

Customizing and Navigating in a Document

PERFORMANCE OBJECTIVES

Upon successful completion of Chapter 4, you will be able to:

- Create custom theme colors, theme fonts, and theme effects
- Save a custom theme
- Apply, edit, and delete custom themes
- Reset to the template theme
- Change the Quick Styles set default
- Apply styles
- Navigate in a document using the Navigation pane, thumbnails, bookmarks, hyperlinks, and cross-references
- Insert hyperlinks to a location in the same document, a different document, and a file in another program

Tutorials

4.1 Creating Custom Theme Colors and Theme Fonts

4.2 Applying Theme Effects

4.3 Changing the Quick Styles Set Default

4.4 Creating and Modifying Styles

4.5 Navigating with Bookmarks

4.6 Creating and Editing Hyperlinks

4.7 Linking to a File in Another Program, a New Document, or an Email Address

4.8 Creating a Cross-Reference

The Office suite offers themes to provide you with consistent formatting for documents to give them a professional and polished look. You can use the themes provided by Office or create your own custom themes. Word provides a number of predesigned styles, grouped into Quick Styles sets, you can use to apply consistent formatting to text in documents. In this chapter, you will learn about customizing themes and learn how to insert hyperlinks, bookmarks, and cross-references to provide additional information for readers and to allow for more efficient navigation within a document. Model answers for this chapter's projects appear on the following pages.

Word2010L2C4

Note: Before beginning the projects, copy to your storage medium the Word2010L2C4 subfolder from the Word2010L2 folder on the CD that accompanies this textbook and then make Word2010L2C4 the active folder.

Northland Security Systems

Northland Security Systems Mission
We are a full-service computer information security management and consulting firm offering a comprehensive range of services to help businesses protect electronic data.

Security Services
Northland Security Systems is dedicated to helping business, private and public, protect vital company data through on-site consultation, product installation and training, and 24-hour telephone support services. We show you how computer systems can be compromised, and we walk you through the steps you can take to protect your company's computer system.

Security Software
We offer a range of security management software to protect your business against viruses, spyware, adware, intrusion, spam, and policy abuse.

- Security Management Software
- Security Software Training
- On-Site Consultation
- 24-Hour Telephone Support

Project 1 Apply Custom Themes to Documents

WL2-C4-P1-NSSServices.docx

Northland Security Systems

Security and Privacy
We partner with you to assess, plan, design, implement, and manage a security-rich environment to protect you, your systems, and your customers.

Specialized Services

- Firewall Implementation
- Internal Security Assessment
- Secured Remote Access
- Two-Factor Authentication
- Antivirus Solutions

WL2-C4-P1-NSSSecurity.docx

African Study Adventure

The African Study Adventure program provide travelers with a unique opportunity to travel to African countries and make connections with local people, visit cultural institutions, and travel with knowledgeable tour guides who will provide insightful information about the countries, peoples, and customs.

Small Groups
The size of each group is limited so that African Study Adventure tour guides can deliver personal service and ensure that you feel comfortable in your surroundings. All tours are limited to a maximum of 25 participants.

Comprehensive Itineraries
Each program in the African Study Adventure program offers comprehensive sightseeing, exciting activities, and direct encounters with the people of the area you are visiting. Tour guides have developed a range of tours, each with its own principal theme and special highlights.

Custom Groups
For those who cannot fit African Study Adventure program scheduled departures into their calendars or who prefer to travel with their own friends and family, Bayside Travel has developed custom programs to suit your specific needs.

Accommodations and Meals
Accommodations will vary with the particular trip. However, Bayside Travel staff has selected accommodations with great care to make sure you will be as comfortable as local conditions allow and that you will enjoy the unique atmosphere of each destination. Most meals are included in the tour package.

"Travel is fatal to prejudice, bigotry and narrow-mindedness." Mark Twain

Project 2 Format a Travel Document with Styles

WL2-C4-P2-TTSAfrica.docx

CHAPTER 1: UNAUTHORIZED ACCESS

Like uncharted wilderness, the Internet lacks borders. This inherent openness is what makes the Internet so valuable and yet so vulnerable. Over its short life, the Internet has grown so quickly that the legal system has not been able to keep pace. The security risks posed by networks and the Internet can be grouped into three categories: unauthorized access, information theft, and denial of service.

Hackers, individuals who gain access to computers and networks illegally, are responsible for most cases of unauthorized access. Hackers tend to exploit sites and programs that have poor security measures in place. However, they also gain access to more challenging sites by using sophisticated programs and strategies. Many hackers claim they hack merely because they like the challenge of trying to defeat security measures. They rarely have a more malicious motive, and they generally do not aim to destroy or damage the sites that they invade. In fact, hackers dislike being identified with those who seek to cause damage. They refer to hackers with malicious or criminal intent as crackers. Methods of Virus Operation

USER IDS AND PASSWORDS

To gain entry over the Internet to a secure computer system, most hackers focus on finding a working user ID and password combination. User IDs are easy to come by and are generally not secure information. Sending an email, for example, displays the sender's user ID in the return address, making it very public. The only missing element is the password. Hackers know from experience which passwords are common; they have programs that generate thousands of likely passwords and they try them systematically over a period of hours or days. Password Suggestions

SYSTEM BACKDOORS

Programmers can sometimes inadvertently aid hackers by providing unintentional entrance to networks and information systems. One such unintentional entrance is a system "backdoor," which is a user ID and password that provides the highest level of authorization. Programmers innocently create a "backdoor" in the early days of system development to allow other programmers and team members to access the system to fix problems. Through negligence or by design, the user ID and password are sometimes left behind in the final version of the system. People who know about them can then enter the system, bypassing the security, perhaps years later, when the backdoor has been forgotten.

SPOOFING

A sophisticated way to break into a network via the Internet involves spoofing, which is the process of fooling another computer by pretending to send information from a legitimate source. It works

Project 3 Navigate and Insert Hyperlinks in a Computer Viruses Report

WL2-C4-P3-VirusesSecurity.docx

Model Answers

by altering the address that the system automatically puts on every message sent. The address is changed to one that the receiving computer is programmed to accept as a trusted source of information.

SPYWARE

Spyware is a type of software that allows an intruder to spy upon someone else's computer. This alarming technology takes advantage of loopholes in the computer's security systems and allows a stranger to witness and record another person's every mouse click or keystroke on the monitor as it occurs. The spy can record activities and gain access to passwords and credit card information. Spyware generally requires the user to install it on the machine that is being spied upon, so it is highly unlikely that random strangers on the Internet could simply begin watching your computer. In the workplace, however, someone might be able to install the software without the victim's knowledge. Disguised as an email greeting, for example, the program can operate like a virus that gets the unwary user to install the spyware unknowingly.

CHAPTER 2: INFORMATION THEFT

Information can be a company's most valuable possession. Stealing corporate information, a crime included in the category of industrial espionage, is unfortunately both easy to do and difficult to detect. This is due in part to the invisible nature of software and data. If a cracker breaks into a company network and manages to download the company database from the network onto a disk, there is no visible sign to the company that anything is amiss. The original database is still in place, working the same way it always has.

WIRELESS DEVICE SECURITY

The growing number of wireless devices has created a new opportunity for data theft. Wireless devices such as cameras, Web phones, networked computers, PDAs, and input and output peripherals are inherently less secure than wired devices. Security is quite lax, and in some cases nonexistent, in new wireless technologies for handheld computers and cell phone systems. In a rush to match competition, manufacturers have tended to sacrifice security to move a product to the marketplace faster. Already, viruses are appearing in emails for cell phones and PDAs. With little protection available for these new systems, hackers and spies are enjoying a free hand with the new technology. One of the few available security protocols for wireless networks is Wired Equivalent Privacy (WEP), developed in conjunction with the standard for wireless local area networks. Newer versions of WEP with enhanced security features make it more difficult for hackers to intercept and modify data transmissions sent by radio waves or infrared signals.

DATA BROWSING

Data browsing is a less damaging form of information theft that involves an invasion of privacy. Workers in many organizations have access to networked databases that contain private information about people. Accessing this information without an official reason is against the law. The IRS had a particularly large problem with data browsing in the late 1990s. Some employees were fired and the rest were given specialized training in appropriate conduct.

CHAPTER 3: COMPUTER VIRUSES

One of the most familiar forms of risk to computer security is the computer virus. A computer virus is a program written by a hacker or cracker designed to perform some kind of trick upon an unsuspecting victim. The trick performed in some cases is mild, such as drawing an offensive image on the screen, or changing all of the characters in a document to another language. Sometimes the trick is much more severe, such as reformatting the hard drive and erasing all the data, or damaging the motherboard so that it cannot operate properly. Computer Virus Presentation

TYPES OF VIRUSES

Viruses can be categorized by their effect, which include nuisance, data-destructive, espionage, and hardware-destructive. A nuisance virus usually does no real damage, but is rather just an inconvenience. The most difficult part of a computer to replace is the data on the hard drive. The installed programs, the documents, databases, and saved emails form the heart of a personal computer. A data-destructive virus is designed to destroy this data. Some viruses are designed to create a backdoor into a system to bypass security. Called espionage viruses, they do no damage, but rather allow a hacker or cracker to enter the system later for the purpose of stealing data or spying on the work of the competitor. Very rarely, a virus is created that attempts to damage the hardware of the computer system itself. Called hardware-destructive viruses, these bits of programming can weaken or destroy chips, drives, and other components. (For more information, refer to **Spyware**.)

METHODS OF VIRUS OPERATION

Viruses can create effects that range from minor and annoying to highly destructive, and are operated and transmitted by a variety of methods. An email virus is normally transmitted as an attachment to a message sent over the Internet. Email viruses require the victim to click on the attachment and cause it to execute. Another common form of virus transmission is by a macro, a small subprogram that allows users to customize and automate certain functions. A macro virus is written specifically for one program, which then becomes infected when it opens a file with the virus stored in its macros. The boot sector of a floppy disk or hard disk contains a variety of information, including how the disk is organized and whether it is capable of loading an operating system. When a disk is left in a drive and the computer reboots, the operating system automatically

reads the boot sector to learn about that disk and to attempt to start any operating system on that disk. A boot sector virus is designed to alter the boot sector of a disk, so that whenever the operating system reads the boot sector, the computer will automatically become infected.

Other methods of virus infection include the Trojan horse virus, which hides inside another legitimate program or data file, and the stealth virus, which is designed to hide itself from detection software. Polymorphic viruses alter themselves to prevent antivirus software from detecting them by examining familiar patterns. Polymorphic viruses alter themselves randomly as they move from computer to computer, making detection more difficult. Multipartite viruses alter their form of attack. Their name derives from their ability to attack in several different ways. They may first infect the boot sector and then later move on to become a Trojan horse type by infecting a disk file. These viruses are more sophisticated, and therefore more difficult to guard against. Another type of virus is the logic bomb, which generally sits quietly dormant waiting for a specific event or set of conditions to occur. A famous logic bomb was the widely publicized Michelangelo virus, which infected personal computers and caused them to display a message on the artist's birthday.

CHAPTER 4: SECURITY RISKS

Although hackers, crackers, and viruses garner the most attention as security risks, a company faces a variety of other dangers to its hardware and software systems. Principally, these risks involve types of system failure, employee theft, and the cracking of software for copying. Click to view types of viruses

SYSTEMS FAILURE

A fundamental element in making sure that computer systems operate properly is protecting the electrical power that runs them. Power interruptions such as blackouts and brownouts have very adverse effects on computers. An inexpensive type of power strip called a surge protector can guard against power fluctuations and can also serve as an extension cord and splitter. A much more vigorous power protection system is an uninterruptible power supply (UPS), which provides a battery backup. Similar in nature to a power strip, but much more bulky and a bit more expensive, a UPS provides not only steady spike-free power, but also keeps computers running during a blackout.

EMPLOYEE THEFT

Although accurate estimates are difficult to pinpoint, businesses certainly lose millions of dollars a year in stolen computer hardware and software. Often, in large organizations, such theft goes unnoticed or unreported. Someone takes a hard drive or a scanner home for legitimate use, then leaves the job sometime later, and keeps the machine. Sometimes, employees take components to add to their home PC systems or a thief breaks into a business and hauls away computers. Such thefts cost far more than the price of the stolen computers because they also involve the cost of

replacing the lost data, the cost of the time lost while the machines are gone, and the cost of installing new machines and training people to use them.

CRACKING SOFTWARE FOR COPYING

A common goal of hackers is to crack a software protection scheme. A crack is a method of circumventing a security scheme that prevents a user from copying a program. A common protection scheme for software is to require that the installation CD be resident in the drive whenever the program runs. Making copies of the CD with a burner, however, easily fools this protection scheme. Some game companies are taking the extra step of making duplication difficult by scrambling some of the data on the original CDs, which CD burners will automatically correct when copying. When the copied and corrected CD is used, the software checks for the scrambled track information. If the error is not found, the software will not run.

Hold down the Ctrl key and then click the logo shown below to display a list of training courses offered by Northland Security Systems

Click to send an email

Project **1** **Apply Custom Themes to Documents**   **5 Parts**

You will create custom theme colors, theme fonts, and then apply theme effects. You will save the changes as a custom theme, which you will apply to a company services and a company security document.

Customizing Themes

HINT

Document themes are shared across Office programs such as Word, Excel, Access, PowerPoint, and Outlook.

HINT

Every document created in Word 2010 has a theme applied to it.

Themes

Theme Colors

Theme Fonts

A document you create in Word is based on the Normal.dotm template. This template provides your document with default layout, formatting, styles, and theme formatting. The default template provides a number of built-in or predesigned themes. You have been using some of these built-in themes to apply colors, fonts, and effects to content in documents. The same built-in themes are available in Microsoft Word, Excel, Access, PowerPoint, and Outlook. With the availability of the themes across these applications, you can "brand" your business files such as documents, workbooks, and presentations with a consistent and uniform appearance.

A theme is a combination of theme colors, theme fonts, and theme effects. Within a theme, you can change any of the three elements that make a theme with the additional buttons in the Themes group. Along with the default theme, named *Office*, you can change to one of the built-in themes or create your own custom theme. A theme you create will display in the Themes drop-down gallery under the *Custom* section. To create a custom theme, change the theme color, theme font, and/or theme effects.

The buttons in the Themes group in the Page Layout tab display a visual representation of the current theme. For example, the Themes button displays an uppercase and lowercase A with color squares below. If you change the theme colors, the colors are reflected in the small color squares on the Themes button as well as the four squares in the Theme Colors button. If you change the theme fonts, the As on the Themes button as well as the uppercase A on the Theme Fonts button reflect the change.

Creating Custom Theme Colors

▼ Quick Steps

Create Custom Theme Colors
1. Click Page Layout tab.
2. Click Theme Colors button.
3. Click *Create New Theme Colors*.
4. Change to desired background, accent, and hyperlink colors.
5. Type name for custom theme colors.
6. Click Save button.

To create custom theme colors, click the Page Layout tab, click the Theme Colors button, and then click *Create New Theme Colors* at the drop-down gallery. This displays the Create New Theme Colors dialog box similar to the one shown in Figure 4.1. Theme colors contain four text and background colors, six accent colors, and two hyperlink colors as shown in the *Themes color* section of the dialog box. Change a color in the list box by clicking the color button at the right side of the color option and then clicking the desired color at the color palette.

After you have made all desired changes to colors, click in the *Name* text box, type a name for the custom color theme, and then click the Save button. This saves the custom theme colors and also applies the color changes to the currently open document. Display the custom theme by clicking the Theme Colors button in the Themes group in the Page Layout tab. Your custom theme will display toward the top of the drop-down gallery in the Custom section.

Figure 4.1 Create New Theme Colors Dialog Box

Change a theme color by clicking the color button and then clicking the desired color at the drop-down palette.

Click the Reset button to reset color back to the defult.

Resetting Custom Theme Colors

If you make changes to colors at the Create New Theme Colors dialog box and then decide you do not like the color changes, click the Reset button located in the lower left corner of the dialog box. Clicking this button resets the colors back to the default *Office* template colors.

Project 1a   **Creating Custom Theme Colors**   Part 1 of 5

Note: If you are running Word 2010 on a computer connected to a network in a public environment such as a school, you may need to complete all parts of Project 1 during the same session. Network system software may delete your custom themes when you exit Word. Check with your instructor.

1. At a blank document, click the Page Layout tab.
2. Click the Theme Colors button in the Themes group and then click the *Create New Theme Colors* option at the drop-down gallery.
3. At the Create New Theme Colors dialog box, click the color button that displays at the right side of the *Text/Background - Light 1* option and then click the *Dark Red* color at the color palette (first color from the left in the *Standard Colors* section).

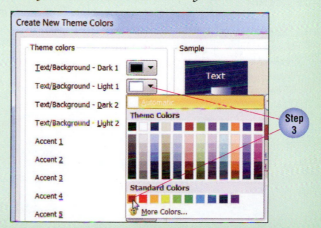

4. Click the color button that displays at the right side of the *Accent 1* option and then click the *Yellow* color at the color palette (fourth color from the left in the *Standard Colors* section).

5. You determine that you do not like the colors you have chosen so you decide to start over. To do this, click the Reset button located in the lower left corner of the dialog box.

6. Click the color button that displays at the right side of the *Text/Background - Dark 2* option and then click the *Blue* color in the color palette (third color from the *right* in the *Standard Colors* section).

7. Change the color for the *Accent 1* option by completing the following steps:
   a. Click the color button that displays at the right side of the *Accent 1* option.
   b. Click the *More Colors* button in the color palette.
   c. At the Colors dialog box, click the Standard tab.
   d. Click the dark green color shown at the right.
   e. Click OK to close the dialog box.

8. Save the custom colors by completing the following steps:
   a. Select the current text in the *Name* text box.
   b. Type your first and last names.
   c. Click the Save button.

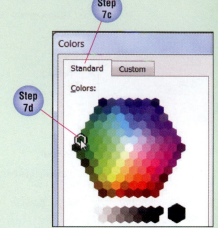

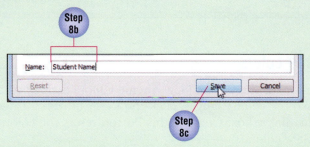

9. Close the document without saving it.

▼ **Quick Steps**

Create Custom Fonts
1. Click Page Layout tab.
2. Click Theme Fonts button.
3. Click *Create New Theme Fonts.*
4. Choose desired fonts.
5. Type name for custom theme fonts.
6. Click Save button.

Creating Custom Fonts

To create a custom theme font, click the Page Layout tab, click the Theme Fonts button, and then click *Create New Theme Fonts* at the drop-down gallery. This displays the Create New Theme Fonts dialog box. At this dialog box, choose a heading font and a font for body text. Type a name for the custom fonts in the *Name* box and then click the Save button.

1. At a blank document, click the Page Layout tab.
2. Click the Theme Fonts button in the Themes group and then click the *Create New Theme Fonts* option at the drop-down gallery.
3. At the Create New Theme Fonts dialog box, click the down-pointing arrow at the right side of the *Heading font* option box, scroll up the drop-down list, and then click *Arial*.
4. Click the down-pointing arrow at the right side of the *Body font* option box, scroll down the drop-down list, and then click *Cambria*.
5. Save the custom fonts by completing the following steps:
   a. Select the current text in the *Name* text box.
   b. Type your first and last names.
   c. Click the Save button.
6. Close the document without saving it.

Step 3

Create New Theme Fonts

Heading font:
Arial

Body font:
Cambria

Step 4

Name: Student Name

Sample

Heading
Body text body text body text. Body text body text.

Save   Cancel

Step 5b

Step 5c

Applying Custom Theme Colors and Fonts

When you create custom theme colors, you can apply them to your document by clicking the Theme Colors button in the Themes group in the Page Layout tab and then clicking the custom theme colors option that displays toward the top of the drop-down gallery in the *Custom* section. Complete similar steps to apply custom theme fonts.

Applying Theme Effects

The options in the Theme Effects button drop-down gallery apply sets of lines and fill effects to graphics in a document. You cannot create your own theme effects but you can apply a theme effect and then save the formatting as your own document theme.

Saving a Document Theme

When you have customized theme colors and fonts and applied theme effects to a document, you can save these in a custom document theme. To do this, click the Themes button in the Themes group in the Page Layout tab and then click *Save Current Theme* at the drop-down gallery. This displays the Save Current Theme dialog box with many of the same options as the Save As dialog box. Type a name for your custom document theme in the *File name* text box and then click the Save button.

▼ **Quick Steps**

Save a Document Theme
1. Click Page Layout tab.
2. Click Themes button.
3. Click *Save Current Theme*.
4. Type name for theme.
5. Click Save button.

1. Open **NSSServices.docx** and then save the document with Save As and name it **WL2-C4-P1-NSSServices**.
2. Make the following changes to the document:
   a. Apply the Title style to the company name *Northland Security Systems*. (Click the More button at the right side of the style thumbnails in the Styles group in the Home tab to display the Title style.)
   b. Apply the Heading 1 style to the heading *Northland Security Systems Mission*.
   c. Apply the Heading 2 style to the remaining headings *Security Services* and *Security Software*.
3. Apply the custom theme colors you saved by completing the following steps:
   a. Click the Page Layout tab.
   b. Click the Theme Colors button in the Themes group.
   c. Click the theme colors option with your name that displays toward the top of the drop-down gallery in the *Custom* group.
4. Apply the custom theme fonts you saved by clicking the Theme Fonts button in the Themes group and then clicking the custom theme font with your name.
5. Apply a theme effect by clicking the Theme Effects button in the Themes group and then clicking *Concourse* at the drop-down gallery.
6. Make the following changes to the SmartArt diagram:
   a. Click near the diagram to select it. (When the diagram is selected, a light gray border displays around the diagram.)
   b. Click the SmartArt Tools Design tab.
   c. Click the Change Colors button and then click the third color option from the left in the *Colorful* section (*Colorful Range - Accent Colors 3 to 4*).
   d. Click the More button at the right side of the SmartArt Styles group and then click the third option from the left in the top row in the *3-D* section (*Cartoon*).
   e. Click outside the diagram to deselect it.
7. Save the custom theme colors and font as well as the Concourse theme effect into a custom document theme by completing the following steps:
   a. Click the Page Layout tab.
   b. Click the Themes button in the Themes group.
   c. Click the *Save Current Theme* option that displays at the bottom of the drop-down gallery.

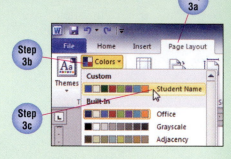

d. At the Save Current Theme dialog box, type your first and last names in the *File name* text box and then click the Save button.

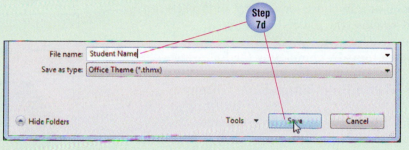

Step 7d

| File name: | Student Name | |
| Save as type: | Office Theme (*.thmx) | |

Hide Folders   Tools ▼   Save   Cancel

8. Save and then print **WL2-C4-P1-NSSServices.docx**.

Editing Custom Themes

You can edit the custom theme colors and theme fonts. To edit the custom theme colors, click the Page Layout tab and then click the Theme Colors button in the Themes group. At the drop-down gallery of custom and built-in themes, right-click your custom theme and then click *Edit* at the shortcut menu. This displays the Edit Theme Colors dialog box that contains the same options as the Create New Theme Colors dialog box. Make the desired changes to theme colors and then click the Save button.

To edit custom theme fonts, click the Theme Fonts button in the Themes group in the Page Layout tab, right-click your custom theme, and then click *Edit* at the shortcut menu. This displays the Edit Theme Fonts dialog box that contains the same options as the Create New Theme Fonts dialog box. Make the desired changes and then click the Save button.

▼ **Quick Steps**

Edit Custom Theme Colors
1. Click Page Layout tab.
2. Click Theme Colors button.
3. Right-click desired custom theme.
4. Click *Edit*.
5. Make desired changes.
6. Click Save button.

Edit Custom Theme Fonts
1. Click Page Layout tab.
2. Click Theme Fonts button.
3. Right-click desired custom theme.
4. Click *Edit*.
5. Make desired changes.
6. Click Save button.

Project 1d   Editing Custom Themes   **4 of 5**

1. With **WL2-C4-P1-NSSServices.docx** open, edit the theme colors by completing the following steps:
   a. Click the Page Layout tab.
   b. Click the Theme Colors button.
   c. Right-click the custom theme named with your first and last names and then click *Edit* at the shortcut menu.
   d. At the Edit Theme Colors dialog box, click the color button that displays at the right side of the *Text/Background - Dark 2* option.
   e. Click the *More Colors* button in the color palette.

Step 1b   Step 1a

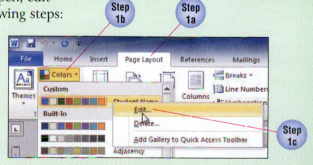

Step 1c

f. At the Colors dialog box, click the Standard tab.

g. Click the dark green color shown below. (This is the same color you chose for *Accent 1* in Project 1a.)

h. Click OK to close the dialog box.

i. Click the Save button.

2. Edit the theme fonts by completing the following steps:

a. Click the Theme Fonts button in the Themes group.

b. Right-click the custom theme that is named with your first and last names and then click *Edit* at the shortcut menu.

c. At the Edit Theme Fonts dialog box, click the down-pointing arrow at the right side of the *Body font* option box, scroll down the drop-down list, and then click *Constantia*.

d. Click the Save button.

3. Apply a different theme effect by clicking the Theme Effects button in the Themes group and then clicking *Apex* at the drop-down gallery. (This applies a shadow behind the shapes.)

4. Save the changes to the custom theme by completing the following steps:

a. Click the Themes button and then click *Save Current Theme* at the drop-down gallery.

b. At the Save Current Theme dialog box, click the theme document that is named with your first and last names.

c. Click the Save button.

d. At the replace question, click Yes.

5. Save, print, and then close **WL2-C4-P1-NSSServices.docx**.

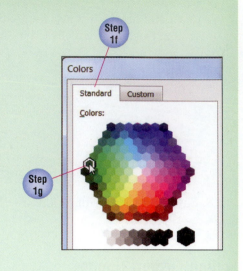

Step 1f

Step 1g

▼ **Quick Steps**

Reset Template Theme
1. Click Page Layout tab.
2. Click Themes button.
3. Click *Reset to Theme from Template*.

Delete Custom Theme Colors or Fonts
1. Click Page Layout tab.
2. Click Theme Colors or Theme Fonts button.
3. Right-click desired custom theme.
4. Click *Delete*.
5. Click Yes.

Delete Custom Theme
1. Click Page Layout tab.
2. Click Themes button.
3. Click *Save Current Theme*.
4. Click custom theme.
5. Click Organize button.
6. Click Delete.
7. Click Yes.

Resetting a Template Theme

If you apply a built-in theme other than the *Office* default or you apply a custom theme, you can reset the theme back to the template default. To do this, click the Themes button and then click the *Reset to Theme from Template* at the drop-down gallery. If you are working in the default template provided by Word, clicking this option resets the themes to *Office*.

Deleting Custom Themes

You can delete custom theme colors from the Theme Colors button drop-down gallery, delete custom theme fonts from the Theme Fonts drop-down gallery, and delete custom themes from the Save Current Theme dialog box.

To delete custom theme colors, click the Theme Colors button, right-click the theme you want to delete, and then click *Delete* at the shortcut menu. At the message asking if you want to delete the theme colors, click Yes. To delete custom theme fonts, click the Theme Fonts button, right-click the theme you want to delete, and then click *Delete* at the shortcut menu. At the message asking if you want to delete the theme fonts, click Yes.

Delete a custom theme (includes custom colors, fonts, and effects) at the Save Current Theme dialog box. To display this dialog box, click the Themes button and then click *Save Current Theme* at the drop-down gallery. At the dialog box, click the custom theme document name, click the Organize button on the dialog box toolbar, and then click *Delete* at the drop-down list. At the message asking if you are sure you want to send the theme document to the Recycle Bin, click Yes.

Project 1e Applying and Deleting Custom Themes

Part 5 of 5

1. Open **NSSSecurity.docx** and then save the document with Save As and name it **WL2-C4-P1-NSSSecurity**.
2. Apply the Title style to the company name and apply the Heading 1 style to the two headings in the document.
3. Apply your custom theme by completing the following steps:
   a. Click the Page Layout tab.
   b. Click the Themes button.
   c. Click the custom theme named with your first and last names that displays at the top of the drop-down gallery in the *Custom* section.
4. Save and then print **WL2-C4-P1-NSSSecurity.docx**.
5. Reset the theme to the *Office* default by clicking the Themes button and then clicking *Reset to Theme from Template* at the drop-down gallery. (This returns the theme to the *Office* default.)
6. Save and then close **WL2-C4-P1-NSSSecurity.docx**.
7. Press Ctrl + N to display a new blank document.
8. Delete the custom theme colors by completing the following steps:
   a. Click the Page Layout tab.
   b. Click the Theme Colors button in the Themes group.
   c. Right-click the custom theme named with your first and last names.
   d. Click *Delete* at the shortcut menu.
   e. At the question asking if you want to delete the theme colors, click Yes.

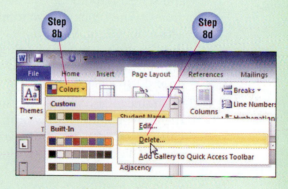

9. Complete steps similar to those in Step 8 to delete the custom theme fonts named with your first and last names.
10. Delete the custom theme by completing the following steps:
    a. Click the Themes button.
    b. Click *Save Current Theme* located toward the bottom of the drop-down gallery.
    c. At the Save Current Theme dialog box, click the theme document in the content pane that is named with your first and last names.
    d. Click the Organize button and then click *Delete* at the drop-down list.
    e. At the message asking if you are sure you want to send the theme to the Recycle Bin, click Yes.
    f. Click the Cancel button to close the Save Current Theme dialog box.
11. Close the document without saving it.

Project **2** **Format a Travel Document with Styles**   **2 Parts**

You will open a First Choice Travel document, change the Quick Styles set default, and apply styles.

Formatting with Styles ■■■■■■■■■■■■■■■■■■■■■■

A **style** is a set of formatting instructions that you can apply to text. Word provides a number of predesigned styles and groups those that apply similar formatting into sets called Quick Styles sets. Whereas a theme changes the overall colors, fonts, and effects used in a document, a Quick Styles set changes how the colors, fonts, and effects are combined and which color, font, and effect are dominant. Using the styles within a Quick Styles set, you can apply formatting that gives your document a uniform and professional appearance.

HINT

Themes change the overall colors, fonts, and effects used in a document while Quick Styles change how the colors, fonts, and effects are combined and which color, font, and effect are dominant.

Displaying Styles in a Quick Styles Set

The default Quick Styles set is named *Word 2010,* and the styles in this set are available in the Quick Style list in the Styles group in the Home tab. Several styles display as *thumbnails,* or miniature representations in the Quick Style list in the Styles group. Generally, these style thumbnails include the Normal, No Spacing, Heading 1, Heading 2, and Title styles. (Depending on your monitor and screen resolution, you may see more or fewer style thumbnails in the Styles group.) The styles change to reflect the styles that have been applied to the active document. Click the More button to the right of the style thumbnails in the Quick Style list, and a drop-down gallery displays containing all of the styles available in the default set. Hover your mouse over a style in the Quick Style list drop-down gallery to see how the style will format text in your document.

You can also display the styles available in a Quick Styles set by clicking either the down-pointing arrow or up-pointing arrow to the right of the style thumbnails. Clicking the down-pointing arrow scrolls down the style set, displaying the next styles. Clicking the up-pointing arrow scrolls up the set of styles.

Changing the Quick Styles Set Default

Along with the default Quick Styles set, Word provides a number of other Quick Styles sets. You have used some of these sets in previous chapters to apply formatting to your documents. To view all available Quick Styles sets, click the Change Styles button in the Styles group in the Home tab and then point to *Style Set.* Each Quick Styles set has a name, such as *Distinctive, Formal,* or *Thatch,* that provides a general description of the type of formatting the styles apply.

▼ Quick Steps

Change Quick Styles Set Default
1. Change desired Quick Styles set, colors, fonts, and/or paragraph spacing.
2. Click Change Styles button.
3. Click *Set as Default.*

The styles in a Quick Styles set apply formatting that includes colors and fonts. You can change the colors or fonts applied by styles in a set with the *Colors* and *Fonts* options at the Change Styles drop-down list. However, because the styles in a set are designed to complement one another, in most situations you will not change them. To change style set colors, click the Change Styles button, point to *Colors,* and then click the desired theme colors. The theme colors available with the *Colors* option are the same as those available with the Themes button and Theme Colors button. Change style set fonts by clicking the Change Styles button, pointing to *Fonts,* and then clicking the desired theme fonts. The theme fonts available with the *Fonts* option are the same as those available with the Themes button and Theme Fonts button. Customize the paragraph spacing in a document with styles at the Paragraph Spacing side menu. Display the paragraph spacing styles by clicking the Change Styles button and then pointing to *Paragraph Spacing.*

Change
Styles

Word 2010 is the Quick Styles set default and is available when you open a blank Word document. If you consistently format your documents with a different Quick Styles set, you may want to make that set the default. To do this, change to the Quick Styles set that you want as the default and make any desired changes to the set colors, fonts, and paragraph spacing. Click the Change Styles button and then click *Set as Default* at the drop-down list. The new default Quick Styles set applies to new documents you create, but it is not the default for any existing documents.

In most situations, you will not change styles in a Quick Styles set because the styles are designed to complement one another.

Project 2a **Change the Quick Styles Default**   **Part 1 of 2**

Note: If you are running Word 2010 on a computer connected to a network in a public environment such as a school, you may not be able to save styles to the hard drive. Before beginning Project 2a, check with your instructor.

1. Suppose you format many of your documents with the *Thatch* Quick Styles set using the *Flow* colors and the *Paper* fonts with relaxed paragraph spacing, and you want to make it the default. To do this, complete the following steps:
   a. At a blank document, click the Change Styles button in the Styles group in the Home tab, point to *Style Set*, and then click *Thatch* at the drop-down gallery.
   b. Click the Change Styles button, point to *Colors*, and then click *Flow* at the drop-down gallery.
   c. Click the Change Styles button, point to *Fonts*, scroll down the fonts drop-down gallery, and then click *Paper*.
   d. Click the Change Styles button, point to *Paragraph Spacing*, and then click *Relaxed* at the side menu.
   e. Click the Change Styles button and then click *Set as Default*.

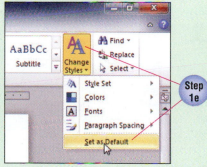

2. Close the document without saving it.
3. Press Ctrl + N to display a blank document.
4. At the blank document, notice the thumbnails in the Quick Style list in the Styles group. The formatting reflects the default Quick Styles set, colors, and font.
5. Click the Change Styles button and then point to *Paragraph Spacing* and then notice that the Relaxed style is selected.
6. Click the Page Layout tab and then notice the Themes group buttons. They reflect the colors and fonts of the default Quick Styles set.
7. Suppose you want a previously created document formatted with the styles in the *Word 2010* Quick Styles set to display with the new default styles applied. To do this, you must insert the file in the current document (rather than open it) by completing the following steps:

a. Click the Insert tab.
b. Click the Object button arrow in the Text group and then click *Text from File*.
c. Navigate to the Word2010L2C4 folder on your storage medium and then double-click **TTSAfrica.docx**. (Notice that the new default Quick Styles set formatting is applied to the document.)
8. Save the document with the name **WL2-C4-P2-TTSAfrica**.

▼ **Quick Steps**

Apply Style
Click style in Styles group.
OR
1. Click More button in Quick Style list in Styles group.
2. Click desired style.
OR
1. Display Styles task pane.
2. Click desired style in task pane.
OR
1. Click More button in Quick Style list in Styles group.
2. Click *Apply Styles* at drop-down gallery.
3. Click down-pointing arrow at right of *Style Name* option box.
4. Click desired style at drop-down list.

HINT

You can also display the Styles task pane by pressing Alt + Ctrl + Shift + S.

Applying Styles

You can use a variety of methods to apply styles to text in a document. You can apply a style by clicking the style thumbnail in the Quick Style list in the Styles group or by clicking the More button and then clicking the style at the drop-down gallery. The Styles task pane provides another method for applying a style. Display the Styles task pane, shown in Figure 4.2, by clicking the Styles group dialog box launcher. The styles in the currently selected Quick Styles set display in the task pane followed by the paragraph symbol (¶), indicating that the style applies paragraph formatting, or the character symbol (**a**), indicating that the style applies character formatting. If both characters display to the right of a style, the style applies both paragraph and character formatting. In addition to displaying styles that apply formatting, the Styles task pane also displays a *Clear All* style that clears all formatting from the selected text.

Figure 4.2 Styles Task Pane

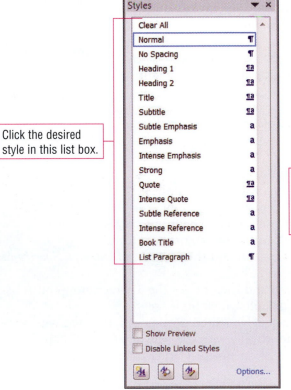

Click the desired style in this list box.

The ¶ and the **a** symbols indicate whether the style applies paragraph formatting, character formatting, or both.

If you hover the mouse pointer on a style in the Styles task pane, a ScreenTip displays with information about the formatting applied by the style. Apply a style in the Styles task pane by clicking the style. Close the Styles task pane by clicking the Close button located in the upper right corner of the task pane.

You can also apply styles at the Apply Styles window, shown in Figure 4.3. Display this window by clicking the More button at the right of the thumbnails in the Quick Style list in the Styles group and then clicking *Apply Styles* at the drop-down gallery. Like the Styles task pane, the Apply Styles window contains the styles of the currently selected Quick Styles set. Click the down-pointing arrow at the right of the *Style Name* option box and then click the desired style at the drop-down list. You can also type the name of the style in the *Style Name* option box and then press the Enter key.

You can also display the Apply Styles window by pressing Ctrl + Shift + S.

Figure 4.3 Apply Styles Window

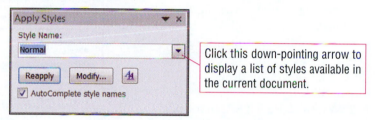

Click this down-pointing arrow to display a list of styles available in the current document.

Project 2b **Applying Styles** **Part 2 of 2**

1. With **WL2-C4-P2-TTSAfrica.docx** open, apply styles using the Styles task pane by completing the following steps:
   a. Select the heading text *Small Groups*.
   b. Click the Home tab and then click the Styles group dialog box launcher. (This displays the Styles task pane.)
   c. Click the *Subtle Emphasis* style in the Styles task pane. (Notice that the style is followed by the character symbol (**a**) indicating that the style applies character formatting.)

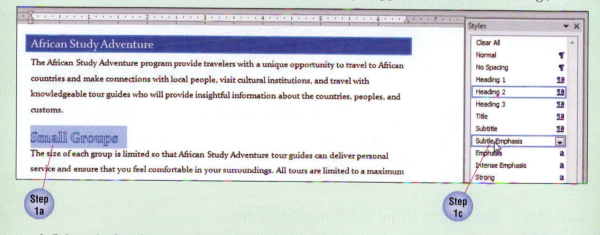

   d. Select the heading text *Comprehensive Itineraries*.
   e. Click the *Subtle Emphasis* style in the Styles task pane.
   f. Complete steps similar to those in Step 1d and 1e to apply the Subtitle Emphasis style to the remaining headings (*Custom Groups* and *Accommodations and Meals*).

g. Select the last line of text in the document (the Mark Twain quote) and then click the *Quote* style in the Styles task pane.

h. After noticing the formatting of the quote, remove it by making sure the text is selected and then clicking the *Clear All* style located toward the top of the Styles task pane.

i. Click anywhere in the heading *Small Groups* and notice that the Subtle Emphasis style is selected in the Styles task pane. Hover the mouse pointer over the Subtle Emphasis style and read the information in the ScreenTip about the formatting applied by the style.

j. Close the Styles task pane by clicking the Close button located in the upper right corner of the task pane.

2. Display the Apply Styles window by clicking the More button at the right of the style thumbnails in the Quick Style list in the Styles group and then clicking *Apply Styles* at the drop-down gallery.

3. Select the quote text located at the end of the document, click the down-pointing arrow at the right of the *Style Name* option box, and then click *Intense Quote* at the drop-down list. (You will need to scroll down the list box to display this option.)

4. Close the Apply Styles window by clicking the Close button located in the upper right corner of the window.

5. Center the title *African Study Adventure*.

6. Save, print, and then close **WL2-C4-P2-TTSAfrica.docx**.

7. Change to the original default Quick Styles set, colors, fonts, and paragraph spacing by completing the following steps:

a. Open **KLHPlan.docx**. (This document was created with the original Quick Styles set.)

b. Click the Change Styles button and then click *Set as Default* at the drop-down list.

8. Close **KLHPlan.docx** without saving it.

Project 3 Navigate and Insert Hyperlinks in a Computer Viruses Report   5 Parts

You will open a report on computer viruses and computer security and insert and then navigate in the report with the Navigation pane, bookmarks, hyperlinks, and cross-references.

Navigating in a Document ■■■■■ ■ ■ ■ ■ ■ ■ ■ ■■■

Word includes a number of features you can use to navigate in a document. Along with the navigating features you have already learned, you can also navigate using the Navigation pane and by inserting bookmarks, cross-references, and hyperlinks.

▼ Quick Steps
Display Navigation Pane
1. Click View tab.
2. Click *Navigation Pane* check box.

Navigating Using the Navigation Pane

To navigate using the Navigation pane shown in Figure 4.4, click the View tab and then click the *Navigation Pane* check box in the Show group. The Navigation pane displays at the left side of the screen and includes a Search text box and a pane with three tabs. Click the first tab and titles and headings with styles applied display in the Navigation pane. Click a title or heading in the pane and the insertion point moves to that title or heading. Click the second tab and thumbnails of each page display in the pane. Click a thumbnail to move the insertion point to the specific page. Click the third tab to browse the current search results in the document. Close the Navigation pane by clicking the *Navigation Pane* check box in the Show group in the View tab or by clicking the Close button located in the upper right corner of the pane.

Figure 4.4 Navigation Pane

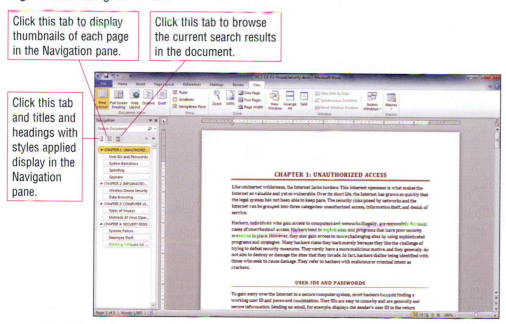

Click this tab to display thumbnails of each page in the Navigation pane.

Click this tab to browse the current search results in the document.

Click this tab and titles and headings with styles applied display in the Navigation pane.

Project 3a **Navigating Using the Navigation Pane** Part 1 of 5

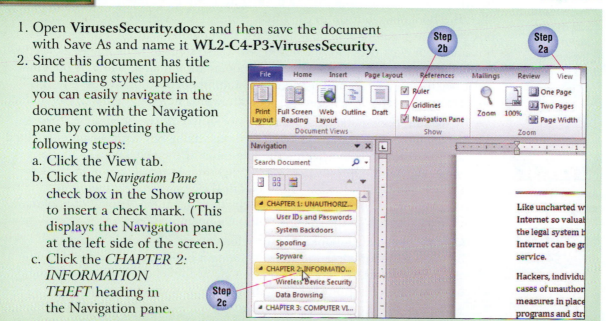

1. Open **VirusesSecurity.docx** and then save the document with Save As and name it **WL2-C4-P3-VirusesSecurity**.
2. Since this document has title and heading styles applied, you can easily navigate in the document with the Navigation pane by completing the following steps:
   a. Click the View tab.
   b. Click the *Navigation Pane* check box in the Show group to insert a check mark. (This displays the Navigation pane at the left side of the screen.)
   c. Click the *CHAPTER 2: INFORMATION THEFT* heading in the Navigation pane.

Step 2a

Step 2b

Step 2c

d. Click *CHAPTER 3: COMPUTER VIRUSES* in the Navigation pane.

e. Click *Systems Failure* in the Navigation pane.

3. Navigate in the document using thumbnails by completing the following steps:

a. Click the middle tab in the Navigation pane. (This displays page thumbnails in the pane.)

b. Click the page 1 thumbnail in the Navigation pane. (You may need to scroll up the Navigation pane to display this thumbnail.)

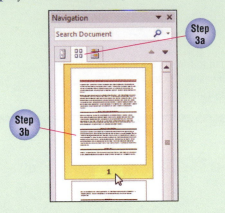

c. Click the page 3 thumbnail in the Navigation pane.

4. Close the Navigation pane by clicking the Close button located in the upper right corner of the Navigation pane.

5. Save **WL2-C4-P3-VirusesSecurity.docx**.

Navigating with Bookmarks

Quick Steps

Create a Bookmark
1. Position insertion point at desired location.
2. Click Insert tab.
3. Click Bookmark button.
4. Type name for bookmark.
5. Click Add button.

Bookmark brackets do not print.

Bookmark

In a long document, you may find marking a location in the document useful so you can quickly move the insertion point to the location. Create bookmarks for locations in a document at the Bookmark dialog box. To create a bookmark, position the insertion point at the desired location, click the Insert tab, and then click the Bookmark button in the Links group. This displays the Bookmark dialog box shown in Figure 4.5. Type a name for the bookmark in the *Bookmark name* text box and then click the Add button. Repeat these steps as many times as needed to insert the desired bookmarks. Give each bookmark a unique name. A bookmark must begin with a letter and it can contain numbers but not spaces. Use the underscore character if you want to separate words in a bookmark name.

By default, bookmarks you insert are not visible in the document. Turn on the display of bookmarks at the Word Options dialog box with *Advanced* selected. Display this dialog box by clicking the File tab and then clicking the Options button. At the Word Options dialog box, click the *Advanced* option in the left panel. Click the *Show bookmarks* check box in the *Show document content* section to insert a check mark. Complete similar steps to turn off the display of bookmarks. A bookmark displays in the document as an I-beam marker.

You can also create a bookmark for selected text. To do this, select the text first and then complete the steps to create a bookmark. When you create a bookmark for selected text, a left bracket ([) indicates the beginning of the selected text and a right bracket (]) indicates the end of selected text.

Figure 4.5 Bookmark Dialog Box

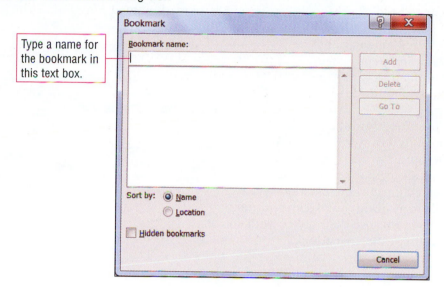

Type a name for the bookmark in this text box.

After you insert bookmarks in a document, you can move the insertion point to a specific bookmark. To do this, display the Bookmark dialog box, and then double-click the bookmark name. You can also click the Bookmark name and then click the Go To button. When Word stops at the location of the bookmark, click the Close button to close the dialog box. If you move the insertion point to a bookmark created with selected text, Word moves the insertion point to the bookmark and selects the text. Delete bookmarks in the Bookmark dialog box by clicking the bookmark name in the list box and then clicking the Delete button.

▼ **Quick Steps**

Navigate with Bookmarks
1. Click Insert tab.
2. Click Bookmark button.
3. Double-click desired bookmark name.

Project 3b   **Inserting and Navigating with Bookmarks**   **Part 2 of 5**

1. With **WL2-C4-P3-VirusesSecurity.docx** open, turn on the display of bookmarks by completing the following steps:
   a. Click the File tab and then click the Options button.
   b. At the Word Options dialog box, click *Advanced* in the left panel.
   c. Click the *Show bookmarks* check box in the *Show document content* section to insert a check mark.
   d. Click OK to close the dialog box.
2. Insert a bookmark by completing the following steps:
   a. Move the insertion point to the beginning of the paragraph in the *TYPES OF VIRUSES* section (the paragraph that begins *Viruses can be categorized . . .*).
   b. Click the Insert tab.
   c. Click the Bookmark button in the Links group.
   d. At the Bookmark dialog box, type **Viruses** in the *Bookmark name* text box.
   e. Click the Add button.

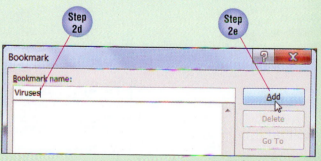

Step 2d

Step 2e

3. Using steps similar to Steps 2a through 2e, insert a bookmark named *Electrical* at the beginning of the paragraph in the *SYSTEMS FAILURE* section.

4. Navigate to the Viruses bookmark by completing the following steps:
   a. If necessary, click the Insert tab.
   b. Click the Bookmark button in the Links group.
   c. At the Bookmark dialog box, click *Viruses* in the list box.
   d. Click the Go To button.

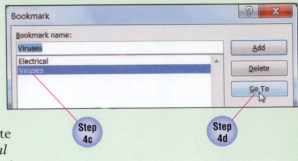

5. With the Bookmark dialog box open, delete the *Electrical* bookmark by clicking *Electrical* in the list box and then clicking the Delete button.

6. Click the Close button to close the Bookmark dialog box.

7. Save **WL2-C5-P3-VirusesSecurity.docx**.

Inserting Hyperlinks ■■■■■■ ■■ ■ ■ ■ ■ ■ ■ ■ ■ ■ ■ ■

A hyperlink in a document can serve a number of purposes. You can use a hyperlink to navigate to a specific location in the document, to display a different document, to open a file in a different program, to create a new document, or to link to an email address. Insert a hyperlink by clicking the Hyperlink button located in the Links group in the Insert tab. This displays the Insert Hyperlink dialog box, shown in Figure 4.6. You can also display the Insert Hyperlink dialog box by pressing Ctrl + K. At this dialog box, identify what you want to link to and the location of the link. Click the ScreenTip button to customize the hyperlink ScreenTip.

Hyperlink

Figure 4.6 Insert Hyperlink Dialog Box

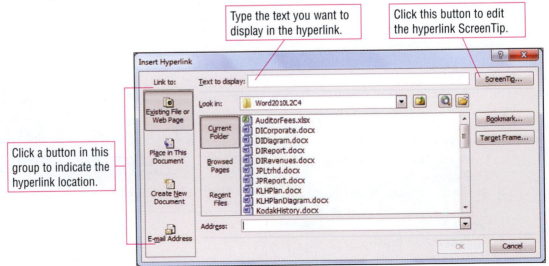

Type the text you want to display in the hyperlink.

Click this button to edit the hyperlink ScreenTip.

Click a button in this group to indicate the hyperlink location.

Linking to a Place in the Document

To create a hyperlink to another location in the document, you need to mark the location either by applying heading styles to text or by inserting bookmarks. To hyperlink to a heading or bookmark in a document, display the Insert Hyperlink dialog box and then click the Place in This Document button in the *Link to* section. This displays text with heading styles applied and bookmarks in the *Select a place in this document* list box. Click the desired heading style or bookmark name, and the heading or bookmark name displays in the *Text to display* text box. You can leave the text as displayed or you can select the text and then type the text you want to appear in the document.

Navigating Using Hyperlinks

Navigate to a hyperlink by hovering the mouse over the hyperlink text, holding down the Ctrl key, and then clicking the left mouse button. When you hover the mouse over hyperlink text, a ScreenTip displays with the name of the heading or bookmark. If you want specific information to display in the ScreenTip, click the ScreenTip button in the Insert Hyperlink dialog box, type the desired text in the Set Hyperlink ScreenTip dialog box, and then click OK.

 Inserting Hyperlinks   **Part 3 of 5**

1. With **WL2-C4-P3-VirusesSecurity.docx** open, insert a hyperlink to a bookmark in the document by completing the following steps:
   a. Position the insertion point at the immediate right of the period that ends the first paragraph of text in the *CHAPTER 4: SECURITY RISKS* section (located on page 4).
   b. Press the spacebar once.
   c. If necessary, click the Insert tab.
   d. Click the Hyperlink button in the Links group.
   e. At the Insert Hyperlink dialog box, click the Place in This Document button in the *Link to* section.
   f. Scroll down the *Select a place in this document* list box and then click *Viruses*, which displays below *Bookmarks* in the list box.
   g. Select the text that displays in the *Text to display* text box and then type **Click to view types of viruses**.
   h. Click the ScreenTip button located in the upper right corner of the dialog box. At the Set Hyperlink ScreenTip dialog box, type **View types of viruses** and then click OK.
   i. Click OK to close the Insert Hyperlink dialog box.

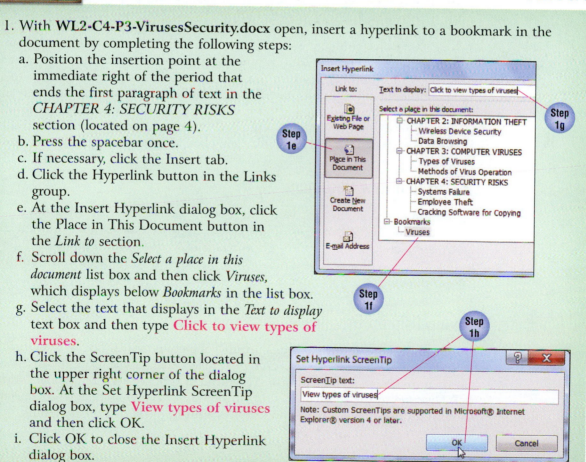

2. Navigate to the hyperlinked location by hovering the mouse over the <u>Click to view types of viruses</u> hyperlink, holding down the Ctrl key, and then clicking the left mouse button.
3. Insert a hyperlink to a heading in the document by completing the following steps:
   a. Press Ctrl + Home to move the insertion point to the beginning of the document.
   b. Move the insertion point to the immediate right of the period that ends the second paragraph in the document and then press the spacebar.
   c. Click the Hyperlink button in the Insert tab.
   d. At the Insert Hyperlink dialog box with the Place in This Document button selected in the *Link to* section, click the *Methods of Virus Operation* heading in the *Select a place in this document* list box.
   e. Click OK to close the Insert Hyperlink dialog box.
4. Navigate to the hyperlinked heading by hovering the mouse over the <u>Methods of Virus Operation</u> hyperlink, holding down the Ctrl key, and then clicking the left mouse button.
5. Save **WL2-C4-P3-VirusesSecurity.docx**.

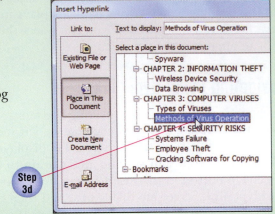

Step 3d

Linking to a File in Another Program

In some situations, you may want to provide information to your readers from a variety of sources. You may want to provide information in a Word document, an Excel spreadsheet, or a PowerPoint presentation. To link a Word document to a file in another application, display the Insert Hyperlink dialog box and then click the Existing File or Web Page button in the *Link to* section. Use the *Look in* option to navigate to the folder containing the desired file and then click the file. Make other changes in the Insert Hyperlink dialog box as needed and then click OK.

Linking to a New Document

In addition to linking to an existing document, you can create a hyperlink to a new document. To do this, display the Insert Hyperlink dialog box and then click the Create New Document button in the *Link to* section. Type a name for the new document in the *Name of new document* text box and then specify if you want to edit the document now or later.

Linking Using a Graphic

You can use a graphic such as a clip art image, picture, or text box to hyperlink to a file or website. To hyperlink with a graphic, select the graphic, click the Insert tab, and then click the Hyperlink button. (You can also right-click the graphic and then click *Hyperlink* at the shortcut menu.) At the Insert Hyperlink dialog box, specify where you want to link to and the text you want to display in the hyperlink.

Linking to an Email Address

You can insert a hyperlink to an email address at the Insert Hyperlink dialog box. To do this, click the E-Mail Address button in the *Link to* group, type the desired address in the *E-mail address* text box, and type a subject for the email in the *Subject* text box. Click in the *Text to display* text box and then type the text you want to display in the document. To use this feature, the email address you use must be set up in Outlook 2010.

Project 3d Inserting a Hyperlink to Another Program, a New Document, and Using a Graphic

Part 4 of 5

1. The file **WL2-C4-P3-VirusesSecurity.docx** contains information used by Northland Security Systems. The company also has a PowerPoint presentation that contains similar information. Link the document with the presentation by completing the following steps:
    a. Move the insertion point to the immediate right of the period that ends the first paragraph in the *CHAPTER 3: COMPUTER VIRUSES* section and then press the spacebar.
    b. If necessary, click the Insert tab.
    c. Click the Hyperlink button in the Links group.
    d. At the Insert Hyperlink dialog box, click the Existing File or Web Page button in the *Link to* section.
    e. Click the down-pointing arrow at the right side of the *Look in* list box and then navigate to the Word2010L2C4 folder on your storage medium.
    f. Click the presentation named **NSSPres.pptx** in the list box.
    g. Select the text in the *Text to display* text box in the dialog box and then type **Computer Virus Presentation**.
    h. Click OK to close the Insert Hyperlink dialog box.

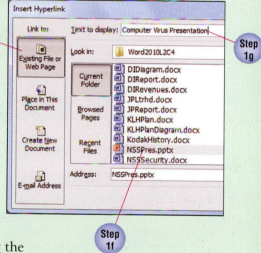

Step 1d

Step 1g

Step 1f

2. View the PowerPoint presentation by completing the following steps:
    a. Position the mouse pointer over the <u>Computer Virus Presentation</u> hyperlink, hold down the Ctrl key, and then click the left mouse button.
    b. At the PowerPoint presentation, click the Slide Show button in the view area on the Status bar.
    c. Click the left mouse button to advance each slide.
    d. Click the left mouse button at the black screen that displays the message *End of slide show, click to exit*.
    e. Close the presentation and PowerPoint by clicking the Close button (contains an X) that displays in the upper right corner of the screen.

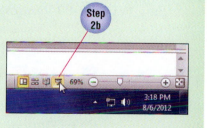

Step 2b

3. Insert a hyperlink with a graphic by completing the following steps:
    a. Press Ctrl + End to move the insertion point to the end of the document.
    b. Click the compass image to select it.

---

c. Click the Hyperlink button in the Insert tab.

d. At the Insert Hyperlink dialog box, make sure the Existing File or Web Page button is selected in the *Link to* group.

e. Navigate to the Word2010L2C4 folder on your storage medium and then double-click the document named **NSSTraining.docx**. (This selects the document name and closes the dialog box.)

f. Click outside the clip art image to deselect it.

4. Navigate to the **NSSTraining.docx** document by hovering the mouse pointer over the compass image, holding down the Ctrl key, and then clicking the left mouse button.

5. Close the document by clicking the File tab and then clicking the Close button.

6. Insert a hyperlink to a new document by completing the following steps:

a. Move the insertion point to the immediate right of the period that ends the paragraph in the *USER IDS AND PASSWORDS* section and then press the spacebar.

b. Click the Hyperlink button in the Insert tab.

c. Click the Create New Document button in the *Link to* section.

d. In the *Name of new document* text box, type **PasswordSuggestions**.

e. Edit the text in the *Text to display* text box so it displays as *Password Suggestions*.

f. Make sure the *Edit the new document now* option is selected and then click OK.

g. At the blank document, turn on bold, type **Please type any suggestions you have for creating secure passwords:**, turn off bold and then press the Enter key.

h. Save and then close the document.

7. Press Ctrl + End to move the insertion point to the end of the document and then press the Enter key four times.

8. Insert a hyperlink to your email or your instructor's email address by completing the following steps:

a. Click the Hyperlink button.

b. At the Insert Hyperlink dialog box, click the E-mail Address button in the *Link to* group.

c. Type your email address or your instructor's email address in the *E-mail address* text box.

d. Select the current text in the *Text to display* text box and then type **Click to send an email**.

e. Click OK to close the dialog box.

Optional: If you have Outlook set up, hold down the Ctrl key, click the Click to send an email hyperlink, and then send a message indicating that you have completed inserting hyperlinks in the WL2-C4-P3-VirusesSecurity.docx documents.

9. Save **WL2-C4-P3-VirusesSecurity.docx**.

Creating a Cross-Reference ■■■■■■■■■■■■■■■■■■ ■■

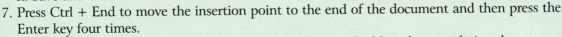

Cross-Reference

A *cross-reference* in a Word document refers the reader to another location within the document. This feature is useful in a long document or a document containing related information. You can insert a reference to an item such as a heading, figure, or table. For example, you can insert a cross-reference that refers readers to another location with more information about the topic, refers readers to a specific table, or refers readers to a specific page. Cross-references are inserted in a document as hyperlinks.

To insert a cross-reference, type introductory text, click the Insert tab, and then click the Cross-reference button in the Links group. This displays the Cross-reference dialog box. At the Cross-reference dialog box, identify the reference type, where to refer, and the specific text.

The reference identified in the Cross-reference dialog box displays immediately after the introductory text. To move to the specified reference, hold down the Ctrl key, position the mouse pointer over the introductory text (pointer turns into a hand), and then click the left mouse button.

▼ **Quick Steps**

Insert a Cross-Reference
1. Type introductory text.
2. Click Insert tab.
3. Click Cross-reference button.
4. Identify reference type, where to refer, and specific text.
5. Click Insert.
6. Click Close.

Project 3e **Inserting and Navigating with Cross-References** **Part 5 of 5**

1. With **WL2-C4-P3-VirusesSecurity.docx** open, insert a cross-reference in the document by completing the following steps:
   a. Move the insertion point so it is positioned immediately right of the period that ends the paragraph in the *TYPES OF VIRUSES* section.
   b. Press the spacebar once and then type **(For more information, refer to**.
   c. Press the spacebar once.
   d. If necessary, click the Insert tab.
   e. Click the Cross-reference button in the Links group.
   f. At the Cross-reference dialog box, click the down-pointing arrow at the right side of the *Reference type* list box and then click *Heading* at the drop-down list.
   g. Click *Spyware* in the *For which heading* list box.
   h. Click the Insert button.
   i. Click the Close button to close the dialog box.
   j. At the document, type a period followed by the right parenthesis.

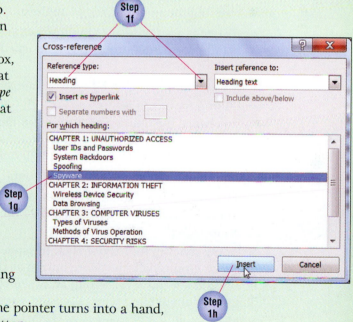

2. Move to the reference text by holding down the Ctrl key, positioning the mouse pointer over *Spyware* until the pointer turns into a hand, and then clicking the left mouse button.
3. Save **WL2-C4-P3-VirusesSecurity.docx**.
4. Print the document.
5. Turn off the display of bookmarks by completing the following steps:
   a. Click the File tab and then click the Options button.
   b. At the Word Options dialog box, click *Advanced* in the left panel.
   c. Click the *Show bookmarks* check box in the *Show document content* section to remove the check mark.
   d. Click OK to close the dialog box.
6. Close **WL2-C4-P3-VirusesSecurity.docx**.

Chapter Summary

- Create custom theme colors with options at the Create New Theme Colors dialog box and create custom theme fonts with options at the Create New Theme Fonts dialog box.

- Click the Reset button in the Create New Theme Colors dialog box to reset colors back to the default *Office* template colors.

- Create custom theme colors and custom theme fonts, apply a theme effect, and then save the changes in a custom theme. Save a custom theme at the Save Current Theme dialog box. Display this dialog box by clicking the Themes button in the Themes group and then clicking *Save Current Theme* at the drop-down gallery.

- Apply custom theme colors by clicking the Theme Colors button and then clicking the custom theme that displays toward the top of the drop-down gallery. Complete similar steps to insert custom theme fonts and a custom theme.

- You can edit and also delete custom themes. Delete a custom theme at the Save Current Theme dialog box.

- Click the *Reset to Theme from Template* at the Themes button drop-down gallery to reset the theme to the template default.

- A style is a set of formatting instructions you can apply to text in a document. Word provides a number of predesigned styles grouped into sets called Quick Styles sets.

- Styles within the Quick Styles set are available in the Styles group in the Home tab.

- To change the Quick Styles set, click the Change Styles button in the Styles group in the Home tab, point to *Style Set*, and then click the desired style set at the drop-down gallery.

- You can change the colors and/or fonts applied by styles in style sets.

- The Word 2010 Quick Styles set is the default. To change this default, change to the desired Quick Styles set, click the Change Styles button, and then click *Set as Default*.

- Apply styles in four ways: click the style thumbnail in the Quick Style list in the Styles group, click the More button at the right of the thumbnails in the Quick Style list in the Styles group and then click the style at the drop-down gallery, use options at the Styles task pane, or use options at the Apply Styles window.

- Navigate in a document with the Navigation pane or by inserting bookmarks, hyperlinks, or cross references.

- Insert bookmarks with options at the Bookmark dialog box.

- Insert hyperlinks in a document with options at the Insert Hyperlink dialog box. You can insert a hyperlink to an existing file or web page, a location in the current document, a new document, or an email. You can also use a graphic to link to a file or website.

- Create a cross-reference with options at the Cross-reference dialog box.

Commands Review

FEATURE	RIBBON TAB, GROUP	BUTTON, OPTION	KEYBOARD SHORTCUT
Create New Theme Colors dialog box	Page Layout, Themes	, Create New Theme Colors	
Create New Theme Fonts dialog box	Page Layout, Themes	, Create New Theme Fonts	
Theme effects	Page Layout, Themes		
Save Current Theme dialog box	Page Layout, Themes	, Save Current Theme	
Styles task pane	Home, Styles		Alt + Ctrl + Shift + S
Apply Styles window	Home, Styles	, Apply Styles	Ctrl + Shift + S
Bookmark dialog box	Insert, Links		
Insert Hyperlink dialog box	Insert, Links		Ctrl + K
Cross-reference dialog box	Insert, Links		

Concepts Check Test Your Knowledge

Completion: In the space provided at the right, indicate the correct term, symbol, or command.

1. The Themes button is located in this tab.

2. Create custom theme colors at this dialog box.

3. A theme you save displays in this section in the Themes button drop-down gallery.

4. If you hover the mouse pointer over a style in the Styles task pane, this displays with information about the formatting applied.

5. The Navigation Pane check box is located in the Show group in this tab.

6. Turn on the display of bookmarks in a document with the *Show bookmarks* check box in this dialog box with *Advanced* selected.

7. The Bookmark button is located in this group in the Insert tab. _____

8. Navigate to a hyperlink by hovering the mouse over the hyperlink text, holding down this key, and then clicking the left mouse button. _____

9. To link a Word document to a file in another application, click this button in the *Link to* group in the Insert Hyperlink dialog box. _____

10. By default, cross-references are inserted in a document as this. _____

Skills Check Assess Your Performance

Assessment

1 CREATE AND APPLY CUSTOM THEMES TO A MEDICAL PLANS DOCUMENT

1. At a blank document, create custom theme colors named with your initials that make the following color changes:
   a. Change the *Accent 2* color to *Dark Blue* (the second option from the right in the *Standard Colors* section).
   b. Change the *Accent 5* color to *Olive Green, Accent 3, Darker 50%* (the bottom option in the seventh column in the *Theme Colors* section).
2. Click the Theme Effects button and then click *Paper* at the drop-down gallery.
3. Save the custom theme and name it with your initials. ***Hint: Do this with the*** **Save Current Theme** ***option at the*** **Themes** ***drop-down gallery.***
4. Close the document without saving the changes.
5. Open **KLHPlan.docx** and then save the document with Save As and name it **WL2-C4-A1-KLHPlan**.
6. Make the following changes to the document:
   a. Change the style set to Formal.
   b. With the insertion point positioned at the beginning of the document, type the title Key Life Health Plan.
   c. Apply the Heading 1 style to the title.
   d. Apply the Heading 2 style to the three headings in the document.
7. Move the insertion point to the end of the document, press the Enter key, and then insert the document **KLHPlanDiagram.docx**. ***Hint: Do this with the*** **Object button** ***in the Insert tab.***
8. Apply the custom theme you created by clicking the Page Layout tab, clicking the Themes button, and then clicking the custom theme named with your initials.
9. Save, print, and then close **WL2-C4-A1-KLHPlan.docx**.
10. At a blank document, delete the custom theme colors named with your initials and the custom theme named with your initials.

Assessment

2 FORMAT AND NAVIGATE IN CORPORATE REPORT DOCUMENTS

1. Open **DIReport.docx** and then save the document with Save As and name it **WL2-C4-A2-DIReport**.
2. Change the Quick Styles set to *Formal*.
3. Change the Quick Styles colors to *Elemental*.
4. Change the Quick Styles fonts to *Apothecary*.
5. Change the Quick Styles paragraph spacing to *Compact*.
6. Move the insertion point to any character in the second paragraph in the document (the paragraph that begins *Assist the company's board of directors in fulfilling . . .*), turn on the display of the Styles task pane, apply the *Intense Quote* style to the paragraph, and then turn off the display of the Styles task pane.
7. Turn on the display of bookmarks.
8. Move the insertion point to the end of the third paragraph in the document (the paragraph that begins *The audit committee selects . . .*) and then insert a bookmark named *Audit*.
9. Move the insertion point to the end of the first paragraph in the *FEES TO INDEPENDENT AUDITOR* section, following the *(Excel worksheet)* text, and then insert a bookmark named *Audit_Fees*.
10. Move the insertion point to the end of the last paragraph of text in the document and then insert a bookmark named *Compensation*.
11. Navigate in the document using the bookmarks.
12. Move the insertion point to the end of the first paragraph in the *COMMITTEE RESPONSIBILITIES* section and then insert a hyperlink to the *Audit_Fees* bookmark.
13. Select the text *(Excel worksheet)* that displays at the end of the first paragraph in the *FEES TO INDEPENDENT AUDITOR* section and then insert a hyperlink to the Excel file named **AuditorFees.xlsx** that is located in the Word2010L2C4 folder on your storage medium.
14. Move the insertion point to the end of the document, click the clip art image, and then insert a hyperlink to the Word document named **DIDiagram.docx** located in the Word2010L2C4 folder on your storage medium.
15. Click the *(Excel worksheet)* hyperlink and then print the Excel worksheet that displays by clicking the File tab, clicking the Print tab, and then clicking the Print button in the Print tab Backstage view.
16. Close the Excel program without saving the workbook.
17. Hold down the Ctrl key and then click the clip art to display the Word document containing the diagram, print the diagram document, and then close the document.
18. Save, print, and then close **WL2-C4-A2-DIReport.docx**.

Assessment

3 EXPLORE AND APPLY OFFICE.COM THEMES

1. Open **SoftwareCycle.docx** and then save the document with Save As and name it **WL2-C4-A3-SoftwareCycle**.
2. Additional themes are available from Office.com and should display at the bottom of the Themes button drop-down gallery. To view the Office.com themes, click the Page Layout tab, click the Themes button in the Themes group, and then scroll down to the bottom of the drop-down gallery. You

should see themes with names such as *Decatur*, *Mylar*, *Sketchbook*, and *SOHO*. (If you do not have any Office.com themes available, connect to the Internet and then go to the Office.com website and explore the site to determine if you can download themes.)

3. Hover the mouse over the Office.com themes in the Themes button drop-down gallery to see how the theme changes the document formatting. Apply one of the Office.com themes to the document.

4. Determine the heading font and body font used by the theme by clicking on any character in the title *Application Software*, clicking the Home tab, and then clicking the Font button arrow. The heading font and body font are listed at the beginning of the drop-down list. Make a note of these fonts.

5. With the insertion point positioned on the title *Application Software*, determine the font color by clicking the Font Color button arrow and then checking the color palette to determine which color option is selected (surrounded by an orange border). If no color option is selected, click the *More Colors* option at the bottom of the drop-down gallery. At the Colors dialog box with the Custom tab selected, make a note of the numbers after the *Red*, *Green*, and *Blue* options.

6. After determining the Office.com heading font and font color and the body font, make the following changes:
   a. Press Ctrl + End to move the insertion point to the end of the document.
   b. Type **Theme name:**, press the spacebar, and then type the name of the theme you applied.
   c. Press Shift + Enter to move the insertion point to the next line.
   d. Type **Heading font:**, press the spacebar, type the name of the font you made note of in Step 4, type a comma, press the spacebar, and then type the font color name (or type *Red*, *Green*, and *Blue* followed by the specific numbers).
   e. Press Shift + Enter.
   f. Type **Body font:**, press the spacebar, and then type the name of the font.

7. Save and then print **WL2-C4-A3-SoftwareCycle.docx**.

8. Apply a different Office.com theme to the document and then determine the heading font and font color and the body font. Change the information that displays at the bottom of the document to reflect the new theme.

9. Save, print, and then close **WL2-C4-A3-SoftwareCycle.docx**.

Visual Benchmark Demonstrate Your Proficiency

INSERT SMARTART DIAGRAMS IN A BUSINESS DOCUMENT

1. Open **DIRevenues.docx** and then save the document with Save As and name it **WL2-C4-VB-DIRevenues**.
2. Apply the *Apothecary* theme to the document.
3. Create the following custom theme colors named with your first and last names with the following changes:
    a. Change the Text/Background – Dark 2 color to *Red, Accent 2, Darker 25%*.
    b. Change the Accent 1 color to *Tan, Accent 3, Darker 50%*.
    c. Change the Accent 3 color to *Gold, Accent 5, Darker 25%*.
4. Create the following custom theme fonts name with your first and last names with the following changes:
    a. Change the heading font to *Copperplate Gothic Bold*.
    b. Change the body font to *Constantia*.
5. Apply the *Verve* theme effect.
6. Save the custom theme and name it *WL2C4* followed by your initials. ***Hint: Do this with the* Save Current Theme *option at the* Themes *drop-down gallery.***
7. Using the Change Styles button in the Home tab, change the paragraph spacing to *Double*.
8. Center the title and reposition the SmartArt diagram as shown in Figure 4.7.
9. Save, print, and then close **WL2-C4-VB-DIRevenues.docx**.
10. Open **DICorporate.docx** and then save the document with Save As and name it **WL2-C4-VB-DICorporate**.
11. Apply the *WL2C4* (followed by your initials) custom theme to the document.
12. Using the Change Styles button in the Home tab, change the paragraph spacing to *Double*.
13. Center the title and, if necessary, reposition the SmartArt diagram as shown in Figure 4.8.
14. Save, print, and then close **WL2-C4-VB-DICorporate.docx**.
15. At a blank document, use the Print Screen button to make a screen capture of the Theme Colors drop-down gallery (make sure your custom theme colors display), a screen capture of the Theme Fonts drop-down gallery (make sure your custom theme fonts display), and a screen capture of the Save Current Theme dialog box (make sure your custom themes are visible). Insert all three screen capture images on the same page. (You will need to size the images.)
16. Save the document and name it **WL2-C4-VB-ScreenImages**.
17. Print and then close **WL2-C4-VB-ScreenImages.docx**.
18. At a blank document, delete the custom color theme you created, the custom font theme, as well as the custom themes.

Figure 4.7 Visual Benchmark Document 1

DEARBORN INDUSTRIES

REVENUES

We are evaluating markets for our current and future products. Prior to the fourth quarter of 2011, we recorded revenues as a result of development contracts with government entities focused on the design of flywheel technologies. We have produced and placed several development prototypes with potential customers and shipped preproduction units.

RESEARCH AND DEVELOPMENT

Our cost of research and development consists primarily of the cost of compensation and benefits for research and support staff, as well as materials and supplies used in the engineering design and development process. These costs decreased significantly during 2011 as we focused on reducing our expenditure rate by reducing product design and development activities.

PREFERRED STOCK DIVIDENDS

Prior to our initial public offering of our common stock, we had various classes of preferred stock outstanding, each of which was entitled to receive dividends. We accrued dividend expenses monthly according to the requirements of each class of preferred stock.

Figure 4.8 Visual Benchmark Document 2

DEARBORN INDUSTRIES

CORPORATE VISION

Dearborn Industries will be the leading developer of clean and environmentally friendly products. Building on strong leadership, development, and resources, we will provide superior-quality products and services to our customers and consumers around the world.

CORPORATE VALUES

We value the environment in which we live, and we will work to produce and maintain energy-efficient and environmentally safe products and strive to reduce our carbon footprint on the environment.

CORPORATE LEADERSHIP

Dearborn Industries employees conduct business under the leadership of the chief executive officer, who is subject to the oversight and direction of the board of directors. Four vice presidents work with the chief executive officer to manage and direct business.

Case Study Apply Your Skills

Part 1

You work for Jackson Photography and you want to create a new letterhead for the company. Open **JPLtrd.docx** and then customize the text and clip art to create an attractive and professional-looking letterhead. Save the completed letterhead with the same name (**JPLtrd.docx**). Create a building block with the letterhead.

Part 2

At a blank document, create and then save custom theme colors that match the letterhead you created in Part 1. Create and then save custom theme fonts that apply the Arial font to headings and the Constantia font to body text. Apply a custom theme effect of your choosing. Save the custom theme in the Save Current Theme dialog box and name it with your initials followed by *FP*.

Part 3

At a blank document, insert the company letterhead building block you created in Part 1, type the title *Photography Services*, and then insert a SmartArt of your choosing that contains the following text:

- Wedding Photography
- Sports Portraits
- Senior Portraits
- Family Portraits
- Processing

Apply a heading style to the *Photography Services* title, apply the custom theme to the document, and then save the document and name it **WL2-C4-CS-FPServices**.

Part 4

Open **JPReport.docx** and then save the document with Save As and name it **WL2-C4-CS-JPReport**. Apply or insert the following to the document:

- Apply your custom theme.
- Apply the Intense Quote style to the quote at the beginning and the quote at the end of the document.
- Insert a footer of your choosing in the document.

Apply any other enhancements to improve the visual appeal of the document. Save **WL2-C4-CS-JPReport.docx**.

Part 5

With **WL2-C4-CS-JPReport.docx** open, insert at the end of the third paragraph in the *Photography* section a hyperlink that links to the document **KodakHistory.docx** located in the Word2010L2C4 folder on your storage medium. Using the Internet, research and locate at least one company that sells digital cameras. Insert, at the end of the document, text that tells the reader to click the hyperlink text to link to that particular site on the Internet and then insert the hyperlink to the website you found. Save, print, and then close **WL2-C4-CS-JPReport.docx**.

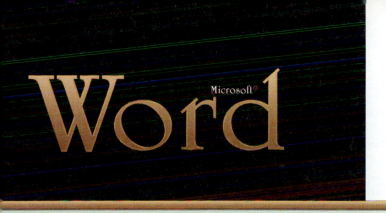

Note: Before beginning unit assessments, copy to your storage medium the Word2010L2U1 subfolder from the Word2010L2 folder on the CD that accompanies this textbook and then make Word2010L2U1 the active folder.

Assessing Proficiency ▪▪■▪■■■■■■■■

In this unit, you have learned to format documents with special features such as customized bullets, numbering, headers, footers, and page numbering. You also learned how to apply and customize building blocks, themes, Quick Styles sets, and styles and how to customize the spelling, grammar, and AutoCorrect features in a document.

Assessment 1 Format Stock Awards Document

1. Open **CMStocks.docx** and then save the document with Save As and name it **WL2-U1-A1-CMStocks**.
2. Apply the Title style to the title *Clearline Manufacturing*.
3. Apply the Heading 1 style to the headings *Stock Awards* and *Employee Stock Plan*.
4. Change the style set to *Traditional*.
5. Select the bulleted paragraphs of text and then define a new picture bullet of your choosing.
6. Select the lines of text below the *Employee Stock Plan* heading and then apply a multilevel list (the middle option in the top row of the *List Library* section of the Multilevel List button drop-down gallery).
7. With the text still selected, define a new multilevel list that inserts capital letters followed by a period (A., B., C.) for level 2 and inserts Arabic numbers followed by a period (1., 2., 3.) for level 3. (Make sure the new multilevel list applies to the selected text.)
8. Save, print, and then close **WL2-U1-A1-CMStocks.docx**.

Assessment 2 Format *Future of Computer Ethics Report*

1. Open **FutureEthics.docx** and then save the document with Save As and name it **WL2-U1-A2-FutureEthics**.
2. Select the entire document and then change the line spacing to 2.0.
3. Apply the Heading 1 style to the two titles in the document, *FUTURE OF COMPUTER ETHICS* and *REFERENCES*.
4. Apply the Heading 2 style to the five headings in the document.
5. Hang indent the paragraphs of text below the title *REFERENCES*.
6. Change the style set to *Modern*.

7. Change the theme fonts to Apex.
8. Insert the *FileName* and *PrintDate* fields at the end of the document.
9. Keep the heading *SELF-REPLICATING ROBOTS* together with the paragraph of text that follows it.
10. Keep the title *REFERENCES* together with the paragraph of text that follows it.
11. Create an odd page footer that prints the document title at the left margin and the page number at the right margin and create an even page footer that prints the page number at the left margin and the document title at the right margin.
12. Save, print, and then close **WL2-U1-A2-FutureEthics.docx**.

Assessment 3 Create and Format a Column Chart

1. At a blank document, use the data in Figure U1.1 to create a column chart with the following specifications:
   a. Change the chart type to *3-D Clustered Column*.
   b. Apply the *Layout 3* chart layout.
   c. Apply the *Style 35* chart style.
   d. Select the chart title text and then type **2011 Sales**.
   e. Insert a small text box in the lower left corner of the chart and then type your first and last names.
   f. Insert major primary vertical gridlines.
   g. Select the chart area, apply *Orange, Accent 6, Lighter 60%* shape fill, and apply the *Offset Bottom* shadow shape effect.
   h. Select the chart title and then apply the *Gradient Fill - Blue, Accent 1* WordArt style.
   i. Change the chart height to 4 inches and the chart width to 6.5 inches.
   j. Position the chart in the middle of the page.
2. Save the document with the name **WL2-U1-A3-SalesChart**.
3. Print **WL2-U1-A3-SalesChart.docx**.
4. With the chart selected, display the Excel worksheet and edit the data in the worksheet by changing the following:
   a. Change the amount in cell C2 from *$285,450* to *$302,500*.
   b. Change the amount in cell C4 from *$180,210* to *$190,150*.
5. Save, print, and then close **WL2-U1-A3-SalesChart.docx**.

Figure U1.1 Assessment 3

Salesperson	First Half	Second Half
Bratton	$235,500	$285,450
Daniels	$300,570	$250,700
Hughes	$170,200	$180,210
Marez	$358,520	$376,400

Assessment 4 Create and Format a Pie Chart

1. At a blank document, use the data in Figure U1.2 to create a pie chart with the following specifications:
   a. Apply the *Layout 6* chart layout.
   b. Apply the *Style 26* chart style.
   c. Select the chart title text and then type **District Expenditures**.
   d. Move the legend to the left side of the chart.
   e. Select the chart area, apply *Purple, Accent 4, Lighter 80%* shape fill, and apply the *Purple, 5 pt glow, Accent color 4* glow shape effect.
   f. Select the legend, apply *Purple, Accent 4, Lighter 40%* shape fill, and apply the *Offset Left* shadow shape effect.
   g. Apply the WordArt style *Gradient Fill - Purple, Accent 4, Reflection* to the chart title text.
   h. Select the plot area and then increase the size of the pie so it better fills the chart area. (You may need to move the pie.)
   i. Select the legend and then move it so it is centered between the left edge of the chart border and the pie.
   j. Position the chart centered at the top of the page.
2. Save the document with the name **WL2-U1-A4-ExpendChart**.
3. Print and then close **WL2-U1-A4-ExpendChart.docx**.

Figure U1.2 Assessment 4

	Percentage
Basic Education	42%
Special Needs	20%
Support Services	19%
Vocational	11%
Compensatory	8%

Assessment 5 Navigate in a Smoke Detector Report

1. Open **SmokeDetectors.docx** and then save the document with Save As and name it **WL2-U1-A5-SmokeDetectors**.
2. If necessary, turn on the display of bookmarks. (Do this at the Word Options dialog box with *Advanced* selected in the left panel.)
3. Move the insertion point to the end of the paragraph in the *TYPE OF SMOKE DETECTORS* section, and then insert a bookmark named *Types*.
4. Move the insertion point to the end of the last paragraph in the *SAFETY TIPS* section and then insert a bookmark named *Resources*.
5. Move the insertion point to the end of the first paragraph in the *TAKING CARE OF SMOKE DETECTORS* section and then insert a bookmark named *Maintenance*.
6. Navigate in the document using the bookmarks.
7. Select the text *(NFPA website)* that displays at the end of the first paragraph in the document and then insert a hyperlink to the website www.nfpa.org.

8. Hold down the Ctrl key and then click the *(NFPA website)* hyperlink. At NFPA home page, navigate to web pages that interest you and then close your browser.

9. Move the insertion point to the end of the document and then create a hyperlink with the clip art image to the Word document named **SmokeDetectorFacts.docx**.

10. Click outside the clip art image to deselect it.

11. Hold down the Ctrl key and then click the clip art image. At the **SmokeDetectorFacts.docx** document, read the information, print the document, and then close the document.

12. Save, print, and then close **WL2-U1-A5-SmokeDetectors.docx**.

Assessment 6 Format *Computer Input Devices* Report

1. Open **CompDevices.docx** and then save the document with Save As and name it **WL2-U1-A6-CompDevices**.

2. With the insertion point positioned at the beginning of the document, press Ctrl + Enter to insert a page break.

3. Change the left and right margins to 1.25" (the *Office 2003 Default*).

4. Apply the Title style to the two titles in the document, *COMPUTER INPUT DEVICES* and *COMPUTER OUTPUT DEVICES*.

5. Apply the Heading 1 style to the six headings in the document.

6. Change the style set to *Formal*.

7. Change the theme to Oriel.

8. Change the theme fonts to Paper.

9. Insert a section break that begins a new page at the title *COMPUTER OUTPUT DEVICES*.

10. Create a footer for the first section in the document that prints *Computer Input Devices* at the left margin, the page number in the middle, and your first and last names at the right margin. (Drag the footer center tab marker to 3". on the ruler and drag the right tab marker to 6".)

11. Edit the footer for the second section so it prints *Computer Output Devices* instead of *Computer Input Devices*.

12. Move the insertion point to the beginning of the document, insert a cover page of your choosing, and then insert the appropriate text in the placeholders. (If your cover page requires a document title, type **Computer Devices** and if your cover page requires a document subtitle, type **Computer Input and Output Devices**.)

13. Move the insertion point to the beginning of the second page (blank page) and then insert a table of contents building block. Select and then apply the Title style to the table of contents title.

14. Scroll through the document and check to make sure that headings remain on the page with the following text.

15. Save, print, and then close **WL2-U1-A6-CompDevices.docx**.

Assessment 7 Format *Building a Website* Document

1. Open **BuildWebsite.docx** and then save the document with Save As and name it **WL2-U1-A7-BuildWebsite**.

2. Display the Word Options dialog box with *Proofing* selected in the left panel, insert a check mark in the *Use contextual spelling* check box, change the *Writing Style* option to *Grammar & Style*, and then close the dialog box.

3. Complete a spelling and grammar check on the document. Proofread the document and make any necessary changes not selected by the spelling and grammar checker.

4. Format the document with the following:
   a. Apply title and/or heading styles to the headings in the document. (*Free Web-Hosting Services*, *Free Hosting from ISPs*, and *Fee-Based Hosting Services* are subheadings within the *Choosing a Host* heading.)
   b. Format the text (except the title) into two evenly spaced columns. Balance the text on the second page.
   c. Apply a style set of your choosing.
   d. Change the theme colors and/or fonts.
   e. Insert a header building block of your choosing.
   f. Insert a footer building block of your choosing.
5. Save, print, and then close **WL2-U1-A7-BuildWebsite.docx**.

Assessment 8 Format *Equipment Rental Agreement*

1. At a blank document, create custom theme colors named with your initials that make the following color changes:
   a. Change the Text/Background - Dark 2 color to *Tan, Text 2, Darker 75%*.
   b. Change the Accent 1 color to *Olive Green, Accent 3, Darker 50%*.
2. Create custom theme fonts named with your initials that apply Verdana to headings and Cambria to body text.
3. Save the custom theme and name it with your initials. (Do this with the *Save Current Theme* option at the Themes drop-down gallery.)
4. Close the document without saving the changes.
5. Open **MRCForm.docx** and then save the document with Save As and name it **WL2-U1-A8-MRCForm**.
6. Search for all occurrences of *mrc* and replace with *Meridian Rental Company*.
7. Add the following text to AutoCorrect:
   a. Insert *mrc* in the *Replace* text box and insert *Meridian Rental Company* in the *With* text box.
   b. Insert *erag* in the *Replace* text box and insert *Equipment Rental Agreement* in the *With* text box.
8. Move the insertion point to the blank line above the *Further Assurances* paragraph located on the third page and then type the text shown in Figure U1.3. Use the Numbering feature to number the paragraphs with the lowercase letter followed by the right parenthesis. (If the AutoCorrect feature capitalizes the first word after the letter and right parenthesis, use the AutoCorrect options button to return the letter to lowercase.)
9. Apply the Title style to the title *Equipment Rental Agreement* and apply the Heading 2 style to the headings in the document (*Lease, Rent, Use and Operation of Equipment, Insurance, Risk of Loss, Maintenance, Return of Equipment, Warranties of Lessee, Default,* and *Further Assurances*).
10. Apply your custom theme to the document.
11. Insert a building block that inserts the word *SAMPLE* as a watermark.
12. Insert a footer that prints the page number at the bottom center of each page.
13. Delete the two entries you made at the AutoCorrect dialog box.
14. Save, print, and then close **WL2-U1-A8-MRCForm.docx**.
15. At a blank document, delete the custom theme colors, custom theme fonts, and custom theme named with your initials.

Default

Upon the occurrence of default, mrc may without any further notice exercise any one or more of the following remedies:

a) declare all unpaid Rentals under this erag to be immediately due and payable;

b) terminate this erag as to any or all items of Equipment;

c) take possession of the Equipment, and for this purpose enter upon any premises of Lessee and remove the Equipment, without any liability, suit, action, or other proceeding by Lessee;

d) cause Lessee at its expense to promptly return the Equipment to mrc in the condition set forth in this erag;

e) use, hold, sell, lease, or otherwise dispose of the Equipment or any item of it on the premises of Lessee or any other location without affecting the obligations of Lessee as provided in this erag;

f) proceed by appropriate action either at law or in equity to enforce performance by Lessee of the applicable covenants of this erag or to recover damages for the breach of them; or

g) exercise any other rights accruing to mrc under any applicable law upon a default by a lessee.

Writing Activities ■■■■■■■■■■■■■■

Activity 1 Create Building Blocks and Compose a Letter

You are the executive assistant to the Human Resources Department Director at Clearline Manufacturing. You are responsible for preparing employee documents, notices, reports, and forms. You decide to create building blocks to increase the efficiency of and consistency in department documents. Create the following:

- Create a letterhead for the company that includes the company name and any other enhancements to improve the visual appeal of the letterhead. Save the letterhead text as a building block.
- Create a building block footer that inserts the company address and telephone number (you determine the address and telephone number). Include a visual element to the footer such as a border line or horizontal line.
- You send documents to the Board of Directors and so you decide to include the following names and addresses as building blocks:

Mrs. Nancy Logan
12301 132nd Avenue East
Warminster, PA 18974

Mr. Dion Jarvis
567 Federal Street
Philadelphia, PA 19093

Dr. Austin Svoboda
9823 South 112th Street
Norristown, PA 18974

- Create a complimentary close building block that includes *Sincerely yours,* your name, and the title *Executive Assistant*.

Write the body of a letter to a member of the board of directors and include at least the following information:

- Explain that the human resources department director has created a new employee handbook and that it will be made available to all new employees. Also mention that the attorney for Clearline Manufacturing has reviewed the handbook document.
- Open the **CMHandbook.docx** document and then use the headings to summarize the contents of the document in a paragraph in the letter. Explain in the letter that a draft of the handbook is enclosed with the letter.
- Include any additional information you feel the directors may want to know.

Save the body of the letter as a separate document. Using the building blocks you created along with the letter document, create a letter to Nancy Logan, Dion Jarvis, and Austin Svoboda. Save each letter individually and then print the letters. Delete the building blocks you created.

Activity 2 Create a Custom Theme

Create a custom theme and/or custom styles for formatting documents that includes the colors and/or fonts you chose for the Clearline Manufacturing letterhead. Open the document named **CMHandbook.docx** and then save the document with Save As and name it **WL2-U1-Act2-CMHandbook**. Apply at least the following formatting to the document:

- The footer building block you created as a footer in the document
- Table of contents building block
- Cover page building block
- Draft watermark building block
- Apply formatting to the title, headings, and subheadings in the document
- Any additional formatting that increases the visual appeal and readability of the document

Select the text *(Click to display Longevity Schedule.)* that displays at the end of the first paragraph in the *Longevity Pay* section and then insert a hyperlink to the Excel file named **CMPaySchedule.xlsx** located in the Word2010L2U1 folder on your storage medium. After inserting the hyperlink, click the hyperlink and make sure the Clearline worksheet displays and then exit Excel.

Save, print, and then close **WL2-U1-Act2-CMHandbook.docx**. Delete the custom themes you created.

Internet Research ■■■■■■■■■■■■■■■

Prepare Information on Printer Specifications

You are responsible for purchasing new color laser printers for the human resources department at Clearline Manufacturing. You need to research printers and then prepare a report to the director of the department. Using the Internet, search for at least two companies that produce color laser printers. Determine information such as printer make and model, printer performance, printer cost, and prices for printer cartridges. Using the information you find, prepare a report to the director, Deana Terril, with the information. Type at least one list in the report and then create and apply a customized bullet to the list. Insert a predesigned header or footer and create and apply a custom theme to the report document. Save the report document and name it **WL2-U1-Act3-Printers**. Save, print, and then close **WL2-U1-Act3-Printers.docx**.

Microsoft® Word

Level 2

Unit 2 ■ Editing and Formatting Documents

Inserting Special Features and References

PERFORMANCE OBJECTIVES

Upon successful completion of Chapter 5, you will be able to:

- Sort text in paragraphs, columns, and tables
- Sort records in a data source file
- Select specific records in a data source file for merging
- Insert nonbreaking spaces
- Find and replace special characters
- Create and use a specialized template
- Create footnotes and endnotes
- Insert and modify sources and citations
- Insert, modify, and format bibliographies

SNAP
Training and Assessment
Simplified.

Tutorials

In Word, you can sort text in paragraphs, columns, and tables and sort records in a data source file. You can also select specific records in a data source file for merging with a main document. If you want to control the line break within text, consider inserting nonbreaking spaces and use the find and replace feature to search for special characters in a document such as nonprinting characters. You can use the default template provided by Word or you can create and use your own specialized template. When you prepare research papers and reports, citing information sources properly is important. In this chapter, you will learn to reference documents and acknowledge sources using footnotes, endnotes, citations, and bibliographies. Model answers for this chapter's projects appear on the following pages.

Word2010L2C5

Note: Before beginning the projects, copy to your storage medium the Word2010L2C5 subfolder from the Word2010L2 folder on the CD that accompanies this textbook and then make Word2010L2C5 the active folder.

Kelly Millerton, Chief Executive Officer
Chris Moreau, President
Danielle Roemer, President
Alexander Rohlman, President
Sanford Singleton, Vice President
Calvin Van Camp, Vice President
Amber Wahlstrom, Vice President
Eugene Whitman, Vice President

Employee	Department	Ext.
Millerton, Kelly	Administrative Services	102
Whitman, Eugene	Administrative Services	105
Langstrom, Jodie	Financial Services	421
Robertson, Jake	Financial Services	409
Holland, Bethany	Marketing	318
Iwami, Kelly	Marketing	322

Salesperson	Sales, First Half	Sales, Second Half
Williams, Sylvia	$543,241	$651,438
Monroe, Nina	$623,598	$630,583
Gresham, Esther	$610,312	$593,412
Kaiser, Michael	$453,483	$510,382
Torres, Edward	$431,568	$486,340

Project 1 Sort Company Information

WL2-C5-P1-Sorting.docx

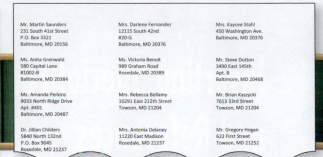

Mr. Martin Saunders
231 South 41st Street
P.O. Box 3321
Baltimore, MD 20156

Mrs. Darlene Fernandez
12115 South 42nd
#20-G
Baltimore, MD 20376

Mrs. Kaycee Stahl
450 Washington Ave.
Baltimore, MD 20376

Ms. Anita Grenwald
580 Capital Lane
#1002-B
Baltimore, MD 20384

Ms. Victoria Benoit
989 Graham Road
Rosedale, MD 20389

Mr. Steve Dutton
3490 East 145th
Apt. B
Baltimore, MD 20468

Ms. Amanda Perkins
9033 North Ridge Drive
Apt. #401
Baltimore, MD 20487

Mrs. Rebecca Bellamy
10291 East 212th Street
Towson, MD 21204

Mr. Brian Kaszycki
7613 33rd Street
Towson, MD 21204

Dr. Jillian Childers
5840 North 132nd
P.O. Box 9045
Rosedale, MD 21237

Mrs. Antonia Delaney
11220 East Madison
Rosedale, MD 21237

Mr. Gregory Hogan
622 First Street
Towson, MD 21252

WL2-C5-P2-Lbls01.docx

Mrs. Antonia Delaney
11220 East Madison
Rosedale, MD 21237

Mr. Gregory Hogan
622 First Street
Towson, MD 21252

Dr. Jillian Childers
5840 North 132nd
P.O. Box 9045
Rosedale, MD 21237

Mrs. Rebecca Bellamy
10291 East 212th Street
Towson, MD 21204

Mr. Brian Kaszycki
7613 33rd Street
Towson, MD 21204

WL2-C5-P2-Lbls02.docx

Mrs. Antonia Delaney
11220 East Madison
Rosedale, MD 21237

Mr. Gregory Hogan
622 First Street
Towson, MD 21252

Dr. Jillian Childers
5840 North 132nd
P.O. Box 9045
Rosedale, MD 21237

Mrs. Rebecca Bellamy
10291 East 212th Street
Towson, MD 21204

Ms. Victoria Benoit
989 Graham Road
Rosedale, MD 20389

Mr. Brian Kaszycki
7613 33rd Street
Towson, MD 21204

Project 2 Sort and Select Records in a Data Source File

WL2-C5-P2-Lbls03.docx

KEYBOARD SHORTCUTS

Microsoft Word includes a number of keyboard shortcuts you can use to access features and commands. The ScreenTip for some buttons displays the keyboard shortcut you can use to access the command. For example, hover the mouse over the Font button and the ScreenTip displays Ctrl + Shift + F as the keyboard shortcut. Additional Home tab Font group keyboard shortcuts include Ctrl + B to bold text, Ctrl + I to italicize text, and Ctrl + U to underline text. You can also press Ctrl + Shift + + to turn on superscript and press Ctrl += to turn on subscript.

Buttons in the Clipboard group include keyboard shortcuts. For example, to cut selected text press Ctrl + X, press Ctrl + C to copy selected text, and use the keyboard shortcut Ctrl + V to insert text. Ctrl + Shift + C is the keyboard command to turn on and off the Format Painter feature.

Project 3 Type a Keyboard Shortcut Document

WL2-C5-P3-Shortcuts.docx

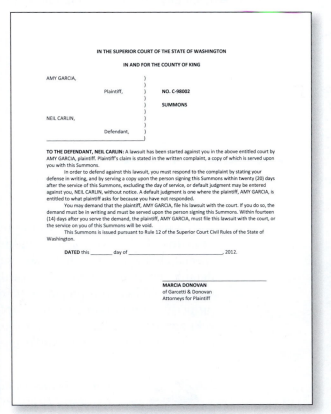

IN THE SUPERIOR COURT OF THE STATE OF WASHINGTON

IN AND FOR THE COUNTY OF KING

AMY GARCIA,   )
)
          Plaintiff,   )   NO. C-98002
)
)   SUMMONS
)
NEIL CARLIN,   )
)
          Defendant,   )
_____)

TO THE DEFENDANT, NEIL CARLIN: A lawsuit has been started against you in the above entitled court by AMY GARCIA, plaintiff. Plaintiff's claim is stated in the written complaint, a copy of which is served upon you with this Summons.

In order to defend against this lawsuit, you must respond to the complaint by stating your defense in writing, and by serving a copy upon the person signing this Summons within twenty (20) days after the service of this Summons, excluding the day of service, or default judgment may be entered against you, NEIL CARLIN, without notice. A default judgment is one where the plaintiff, AMY GARCIA, is entitled to what plaintiff asks for because you have not responded.

You may demand that the plaintiff, AMY GARCIA, file his lawsuit with the court. If you do so, the demand must be in writing and must be served upon the person signing this Summons. Within fourteen (14) days after you serve the demand, the plaintiff, AMY GARCIA, must file this lawsuit with the court, or the service on you of this Summons will be void.

This Summons is issued pursuant to Rule 12 of the Superior Court Civil Rules of the State of Washington.

DATED this _____ day of _____, 2012.

_____
MARCIA DONOVAN
of Garcetti & Donovan
Attorneys for Plaintiff

Project 4 Create and Use a Summons Template

WL2-C5-P4-Summons.docx

NATURAL INTERFACE APPLICATIONS

A major area of artificial intelligence has the goal of creating a more natural interface between human and machine. Currently, computer users are restricted in most instances to using a mouse and keyboard for input. For output, they must gaze at a fairly static, two-dimensional screen. Speakers are used for sound, and a printer for hard copy. The user interface consists of typing, pointing, and clicking. New speech recognition and natural-language technologies promise to change that soon.[1]

Speech Recognition

One of the most immediately applicable improvements comes in the area of speech recognition. Rather than typing information into the computer, users can direct it with voice commands. A computer that can take dictation and perform requested actions is a real step forward in convenience and potential. Speech recognition has developed rather slowly, mainly because the typical PC did not have the necessary speed and capacity until very recently.[2]

Natural-Language Interface

Computers that are able to communicate using spoken English, Japanese, or any of the hundreds of other languages currently in use around the world, would certainly be helpful. In the not-so-distant future, computers will most likely be able to read, write, speak, and understand many human languages. Language translators already exist, and they are getting better all the time.

[1] Novak, Kevin, *Artificial Intelligence*, Home Town Publishing, 2012, pages 45-51.
[2] Everson, Heather and Nicolas Royos, "Integrating Speech Recognition," *Design Technologies*, January/February 2012, pages 24-26.

Page 1

Programmers can look forward to a human-language computer interface. With better interfaces, programmers may be able to describe what they want using natural (human) languages, rather than writing programs in the highly restrictive and rather alien programming languages in use today. Natural-language interfaces are an area of artificial intelligence that is broader in scope than simple speech recognition. The goal is to have a machine that can read a set of news articles on any topic and understand what it has read. Ideally, it could then write its own report summarizing what it has learned.[3]

Virtual Reality

Virtual reality (VR) describes the concept of creating a realistic world within the computer. Online games with thousands of interacting players already exist. In these games people can take on a persona and move about a virtual landscape, adventuring and chatting with other players. The quality of a virtual reality system is typically characterized in terms of its immersiveness, which measures how real the simulated world feels and how well it can make users accept the simulated world as their own and forget about reality. With each passing year, systems are able to provide increasing levels of immersion. Called by some the "ultimate in escapism," VR is becoming increasingly common—and increasingly realistic.[4]

Mental Interface

Although still in the experimental phase, a number of interfaces take things a bit further than VR, and they don't require users to click a mouse, speak a word, or even lift a finger. Mental interfaces use sensors mounted around the skull to read the alpha waves given off by our brains. Thinking of the color blue could be used to move the mouse cursor

[3] Glenovich, James, "Language Interfaces," *Corporate Computing*, November 2011, pages 8-12.
[4] Curtis, William, *Virtual Reality Worlds*, Lilly-Harris Publishers, 2012, pages 53-68.

Page 2

Project 5 Insert Footnotes and Endnotes in Reports

WL2-C5-P5-InterfaceApps.docx

---

to the right, or thinking of the number seven could move it to the left. The computer measures brain activity and interprets it as a command, eliminating the need to physically manipulate a mouse to move the screen cursor. While this technology has obvious applications for assisting people with disabilities, military researchers are also using it to produce a superior form of interface for pilots.[5]

[5] Beal, Marilyn, "Challenges of Artificial Intelligence," *Interface Designs*, April 2012, pages 10-18.

Page 3

FUTURE OF THE INTERNET

The Internet is having trouble keeping up with the rapid increase in users and the increased workload created by the popularity of bandwidth-intensive applications such as music and video files. The broadband connections needed to enjoy these new applications are not evenly distributed. Several ongoing projects promise to provide solutions for these problems in the future. Once these connectivity problems are dealt with, people around the world will be able to enjoy the new web services that are only a few short years away.[1]

Satellite Internet Connections

Many people living in remote or sparsely populated areas are not served by broadband Internet connections. Cable or optical fiber networks are very expensive to install and maintain, and ISPs are not interested in providing service to areas or individuals unless they think it will be profitable. One hope for people without broadband connections is provided by satellite TV networks. Remote ISPs connect to the satellite network using antennae attached to their servers. Data is relayed to and from ISP servers to satellites, which are in turn connected to an Internet backbone access point. While the connection speeds might not be as fast as those offered by regular land-based broadband access, they are faster than the service twisted-pair cable can offer and much better than no access at all.[2]

Second Internet

A remedy for the traffic clogging the information highway is Internet2, a revolutionary new type of Internet currently under development. When fully operational, Internet2 will enable large research universities in the United States to collaborate and share huge amounts of complex scientific information at amazing speeds. Led by over 170 universities working in partnership with industry and government, the Internet2 consortium is developing and deploying advanced network technologies and applications.

Internet2 is a testing ground for universities to work together and develop advanced Internet technologies such as telemedicine, digital libraries, and virtual laboratories. Internet2 universities will be connected to an ultrahigh-speed network called the Abilene backbone. Each university will use state-of-the-art equipment to take advantage of transfer speeds provided by the network.

Internet Services for a Fee

Industry observers predict that large portals such as AOL, MSN, and Yahoo! will soon determine effective structures and marketing strategies to get consumers to pay for Internet services. This new market, called bring-your-own-access (BYOA), will combine essential *content*, for example, news and weather, with *services*, such as search, directory, email, IM, and online

[1] Abrahamson, Joshua, *Future Trends in Computing*, Gleason-Rutherford Publishing, 2012, pages 5-9.
[2] Clements, Aileen, *Satellite Systems*, Robison Publishing House, 2012, pages 23-51.

Page 1

WL2-C5-P5-InternetFuture.docx

shopping, into a new product with monthly access charges. But to entice current and potential customers into the BYOA market, ISP and telecom companies must offer improvements in the areas of security, privacy, and ease of use. Additionally, they are expected to develop new ways to personalize content and add value to the current range of Internet services.[3]

Internet in 2030

Ray Kurzweil, a computer futurist, has looked ahead to the year 2030 and visualized a Web that offers no clear distinctions between real and simulated environments and people. Among the applications he sees as very possible are computerized displays in eyeglasses that could offer simultaneous translations of foreign language conversations, nanobots (microscopic robots) that would work with our brains to extend our mental capabilities, and sophisticated avatars (simulated on-screen persons) that people will interact with online. Technologies that allow people to project their feelings as well as their images and voices may usher in a period when people could "be" with another person even though they are physically hundreds or even thousands of miles apart.

---
[3] Campbell, Jolene, "Fee-Based Internet Services," *Connections*, March/April 2012, pages 5-8.

Page 2

Last Name 1

Student Name

Instructor Name

Course Title

Current Date

Mobile Security

Computing is no longer just a sit-at-your-desk type of activity—it is mobile. Mobile is convenient, but it also brings its own security risks. Various settings and tools can help you keep your portable devices and the information stored on it safer (Suong).

When you bring your computer with you, you are carrying a big investment in both dollars and data, so protecting it from theft and damage is important. Corporations are struggling with protecting information technology assets as their workforces begin to carry smaller devices, which are prone to being left behind by mistake or stolen. Protecting mobile devices is important and several devices and procedures exist to physically secure a laptop computer.

Laptops have a cable device you can use to tie them to an airport chair or desk in a field office to deter potential thieves from stealing them. The determined thief with enough time can cut the cable and get away with the laptop, so it is only a slight deterrent. If you want stronger protection, consider a service that allows you to remotely delete data if your computer is stolen and uses GPS to track your laptop (Jackson).

Many newer laptops include fingerprint readers. Because fingerprints are unique to each individual, being able to authenticate yourself with your own set of prints to gain access to your computer is a popular security feature. If somebody without a fingerprint

Page 1

Project 6 Cite References in a Mobile Security Report

WL2-C5-P6-MobileSecurity.docx

Last Name 2

match tries to get into the computer data, the system locks up. If you travel with a laptop, activating password protection and creating a secure password is a good idea.

Stopping thieves is one concern when you are on the road, but stopping employees from making costly mistakes regarding company data is another area where companies must take precautions. Making sure that employees who take company laptops outside of the office are responsible for safe and secure storage offsite is vital to company security (Nakamura). Policies might require them to keep backups of data on physical storage media or to backup data to a company network.

If you travel and access the Internet using a public location, you have to be very careful not to expose private information (Jackson). Anything you send over a public network can be accessed by malicious hackers and cybercriminals. Limit your use of online accounts to times when it is essential. "Be especially on guard when accessing your bank accounts, investment accounts, and retail accounts that store your credit card for purchases, and avoid entering your social security number" (Miraldi 19).

Page 2

Last Name 3

Works Cited

Jackson, Gabriel. "Securing Laptops and Mobile Devices." Future Computing Technologies (2012): 8-10.

Miraldi, Georgia. Evolving Technology. Houston: Rio Grande Publishing, 2012.

Nakamura, Janet. "Computer Security." Currect Technology Times 6 (2011): 20-28.

Suong, Chay. Securing and Managing Mobile Devices. 20 April 2012. 04 08 2012 <www.emcp.net/publishing>.

Page 3

<table><tr><td></td></tr></table>

Project **1** **Sort Company Information** **2 Parts**

You will open a document containing information on company employees and then sort data in paragraphs, columns, and tables. You will also create a document and insert nonbreaking spaces within keyboard shortcuts.

Sorting Text in Paragraphs ■■■■■■■■■■■■■■■■■■

You can sort paragraphs of text in a document alphanumerically, numerically, or by date. For example, you might want to sort a list of company employees to create an internal telephone directory or to create a list for a company-wide mailing. Other situations in which sorting a Word document is an effective problem-solving method are times when you need to organize a list of customers by ZIP Code or by product purchased (product number).

In an alphanumeric sort, punctuation marks or special symbols are sorted first, followed by numbers, and then text. If you sort paragraphs either alphanumerically or numerically, dates are treated as regular text. Also be aware that during a paragraph sort, any blank lines in a document are moved to the beginning of the document.

To sort text, select the text and then click the Sort button in the Paragraph group in the Home tab. This displays the Sort Text dialog box containing sorting options. The *Sort by* option has a default setting of *Paragraphs*. This default setting changes depending on the text in the document. For example, if you are sorting a table, the *Sort by* option has a default setting of *Column 1*. The *Sort by* options will also vary depending on selections at the Sort Options dialog box shown in Figure 5.1. To display this dialog box, click the Options button in the Sort Text dialog box. At the Sort Options dialog box, specify how fields are separated.

Quick Steps

Sort Text in Paragraph
1. Click Sort button.
2. Make any needed changes at the Sort Text dialog box.
3. Click OK.

Display Sort Options Dialog Box
1. Click Sort button.
2. Click Options button.

Sort

Figure 5.1 Sort Options Dialog Box

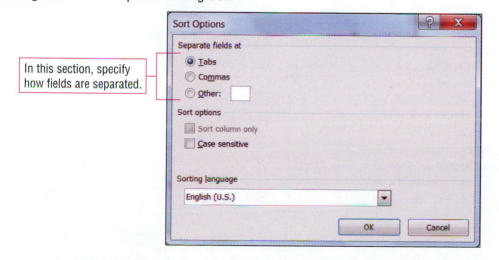

In this section, specify how fields are separated.

Sort Text in Columns
1. Select specific text.
2. Click Sort button.
3. Click Options button.
4. Specify *Tabs* as separator.
5. Click OK.
6. Make any needed changes at Sort Text dialog box.
7. Click OK.

Sorting Text in Columns

To sort text set in columns, the text must be separated with tabs. When sorting text in columns, Word considers the left margin *Field 1*, text typed at the first tab is considered *Field 2*, and so on. When sorting text in columns, make sure columns of text are separated by only one tab. If you press the Tab key more than once between columns, Word recognizes each tab as a separate column. Thus pressing the Tab key more than once may result in a field number that corresponds to an empty column rather than the desired column.

Sorting on More Than One Field

HINT

When sorting on two fields, Word sorts on the first field and then sorts the second field within the first.

When sorting text, you can sort on more than one field. For example, in Project 1a, Step 6, you will sort the department entries alphabetically and then sort the employee names alphabetically within the departments. To do this, you specify the department column in the *Sort by* option and then specify the employee column in the *Then by* option. If a document contains columns with heading text, click the *Header row* option in the *My list has* section.

Project 1a **Sorting Text** Part 1 of 2

1. Open **Sorting.docx** and then save the document with Save As and name it **WL2-C5-P1-Sorting**.
2. Sort the text alphabetically by first name by completing the following steps:
   a. Select the eight lines of text at the beginning of the document.
   b. Click the Sort button in the Paragraph group in the Home tab.
   c. At the Sort Text dialog box, click OK.
3. Sort the text by last name by completing the following steps:
   a. With the eight lines of text still selected, click the Sort button.
   b. At the Sort Text dialog box, click the Options button.
   c. At the Sort Options dialog box, click *Other* and then press the spacebar. (This indicates that the first and last names are separated by a space.)
   d. Click OK.
   e. At the Sort Text dialog box, click the down-pointing arrow at the right side of the *Sort by* option and then click *Word 2* at the drop-down list.
   f. Click OK.

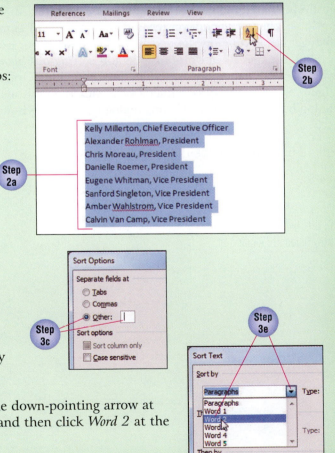

4. Sort text in columns by completing the
   following steps:
   a. Select the seven lines of text set in
      columns.
   b. Click the Sort button in the
      Paragraph group in the Home tab.
   c. Click the Options button.
   d. At the Sort Options dialog box,
      make sure the *Separate fields at*
      option is set at *Tabs* and then click
      OK to close the dialog box.
   e. At the Sort Text dialog box, make
      sure *Employee* is selected in the *Sort by*
      option box.
   f. Click OK.
5. With the columns of text still selected, sort the third column of text numerically by
   completing the following steps:
   a. Click the Sort button.
   b. Click the down-pointing arrow at the right side of the *Sort by* option and then click *Ext.*
      at the drop-down list.
   c. Click OK.
6. Sort two columns by completing the following steps:
   a. Make sure the seven lines of text set in
      columns are still selected.
   b. Click the Sort button.
   c. At the Sort Text dialog box, if
      necessary, click the *Header
      row* option in the *My list has*
      section of the dialog box.
   d. Click the down-pointing
      arrow at the right side of the
      Sort by option and then click
      Department.
   e. Click the down-pointing arrow at
      the right side of the *Then by*
      option and then click *Employee*
      at the drop-down list.
   f. Click OK.
7. Save **WL2-C5-P1-Sorting.docx**.

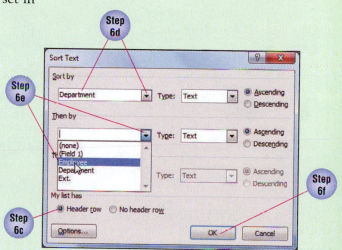

Sorting Text in Tables

Sorting text in columns within tables is similar to sorting columns of text separated
by tabs. If a table contains a header, you can tell Word not to include the header
row when sorting by clicking the *Header row* option at the Sort dialog box. The Sort
Text dialog box becomes the Sort dialog box when sorting a table. If you want to
sort only specific cells in a table, select the cells and then complete the sort.

▼ **Quick Steps**

Sort Text in Table
1. Position insertion
   point in table.
2. Click Sort button.
3. Make any needed
   changes at Sort dialog
   box.
4. Click OK.

1. With **WL2-C5-P1-Sorting.docx** open, sort text in the first column in the table by completing the following steps:
   a. Position the insertion point in any cell in the table.
   b. Click the Sort button.
   c. At the Sort dialog box, make sure the *Header row* option is selected in the *My list has* section.
   d. Click the down-pointing arrow at the right side of the *Sort by* option and then click *Sales, First Half* at the drop-down list.
   e. Click OK.
2. Sort the numbers in the third column in descending order by completing the following steps:
   a. Select all of the cells in the table except the cells in the first row.
   b. Click the Sort button.
   c. Click the down-pointing arrow at the right side of the *Sort by* option and then click *Column 3* at the drop-down list.
   d. Click *Descending*.
   e. Click OK.
3. Save, print, and then close **WL2-C5-P1-Sorting.docx**.

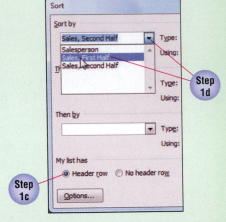

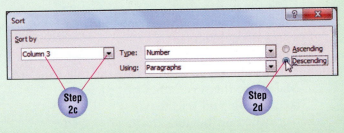

P**roject** **2**   **Sort and Select Records in a Data Source File**   **3 Parts**

You will sort data in a data source file and then create labels and select specific records in a data source file and then create labels.

Sorting Records in a Data Source ■■■■■■ ■■■ ■■■■

When you are working on a project that requires sorting data and merging documents, consider the order in which you want your merged documents printed and then sort the data before merging. To sort records in a data source, click the Mailings tab, click the Select Recipients button, and then click *Use Existing List*. At the Select Data Source dialog box, navigate to the folder containing the data source file and then double-click the file. Click the Edit Recipient List button in the Start Mail Merge group in the Mailings tab and the Mail Merge Recipients dialog box displays similar to the one shown in Figure 5.2.

Click the column heading to sort data in a specific column in ascending order. To perform additional sorts, click the down-pointing arrow at the right side of the column heading and then click the desired sort order. You can also click the *Sort* hyperlink located in the *Refine recipient list* section of the Mail Merge Recipients dialog box. Clicking this hyperlink displays the Filter and Sort dialog box with the Sort Records tab selected as shown in Figure 5.3. The options at the dialog box are similar to the options available at the Sort Text (and Sort) dialog box.

Figure 5.2 Mail Merge Recipients Dialog Box

To sort on a specific field, click the column heading.

Click this hyperlink to display the Filter and Sort dialog box.

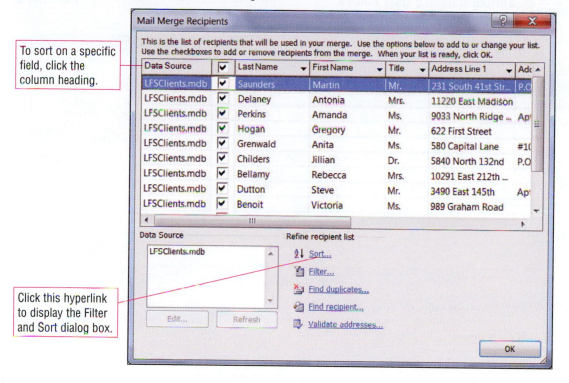

Figure 5.3 Filter and Sort Dialog Box with Sort Records Tab Selected

Use options at this dialog box to specify sort options.

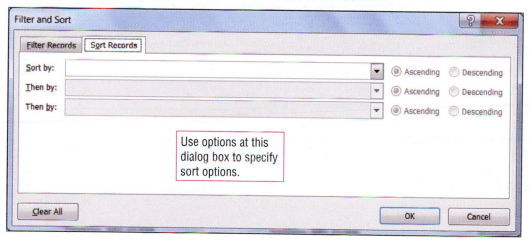

Select Recipients

Edit Recipient List

1. At a blank document, click the Mailings tab, click the Start Mail Merge button in the Start Mail Merge group, and then click *Labels* at the drop-down list.
2. At the Label Options dialog box, click the down-pointing arrow at the right side of the *Label vendors* option and then click *Avery US Letter* at the drop-down list. Scroll down the *Product number* list box, click *5160 Easy Peel Address Labels*, and then click OK.

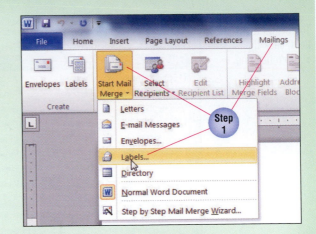

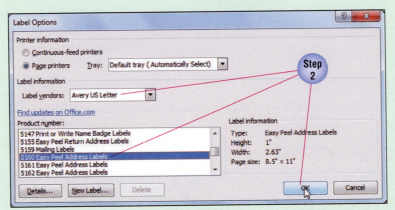

3. Click the Select Recipients button in the Start Mail Merge group and then click *Use Existing List* at the drop-down list.
4. At the Select Data Source dialog box, navigate to the Word2010L2C5 folder on your storage medium and then double-click the data source file named **LFSClients.mdb**.
5. Click the Edit Recipient List button in the Start Mail Merge group in the Mailings tab.
6. At the Mail Merge Recipients dialog box, click the *Last Name* column heading. (This sorts the last names in ascending alphabetical order.)
7. Scroll to the right to display the *City* field and then click the *City* column heading.
8. Sort records by ZIP Codes and then by last name by completing the following steps:
   a. Click the Sort hyperlink located in the *Refine recipient list* section of the Mail Merge Recipients dialog box.
   b. At the Filter and Sort dialog box with the Sort Records tab selected, click the down-pointing arrow at the right side of the *Sort by* option box and then click *ZIP Code* at the drop-down list. (You will need to scroll down the list to display the *ZIP Code* field.)
   c. Make sure *Last Name* displays in the *Then by* option box.

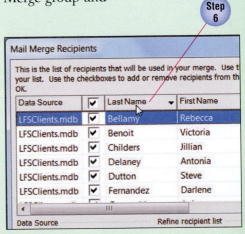

d. Click OK to close the Filter and Sort dialog box.

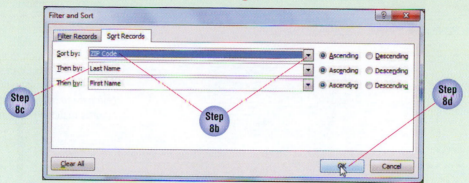

e. Click OK to close the Mail Merge Recipients dialog box.
9. At the labels document, click the Address Block button in the Write & Insert Fields group.
10. At the Insert Address Block dialog box, click the OK button.
11. Click the Update Labels button in the Write & Insert Fields group.
12. Click the Finish & Merge button in the Finish group and then click *Edit Individual Documents* at the drop-down list.
13. At the Merge to New Document dialog box, make sure *All* is selected, and then click OK. (If the labels display with 1.15 line spacing and 10 points of spacing after paragraphs, press Ctrl + A to select the entire document and then click the No Spacing style in the Styles group in the Home tab.)

14. Save the merged labels and name the document **WL2-C5-P2-Lbls01**.
15. Print and then close **WL2-C5-P2-Lbls01.docx**.
16. Close the main labels document without saving it.

Selecting Records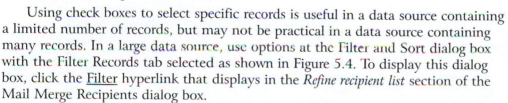

If you have a data source file with numerous records, situations may arise where you want to merge the main document with only specific records in the data source. For example, you may want to send a letter to customers with a specific ZIP code or who live in a particular city. One method for selecting specific records is to display the Mail Merge Recipients dialog box and then insert or remove check marks from specific records.

Using check boxes to select specific records is useful in a data source containing a limited number of records, but may not be practical in a data source containing many records. In a large data source, use options at the Filter and Sort dialog box with the Filter Records tab selected as shown in Figure 5.4. To display this dialog box, click the Filter hyperlink that displays in the *Refine recipient list* section of the Mail Merge Recipients dialog box.

When you select a field from the *Field* drop-down list, Word automatically insets *Equal to* in the *Comparison* option box. You can make other comparisons. Clicking the down-pointing arrow to the right of the *Comparison* option box causes a drop-down list to display with these additional options: *Not equal to, Less than, Greater than, Less than or equal, Greater than or equal, Is blank,* and *Is not blank.* Use one of these options to create a select equation.

HINT
Including or excluding certain records from the merge is referred to as *filtering.*

Figure 5.4 Filter and Sort Dialog Box with Filter Records Tab Selected

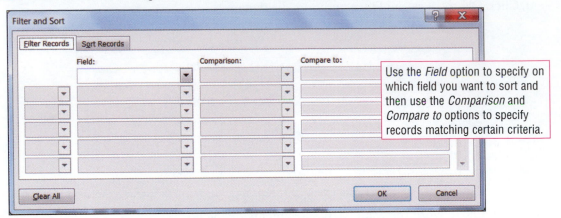

Use the *Field* option to specify on which field you want to sort and then use the *Comparison* and *Compare to* options to specify records matching certain criteria.

Project 2b Selecting Records

Part 2 of 3

1. At a blank document, click the Mailings tab, click the Start Mail Merge button in the Start Mail Merge group, and then click *Labels* at the drop-down list.
2. At the Label Options dialog box, make sure *Avery US Letter* displays in the *Label vendors* option box and *5160 Easy Peel Address Labels* displays in the *Product number* list box and then click OK.
3. Click the Select Recipients button in the Start Mail Merge group and then click *Use Existing List* at the drop-down list.
4. At the Select Data Source dialog box, navigate to the Word2010L2C5 folder on your storage medium and then double-click the data source file named **LFSClients.mdb**.
5. Click the Edit Recipient List button.
6. At the Mail Merge Recipients dialog box, click the <u>Filter</u> hyperlink in the *Refine recipient list* section of the dialog box.
7. At the Filter and Sort dialog box with the Filter Records tab selected, click the down-pointing arrow at the right side of the *Field* option and then click *ZIP Code* at the drop-down list. (You will need to scroll down the list to display *ZIP Code*. When *ZIP Code* is inserted in the *Field* option box, *Equal to* is inserted in the *Comparison* option box and the insertion point is positioned in the *Compare to* text box.)
8. Type 21000 in the *Compare to* text box.
9. Click the down-pointing arrow at the right side of the *Comparison* option box and then click *Greater than* at the drop-down list.

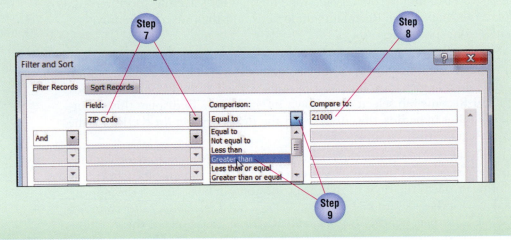

10. Click OK to close the Filter and Sort dialog box.
11. Click OK to close the Mail Merge Recipients dialog box.
12. At the labels document, click the Address Block button in the Write & Insert Fields group and then click OK at the Insert Address Block dialog box.
13. Click the Update Labels button in the Write & Insert Fields group.
14. Click the Finish & Merge button in the Finish group and then click *Edit Individual Documents* at the drop-down list.
15. At the Merge to New Document dialog box, make sure *All* is selected, and then click OK. (If the labels display with 1.15 line spacing and 10 points of spacing after paragraphs, press Ctrl + A to select the entire document and then click the No Spacing style in the Styles group in the Home tab.)
16. Save the merged labels and name the document **WL2-C5-P2-Lbls02**.
17. Print and then close **WL2-C5-P2-Lbls02.docx**.
18. Close the main labels document without saving it.

When a field is selected from the *Field* option box, Word automatically inserts *And* in the first box at the left side of the dialog box. You can change this, if needed, to *Or*. With the *And* and *Or* options, you can specify more than one condition for selecting records. For example, in Project 2c, you will select all records of clients living in the cities of Rosedale or Towson. If the data source file contained another field such as a specific financial plan for each customer, you could select all customers in a specific city that subscribe to a specific financial plan. For this situation, you would use the *And* option.

If you want to clear the current options at the Filter and Sort dialog box with the Filter Records tab selected, click the Clear All button. This clears any text from text boxes and leaves the dialog box on the screen. Click the Cancel button if you want to close the Filter and Sort dialog box without specifying any records.

Project 2c **Selecting Records with Specific Cities** **Part 3 of 3**

1. At a blank document, click the Mailings tab, click the Start Mail Merge button in the Start Mail Merge group, and then click *Labels* at the drop-down list.
2. At the Label Options dialog box, make sure *Avery US Letter* displays in the *Label vendors* option box and *5160 Easy Peel Address Labels* displays in the *Product number* list box and then click OK.
3. Click the Select Recipients button in the Start Mail Merge group and then click *Use Existing List* at the drop-down list.
4. At the Select Data Source dialog box, navigate to the Word2010L2C5 folder on your storage medium and then double-click the data source file named *LFSClients.mdb*.
5. Click the Edit Recipient List button.
6. At the Mail Merge Recipients dialog box, click the Filter hyperlink in the *Refine recipient list* section of the dialog box.
7. At the Filter and Sort dialog box with the Filter Records tab selected, click the down-pointing arrow at the right side of the *Field* option and then click *City* at the drop-down list. (You will need to scroll down the list to display this field.)
8. Type Rosedale in the *Compare to* text box.

9. Click the down-pointing arrow to the right of the option box containing the word *And* (at the left side of the dialog box) and then click *Or* at the drop-down list.

10. Click the down-pointing arrow at the right side of the second *Field* option box, and then click *City* at the drop-down list. (You will need to scroll down the list to display this field.)

11. With the insertion point positioned in the second *Compare to* text box (the one below the box containing *Rosedale*), type **Towson**.

12. Click OK to close the Filter and Sort dialog box.

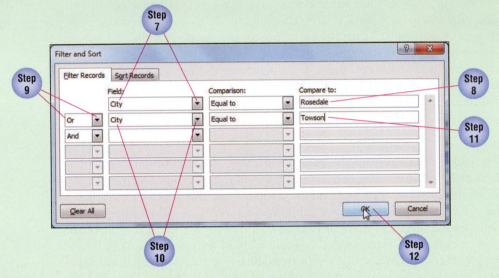

13. Click OK to close the Mail Merge Recipients dialog box.

14. At the labels document, click the Address Block button in the Write & Insert Fields group and then click OK at the Insert Address Block dialog box.

15. Click the Update Labels button in the Write & Insert Fields group.

16. Click the Finish & Merge button in the Finish group and then click *Edit Individual Documents* at the drop-down list.

17. At the Merge to New Document dialog box, make sure *All* is selected and then click OK. (If the labels display with 1.15 line spacing and 10 points of spacing after paragraphs, press Ctrl + A to select the entire document and then click the No Spacing style in the Styles group in the Home tab.)

18. Save the merged labels and name the document **WL2-C5-P2-Lbls03**.

19. Print and then close **WL2-C5-P2-Lbls03.docx**.

20. Close the main labels document without saving it.

Project 3 Type a Keyboard Shortcut Document   2 Parts

You will type a document with information on keyboard shortcuts and use nonbreaking spaces within the shortcuts to keep them from being split between two lines of text. You will then use the find and replace feature to search for all nonbreaking spaces and replace them with regular spaces.

Inserting a Nonbreaking Space ■■■■■■■■■■■■■

As you type text in a document, Word makes line-end decisions and automatically wraps text to the next line. In some situations, word wrap may break up words or phrases on separates lines that should remain together. To control where text is wrapped to the next line, consider inserting a *nonbreaking space* between words. Press Ctrl + Shift + spacebar to insert a nonbreaking space. With the display of nonprinting characters turned on, a normal space displays as a dot and a nonbreaking space displays as a degree symbol.

HINT

You can insert a nonbreaking space at the Symbol dialog box with the (normal text) font selected.

Project 3a	Inserting Nonbreaking Spaces	Part 1 of 2

1. At a blank document, turn on the display of nonprinting characters by clicking the Show/Hide ¶ button in the Paragraph group in the Home tab.
2. Type the text shown in Figure 5.5 and insert nonbreaking spaces in keyboard shortcuts by pressing Ctrl + Shift + spacebar before and after the plus symbol in the keyboard shortcuts.
3. Turn off the display of nonprinting characters.
4. Save the document and name it **WL2-C5-P3-Shortcuts**.

Figure 5.5 Project 3a

KEYBOARD SHORTCUTS

Microsoft Word includes a number of keyboard shortcuts you can use to access features and commands. The ScreenTip for some buttons displays the keyboard shortcut you can use to access the command. For example, hover the mouse over the Font button and the ScreenTip displays Ctrl + Shift + F as the keyboard shortcut. Additional Home tab Font group keyboard shortcuts include Ctrl + B to bold text, Ctrl + I to italicize text, and Ctrl + U to underline text. You can also press Ctrl + Shift + + to turn on superscript and press Ctrl + = to turn on subscript.

Buttons in the Clipboard group include keyboard shortcuts. For example, to cut selected text press Ctrl + X, press Ctrl + C to copy selected text, and use the keyboard shortcut Ctrl + V to insert text. Ctrl + Shift + C is the keyboard command to turn on and off the Format Painter feature.

Finding and Replacing Special Characters ■■■■■■■■

You can use the find feature to find special text and the find and replace feature to find specific text and replace with other text. You can also use these features to find special formatting, characters, or nonprinting elements in a document. To display a list of special characters and nonprinting elements, display the Find and Replace dialog box with either the Find or Replace tab selected, expand the dialog box, and then click the Special button. This displays a pop-up list similar to the one shown in Figure 5.6.

▼ **Quick Steps**

Find and Replace Special Character
1. Click Replace button.
2. Click More button.
3. Click Special button.
4. Click desired character.
5. Click in *Replace with* text box.
6. Click Special button.
7. Click desired character.
8. Click Replace All.

Figure 5.6 Special Button Pop-up List

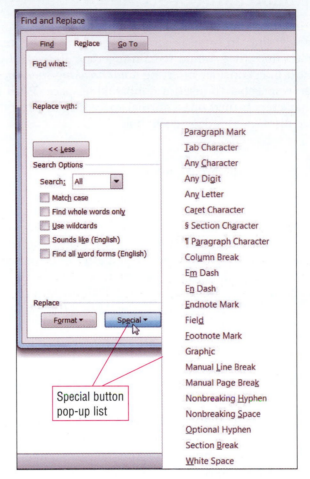

Press Ctrl + H to display the Find and Replace dialog box with the Replace tab selected.

If you are not sure about the name of the special character you want to find or if the names of the special characters in the Special button pop-up list are unclear, you can access Word's list of special characters to see the characters and their names. Click the Symbol button in the Symbols group in the Insert tab and a short list of symbols displays. Click the More Symbols option at the drop-down list and the Symbol dialog box displays. Click the Special Characters tab to see a list of characters and their names. For example, many users may not know the difference between an em dash (—) and an en dash (–). The Special Characters listing shows each type of dash.

Project 3b Finding and Replacing Nonbreaking Spaces   Part 2 of 2

1. With **WL2-C5-P3-Shortcuts.docx** open, find all occurrences of nonbreaking spaces and replace with regular spaces by completing the following steps:
   a. Click the Replace button in the Editing group in the Home tab.
   b. At the Find and Replace dialog box with the Replace tab selected, click the More button.
   c. With the insertion point positioned in the *Find what* text box, click the Special button that displays toward the bottom of the dialog box.

d. At the pop-up list that displays, click *Nonbreaking Space*. (This inserts ^s in the *Find what* text box.)

e. Click in the *Replace with* text box (make sure the text box does not contain any text) and then press the spacebar once. (This tells the Find and Replace feature to find a nonbreaking space and replace it with a regular space.)

f. Click the Replace All button.

g. At the message telling you that Word completed the search and made the replacements, click OK.

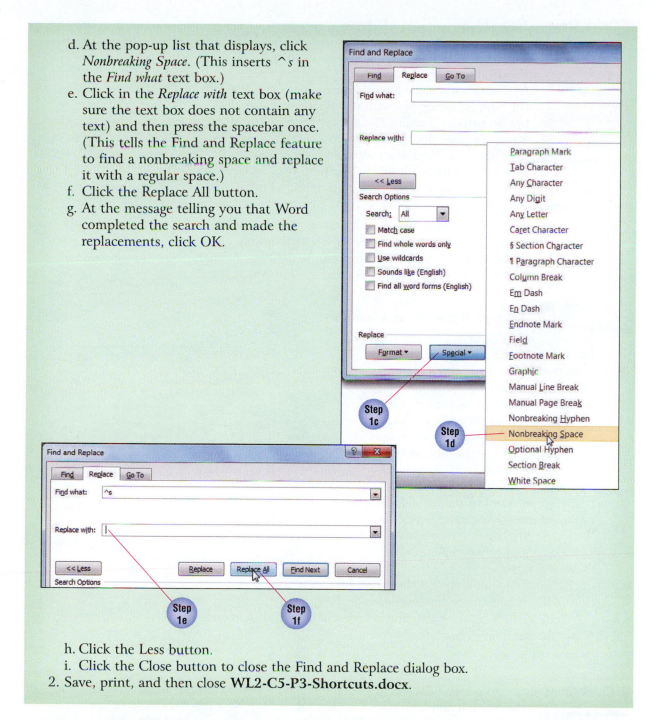

h. Click the Less button.

i. Click the Close button to close the Find and Replace dialog box.

2. Save, print, and then close **WL2-C5-P3-Shortcuts.docx**.

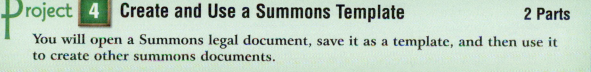

Project **4** **Create and Use a Summons Template**   **2 Parts**

You will open a Summons legal document, save it as a template, and then use it to create other summons documents.

▼ **Quick Steps**

Create a Template
1. Open desired document.
2. Click File tab, Save As button.
3. Click *Templates* in Navigation pane.
4. Change *Save as type* to *Word Template (*.dotx)*.
5. Type template name in *File name* text box.
6. Click Save.

Creating a Template ■■■■■■■■■■■■■■■■■■■■■■■■

If you use the contents of a document to create other documents, consider saving the document as a template. To save a document as a template, display the Save As dialog box. At the Save As dialog box, click *Templates* in the Navigation pane. At the Save As dialog box with the Templates folder selected, change the *Save as type* option to *Word Template (*.dotx)*, type a name for the template, and then press Enter. Word template documents are saved with the *.dotx* file extension. You can also save a template as a Word Macro-Enabled Template with the file extension *.dotm*. You can save a template to a folder other than the *Templates* folder. To do this, display the Save As dialog box, navigate to the desired folder, change the *Save as type* option to *Word Template (*.dotx)*, and then type a name for the template.

Another method for saving a template is to display the Save & Send tab Backstage view, click the *Change File Type* option, click the *Template (*.dotx)* option, and then click the Save As button. At the Save As dialog box, type a name for your template and then click the Save button.

Project 4a   **Saving a Document as a Template**   **Part 1 of 2**

1. Open **Summons.docx**.
2. Save the document as a template in the Templates folder by completing the following steps:
   a. Click the File tab and then click Save As.
   b. At the Save As dialog box, click *Templates* in the Navigation pane.
   c. Click the *Save as type* option box and then click *Word Template (*.dotx)*.
   d. Select the name in the *File name* text box and then type your last name followed by *Summons*.
   e. Press Enter or click the Save button.
3. Save the template document on your storage medium by completing the following steps:
   a. Click the File tab and then click Save As.
   b. At the Save As dialog box, navigate to the Word2010L2C5 folder on your storage medium and then click the Save button.
4. Close the summons template.

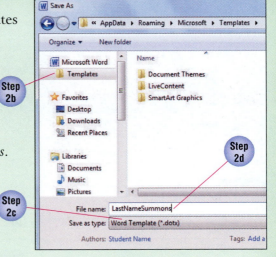

Step 2b

Step 2d

Step 2c

▼ **Quick Steps**

Creating a Document with a Template
1. Click File tab, click New tab.
2. Click *My templates* or *New from existing*.
3. Double-click template.

To create a document with a template you saved to the *Templates* folder, click the File tab and then click the New tab. At the New tab Backstage view, click the *My templates* option in the Available Templates category. At the New dialog box similar to the one shown in Figure 5.7, click the desired template in the list box and then click OK. To create a document with a template from a folder on your storage medium, display the New tab Backstage view and then click the *New from existing* option in the Available Templates category. At the New from Existing Document dialog box, navigate to the desired folder, and then double-click the template.

Figure 5.7 New Dialog Box

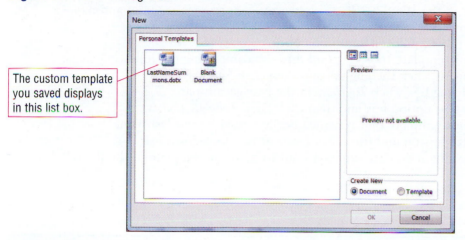

The custom template you saved displays in this list box.

Project 4b Creating a Document Based on a Template

Part 2 of 2

1. Open the summons template as a document by completing the following steps:
   a. Click the File tab and then click the New tab.
   b. At the New tab Backstage view, click the *My templates* option in the Available Templates category.

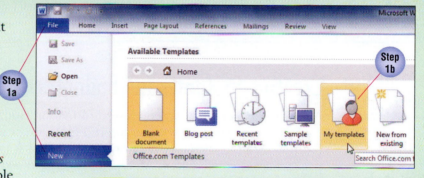

   c. At the New dialog box, click the summons template that is preceded by your last name.
   d. Click OK.
2. Close the summons document.
3. Open the summons template as a document from the folder on your storage medium by completing the following steps:
   a. Click the File tab and then click the New tab.

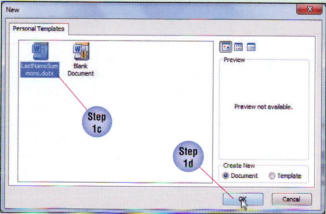

   b. At the New tab Backstage view, click the *New from existing* option in the Available Templates category.
   c. At the New from Existing Document dialog box, navigate to the Word2010L2C5 folder on your storage medium and then double-click the summons template preceded by your last name.
4. With the summons document open, make the following find and replaces:
   a. Find *NAME1* and replace with *AMY GARCIA*.
   b. Find *NAME2* and replace with *NEIL CARLIN*.
   c. Find *NUMBER* and replace with *C-98002*.

5. Save the document in the Word2010L2C5 folder on your storage medium and name it **WL2-C5-P4-Summons**.
6. Print and then close **WL2-C5-P4-Summons.docx**.
7. Delete the summons template from the hard drive by completing the following steps:
    a. At a blank document, click the File tab and then click *Save As*.
    b. At the Save As dialog box, click *Templates* in the Navigation pane.
    c. Click the *Save as type* option box and then click *Word Template (*.dotx)*.
    d. Click the summons template that is named beginning with your last name.
    e. Click the Organize button and then click *Delete* at the drop-down list.
    f. At the message asking if you are sure you want to send the template to the Recycle Bin, click Yes.
8. Close the Save As dialog box.

Project 5 Insert Footnotes and Endnotes in Reports   3 Parts

You will open a report on artificial intelligence and then insert, format, and modify footers. You will also open a report on the future of the Internet and then insert endnotes.

▼ **Quick Steps**

Insert Footnote
1. Click References tab.
2. Click Insert Footnote button.
3. Type footnote text.

Insert Endnote
1. Click References tab.
2. Click Insert Endnote button.
3. Type endnote text.

Insert Footnote

Insert Endnote

Creating Footnotes and Endnotes ■■■■■■■■■■■■■

A research paper or report contains information from a variety of sources. To give credit to those sources, you can insert a footnote or endnote in a document. A footnote is an explanatory note or reference that is printed at the bottom of the page where it is referenced. An endnote is also an explanatory note or reference, but it prints at the end of the document.

Two steps are involved in creating a footnote or endnote. First, the note reference number is inserted in the document at the location where the note is referenced. The second step is to type the note entry text. Footnotes and endnotes are created in a similar manner. To create a footnote, position the insertion point at the location where the reference number is to appear, click the References tab, and then click the Insert Footnote button in the Footnotes group. This inserts a number in the document and also inserts a separator line at the bottom of the page with a superscript number below. With the insertion point positioned immediately right of the superscript number, type the footnote entry text. Word automatically numbers footnotes with superscript Arabic numbers and endnotes with superscript lowercase Roman numerals.

Project 5a Creating Footnotes   Part 1 of 3

1. Open **InterfaceApps.docx** and then save the document with Save As and name it **WL2-C5-P5-InterfaceApps**.
2. Create the first footnote shown in Figure 5.8 by completing the following steps:
    a. Position the insertion point at the end of the first paragraph of text in the document.

---

b. Click the References tab.

c. Click the Insert Footnote button in the Footnotes group.

d. With the insertion point positioned at the bottom of the page immediately following the superscript number, type the first footnote shown in Figure 5.8.

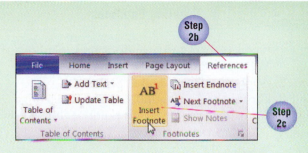

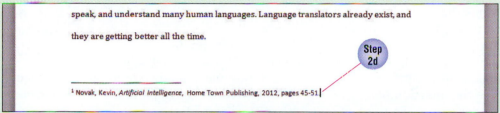

3. Move the insertion point to the end of the paragraph in the *Speech Recognition* section and, using steps similar to Steps 2b through 2d, create the second footnote shown in Figure 5.8.

4. Move the insertion point to the end of the second paragraph in the *Natural-Language Interface* section and then create the third footnote shown in Figure 5.8.

5. Move the insertion point to the end of the paragraph in the *Virtual Reality* section and then create the fourth footnote shown in Figure 5.8.

6. Move the insertion point to the end of the last paragraph in the document and then create the fifth footnote shown in Figure 5.8.

7. Save, print, and then close **WL2-C5-P5-InterfaceApps.docx**.

Figure 5.8 Project 5a

Novak, Kevin, *Artificial Intelligence*, Home Town Publishing, 2012, pages 45-51.

Everson, Heather and Nicolas Reyes, "Integrating Speech Recognition," *Design Technologies*, January/February 2012, pages 24-26.

Glenovich, James, "Language Interfaces," *Corporate Computing*, November 2011, pages 8-12.

Curtis, William, *Virtual Reality Worlds*, Lilly-Harris Publishers, 2012, pages 53-68.

Beal, Marilyn, "Challenges of Artificial Intelligence," *Interface Designs*, April 2012, pages 10-18.

Printing Footnotes and Endnotes

When you print a document containing footnotes, Word automatically reduces the number of text lines on a page by the number of lines in the footnote plus the separator line. If the page does not contain enough space, the footnote number and footnote entry text are taken to the next page. Word separates the footnotes from the text with a 2-inch separator line that begins at the left margin. When endnotes are created in a document, Word prints all endnote references at the end of the document separated from the text by a 2-inch separator line.

Ctrl + Alt + F is the keyboard shortcut to insert a footnote.

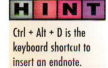

Ctrl + Alt + D is the keyboard shortcut to insert an endnote.

1. Open **InternetFuture.docx** and then save the document with Save As and name it **WL2-C5-P5-InternetFuture**.
2. Apply the *Simple* Quick Styles set.
3. Create the first endnote shown in Figure 5.9 by completing the following steps:
   a. Position the insertion point at the end of the first paragraph of text in the document.
   b. Click the References tab.
   c. Click the Insert Endnote button.
   d. Type the first endnote shown in Figure 5.9.
4. Move the insertion point to the end of the paragraph in the *Satellite Internet Connection* section and then, completing steps similar to those in Steps 3b through 3d, create the second endnote shown in Figure 5.9.
5. Move the insertion point to the end of the second paragraph in the *Second Internet* section and then create the third endnote shown in Figure 5.9.
6. Move the insertion point to the end of the paragraph in the *Internet Services for a Fee* section and then create the fourth endnote shown in Figure 5.9.
7. Save **WL2-C5-P5-InternetFuture.docx**.

Figure 5.9 Project 5b

Abrahamson, Joshua, *Future Trends in Computing*, Gleason-Rutherford Publishing, 2012, pages 8-12.

Clements, Aileen, *Satellite Systems*, Robison Publishing House, 2012, pages 23-51.

Ventrella, Terry, "Future of the Internet," *Computing Today*, October 2012, pages 29-33.

Campbell, Jolene, "Fee-Based Internet Services," *Connections*, March/April 2012, pages 5-8.

Viewing and Editing Footnotes and Endnotes

HINT
Position the mouse pointer on a footnote or endnote reference mark, and the footnote or endnote text displays in a box above the mark.

Next Footnote

Show Notes

To view footnotes in a document, click the Next Footnote button in the Footnotes group in the References tab. This moves the insertion point to the location of the footnote reference number. To view an endnote in a document, click the Next Footnote button arrow and then click *Next Endnote* at the drop-down list. With other options at the Next Footnote button drop-down list, you can view the next footnote, previous footnote, or previous endnote. You can move the insertion point to specific footnote text with the Show Notes button.

When you move, copy, or delete footnote or endnote reference numbers, all remaining footnotes or endnotes are automatically renumbered. To move a footnote or endnote, select the reference number and then click the Cut button in the Clipboard group in the Home tab. Position the insertion point at the location where you want the footnote or endnote inserted and then click the Paste button. To delete a footnote or endnote, select the reference number and then press the Delete key. This deletes the reference number as well as the footnote or endnote text. Click the Footnotes group dialog box launcher and the Footnote and Endnote dialog box displays. At this dialog box, you can convert footnotes to endnotes and endnotes to footnotes, change the location of footnotes or endnotes, change the number formatting; start footnote or endnote numbering with a specific number, letter, or symbol; or change numbering within sections in a document.

1. With **WL2-C5-P5-InternetFuture.docx** open, edit the endnotes by completing the following steps:
   a. Click the References tab.
   b. Click the Next Footnote button arrow and then click *Next Endnote* at the drop-down list.
   c. Click the Show Notes button. (This displays the endnote text.)
   d. Change the pages numbers for the Joshua Abrahamson entry from *8-12* to *5-9*.
   e. Click the Show Notes button again to return to the reference number in the document.

2. Press Ctrl + A to select the document (this does not select the endnote reference text) and then change the font to Constantia.
3. Change the fonts for the endnotes by completing the following steps:
   a. Press Ctrl + End to move the insertion point to the end of the document.
   b. Click on any endnote entry and then press Ctrl + A to select all of the endnote entries.
   c. Change the font to Constantia.
   d. Press Ctrl + Home.
4. Convert the endnotes to footnotes by completing the following steps:
   a. Click the References tab and then click the Footnotes group dialog box launcher.
   b. At the Footnote and Endnote dialog box, click the Convert button.
   c. At the Convert Notes dialog box with the *Convert all endnotes to footnotes* option selected, click the OK button.
   d. Click the Close button to close the dialog box.
5. Change footnote number by completing the following steps:
   a. Click the Footnotes group dialog box launcher.
   b. Click the *Footnotes* option in the *Location* section of the dialog box.
   c. Click the down-pointing arrow at the right side of the *Number format* option box and then click *a, b, c, ...* at the drop-down list.
   d. Change the starting number by clicking the up-pointing arrow at the right side of the *Start at* option until *d* displays in the option box.
   e. Click the Apply button and then scroll through the document and notice the footnotes.
6. Change the footnote number format back to Arabic numbers by completing the following steps:
   a. With the References tab active, click the Footnotes group dialog box launcher.
   b. At the Footnote and Endnote dialog box, click the *Footnotes* option in the *Location* section.
   c. Click the down-pointing arrow at the right side of the *Number format* option box and then click *1, 2, 3, ...* at the drop-down list.

d. Change the starting number back to 1 by clicking the down-pointing arrow at the right side of the *Start at* option until *1* displays in the option box.

e. Click the Apply button.

7. Delete the third footnote by completing the following steps:

a. Press Ctrl + Home.

b. Make sure the References tab is active and then click three times on the Next Footnote button in the Footnotes group.

c. Select the third footnote reference number (superscript number) and then press the Delete key.

8. Save, print, and then close **WL2-C5-P5-InternetFuture.docx**.

Project **Cite References in a Mobile Security Report**   **8 Parts**

You will open a report on securing mobile devices, add information and insert citations and a bibliography, and then modify and customize citation styles.

Creating Citations and Bibliographies ■■■■■■■■■■■■

In addition to using footnotes and endnotes to credit sources in a research paper or manuscript, consider inserting in-text citations and a works cited page to identify sources of quotations, ideas, and borrowed or summarized material. An in-text citation acknowledges that you are borrowing information from a source rather than plagiarizing (stealing) the words or ideas of another.

Word provides three commonly used editorial styles for citing references in research papers and reports: the American Psychological Association (APA) reference style, which is generally used in the social sciences and research fields; the Modern Language Association (MLA) style, which is generally used in the humanities and English composition; and the Chicago Manual of Style (CMS), which is used both in the humanities and social sciences and is considered more complex than either the APA or MLA style.

If you prepare a research paper or report in APA or MLA style, format your document according to the following general guidelines. Use standard-sized paper (8.5 × 11 inches); set one-inch top, bottom, left, and right margins; set text in a 12-point serif typeface (such as Cambria or Times New Roman); double-space text; indent the first line of each paragraph one-half inch; and insert page numbers in the upper right corner of pages.

When formatting a research paper or report in MLA or APA standards, you will need to follow certain guidelines for properly formatting the first page of the document. With the MLA style, in the upper left corner of the first page of the document, you will need to insert your name, your instructor's name, the course title, and the current date, all double-spaced. Type the title of the document a double-space below the current date, and then center the document title. You will then need a double-space between the title and the first line of the text. Insert a header located in the upper right corner of the document that includes your last name followed by the current page number.

When using APA style, the title page is located on a separate page from the body of the document. On the title page, you need to include the title of your paper, your name, and your school's name, all double-spaced, centered, and located in the upper half of the title page. The title page also needs to include a header with the text *Running Head:* followed by the title of your paper in uppercase letters at the left margin, and the page number at the right margin.

Project 6a   **Formatting the First Page of a Research Paper**   **Part 1 of 8**

1. Open **MobileSecurity.docx** and then save the document with Save As and name it **WL2-C5-P6-MobileSecurity**.
2. Format the first page of the document by completing the following steps:
   a. Press Ctrl + A to select the entire document.
   b. Change the font to Cambria and the font size to 12 point.
   c. Change the line spacing to 2.0.
   d. Remove spacing after paragraphs by clicking the Page Layout tab, clicking in the *After* text box in the *Spacing* section in the Paragraph group, typing **0**, and then pressing the Enter key.
   e. Press Ctrl + Home to position the insertion point at the beginning of the document, type your first and last names, and then press the Enter key.
   f. Type your instructor's name and then press the Enter key.
   g. Type the title of your course and then press the Enter key.
   h. Type the current date and then press the Enter key.
   i. Type the document title **Mobile Security** and then center the title.

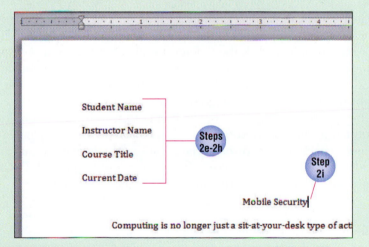

3. Insert a header in the document by completing the following steps:
   a. Click the Insert tab.
   b. Click the Header button in the Header & Footer group and then click *Edit Header* at the drop-down list.
   c. Press the Tab key twice to move the insertion point to the right margin in the Header pane.
   d. Type your last name and then press the spacebar.

e. Click the Page Number button in the Header & Footer group in the Header & Footer Tools Design tab, point to *Current Position*, and then click the *Plain Number* option.

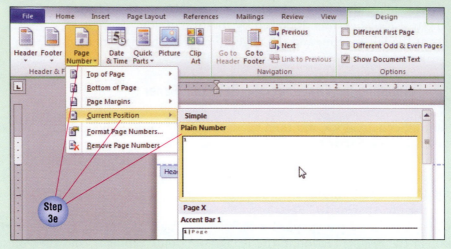

f. Select the header text and change the font to 12-point Cambria.

g. Double-click in the body of the document.

4. Save **WL2-C5-P6-MobileSecurity.docx**.

Inserting Sources and Citations

▼ **Quick Steps**

Insert New Citation
1. Click References tab.
2. Click Insert Citation button.
3. Click *Add New Source* at drop-down list.
4. Type necessary source information.
5. Click OK.

Citation

When you create an in-text citation, Word requires you to enter information about the source in required fields at the Create Source dialog box. To insert a citation in a Word document, click the References tab, click the Insert Citation button in the Citations & Bibliography group, and then click *Add New Source* at the drop-down list. At the Create Source dialog box, shown in Figure 5.10, select the type of reference you want to cite, such as a book, journal article, or report, and then type the bibliographic information in the required fields. If you want to include more information than required in the displayed fields, click the *Show All Bibliography Fields* check box to insert a check mark and then type additional bibliographic information in the extra fields. After filling in the necessary source information, click OK. The citation is automatically inserted in the document at the location of the insertion point.

Figure 5.10 Create Source Dialog Box

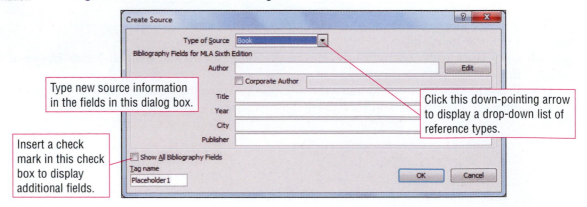

1. With **WL2-C5-P6-MobileSecurity.docx** open, press Ctrl + End to move the insertion point to the end of the document and then type the text shown in Figure 5.11 up to the first citation [the text *(Jefferson)*]. To insert the citation, complete these steps:

   a. Press the spacebar once after typing the text *laptop*.

   b. Click the References tab.

   c. Make sure the *Style* option is set at MLA Sixth Edition. If not, click the down-pointing arrow at the right of the *Style* option in the Citations & Bibliography group and then click *MLA Sixth Edition* at the drop-down list.

   d. Click the Insert Citation button in the Citations & Bibliography group and then click *Add New Source* at the drop-down list.

   e. At the Create Source dialog box, click the down-pointing arrow at the right of the *Type of Source* option and then click *Journal Article* at the drop-down list.

   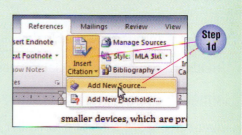

   f. Click in the *Author* text box, type **Gabe Jefferson**, and then press the Tab key three times.

   g. Type **Securing Laptops and Mobile Devices** in the *Title* text box and then press the Tab key.

   h. Type **Future Computing Technologies** in the *Journal Name* text box and then press the Tab key.

   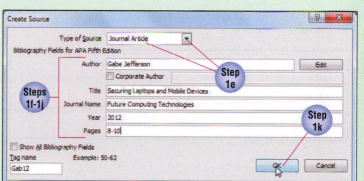

   i. Type **2012** in the *Year* text box and then press the Tab key.

   j. Type **8-10** in the *Pages* text box.

   k. Click OK.

   l. Type the period to end the sentence.

2. Continue typing the text up to the next citation [the text *(Lopez)*] and insert the following source information from a book (click the down-pointing arrow at the right of the *Type of Source* option and then click *Book* at the drop-down list):

Author =	**Rafael Lopez**
Title =	**Technology World**
Year =	**2012**
City =	**Chicago**
Publisher =	**Great Lakes Publishing House**

3. Continue typing the text up to the next citation [the text *(Nakamura)*] and insert the following source information from a journal article (make sure you change the *Type of Source* to *Journal Article*):

Author =	Janet Nakamura
Title =	Computer Security
Journal Name =	Current Technology Times
Year =	2011
Pages =	20-28
Volume =	6 (Display the *Volume* field by clicking the *Show All Bibliography Fields* check box and then scroll down the options list.)

4. Type the remaining text in Figure 5.11.
5. Save **WL2-C5-P6-MobileSecurity.docx**.

Figure 5.11 Project 6b

Laptops have a cable device you can use to tie them to an airport chair or desk in a field office to deter potential thieves from stealing them. The determined thief with enough time can cut the cable and get away with the laptop, so it is only a slight deterrent. If you want stronger protection, consider a service that allows you to remotely delete data if your computer is stolen and uses GPS to track your laptop (Jefferson).

Many newer laptops include fingerprint readers. Because fingerprints are unique to each individual, being able to authenticate yourself with your own set of prints to gain access to your computer is a popular security feature. If somebody without a fingerprint match tries to get into the computer data, the system locks up. If you travel with a laptop, activating password protection and creating a secure password is a good idea. If somebody steals your laptop and cannot get past the password feature, he or she cannot immediately get at your valuable data (Lopez).

Stopping thieves is one concern when you are on the road, but stopping employees from making costly mistakes regarding company data is another area where companies must take precautions. Making sure that employees who take company laptops outside of the office are responsible for safe and secure storage offsite is vital to company security (Nakamura). Policies might require them to keep backups of data on physical storage media or to backup data to a company network.

Inserting a Citation with an Existing Source

Once you insert source information at the Create Source dialog box, Word automatically saves it. To insert a citation in a document for source information that has already been saved, click the Insert Citation button in the Citations & Bibliography group and then click the desired source at the drop-down list.

▼ **Quick Steps**

Insert Citation with Existing Source
1. Click References tab.
2. Click Insert Citation button.
3. Click desired source at drop-down list.

Project 6c　**Inserting an Existing Source**　　　　　　　**Part 3 of 8**

1. With **WL2-C5-P6-MobileSecurity.docx** open, press Ctrl + End to move the insertion point to the end of the document and then press the Enter key once.
2. Type the text in Figure 5.12 up to the citation text *(Jefferson)* and insert a citation from an existing source by completing the following steps:
   a. If necessary, click the References tab.
   b. Click the Insert Citation button in the Citations & Bibliography group.
   c. Click the Gabe Jefferson reference at the drop-down list.
   d. Type the remaining text in Figure 5.12.
3. Save **WL2-C5-P6-MobileSecurity.docx**.

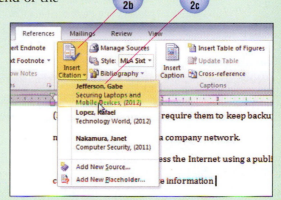

Figure 5.12　Project 6c

> If you travel and access the Internet using a public location, you have to be very careful not to expose private information (Jefferson). Anything you send over a public network can be accessed by malicious hackers and cybercriminals. Limit your use of online accounts to times when it is essential.

Modifying Sources

After you have inserted information about a source into a document, you may need to modify the citation to correct errors or change data. To modify source information, click the References tab and then click the Manage Sources button in the Citations & Bibliography group. This displays the Source Manager dialog box, shown in Figure 5.13. In the *Master List* section, the Source Manager dialog box displays all of the citations you have created in Word. The *Current List* section of the dialog box displays all of the citations included in the currently open document. At the Source Manager dialog box, click the desired source in the *Current List* section. Click the Edit button that displays between the list boxes and then make any desired changes at the Edit Source dialog box. The Edit Source dialog box contains the same options that

▼ **Quick Steps**

Modify Sources
1. Click References tab.
2. Click Manage Sources button.
3. Edit, add, and/or delete sources.
4. Click Close.

Modifying Sources

Figure 5.13 Source Manager Dialog Box

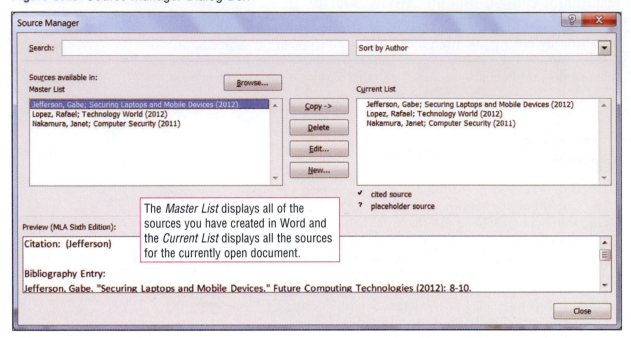

The *Master List* displays all of the sources you have created in Word and the *Current List* displays all the sources for the currently open document.

HINT

Click the Browse button in the Source Manager dialog box to select another master list.

▼ **Quick Steps**

Insert Page Number in Citation
1. Click citation to display placeholder.
2. Click Citation Options arrow.
3. Click *Edit Citation*.
4. Type page number(s).
5. Click OK.

are available at the Create Source dialog box. You can also edit a source by clicking the desired citation in the document to select the citation placeholder, clicking the Citation Options arrow, and then clicking *Edit Source* at the drop-down list.

You may also want to add new sources or delete existing sources in a document. To insert a new source, click the New button at the Source Manager dialog box and then insert the source information in the required fields. To delete a source from a document, click the source you wish to delete in the *Current List* section and then click the Delete button.

Inserting Page Numbers in a Citation

If you include a direct quote from a source, you will want to include quotation marks around all of the text borrowed from that source and insert in the citation the page number(s) of the quoted material. To insert specific page numbers into a citation, click the citation in the document to select the citation placeholder. Click the Citation Options arrow and then click *Edit Citation* at the drop-down list. At the Edit Citation dialog box, type in the page or page numbers of the source where the quote was borrowed and then click OK.

Project 6d **Modifying Sources**   **Part 4 of 8**

1. With **WL2-C5-P6-MobileSecurity.docx** open, edit a source by completing the following steps:
   a. If necessary, click the References tab.
   b. Click the Manage Sources button in the Citations & Bibliography group.

c. At the Source Manager dialog box, click the source entry for Gabe Jefferson in the *Master List* section.

d. Click the Edit button.

e. At the Edit Source dialog box, delete the text in the *Author* text box and then type **Gabriel Jackson**.

f. Click OK to close the Edit Source dialog box.

g. At the message asking if you want to update both the master list and the current list with the changes, click Yes.

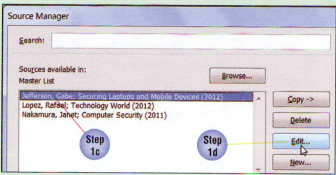

h. Click the Close button to close the Source Manager dialog box. (Notice the last name changed in both of the Jefferson citations to reflect the edit.)

2. Delete a source by completing the following steps:

a. Select and then delete the last sentence in the fourth paragraph in the document including the citation (the sentence beginning *If somebody steals your laptop…*).

b. Click the Manage Sources button in the Citations & Bibliography group in the References tab.

c. At the Source Manager dialog box, click the Rafael Lopez entry in the *Current List* section. (This entry in the list will not contain a check mark because you deleted the citation from the document.)

d. Click the Delete button.

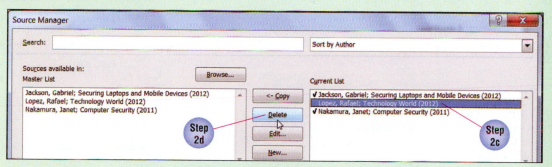

e. Click the Close button to close the Source Manager dialog box.

3. Create and insert a new source in the document by completing the following steps:

a. Click the Manage Sources button in the Citations & Bibliography group in the References tab.

b. Click the New button in the Source Manager dialog box.

c. Type the following book information in the Create Source dialog box (change the *Type of Source* option to *Book*):

Author =	**Georgia Miraldi**
Title =	**Evolving Technology**
Year =	**2012**
City =	**Houston**
Publisher =	**Rio Grande Publishing**

d. Click OK to close the Create Source dialog box.

e. Click the Close button to close the Source Manager dialog box.

f. Position the insertion point one space after the period that ends the last sentence in the document and then type the sentence "**Be especially on guard when accessing your bank accounts, investment accounts, and retail accounts that store your credit card for purchases, and avoid entering your social security number**". (Press the spacebar once after typing the quotation mark after *number*.)

g. Insert a citation at the end of the sentence for Georgia Miraldi by clicking the Insert Citation button in the Citations & Bibliography group and then clicking the Georgia Miraldi reference at the drop-down list.

h. Type the period to end the sentence.

Step 3g

4. Because you inserted a direct quote from Georgia Miraldi, you will need to include the page number of the book where you found the quote. Insert the page number within the citation by completing the following steps:

a. Click anywhere in the Miraldi citation. (This displays the citation placeholder.)

b. Click the Citation Options arrow that displays at the right of the citation placeholder and then click *Edit Citation* at the drop-down list.

c. At the Edit Citation dialog box, type **19** in the *Pages* text box.

d. Click OK.

5. Save **WL2-C5-P6-MobileSecurity.docx**.

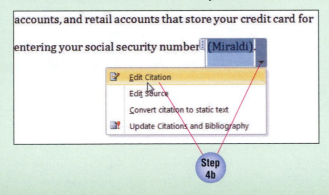

Step 4b

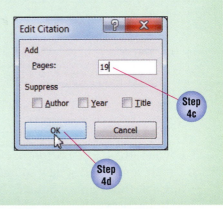

Step 4c

Step 4d

Inserting a Works Cited Page or Bibliography

If you include citations in a report or research paper, you need to insert as a separate page a works cited page or bibliography at the end of the document. A works cited page or bibliography is an alphabetic list of the books, journal articles, reports, or other sources referenced in the document. When you type source information for citations, Word automatically saves information from all of the fields into a bibliography and works cited list, alphabetized by author's last name or the title of the work. Insert a works cited page for a document formatted in the MLA style and insert a bibliography for a document formatted in the APA style.

To insert a works cited page, move the insertion point to the end of the document and then insert a new page. Click the References tab and make sure the Style option is set at *MLA Sixth Edition*. Click the Bibliography button in the Citations & Bibliography group and then click the predesigned works cited option. Complete similar steps to insert a bibliography in an APA-style document except click the predesigned bibliography option.

Bibliography

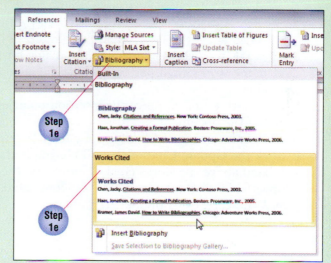

Project 6e   **Inserting a Works Cited Page**   **Part 5 of 8**

1. With **WL2-C5-P6-MobileSecurity.docx** open, insert a works cited page at the end of the document by completing these steps:
   a. Press Ctrl + End to move the insertion point to the end of the document.
   b. Press Ctrl + Enter to insert a page break.
   c. If necessary, click the References tab.
   d. Click the Bibliography button in the Citations & Bibliography group.
   e. Click the *Works Cited* option in the *Built-In* section of the drop-down list.
2. Save **WL2-C5-P6-MobileSecurity.docx**.

Modifying and Updating a Works Cited Page or Bibliography

If you insert a new source at the Source Manager dialog box or modify an existing source, Word automatically inserts the source information in the works cited page or bibliography. If you insert a new citation, which requires you to add a new source, Word will not automatically update the works cited page or bibliography. To update the works cited page or bibliography, click anywhere in the works cited page or bibliography and then click the Update Citations and Bibliography tab. The updated works cited page or bibliography will reflect any changes made to the citations and source information in the document.

▼ **Quick Steps**

Update Works Cited Page or Bibliography
1. Click anywhere in the works cited page or bibliography.
2. Click Update Citations and Bibliography tab.

Project 6f   **Modifying and Updating a Works Cited Page**   **Part 6 of 8**

1. With **WL2-C5-P6-MobileSecurity.docx** open, create a new source and citation by completing the following steps:
   a. Position the insertion point immediately left of the period that ends the last sentence in the first paragraph of the document.
   b. Press the spacebar once.
   c. If necessary, click the References tab.

d. Click the Insert Citation button in the Citations & Bibliography group and then click *Add New Source* at the drop-down list.

e. At the Create Source dialog box, insert the following source information from a website (change the *Type of Source* option to *Web site*):

Author =	**Chay Suong**
Name of Web Page =	**Securing and Managing Mobile Devices**
Year =	**2012**
Month =	**April**
Day =	**20**
Year Accessed =	(type current year in numbers)
Month Accessed =	(type current month in letters)
Day Accessed =	(type current day in numbers)
URL =	**www.emcp.net/publishing**

f. Click OK to close the Create Source dialog box.

2. Update the works cited page to include the new source by completing the following steps:

a. Press Ctrl + End to move the insertion point to the end of the document.

b. Click anywhere in the bibliography text.

c. Click the Update Citations and Bibliography tab located above the works cited. (Notice that the updated bibliography includes the Suong reference.)

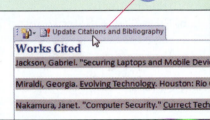

3. Save **WL2-C5-P6-MobileSecurity.docx**.

Formatting a Works Cited Page or Bibliography

Reference styles have specific formatting guidelines. The formatting applied by Word to the works cited page or bibliography may need to be changed to meet specific guidelines of the MLA, APA, or Chicago style. For example, MLA and APA styles require the following formatting guidelines for the works cited page or bibliography:

- Begin works cited or bibliography on a separate page after the text of the report.
- Include the title "Works Cited" or "Bibliography" and center the title.
- Double space between and within entries.
- Begin each entry at the left margin and hang-indent second and subsequent lines in each entry.
- Alphabetize the entries.

The general formatting requirements for the Chicago style are similar except entries are single-spaced within and double-spaced between.

Project 6g **Formatting a Works Cited Page**   **Part 7 of 8**

1. With **WL2-C5-P6-MobileSecurity.docx** open, make the following formatting changes to the works cited page:

a. Select the *Works Cited* heading and the entries below the heading.

b. Click the Home tab and then click the *No Spacing* style in the Styles group.

c. With the text still selected, change the font to Cambria, the font size to 12, and the line spacing to 2.0.

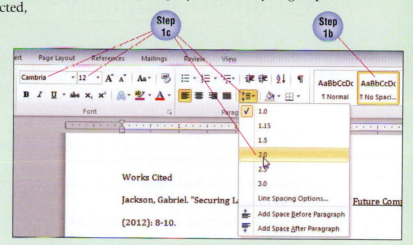

d. Click anywhere in the title *Works Cited* and then click the Center button in the Paragraph group.

e. Select only the works cited entries and then press Ctrl + T. (This hang-indents the entries.)

2. Press Ctrl + Home to move the insertion point to the beginning of the document.

3. Save and then print **WL2-C5-P6-MobileSecurity.docx**.

Choosing a Citation Style

Instructors or professors may require different forms of citation or reference styles. You can change the citation or reference style before beginning a new document or in an existing document. To do this, click the References tab, click the down-pointing arrow at the right of the *Style* option, and then click the desired style at the drop-down list.

▼ **Quick Steps**

Change Citation Style
1. Click References tab.
2. Click down-pointing arrow at right of *Style* option.
3. Click desired style.

Project 6h   Choosing a Citation Style   **Part 8 of 8**

1. With **WL2-C5-P6-MobileSecurity.docx** open, change the document and the works cited page from MLA style to APA style by completing the following steps:

   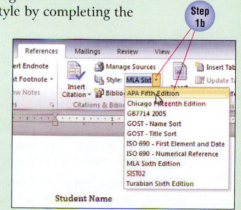

   a. With the insertion point positioned at the beginning of the document, click the References tab.

   b. Click the down-pointing arrow at the right of the *Style* option in the Citations & Bibliography group and then click *APA Fifth Edition* at the drop-down list.

   c. Scroll through the document and notice the changes in the style of the citations and the works cited page.

2. Save the document and then print only the works cited page.

3. Close **WL2-C5-P6-MobileSecurity.docx**.

4. Display a blank document, click the References tab, change the style to *MLA Sixth Edition*, and then close the document without saving it.

Chapter Summary

- You can sort text in paragraphs, columns, and tables and sort records in a data source file. You can also select specific records in a data source file for merging with a main document.

- Use the Sort button in the Paragraph group in the Home tab to sort text in paragraphs, columns, and tables.

- When sorting text set in columns, Word considers the left margin *Field 1*, text typed at the first tab *Field 2*, and so on.

- You can sort on more than one field with the *Sort by* and *Then by* options at the Sort dialog box.

- Use the *Header row* option in the *My list has* section in the Sort Text dialog box to sort all text in columns except the first row.

- Sort records in a data source file at the Mail Merge Recipients dialog box. Sort by clicking the column heading or with options at the Filter and Sort dialog box with the Sort Records tab selected.

- Select specific records in a data source file with options at the Filter and Sort dialog box with the Filter Records tab selected.

- When a nonbreaking space is inserted between words, Word considers these words as one unit and will not divide them when wrapping text to the next line. Insert a nonbreaking space with the keyboard shortcut, Ctrl + Shift + spacebar.

- Use the find and replace feature to find special formatting, characters, or nonprinting elements, and replace with nothing or other special text.

- Save a document as a template by changing the *Save as type* option at the Save As dialog box to *Word Template (*.dotx)* and then saving the template in the Templates folder or another folder of your choosing.

- Word adds the extension *.dotx* to a template.

- Open a template located in the Templates folder by displaying the New tab Backstage view, clicking the *My Templates* option, and then clicking the desired template at the New dialog box. Open a template from a folder other than the Templates folder by displaying the New tab Backstage view, clicking the *New from existing* option, navigating to the desired folder at the New from Existing Document dialog box, and then double-clicking the template.

- Footnotes and endnotes are explanatory notes or references. Footnotes are inserted and printed at the bottom of the page and endnotes are printed at the end of the document. Type footnote/endnote text at the footnote or endnote pane.

- By default, footnotes are numbered with Arabic numbers and endnotes are numbered with lowercase Roman numerals.

- Move, copy, or delete a reference number in a document and all other footnotes or endnotes are automatically renumbered.

- Delete a footnote or endnote by selecting the reference number and then pressing the Delete key.

- Consider using in-text citations to acknowledge sources in a paper. Commonly used citation and reference styles include American Psychological Association (APA), Modern Language Association (MLA), and Chicago Manual of Style (CMS).

- Use the Insert Citation button in the Citations & Bibliography group in the References tab to insert a citation. Specify source information at the Create Source dialog box.
- Modify a source by clicking the References tab, clicking the Manage Sources button, clicking the source you want to modify in the Source Manager dialog box, clicking the Edit button, and then making any desired changes at the Edit Source dialog box.
- To insert a new source, click the New button at the Source Manager dialog box and then insert the information in the required fields. To delete a source, click the source in the *Current List* section in the Source Manager dialog box and then click the Delete button.
- Insert a works cited page or bibliography at the end of the document on a separate page. Insert a works cited page or bibliography with the Bibliography button in the Citations & Bibliography group in the References tab.
- To update a works cited page or bibliography, click anywhere in the works cited page or bibliography and then click the Update Citations and Bibliography tab.
- Change the reference style with the Style option in the Citations & Bibliography group in the References tab.

Commands Review

FEATURE	RIBBON TAB, GROUP	BUTTON, OPTION	KEYBOARD SHORTCUT
Sort Text dialog box	Home, Paragraph		
Sort Options dialog box	Home, Paragraph	, Options	
Filter and Sort dialog box with Sort Records tab selected	Mailings, Start Mail Merge	, Sort	
Filter and Sort dialog box with Select Records tab selected	Mailings, Start Mail Merge	, Filter	
Nonbreaking space			Ctrl + Shift + Spacebar
Find and Replace dialog box	Home, Editing		Ctrl + H
Footnote	References, Footnotes		Alt + Ctrl + F
Endnote	References, Footnotes		Alt + Ctrl + D
Create Source dialog box	References, Citations & Bibliography		
Source Manager dialog box	References, Citations & Bibliography		
Bibliography	References, Citations & Bibliography		
Style	References, Citations & Bibliography		

Concepts Check Test Your Knowledge

Completion: In the space provided at the right, indicate the correct term, symbol, or command.

1. The Sort button is located in this group in the Home tab. _____

2. When sorting text in columns, Word considers the first tab this field number. _____

3. Click this option at the Sort Text dialog box to tell Word not to include the column headings in the sort. _____

4. Click the Filter hyperlink at this dialog box to display the Filter and Sort dialog box with the Filter Records tab selected. _____

5. This is the keyboard shortcut to insert a nonbreaking space. _____

6. Click this button at the expanded Find and Replace dialog box to display a pop-up list of special characters and nonprinting elements. _____

7. Word saves template documents with this file extension. _____

8. Click the *My templates* option at the New tab Backstage view and this dialog box displays. _____

9. Word numbers footnotes with this type of number. _____

10. Word numbers endnotes with this type of number. _____

11. Three of the most popular styles for preparing a report are APA (American Psychological Association), CMS *Chicago Manual of Style*), and this. _____

12. Click this tab to display the Citations & Bibliography group. _____

13. Create a new source for a document with options at this dialog box. _____

14. To modify a source, click this button in the Citations & Bibliography group. _____

15. To update a bibliography, click anywhere in the bibliography and then click this tab. _____

Skills Check Assess Your Performance

Assessment

1 CREATE KEYBOARD SHORTCUTS WITH NONBREAKING SPACES

1. Open **SFSSorting.docx** and then save the document with Save As and name it **WL2-C5-A1-SFSSorting**.
2. Select the nine lines of text below the *Executive Team* heading and then sort the text alphabetically by last name.
3. Sort the three columns of text below the title *New Employees* by the date of hire in ascending order.
4. Sort the text in the *First Qtr.* column in the table numerically in descending order.
5. Press Ctrl + End to move the insertion point to the end of the document and then type the text shown in Figure 5.14. Insert nonbreaking spaces within keyboard shortcuts.
6. Save, print, and then close **WL2-C5-A1-SFSSorting.docx**.

Figure 5.14 Assessment 1

Keyboard Shortcuts

Word includes keyboard shortcuts you can use for creating, viewing, and saving documents. Press Ctrl + N to display a new blank document or press Ctrl + O to open a document. Use the shortcut Ctrl + W to close the currently open document. Additional keyboard shortcuts include pressing Alt + Ctrl + S to split the document window and pressing Alt + Shift + C to remove the document window split.

Assessment

2 INSERT FOOTNOTES IN DESIGNING A NEWSLETTER REPORT

1. Open **DesignNwsltr.docx** and then save the document with Save As and name it **WL2-C5-A2-DesignNwsltr**.
2. Create the first footnote shown in Figure 5.15 at the end of the first paragraph in the *Applying Guidelines* section.
3. Create the second footnote shown in Figure 5.15 at the end of the third paragraph in the *Applying Guidelines* section.
4. Create the third footnote shown in Figure 5.15 at the end of the last paragraph in the *Applying Guidelines* section.
5. Create the fourth footnote shown in Figure 5.15 at the end of the only paragraph in the *Choosing Paper Size and Type* section.
6. Create the fifth footnote shown in Figure 5.15 at the end of the only paragraph in the *Choosing Paper Weight* section.
7. Save and then print **WL2-C5-A2-DesignNwsltr.docx**.
8. Select the entire document and then change the font to Constantia.

9. Select all of the footnotes and change the font to Constantia.
10. Delete the third footnote.
11. Save, print, and then close **WL2-C5-A2-DesignNwsltr.docx**.

Figure 5.15 Assessment 2

Habermann, James, "Designing a Newsletter," *Desktop Designs*, January/February 2012, pages 23-29.

Pilante, Shirley G., "Adding Pizzazz to Your Newsletter," *Desktop Publisher*, September 2011, pages 32-39.

Maddock, Arlita G., "Guidelines for a Better Newsletter," *Business Computing*, June 2012, pages 9-14.

Alverso, Monica, "Paper Styles for Newsletters," *Design Technologies*, March 14, 2011, pages 45-51.

Sutton, Keith, "Choosing Paper Styles," *Design Techniques*, March/April 2011, pages 8-11.

Assessment

3 INSERT SOURCES AND CITATIONS IN A PRIVACY RIGHTS REPORT

1. Open **PrivRights.docx** and then save the document with Save As and name it **WL2-C5-A3-PrivRights**.
2. Make sure the MLA style is selected in the Citations & Bibliography group in the References tab.
3. Format the title page to meet MLA requirements with the following changes:
   a. Select the entire document, change the font to 12-point Cambria, the line spacing to 2.0, and remove the spacing after paragraphs.
   b. Move the insertion point to the beginning of the document, type your name, press the Enter key, type your instructor's name, press the Enter key, type the title of your course, press the Enter key, type the current date, and then press the Enter key.
   c. Type the title **Privacy Rights** and then center the title.
   d. Insert a header that displays your last name and the page number at the right margin and change the font to 12-point Cambria.
4. Press Ctrl + End to move the insertion point to the end of the document and then type the text shown in Figure 5.16 up to the first citation [the text *(Hartley)*]. Insert the source information from a journal article written by Kenneth Hartley using the following information:

Author =	**Kenneth Hartley**
Title =	**Privacy Laws**
Journal Name =	**Business World**
Year =	**2011**
Pages =	**24-46**
Volume =	**12**

Figure 5.16 Assessment 3

An exception to the ability of companies to monitor their employees does exist. If the company has pledged to respect any aspect of employee privacy, it must keep that pledge. For example, if a business states that it will not monitor employee email or phone calls, by law, it must follow this stated policy (Hartley). However, no legal requirement exists mandating that companies notify their employees when and if monitoring takes place (Ferraro). Therefore, employees should assume they are always monitored and act accordingly.

Privacy advocates are calling for this situation to change. "They acknowledge that employers have the right to ensure that their employees are doing their jobs, but they question the need to monitor employees without warning and without limit" (Aldrich 20). The American Civil Liberties Union has, in fact, proposed a Fair Electronic Monitoring Policy to prevent abuses of employee privacy.

5. Continue typing the text up to the next citation [the text *(Ferraro)*] and insert the following source information from a book:

Author =	Ramona Ferraro
Title =	Business Employee Rights
Year =	2012
City =	Tallahassee
Publisher =	Everglades Publishing House

6. Continue typing the text up to the next citation [the text *(Aldrich)*] and insert the following information from an article in a periodical:

Author =	Kelly Aldrich
Title =	What Rights Do Employees Have?
Periodical Title =	Great Plains Times
Year =	2010
Month =	May
Day =	6
Pages =	18-22

7. Insert the page number in the Kelly Aldrich citation using the Edit Citation dialog box.
8. Type the remaining text in Figure 5.16.
9. Edit the Kenneth Hartley source title to read *Small Business Privacy Laws* in the *Master List* section of the Source Manager dialog box.
10. Select and delete the last two sentences in the second paragraph and then delete the Ramona Ferraro source in the *Current List* section of the Source Manager dialog box.
11. Insert a works cited page at the end of the document on a separate page.

12. Create a new source in the document using the Source Manager dialog box and include the following source information from a website:

Author =	**Harold Jefferson**
Name of Web Page =	**Small Business Policies and Procedures**
Year =	**2011**
Month =	**December**
Day =	**12**
Year Accessed =	(type current year)
Month Accessed =	(type current month)
Day Accessed =	(type current day)
URL =	**www.emcp.net/policies**

13. Insert a citation for Harold Jefferson at the end of the last sentence in the first paragraph.
14. Update the works cited page.
15. Format the works cited page to meet MLA requirements with the following changes:
    a. Select the *Works Cited* heading and all the entries and click the *No Spacing* style.
    b. Change the font to 12-point Cambria and change the spacing to 2.0.
    c. Center the title *Works Cited*.
    d. Hang-indent the works cited entries.
16. Save and then print **WL2-C5-A3-PrivRights.docx**.
17. Change the document and works cited page from MLA to APA style.
18. Save, print page two, and then close **WL2-C5-A3-PrivRights.docx**.

Assessment

4 DOWNLOADING AN INVITATION TEMPLATE

1. Display the New tab Backstage view and then search Office.com for business invitations.
2. Download a business invitation of your choosing.
3. Insert text in the appropriate locations in the invitation.
4. Save the invitation document and name it **WL2-C5-A4-Invitation**.
5. Print and then close **WL2-C5-A4-Invitation.docx**.

Visual Benchmark Demonstrate Your Proficiency

FORMAT A REPORT IN MLA STYLE

1. Open **SecurityDefenses.docx** and then save the document with Save As and name it **WL2-C5-VB-SecurityDefenses**.
2. Format the document so it displays as shown in Figure 5.17 with the following specifications:
   a. Change the document font to 12-point Cambria.
   b. Use the information from the works cited page when inserting citations into the document. The Hollingsworth citation is from a journal article, the Montoya citation is from a book, and the Gillespie citation is from a website.
   c. Format the works cited page to meet MLA requirements.
3. Save, print, and then close **WL2-C5-VB-SecurityDefenses.docx**.

Figure 5.17 Visual Benchmark

Last Name 3

Works Cited

Gillespie, Julietta. Creating Computer Security Systems. 22 August 2012. 5 September 2012

<www.emcp.net/publishing>.

Hollingsworth, Melanie. "Securing Vital Company Data." Corporate Data Management

(2012): 8-11.

Montoya, Paul. Designing and Building Secure Systems. San Francisco: Golden Gate

Publishing House, 2011.

Page 3

Last Name 2

More and more people are using software products that deal with both viruses and

spyware in one package. Some can be set to protect your computer in real time, meaning

that they detect an incoming threat, alert you, and stop it before it is downloaded to your

computer. In addition to using antivirus and antispyware software, consider allowing

regular updates to your operating system. Companies release periodic updates that

address flaws in their shipped software or new threats that have come on the scene since

their software shipped (Hollingsworth).

Last Name 1

Student Name

Instructor Name

Course Title

Current Date

Security Defenses

Whether protecting a large business or your personal laptop, security defenses are

available that help to prevent attacks and avoid data loss, including firewalls and software

that detects and removes malware.

A firewall is a part of your computer system that blocks unauthorized access to your

computer or network even as it allows authorized access. You can create firewalls using

software, hardware, or a combination of software and hardware (Hollingsworth). Firewalls

are like guards at the gate of the Internet. Messages that come into or leave a computer or

network go through the firewall, where they are inspected. Any message that does not meet

preset criteria for security is blocked. "You can set up trust levels that allow some types of

communications through and block others, or designate specific sources of

communications that should be allowed access" (Montoya 15).

All computer users should consider using antivirus software and antispyware

software to protect their computers, data, and privacy. Antivirus products require that you

update the virus definitions on a regular basis to ensure that you have protection from new

viruses as they are introduced. Once you have updated definitions, you run a scan and have

several options: to quarantine viruses to keep your system safe from them, to delete a virus

completely, and to report viruses to the antivirus manufacturer to help keep their

definitions current. Antispyware performs a similar function regarding spyware (Gillespie).

Page 2

Page 1

Case Study   Apply Your Skills

Part 1

You are the office manager for Lincoln Freelance Services. You have been compiling information on keyboard shortcuts for an employee training manual. Using the Help feature, find information on keyboard shortcuts for finding, replacing, and browsing through text as well as keyboard shortcuts for references, footnotes, and endnotes. Type the information you find on the keyboard shortcuts in a Word document. Use nonbreaking spaces within keyboard shortcuts. Provide a title for the document and insert any other formatting to improve the visual appeal of the document. Save the document and name it **WL2-C5-CS-Shortcuts**. Print and then close the document.

Part 2

Lincoln Freelance Services provides freelance employees for businesses in Baltimore and surrounding communities. A new industrial park has opened in Baltimore and you need to fill a number of temporary positions. You decide to send a letter to current clients living in Baltimore to let them know about the new industrial park and the temporary jobs that are available. Create a letter main document and include in the letter the information that a new industrial park is opening in a few months, the location of the park (you determine a location), and that Lincoln Freelance Services will be providing temporary employees for many of the technology jobs. Include a list of at least five technology jobs (find job titles on the Internet) for which you will be placing employees. Include any additional information in the letter. Merge the letter main document with only those clients in the **LFSClients.mdb** data source file living in Baltimore. Save the merged letters and name the document **WL2-C5-CS-LFSLtrs**. Print and then close **WL2-C5-CS-LFSLtrs.docx**. Save the letter main document and name it **WL2-C5-CS-LFSMD** and then close the document.

Part 3

Your supervisor has given you a report on newsletter guidelines and asked you to reformat it into the APA reference style. Open the **WL2-C5-A2-DesignNwsltr. docx** document and then save it and name it **WL2-C5-CS-DesignNwsltr**. Change the title to *DESIGNING A NEWSLETTER* and remove the title *SECTION 2: CREATING NEWSLETTER LAYOUT*. Remove the footnotes and instead insert the information as citations and insert a bibliography on a separate page. Save **WL2-C5-CS-DesignNwsltr.docx**.

Part 4

Your supervisor has asked you to include some additional information on newsletter guidelines. Using the Internet, look for sites that provide information on desktop publishing and/or newsletter design guidelines. Include in the **WL2-C5-CS-DesignNwsltr.docx** report document at least one additional paragraph with information you found on the Internet and include a citation to the source(s). Save, print, and then close the report.

Creating Specialized Tables and Indexes

PERFORMANCE OBJECTIVES

Upon successful completion of Chapter 6, you will be able to:
- Create, insert, and update a table of contents
- Create, insert, and update an index
- Create, insert, and update a table of figures

Tutorials

6.1 Creating a Table of Contents

6.2 Customizing and Updating a Table of Contents

6.3 Assigning Levels to Table of Content Entries

6.4 Creating a Table of Figures

6.5 Creating Captions

6.6 Marking Index Entries and Inserting an Index

6.7 Creating a Concordance File

6.8 Updating and Deleting an Index

A book, textbook, report, or manuscript often includes sections such as a table of contents, index, and table of figures in the document. Creating these sections can be tedious when done manually. With Word, these functions can be automated to create the sections quickly and easily. In this chapter, you will learn the steps to mark text for a table of contents, a table of figures, and an index and then insert the table or index. Model answers for this chapter's projects appear on the following pages.

Word2010L2C6

Note: Before beginning the projects, copy to your storage medium the Word2010L2C6 subfolder from the Word2010L2 folder on the CD that accompanies this textbook and then make Word2010L2C6 the active folder.

Project 1 Create a Table of Contents for a Computer Interface Report

CONTENTS

i

Project 1 Create a Table of Contents for a Computer Interface Report

WL2-C6-P1-AIReport.docx

Project 2 Mark Text for and Insert a Table of Contents in an Internet Report

TABLE OF CONTENTS

i

Project 2 Mark Text for and Insert a Table of Contents in an Internet Report

WL2-C6-P2-CompComm.docx

Project 3 Create a Table of Figures for a Technology Report

TABLE OF FIGURES

Project 3 Create a Table of Figures for a Technology Report

WL2-C6-P3-TechRpt.docx

Productivity Software

Productivity software includes software that people typically use to complete work, such as word processing software (working with words), spreadsheet software (working with data, numbers, and calculations), database software (organizing and retrieving data records), or presentation software (creating slide shows with text and graphics).

WORD PROCESSING SOFTWARE

With word processing software, you can create documents that include sophisticated formatting; change text fonts; add special effects such as bold, italics, and underlining; add shadows, background colors, and other effects to text and objects; and include tables, photos, drawings, and links to online content.

Figure 1 Word Document

With a mail merge feature, you can take a list of names and addresses and print personalized letters and envelopes or labels. Figure 1 shows the application of some of the word processing features and tools Microsoft Word offers.

SPREADSHEET SOFTWARE

Using spreadsheet software, such as Microsoft Excel, you can perform calculations that range from simple (adding, averaging, and multiplying) to complex (estimating standard deviations based on a range of numbers, for example). In addition, spreadsheet software offers sophisticated charting and graphing capabilities. Formatting tools help you create polished looking documents such as budgets, invoices, schedules, attendance records, and purchase orders. With spreadsheet software you can also keep track of data such as your holiday card list and sort that list or search for

Figure 2 Excel Worksheet

Model Answers

specific names or other data. Figure 2 shows a typical Excel spreadsheet making use of several key features.

Output Devices

To get information into a computer, a person uses an input device. To get information out, a person uses an output device. Some common output devices include monitors and printers.

MONITOR

A monitor, or screen, is the most common output device used with a personal computer. The most common monitors use either a thin film transistor (TFT) active matrix liquid crystal display (LCD) or a plasma display. Plasma displays have a very true level of color reproduction compared with LCDs. Emerging display technologies include surface-conduction electron-emitter displays (SED) and organic light emitting diodes (OLED).

Figure 3 Monitor

PRINTERS

After monitors, printers are the most important output devices. The print quality produced by these devices is measured in dpi, or dots per inch. As with screen resolution, the greater the number of dots per inch, the better the quality. The earliest printers for personal computers were dot matrix printers that used perforated computer paper. These impact printers worked something like typewriters, transferring the image of a character by using pins to strike a ribbon.

A laser printer uses a laser beam to create points of electrical charge on a cylindrical drum. Toner, composed of particles of ink with a negative electrical charge, sticks to the charged points on the positively charged drum. As the page moves past the drum, heat and pressure fuse the toner to the page. Inkjet printers generally provide at least 300 dpi resolution, although high-resolution inkjets are available. Inkjet printers use a print head that moves across the page that sprays a fine mist of ink when an

Figure 4 Laser Printer

Page 3

---

electrical charge moves through the print cartridge. An inkjet printer can use color cartridges and so provides affordable color printing suitable for home and small office use.

Developing Software

Through the years, some software products have become incredibly sophisticated as new features are added in each version. The *software development life cycle* (SDLC) has evolved over time. This procedure dictates the general flow of creating a new software product as shown in the figure below. The SDLC involves performing market research to ensure a need or demand for the product exists; completing a business analysis to match the solution to the need; creating a plan for implementing the software, which involves creating a budget and schedule for the project; writing the software program; testing the software; deploying the software to the public, either by selling the product in a package or online; and performing maintenance and bug fixes to keep the product functioning optimally.

Figure 5 Software Life Cycle

Page 4

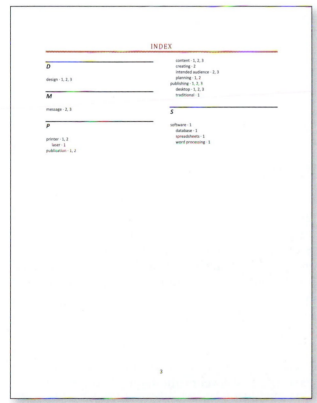

INDEX

D

design · 1, 2, 3

M

message · 2, 3

P

printer · 1, 2
  laser · 1
publication · 1, 2

content · 1, 2, 3
  creating · 2
  intended audience · 2, 3
  planning · 1, 2
publishing · 1, 2, 3
  desktop · 1, 2, 3
  traditional · 1

S

software · 1
  database · 1
  spreadsheets · 1
  word processing · 1

3

---

newsletters	Newsletters
Newsletters	Newsletters
Software	Software
Desktop publishing	Software: desktop publishing
word processing	Software: word processing
Printers	Printers
Laser	Printers: laser
Design	Design
Communication	Communication
Consistency	Design: consistency
Elements	Elements
Nameplate	Elements: nameplate
Logo	Elements: logo
Subtitle	Elements: subtitle
Folio	Elements: folio
Headlines	Elements: headlines
Subheads	Elements: subheads
Byline	Elements: byline
Body Copy	Elements: body copy
Graphics Images	Elements: graphics images
Audience	Newsletters: audience
Purpose	Newsletters: purpose
focal point	Newsletters: focal point

Project 4 Create an Index for a Desktop Publishing Report
WL2-C6-P4-DTP.docx

Project 5 Create an Index with a Concordance File for a Newsletter Report
WL2-C6-P5-CFile.docx

WL2-C6-P5-PlanNwsltr.docx

Project 1 — Create a Table of Contents for a Computer Interface Report

2 Parts

You will open a report on computer interfaces, mark text for a table of contents, and then insert the table of contents in the document. You will also make, customize, and update the table of contents.

Creating a Table of Contents

You can use a table of contents to quickly navigate in a document and to get an overview of the topics covered in the document.

A table of contents appears at the beginning of a book, manuscript, or report and contains headings and subheadings with page numbers. In a previous chapter, you created a table of contents using the Quick Parts button in the Text group in the Insert tab. You can also create a table of contents using the Table of Contents button in the Table of Contents group in the References tab. You can identify text to be included in a table of contents by applying built-in heading styles, custom styles, assigning levels, or marking text.

Apply heading styles to text in a document and you can easily insert a table of contents.

Applying Styles

To create a table of contents with built-in styles, open the document and then apply the desired styles. Word uses as the first level of the table of contents text with the Heading 1 style applied, Heading 2 text for the second level, and so on. Apply the built-in style with options in the Styles group in the Home tab.

Inserting a Table of Contents

After you have applied styles to the headings in the document, insert the table of contents in the document. To do this, position the insertion point where you want the table to appear, click the References tab, click the Table of Contents button, and then click the desired option at the drop-down list.

Numbering the Table of Contents Page

Generally, a table of contents page is numbered with lowercase Roman numerals (*i, ii, iii*). Change the page number to lowercase Roman numerals at the Page Number Format dialog box shown in Figure 6.1. Display this dialog box by clicking the Insert tab, clicking the Page Number button in the Header & Footer group, and then clicking *Format Page Numbers* at the drop-down list. The first page of the document, other than the Table of Contents page, should begin with number 1. To insert these two types of page numbering, separate the Table of Contents from the beginning of the document with a section break that begins a new page.

Navigating Using a Table of Contents

When you insert a table of contents in a document, you can use the table of contents headings to navigate in a document. Table of contents headings are hyperlinks that are connected to the heading in the document. To navigate in a document using table of contents headings, click in the table of contents to select it. Position the mouse pointer over the desired heading and a box will display with the path and file name as well as the text *Ctrl+Click to follow link*. Hold down the Ctrl key and then click the left mouse button and the insertion point is positioned in the document at the location of the heading.

▼ **Quick Steps**

Insert a Table of Contents
1. Apply heading styles.
2. Click References tab.
3. Click Table of Contents button.
4. Click desired option at drop-down list.

Number Table of Contents Page
1. Click Insert tab.
2. Click Page Number button.
3. Click *Format Page Numbers* at drop-down list.
4. Change number format to lowercase Roman numerals at Page Number Format dialog box.
5. Click OK.

Table of Contents

Page Number

Figure 6.1 Page Number Format Dialog Box

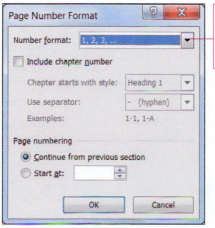

Change the number format to lowercase Roman numerals when numbering table of contents pages.

1. Open **AIReport.docx** and then save the document with Save As and name it **WL2-C6-P1-AIReport**. (This document contains headings with headings styles applied.)

2. Position the insertion point immediately left of the *N* in *NATURAL INTERFACE APPLICATIONS* and then insert a section break by completing the following steps:

   a. Click the Page Layout tab.

   b. Click the Breaks button in the Page Setup group.

   c. Click the *Next Page* option in the *Section Breaks* section.

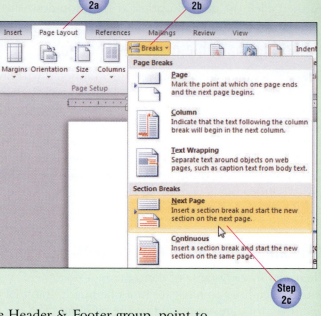

Step 2a

Step 2b

Step 2c

3. With the insertion point positioned below the section break, insert page numbering and change the beginning number to 1 by completing the following steps:

   a. Click the Insert tab.

   b. Click the Page Number button in the Header & Footer group, point to *Bottom of Page*, and then click *Plain Number 2*.

   c. Click the Page Number button in the Header & Footer group in the Header & Footer Tools Design tab and then click *Format Page Numbers* at the drop-down list.

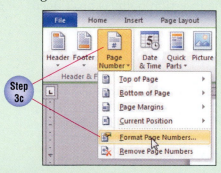

Step 3c

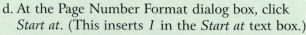

Step 3d

Step 3e

   d. At the Page Number Format dialog box, click *Start at*. (This inserts *1* in the *Start at* text box.)

   e. Click OK to close the Page Number Format dialog box.

   f. Double-click in the document to make it active.

4. Insert a table of contents at the beginning of the document by completing the following steps:

   a. Press Ctrl + Home to move the insertion point to the beginning of the document.

b. Click the References tab.

c. Click the Table of Contents button and then click the *Automatic Table 1* option in the *Built-In* section of the drop-down list.

5. Insert page numbering in the table of contents page by completing the following steps:

a. With the insertion point positioned on any character in the CONTENTS title, click the Insert tab.

b. Click the Page Number button in the Header & Footer group and then click *Format Page Numbers* at the drop-down list.

c. At the Page Number Format dialog box, click the down-pointing arrow at the right side of the *Number format* option box and then click *i, ii, iii, . . .* at the drop-down list.

d. Click OK to close the dialog box.

e. Double-click in the document to make it active.

6. Navigate in the document using the table of contents by completing the following steps:

a. Click on any character in the table of contents.

b. Position the mouse pointer on the *Virtual Reality* heading, hold down the Ctrl key, click the left mouse button, and then release the Ctrl key. (This moves the insertion point to the beginning of the *Virtual Reality* heading in the document.)

c. Press Ctrl + Home to move the insertion point to the beginning of the document.

7. Save the document and then print only the table of contents page.

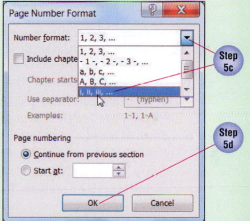

Customizing the Table of Contents ■■■■■■■■■■■■■■

You can customize the table of contents in a document with options at the Table of Contents dialog box as shown in Figure 6.2. Display this dialog box by clicking the Table of Contents button in the References tab and then clicking *Insert Table of Contents* at the drop-down list.

At the Table of Contents dialog box, a sample table of contents displays in the *Print Preview* section. You can change the table of contents format by clicking the down-pointing arrow at the right side of the *Formats* option box (located in the *General* section). At the drop-down list that displays, click the desired format. When you select a different format, that format displays in the *Print Preview* section. Page numbers in a table of contents will display after the text or aligned at the right

Figure 6.2 Table of Contents Dialog Box

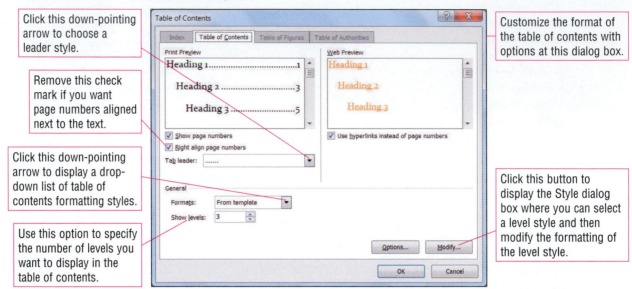

Click this down-pointing arrow to choose a leader style.

Remove this check mark if you want page numbers aligned next to the text.

Click this down-pointing arrow to display a drop-down list of table of contents formatting styles.

Use this option to specify the number of levels you want to display in the table of contents.

Customize the format of the table of contents with options at this dialog box.

Click this button to display the Style dialog box where you can select a level style and then modify the formatting of the level style.

margin depending on what options are selected. You can also specify page number alignment with the *Right align page numbers* option. The number of levels that display depends on the number of heading levels specified in the document. You can control the number of levels that display in a table of contents with the *Show levels* option.

Tab leaders help guide the reader's eyes from the table of contents heading to the page number. The default tab leader is a period. To choose a different leader, click the down-pointing arrow at the right side of the *Tab leader* option box, and then click the desired leader character from the drop-down list.

Word automatically identifies headings in a table of contents as hyperlinks and inserts page numbers. You can use these hyperlinks to move the insertion point to a specific location in the document. If you are going to post your document to the Web, consider removing the page numbers since the reader will only need to click the hyperlink to view a specific page.

You can modify the formatting of a level style by clicking the Modify button. At the Style dialog box that displays, click the level in the *Styles* list box that you want to modify and then click the Modify button. At the Modify Style dialog box, apply the desired formatting for each level of the table of contents and then click OK. The Modify Style dialog box contains a number of options for specifying formatting for table of content level. Use options in the *Formatting* section to apply character and paragraph formatting such as changing the font, font size, font color, and font effects and changing paragraph alignment, spacing, and indenting.

If you make changes to the options at the Table of Contents dialog box and then click OK, a message will display asking if you want to replace the selected table of contents. At this message click Yes.

Updating a Table of Contents

If you add, delete, move, or edit headings or other text in a document after inserting a table of contents, update the table of contents. To do this, click anywhere within the current table of contents and then click the Update Table

▼ **Quick Steps**

Update Table of Contents
1. Click anywhere within table of contents.
2. Click References tab.
3. Click Update Table button.
4. Select *Update page numbers only* or *Update entire table* at Update Table of Contents dialog box.
5. Click OK.

button or press F9 (the Update Field key). At the Update Table of Contents dialog box shown in Figure 6.3, click *Update page numbers only* if changes occur only to the page numbers, or click *Update entire table* if changes were made to headings or subheadings within the table. Click OK or press Enter to close the dialog box.

Removing a Table of Contents

Remove a table of contents from a document by clicking the Table of Contents button in the References tab and then clicking *Remove Table of Contents* at the drop-down list. You can also remove a table of contents by clicking on any character in the table of contents, clicking the Table of Contents tab located in the upper left corner of the table of contents (immediately left of the Update Table tab), and then clicking *Remove Table of Contents* at the drop-down list.

Quick Steps

Remove Table of Contents
1. Click References tab.
2. Click Table of Contents button.
3. Click *Remove Table of Contents* at drop-down list.
OR
1. Click on any character in table of contents.
2. Click the Table of Contents tab.
3. Click *Remove Table of Contents* at drop-down list.

Figure 6.3 Update Table of Contents Dialog Box

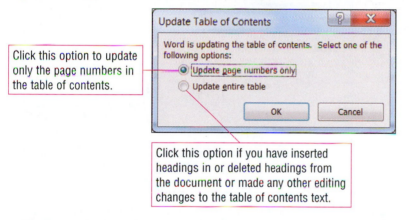

Click this option to update only the page numbers in the table of contents.

Click this option if you have inserted headings in or deleted headings from the document or made any other editing changes to the table of contents text.

HINT

If you add, delete, move, or edit headings or other text in a document, update the table of contents.

Update Table

Project 1b **Customizing and Updating the Table of Contents**   **Part 2 of 2**

1. With **WL2-C6-P1-AIReport.docx** open, press Ctrl + Home and then modify the level 1 and level 2 styles by completing the following steps:
   a. Click the References tab, click the Table of Contents button, and then click *Insert Table of Contents* at the drop-down list.
   b. At the Table of Contents dialog box, click the Modify button that displays in the lower right corner of the dialog box.
   c. At the Style dialog box with *TOC 1* selected in the *Styles* list box, click the Modify button.

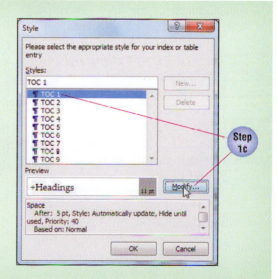

Step 1c

d. At the Modify Style dialog box, change the font size to 12 and then click the Italic button.

e. Click OK to close the Modify Style dialog box.

f. At the Style dialog box, click *TOC 2* in the *Styles* list box and then click the Modify button.

g. At the Modify Style dialog box, change the font size to 12, click the Italic button, and then click OK.

h. Click OK at the Style dialog box.

i. At the Table of Contents dialog box, specify that you only want two levels of the table of contents to display by clicking once on the down-pointing arrow at the right side of the *Show levels* option. (This changes the number to *2*.)

j. Click the *Right align page numbers* option to remove the check mark.

k. Click OK to close the Table of Contents dialog box.

l. At the message asking if you want to replace the selected table of contents, click Yes.

2. Save the document and print only the table of contents page.

3. After looking at the modified table of contents, you decide to apply a different formatting style. With the insertion point positioned in the table of contents, complete the following steps:

a. Click the References tab, click the Table of Contents button, and then click *Insert Table of Contents* at the drop-down list.

b. At the Table of Contents dialog box, click the down-pointing arrow at the right of the *Formats* option in the *General* section and then click *Formal* at the drop-down list.

c. Click the down-pointing arrow at the right of the *Tab leader* option box and then click the solid line option (bottom option) at the drop-down list.

d. Click once on the up-pointing arrow at the right side of the *Show levels* option box to change the number to *3*.

e. Click OK to close the dialog box.

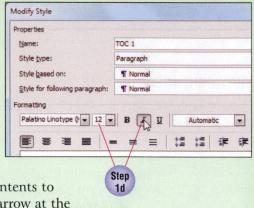

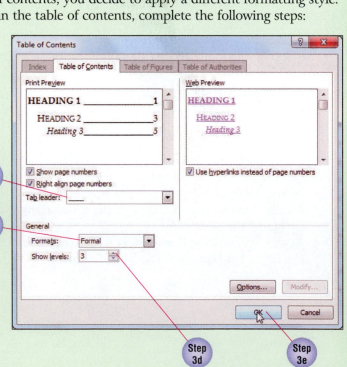

f. At the message asking if you want to replace the selected table of contents, click Yes.

4. Move the insertion point so it is positioned at the beginning of the *NAVIGATION* heading located at the bottom of page 3 and then press Ctrl + Enter to insert a page break.

5. Update the table of contents by completing the following steps:

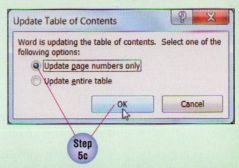

a. Press Ctrl + Home and then click on any character in the table of contents.

b. Click the Update Table tab.

c. At the Update Table of Contents dialog box, make sure *Update page numbers only* is selected and then click OK.

6. Save the document, print only the table of contents page, and then close **WL2-C6-P1-AIReport.docx**.

 **roject 2** **Mark Text for and Insert a Table of Contents in an Internet Report** **2 Parts**

You will open a report on the future of the Internet, mark text as table of contents fields, and then insert the table of contents in the document. You will also insert a file containing additional information on the Internet and then update the table of contents.

Assigning Levels to Table of Contents Entries

Another method for identifying text for the table of contents is to use the Add Text button in the Table of Contents group in the References tab. Click this button and a drop-down list of level options displays. Click the desired level for the currently selected text. After specifying levels, insert the table of contents by clicking the Table of Contents button and then clicking the desired option at the drop-down list.

Add Text

Marking Table of Contents Entries as Fields

Applying styles to text applies specific formatting. If you want to identify titles and/or headings for a table of contents but you do not want heading style formatting applied, mark the text as a field entry. To do this, select the text you want included in the table of contents and then press Alt + Shift + O. This displays the Mark Table of Contents Entry dialog box shown in Figure 6.4.

The text you selected in the document displays in the *Entry* text box. At this dialog box, specify the text level using the *Level* option, and then click the Mark button. This turns on the display of nonprinting symbols in the document and also inserts a field code immediately after the selected text. For example, when you select the first title in Project 2a, the following code is inserted immediately after the title: { TC "FUTURE OF THE INTERNET" \f C \l " 1 " }. The Mark Table of Contents Entry dialog box also remains open. To mark the next entry for the table of contents, select the text, and then click the title bar of the Mark Table

Figure 6.4 Mark Table of Contents Entry Dialog Box

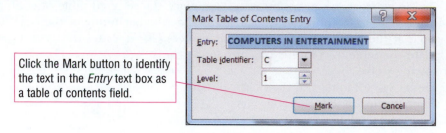

Click the Mark button to identify the text in the *Entry* text box as a table of contents field.

of Contents Entry dialog box. Specify the level and then click the Mark button. Continue in this manner until all table of contents entries have been marked.

If you mark table of content entries as fields, you will need to activate the *Table entry fields* option when inserting the table of contents. To do this, display the Table of Contents dialog box and then click the Options button. At the Table of Contents Options dialog box shown in Figure 6.5, click the *Table entry fields* check box to insert a check mark and then click OK.

Figure 6.5 Table of Contents Options Dialog Box

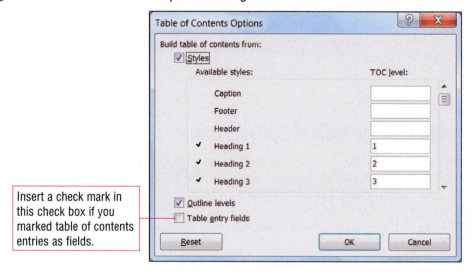

Insert a check mark in this check box if you marked table of contents entries as fields.

Project 2a **Marking Headings as Fields** Part 1 of 2

1. Open **CompComm.docx** and then save the document with Save As and name it **WL2-C6-P2-CompComm**.
2. Position the insertion point immediately left of the *C* in the title *COMPUTERS IN ENTERTAINMENT* and then insert a section break that begins a new page.
3. Mark the titles and headings as fields for insertion in a table of contents by completing the following steps:
   a. Select the title *COMPUTERS IN ENTERTAINMENT*.
   b. Press Alt + Shift + O.

c. At the Mark Table of Contents Entry dialog box, make sure the *Level* is set at *1* and then click the Mark button. (This turns on the display of nonprinting characters.)

d. Click in the document, scroll down the document, and then select the title *COMPUTERS IN COMMUNICATION*.

e. Click the dialog box title bar and then click the Mark button.

f. Click in the document, scroll up the document, and then select the heading *Television and Film*.

g. Click the dialog box title bar and then click the up-pointing arrow at the right of the *Level* text box in the Mark Table of Contents Entry dialog box until *2* displays.

h. Click the Mark button.

i. Mark the following headings as level 2:
    Home Entertainment
    Telecommunications
    Publishing
    News Services

j. Click the Close button to close the Mark Table of Contents Entry dialog box.

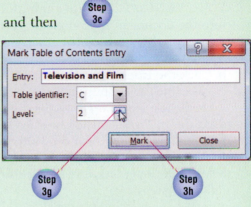

Step 3c

Step 3g   Step 3h

4. Position the insertion point below the section break and then insert page numbering at the bottom center of each page of the section and change the starting number to 1. ***Hint: Refer to Project 1a, Step 3.***

5. Double-click in the document.

6. Insert a table of contents at the beginning of the document by completing the following steps:

a. Position the insertion point at the beginning of the document (on the new page).

b. Type the title *TABLE OF CONTENTS*, centered and bolded, and then press the Enter key. (The insertion point may not move down to the next line.)

c. Click the References tab.

d. Click the Table of Contents button and then click *Insert Table of Contents* at the drop-down list.

e. At the Table of Contents dialog box, click the Options button.

f. At the Table of Contents Options dialog box, click *Table entry fields* to insert a check mark in the check box. (This option is located in the bottom left corner of the dialog box.)

g. Click OK to close the Table of Contents Options dialog box.

h. Click OK to close the Table of Contents dialog box.

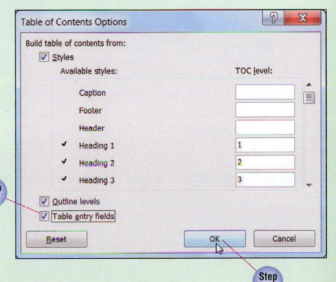

Step 6f

Step 6g

7. Insert lowercase Roman numeral page numbering on the table of contents page. ***Hint: Refer to Project 1a, Step 5.***

8. Click the Show/Hide ¶ button to turn off the display of nonprinting characters.

9. Save the document and then print only the table of contents page.

You can insert additional information in a document and update the table. To do this, insert the text and then mark the text with options at the Mark Table of Contents Entry dialog box. Click anywhere in the table of contents and then click the Update Table tab. At the Update Table of Contents dialog box, click the *Update entire table* option and then click OK.

Project 2b **Updating the Entire Table of Contents** **Part 2 of 2**

1. With **WL2-C6-P2-CompComm.docx** open, insert a file into the document by completing the following steps:
   a. Press Ctrl + End to move the insertion point to the end of the document.
   b. Click the Insert tab.
   c. Click the Object button arrow in the Text group and then click *Text from File* at the drop-down list.
   d. At the Insert File dialog box, navigate to the Word2010L2C6 folder on your storage medium and then double-click *CommMedia.docx*.

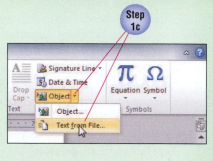

2. Select and then mark text for inclusion in the table of contents by completing the following steps:
   a. Select the heading *Communications Media*.
   b. Press Alt + Shift + O.
   c. At the Mark Table of Contents Entry dialog box, click the up-pointing arrow at the right of the *Level* text box in the Mark Table of Contents Entry dialog box until *2* displays.
   d. Click the Mark button.
   e. Click the Close button to close the Mark Table of Contents Entry dialog box.
3. Insert a page break at the beginning of the title *COMPUTERS IN COMMUNICATION*.
4. Update the table of contents by completing the following steps:
   a. Select the entire table of contents text (excluding the title).
   b. Click the References tab.
   c. Click the Update Table button in the Table of Contents group.
   d. At the Update Table of Contents dialog box, click the *Update entire table* option.
   e. Click OK.

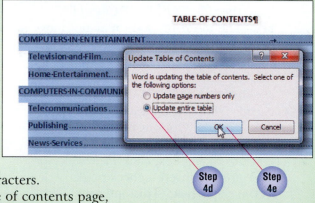

5. Turn off the display of nonprinting characters.
6. Save the document, print only the table of contents page, and then close **WL2-C6-P2-CompComm.docx**.

Project 3 **Create a Table of Figures for a Technology Report** **2 Parts**

You will open a report containing information on software, output devices, and the software development cycle as well as images and a SmartArt diagram; insert captions; and then create a table of figures.

Creating a Table of Figures ■■■■■■■■■■■■■■■■■■

A document that contains figures should include a list (table) of figures so a reader can quickly locate a specific figure. Figure 6.6 shows an example of a table of figures. Create a table of figures by marking figures or images as captions and then using the caption names to create the table of figures.

Creating Captions

A caption is text that describes a figure or picture. You can create a caption by selecting the figure text or image, clicking the References tab, and then clicking the Insert Caption button in the Captions group. This displays the Caption dialog box shown in Figure 6.7. At the dialog box, make sure *Figure 1* displays in the *Caption* text box and the insertion point is positioned after *Figure 1*. Type a name for the caption and then press the Enter key. Word inserts *Figure 1 (caption name)* below the selected text or image. Click the down-pointing arrow at the right of the *Label* option to specify the caption label. The default is Figure, which you can change to Equation or Table.

▼ **Quick Steps**

Create a Caption
1. Select text or image.
2. Click References tab.
3. Click Insert Caption button.
4. Type caption name.
5. Click OK.

H I N T

A caption is text that describes an object and generally displays below the object.

Figure 6.6 Table of Figures

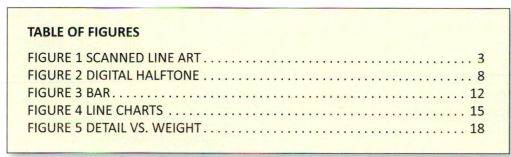

TABLE OF FIGURES

Insert Caption

Figure 6.7 Caption Dialog Box

Type a caption in this text box after *Figure 1*.

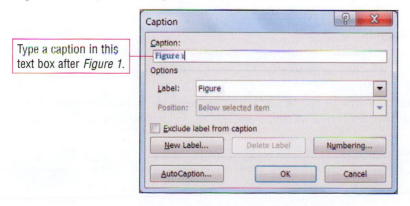

Insert a Table of Figures
1. Click References tab.
2. Click Insert Table of Figures button.
3. Select desired format.
4. Click OK.

A table of figures includes a list of all figures, tables, and equations in the document.

Insert Table
of Figures

Inserting a Table of Figures

After you have marked figure text or images as captions, insert the table of figures. A table of figures generally displays at the beginning of the document, after the table of contents and on a seperate page. To insert the table of figures, click the Insert Table of Figures button in the Captions group in the References tab. At the Table of Figures dialog box shown in Figure 6.8, make any necessary changes and then click OK.

The options at the Table of Figures dialog box are similar to those options available at the Table of Contents dialog box. For example, you can choose a format for the table of figures from the *Formats* option box, change the alignment of the page number, or add leaders before page numbers.

Figure 6.8 Table of Figures Dialog Box

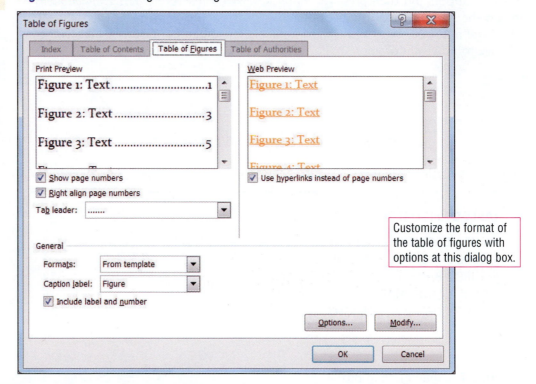

Customize the format of the table of figures with options at this dialog box.

Project 3a **Creating a List of Figures** Part 1 of 2

1. Open **TechRpt.docx** and then save the document with Save As and name it **WL2-C6-P3-TechRpt**.
2. Add the caption *Figure 1 Word Document* to the image by completing the following steps:
   a. Click the screen image that displays in the *WORD PROCESSING SOFTWARE* section.
   b. Click the References tab.
   c. Click the Insert Caption button in the Captions group.
   d. At the Caption dialog box, press the spacebar once and then type **Word Document**.

e. Click OK or press Enter.

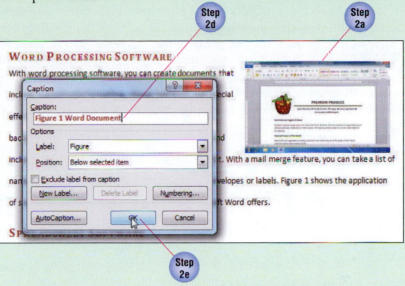

Step 2d

Step 2a

Step 2e

f. Press Ctrl + E to center the caption in the text box.

3. Complete steps similar to those in Step 2 to create the caption *Figure 2 Excel Worksheet* for the image in the SPREADSHEET SOFTWARE section.

4. Complete steps similar to those in Step 2 to create the caption *Figure 3 Monitor* for the image in the MONITOR section.

5. Complete steps similar to those in Step 2 to create the caption *Figure 4 Software Life Cycle* for the SmartArt diagram in the *Developing Software* section.

6. Insert a table of figures at the beginning of the document by completing the following steps:

a. Press Ctrl + Home to move the insertion point to the beginning of the document.

b. Press Ctrl + Enter to insert a page break.

c. Move the insertion point to the blank page above the page break and then type TABLE OF FIGURES bolded and centered.

d. Press the Enter key, turn off bold, and then change the paragraph alignment back to left.

e. Click the References tab.

f. Click the Insert Table of Figures button in the Captions group.

g. At the Table of Figures dialog box, click the down-pointing arrow at the right side of the *Formats* option box and then click *Formal* at the drop-down list.

h. Click OK.

7. Save **WL2-C6-P3-TechRpt.docx**.

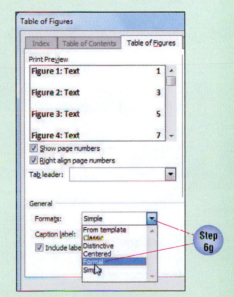

Step 6g

▼ **Quick Steps**

Update Table of Figures
1. Click in table of figures.
2. Click References tab.
3. Click Update Table button or press F9.
4. Click OK at the Update Table of Figures dialog box.

Delete Table of Figures
1. Select entire table of figures.
2. Press Delete key.

Updating or Deleting a Table of Figures

If you make changes to a document after inserting a table of figures, update the table. To do this, click anywhere within the table of figures and then click the Update Table button in the Captions group in the References tab or press F9. At the Update Table of Figures dialog box, click *Update page numbers only* if the changes occur only to the page numbers or click *Update entire table* if changes were made to caption text. Click OK or press Enter to close the dialog box. To delete a table of figures, select the entire table using either the mouse or the keyboard and then press the Delete key.

Project 3b **Updating the Table of Figures** **Part 2 of 2**

1. With **WL2-C6-P3-TechRpt.docx** open, insert a clip art image of a laser printer by completing the following steps:
   a. Move the insertion point to the beginning of the second paragraph of text in the *PRINTERS* section.
   b. Click the Insert tab and then click the Clip Art button in the Illustrations group.
   c. At the Clip Art task pane, click the down-pointing arrow at the right of the *Results should be* option box and then click in the *Photographs*, *Videos*, and *Audio* check boxes to remove the check marks. (The *Illustrations* check box should be the only one with a check mark.)

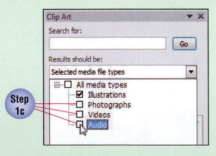

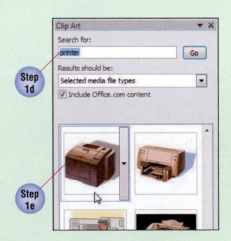

   d. Select any text that displays in the *Search for* text box, type **printer**, and then press the Enter key.
   e. Click the printer image in the list box as shown at the right. (You will need to scroll down the list box to display this image.)
   f. Close the Clip Art task pane.
   g. Change the height of the clip art image to 1.5 inches.
   h. Change the text wrapping to *Tight*.

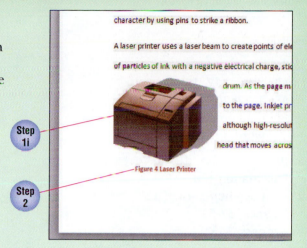

i. Move the laser printer image so it is positioned at the left side of the second paragraph of text in the *PRINTERS* section as shown at the right.

2. Add the caption *Figure 4 Laser Printer* to the printer image and then center the caption.

3. Click on any character in the table of figures.

4. Press the F9 function key on your keyboard.

5. At the Update Table of Figures dialog box, click the *Update entire table* option and then click OK.

6. Save and then print **WL2-C6-P3-TechRpt.docx**.

7. Close **WL2-C6-P3-TechRpt.docx**.

Project 4 Create an Index for a Desktop Publishing Report   2 Parts

You will open a report containing information on desktop publishing, mark specific text for an index, and then insert the index in the document. You will also make changes to the document and then update the index.

Creating an Index

An index is a list of topics contained in a publication, and the pages where those topics are discussed. Word lets you automate the process of creating an index in a manner similar to that used for creating a table of contents. When creating an index, you mark a word or words that you want included in the index. Creating an index takes some thought and consideration. The author of the book, manuscript, or report must determine the main entries desired and what subentries will be listed under main entries. An index may include such items as the main idea of a document, the main subject of a chapter or section, variations of a heading or subheading, and abbreviations. Figure 6.9 shows an example of an index.

Marking Text for an Index

A selected word or words can be marked for inclusion in an index. Before marking words for an index, determine what main entries and subentries are to be included in the index. Selected text is marked as an index entry at the Mark Index Entry text box. To mark text for an index, select the word or words, click the References tab, and then click the Mark Entry button in the Index group. You can also press Alt + Shift + X. At the Mark Index Entry dialog box, shown in Figure 6.10, the selected word(s) appears in the *Main entry* text box. Make any necessary changes to the dialog box and then click the Mark button. (When you click the Mark button, Word automatically turns on the display of nonprinting symbols and displays the index field code.) Click the Close button to close the Mark Index Entry dialog box.

Figure 6.9 Sample Index

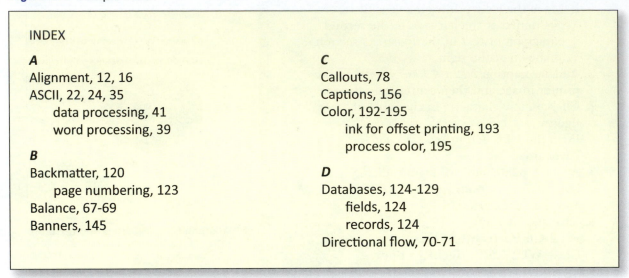

INDEX

A
Alignment, 12, 16
ASCII, 22, 24, 35
    data processing, 41
    word processing, 39

B
Backmatter, 120
    page numbering, 123
Balance, 67-69
Banners, 145

C
Callouts, 78
Captions, 156
Color, 192-195
    ink for offset printing, 193
    process color, 195

D
Databases, 124-129
    fields, 124
    records, 124
Directional flow, 70-71

Figure 6.10 Mark Index Entry Dialog Box

Specify text as a main entry and/or subentry in an index with these two options.

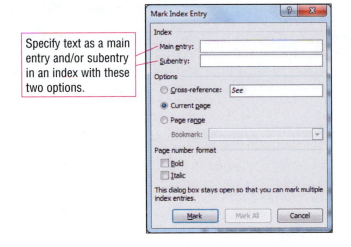

At the Mark Index Entry dialog box, the selected word or words displays in the *Main entry* text box. If the text is a main entry, leave it as displayed. If, however, the selected text is a subentry, type the main entry in the *Main entry* text box, click in the *Subentry* text box, and then type the selected text. For example, suppose a publication includes the terms *Page layout* and *Portrait*. The words *Page layout* are to be marked as a main entry for the index and *Portrait* is to be marked as a subentry below *Page layout*. To mark these words for an index, you would complete the following steps:

1. Select *Page layout*.
2. Click the References tab and then click the Mark Entry button or press Alt + Shift + X.
3. At the Mark Index Entry dialog box, click the Mark button. (This turns on the display of nonprinting symbols.)
4. With the Mark Index Entry dialog box still displayed on the screen, click in the document to make the document active, and then select *Portrait*.

5. Click the Mark Index Entry dialog box title bar to make it active.
6. Select *Portrait* in the *Main entry* text box and then type **Page layout**.
7. Click in the *Subentry* text box and then type **Portrait**.
8. Click the Mark button.
9. Click the Close button.

The main entry and subentry do not have to be the same as the selected text. You can select text for an index, type the text you want to display in the *Main entry* or *Subentry* text box, and then click the Mark button. At the Mark Index Entry dialog box, you can apply bold and/or italic formatting to the page numbers that will appear in the index. To apply formatting, click *Bold* and/or *Italic* to insert a check mark in the check box.

The *Options* section of the Mark Index Entry dialog box contains several options, with *Current page* the default. At this setting, the current page number will be listed in the index for the main and/or subentry. If you click *Cross-reference*, you would type the text you want to use as a cross-reference for the index entry in the *Cross-reference* text box. For example, you could mark the word *Serif* and cross reference it to *Typefaces*.

Click the Mark All button at the Mark Index Entry dialog box to mark all occurrences of the text in the document as index entries. Word marks only those entries whose uppercase and lowercase letters exactly match the index entry.

To include a third-level index entry, type the subentry text, type a colon, and then type the third-level entry text.

To delete an index entry, select the entire entry field including the braces ({}) and then press the Delete key.

Project 4a **Marking Words for an Index** Part 1 of 2

1. Open **DTP.docx** and then save the document with Save As and name it **WL2-C6-P4-DTP**.
2. Number pages at the bottom center of each page.
3. Mark the word *software* in the first paragraph for the index as a main entry and mark *word processing* in the first paragraph as a subentry below *software* by completing the following steps:
   a. Select *software* (located in the second sentence of the first paragraph).
   b. Click the References tab and then click the Mark Entry button in the Index group.
   c. At the Mark Index Entry dialog box, click the Mark All button. (This turns on the display of nonprinting symbols.)

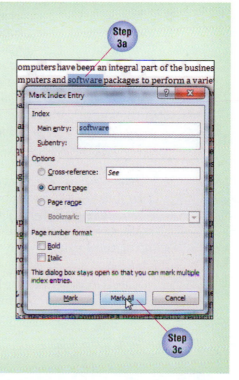

Step 3a

Step 3c

d. With the Mark Index Entry dialog box still displayed, click in the document to make the document active and then select *word processing* (located in the last sentence of the first paragraph). (You may want to drag the dialog box down the screen so more of the document text is visible.)

e. Click the Mark Index Entry dialog box title bar to make it active.

f. Select *word processing* in the *Main entry* text box and then type **software**.

g. Click in the *Subentry* text box and then type **word processing**.

h. Click the Mark All button.

i. With the Mark Index Entry dialog box still displayed, complete steps similar to those in 3d through 3h to mark the *first* occurrence of the following words as main entries or subentries for the index:

    In the first paragraph in the *Defining Desktop Publishing* section:

spreadsheets	=	subentry (main entry = *software*)
database	=	subentry (main entry = *software*)

    In the second paragraph in the *Defining Desktop Publishing* section:

publishing	=	main entry
desktop	=	subentry (main entry = *publishing*)
printer	=	main entry
laser	=	subentry (main entry = *printer*)

    In the third paragraph in the *Defining Desktop Publishing* section:

design	=	main entry

    In the fourth paragraph in the *Defining Desktop Publishing* section:

traditional	=	subentry (main entry = *publishing*)

    In the only paragraph in the *Initiating the Process* section:

publication	=	main entry
planning	=	subentry (main entry = *publication*)
creating	=	subentry (main entry = *publication*)
intended audience	=	subentry (main entry = *publication*)
content	=	subentry (main entry = *publication*)

    In the third paragraph in the *Planning the Publication* section:

message	=	main entry

j. Click Close to close the Mark Index Entry dialog box.

4. Turn off the display of nonprinting characters.

5. Save **WL2-C6-P4-DTP.docx**.

Inserting an Index

After you have marked all of the words that you want to include in an index as either main entries or subentries, the next step is to insert the index. An index should appear at the end of a document, generally beginning on a separate page. To insert the index, position the insertion point at the end of the document and then insert a page break. With the insertion point positioned below the page break, type **INDEX** centered and bolded and then press the Enter key. With the insertion point positioned at the left margin, click the References tab and then click the Insert Index button in the Index group. At the Index dialog box shown in Figure 6.11, select the desired formatting and then click OK. Word inserts the index at the location of the insertion point with the formatting selected at the Index dialog box. Word also inserts a section break above and below the index text.

At the Index dialog box, you can specify how the index entries will appear. The *Print Preview* section shows how the index will display in the document. The *Columns* option has a default setting of *2*. At this setting, the index will display in two newspaper columns. You can increase or decrease this number.

By default, numbers are right-aligned in the index. If you do not want numbers right-aligned, click the *Right align page numbers* check box to remove the check mark. The *Tab leader* option is dimmed for all formats except *Formal*. If you click *Formal* in the *Formats* option box, the *Tab leader* option displays in black. The default tab leader character is a period. To change to a different character, click the down-pointing arrow at the right of the option box and then click the desired character.

In the *Type* section, the *Indented* option is selected by default. At this setting, subentries will appear indented below main entries. If you click *Run-in*, subentries will display on the same line as main entries.

Click the down-pointing arrow at the right side of the *Formats* option box and a list of formatting choices displays. At this list, click the desired formatting and the *Print Preview* box will display how the index will appear in the document.

▼ **Quick Steps**

Insert an Index
1. Click References tab.
2. Click Insert Index button.
3. Select desired format.
4. Click OK.

Insert Index

Figure 6.11 Index Dialog Box

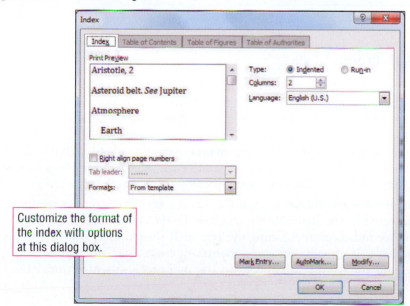

Customize the format of the index with options at this dialog box.

1. With **WL2-C6-P4-DTP.docx** open, insert the index in the document by completing the following steps:
   a. Press Ctrl + End to position the insertion point at the end of the document.
   b. Insert a page break.
   c. With the insertion point positioned below the page break, press Ctrl + E and then type **INDEX**.
   d. Press the Enter key and then change the paragraph alignment back to left.
   e. Click the References tab.
   f. Click the Insert Index button in the Index group.
   g. At the Index dialog box, click the down-pointing arrow at the right side of the *Formats* option box and then click *Modern* at the drop-down list.
   h. Click OK to close the dialog box.
   i. Select the title *INDEX* and then apply the Heading 1 style.
2. Save and then print the last page (the Index page) of the document.
3. Close **WL2-C6-P4-DTP.docx**.

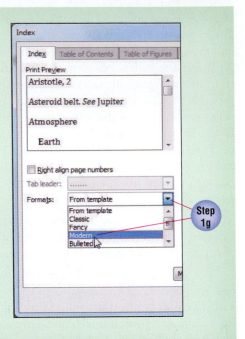

Project **5**   **Create an Index with a Concordance File for a Newsletter Report**   **3 Parts**

You will create and then save a concordance file. You will then open a report containing information on designing newsletters and use the concordance file to create an index.

Creating a Concordance File

▼ Quick Steps

Create a Concordance File
1. Click Insert tab.
2. Click Table button and drag to create table.
3. In first column, type words you want in index.
4. In second column, type the main entry and subentry.
5. Save document.

You can save words that appear frequently in a document as a concordance file. This saves you from having to mark each reference in a document. A *concordance file* is a regular Word document containing a single two-column table with no text outside the table. In the first column of the table, you enter words you want to index. In the second column, you enter the main entry and subentry that should appear in the index. To create a subentry, separate each main entry from a subentry by a colon. Figure 6.12 shows an example of a completed concordance file.

In the concordance file shown in Figure 6.12, the text as it appears in the document is inserted in the first column (such as *World War I*, *Technology*, and *technology*). The second column contains the text as it should appear in the index specifying whether it is a main entry or subentry. For example, the text *motion pictures* in the concordance file will appear in the index as a subentry under the main entry *Technology*.

After you have created a concordance file, you can use it to quickly mark text for an index in a document. To do this, open the document containing text you want marked for the index, display the Index and Tables dialog box with the Index tab selected, and then click the AutoMark button. At the Open Index AutoMark File dialog box, double-click the concordance file name in the list box. Word turns on the display of nonprinting symbols, searches through the document for text that matches the text in the concordance file, and then marks it accordingly. After marking text for the index, insert the index in the document as described earlier.

As you create the concordance file in Project 5a, Word's AutoCorrect feature will automatically capitalize the first letter of the first word entered in each cell. In Figure 6.12, you can see that several of the first words in the first column do not begin with a capital letter. Before beginning the project, consider turning off this AutoCorrect capitalization feature. To do this, click the File tab and then click the Options button. At the Word Options dialog box, click *Proofing* at the left side of the dialog box and then click the AutoCorrect Options button. At the AutoCorrect dialog box with the AutoCorrect tab selected, click the *Capitalize first letter of table cells* check box to remove the check mark. Click OK to close the dialog box and then click OK to close the Word Options dialog box.

Figure 6.12 Concordance File

World War I	World War I
Technology	Technology
technology	Technology
Teletypewriters	Technology: teletypewriters
motion pictures	Technology: motion pictures
Television	Technology: television
Radio Corporation of America	Radio Corporation of America
coaxial cable	Coaxial cable
Telephone	Technology: telephone
Communications Act of 1934	Communications Act of 1934
World War II	World War II
radar system	Technology: radar system
Computer	Computer
Atanasoff Berry Computer	Computer: Atanasoff Berry Computer
Korean War	Korean War
Columbia Broadcasting System	Columbia Broadcasting System
Cold War	Cold War
Vietnam	Vietnam
artificial satellite	Technology: artificial satellite
Communications Satellite Act of 1962	Communications Satellite Act of 1962

1. At a blank document, create the text shown in Figure 6.13 as a concordance file by completing the following steps:
   a. Click the Insert tab.
   b. Click the Table button in the Tables group.
   c. Drag down and to the right until *2 × 1 Table* displays at the top of the grid and then click the left mouse button.
   d. Type the text in the cells as shown in Figure 6.13. Press the Tab key to move to the next cell. (If you did not remove the check mark before the *Capitalize first letter of table cells* option at the AutoCorrect dialog box, the *n* in the first word in the first cell, *newsletters*, is automatically capitalized. Hover the mouse over the *N*, click the blue rectangle that displays below the *N*, and then click *Stop Auto-capitalizing First Letter of Table Cells*.)
2. Save the document and name it **WL2-C6-P5-CFile**.
3. Print and then close **WL2-C6-P5-CFile.docx**.

Figure 6.13 Project 5a

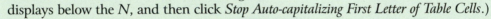

newsletters	Newsletters
Newsletters	Newsletters
Software	Software
Desktop publishing	Software: desktop publishing
word processing	Software: word processing
Printers	Printers
Laser	Printers: laser
Design	Design
Communication	Communication
Consistency	Design: consistency
Elements	Elements
Nameplate	Elements: nameplate
Logo	Elements: logo
Subtitle	Elements: subtitle
Folio	Elements: folio
Headlines	Elements: headlines
Subheads	Elements: subheads
Byline	Elements: byline
Body Copy	Elements: body copy
Graphics Images	Elements: graphics images
Audience	Newsletters: audience
Purpose	Newsletters: purpose
focal point	Newsletters: focal point

If you removed the check mark before the *Capitalize first letter of table cells* option at the AutoCorrect dialog box, you may need to turn this feature back on. To do this, click the File tab and then click the Options button. At the Word Options dialog box, click *Proofing* at the left side of the dialog box and then click the AutoCorrect Options button. At the AutoCorrect dialog box with the AutoCorrect tab selected, click the *Capitalize first letter of table cells* check box to insert the check mark. Click OK to close the dialog box and then click OK to close the Word Options dialog box.

Project 5b **Inserting an Index Using a Concordance File** **Part 2 of 3**

1. Open **PlanNwsltr.docx** and then save the document with Save As and name it **WL2-C6-P5-PlanNwsltr**.
2. Mark text for the index using the concordance file by completing the following steps:
   a. Click the References tab.
   b. Click the Insert Index button in the Index group.
   c. At the Index dialog box, click the AutoMark button.
   d. At the Open Index AutoMark File dialog box, double-click **WL2-C6-P5-CFile.docx** in the Content pane. (This turns on the display of the nonprinting symbols.)
3. Insert the index in the document by completing the following steps:
   a. Position the insertion point at the end of the document.
   b. Insert a page break.
   c. Type **INDEX**.
   d. Press the Enter key.
   e. Click the Insert Index button in the Index group.
   f. At the Index dialog box, click the down-pointing arrow at the right side of the *Formats* option box and then click *Formal* at the drop-down list.
   g. Click OK to close the dialog box.
4. Apply the Heading 1 style to the *INDEX* title and then center the title.
5. Turn off the display of nonprinting characters.
6. Save **WL2-C6-P5-PlanNwsltr.docx** and then print only the Index page.

Updating and Deleting an Index

If you make changes to a document after inserting an index, update the index. To do this, click anywhere within the current index and then click the Update Index button in the Index group or press F9. To delete an index, select the entire index using either the mouse or the keyboard and then press the Delete key.

▼ **Quick Steps**

Update an Index
1. Click in index.
2. Click Update Index button or press F9.

Delete an Index
1. Select entire index.
2. Press Delete key.

Update Index

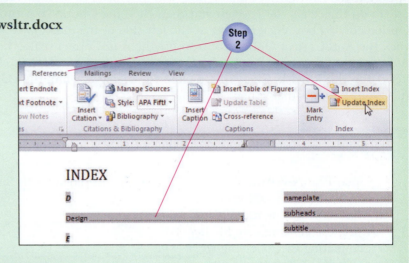

1. With **WL2-C6-P5-PlanNwsltr.docx** open, insert a page break at the beginning of the title *PLANNING A NEWSLETTER*.
2. Update the index by clicking anywhere in the index, clicking the References tab, and then clicking the Update Index button in the Index group.
3. Save **WL2-C6-P5-PlanNwsltr.docx** and then print only the Index page.
4. Close **WL2-C6-P5-PlanNwsltr.docx**.

Chapter Summary

- Word provides options for automating the creation of a table of contents, table of figures, and index.

- Text to be included in a table of contents can be identified by applying a heading style, assigning a level, or marking text as a field entry.

- Mark text as a field entry at the Mark Table of Contents dialog box. Display this dialog box by pressing Alt + Shift + O.

- Creating a table of contents involves two steps: applying the appropriate styles to mark text that will be included and inserting the table of contents in the document.

- To insert the table of contents, position the insertion point where you want the table to appear, click the References tab, click the Table of Contents button, and then click the desired option at the drop-down list.

- If you want the table of contents to print on a page separate from the document text, insert a section break that begins a new page between the table of contents and the title of the document.

- If you make changes to a document after inserting a table of contents, update the table of contents by clicking anywhere in the table and then clicking the Update Table button in the References tab or pressing F9. Update a table of figures or index in a similar manner.

- Remove a table of contents by clicking the Table of Contents button in the References tab and then clicking *Remove Table of Contents* at the drop-down list.

- Create a table of figures by marking specific text or images as captions and then using the caption names to create the table of figures. Mark captions at the Caption dialog box. Display this dialog box by clicking the Insert Caption button in the References tab.

- Insert a table of figures in a document in a manner similar to a table of contents. A table of figures generally displays at the beginning of the document, after the table of contents.

- An index is a list of topics contained in a publication and the pages on which those topics are discussed. Word automates the process of creating an index in a manner similar to that for creating a table of contents.

- Mark text for an index at the Mark Index Entry dialog box. Display this dialog box by clicking the Mark Entry button in the References tab or pressing Alt + Shift + X.

- After all necessary text has been marked as a main entry or subentry for the index, insert the index, placing it on a separate page at the end of the document.

- Word provides seven formatting choices for an index at the *Formats* option box at the Index dialog box.

- Words that appear frequently in a document can be saved as a concordance file so that you need not mark each reference in a document. A concordance file is a regular document containing a single two-column table.

Commands Review

FEATURE	RIBBON TAB, GROUP	BUTTON, OPTION	KEYBOARD SHORTCUT
Page Number Format dialog box	Insert, Header & Footer	, Format Page Numbers	
Table of Contents dialog box	References, Table of Contents	, Insert Table of Contents	
Update Table of Contents	References, Table of Contents		F9
Mark Table of Contents Entry dialog box			Alt + Shift + O
Table of Contents Options dialog box	References, Table of Contents	, Insert Table of Contents, Options	
Caption dialog box	References, Captions		
Table of Figures dialog box	References, Captions		
Mark Index Entry dialog box	References, Index		Alt + Shift + X
Index dialog box	References, Index		
Open Index AutoMark File dialog box	References, Index		

Concepts Check Test Your Knowledge

Completion: In the space provided at the right, indicate the correct term, symbol, or command.

1. In a built-in table of contents, Word uses as the first level, text with this heading applied. _____

2. A table of contents generally appears in this location in the document. _____

3. A table of contents is generally numbered with this type of number. _____

4. This is the keyboard shortcut to update a table of contents. _____

5. This is the keyboard shortcut to display the Mark Table of Contents Entry dialog box. _____

6. If you mark table of contents entries as fields, you will need to activate this option at the Table of Contents Options dialog box. _____

7. Create a table of figures by marking figure names as these. _____

8. This is the keyboard shortcut to display the Mark Index Entry dialog box. _____

9. An index generally appears at this location in the document. _____

10. Create this type of file and then use it to save time when marking text for an index. _____

Skills Check Assess Your Performance

Assessment

1 CREATE AND UPDATE A TABLE OF CONTENTS FOR A PHOTOGRAPHY REPORT

1. Open **PhotoRpt.docx** and then save the document with Save As and name it **WL2-C6-A1-PhotoRpt**.
2. Insert at the beginning of the heading *Photography* a section break that begins a new page.
3. With the insertion point positioned below the section break, insert page numbering at the bottom center of pages and change the beginning number to 1.
4. Press Ctrl + Home to move the insertion point to the beginning of the document (on the blank page) and then create a table of contents with the *Automatic Table 1* option at the Table of Contents button drop-down list.

5. Change the page number format on the Table of Contents page to lowercase Roman numerals.
6. Save the document and then print only the table of contents page.
7. Insert a page break at the beginning of the heading *Camera Basics*.
8. Update the table of contents.
9. Save the document and then print only the table of contents page.
10. Close **WL2-C6-A1-PhotoRpt.docx**.

Assessment

2 INSERT CAPTIONS AND A TABLE OF FIGURES IN A REPORT

1. Open **InputDevices.docx** and then save the document with Save As and name it **WL2-C6-A2-InputDevices**.
2. Insert a caption for each of the three images in the document and center each caption. (You determine the name of each caption.)
3. Move the insertion point to the beginning of the title *Computer Input Devices* and then insert a section break that begins a new page.
4. Press Ctrl + Home and then insert a table of figures with the title *Table of Figures*. (You determine the Table of Figures format.)
5. Apply the Heading 1 style to the title *Table of Figures*.
6. Move the insertion point to the title *Computer Input Devices* and then insert page numbering at the bottom center of each page and change the starting number to 1.
7. Move the insertion point to the title *TABLE OF FIGURES* and then change the page numbering style to lowercase Roman numerals.
8. Insert a page break at the beginning of the *TRACKBALL* heading.
9. Update the table of figures.
10. Save, print, and then close **WL2-C6-A2-InputDevices.docx**.

Assessment

3 CREATE AND UPDATE A TABLE OF CONTENTS AND INDEX FOR A NEWSLETTER REPORT

1. At a blank document, create the text shown in Figure 6.14 as a concordance file.
2. Save the document and name it **WL2-C6-A3-CFile**.
3. Print and then close **WL2-C6-A3-CFile.docx**.
4. Open **DesignNwsltr.docx**.
5. Save the document with Save As and name it **WL2-C6-A3-DesignNwsltr**.
6. Make the following changes to the document:
   a. Mark text for an index using the concordance file **WL2-C6-A3-CFile.docx**.
   b. Insert the index at the end of the document on a separate page.
   c. Apply the Heading 1 style to the index title and then center the title.
7. Number the pages at the bottom center of each page.
8. Change the paragraph spacing to *Double* using the Change Styles button in the Home tab. (The index will not be double-spaced.)
9. Insert a page break at the beginning of the title *CREATING NEWSLETTER LAYOUT*.
10. Update the index.
11. Save the document, print the index, and then close **WL2-C6-A3-DesignNwsltr.docx**.

Figure 6.14 Assessment 3

NEWSLETTER	Newsletter
newsletter	Newsletter
consistency	Newsletter: consistency
element	Elements
margins	Elements: margins
column layout	Elements: column layout
nameplate	Elements: nameplate
location	Elements: location
logos	Elements: logo
color	Elements: color
ruled lines	Elements: ruled lines
Focus	Elements: focus
balance	Elements: balance
graphics	Graphics
images	Images
photos	Photos
Headlines	Newsletter: headlines
subheads	Newsletter: subheads
White space	White space
directional flow	Newsletter: directional flow
paper	Paper
Size	Paper: size
type	Paper: type
weight	Paper: weight
stock	Paper: stock
margin size	Newsletter: margin size

Assessment

 4 **CUSTOMIZE AN INDEX**

1. You can customize an index with options at the Index dialog box. At a blank document, display this dialog box by clicking the References tab and then clicking the Insert Index button in the Index group. Look at the options offered by the dialog box and determine how to change leaders and number of columns. Close the blank document.
2. Open **WL2-C6-A3-DesignNwsltr.docx** and then save the document with Save As and name it **WL2-C6-A4-DesignNwsltr**.
3. Apply the Adjacency theme.
4. Remove the page break that you inserted before the title *CREATING NEWSLETTER LAYOUT*. ***Hint: Do this by positioning the insertion point after the period that ends the paragraph that displays before the title and then pressing the Delete key two times.***

5. Make the following changes to the index:
   a. Display the Index dialog box for the index.
   b. Change to a format that contains leaders.
   c. Change the leaders to hyphens (rather than periods).
   d. Specify three columns.
   e. Close the Index dialog box. When asked if you want to replace the selected index, click OK.
6. Save **WL2-C6-A4-DesignNwsltr.docx**.
7. Print only the index and then close the document.

Visual Benchmark Demonstrate Your Proficiency

CREATE A TABLE OF CONTENTS AND TABLE OF FIGURES

1. Open **Networks.docx** and then save the document with Save As and name it **WL2-C6-VB-Networks**.
2. Format the document so it appears as shown in Figure 6.15 with the following specifications:
   a. Insert the captions for the figures as shown in Figure 6.15.
   b. Insert the table of contents as shown in Figure 6.15.
   c. Insert the table of figures as shown on the second page.
   d. Insert page numbering as shown.
   e. Apply any other formatting so your document appears as shown in Figure 6.15.
3. Save, print, and then close **WL2-C6-VB-Networks.docx**.

Figure 6.15 Visual Benchmark

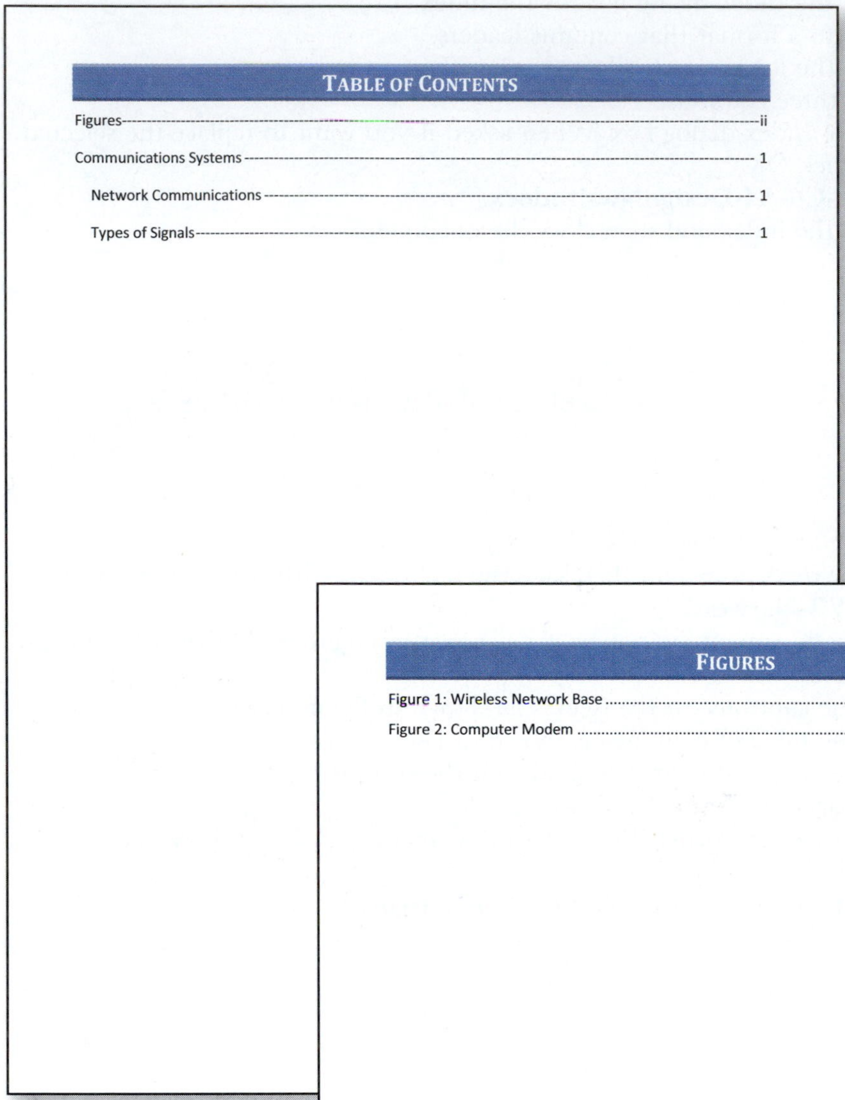

Table of Contents

Page 1

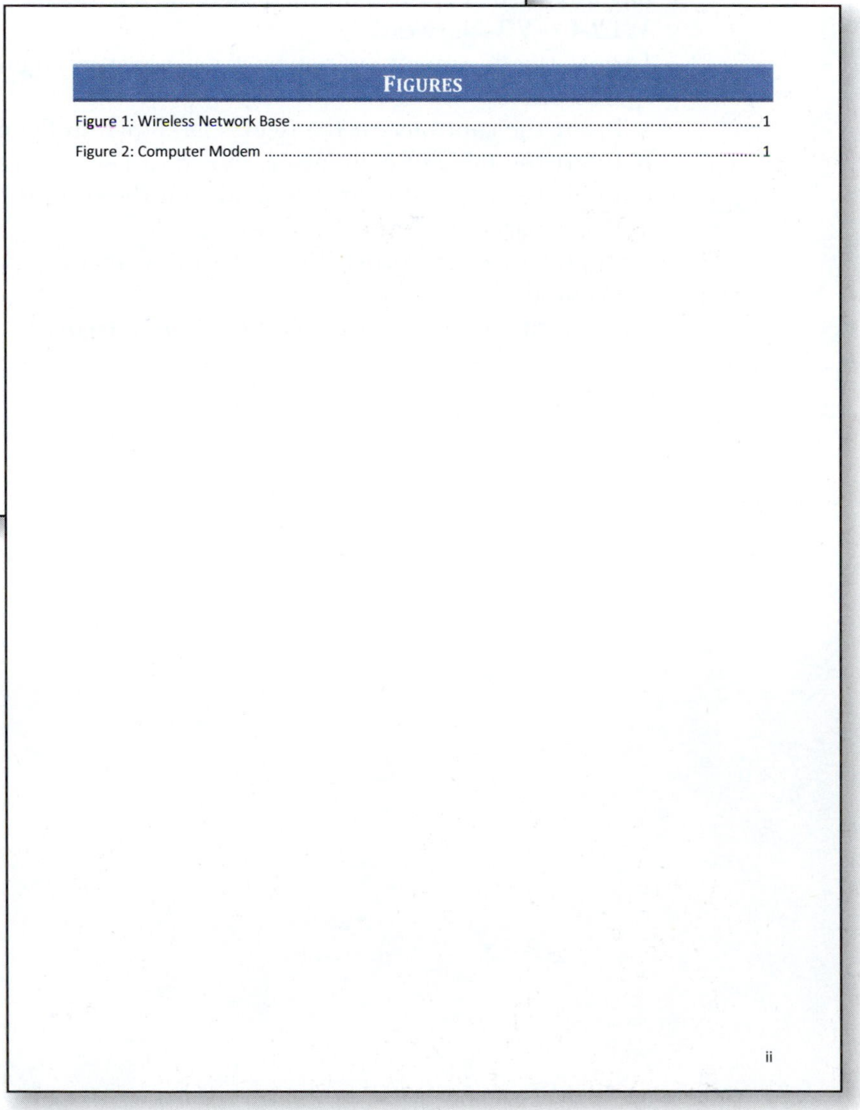

Figures

ii

Page 2

Figure 6.15 Visual Benchmark—*Continued*

COMMUNICATIONS SYSTEMS

A computer network is one kind of communications system. This system includes sending and receiving hardware, transmission and relay systems, common sets of standards so all the equipment can "talk" to each other, and communications software.

NETWORK COMMUNICATIONS

You use such a networked communications system whenever you send/receive IM or email messages, pay a bill online, shop at an Internet store, send a document to a shared printer at work or at home, or download a file.

The world of computer network communications systems is made up of:

- Transmission media upon which the data travels to/from its destination.
- A set of standards and network protocols (rules for how data is handled as it travels along a communications channel). Devices use these to send and receive data to and from each other.
- Hardware and software to connect to a communications pathway from the sending and receiving ends

The first step in understanding a co... transmission signals and transmissi...

TYPES OF SIGNALS

Two types of signals are used to tra... digital. An analog signal is formed b... voice is transmitted as an analog sig... signal uses a discrete signal that is e... 1, and low represents the digital bit...

Telephone lines carry your voice us...

rather, th... signals. If... phone lin... (modulate...

Figure 2: Computer Modem

computer on the receiving end. The piece of hardware that sends and receives data from a transmission source such as your telephone line or cable television connection is a modem. The word modem comes from the combination of the words *modulate* and *demodulate*.

Today, most new communications technologies simply use a digital signal, saving the trouble of converting transmissions. An example of this trend is the demise in 2009 of analog television transmissions as the industry switched to digital signals. Many people were sent scrambling to either buy a newer television set or buy a converter to convert digital transmissions back to analog to work with their older equipment. Newer computer networks, too, use a pure digital signal method of sending and receiving data over a network.

2

Page 3

Page 4

Case Study   Apply Your Skills

Part 1

You work in the Human Resources Department at Brennan Distributors. You are responsible for preparing an employee handbook. Open the **BDEmpHandbook.docx** document and then save the document with Save As and name it **WL2-C6-CS-BDEmpHandbook**. Apply the following to the document:

- Insert page breaks before each centered title (except first title, *Introduction*).
- Apply heading styles to the titles and headings.
- Change to a style set of your choosing.
- Apply a theme that makes the handbook easy to read.
- Insert a table of contents.
- Create a concordance file and then insert an index.
- Insert appropriate page numbering in the document.
- Insert a cover page.
- Add any other elements to improve the visual appeal of the document.

Save and then print **WL2-C6-CS-BDEmpHandbook.docx**.

Part 2

Your supervisor wants you to determine how to insert a caption for a table rather than a figure. ***Hint: Do this with the Label option in the Caption dialog box***. Open **NavigateWeb.docx** and then save the document with Save As and name it **WL2-C6-CS-NavigateWeb**. Apply the following to the document:

- Move the insertion point to the blank line above the first table in the document and then use the caption feature to create the caption *Table 1: Common Top-Level Domain Suffixes*.
- Move the insertion point to the blank line above the second table and then create the caption *Table 2: Common Search Tools*.
- Move the insertion point to the blank line above the third table and then create the caption *Table 3: Advanced Search Parameters*.
- Insert a table of contents at the beginning of the document.
- Insert a table of figures on the page following the table of contents.
- Insert appropriate page numbering in the document.
- Check the page breaks in the document and if a heading displays at the bottom of a page and the paragraph of text that follows displays at the top of the next page, format the heading so it stays with the paragraph of text that follows. ***Hint: Do this at the Paragraph dialog box with the Line and Page Breaks tab selected***.
- If necessary, update the entire table of contents and the table of figures.

Save, print, and then close **WL2-C6-CS-NavigateWeb.docx**.

Part 3

Send an email to your instructor detailing the steps you followed to create table captions. Attach **WL2-C6-CS-NavigateWeb.docx** to the email.

Microsoft® Word

CHAPTER 7

Working with Shared Documents

PERFORMANCE OBJECTIVES

Upon successful completion of Chapter 7, you will be able to:

- Insert, edit, and delete comments
- Track changes to a document and customize tracking
- Compare documents
- Combine documents
- Display a document in Web Layout view and Outline view
- Assign levels in Outline view
- Create a master document and subdocuments
- Open a new window

Tutorials

7.1 Inserting and Editing Comments

7.2 Inserting Comments in the Reviewing Pane; Distinguishing Comments from Other Users

7.3 Tracking Changes to a Document

7.4 Displaying for Review and Showing Markup

7.5 Customizing Track Changing and Compare Options

7.6 Comparing Documents

7.7 Combining Documents

7.8 Viewing and Sharing Documents

In a company environment, you may work with other employees and you may need to share and distribute documents to members of the company. You may be part of a workgroup in a company, which is a networked collection of computers sharing files, printers, and other resources. As a member of a workgroup, you can collaborate with other members of the workgroup and distribute documents for review and/ or revision. In this chapter, you will perform workgroup activities such as inserting comments, tracking changes in a document from multiple users, comparing documents, and combining documents from multiple users. Model answers for this chapter's projects appear on the following pages.

If a Word 2010 document (in the .docx format) is located on a server running Microsoft SharePoint Server 2010, multiple users can edit the document concurrently. Concurrent editing allows a group of users to work on a document at the same time or a single user to work on the same document from different computers. If a document is not located on a server running SharePoint Server 2010, Word 2010 supports only single-user editing. Exercises and assessments in this chapter assume that the files you are editing are not located on a server running SharePoint Server 2010.

Word2010L2C7

Note: Before beginning the projects, copy to your storage medium the Word2010L2C7 subfolder from the Word2010L2 folder on the CD that accompanies this textbook and then make Word2010L2C7 the active folder.

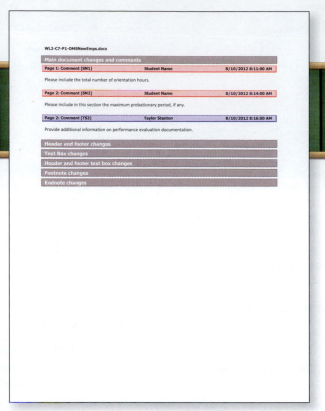

WL2-C7-P1-OMSNewEmps.docx

Main document changes and comments

| Page 1: Comment [SN1] | Student Name | 8/10/2012 8:11:00 AM |

Please include the total number of orientation hours.

| Page 2: Comment [SN2] | Student Name | 8/10/2012 8:14:00 AM |

Please include in this section the maximum probationary period, if any.

| Page 2: Comment [TS3] | Taylor Stanton | 8/10/2012 8:16:00 AM |

Provide additional information on performance evaluation documentation.

Header and footer changes

Text Box changes

Header and footer text box changes

Footnote changes

Endnote changes

Project 1 Insert Comments in a New Employees Document

WL2-C7-P1-OMSNewEmps.docx

BUILDING CONSTRUCTION AGREEMENT

THIS AGREEMENT made this _____ day of _____, 2012, by and between _____, hereinafter referred to as "builder," and _____, hereinafter referred to as "owner," the builder and the owner, for the considerations hereinafter named, agree as follows:

Construction Loan and Financing Arrangements: The owner either has or will obtain a construction loan to finance the work to be performed under this Agreement. If adequate financing has not been arranged within sixty (60) days of the date of this Agreement, or the owner cannot provide evidence to the builder of other financial ability to pay the full amount of the contract, then the builder at his option may treat this Agreement as null and void, and retain the down payment made on the execution of this Agreement.

Supervision of Work: Owner agrees that the direction and supervision of the working force including subcontractor, rests exclusively with the builder or his/her duly designated agent, and owner agrees not to issue any instructions to, or otherwise interfere with, same.

Start of Construction: The builder shall commence construction of the residence as soon as practical after signing of this Agreement and adequate financial arrangements satisfactory to the builder have been made.

Changes and Alterations: All changes in or departures from the plans and/or specifications shall be in writing. Where changes in or departures from plans and specifications requested in writing by owner will result in furnishing of additional labor and materials, the owner shall pay the builder for such extras at a price agreed upon in writing before commencement of said change. Where such change results in the omitting of any labor or materials, the builder shall allow the owner a credit therefore at a price agreed to in writing before commencement of said changes.

Possession of Residence: On final payment by owner and upon owner's request, builder will provide owner with affidavit stating that all labor, materials, and equipment used in the construction have been paid for or will be paid for in full by the builder unless otherwise noted. Builder shall not be required to give possession of the residence to the owner before final payment by owner. Final payment constitutes acceptance of the residence as being satisfactorily completed unless a separate escrow agreement is executed between the parties stipulating the unfinished items.

Exclusions: The owner is solely responsible for the purchase and installation of any septic tank or other individual subsurface sewage disposal system that may be required on the property.

Builder's Right to Terminate the Contract: Should the work be stopped by any public authority for a period of sixty (60) days or more, through no fault of the builder, or should the work be stopped through act or neglect of the owner for a period of seven days, or should the owner fail to pay the builder any payment within seven days after it is due, then the builder upon seven days written notice to the owner,

Page 1

Project 2 Track Changes in a Building Construction Agreement

WL2-C7-P2-Agreement.docx

---

may stop work or terminate the contract and recover from the owner payment for all work executed and any loss sustained and reasonable profit and damages.

The owner acknowledges that she/he has read and fully understands the provisions of this Agreement.

IN WITNESS WHEREOF, the builder and owner have hereunto set their hands this _____ day of _____, 20____.

_____   _____
BUILDER   OWNER

Page 2

COMMERCIAL LEASE AGREEMENT

This Commercial Lease Agreement ("Lease") is made by and between _____ ("Landlord") and _____ ("Tenant"). Landlord is the owner of land and improvements commonly known and numbered as _____ and legally described as follows (the "Building"): _____ _____. Landlord makes available for lease a portion of the Building designated as _____ (the "Leased Premises").

Landlord desires to lease the Leased Premises to Tenant, and Tenant desires to lease the Leased Premises from Landlord for the term at the rental, and upon the covenants, conditions, and provisions herein set forth.

THEREFORE, in consideration of the mutual promises herein contained, and other good and valuable consideration, it is agreed:

Term

A. Landlord hereby leases the Leased Premises to Tenant, and Tenant hereby leases the same from Landlord, for an "Initial Term" beginning _____ and ending _____. Landlord shall use his/her best efforts to give Tenant possession as nearly as possible at the beginning of the Lease term. If Landlord is unable to timely provide the Leased Premises, rent shall abate for the period of delay. Tenant shall make no other claim against Landlord for any such delay.

B. Tenant may renew the Lease for one extended term of _____. Tenant shall exercise such renewal option by giving written notice to Landlord not less than ninety (90) days prior to the expiration of the Initial Term. The renewal term shall be at the rental set forth below and otherwise upon the same covenants, conditions, and provisions as provided in this Lease.

Rental

A. Tenant shall pay to Landlord during the Initial Term rental of _____ per year, payable in installments of _____ per month. Each installment payment shall be due in advance on the first day of each calendar month during the lease term to Landlord at _____ or at such other place designated by written notice from Landlord or Tenant. The rental payment amount for any partial calendar months included in the lease term shall be prorated on a daily basis. Tenant shall also pay to Landlord a "Security Deposit" in the amount of _____.

B. The rental for any renewal lease term, if created as permitted under this Lease, shall be _____ per year payable in installments of _____ per month.

Page 1

Project 3 Compare Lease Agreement Documents

WL2-C7-P3-ComAgrmnt.docx

Model Answers

Use

Notwithstanding the forgoing, Tenant shall not use the Leased Premises for the purposes of storing, manufacturing, or selling any explosives, flammables, or other inherently dangerous substance, chemical, item, or device.

Repairs

During the Lease term, Tenant shall make, at Tenant's expense, all necessary repairs to the Leased Premises. Repairs shall include such items as routine repairs of floors, walls, ceilings, and other parts of the Leased Premises damaged or worn through normal occupancy, except for major mechanical systems or the roof, subject to the obligations of the parties otherwise set forth in this Lease.

Sublease and Assignment

Tenant shall have the right, without Landlord's consent, to assign this Lease to a corporation with which Tenant may merge or consolidate, to any subsidiary of Tenant, to any corporation under common control with Tenant, or to a purchaser of substantially all of Tenant's assets. Except as set forth above, Tenant shall not sublease all or any part of the Leased Premises, or assign this Lease in whole or in part without Landlord's consent, such consent not to be unreasonably withheld or delayed.

Property Taxes

Landlord shall pay all general real estate taxes and installments of special assessments coming due during the Lease term on the Leased Premises, and all personal property taxes with respect to Landlord's personal property, if any, on the Leased Premises. Tenant shall be responsible for paying all personal property taxes with respect to Tenant's personal property at the Leased Premises.

Landlord _____

Tenant _____

Page 2

LEASE AGREEMENT

THIS LEASE AGREEMENT (hereinafter referred to as the "Agreement") is made and entered into this ___ day of _____, 2012, by and between Lessor and Lessee.

Term

Lessor leases to Lessee and Lessee leases from Lessor the described Premises together with any and all appurtenances thereto, for a term of ____ year(s), such term beginning on _____ and ending at midnight on _____.

Damage Deposit

Upon the signing of this Agreement, Lessee shall deposit with Lessor the sum of _____ DOLLARS ($_____) receipt of which is hereby acknowledged by Lessor, as security for any damage caused to the Premises during the leasing term. Such deposit shall be returned to Lessee, without interest ,upon the termination of this leasing Agreement.

Rent

The total rent for the term hereof is the sum of _____ DOLLARS ($ _____) less any reimbursements and payable on the _____ day of each month of the term. All such payments shall be made to Lessor at Lessor's address on or before the due date and without demand.

Use of Premises

The Premises shall be used and occupied by Lessee and Lessee's immediate family, exclusively, as a private, single-family dwelling, and no part of the Premises shall be used at any time during the term of this Agreement by Lessee for the purpose of carrying on any business, profession, or trade of any kind, or for any purpose other than as a private, single-family dwelling. Lessee shall not allow any other person, other than Lessee's immediate family or transient relatives and friends who are guests of Lessee, to use or occupy the Premises without first obtaining Lessor's written consent to such use.

Condition of Premises

Lessee stipulates, represents, and warrants that Lessee has examined the Premises, and that they are at the time of this Agreement in good order, repair, and in a safe, clean, and tenantable condition.

Alterations and Improvements

Lessee shall make no alterations to or improvements on the Premises without the prior written consent of Lessor. Any and all alterations, changes, and/or improvements built, constructed, or placed on the Premises by Lessee shall be and become the property of the Lessor and remain on the Premises at the expiration or earlier termination of this Agreement.

Page 1

Project 4 Combine Documents

WL2-C7-P4-CombinedLease.docx

Damage to Premises

In the event Premises are destroyed or rendered wholly unlivable by fire, storm, earthquake, or other casualty not caused by the negligence of Lessee, this Agreement shall terminate from such time except for the purpose of enforcing rights that may have accrued hereunder.

LESSEE _____

LESSOR _____

Page 2

CHAPTER 1: SECURITY RISKS

Although hackers, crackers, and viruses garner the most attention as security risks, companies face a variety of other dangers to their hardware and software systems. Principally, these risks involve types of system failure, employee theft, and the cracking of software for copying.

EMPLOYEE THEFT

Although accurate estimates are difficult to pinpoint, businesses certainly lose millions of dollars a year in stolen computer hardware and software. In large organizations, such theft often goes unnoticed or unreported. Someone takes a hard drive or a scanner home for legitimate use, then leaves the job sometime later and keeps the machine. Sometimes, employees take components to add to their home PC systems, or thieves break into businesses and haul away computers. Such thefts cost far more than the price of the stolen computers because they also involve the cost of replacing the lost data, the cost of time lost while the machines are gone, and the cost of installing new machines and training people to use them.

SYSTEMS FAILURE

A fundamental element in making sure that computer systems operate properly is protecting the electrical power that runs them. Power interruptions such as blackouts and brownouts have very adverse effects on computers. An inexpensive type of power strip called a surge protector can guard against power fluctuations and can also serve as an extension cord and splitter. A much more vigorous power protection system is an uninterruptible power supply (UPS), which provides a battery backup. Similar in nature to a power strip but much bulkier and a bit more expensive, a UPS provides steady, spike-free power and keeps a computer running during a blackout.

CRACKING SOFTWARE FOR COPYING

A common goal of hackers is to crack a software protection scheme. A crack is a method of circumventing a security scheme that prevents a user from copying a program. A common protection scheme for software is to require the installation CD to be resident in the drive whenever the program runs. Making copies of the CD with a burner, however, easily fools this protection scheme. Some game companies are taking an extra step to make duplication difficult by scrambling some of the data on the original CDs, which CD burners will automatically correct when copying. When the copied and corrected CD is used, the software checks for the scrambled track information. If the error is not found, the software will not run.

CHAPTER 2: COMPUTER VIRUSES

One of the most familiar forms of risk to computer security is the computer virus. A computer virus is a program written by a hacker or a cracker, designed to perform some kind of trick upon an unsuspecting victim's computer. In some cases, the trick performed is mild, such as drawing an offensive image on the victim's screen or changing all of the characters in a document to another language. Sometimes the trick

Project 5 Organize and Edit Documents in Different Views

WL2-C7-P5-OutlineChapters.docx

SECTION A: NEWSLETTERS

Preparing a newsletter requires a number of preliminary steps. Before determining the contents of the newsletter, determine the basic elements to be included in the newsletter, study newsletter design, and determine the purpose of the newsletter.

G:\Word2010L2C7\MODULE 1.docx

G:\Word2010L2C7\MODULE 2.docx

G:\Word2010L2C7\MODULE 4.docx

WL2-C7-P5-Newsletters.docx

SECTION A: NEWSLETTERS

Preparing a newsletter requires a number of preliminary steps. Before determining the contents of the newsletter, determine the basic elements to be included in the newsletter, study newsletter design, and determine the purpose of the newsletter.

MODULE 1: DEFINING NEWSLETTER ELEMENTS

Designing a Newsletter

The demand for newsletters in the private and business sectors has helped to promote the desktop publishing revolution. Affordable word processing and desktop publishing software, along with laser printers, significantly reduced the cost of producing professional-quality newsletters. Now, users with limited budgets can create multiple-page documents in-house, providing organizations, businesses, or individuals with a cost-effective means of communicating.

Designing a newsletter may seem like a simple task, but newsletters are more complex than they appear. Producing one may be the ultimate test of your desktop publishing skills. Remember that your goal is to get a message across. Design is important because it increases the overall appeal of your newsletter, but content is still the most important consideration. Whether your purpose for creating a newsletter is to develop better communication within your company or to develop awareness of a product or service, your newsletter must give the appearance of being well planned, orderly, and consistent. To establish consistency from one issue of a newsletter to the next, carefully plan your document.

Newsletters are one of the most common means of communicating information and ideas to other people. Newsletters may be published by individuals, associations, clubs, churches, schools, businesses, consultants, service organizations, political organizations, government offices, and other organizations all over the world.

Defining Basic Newsletter Elements

Successful newsletters contain consistent elements in every issue. Basic newsletter elements divide the newsletter into organized sections to help the reader understand the text, as well as entice the reader to continue reading. Basic newsletter elements include the following:

- **Nameplate:** The nameplate, or banner, consists of the newsletter's title and is usually located on the front page. Nameplates may include a company logo, a unique typeface, or a graphics element to help create or reinforce a company identity.
- **Logo:** A graphic symbol of a company.
- **Subtitle:** A subtitle is a short phrase describing the purpose or audience of the newsletter. A subtitle may also be called a *tag line*. The information in the subtitle is usually located below the nameplate near the folio.
- **Folio:** A folio is the publication information including the volume, issue number, and current date of the newsletter.

Page 1

WL2-C7-P5-EditedNewsletters.docx

- **Headlines:** Headlines are titles to articles that are frequently created to attract the reader's attention. The headline may be set in 36- to 72-point type or larger and is generally keyed in a sans serif typeface.
- **Subheads:** Subheads are secondary headings that provide the transition from headlines to body copy. Subheads break up the text into organized sections.
- **Byline:** The byline identifies the author of the article.
- **Body Copy:** The main part of the newsletter is the body copy or text.
- **Graphics Images:** Graphics images are added to newsletters to help stimulate ideas and add interest to the document. They provide visual clues and visual relief to text-intensive copy.

MODULE 4: CREATING NEWSLETTER LAYOUT

Choosing Paper Size and Type

Among the first considerations in designing a newsletter page layout are paper size and type. These decisions may be affected by the number of copies needed and the equipment available for creating, printing, and distributing the newsletters. Most newsletters are created on standard-sized, 8.5-by-11-inch paper. However, some newsletters are printed on larger sheets, such as 11 by 14 inches. Standard 8.5-by-11-inch paper is the most economical choice for printing. Another consideration is that 8.5-by-11-inch paper is easier to hold and read. In addition, standard-sized paper is cheaper to mail and fits easily in standard file folders.

Choosing Paper Weight

The weight of the paper used for a newsletter is determined by the cost, the quality desired, and the graphics or photographs included. The heavier the stock, the more expensive the paper. In addition, pure white paper is more difficult to read because of glare. If possible, investigate other subtle colors. Another option is to purchase predesigned newsletter paper from a paper supply company. Predesigned papers come in many colors and designs. Several have different blocks of color created on a page to help separate and organize your text.

Creating Margins for Newsletters

After considering the paper size, type, and weight, determine the margins of your newsletter pages. Margin size is linked to the number of columns needed, the formality desired, the visual elements used, and the amount of text available. Keep all margins consistent throughout your newsletter. Listed here are a few generalizations about margins in newsletters:

- A wide right margin is considered formal. This approach positions the text at the left side of the page—the side where most readers tend to look first. If the justification is set at full, the newsletter will appear even more formal.
- A wide left margin is less formal. A table of contents or marginal subheads can be placed in the left margin giving the newsletter an airy, open appearance.
- Equal margins tend to create an informal look.

Page 2

Project 1 Insert Comments in a New Employees Document **4 Parts**

You will open a report containing company information for new employees and then insert and edit comments from multiple users.

Inserting and Managing Comments

You can provide feedback and suggest changes to a document that someone else has written by inserting comments into it. Similarly, you can obtain feedback on a document that you have written by distributing it electronically to others and having them insert their comments into it. To insert a comment in a document, select the text or item on which you want to comment or position the insertion point at the end of the text, click the Review tab, and then click the New Comment button in the Comments group. This displays a comment balloon at the right margin as shown in Figure 7.1.

Depending on any previous settings applied, clicking the New Comment button may cause the Reviewing pane to display at the left side of the document rather than the comment balloon. If this happens, click the Show Markup button in the Tracking group in the Review tab, point to *Balloons*, and then click *Show Only Comments and Formatting in Balloons* at the side menu.

New Comment

Figure 7.1 Comment Balloon

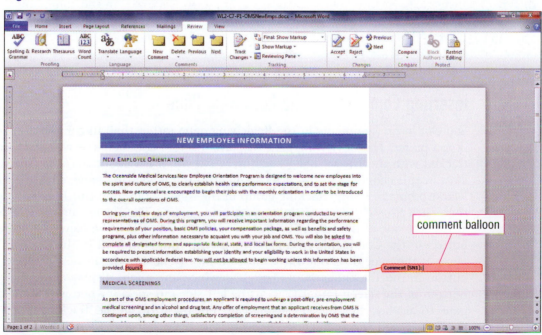

1. Open **OMSNewEmps.docx** and then save the document with Save As and name it **WL2-C7-P1-OMSNewEmps**.
2. Insert a comment by completing the following steps:
   a. Position the insertion point at the end of the second paragraph in the NEW EMPLOYEE ORIENTATION section.
   b. Press the spacebar once and then type **Hours?**.
   c. Select *Hours?*.
   d. Click the Review tab and then click the New Comment button in the Comments group.
   e. Type **Please include the total number of orientation hours.** in the comment balloon.

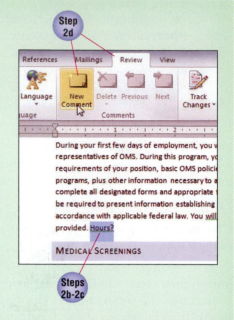

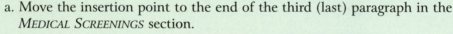

3. Insert another comment by completing the following steps:
   a. Move the insertion point to the end of the third (last) paragraph in the MEDICAL SCREENINGS section.
   b. Press the spacebar, type **Locations**, and then select *Locations*.
   c. Click the New Comment button in the Comments group.
   d. Type **Specify the locations where drug tests are administered.** in the comment balloon.
4. Save **WL2-C7-P1-OMSNewEmps.docx**.

▼ **Quick Steps**

Insert Comment in Reviewing Pane
1. Click Review tab.
2. Click Show Markup button.
3. Point to *Balloons*.
4. Click *Show All Revisions Inline* at side menu.
5. Click the New Comment button.
6. Type comment.

Inserting Comments in the Reviewing Pane

You can insert comments in the Reviewing pane rather than in comment balloons, if you prefer. The Reviewing pane displays inserted comments as well as changes tracked with the Track Changes feature. (You will learn about tracking changes later in this chapter.) To insert a comment in the Reviewing pane, click the Show Markup button in the Tracking group in the Review tab, point to *Balloons*, and then click *Show All Revisions Inline* at the side menu. The Reviewing pane displays at the left side of the screen, as shown in Figure 7.2. Click the New Comment button in the Comments group and then type your comment in the Reviewing pane. If the pane does not display, turn it on by clicking the Reviewing Pane button in the Tracking group. (The Reviewing pane might display along the bottom of the screen rather than at the left side. To specify where you want the pane to display, click the Reviewing Pane button arrow in the Tracking group in the Review tab and then click *Reviewing Pane Vertical* or *Reviewing Pane Horizontal*.)

The summary section at the top of the Reviewing pane provides a count of the number of comments inserted and a count of various types of changes that have been made to the document. After typing your comment in the Reviewing pane, close the pane by clicking the Reviewing Pane button in the Tracking group or clicking the Close button (the button marked with an X) located in the upper right corner of the pane.

Reviewing Pane

Figure 7.2 Vertical Reviewing Pane

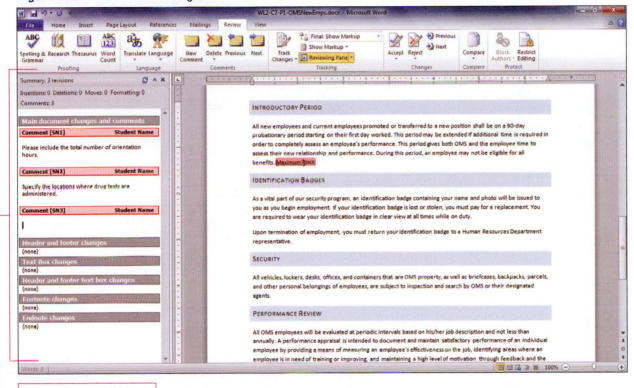

Comments inserted into a document display in the Reviewing pane.

Project 1b **Inserting a Comment in the Reviewing Pane** **Part 2 of 4**

1. With **WL2-C7-P1-OMSNewEmps.docx** open, show comments in the Reviewing pane rather than in comment balloons by completing the following steps:
   a. If necessary, click the Review tab.
   b. Click the Show Markup button in the Tracking group.
   c. Point to *Balloons* at the drop-down list.
   d. Click *Show All Revisions Inline* at the side menu.

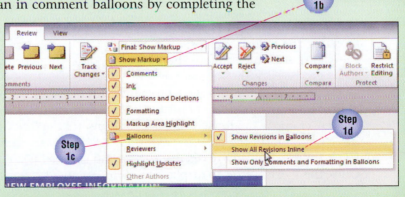

2. Make sure the Reviewing pane displays. If not, click the Reviewing Pane button in the Tracking group.
3. Insert a comment by completing the following steps:
   a. Move the insertion point to the end of the paragraph of text in the *INTRODUCTORY PERIOD* section.
   b. Press the spacebar once, type **Maximum?**, and then select *Maximum?*.
   c. Click the New Comment button in the Comments group in the Review tab.
   d. With the insertion point positioned in the Reviewing pane, type **Please include in this section the maximum length of the probationary period.**
4. Click the Reviewing Pane button in the Tracking group to turn off the display of the Reviewing pane.

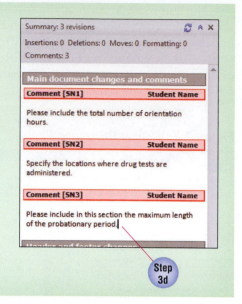

Step 3d

Next

Previous

Navigating between Comments

When you are working in a long document with many inserted comments, the Previous and Next buttons in the Comments group in the Review tab can be useful. Click the Next button to move the insertion point to the next comment or click the Previous button to move the insertion point to the preceding comment.

Editing a Comment

You can edit a comment in the Reviewing pane or in a comment balloon. To edit a comment in the Reviewing pane, click the Reviewing Pane button to turn on the pane and then click in the comment that you want to edit. Make the desired changes to the comment and then close the Reviewing pane. To edit a comment in a comment balloon, turn on the display of comment balloons, click in the comment balloon, and then make the desired changes.

▼ **Quick Steps**

Edit a Comment
1. Click Review tab.
2. Click Reviewing Pane button.
3. Click in desired comment in pane.
4. Make desired changes.
OR
1. Click Review tab.
2. Turn on display of comment balloons.
3. Click in comment balloon.
4. Make desired changes.

Project 1c **Editing Comments** **Part 3 of 4**

1. With **WL2-C7-P1-OMSNewEmps.docx** open, navigate from one comment to another by completing the following steps:
   a. Press Ctrl + Home to move the insertion point to the beginning of the document.
   b. If necessary, click the Review tab.
   c. Click the Next button in the Comments group. (This moves the insertion point to the first comment reference, opens the Reviewing pane, and inserts the insertion point in the pane.)
   d. Click the Next button to display the second comment.
   e. Click the Next button to display the third comment.

Step 1c

f. Click the Previous button to display the second comment.
2. With the insertion point positioned in the Reviewing pane, edit the second comment to read *Specify the locations within OMS where drug tests are administered as well as any off-site locations.*
3. Click the Reviewing Pane button to close the pane.
4. Edit a comment in a comment balloon by completing the following steps:
   a. Click the Show Markup button in the Tracking group, point to *Balloons*, and then click *Show Only Comments and Formatting in Balloons* at the side menu.
   b. Move the insertion point to the paragraph of text in the *INTRODUCTORY PERIOD* section and then click in the comment balloon that displays at the right.
   c. Edit the comment so it displays as *Please include in this section the maximum probationary period, if any.*

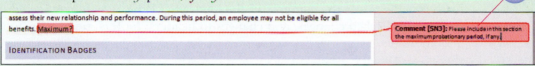

Step 4c

   d. Click in the document.
   e. Click the Show Markup button, point to *Balloons*, and then click *Show All Revisions Inline.*
5. Save **WL2-C7-P1-OMSNewEmps.docx.**

Distinguishing Comments from Different Users

More than one user can make comments in a document. Word uses color to distinguish comments made by different users, generally displaying the first user's comments in red and the second user's comments in blue (these colors may vary). You can change the user name and initials at the Word Options dialog box with *General* selected, as shown in Figure 7.3. To change the user name, select the name that displays in the *User name* text box and then type the desired name. Complete similar steps to change the user initials in the *Initials* text box.

Figure 7.3 Word Options Dialog Box with General Selected

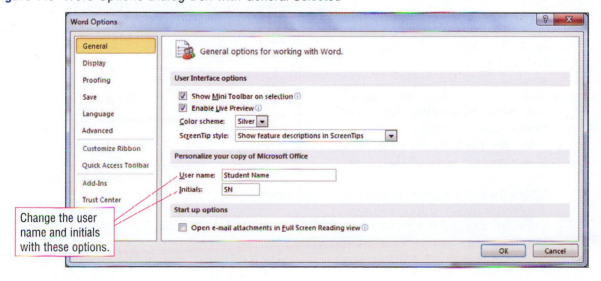

Change the user name and initials with these options.

Quick Steps

Print Document with Comments
1. Click File tab, Print tab.
2. Click first gallery in Settings category.
3. If necessary, click *Print Markup* to insert check mark.
4. Click Print button.

Print Only Comments
1. Click File tab, Print tab.
2. Click first gallery in Settings category.
3. Click *List of Markup* in drop-down list box.
4. Click Print button.

Delete a Comment
1. Click Review tab.
2. Click Next button until desired comment is selected.
3. Click Delete button.

Printing Comments

To print a document with the comments, display the Print tab Backstage view, and then click the first gallery in the Settings category (this is the gallery containing the text *Print All Pages*). A drop-down list displays with a list box as well as options below the list box. The option *Print Markup* is one of the options that displays below the drop-down list box. Insert a check mark before this option if you want the document to print with the comments. If you want to print the document without the comments, remove the check mark from the *Print Markup* option at the Print tab Backstage view gallery drop-down list. If you want to print only the comments and not the document, click the first gallery in the Settings category in the Print tab Backstage view and then click *List of Markup* in the drop-down list box. This prints the contents of the Reviewing Pane, which may include comments, tracked changes, and changes to headers, footers, text boxes, footnotes, and endnotes.

Deleting a Comment

You can delete a comment by clicking the Next button in the Comments group in the Review tab until the desired comment is selected and then clicking the Delete button in the Comments group. If you want to delete all comments in a document, click the Delete button arrow and then click *Delete All Comments in Document* at the drop-down list.

Delete

Project 1d   Changing User Information and Inserting and Deleting Comments   **Part 4 of 4**

1. With **WL2-C7-P1-OMSNewEmps.docx** open, change the user information by completing the following steps:
   a. Click the File tab.
   b. Click the Options button located below the Help tab.
   c. At the Word Options dialog box, make sure *General* is selected in the left panel.
   d. Make a note of the current name and initials in the *Personalize your copy of Microsoft Office* section.
   e. Select the name displayed in the *User name* text box and then type **Taylor Stanton**.
   f. Select the initials displayed in the *Initials* text box and then type **TS**.
   g. Click OK to close the Word Options dialog box.

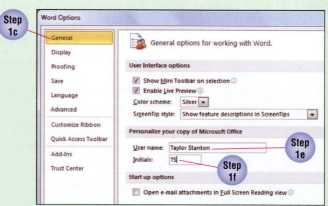

2. Insert a comment by completing the following steps:
   a. Move the insertion point to the end of the first paragraph of text in the PERFORMANCE REVIEW section.
   b. Press the spacebar once and then type Documentation?
   c. Make sure the Review tab is active and then select *Documentation?*.
   d. Click the New Comment button in the Comments group.
   e. Type Provide additional information on performance evaluation documentation. in the Reviewing pane. (The color may vary from what you see in the image at the right.)
   f. Click the Reviewing Pane button to close the pane.
3. Print only the information in the Reviewing pane by completing the following steps:
   a. Click the File tab and then click the Print tab. (You can also display the Print tab Backstage view by pressing Ctrl + P.)
   b. At the Print tab Backstage view, click the first gallery in the Settings category and then click *List of Markup* in the drop-down list box.
   c. Click the Print button.
4. Delete a comment by completing the following steps:
   a. Press Ctrl + Home.
   b. If necessary, click the Review tab.
   c. Click the Next button in the Comments group.
   d. Click the Next button again.
   e. Click the Delete button in the Comments group.
5. Print only the information in the Reviewing pane by completing Step 3.
6. Close the Reviewing pane.
7. Change the user information back to the default by completing the following steps:
   a. Click the File tab and then click the Options button.
   b. At the Word Options dialog box with *General* selected, select *Taylor Stanton* in the *User name* text box and then type the original name.
   c. Select the initials *TS* in the *Initials* text box and then type the original initials.
   d. Click OK to close the dialog box.
8. Save and then close **WL2-C7-P1-OMSNewEmps.docx**.

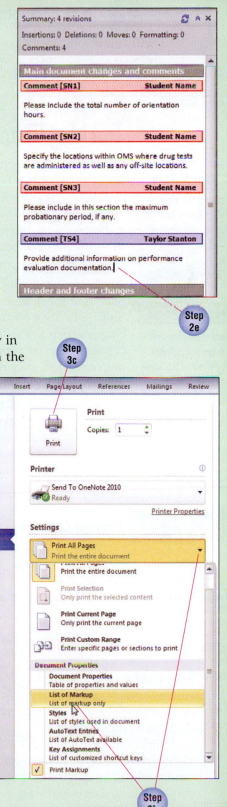

You will open a building construction agreement, turn on tracking, and then make changes to the document. You will also customize tracking and accept and reject changes.

Tracking Changes in a Document ■ ■ ■ ■ ■ ■ ■ ■ ■ ■ ■ ■ ■ ■

▼ **Quick Steps**

Turn on Tracking
1. Click Review tab.
2. Click Track Changes button.
OR
Press Ctrl + Shift + E.

Word displays tracked changes and comments by default so you know what your document contains before distributing it to others.

Track Changes

If more than one person in a work group needs to review and edit a document, consider using the Track Changes feature in Word. When Track Changes is turned on, Word tracks each deletion, insertion, or formatting change made in a document. For example, when you delete text, it is not removed from the document. Instead, it displays in a different color with a line through it. Word uses a different color (up to eight) for each person who makes changes to the document. In this way, anyone looking at the document can identify which user made which changes.

Turn on tracking by clicking the Review tab and then clicking the Track Changes button in the Tracking group. You can also turn on tracking by pressing Ctrl + Shift + E. Turn off tracking by completing the same steps. By default, Word displays changes such as deletions and insertions in the document. Word displays formatting changes, such as a change of font or font size, in the text and also inserts a vertical line at the left margin to indicate where a formatting change has been made.

You can specify what tracking information displays in a document with options at the Balloons side menu. To show all revisions in balloons at the right margin, click the Show Markup button, point to *Balloons*, and then click *Show Revisions in Balloons* at the side menu. Click the *Show Only Comments and Formatting in Balloons* option at the side menu, and insertions and deletions display in the text while comments and formatting changes display in balloons at the right margin.

Project **2a** **Tracking Changes in a Document** **Part 1 of 5**

1. Open **Agreement.docx** and then save the document with Save As and name it **WL2-C7-P2-Agreement**.
2. Turn on tracking by clicking the Review tab and then clicking the Track Changes button in the Tracking group.
3. Type the word **BUILDING** between the words *THIS* and *AGREEMENT* in the first paragraph of text in the document. (The text you type displays in the document underlined and in red.)
4. Delete *thirty (30)* in the second paragraph. (The deleted text displays as strikethrough text in the document.)
5. Type **sixty (60)**.

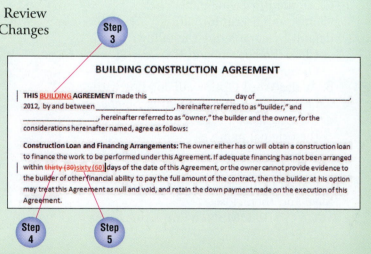

6. Move a paragraph of text by completing the following steps:
   a. Select the paragraph of text that begins with *Supervision of Work*.
   b. Press Ctrl + X to cut the text. (The text stays in the document and displays in red with strikethrough characters.)
   c. Position the insertion point at the beginning of the word *Start* (in the paragraph that begins *Start of Construction and Completion:*).
   d. Press Ctrl + V to insert the cut text. (This inserts the text in green and double underlined in the new location and also changes the text in the original location to green with double-strikethrough characters. If necessary, press the Enter key to separate the paragraphs.)
7. Turn off tracking by clicking the Track Changes button in the Tracking group.
8. Display revisions in balloons by clicking the Show Markup button, pointing to *Balloons*, and then clicking *Show Revisions in Balloons* at the drop-down list.
9. After looking at the revisions in balloons, click the Show Markup button, point to *Balloons*, and then click *Show All Revisions Inline* at the side menu.
10. Save **WL2-C7-P2-Agreement.docx**.

You can display information about tracked changes by positioning the mouse pointer on a change. After approximately one second, a box displays above the change containing the author's name, date, time, and the type of change (for example, whether it was a deletion or insertion). You can also display information on tracking changes by displaying the Reviewing pane. Each change is listed separately in the Reviewing pane. Use the arrow keys at the right side of the Reviewing pane to scroll through the pane and view each change.

Changing User Information

In the "Distinguishing Comments from Different Users" section earlier in this chapter, you learned how to change the user name and initials at the Word Options dialog box. You can also display the Word Options dialog box with *General* selected by clicking the Track Changes button arrow and then clicking *Change User Name* at the drop-down list.

▼ **Quick Steps**

Change User Information
1. Click Review tab.
2. Click Track Changes button arrow.
3. Click *Change User Name* at drop-down list.
4. Type desired name in *User name* text box.
5. Type desired initials in *Initials* text box.
6. Click OK.

Project 2b   **Changing User Information and Tracking Changes**   **Part 2 of 5**

1. With **WL2-C7-P2-Agreement.docx** open, change the user information by completing the following steps:
   a. If necessary, click the Review tab.
   b. Click the Track Changes button arrow and then click *Change User Name*.
   c. At the Word Options dialog box with *General* selected, select the current name in the *User name* text box and then type **Julia Moore**.
   d. Select the initials in the *Initials* text box and then type **JM**.
   e. Click OK to close the dialog box.

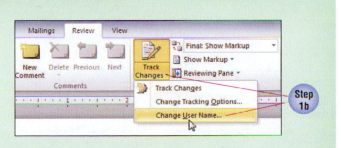

2. Make additional changes to the contract and track the changes by completing the following steps:

   a. Click the Track Changes button to turn on tracking.

   b. Select the title *BUILDING CONSTRUCTION AGREEMENT* and then change the font size to 14.

   c. Delete the text *at his option* located in the second sentence in the second paragraph.

   d. Delete the text *and Completion* that displays in the beginning text in the fourth paragraph.

Construction Loan and Financing Arrangements: The owner either has or will obtain a construction loan to finance the work to be performed under this Agreement. If adequate financing has not been arranged within ~~thirty (30)~~sixty (60) days of the date of this Agreement, or the owner cannot provide evidence to the builder of other financial ability to pay the full amount of the contract, then the builder ~~at his option~~ may treat this Agreement as null and void, and retain the down payment made on the execution of this Agreement. Step 2c

Supervision of Work: Owner agrees that the direction and supervision of the working force including subcontractor, rests exclusively with the builder or his/her duly designated agent, and owner agrees not to issue any instructions to, or otherwise interfere with, same.

 Step 2d **Start of Construction** ~~and Completion~~: The builder shall commence construction of the residence as soon as practical after signing of this Agreement and adequate financial arrangements satisfactory to the builder have been made.

   e. Delete *thirty (30)* in the paragraph that begins *Builder's Right to Terminate the Contract:* (located on the second page).

   f. Type **sixty (60)**.

   g. Select the text *IN WITNESS WHEREOF* that displays toward the bottom of the document and then turn on bold.

3. Click the Review tab and then click the Track Changes button to turn off tracking.

4. Click the Reviewing Pane button to turn on the display of the pane and then use the vertical scroll bar at the right side of the Reviewing pane to review the changes.

5. View the changes in balloons by clicking the Show Markup button, pointing to *Balloons*, and then clicking *Show Revisions in Balloons*.

6. Click the Reviewing Pane button to turn off the display of the pane. Scroll through the document and view the changes in the balloons.

7. Click the Show Markup button, pointing to *Balloons*, and then click *Show All Revisions Inline* at the side menu.

8. Change the user information back to the information that displayed before you typed *Julia Moore* and the initials *JM* by completing the following steps:

   a. Click the Track Changes button arrow and then click *Change User Name*.

   b. At the Word Options dialog box, select *Julia Moore* in the *User name* text box and then type the original name.

   c. Select the initials *JM* in the *Initials* text box and then type the original initials.

   d. Click OK to close the dialog box.

9. Print the document with the markups by completing the following steps:

   a. Click the File tab and then click the Print tab.

   b. At the Print tab Backstage view, click the first gallery in the Settings category, and then make sure a check mark displays before the *Print Markup* option that displays below the drop-down list box. (If the *Print Markup* option is not preceded by a check mark, click the option.)

   c. Click the Print button.

10. Save **WL2-C7-P2-Agreement.docx**.

Displaying Changes for Review

By default, Word displays all tracked changes and comments in a document. You can change this default setting at the Display for Review button drop-down list. If you change the default setting *Final: Show Markup* to *Final*, the document displays with all changes incorporated in it. If you select *Original: Show markup*, the original document displays with the changes tracked. Select *Original*, and the original document displays without any changes. These four options at the Display for Review button drop-down list allow you to view a document at various stages in the editing process.

Showing Markup

You can customize which tracked changes display in a document with options at the Show Markup button drop-down list. If you want to show only one particular type of tracked change, remove the check marks before all options except the desired one. For example, if you want to view only formatting changes and not other types of changes such as insertions and deletions, remove the check mark before each option except *Formatting*. If the changes of more than one reviewer have been tracked in a document, you can choose to view only the changes of a particular reviewer. To do this, click the Show Markup button, point to *Reviewers* at the drop-down list, and then click the *All Reviewers* check box to remove the check mark. Click the Show Markup button, point to *Reviewers*, and then click the check box of the desired reviewer.

HINT

Each of the four options at the Display for Review button drop-down list displays a document at various stages in the editing process.

HINT

If the *Markup Area Highlight* option is active, the margin area where all balloons appear is highlighted.

Display for Review

Show Markup

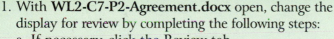 **Changing the Display for Review and Showing Markup** Part 3 of 5

1. With **WL2-C7-P2-Agreement.docx** open, change the display for review by completing the following steps:
   a. If necessary, click the Review tab.
   b. Click the Display for Review button arrow and then click *Final*. (This displays the document with the changes included.)
   c. Click the Display for Review button and then click *Original*. (This displays the original document before changes.)
   d. Click the Display for Review button and then click *Final: Show Markup*.

2. Display only those changes made by Julia Moore by completing the following steps:
   a. Click the Show Markup button in the Tracking group and then point to *Reviewers*.
   b. Click the *All Reviewers* check box to remove the check mark. (This also removes the drop-down list.)

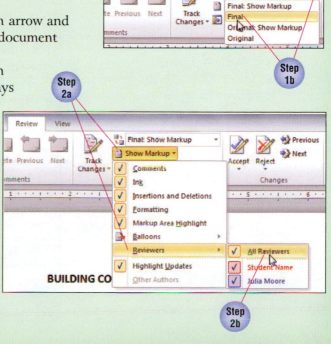

Customizing Track Changes Options

Default settings determine how tracked changes display in a document. For example, inserted text displays in red with an underline below the text and deleted text displays in red with strikethrough characters. Moved text displays in the original location in green with double strikethrough characters and the text in the new location displays in green with double-underline below the text. You can customize these options along with others at the Track Changes Options dialog box shown in Figure 7.4. With options at this dialog box, you can customize the display of markup text, moved text, table cell highlighting, formatting, and balloons. Display this dialog box by clicking the Track Changes button arrow and then clicking *Change Tracking Options* at the drop-down list.

Figure 7.4 Track Changes Options Dialog Box

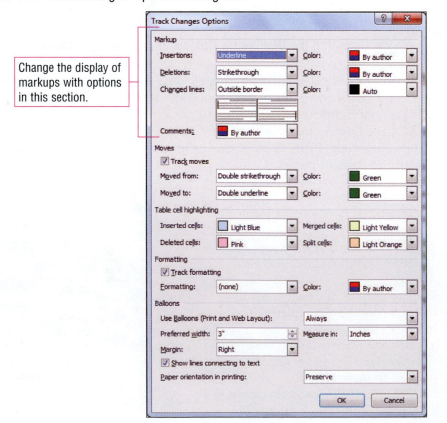

Change the display of markups with options in this section.

1. With **WL2-C7-P2-Agreement.docx** open, customize the track changes options by completing the following steps:
   a. If necessary, click the Review tab.
   b. Click the Track Changes button arrow in the Tracking group and then click *Change Tracking Options*.
   c. At the Track Changes Options dialog box, click the down-pointing arrow at the right side of the *Insertions* option and then click *Double underline* at the drop-down list.
   d. Click the down-pointing arrow at the right side of the *Insertions* color option box and then click *Green* at the drop-down list. (You will need to scroll down the list to display this color.)
   e. Click the down-pointing arrow at the right side of the *Moved from* color option box and then click the *Dark Blue* color at the drop-down list.
   f. Click the down-pointing arrow at the right side of the *Moved to* color option box and then click the *Violet* color at the drop-down list. (You will need to scroll down the list to display this color.)
   g. Click OK to close the dialog box.
2. Save **WL2-C7-P2-Agreement.docx**.

Navigating to Revisions

Navigate to revisions in a document using the Next and Previous buttons in the Changes group in the Review tab. Click the Next button and Word selects the next revision in the document or click the Previous button to select the previous revision. If you turn on Track Changes and then move text, revision balloons that contain a small Go button display in the lower right corner of the balloon identifying the deleted (cut) text and the inserted (pasted) text. Click the Go button in one of the balloons to move the insertion point to the other balloon.

Next

Previous

Accepting or Rejecting Revisions

You can accept or reject changes made to a document. Click the Accept button to accept the change and move to the next change. Click the Reject button to reject the change and move to the next. Click the Reject button arrow and a drop-down list displays with options to reject the change and move to the next change, reject the change, reject all changes shown, and reject all changes in the document. Similar options are available at the Accept button arrow drop-down list.

Accept

Reject

1. With **WL2-C7-P2-Agreement.docx** open, display all tracked changes *except* formatting changes by completing the following steps:
   a. Click the Show Markup button in the Tracking group and then click *Formatting* at the drop-down list. (This removes the check mark from the option.)
   b. Scroll through the document and notice that the vertical line at the left side of the formatting locations has been removed.
   c. Click the Show Markup button and then click *Formatting* at the drop-down list. (This inserts a check mark in the check box.)
2. Navigate to tracked changes by completing the following steps:
   a. Press Ctrl + Home to move the insertion point to the beginning of the document.
   b. Click the Next button in the Changes group to select the first change.
   c. Click the Next button again to select the second change.
   d. Click the Previous button to select the first change.
3. Navigate between the original location of the moved text and the new location by completing the following steps:
   a. Press Ctrl + Home to move the insertion point to the beginning of the document.
   b. Click the Show Markup button, point to *Balloons*, and then click *Show Revisions in Balloons*.
   c. Scroll to the right to display the right edge of the balloons and then click the Go button that displays in the lower right corner of the Moved balloon. (This selects the text in the Moved up balloon.)
   d. Click the Go button in the lower right corner of the Moved up balloon. (This selects the text in the Moved balloon.)
   e. Click the Show Markup button, point to *Balloons*, and then click *Show All Revisions Inline*.

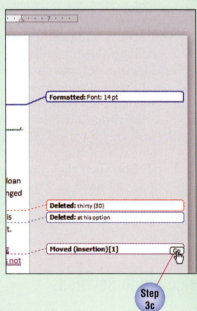

Step 3c

4. Press Ctrl + Home to move the insertion point to the beginning of the document.
5. Display and then accept only formatting changes by completing the following steps:
   a. Click the Show Markup button in the Tracking group and then click *Comments* at the drop-down list. (This removes the check mark and the drop-down list.)
   b. Click the Show Markup button and then click *Ink*.
   c. Click the Show Markup button and then click *Insertions and Deletions*.
   d. Click the Show Markup button and then click *Markup Area Highlight* (*Formatting* is now the only option containing a check mark.)
   e. Click the Accept button arrow and then click *Accept All Changes Shown* at the drop-down list. (This accepts only the formatting changes in the document since those are the only changes showing.)

Step 5e

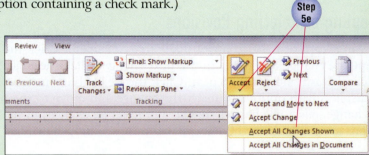

6. Display all changes by completing the following steps:
   a. Click the Show Markup button and then click *Comments* at the drop-down list.
   b. Click the Show Markup button and then click *Ink*.
   c. Click the Show Markup button and then click *Insertions and Deletions*.
   d. Click the Show Markup button and then click *Markup Area Highlight*.
7. Press Ctrl + Home to move the insertion point to the beginning of the document.
8. Reject the change inserting the word *BUILDING* by clicking the Next button in the Changes group and then clicking the Reject button. (This rejects the change and moves to the next revision in the document.)
9. Click the Accept button to accept the change deleting *thirty (30)*.
10. Click the Accept button to accept the change inserting *sixty (60)*.
11. Click the Reject button to reject the change deleting the words *at his option*.
12. Accept all remaining changes by clicking the Accept button arrow and then clicking *Accept All Changes in Document* at the drop-down list.
13. Return track changes options to the default settings by completing the following steps:
    a. If necessary, click the Review tab.
    b. Click the Track Changes button arrow and then click *Change Tracking Options*.
    c. At the Track Changes Options dialog box, click the down-pointing arrow at the right side of the *Insertions* option and then click *Underline* at the drop-down list.
    d. Click the down-pointing arrow at the right side of the *Insertions* color option box and then click *By author* at the drop-down list. (You will need to scroll up the list to display this color.)
    e. Click the down-pointing arrow at the right side of the *Moved from* color option box and then click the *Green* color at the drop-down list. (You may need to scroll down the list to display this color.)
    f. Click the down-pointing arrow at the right side of the *Moved to* color option box and then click the *Green* color at the drop-down list.
    g. Click OK to close the dialog box.
14. Check to make sure all tracking changes are accepted or rejected by completing the following steps:
    a. Click the Reviewing Pane button in the Tracking group.
    b. Check the summary information that displays at the top of the Reviewing pane and make sure that a zero follows all of the options.
    c. Click the Reviewing Pane button.
15. Save, print, and then close **WL2-C7-P2-Agreement.docx**.

Project 3 Compare Lease Agreement Documents   **2 Parts**

You will compare the contents of a lease agreement and an edited version of the lease agreement. You will then customize compare options and then compare the documents again.

Comparing Documents ■ ■■ ■ ■■■■■■■ ■ ■■■■■■ ■ ■■■■■

▼ Quick Steps

Compare Documents
1. Click Review tab.
2. Click Compare button.
3. Click *Compare* at drop-down list.
4. Click Browse for Original button.
5. Double-click desired document.
6. Click Browse for Revised button.
7. Double-click desired document.

Word contains a legal blackline option you can use to compare two documents and display the differences as tracked changes in a third document. To use this option, click the Review tab, click the Compare button in the Compare group, and then click *Compare* at the drop-down list. This displays the Compare Documents dialog box shown in Figure 7.5. At this dialog box, click the Browse for Original button and then, at the Open dialog box, navigate to the folder that contains the first of the two documents you want to compare and double-click the document. Click the Browse for Revised button in the Compare Documents dialog box, navigate to the folder containing the second of the two documents you want to compare, and then double-click the document.

HINT

Word does not change the documents you are comparing.

Compare

Figure 7.5 Compare Documents Dialog Box

Click the Browse for Original button to locate the original document.

Click the Browse for Revised button to locate the revised document.

Viewing Compared Documents

When you click OK at the Compare Documents dialog box, the compared document displays with the changes tracked. Other windows may also display, depending on the option selected at the Show Source Documents side menu. Display this side menu by clicking the Compare button and then pointing to *Show Source Documents*. You may see just the compared document, or you may see the compared document plus the Reviewing pane, original document, and/or revised document.

Project 3a **Comparing Documents** **Part 1 of 2**

1. Close any open documents.
2. Click the Review tab.
3. Click the Compare button and then click *Compare* at the drop-down list.

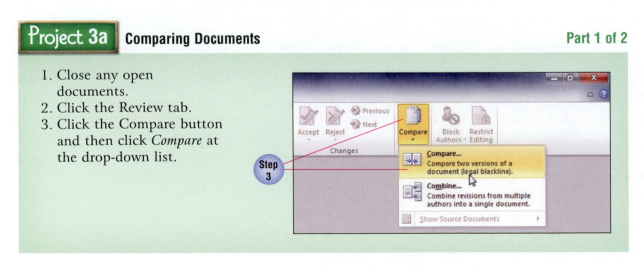

Step 3

4. At the Compare Documents dialog box, click the Browse for Original button.

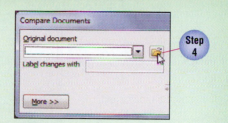

5. At the Open dialog box, navigate to the Word2010L2C7 folder on your storage medium and then double-click **ComAgrmnt.docx**.

6. At the Compare Documents dialog box, click the Browse for Revised button.

7. At the Open dialog box, double-click **EditedComAgrmnt.docx**.

8. Click the OK button. (If the original and revised documents display along with the compared document, click the Compare button, point to *Show Source Documents* at the drop-down list, and then click *Hide Source Documents* at the side menu.)

9. With the compared document active, print the document showing markups.

10. Click the File tab and then click *Close*. At the message asking if you want to save changes, click the Don't Save button.

Customizing Compare Options

By default, Word compares the original document with the revised document and displays the differences as tracked changes in a third document. You can change this default along with others by expanding the Compare Documents dialog box. Expand the dialog box by clicking the More button and additional options display as shown in Figure 7.6.

Control the level of comparisons that Word makes to the original and revised document with options in the *Comparison settings* section of the dialog box. The *Show changes at* option in the *Show changes* section of the dialog box has a default setting of *Word level*. At this setting, Word shows changes to whole words rather than individual characters within the word. For example, if you deleted the letters *ed* from the end of a word, Word would display the entire word as a change rather than just the *ed*. If you want to show changes by character, click the *Character level* option.

By default, Word displays differences between compared documents in a new document. With options in the *Show changes in* section, you can change this to *Original document* or *Revised document*. If you change options in the expanded Compare Documents dialog box, the selected options will be the defaults the next time you open the dialog box.

Figure 7.6 Expanded Compare Documents Dialog Box

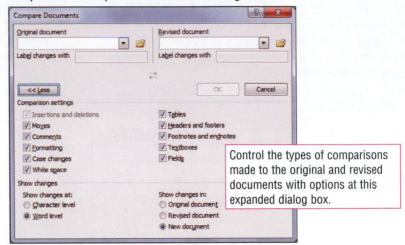

Control the types of comparisons made to the original and revised documents with options at this expanded dialog box.

Project 3b Customizing Compare Options and Then Comparing Documents   **Part 2 of 2**

1. Close any open documents.
2. Click the Review tab.
3. Click the Compare button and then click *Compare* at the drop-down list.
4. At the Compare Documents dialog box, click the Browse for Original button.
5. At the Open dialog box, navigate to the Word2010L2C7 folder on your storage medium and then double-click *ComAgrmnt.docx*.
6. At the Compare Documents dialog box, click the Browse for Revised button.
7. At the Open dialog box, double-click *EditedComAgrmnt.docx*.
8. At the Compare Documents dialog box, click the More button. (Skip this step if the dialog box displays expanded and a Less button displays above the *Comparison settings* section.)
9. Click the *Moves* check box and then click the *Formatting* check box to remove the check marks.
10. Click the OK button.
11. Print the document showing markups.
12. Close the document without saving it.
13. Return the options to the default settings by completing the following steps:
    a. Close any open documents.
    b. Click the Review tab.
    c. Click the Compare button and then click *Compare* at the drop-down list.
    d. At the Compare Documents dialog box, click the Browse for Original button.
    e. At the Open dialog box, double-click *ComAgrmnt.docx*.
    f. At the Compare Documents dialog box, click the Browse for Revised button.
    g. At the Open dialog box, double-click *EditedComAgrmnt.docx*.
    h. At the Compare Documents dialog box, click the *Moves* check box to insert a check mark and then click the *Formatting* check box to insert a check mark.
    i. Click the Less button.
    j. Click the OK button.
14. At the new document, accept all of the changes.
15. Save the document and name it **WL2-C7-P3-ComAgrmnt**.
16. Print and then close the document.

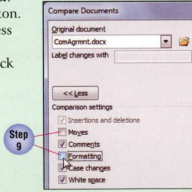

Step 9

You will open a lease agreement document and then combine edited versions of the agreement into the original document.

Combining Documents ▪■■■■■■■■■■■■■■■■■

If you send a document for reviewing to several people, you can combine changes made by each person into the original document. You can combine each document with the original until you have incorporated all changes in the original document. To do this, click the Compare button in the Review tab and then click *Combine* at the drop-down list. This displays the Combine Documents dialog box as shown in Figure 7.7. The Combine Documents dialog box contains many of the same options as the Compare Documents dialog box.

Figure 7.7 Combine Documents Dialog Box

Click the Browse for Original button to locate the original document.

Click the Browse for Revised button to locate the revised document.

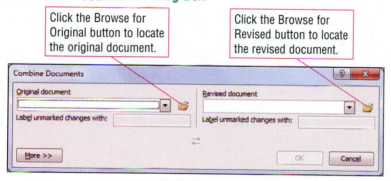

To combine documents at the Combine Documents dialog box, click the Browse for Original button, navigate to the desired folder, and then double-click the original document. Click the Browse for Revised button, navigate to the desired folder, and then double-click one of the documents containing revisions. You can also click the down-pointing arrow at the right side of the *Original document* text box or the *Revised document* text box and a drop-down list displays with the most recently selected documents.

Combining and Merging Documents

Control how changes are combined with options in the expanded Combine Documents dialog box. This document contains many of the same options as the expanded Compare Documents dialog box. By default, Word merges the changes in the revised document into the original document. You can change this default setting with options in the *Show changes in* section. You can choose to merge changes into the revised document or to merge changes into a new document.

▼ **Quick Steps**

Combine Multiple Versions of a Document
1. Click Review tab.
2. Click Compare button.
3. Click *Combine* at drop-down list.
4. Click Browse for Original button.
5. Double-click desired document.
6. Click Browse for Revised button.
7. Double-click desired document.
8. Click OK.

1. Close all open documents.
2. Click the Review tab.
3. Click the Compare button in the Compare group and then click *Combine* at the drop-down list.

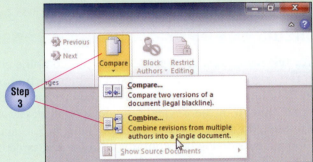

4. At the Combine Documents dialog box, click the More button to expand the dialog box.
5. Click the *Original Document* option in the *Show changes in* section.
6. Click the Browse for Original button.
7. At the Open dialog box, navigate to the Word2010L2C7 folder on your storage medium and then double-click *OriginalLease.docx*.
8. At the Combine Documents dialog box, click the Browse for Revised button.
9. At the Open dialog box, double-click *LeaseReviewer1.docx*.
10. Click the OK button.
11. Save the document with Save As and name it **WL2-C7-P4-CombinedLease**.

Showing Source Documents

With options in the Show Source Documents side menu, you can specify which source documents to display. Display this side menu by clicking the Compare button and then pointing to *Show Source Documents*. Four options display at the side menu including *Hide Source Documents*, *Show Original*, *Show Revised*, and *Show Both*. With the *Hide Source Documents* option selected, the original and revised documents do not display on the screen; only the combined document displays. If you choose the *Show Original* option, the original document displays in a side pane at the right side of the document. Synchronous scrolling is selected, so scrolling in the combined document results in scrolling in the other. Choose the *Show Revised* option, and the revised document displays in the panel at the right. Choose the *Show Both* option to display the original document in a panel at the right side of the screen and the revised document in a panel below the original document panel.

1. With **WL2-C7-P4-CombinedLease.docx** open, click the Compare button, point to *Show Source Documents*, and then, if necessary, click *Hide Source Documents* at the side menu. (This displays the original document with the combined document changes shown as tracked changes.)

2. Click the Compare button, point to *Show Source Documents*, and then click *Show Original* at the side menu. (This displays the original document at the right and the original document with tracked changes in the middle.)

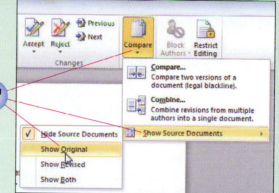

3. Click the Compare button, point to *Show Source Documents*, and then click *Show Revised*.

4. Click the Compare button, point to *Show Source Documents*, and then click *Show Both*. Scroll in the combined document and notice that the original document and the revised document also scroll simultaneously.

5. Click the Compare button point to *Show Source Documents*, and then click *Hide Source Documents*.

6. If the Reviewing pane displays, close it.

7. Click the Compare button and then click *Combine* at the drop-down list.

8. At the Combine Documents dialog box, click the Browse for Original button.

9. At the Open dialog box, double-click **WL2-C7-P4-CombinedLease.docx**.

10. At the Combine Documents dialog box, click the Browse for Revised button.

11. At the Open dialog box, double-click **LeaseReviewer2.docx**.

12. At the Combine Documents dialog box, click the OK button.

13. Save **WL2-C7-P4-CombinedLease.docx**.

14. Print the document showing markups.

15. Accept all changes to the document. (Look through the document and notice that the *Rent* heading displays in blue. Select *Rent* and then change the font color to dark red.)

16. Save, print, and then close **WL2-C7-P4-CombinedLease.docx**.

Project 5 **Organize and Edit Documents in Different Views**   **3 Parts**

You will open documents in various views, organize a document in Outline view, create a master document and subdocuments, and edit and manage the same document in two windows.

Viewing and Sharing Documents ▪▪▪▪▪▪▪▪▪▪▪▪▪

Microsoft Word provides a number of views for working with and managing documents. The default view is Print Layout. It is used to create and edit documents and displays the document as it will appear when printed. You can change views with buttons in the View tab or with buttons in the view area on the Status bar. In an earlier chapter, you learned about Print Layout view, Full Screen Reading view, and Draft view. Word also includes Web Layout view and Outline view.

Displaying a Document in Web Layout View

Web Layout

Use Web Layout view to see how the document displays as a web page. In Web Layout view, text is wrapped to fit the window, backgrounds are visible, and graphics appear as they would display in a browser. Display a document in Web Layout view by clicking the View tab and then clicking the Web Layout button in the Document Views group or by clicking the Web Layout button in the view area on the Status bar.

Using Outline View

In Outline view, you can collapse a document to only headings, letting you view the document's organization and rearrange or delete headings and text in the document. You can collapse text in a document that has been formatted with heading styles or with outline levels. To switch to Outline view, click the View tab and then click the Outline button in the Document Views group (or click the Outline button in the view area on the Status bar). In Outline view, the Outlining tab displays containing buttons for promoting or demoting a heading (and the body text below the heading), moving a selected heading up or down in the outline, collapsing or expanding the outline, and specifying what level of headings you want displayed in the outline.

If a heading style is not applied to headings in a document, all text in the outline is identified as body text. In Outline view, you can assign levels to text with the Promote and Demote buttons in the Outline Tools group in the Outlining tab. One of the major benefits of working in Outline view is the ability to see a condensed outline of your document without all of the text in between titles, headings, and subheadings. Use the Show Level button in the Outline Tools group in the Outlining tab to specify the levels you want to view. Click the Expand button in the Outlining Tools group to display the headings below the title or heading where the insertion point is positioned or click the Collapse button to hide the headings below the title or heading where the insertion point is positioned.

In Outline view, you can move a heading and any text below the heading by selecting the heading and then clicking the Move Up or Move Down button in the Outline Tools group. You can also select a heading and then use the mouse to drag it to the desired position. Select a heading by clicking the selection symbol (gray circle with a white plus symbol) that displays before the heading.

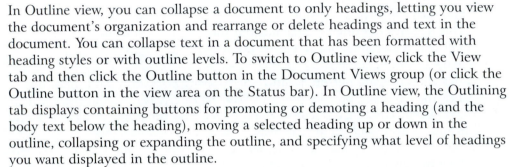

| **Project 5a** | **Viewing Documents in Web Layout View and Viewing and Editing a Document in Outline View** | **Part 1 of 3** |

1. Open **NSSEmpPerf.docx**.
2. View the document in Web Layout view by clicking the Web Layout button in the view area on the Status bar. (Notice how text in the document wraps to fit the window and that the letterhead does not display.)
3. Close **NSSEmpPerf.docx**.
4. Open **OutlineChapters.docx** and then save the document with Save As and name it **WL2-C7-P5-OutlineChapters**.

5. View the document in Web Layout view by clicking the View tab and then clicking the Web Layout button in the Document Views group. (Scroll through the document and notice that it does not contain page breaks.)

6. Change to Outline view by clicking the Outline button in the Document Views group.

7. In Outline view, make sure the Show Level button is set to *All Levels* and the *Show First Line Only* check box contains a check mark.

8. Promote or demote headings by completing the following steps:

   a. Click in the heading *TYPES OF VIRUSES* and then click the Demote button in the Outline Tools group in the Outlining tab.

   b. Click in the heading *METHODS OF VIRUS OPERATIONS* and then click the Promote button in the Outline Tools group.

   c. Click in the heading *CHAPTER 2: SECURITY RISKS* and then click the Promote button.

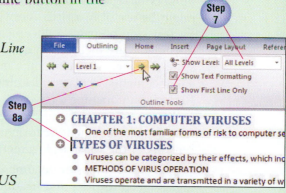

9. Display only the first level by clicking the down-pointing arrow at the right side of the Show Level button in the Outline Tools group and then clicking *Level 1* at the drop-down list.

10. Click in the title *CHAPTER 1: COMPUTER VIRUSES* and then click the Expand button in the Outline Tools group. (This displays the two headings below the title.)

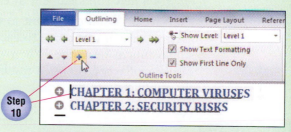

11. Click the Collapse button in the Outline Tools group to hide the two headings.

12. Move down the title *CHAPTER 1: COMPUTER VIRUSES* (along with the headings and text below the title) by clicking the selection symbol that displays before the title and then clicking the Move Down button in the Outline Tools group.

13. Edit the chapter titles so the first title displays as *CHAPTER 1: SECURITY RISKS* and the second title displays as *CHAPTER 2: COMPUTER VIRUSES*.

14. Show two levels by clicking the down-pointing arrow at the right side of the Show Level button in the Outline Tools group and then clicking *Level 2* at the drop-down list.

15. Move up the heading *EMPLOYEE THEFT* by clicking the selection symbol (gray circle with a white plus symbol) that displays before the heading and then clicking the Move Up button in the Outline Tools groups.

16. Click the Close Outline View button.

17. At the document, deselect the text and then print only page 1 of the document.

18. Save and then close **WL2-C7-P5-OutlineChapters.docx**.

Creating a Master Document and Subdocuments

For projects containing a variety of parts or sections, such as a reference guide or book, consider using a *master document*. A master document contains a number of separate documents referred to as *subdocuments*. A master document might be useful in a situation where several people are working on one project. Each person prepares a document for his or her part of the project and then the documents are included in a master document. In a work environment, you can store a master document on a network and then individuals can work on specific subdocuments. A master document allows for easier editing of subdocuments. Rather than opening a large document for editing, you can open a subdocument, make changes, and those changes are reflected in the master document. Create a new master document or format an existing document as a master document with buttons in the Master Document group in the Outlining tab.

To create a master document, switch to Outline view, make sure heading levels are assigned to titles and headings, and then click the Show Document button in the Master Document group in the Outlining tab. Select the headings and text you want divided into a subdocument and then click the Create button in the Master Document group. Text specified as a subdocument displays surrounded by a thin, gray line frame and a subdocument icon displays in the upper left corner of the frame. Word creates a subdocument for each heading at the top level within the selected text. For example, if selected text begins with Heading 1 text, Word creates a new subdocument at each Heading 1 in the selected text.

Save a master document in the normal manner and Word automatically assigns a document name to each subdocument using the first characters in the subdocument headings. When you open a master document, subdocuments display collapsed. To open a subdocument, hold down the Ctrl key and then click the subdocument hyperlink.

Project 5b | **Creating a Master Document and Subdocuments** | **Part 2 of 3**

1. Open **Newsletters.docx** and then save the document with Save As and name it **WL2-C7-P5-Newsletters**.
2. Create subdocuments with the module text by completing the following steps:
   a. Click the View tab and then click the Outline button in the Document Views group.
   b. Position the mouse pointer on the selection symbol that displays immediately left of the heading *MODULE 1: DEFINING NEWSLETTER ELEMENTS* until the pointer turns into a four-headed arrow and then click the left mouse button.
   c. Scroll through the document until the *MODULE 4: CREATING NEWSLETTER LAYOUT* heading displays.
   d. Hold down the Shift key, position the mouse pointer on the selection symbol immediately left of the heading *MODULE 4: CREATING NEWSLETTER LAYOUT* until the pointer turns into a four-headed arrow, and then click the left mouse button. (This selects all of the text in modules 1, 2, 3, and 4.)

e. With the text selected, click the Show Document button in the Master Document group in the Outlining tab.

f. Click the Create button in the Master Document group.

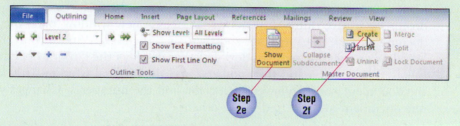

3. Save and then close **WL2-C7-P5-Newsletters.docx**.

4. Open **WL2-C7-P5-Newsletters.docx**. (Notice the subdocuments created by Word.)

5. Edit the MODULE 1 subdocument by completing the following steps:

a. Hold down the Ctrl key and then click the G:\Word2010L2C7\MODULE 1.docx hyperlink.

b. With the **MODULE 1.docx** document displayed, edit the title so it reads *MODULE 1: DEFINING ELEMENTS*.

c. Change the heading *Designing a Newsletter* so it displays as *Designing*.

d. Change the heading *Defining Basic Newsletter Elements* so it displays as *Defining Basic Elements*.

6. Save the subdocument by clicking the Save button on the Quick Access toolbar.

7. Close the subdocument.

8. Move the Module 4 subdocument above the Module 3 subdocument by completing the following steps:

a. Position the arrow pointer on the subdocument icon that displays to the left of the G:\Word2010L2C7\MODULE 4.docx subdocument. (The pointer turns into an arrow pointing up and to the right.)

b. Hold down the left mouse button, drag up so the dark gray, horizontal line displays between the MODULE 2 and MODULE 3 subdocuments (above the gray circle between the modules), and then release the mouse button.

9. Delete the G:\Word2010L2C7\MODULE 3.docx subdocument by completing the following steps:

a. Click the subdocument icon that displays to the left of the G:\Word2010L2C7\MODULE 3.docx subdocument.

b. Press the Delete key.

10. Save and then print **WL2-C7-P5-Newsletters.docx**. At the message that displays asking if you want to open subdocuments, click the No button. (The master document will print with the subdocuments collapsed.)

11. Close **WL2-C7-P5-Newsletters.docx**.

Opening a New Window

New Window

Another useful method for viewing and managing documents is to open a new window containing the contents of the current document. With two versions of the same document, you can be viewing and editing different parts of the document in two different windows. To open a new window, open the desired document, click the View tab, and then click the New Window button in the Window group. The new window Title bar displays the current document name followed by a colon and the number 2 and the original window Title bar displays the document name followed by a colon and the number 1. Changes you make to one document are reflected in the other.

If you want to work in a different location in each window, click the View Side by Side button. This arranges the two windows side by side on the screen. To move to different locations in each window, click the Synchronous Scrolling button to turn the feature off. When all edits are complete, save either document and then close one of the documents. When you close one window the other also closes.

Project 5c   Editing a Document in Two Windows   Part 3 of 3

1. Open **Newsletters.docx** and then save the document with Save As and name it **WL2-C7-P5-EditedNewsletters**.
2. Open a new window by clicking the View tab and then clicking the New Window button in the Window group. (Notice the document name displays in the Title bar followed by a colon and the number 2.)
3. Click the View tab and then click the View Side by Side button in the Window group to display both windows on the screen.
4. Click the Synchronous Scrolling button in the Window group in the View tab in the window at the left side of the screen.

Step 4

5. Move a paragraph in the window at the left side of the screen by completing the following steps:
   a. Scroll down the document in the left window until the third paragraph in the *Designing a Newsletter* section is visible.
   b. Position the mouse pointer in the third paragraph in the *Designing a Newsletter* section and then triple-click the mouse. (Triple-clicking selects the entire paragraph.)
   c. Press Ctrl + X to cut the paragraph from the document.
   d. Position the insertion point at the beginning of the second paragraph in the *Designing a Newsletter* section (the paragraph that begins *Newsletters are one of the most . . .*).
   e. Press Ctrl + V to insert the cut paragraph into the document.
6. Click the title bar of the window at the right side of the screen and then select and move a section by completing the following steps:
   a. Press Ctrl + End to display the end of the document.
   b. Scroll up the document until the module 4 title is visible.
   c. Position the insertion point at the beginning of the title *MODULE 4: CREATING NEWSLETTER LAYOUT*, press the F8 function key (this turns on the Select mode), and then press Ctrl + End. (This should select all of the module 4 text.)

d. Press Ctrl + X to cut the section from the document.

e. Click in the window at the left side of the screen.

f. Scroll down the document until the module 2 title is visible.

g. Position the insertion point at the beginning of the title *MODULE 2: PLANNING A NEWSLETTER* and then press Ctrl + V to insert the module into the document.

7. Click the Maximize button that displays in the upper right corner of the current window.

8. Print pages 1 and 2 of the document.

9. Save and then close **WL2-C7-P5-EditedNewsletters.docx**. (When you close the document, the other document window also closes.)

Chapter Summary

■ Insert a comment in a document by clicking the New Comment button in the Comments group in the Review tab. When you click the New Comment button, a comment balloon displays at the right margin. If any previous settings have been applied, the Reviewing pane, rather than a comment balloon, may display.

■ Turn the display of the Reviewing pane on and off with the Reviewing Pane button in the Tracking group in the Review tab.

■ You can insert comments in the Reviewing pane or in comment balloons. Insert a comment in a balloon by clicking the Show Markup button in the Tracking group in the Review tab, pointing to *Balloons*, and then clicking *Show Only Comments and Formatting in Balloons* at the side menu.

■ Navigate through comments using the Previous and Next buttons in the Comments group in the Review tab.

■ Edit a comment in the Reviewing pane by displaying the pane and then making desired changes to the comment. Edit a comment in a comment balloon by turning on the display of balloons, clicking in the desired comment balloon, and then making desired changes.

■ If changes are made to a document by another person with different user information, the changes display in a different color. Change user name and initials at the Word Options dialog box with *General* selected.

■ Print a document along with the inserted comments or choose to print just the comments and not the document.

■ Delete a comment by clicking the Next button in the Comments group in the Review tab until the desired comment is selected and then clicking the Delete button in the Comments group.

■ Use the Track Changes feature when more than one person is reviewing a document and making editing changes to it. Turn on tracking by clicking the Track Changes button in the Tracking group in the Review tab.

- Display information about tracked changes, such as author's name, date, time, and the type of change, by positioning the mouse pointer on a change. After approximately one second, a box displays with the information. You can also display information on tracked changes by displaying the Reviewing pane.

- Control how editing markings display in a document with the Display for Review button in the Tracking group in the Review tab. Control the marking changes that Word displays in a document with options at the Show Markup button drop-down list.

- Change Track Changes default settings with options at the Track Changes Options dialog box. Display this dialog box by clicking the Track Changes button arrow in the Tracking group and then clicking *Change Tracking Options* at the drop-down list.

- Move to the next change in a document by clicking the Next button in the Changes group in the Review tab or click the Previous button to move to the previous change.

- Use the Accept and Reject buttons in the Changes group in the Review tab to accept or reject revisions made in a document.

- Use the Compare button in the Compare group in the Review tab to compare two documents and display the differences between the documents as tracked changes.

- Customize options for comparing documents at the expanded Compare Documents dialog box. Click the More button to expand the dialog box.

- If you send a document to several people for review, you can combine changes made by each person with the original document until all changes are incorporated in the original document. Combine documents with options at the Combine Documents dialog box.

- Customize options for combining documents at the expanded Combine Documents dialog box. Click the More button to expand the dialog box.

- Specify which source documents to display by clicking the Compare button in the Compare group in the Review tab, pointing to *Show Source Documents*, and then clicking the desired option at the side menu.

- Use Web Layout view to see how a document displays as a web page.

- Use Outline view to collapse a document to only headings to organize headings and text. Use buttons on the Outlining tab that displays in Outline view to promote or demote a heading, move a heading up or down, collapse or expand the outline, and specify levels you want to display.

- A master document contains a number of separate documents called subdocuments. Create a master document or format an existing document as a master document in Outline view. Use buttons in the Master Document group in the Outlining tab to create and edit subdocuments.

Commands Review

FEATURE	RIBBON TAB, GROUP	BUTTON, OPTION	KEYBOARD SHORTCUT
Comment	Review, Comments		
Reviewing pane	Review, Tracking		
Balloons	Review, Tracking	, Balloons	
Delete comment	Review, Comments		
Next comment	Review, Comments		
Previous comment	Review, Comments		
Track changes	Review, Tracking		Ctrl + Shift + E
Display for review	Review, Tracking		
Show markup	Review, Tracking		
Track Changes Options dialog box	Review, Tracking	, Change Tracking Options	
Next revision	Review, Changes		
Previous revision	Review, Changes		
Accept changes	Review, Changes		
Reject changes	Review, Changes		
Compare Documents dialog box	Review, Compare	, Compare	
Combine Documents dialog box	Review, Compare	, Combine	
Show source documents	Review, Compare	, Show Source Documents	
Web Layout view	View, Document Views		
Outline view	View, Document Views		
New window	View, Window		

Concepts Check Test Your Knowledge

Completion: In the space provided at the right, indicate the correct term, command, or number.

1. Insert a comment into a document by clicking this button in the Comments group in the Review tab. _____

2. Navigate to comments by using these two buttons in the Comments group in the Review tab. _____

3. Change user information with options at this dialog box. _____

4. If a document contains comments, print only the comments by displaying the Print tab Backstage view, clicking the first gallery in the Settings category, clicking this option, and then clicking the Print button. _____

5. This is the keyboard shortcut to turn on tracking. _____

6. Turn on the tracking feature by clicking the Track Changes button in this group in the Review tab. _____

7. Display information on tracking changes in this pane. _____

8. This is the default setting for the Display for Review button. _____

9. With track changes on, moved text displays, by default, in this color. _____

10. Customize tracking options at this dialog box. _____

11. Click the *Combine* option at the Compare button drop-down list and this dialog box displays. _____

12. Specify which source document to display by clicking the Compare button, pointing to this option, and then clicking the desired option at the side menu. _____

13. The Outline button is located in this tab. _____

14. Use this button in the Outlining tab to switch between displaying all headings through the lowest level chosen. _____

15. The Show Document button is located in this group in the Outlining tab. _____

16. Click the Expand Subdocuments button and the name of the button changes to this. _____

Skills Check Assess Your Performance

Assessment

1 INSERT COMMENTS AND TRACK CHANGES IN COMPUTER VIRUSES REPORT

1. Open **CompChapters.docx** and then save the document with Save As and name it **WL2-C7-A1-CompChapters**.
2. Insert a comment at the end of the paragraph in the *TYPES OF VIRUSES* section. To do this, type the word **Update**, select it, and then create a comment with the following text: *Insert information on the latest virus*.
3. Insert a comment at the end of the last paragraph in the *METHODS OF VIRUS OPERATION* section. To do this, type the words **Company Example**, select the words, and then create a comment with the following text: *Include information on the latest virus to affect our company*.
4. Insert a comment at the end of the last paragraph in the document. To do this, type the word **Information**, select it, and then create a comment with the following text: *Include information about laws related to copying software*.
5. Turn on tracking and then make the following changes:
   a. Edit the first sentence in the document so it displays as *The computer virus is one of the most familiar forms of risk to computer security.*
   b. Insert the word **computer's** between *the* and *motherboard* in the last sentence in the first paragraph of the document.
   c. Delete the word *real* in the second sentence of the *TYPES OF VIRUSES* section and then type **significant**.
   d. Select and then delete the last sentence in the *Methods of Virus Operation* section (the sentence that begins *A well-known example of the logic bomb was the...*). (Do not delete the comment.)
   e. Turn off tracking.
6. Display the Word Options dialog box with *General* selected and then change the *User name* to **Stacey Phillips** and the *Initials* to **SP**.
7. Turn on tracking and then make the following changes:
   a. Delete the words *or cracker* located in the seventh sentence in the *TYPES OF VIRUSES* section.
   b. Delete the word *garner* in the first sentence in the CHAPTER 2: SECURITY RISKS section and then type **generate**.
   c. Select and then move the *EMPLOYEE THEFT* section below the *CRACKING SOFTWARE FOR COPYING* section.
   d. Turn off tracking.
8. Display the Word Options dialog box with *General* selected and then change the *User name* back to the original name and *Initials* back to the original initials.
9. Print the document showing markups.
10. Accept all of the changes in the document *except* the change moving the *EMPLOYEE THEFT* section below the *CRACKING SOFTWARE FOR COPYING* section.
11. Save, print, and then close **WL2-C7-A1-CompChapters.docx**.

Assessment

2 COMPARE ORIGINAL AND REVISED DISASTER RECOVERY PLAN REPORT

1. Compare **Security.docx** with **EditedSecurity.docx** and insert the changes into a new document. *Hint: Choose **New** document at the expanded Compare Documents dialog box.*
2. Save the compared document and name it **WL2-C7-A2-Security.docx**.
3. Print the list of markups only (not the document).
4. Reject the changes made to the bulleted text and the changes made to the last paragraph in the *DISASTER RECOVERY PLAN* section and accept all other changes.
5. Number the pages at the bottom center of each page.
6. Save the document, print only the document, and then close **WL2-C7-A2-Security.docx**.

Assessment

3 COMBINE ORIGINAL AND REVISED LEGAL DOCUMENTS

1. Open **LegalSummons.docx** and then save the document with Save As and name it **WL2-C7-A3-LegalSummons**.
2. Close **WL2-C7-A3-LegalSummons.docx**.
3. At a blank screen, combine **WL2-C7-A3-LegalSummons** (the original document) with **Review1-LegalSummons.docx** (the revised document) into the original document. *Hint: Choose **Original** document at the Combine Documents expanded dialog box.*
4. Accept all changes to the document.
5. Save and then close **WL2-C7-A3-LegalSummons.docx**.
6. At a blank screen, combine **WL2-C7-A3-LegalSummons.docx** (the original document) with **Review2-LegalSummons.docx** (the revised document) into the original document.
7. Print only the list of markups.
8. Accept all changes to the document.
9. Save the document, print only the document, and then close **WL2-C7-A3-LegalSummons.docx**.

Assessment

4 TRACK CHANGES IN A TABLE

1. Open **SalesTable.docx** and then save the document with Save As and name it **WL2-C7-A4-SalesTable**.
2. You can track changes made to a table and customize the track changes options for a table. Display the Track Changes Options dialog box and experiment with the options in the *Table cell highlighting* section and then make the following changes:
   a. Change the color for inserted cells to light purple.
   b. Change the color for deleted cells to light green.
3. Turn on track changes and then make the following changes:
   a. Insert a new row at the beginning of the table.
   b. Merge the cells in the new row. (At the message saying the action will not be marked as a change, click OK.)

c. Type **Clearline Manufacturing** in the merged cell.

d. Delete the *Fanning, Andrew* row.

e. Insert a new row below *Barnett, Jacqueline* and then type **Montano, Neil** in the first cell, **$530,678** in the second cell, and **$550,377** in the third cell.

f. Turn off track changes.

4. Save and then print the document with markups.

5. Accept all of the changes.

6. Display the Track Changes Options dialog box and then return the inserted cells color back to *Light Blue* and the deleted cells color back to *Pink*.

7. Save, print, and then close **WL2-C7-A4-SalesTable.docx**.

Assessment

5 **INSERT COMMENTS AND TRACK CHANGES IN A TRAVEL DOCUMENT**

1. Open **TTSTravel.docx** and then save the document with Save As and name it **WL2-C7-A5-TTSTravel**.

2. Display the Track Changes Options dialog box and make a note of the default settings. Change the *Use Balloons (Print and Web Layout)* option to *Always* and then make the following changes:

a. Change the balloon width to 2 inches.

b. Display balloons at the left margin.

c. Change the paper orientation to *Forced Landscape*.

3. Insert the following comments:

a. Type the text **Country names** at the end of the paragraph in the *African Study Adventure* section, select the text, and then insert the comment **Ask Jan if she wants to include specific country names.**

b. Type the word **Examples** at the end of the paragraph in the *Custom Groups* section, select the word, and then insert the comment **Please provide custom program examples.**

4. Turn on tracking and then make the following changes:

a. Insert the word *TRAVEL* between *COMPREHENSIVE* and *ITINERARIES* in the *COMPREHENSIVE ITINERARIES* heading.

b. Change the number *25* in the *SMALL GROUPS* section to *20*.

c. Delete the words *make sure* in the *ACCOMMODATIONS AND MEALS* section and then type **ensure**.

d. Turn off tracking.

5. Save and then print the list of markups only.

6. Accept the changes.

7. Return the options at the Track Changes Option dialog box back to the default settings.

8. Save the document, print only the document, and then close the document.

6 **ASSIGN LEVELS AND EDIT A DOCUMENT IN OUTLINE VIEW**

1. Open **Computers.docx** and then save the document with Save As and name it **WL2-C7-A6-Computers**.
2. Change to Outline view and then make the following changes:
   a. Demote the heading *Home Entertainment* to level 2.
   b. Promote the title *COMPUTERS IN EDUCATION* to level 1.
   c. Show only two levels.
   d. Move the *COMPUTERS IN EDUCATION* section above the *COMPUTERS IN ENTERTAINMENT* section.
   e. Move the *Television and Film* heading below the *Home Entertainment* heading.
3. Print **WL2-C7-A6-Computers.docx**. (The document will print collapsed.)
4. Close the Outline view.
5. Save and then close **WL2-C7-A6-Computers.docx**.

Visual Benchmark Demonstrate Your Proficiency

TRACK CHANGES IN AN EMPLOYEE PERFORMANCE DOCUMENT

1. Open **NSSEmpPerf.docx** and then save the document with Save As and name it **WL2-C7-VB-NSSEmpPerf**.
2. Turn on track changes and then make the changes shown in Figure 7.8. (Make the editing changes before you move the Employment Records information below the Performance Evaluation information.)
3. Turn off track changes and then print only the list of markups.
4. Accept all changes to the document.
5. Save the document, print only the document, and then close **WL2-C7-VB-NSSEmpPerf.docx**.
6. At a blank screen, combine **WL2-C7-VB-NSSEmpPerf.docx** (the original document) with **EditedNSSEmpPerf.docx** (the revised document) into the original document.
7. Accept all changes to the document.
8. Save, print, and then close **WL2-C7-VB-NSSEmpPerf.docx**.

Figure 7.8 Visual Benchmark

Northland Security Systems
3200 North 22nd Street ✦ Springfield ✦ IL ✦ 62102

EMPLOYEE PERFORMANCE

and/or behavior

Work Performance Standards

Some work performance standards are written statements of the results expected of an employee when his or her job elements are satisfactorily performed under existing working conditions. Each employee in a permanent position must be provided with a current set of work performance standards for his or her position.

Employment Records

Your personnel file is maintained in the human resources department at the main office of Northland Security Systems. The human resources department maintains a file with copies of the documentation in your particular department. Your file includes personnel action documents, mandatory employment forms, your performance evaluations, and documentation of disciplinary action. Your file may include letters of commendation, training certificates, or other work-related documents that your supervisor has requested to be included in your file.

working

Performance Evaluation

(full-time equivalent)

If you are serving a six-month probationary period, your supervisor will evaluate your performance at the end of the second and fifth months. If you are completing a one-year probationary period, your evaluations will be conducted at the end of the third, seventh, and eleventh month. You will receive a copy of each performance report. Once you have attained permanent employee status, your performance will be evaluated annually during the month prior to your pay progression date. Each evaluation will include a discussion between you and your supervisor to review and clarify goals and methods to achieve them. The evaluation will also include a report of your progress on the job. Evaluations will be made with reference to established work performance standards.

written

1-888-555-2200 ✦ www.emcp.net/nss

Case Study   Apply Your Skills

Part 1

You work in the Training Department at Hart International. Your department is responsible for preparing training material and for training employees on how to use software applications within the company. Your supervisor, Nicole Sweeney, has asked you to help her prepare a Microsoft Word training manual. She has written a portion of the manual and has had two employees, Terry Oberman and Gina Singh, review the contents and make tracked changes. She has asked you to combine the two reviewers' changes into the original document. Combine **HITraining.docx** with **HITrainingTO.docx** and then combine **HITraining.docx** with **HITrainingGS.docx**. Go through the original document with the tracked changes and accept and/or reject revisions. Not all revisions made by Terry Oberman or Gina Singh are correct so check each revision before accepting it. Save the combined document with Save As and name it **WL2-C7-CS-HITraining**.

Part 2

Ms. Sweeney has asked you to prepare training materials on how to check the spelling and grammar in a document and how to customize spelling and grammar options. Using the **WL2-C7-CS-HITraining.docx** document as a guideline, write information (including steps) on how to complete a spelling and grammar check in a document and how to change spelling and grammar options at the Word Options dialog box with *Proofing* selected. Include in the document a table that presents the names of the buttons available at the Spelling and Grammar dialog box and a brief description of what tasks the buttons complete. Save the completed document and name it **WL2-C7-CS-HISpelling**.

Part 3

If possible, send a copy of your document to one or two classmates and have him or her edit the document with track changes turned on. Combine the edited documents with your original **WL2-C7-CS-HISpelling** document. Save, print, and then close the document.

Part 4

Open **WL2-C7-CS-HITraining.docx**, move the insertion point to the end of the document, and then insert **WL2-C7-CS-HISpelling.docx**. Apply at least the following to the document:

- Heading styles
- Quick Styles set
- Theme
- Table of contents
- Page numbering
- Cover page

Save, print, and then close the document.

Protecting and Preparing Documents

PERFORMANCE OBJECTIVES

Upon successful completion of Chapter 8, you will be able to:

- Restrict formatting and editing in a document and allow exceptions to restrictions
- Protect a document with a password
- Open a document in different views
- Modify document properties
- Inspect and encrypt a document
- Restrict permission to a document
- Create and apply a digital signature
- Insert a signature line
- Mark a document as final
- Check a document for accessibility and compatibility issues
- Manage versions

Tutorials

8.1 Restricting Formatting and Editing in a Document

8.2 Protecting a Document with a Password and Making a Document Read-only

8.3 Modifying Document Properties; Running the Compatibility Checker

8.4 Inspecting and Encrypting a Document

8.5 Creating a Digital Signature and Inserting a Signature Line

8.6 Checking the Accessibility of a Document

8.7 Managing Versions

In Chapter 7, you learned to perform workgroup activities such as inserting comments into a document, tracking changes made by other users, comparing documents, and combining documents from multiple users. In this chapter, you will learn how to protect the integrity of shared documents, limit the formatting or editing changes that other users can make, and prepare documents for distribution. Model answers for this chapter's projects appear on the following pages.

Word2010L2C8

Note: Before beginning the projects, copy to your storage medium the Word2010L2C8 subfolder from the Word2010L2 folder on the CD that accompanies this textbook and then make Word2010L2C8 the active folder.

TERRA ENERGY CORPORATION

OVERVIEW

Terra Energy Corporation is a development stage company that was incorporated on May 1, 2009. The corporation and its subsidiary (collectively referred to as the "Company") designs, develops, configures, and offers for sale power systems that provide highly reliable, high-quality, environmentally friendly power. The Company has segmented the potential markets for its products into two broad categories: high-energy, high-power, uninterruptible power system (UPS), and high-power distributed generation and utility power-grid energy storage system. We have available for sale several high-energy products that deliver a low level of power over a long period of time (typically measured in hours). These products are tailored to the telecommunications, cable systems, computer networks, and Internet markets.

We are developing a new high-energy product for potential applications in the renewable energy market for both photovoltaic and wind turbine uses. As part of exploring these markets, we have committed to invest $2 million in Clear Sun Energies and we have purchased the inverter electronics technology of Technology Pacific[SN1].

We have taken significant actions over the last eighteen months to reduce our expenditures for product development, infrastructure, and production readiness. Our headcount, development spending, and capital expenditures have been significantly reduced. We have continued the preliminary design and development of potential products for markets under consideration and with specific approval by the Company's board of directors.

RESEARCH AND DEVELOPMENT

We believe that our research and development efforts are essential to our ability to successfully design and deliver our products to our targeted customers, as well as to modify and improve them to reflect the evolution of markets and customer needs. Our research and development team has worked closely with potential customers to define product features and performance to address specific needs. Our research and development expenses, including engineering expenses, were approximately $8,250,000 in 2011, $15,525,000 in 2010, and $7,675,000 in 2009. We expect research and development expenses in 2012 to be lower than in 2011. As we determine market opportunities, we may need to make research and development expenditures in the future. As of December 31, 2011, we employed twenty-five engineers and technicians who were engaged in research and development.

MANUFACTURING

Historically, our manufacturing has consisted of the welding and assembly of our products. We have previously contracted out the manufacture of our high-energy flywheel components, using our design drawings and processes to facilitate more rapid growth by taking advantage of third-party installed manufacturing capacity. For a limited number of non-proprietary components, we generate performance specifications and obtain either standard or custom components.

Project 1 Restrict Formatting and Editing in an Annual Report

WL2-C8-P1-TECRpt.docx

WL2-C8-P1-TECRpt.docx

Main document changes and comments		
Page 1: Comment [SN1]	Student Name	8/10/2012 8:35:00 AM

Include additional information on the impact of this purchase.

Header and footer changes

Text Box changes

Header and footer text box changes

Footnote changes

Endnote changes

1

REAL ESTATE SALE AGREEMENT

The Buyer, BUYER, and Seller, SELLER, hereby agree that SELLER will sell and BUYER will buy the following property, with such improvements as are located thereon, and is described as follows: All that tract of land lying and being in Land Lot _____ of the _____ District, Section _____ of _____ County, and being known as Address: _____
City:_____ State: _____ Zip:_____, together with all light fixtures, electrical, mechanical, plumbing, air-conditioning, and any other systems or fixtures as are attached thereto; all plants, trees, and shrubbery now a part thereof, together with all the improvements thereon, and all appurtenances thereto, all being hereinafter collectively referred to as the "Property." The full legal description of said Property is the same as is recorded with the Clerk of the Superior Court of the County in which the Property is located and is made a part of this Agreement by reference.

SELLER will sell and BUYER will buy upon the following terms and conditions, as completed or marked. On any conflict of terms or conditions, that which is added will supersede that which is printed or marked. It is understood that the Property will be bought by Warranty Deed, with covenants, restrictions, and easements of record.

Financing: The balance due to SELLER will be evidenced by a negotiable Promissory Note of Borrower, secured by a Mortgage or Deed to Secure Debt on the Property and delivered by BUYER to SELLER dated the date of closing.

New financing: If BUYER does not obtain the required financing, the earnest money deposit shall be forfeited to SELLER as liquidated damages. BUYER will make application for financing within five days of the date of acceptance of the Agreement and in a timely manner furnish any and all credit, employment, financial, and other information required by the lender.

Closing costs: BUYER will pay all closing costs to include: Recording Fees, Intangibles Tax, Credit Reports, Funding Fees, Loan Origination Fee, Document Preparation Fee, Loan Insurance Premium, Title Insurance Policy, Attorney's Fees, Courier Fees, Overnight Fee, Appraisal Fee, Survey, Transfer Tax, Satisfaction and Recording Fees, Wood Destroying Organism Report, and any other costs associated with the funding or closing of this Agreement.

Prorations: All taxes, rentals, condominium or association fees, monthly mortgage insurance premiums, and interest on loans will be prorated as of the date of closing.

Title insurance: Within five (5) days of this Agreement SELLER will deliver to BUYER or closing attorney: Title insurance commitment for an owner's policy in the amount of the purchase price. Any expense of securing title, including but not limited to legal fees, discharge of liens, and recording fees will be paid by SELLER.

WL2-C8-P3-REAgrmnt.docx

2

Survey: Within ten (10) days of acceptance of this Agreement, BUYER or closing attorney, may, at BUYER's expense, obtain a new staked survey showing any improvements now existing thereon and certified to BUYER, lender, and the title insurer.

Default and attorney's fees: Should BUYER elect not to fulfill obligations under this Agreement, all earnest monies will be retained by SELLER as liquidated damages and fund settlement of any claim, whereupon BUYER and SELLER will be relieved of all obligations under this Agreement. If SELLER defaults under this agreement, the BUYER may seek specific performance in return of the earnest money deposit. In connection with any litigation arising out of this Agreement, the prevailing party shall be entitled to recover all costs including reasonable attorney's fees.

IN WITNESS WHEREOF, all of the parties hereto affix their hands and seals this _____ day of _____, 20_____.

WL2-C8-P3-REAgrmnt.docx

Project 3 Prepare a Real Estate Agreement for Distribution

WL2-C8-P3-REAgrmnt.docx

Model Answers

Project 4 Prepare and Inspect a Lease Agreement

WL2-C8-P4-Lease.docx

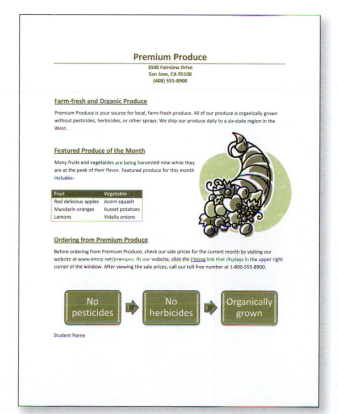

Project 5 Check the Accessibility and Compatibility of a Produce Document

WL2-C8-P5-PremPro.docx

Project **1** **Restrict Formatting and Editing in an Annual Report**   **3 Parts**

You will open an annual report document, restrict formatting and editing in the document, insert a password, and allow exceptions to restrictions for specific users.

Protecting Documents ▪▪▪▪▪▪▪▪▪▪▪▪▪▪▪▪▪▪▪▪

In a company or organization, you may want to distribute copies of a document among members of your group. In some situations, you may want to protect your document and limit the changes that can be made to the document. If you create a document containing sensitive, restricted, or private information, consider protecting the document by saving it as a read-only document or securing it with a password.

With options at the Restrict Formatting and Editing task pane, you can limit what formatting and editing users can perform on text in a document. Limiting formatting and editing is especially useful in a workgroup environment where a number of people in an organization will be reviewing and editing the same document. For example, suppose you are responsible for preparing the yearly corporate report for your company. This corporate report contains information from a variety of departments such as finance, human resources, and sales and marketing. You can prepare the report and then specify what portion of the report document an individual is allowed to edit. For example, you can specify that a person in the finance department would only be able to edit that portion of the report containing information on finances and someone in human resources would only be able to edit data pertinent to the human resources department. In this way, you can protect the integrity of the document.

To protect a document, display the Restrict Formatting and Editing task pane shown in Figure 8.1 by clicking the Review tab and then clicking the Restrict

Figure 8.1 Restrict Formatting and Editing Task Pane

Use options in this section to limit formatting to specific styles.

Use options in this section to specify the type of editing allowed in the document.

After specifying formatting and editing restrictions, click this button to display the Start Enforcing Protection dialog box with protection options.

Editing button in the Protect group. Use options in the *Formatting restrictions* section to limit formatting to specific styles and use options in the *Editing restrictions* section to specify the type of editing allowed in the document.

Note: The Protect group in the Review tab contains a Block Authors button. This button is available only when a document is saved to a Microsoft SharePoint Foundation 2010 site that supports Workspaces. If the button is active, select the portion of the document you want to block from editing and then click the Block Authors button. To unblock authors, click in the locked section of the document and then click the Block Authors button.

Restricting Formatting

With options in the *Formatting restrictions* section of the Restrict Formatting and Editing task pane, you can lock specific styles used in a document, thus allowing the use of only those styles and prohibiting a user from making other formatting changes. Click the <u>Settings</u> hyperlink in the *Formatting restrictions* section, and the Formatting Restrictions dialog box displays as shown in Figure 8.2.

Insert a check mark in the *Limit formatting to a selection of styles* check box and the styles become available in the *Checked styles are currently allowed* list box. In this list box, insert a check mark in the check box preceding the styles you want to allow and remove the check mark in the check box preceding the styles you do not want allowed. You can limit formatting to a minimum number of styles by clicking the Recommended Minimum button. This allows formatting with styles that Word uses for certain features such as bulleted or numbered lists. Click the None button to remove all check marks and allow no styles to be used in the document. Click the All button to insert a check mark in all the check boxes and allow all styles to be used in the document.

With options in the *Formatting* section of the dialog box, you can allow or not allow AutoFormat to make changes in a document and allow or not allow users to switch themes or Quick Styles sets.

▼ **Quick Steps**

Display Formatting Restrictions Dialog Box
1. Click Review tab.
2. Click Restrict Editing button.
3. Click the <u>Settings</u> hyperlink.

Figure 8.2 Formatting Restrictions Dialog Box

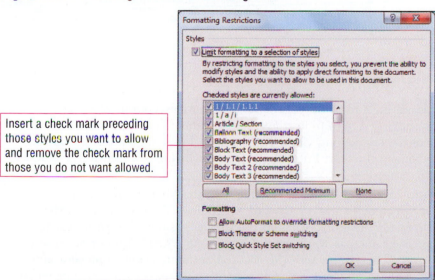

Insert a check mark preceding those styles you want to allow and remove the check mark from those you do not want allowed.

1. Open **TECRpt.docx** and then save the document with Save As and name it **WL2-C8-P1-TECRpt**.
2. Restrict formatting to Heading 1 and Heading 2 styles by completing the following steps:
   a. Click the Review tab.
   b. Click the Restrict Editing button in the Protect group.

Step 2a

Step 2b

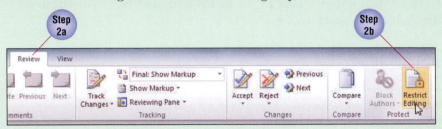

c. At the Restrict Formatting and Editing task pane, click the *Limit formatting to a selection of styles* check box to insert a check mark. (Skip this step if the check box already contains a check mark.)
d. Click the <u>Settings</u> hyperlink.
e. At the Format Restrictions dialog box, click the None button.
f. Scroll down the list box and then insert a check mark in the *Heading 1* check box and also the *Heading 2* check box.
g. Click OK.
h. At the message telling you that the document may contain direct formatting or styles that are not allowed and asking if you want to remove them, click Yes.
3. Save **WL2-C8-P1-TECRpt.docx**.

Step 2c

Step 2d

Step 2f

Step 2e

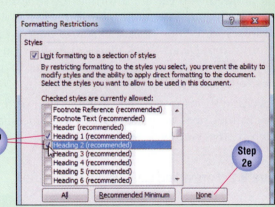

▼ **Quick Steps**

Display Start Enforcing Protection Dialog Box
1. Click Review tab.
2. Click Restrict Editing button.
3. Specify formatting and/or editing options.
4. Click Yes, Start Enforcing Protection button.
5. Type password.
6. Press Tab key, type password again.
7. Click OK.

Enforcing Restrictions

Specifying formatting and editing restrictions and any exceptions to those restrictions is the first step to protecting your document. The next step is to start enforcement of the restrictions. Click the Yes, Start Enforcing Protection button in the task pane and the Start Enforcing Protection dialog box shown in Figure 8.3 displays.

At the Start Enforcing Protection dialog box, the *Password* option is automatically selected. To add a password, type the desired password in the *Enter new password (optional)* text box. Click in the *Reenter password to confirm* text box and then type the same password again. Choose the *User authentication* option if you want to use encryption and SSL-secured authentication to prevent any unauthorized changes. If Word does not recognize the password you type when opening a password-protected document, check to make sure Caps Lock is off and then try typing the password again.

Figure 8.3 Start Enforcing Protection Dialog Box

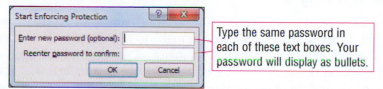

Type the same password in each of these text boxes. Your password will display as bullets.

Project 1b **Protecting a Document**   **Part 2 of 3**

1. With **WL2-C8-P1-TECRpt.docx** open, click the Yes, Start Enforcing Protection button (located toward the bottom of the task pane).

2. At the Start Enforcing Protection dialog box, type **formatting** in the *Enter new password (optional)* text box. (Bullets will display in the text box rather than the letters you type.)

3. Press the Tab key (this moves the insertion point to the *Reenter password to confirm* text box) and then type **formatting**. (Bullets will display in the text box rather than the letters you type.)

4. Click OK to close the dialog box.

5. Read the information in the task pane telling you that the document is protected and special restrictions are in effect and that you may format text only with certain styles. Click the Available styles hyperlink. (This displays the Styles task pane with only four styles in the list box: *Clear All*, *Normal*, *Heading 1*, and *Heading 2*.)

6. Apply the Heading 1 style to the title TERRA ENERGY CORPORATION and apply the Heading 2 style to the following headings: *Overview*, *Research and Development*, *Manufacturing*, and *Sales and Marketing*.

7. Close the Styles task pane.

8. Change the Quick Styles set to *Formal*.

9. At the message indicating that some of the Quick Styles could not be updated, click OK.

10. Save the document.

11. Remove the password protection from the document by completing the following steps:
    a. Click the Stop Protection button located at the bottom of the task pane.
    b. At the Unprotect Document dialog box, type **formatting** in the text box.
    c. Click OK.

12. Save **WL2-C8-P1-TECRpt.docx**.

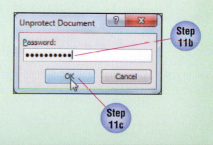

Restricting Editing

Use the *Editing restrictions* option at the Restrict Formatting and Editing task pane to limit the types of changes a user can make to a document. Insert a check mark in the *Allow only this type of editing in the document* option and the drop-down list below the option becomes active. Click the down-pointing arrow at the right of the option box and these options are available: *Tracked changes, Comments, Filling in forms,* and *No changes (Read only).*

If you do not want a user to be able to make any changes to a document, choose the *No changes (Read only)* option. If you want the user to be able to make tracked changes in a document, choose the *Tracked changes* option and choose the *Comments* option if you want the user to be able to make comments in a document. These two options are useful in a workgroup environment where a document for review is routed to various members of the group. Choose the *Filling in forms* option and a user will be able to fill in fields in a form but will not be able to make any other editing changes.

Project 1c   **Restricting Editing of a Document**   **Part 3 of 3**

1. With **WL2-C8-P1-TECRpt.docx** open, restrict editing to only comments by completing the following steps:
   a. Make sure the Restrict Formatting and Editing task pane displays.
   b. Click the *Allow only this type of editing in the document* check box to insert a check mark.
   c. Click the down-pointing arrow at the right of the option box below *Allow only this type of editing in the document* and then click *Comments* at the drop-down list.
2. Click the Yes, Start Enforcing Protection button located toward the bottom of the task pane.
3. At the Start Enforcing Protection dialog box, click OK. (Adding a password is optional.)
4. Read the information in the task pane telling you that the document is protected and that you may only insert comments.
5. Click each of the ribbon tabs and notice the buttons and options that are dimmed and unavailable.
6. Insert a comment by completing the following steps:
   a. Move the insertion point immediately right of the period that ends the last sentence in the second paragraph of the *Overview* section.
   b. Click the Review tab (if necessary), click the Show Markup button in the Tracking group, point to *Balloons*, and then click the *Show All Revisions Inline* option.
   c. If necessary, click the Reviewing Pane button to turn on the display of the Reviewing pane.
   d. Click the New Comment button in the Comments group in the Review tab.

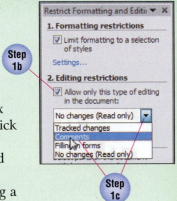

Step 1b

Step 1c

e. Type the following in the Reviewing pane: **Include additional information on the impact of this purchase.**
f. Close the Reviewing pane.
g. Click the Stop Protection button located at the bottom of the Restrict Formatting and Editing task pane.
h. Close the Restrict Formatting and Editing task pane.

7. Save the document and then print only page 1.
8. Print only the comment. (To do this, display the Print tab Backstage view, click the first gallery in the Settings category, click the *List of Markup* option, and then click the Print button.)
9. Close **WL2-C8-P1-TECRpt.docx**.

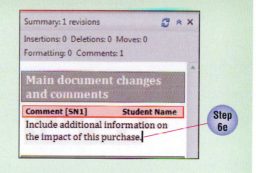

Step 6e

---

roject **2** **Protect a Contract Document and Identify a Training Document as Read-Only**   **2 Parts**

You will open a contract document and then protect the document with a password. You will also open documents in different views.

Protecting a Document with a Password

In the previous section of this chapter, you learned how to protect a document with a password using options at the Start Enforcing Protection dialog box. You can also protect a document with a password using options at the General Options dialog box shown in Figure 8.4. To display this dialog box, click the File tab and then click Save As. At the Save As dialog box, click the Tools button located toward the bottom of the dialog box next to the Save button and then click *General Options* at the drop-down list.

At the General Options dialog box, you can assign a password to open the document, modify the document, or both. To insert a password to open the document, click in the *Password to open* text box and then type the password. A password can contain up to 15 characters, should be eight characters or more in length, and is case sensitive. Consider combining uppercase letters, lowercase letters, numbers, and/or symbols in your password to make it more secure. Use the *Password to modify* option to create a password that a person must enter before being able to make edits to the document.

At the General Options dialog box, insert a check mark in the *Read-only recommended* check box to save a document as a read-only document. If you open a document that is saved as a read-only document and then make changes to it, you have to save the document with a new name. Use this option if you do not want the contents of the original document changed.

▼ **Quick Steps**

Add a Password to a Document
1. Click File tab, click Save As button.
2. Click Tools button, *General Options*.
3. Type a password in the *Password to modify* text box.
4. Press Enter.
5. Type the same password again.
6. Press Enter.

A strong password contains a mix of uppercase and lowercase letters as well as numbers and symbols.

Figure 8.4 General Options Dialog Box

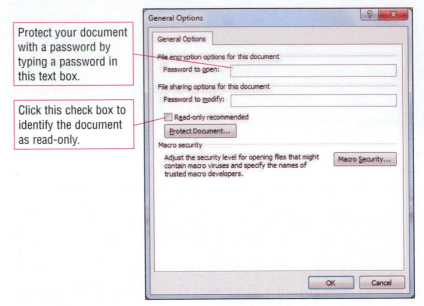

Protect your document with a password by typing a password in this text box.

Click this check box to identify the document as read-only.

1. Open **TECContract.docx**.
2. Save the document with Save As and name it **WL2-C8-P2-TECContract**.
3. Save the document and protect it with a password by completing the following steps:
   a. Display the Save As dialog box.
   b. Click the Tools button located toward the bottom of the dialog box (next to the Save button) and then click *General Options* at the drop-down list.
   c. At the General Options dialog box, type your first name in the *Password to open* text box. (If it is longer than 15 characters, abbreviate it. You will not see your name—instead Word inserts bullets.)

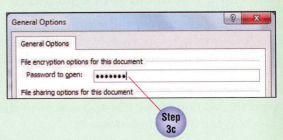

Step 3c

   d. After typing your name, press the Enter key.
   e. At the Confirm Password dialog box, type your name again (be sure to type it exactly as you did in the *Password to open* text box—including uppercase or lowercase letters) and then press Enter.
   f. Click the Save button at the Save As dialog box.
4. Close **WL2-C8-P2-TECContract.docx**.
5. Open **WL2-C8-P2-TECContract.docx** and type your password when prompted.
6. Close the document.

Opening a Document in Different Views

With the Open button in the Open dialog box, you can open a document in different views. At the Open dialog box, click the Open button arrow and a drop-down list of options displays. Click the *Open Read-Only* option and the document opens in read-only mode. In this mode, you can make changes to the document but you cannot save the document with the same name. Click the *Open as Copy* option and a copy of the document opens and the text *Copy (1)* displays at the beginning of the document name in the Title bar. If you click the *Open in Protected View* option, the document opens and the text *(Protected View)* displays after the document name in the Title bar. Also, a message bar displays telling you that the file was opened in *Protected View*. If you want to edit the document, click the Enable Editing button in the message bar. You can open a document with the *Open and Repair* option and Word will open a new version of the document and repair any issues with the document.

▼ **Quick Steps**

Open Document in Different Views
1. Display Open dialog box.
2. Click desired document name.
3. Click Open button arrow.
4. Click desired open option at drop-down list.

Project 2b   **Opening a Document in Different Views**   **Part 2 of 2**

1. Open **TECTraining.docx** and then save the document with Save As and name it **WL2-C8-P2-TECTraining**.
2. Close **WL2-C8-P2-TECTraining.docx**.
3. Open a document as a read-only document by completing the following steps:
   a. Display the Open dialog box with the Word2010L2C8 folder on your storage medium the active folder.
   b. Click once on the document name **WL2-C8-P2-TECTraining.docx**.
   c. Click the Open button arrow (located toward the bottom right corner of the dialog box) and then click *Open Read-Only* at the drop-down list. (Notice that the text *(Read Only)* displays after the name of the document in the Title bar.)

   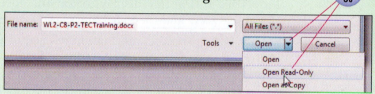

   Step 3c

   d. Close the document.
4. Open a document in protected view by completing the following steps:
   a. Display the Open dialog box.
   b. Click once on the document name **PremPro.docx**.
   c. Click the Open button arrow and then click *Open in Protected View* at the drop-down list. (Notice that the text *(Protected View)* displays after the name in the Title bar and the message bar displays telling you that the file was opened in *Protected View*.)
   d. Click each of the tabs and notice that most formatting options are dimmed.
   e. Click in the document and then click the Enable Editing button in the message bar. (This removes *(Protected View)* after the document name in the Title bar and makes available the options in the tabs.)

   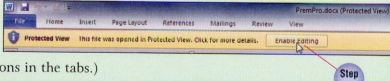

   Step 4e

   f. Close the document.

Project 3   **Prepare a Real Estate Agreement for Distribution**   **3 Parts**

You will open a real estate agreement and then prepare it for distribution by inserting document properties, marking it as final, and encrypting it with a password.

Managing Document Properties ■■■■■■■■■■■■■■■■■

Each document you create has properties associated with it such as the type of document, its location, and when it was created, modified, and accessed. You can view and modify document properties at the Info tab Backstage view and modify document properties at the document information panel. Display information about the document by clicking the File tab and then clicking the Info tab. The Info tab Backstage view displays information about the document in the pane at the right side as shown in Figure 8.5.

The document property information that displays in the pane at the right includes the file size, number of pages and words, total editing time, and any tags or comments you added. You can add or update a document property by hovering your mouse over the information that displays at the right of the property (a rectangular text box with a light yellow border displays), clicking in the text box, and then typing the desired information. In the *Related Dates* section, dates display for when the document was created and when it was last modified and printed. The *Related People* section displays the name of the author of the document and also contains options for adding additional author names. Display additional document properties by clicking the <u>Show All Properties</u> hyperlink.

Properties ▾

Properties

You also can add information to a document's properties at the document information panel shown in Figure 8.6. Display this panel by clicking the Properties button that displays below the document thumbnail in the Info tab Backstage view and then clicking *Show Document Panel* at the drop-down list.

By typing specific information in each of the text boxes in the document information panel, you can describe a document. Inserting text in some of the text boxes can help you organize and identify your documents. For example, insert specific words contained in the document in the *Keywords* text box, and you can search for all documents containing the specific keywords. Text you type in

Figure 8.5 Info Tab Backstage View

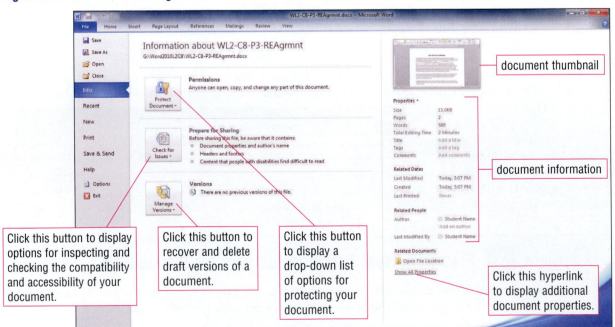

Figure 8.6 Document Information Panel

Type document information in the text boxes in the document information panel.

the document information panel is saved with the document. You can print the document properties for a document by displaying the Print tab Backstage view, clicking the first gallery in the Settings category, clicking *Document Properties* at the drop-down list, and then clicking the Print button.

In addition to inserting information about a document in the document information panel, you can insert specific information with options at the Properties dialog box shown in Figure 8.7. The name of the dialog box reflects the currently open document. Display this dialog box by clicking the Document Properties button that displays in the upper left corner of the document information panel and then clicking *Advanced Properties* at the drop-down list. You can also display this dialog box by displaying the Info tab Backstage view, clicking the Properties button, and then clicking *Advanced Properties* at the drop-down list. Another method for displaying the Properties dialog box is to display the Open dialog box, click the desired document, click the Organize button, and then click *Properties* at the drop-down list. You can also right-click on the desired file name and then click *Properties* at the shortcut menu.

The Properties dialog box with the General tab selected displays information about the document type, size, and location. Click the Summary tab and fields display such as title, subject, author, company, category, keywords, and comments. Some fields may contain data and others may be blank. You can insert, edit, or delete text in the fields. With the Statistics tab selected, information displays such as the number of pages, paragraphs, lines, words, and characters. You can view the document without opening it by clicking the Contents tab. This displays a portion of the document in the viewing window. Click the Custom tab to add custom

▼ **Quick Steps**

Display Properties Dialog Box
1. Click File tab.
2. Click Properties button at Info tab Backstage view.
3. Click *Advanced Properties.*

Figure 8.7 Properties Dialog Box with General Tab Selected

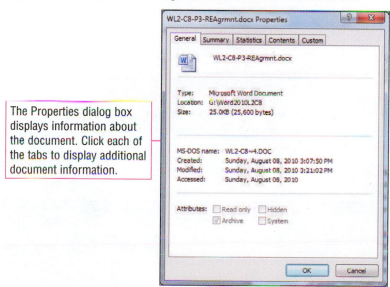

The Properties dialog box displays information about the document. Click each of the tabs to display additional document information.

properties to the document. For example, you can add a property that displays the date the document was completed, information on the department in which the document was created, and much more.

Project 3a   **Inserting Document Properties** **Part 1 of 3**

1. Open **REAgrmnt.dox** and then save the document with Save As and name it **WL2-C8-P3-REAgrmnt**.
2. Make the following changes to the document:
   a. Insert page numbers that print at the top of each page at the right margin.
   b. Insert the footer *WL2-C8-P3-REAgrmnt.docx* centered on each page.
3. Insert document properties by completing the following steps:
   a. Click the File tab. (Make sure the Info tab is selected.)
   b. Hover your mouse over the text *Add a title* that displays at the right of the *Title* document property, click in the text box that displays, and then type **Real Estate Sale Agreement**.

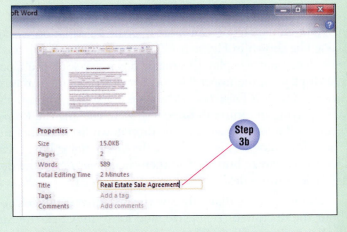

   c. Display the document information panel by clicking the Properties button that displays below the document thumbnail, and then clicking *Show Document Panel* at the drop-down list.
   d. Select any text that appears in the *Author* text box and then type your first and last names.
   e. Press the Tab key twice (this makes the *Subject* text box active) and then type **Real Estate Sale Agreement**.
   f. Press the Tab key and then type the following words in the *Keywords* text box: **real estate, agreement, contract, purchasing**.

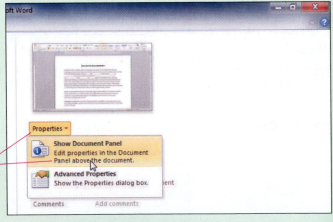

   g. Press the Tab key and then type **Agreement** in the *Category* text box.
   h. Press the Tab key twice and then type the following text in the *Comments* text box: **This is a real estate sale agreement between two parties.**

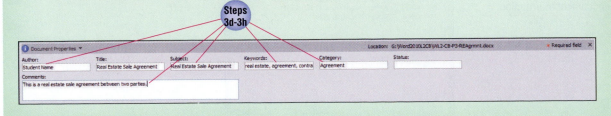

---

4. Click the Close button that displays in the upper right corner of the document information panel.
5. Save **WL2-C8-P3-REAgrmnt.docx** and then print only the document properties by completing the following steps:
   a. Click the File tab and then click the Print tab.
   b. At the Print tab Backstage view, click the first gallery in the Settings category and then click *Document Properties* at the drop-down list.
   c. Click the Print button.
6. Save **WL2-C8-P3-REAgrmnt.docx**.

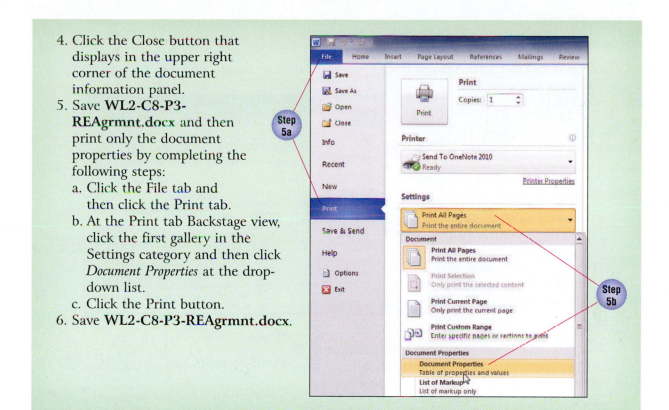

Restricting Documents

The middle panel in the Info tab Backstage view contains buttons for protecting a document, checking for issues in a document, and managing versions of a document. Click the Protect Document button in the middle panel and a drop-down list displays with the following options: *Mark as Final, Encrypt with Password, Restrict Editing, Restrict Permission by People,* and *Add a Digital Signature.*

Protect Document

Marking a Document as Final

Click the *Mark as Final* option to save the document as a read-only document. When you click this option, a message displays telling you that the document will be marked and then saved. At this message, click OK. This displays another message telling you that the document has been marked as final to indicate that editing is complete and that it is the final version of the document. The message further indicates that when a document is marked as final, the status property is set to "Final," typing, editing commands, and proofing marks are turned off, and that the document can be identified by the Mark as Final icon, which displays toward the left side of the Status bar. At this message, click OK. After a document is marked as final, the message "This document has been marked as final to discourage editing." displays to the right of the Protect Document button in the Info tab Backstage view.

1. With **WL2-C8-P3-REAgrmnt.docx** open, mark the document as final by completing the following steps:
   a. Click the File tab.
   b. Click the Protect Document button at the Info tab Backstage view and then click *Mark as Final* at the drop-down list.
   c. At the message telling you the document will be marked and saved, click OK.
   d. At the next message that displays, click OK. (Notice the message that displays to the right of the Protect Document button.)

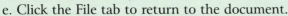

   e. Click the File tab to return to the document.
2. At the document, notice the message bar that displays above the Ruler and then close the document.
3. Open **WL2-C8-P3-REAgrmnt.docx** and then click the Edit Anyway button on the yellow message bar.

4. Save **WL2-C8-P3-REAgrmnt.docx**.

Encrypting a Document

Word provides a number of methods for protecting a document with a password. Previously in this chapter, you learned how to protect a document with a password using options at the Start Enforcing Protection dialog box and how to protect a document with a password using options at the General Options dialog box. In addition to these two methods, you can protect a document with a password by clicking the Protect Document button at the Info tab Backstage view and then clicking *Encrypt with Password* option at the drop-down list. At the Encrypt Document dialog box that displays, type your password in the text box (the text will display as round bullets) and then press the Enter key (or click OK). At the Confirm Password dialog box, type your password again (the text will display as round bullets) and then press the Enter key (or click OK). When you apply a password, the message "A password is required to open this document." displays to the right of the Protect Document button.

1. With **WL2-C8-P3-REAgrmnt.docx** open, encrypt the document with a password by completing the following steps:

   a. Click the File tab, click the Protect Document button at the Info tab Backstage view, and then click *Encrypt with Password* at the drop-down list.

   b. At the Encrypt Document dialog box, type your initials in uppercase letters (your text will display as round bullets).

   c. Press the Enter key.

   d. At the Confirm Password dialog box, type your initials again in uppercase letters (your text will display as bullets) and then press the Enter key.

2. Click the File tab to return to the document.

3. Save and then close the document.

4. Open **WL2-C8-P3-REAgrmnt.docx**. At the Password dialog box, type your initials in uppercase letters and then press the Enter key.

5. Save, print, and then close **WL2-C8-P3-REAgrmnt.docx**.

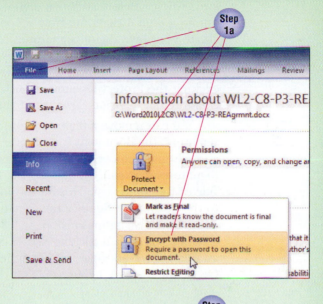

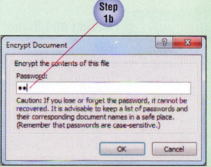

---

 roject 4   **Prepare and Inspect a Lease Agreement**   **3 Parts**

You will open a lease agreement document, apply a digital signature, insert signature lines, and then inspect the document.

Restricting Editing

Click the Protect Document button at the Info tab Backstage view and then click the *Restrict Editing* option at the drop-down list and the document displays with the Restrict Formatting and Editing task pane. This is the same task pane you learned about previously in this chapter.

Restrict
Editing

Adding and Removing a Digital Signature

You can add a digital signature to a document to authenticate it and indicate that you agree with its contents. When you add a digital signature, the document is locked so that it cannot be edited or changed unless you remove the digital signature. A digital signature is an electronic stamp that vouches for a document's authenticity. Before adding a digital signature, you must obtain one. You can obtain a digital signature from a commercial certification authority, or you can create your own digital signature. When you create a digital signature, it is saved on the hard drive or the network. Depending on how your system is set up, you might be prevented from using a digital signature. Insert a digital signature by clicking the Protect Document button at the Info tab Backstage view and then clicking *Add a Digital Signature* at the drop-down list.

Signatures

You can remove a digital signature from a document. When you remove the signature, the document is no longer authenticated, and it is available for formatting and editing. Remove the digital signature at the Signatures task pane. Display the Signatures task pane by clicking the Signatures button that displays toward the left side of the Status bar. This button indicates that a digital signature has been applied to the document. Remove the signature by hovering the mouse pointer over the name in the Signatures task pane, clicking the down-pointing arrow at the right of the name, and then clicking *Remove Signature* at the drop-down list. At the message asking if you want to permanently remove the signature, click Yes and then click OK at the message telling you that the signature has been removed.

Project 4a   Adding and Removing a Digital Signature   Part 1 of 3

1. Open **Lease.docx** and save the document with the name **WL2-C8-P4-Lease**.
2. Create and add a digital signature by completing the following steps:
   a. Click the File tab, click the Protect Document button at the Info tab Backstage view, and then click *Add a Digital Signature* at the drop-down list.
   b. At the Microsoft Word digital signature information message, click OK.
   c. At the Get a Digital ID dialog box, click the *Create your own digital ID* option and then click OK. (If this dialog box does not display, skip to Step 2e.)
   d. At the Create a Digital ID dialog box, insert the following information:
      1) Type your name in the *Name* text box.
      2) Type your actual email address or a fictitious email address in the *E-mail address* text box.
      3) Type your school's name in the *Organization* text box.
      4) Type the city in which your school is located in the *Location* text box.
      5) Click the Create button.
   e. At the Sign dialog box, type **Agreeing to the terms of the lease.** in the *Purpose for signing this document* text box.
   f. Click the Sign button.
   g. At the message saying your signature has been successfully saved, click OK.

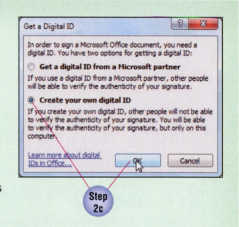

Step 2c

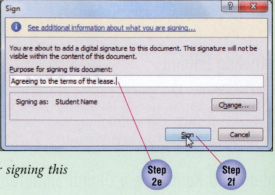

Step 2e

Step 2f

3. Click the File tab to return to the document and then click each of the tabs and notice the commands and buttons that are inactive or dimmed.

4. Click the Signatures button located toward the left side of the Status bar. (This displays the Signatures task pane at the right side of the screen.)

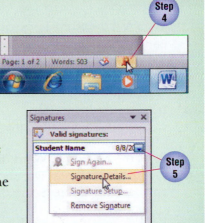

5. View the invisible digital signature details by hovering the mouse pointer over your name in the Signatures task pane, clicking the down-pointing arrow that displays to the right of your name, and then clicking *Signature Details* at the drop-down list.

6. Notice the signature details, including the information on the inserted digital signature and the purpose of the signature.

7. Click the Close button to close the Signature Details dialog box.

8. Remove the digital signature by completing the following steps:
   a. Hover the mouse pointer over your name in the Signatures task pane and then click the down-pointing arrow that displays to the right of your name.
   b. Click *Remove Signature* at the drop-down list.
   c. At the message asking if you want to permanently remove the signature, click Yes.
   d. At the message telling you the signature has been removed and the document has been saved, click OK.

9. Close the Signatures task pane.

Inserting and Signing on a Signature Line

You can insert a signature line in a document that specifies who should sign it. The signature line can include information about the intended signer, such as the person's name, title, and email address. It can also provide instructions for the intended signer. If you send an electronic copy of the document to the intended signer, the person sees the signature line as well as the instructions. To add a signature line in a document, position the insertion point where you want the signature line to display, click the Insert tab, and then click the Signature Line button in the Text group. At the Signature Setup dialog box, type the desired information about the intended signer and then click OK to close the dialog box.

When you insert a signature line, the signer can type his or her name on the line, select a digital image of his or her signature, or write a signature using a tablet PC. When the signer signs the document, a digital signature is added simultaneously that authenticates the identity of the signer. When the document is signed, it becomes a read-only document.

▼ **Quick Steps**

Insert a Signature Line
1. Click Insert tab.
2. Click Signature Line button.
3. At Microsoft Word dialog box, click OK.
4. Type desired signature information.
5. Click OK.

Insert Signature on Signature Line
1. Double-click signature line.
2. At Microsoft Word message, click OK.
3. Type signature in Sign dialog box.
4. Click Sign.
5. Click OK.

1. With **WL2-C8-P4-Lease.docx** open, insert a signature line at the end of the document by completing the following steps:

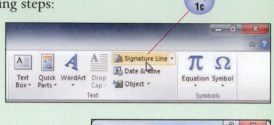

a. Press Ctrl + End to move the insertion point to the end of the document and then press the Enter key.
b. Click the Insert tab.
c. Click the Signature Line button in the Text group.
d. At the Microsoft Word digital signature information message, click OK.
e. At the Signature Setup dialog box, type your first and last names in the *Suggested signer* text box.
f. Type Assistant Manager in the *Suggested signer's title* text box.
g. Click OK.

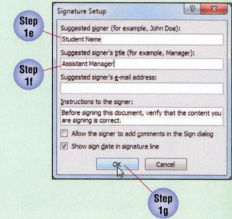

2. Insert a second signature line for a lessee to sign by completing the following steps:
a. Press the Enter key.
b. If necessary, click the Insert tab.
c. Click the Signature Line button in the Text group.
d. At the Microsoft Word digital signature information message, click OK.
e. At the Signature Setup dialog box, type Jaden Cowell in the *Suggested signer* text box and then press the Tab key.
f. Type Lessee in the *Suggested signer's title* text box.
g. Click OK.

3. Insert a signature on the top signature line by completing the following steps:
a. Double-click the top signature line.
b. At the Microsoft Word digital signature information message, click OK.
c. At the Sign dialog box, type your first and last names in the text box following the *X*.
d. Click the Sign button.
e. At the message telling you that your signature has been successfully saved, click OK.

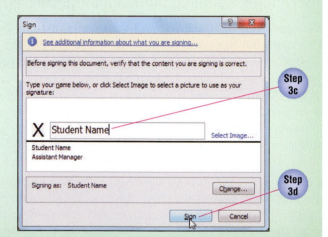

Inspecting a Document ■■■■■■■■■■■■■■■■■■■

Use options from the Check for Issues button drop-down list at the Info tab Backstage view to inspect a document for personal and hidden data and to check a document for compatibility and accessibility issues. When you click the Check for Issues button, a drop-down list displays with the following options: *Inspect Document*, *Check Accessibility*, and *Check Compatibility*.

Check for
Issues

Using the Document Inspector

Word includes a document inspector that you can use to inspect your document for personal data, hidden data, and metadata. Metadata is data that describes other data, such as document properties. You may want to remove some personal or hidden data before you share a document with other people. To check your document for personal or hidden data, click the File tab, click the Check for Issues button at the Info tab Backstage view, and then click the *Inspect Document* option at the drop-down list. This displays the Document Inspector dialog box shown in Figure 8.8.

By default, the document inspector checks all of the items listed in the dialog box. If you do not want the inspector to check a specific item in your document, remove the check mark preceding the item. For example, if you know your document has headers and footers that you do not need to check, click the *Headers, Footers, and Watermarks* check box to remove the check mark. Click the Inspect button located toward the bottom of the dialog box, and the document inspector scans the document to identify information.

When the inspection is complete, the results display in the dialog box. A check mark before an option indicates that the inspector did not find the specific items. If an exclamation point is inserted before an option, the inspector found items and displays a list of the items. If you want to remove the found items, click the Remove All button that displays at the right of the desired option. Click the Reinspect button to ensure that the specific items were removed and then click the Close button.

Figure 8.8 Document Inspector Dialog Box

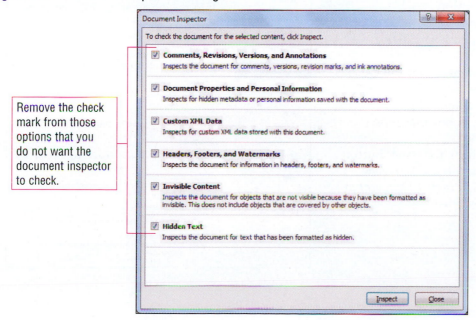

Remove the check mark from those options that you do not want the document inspector to check.

1. With **WL2-C8-P4-Lease.docx** open, remove your signature by completing the following steps:
   a. Click the Edit Anyway button that displays in the yellow message bar located toward the top of the screen.
   b. At the message asking if you want to remove the signature, click Yes.
   c. At the message indicating the signature has been removed and the document has been saved, click OK.
2. Press Ctrl + Home and then make the following changes to the document:
   a. Turn on Track Changes.
   b. Select the title *LEASE AGREEMENT* and then change the font size to 14 points.
   c. Delete the text *first* that displays in the second numbered paragraph (the *RENT* paragraph) and then type **fifteenth**.
   d. Move the insertion point to the beginning of the text *IN WITNESS WHEREOF* (located on page two) and then press the Tab key.
   e. Turn off Track Changes.
3. Hide text by completing the following steps:

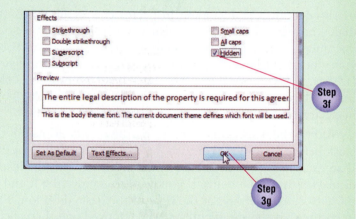

   a. Move the insertion point to the end of the first paragraph of text in the document (one space after the period at the end of the sentence).
   b. Type **The entire legal description of the property is required for this agreement to be valid.**
   c. Select the text you just typed.
   d. Click the Home tab.
   e. Click the Font group dialog box launcher.
   f. At the Font dialog box, click the *Hidden* option in the *Effects* section.
   g. Click OK to close the dialog box.
4. Click the Save button on the Quick Access toolbar.
5. Inspect the document by completing the following steps:
   a. Click the File tab.
   b. Click the Check for Issues button at the Info tab Backstage view and then click *Inspect Document* at the drop-down list.

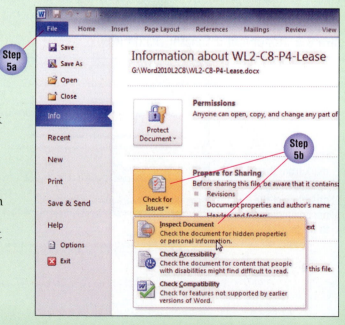

c. At the Document Inspector dialog box, tell the document inspector not to check the document for XML data by clicking the *Custom XML Data* check box to remove the check mark.

d. Click the Inspect button.

e. Read through the inspection results and then remove all hidden text by clicking the Remove All button that displays at the right side of the *Hidden Text* section. (Make sure a message displays below *Hidden Text* indicating that the text was successfully removed.)

f. Click the Reinspect button.

g. To keep the header and footer text in the document, click the *Headers, Footers, and Watermarks* check box to remove the check mark.

h. Click the Inspect button.

i. Read through the inspection results and then remove all revisions by clicking the Remove All button that displays at the right side of the *Comments, Revisions, Versions, and Annotations* section.

j. Click the Reinspect button.

k. To leave the remaining items in the document, click the Close button.

6. Click the File tab to return to the document and then save the document.

7. Insert your signature in the top signature line (located toward the bottom of the document) by completing Step 3 in Project 4b.

8. Print and then close **WL2-C8-P4-Lease.docx**.

 **roject** **5** **Check the Accessibility and Compatibility of a Produce Document**   **3 Parts**

You will open a document containing information on produce, check for accessibility issues, and check the compatibility of elements with previous versions of Word. You will also manage unsaved versions of the document.

Checking the Accessibility of a Document

Word 2010 includes the accessibility checker feature, which checks a document for content that a person with disabilities, such as a visual impairment, might find difficult to read. Check the accessibility of a document by clicking the Check for Issues button at the Info tab Backstage view and then clicking *Check Accessibility*.

The accessibility checker examines the document for the most common accessibility problems in Word documents and groups them into three categories: errors—content that is unreadable to a person who is blind; warnings—content that is difficult to read; and tips—content that may or may not be difficult to read. The accessibility checker examines the document, closes the Info tab Backstage view, and displays the Accessibility Checker task pane.

At the Accessibility Checker task pane, unreadable errors are grouped in the *Errors* section, content that is difficult to read is grouped in the *Warnings* section, and content that may or may not be difficult to read is grouped in the *Tips* section. Select an issue in one of the sections, and an explanation of how to fix the issue and why displays at the bottom of the task pane.

Project 5a   Checking the Accessibility of a Document   Part 1 of 3

1. Open **PremPro.docx** and then save the document with Save As and name it **WL2-C8-P5-PremPro**.
2. Complete an accessibility check by completing the following steps:
   a. Click the File tab.
   b. At the Info tab Backstage view, click the Check for Issues button and then click *Check Accessibility* at the drop-down list.
   c. Notice the Accessibility Checker task pane that displays at the right side of the screen. The task pane displays an *Errors* section and a *Warnings* section. Click *Picture 4* in the *Errors* section and then read the information that displays toward the bottom of the task pane describing why you should fix the error and how to fix it.

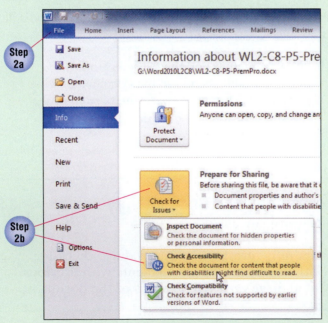
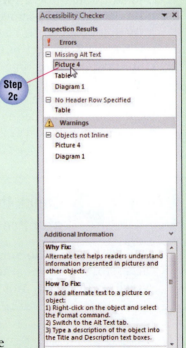

3. Add alternate text (which is a text-based representation of the clip art image) to the clip art by completing the following steps:
   a. Right-click on the clip art image in the document and then click *Format Picture* at the shortcut menu.
   b. At the Format Picture dialog box, click the *Alt Text* option located at the bottom of the left panel.

c. Click in the *Title* text box and then type **Cornucopia**.

d. Select and then delete any text that displays in the *Description* text box and then type **Clip art image of a cornucopia of fruits and vegetables representing Premium Produce.**

e. Click the Close button.

4. Click the first *Table* entry in the *Errors* section and then read the information that displays toward the bottom of the task pane explaining about creating alternate text for a table. Since the table contains text that is easily interpreted, you do not need to include alternate text.

Step 3c

Step 3d

Step 3b

Step 3e

Format Picture

Fill
Line Color
Line Style
Shadow
Reflection
Glow and Soft Edges
3-D Format
3-D Rotation
Picture Corrections
Picture Color
Artistic Effects
Crop
Text Box
Alt Text

Alt Text

Title:
Cornucopia

Description:
Clip art image of a cornucopia of fruits and vegetables representing Premium Produce.

Titles and descriptions provide alternative, text-based representations of the information contained in tables, diagrams, images, and other objects. This information is useful for people with vision or cognitive impairments who may not be able to see or understand the object.

A title can be read to a person with a disability and is used to determine whether they wish to hear the description of the content.

Close

5. Click the *Diagram 1* entry in the *Errors* section and then read the information about alternate text. Since this diagram contains text that is easily interpreted, you do not need to include alternate text.

6. Click the second *Table* entry in the *Errors* section and then read the information that displays toward the bottom of the task pane explaining about header rows. Since the table in the document does not span across pages you can ignore this information.

7. Click *Picture 4* in the *Warning* section and then read the information about objects that are not inline with text. If you made the change suggested, the clip art would move to a different location on the page so do not make the change suggested.

8. Click *Diagram 1* in the *Warning* section and notice it is the same information about objects that are not inline.

9. Close the Accessibility Checker task pane by clicking the Close button located in the upper right corner of the task pane.

10. Save **WL2-C8-P5-PremPro.docx**.

Checking the Compatibility of a Document

Use one of the Check for Issues button drop-down options, *Check Compatibility*, to check your document and identify elements that are either not supported or will act differently in previous versions of Word from Word 97 through Word 2007. To run the compatibility checker, open the desired document, click the Check for Issues button at the Info tab Backstage view, and then click *Check Compatibility* at the drop-down list. This displays the Microsoft Word Compatibility Checker dialog box that displays a summary of the elements in the presentation that are not compatible with previous versions of Word and indicates what will happen when the document is saved and then opened in a previous version.

▼ **Quick Steps**

Check Compatibility
1. Click File tab.
2. Click Check for Issues button.
3. Click *Check Compatibility*.
4. Click OK.

1. With **WL2-C8-P5-PremPro.docx** open, check the compatibility of elements in the document by completing the following steps:

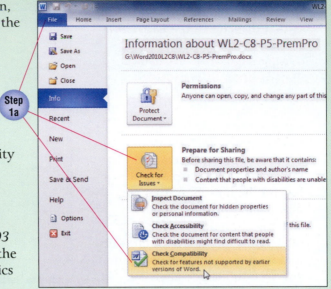

a. Click the File tab, click the Check for Issues button at the Info tab Backstage view, and then click *Check Compatibility* at the drop-down list.

b. At the Microsoft Word Compatibility Checker dialog box, read the information that displays in the *Summary* list box.

c. Click the Select versions to show button and then click *Word 97-2003* at the drop-down list. Notice that the information about SmartArt graphics being converted to a static object disappears from the *Summary* list box. This is because Word 2007 supports SmartArt graphics.

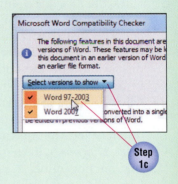

d. Click OK to close the dialog box.

2. Save the document in Word 2003 format by completing the following steps:

a. Click the File tab and then click Save As.

b. At the Save As dialog box, click the *Save as type* option box and then click *Word 97-2003 Document (*.doc)* at the drop-down list.

c. Select the text in the *File name* text box and then type **WL2-C8-P5-PremPro-2003format**.

d. Click the Save button.

e. Click the Continue button at the Microsoft Word Compatibility Checker dialog box.

f. Scroll through the document and notice the changes.

3. Close **WL2-C8-P5-PremPro-2003format.doc**.

Managing Versions ▪▪■▪■▪■▪■▪■▪■▪■

Manage
Versions

As you are working in a document, Word is automatically saving your document every 10 minutes. This automatic backup feature can be very helpful if you accidentally close your document without saving it, or if the power to your computer is disrupted. As Word is automatically saving a backup of your currently open document, the saved documents are listed to the right of the Manage Versions button in the Info tab Backstage view as shown in Figure 8.9. Each autosave document displays with *Today*, followed by the time and *(autosave)*. When you save and then close your document, the autosave backup documents are deleted.

To open an autosave backup document, click the File tab, and then click the backup document you want to open that displays to the right of the Manage Versions button. The document opens as a read-only document, and a yellow message bar displays with a Compare button and a Restore button. Click the

Compare button and the autosave document is compared to the original document. You can then decide which changes you want to accept or reject. Click the Restore button and a message displays indicating that you are about to overwrite the last saved version with the selected version. At this message, click OK.

When you save a document, the autosave backup documents are deleted. However, if you are working in a document that you close without saving (after 10 minutes) or the power is disrupted, Word keeps the backup file in the UnsavedFiles folder on the hard drive. You can access this folder by clicking the Manage Versions button in the Info tab Backstage view and then clicking *Recover Unsaved Documents*. At the Open dialog box that displays, double-click the desired backup file you want to open. You can also display the UnsavedFiles folder by clicking the File tab, clicking the Recent tab, and then clicking the Recover Unsaved Documents button that displays below the Recent Places folders. Files in the UnsavedFiles folder are kept for four days after the creation of the document. After that, they are automatically deleted.

You can manage the backup files by right-clicking a backup file. At the shortcut menu that displays, click the *Open Version* option to open the backup file, click the *Delete This Version* option to delete the backup file, or click the *Compare with Current* option to compare the backup file with the currently open file. If you want to delete all unsaved files, open a blank document, click the File tab, click the Manage Versions button, and then click the *Delete All Unsaved Document* option. At the message asking if you are sure you want to delete the unsaved documents, click Yes.

As mentioned previously, by default, Word automatically saves a backup of your unsaved document every 10 minutes. To change this default setting, click the File tab and then click the Options button below the Help tab. At the Word Options dialog box, click *Save* in the left panel. Notice that the *Save AutoRecover information every* option is set at 10 minutes. To change this number, click the up-pointing arrow to the right of *10* to increase the number of minutes between autosaves or click the down-pointing arrow to decrease the amount of time between autosaves.

▼ **Quick Steps**

Display Unsaved Files Folder
1. Click File tab.
2. Click Manage Versions button.
3. Click *Recover Unsaved Documents.*
OR
1. Click File tab.
2. Click Recent tab.
3. Click Recover Unsaved Documents button.

Delete Backup File
1. Click File tab.
2. Right-click backup file.
3. Click *Delete This Version* at shortcut menu.

Delete All Unsaved Files
1. Open blank document.
2. Click File tab.
3. Click Manage Versions button.
4. Click *Delete All Unsaved Documents.*
5. Click Yes.

Change AutoRecover Time
1. Click File tab.
2. Click Options button.
3. Click *Save.*
4. Type desired minutes in *Save AutoRecover information every* option box.
5. Click OK.

Figure 8.9 Autosave Documents in Info Tab Backstage View

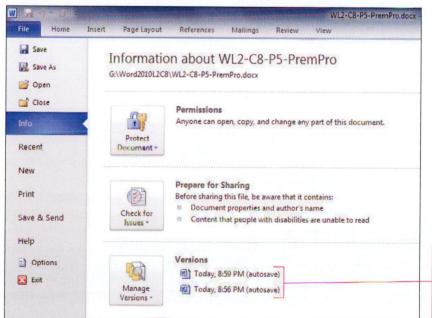

Word automatically creates backups of your document. The backup documents are deleted when you save the document. To open a backup, click the desired version.

1. At a blank document, decrease the autosave time by completing the following steps:
   a. Click the File tab and then click the Options button that displays below the Help tab.
   b. At the Word Options dialog box, click *Save* in the left panel.
   c. Click the down-pointing arrow at the right of the *Save AutoRecover information every* option box until *2* displays.

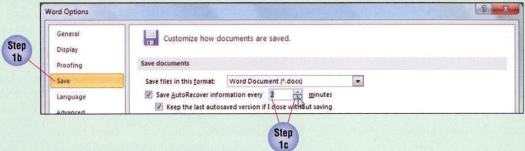

Step 1b

Step 1c

   d. Click OK to close the dialog box.
   e. Close the blank document.
2. Open **WL2-C8-P5-PremPro.docx**.
3. Press Ctrl + End to move the insertion point to the end of the document and then type your first and last names.
4. Leave the document open for over two minutes without making any changes. After a couple of minutes have passed, click the File tab and then check to see if an autosave document displays to the right of the Manage Versions button. (If not, click the File tab to return to the document and wait a few more minutes.)
5. When an autosave document displays in the Info tab Backstage view, click the File tab to return to the document.

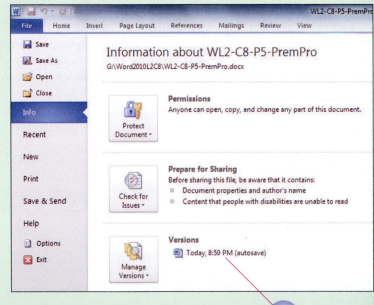

Step 4

6. Scroll to the end of the document, select the SmartArt, and then delete the SmartArt.
7. Click the File tab and then click the autosave document that displays to the right of the Manage Versions button. If more than one autosave document displays, click the one at the bottom of the list. This opens the autosave document as read-only.

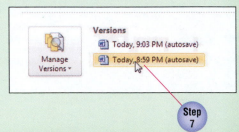

Step 7

8. Restore the document to the autosave document by clicking the Restore button that displays in the yellow message bar.

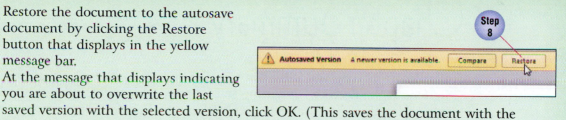

9. At the message that displays indicating you are about to overwrite the last saved version with the selected version, click OK. (This saves the document with the SmartArt.)

10. Check to see what versions of previous documents Word has saved by completing the following steps:

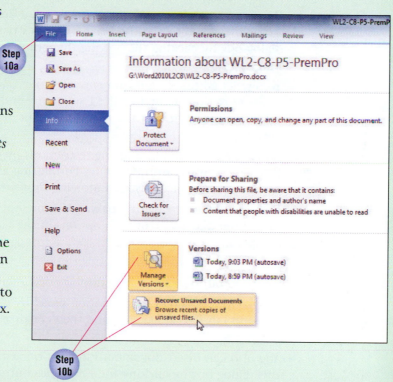

   a. Click the File tab.
   b. Click the Manage Versions button and then click *Recover Unsaved Documents* at the drop-down list.
   c. At the Open dialog box that displays draft documents in the UnsavedFiles folder on your hard drive, check the documents that display in the list box.
   d. Click the Cancel button to close the Open dialog box.

11. Delete a backup file by completing the following steps:
   a. Click the File tab.
   b. Right-click the first autosave backup file name that displays to the right of the Manage Versions button.
   c. Click *Delete This Version* at the shortcut menu.

12. Return the autosave time back to 10 minutes by completing the following steps:
   a. Click the File tab and then click the Options button that displays below the Help tab.
   b. At the Word Options dialog box, click *Save* in the left panel.
   c. Click the up-pointing arrow at the right of the *Save AutoRecover information every* option box until *10* displays.
   d. Click OK to close the dialog box.

13. Save, print, and then close **WL2-C8-P5-PremPro.docx**.

14. Delete all unsaved backup files by completing the following steps:
   a. Press Ctrl + N to display a blank document.
   b. Click the File tab.
   c. Click the Manage Versions button and then click *Delete All Unsaved Documents*.
   d. At the message that displays, click Yes.

15. Click the File tab to return to the blank document.

Chapter Summary

- Restrict formatting and editing in a document and apply a password to it with options at the Restrict Formatting and Editing task pane. Display this task pane by clicking the Review tab and then clicking the Restrict Editing button in the Protect group.

- Restrict formatting by specifying styles that are allowed and not allowed in a document. Do this at the Formatting Restrictions dialog box. Display this dialog box by clicking the Settings hyperlink in the Restrict Formatting and Editing task pane.

- To restrict editing in a document, click the *Allow only this type of editing in the document* option at the Restrict Formatting and Editing task pane, click the down-pointing arrow at the right of the options box, and then click the desired option.

- Enforce editing and formatting restrictions by clicking the Yes, Start Enforcing Protection button in the Restrict Formatting and Editing task pane and make desired changes at the Start Enforcing Protection dialog box.

- Protect a document with a password using options at the Start Enforcing Protection dialog box or with options at the General Options dialog box.

- Open a document in different views with options at the Open button drop-down list in the Open dialog box.

- The Info tab Backstage view displays document properties information.

- Display the document information panel by clicking the Properties button at the Info tab Backstage view and then clicking *Show Document Panel* at the drop-down list.

- You also can insert document information at the Properties dialog box. Display this dialog box by clicking the Properties button at the Info tab Backstage view and then clicking *Advanced Properties* or by clicking the Document Properties button at the document information panel and then clicking *Advanced Properties*.

- Mark a document as final, and the document is saved as a read-only document. Mark a document as final by clicking the Protect Document button at the Info tab Backstage view and then clicking *Mark as Final* at the drop-down list. Typing, editing commands, and proofing marks are turned off when a document is marked as final.

- Protect a document with a password by clicking the Protect Document button at the Info tab Backstage view and then clicking *Encrypt with Password*.

- Another method for displaying the Restrict Formatting and Editing task pane is to click the Protect Document button at the Info tab Backstage view and then click *Restrict Editing* at the drop-down list.

- Add a digital signature to a document to authenticate it and indicate that you agree with its contents. Adding a digital signature locks the document so it cannot be edited or changed unless the digital signature is removed. Create your own digital signature by clicking the Protect Document button at the Info tab Backstage view and then clicking *Add a Digital Signature* at the drop-down list.

- Remove a digital signature by clicking the Signatures button on the Status bar to display the Signatures task pane, hovering the mouse over the name, clicking the down-pointing arrow at the right of the name, and then clicking *Remove Signature* at the drop-down list.

- Insert a signature line in a document to specify who should sign it. To insert a signature line, click the Insert tab and then click the Signature Line button in the Text group.

- Inspect a document for personal data, hidden data, and metadata with options at the Document Inspector dialog box. Display this dialog box by clicking the Check for Issues button at the Info tab Backstage view and then clicking *Inspect Document* at the drop-down list.

- The accessibility checker checks a document for content that a person with disabilities might find difficult to read. Run the accessibility checker by clicking the Check for Issues button at the Info tab Backstage view and then clicking Check Accessibility at the drop-down list.

- Run the compatibility checker to check your document and identify elements that are not supported or will act differently in previous versions of Word. To determine the compatibility of the features in your document, click the Check for Issues button at the Info tab Backstage view and then click Check Compatibility at the drop-down list.

- By default, Word automatically saves a backup of your unsaved document every 10 minutes, and the backup document displays to the right of the Manage Versions button at the Info tab Backstage view. Click the document name to open the backup document.

- When you save a document, Word automatically deletes the backup documents. However, if you close a document without saving it, or if the power to your computer is disrupted, Word keeps the backup document in the UnsavedFiles folder on the hard drive. Display this folder by clicking the Manage Versions button at the Info tab Backstage view and then clicking *Recover Unsaved Documents* at the drop-down list.

- Delete an autosave backup file by displaying the Info tab Backstage view, right-clicking the desired autosave backup file, and then clicking *Delete This Version* at the shortcut menu.

- Delete all unsaved documents by displaying a blank document, clicking the File tab, clicking the Manage Versions button, and then clicking *Delete All Unsaved Documents*. At the message that displays, click Yes.

- By default, Word automatically saves a backup of your unsaved document every 10 minutes. You can change this default setting with the *Save AutoRecover information every* option at the Word Options dialog box with *Save* selected in the left panel.

Commands Review

FEATURE	RIBBON TAB, GROUP	BUTTON, OPTION
Restrict Formatting and Editing task pane	Review, Protect	
Formatting Restrictions dialog box	Review, Protect	, Settings
General Options dialog box	File	Save As, Tools, General Options
Document information panel	File	Properties ▾, Show Document Panel
Properties dialog box	File	Properties ▾, Advanced Properties
Encrypt Document dialog box	File	, Encrypt with Password
Digital signature	File	, Add Digital Signature
Signature Setup dialog box	Insert, Text	
Document Inspector dialog box	File	, Inspect Document
Accessibility checker	File	, Check Accessibility
Compatibility checker	File	, Check Compatibility
UnSavedFiles folder	File	, Recover Unsaved Documents

Concepts Check Test Your Knowledge

Completion: In the space provided at the right, indicate the correct term, command, or number.

1. Limit what formatting users can perform on text in a document with options in this section of the Restrict Formatting and Editing task pane. _____

2. Use options in this section of the Restrict Formatting and Editing task pane to limit the types of changes a user can make to a document. _____

3. Click this button in the Restrict Formatting and Editing task pane to display the Start Enforcing Protection dialog box. _____

4. Protect a document with a password using options at the Start Enforcing Protection dialog box or with options at this dialog box. _____

5. You can add additional information to a document's properties at this panel. _____

6. Display the Properties dialog box by clicking the Properties v button at the Info tab Backstage view and then clicking this option at the drop-down list. _____

7. Mark a document as final by clicking this button at the Info tab Backstage view and then clicking *Mark as Final* at the drop-down list. _____

8. Add this type of signature to a document to vouch for the authenticity of the document. _____

9. Insert a signature line in a document by clicking this tab and then clicking the Signature Line button in the Text group. _____

10. Use this feature to inspect your document for personal data, hidden data, and metadata. _____

11. This feature checks a document for content that a person with disabilities might find difficult to read. _____

12. Create alternate text for an image by clicking the *Alt Text* option in the left panel at this dialog box. _____

13. Use this feature to check your document and identify elements that are not supported in previous versions of Word. _____

14. Word keeps backup files in this folder on the hard drive. _____

Skills Check Assess Your Performance

Assessment

1 **RESTRICT FORMATTING AND EDITING OF A COMPUTER REPORT**

1. Open **WritingProcess.docx** and then save the document with Save As and name it **WL2-C8-A1-WritingProcess**.
2. Display the Restrict Formatting and Editing task pane and then restrict formatting to the Heading 2 and Heading 3 styles. (At the message asking if you want to remove formatting or styles that are not allowed, click No.)
3. Enforce the protection and include the password *writing*.
4. Click the Available styles hyperlink.
5. Apply the Heading 2 style to the two titles: *THE WRITING PROCESS* and *REFERENCES*. (The Heading 3 style may not display until you apply the Heading 2 style to the first title.)
6. Apply the Heading 3 style to the seven headings in the document.

7. Close the Styles pane and then close the Restrict Formatting and Editing task pane.
8. Save the document and then print only page 1.
9. Close **WL2-C8-A1-WritingProcess.docx**.

Assessment

2 INSERT COMMENTS IN A SOFTWARE LIFE CYCLE DOCUMENT

1. Open **CommCycle.docx** and then save the document with Save As and name it **WL2-C8-A2-CommCycle**.
2. Display the Restrict Formatting and Editing task pane, restrict editing to only comments, and then start enforcing the protection (do not include a password).
3. Insert the comment **Create a SmartArt diagram that illustrates the software life cycle.** at the end of the first paragraph of text in the document.
4. Insert the comment **Include the problem-solving steps.** at the end of the paragraph in the *Design* section.
5. Insert the comment **Describe a typical beta testing cycle.** at the end of the paragraph in the *Testing* section.
6. Print only the comments.
7. Save and then close **WL2-C8-A2-CommCycle.docx**.
8. Close the Restrict Formatting and Editing task pane.

Assessment

3 INSERT DOCUMENT PROPERTIES, CHECK COMPATIBILITY, AND SAVE A PRESENTATION DOCUMENT IN A DIFFERENT FORMAT

1. Open **Presentation.docx** and then save the document with Save As and name it **WL2-C8-A3-Presentation**.
2. Make the following changes to the document:
   a. Apply the Heading 1 style to the title *Delivering a How-To Presentation*.
   b. Apply the Heading 2 style to the three headings in the document.
   c. Change the style set to *Thatch*.
   d. Apply the Flow theme and change the theme colors to *Clarity*.
   e. Center the title.
   f. Change the color of the clip art image to *Gray-50%, Accent color 1 Light*.
   g. Change the color of the SmartArt (located at the end of the document) to *Colorful Range – Accent Colors 3 to 4* and apply the *White Outline* SmartArt style.
3. Display the document information panel and then type the following in the specified text boxes:
   a. Author = (type your first and last names)
   b. Title = **Delivering a How-To Presentation**
   c. Subject = **Presentations**
   d. Keywords = **presentation, how-to, delivering, topics**
   e. Comments = **This document describes the three steps involved in developing a how-to presentation.**
   f. Close the document information panel.
4. Save **WL2-C8-A3-Presentation.docx** and then print only the document properties.

5. Run the accessibility checker on the document and then create alternate text for the clip art image. Type the text **Presentation clip art image** for the title and type **Clip art image representing a person giving a presentation.** for the description. Close the accessibility checker.
6. Save and then print **WL2-C8-A3-Presentation.docx**.
7. Run the compatibility checker to determine what features are not supported by earlier versions of Word.
8. Save the document in the *Word 97-2003 Document (*.doc)* format and name it **WL2-C8-A3-Presentation-2003format**.
9. Save, print, and then close **WL2-C8-A3-Presentation-2003format.doc**.

Assessment

4 CREATE A REPORT ON WORD OPTIONS AND CUSTOMIZATION FEATURES

1. Display the Word Help window, type **customize ribbon**, and then click the <u>Customize the Ribbon</u> hyperlink.
2. Watch the video on customizing the ribbon and then read the information that displays and learn specifically how to add, rename, hide, and remove default and custom tabs and how to change the order of tabs.
3. Create a Word document that contains the following information:
   a. An appropriate title for the document.
   b. Specific information on how to add a custom tab.
   c. Specific information on how to rename a default or custom tab.
   d. Specific information on how to hide a default or custom tab.
   e. Specific information on how to change the order of default or custom tabs.
   f. Specific information on how to remove a custom tab.
4. Apply formatting to enhance the visual appeal of the document.
5. Save the document and name it **WL2-C8-A4-Ribbon**.
6. Print and then close **WL2-C8-A4-Ribbon.docx**.

Visual Benchmark Demonstrate Your Proficiency

FORMAT, INSERT DOCUMENT PROPERTIES, CHECK COMPATIBILITY, AND SAVE A DOCUMENT IN A DIFFERENT FORMAT

1. Open **InfoSystem.docx** and then save the document with Save As and name it **WL2-C8-VB-InfoSystem**.
2. Format the document so it appears as shown in Figure 8.10 with the following specifications:
   a. Apply the *Paper* theme and change the theme colors to *Hardcover*.
   b. Insert page numbers that print in the upper right corner of the page.
   c. Insert the Puzzle (Odd Page) footer. (Click the *[Type the company name]* placeholder and then type your first and last names.)
   d. Insert the SmartArt Continuous Cycle diagram and change the colors to *Colorful – Accent Colors* and apply the *Metallic Scene* style.
   e. Recolor the clip art image as shown in the figure.
   f. Make any other changes so your document displays as shown in Figure 8.10.
3. Display the document information panel and then type the following in the specified text boxes:
   a. Author = (type your first and last names)
   b. Title = **Developing an Information System**
   c. Subject = **Software Development**
   d. Keywords = **software, design, plan**
   e. Category = **Software**
   f. Status = **Draft**
   g. Comments = **This document describes the four steps involved in developing an information system.**
4. Save the document and then print only the document properties.
5. Inspect the document and remove any hidden text.
6. Run the accessibility checker and then create alternate text for the clip art image.
7. Run the compatibility checker to determine what features are not supported by earlier versions of Word.
8. Save the document in the *Word 97-2003 Document (*.doc)* format and name it **WL2-C8-VB-InfoSystem-2003format**.
9. Save, print, and then close **WL2-C8-VB-InfoSystem-2003format.docx**.

Figure 8.10 Visual Benchmark

DEVELOPING AN INFORMATION SYSTEM

Identifying and assembling a team of employees with the required skills and expertise is a necessary first step in developing a new in-house information system. A management group may be involved in answering questions and providing information in the early planning phases of the project, but programmers and/or software engineers handle the design and implementation of any new system.

Programmers specialize in the development of new software, while software engineers are highly skilled professionals with programming and teamwork training. Their organized, professional application of the software development process is called software engineering.

PROJECT TEAM

Because of their large size, information systems require the creation of a project team. A project team usually includes a project manager, who acts as the team leader. Sometimes the project manager also functions as a systems analyst, responsible for completing the systems analysis and making design recommendations. Other project team members include software engineers and technicians. The software engineers deal with programming software, while technicians handle hardware issues. The comprehensive process software engineers initiate is called the system development life cycle (SDLC), a series of steps culminating in a completed information system.

PROJECT PLAN

The first step in the system development cycle is planning. The planning step involves preparing a needs analysis and conducting feasibility studies. During this step, a company usually establishes a project team and the team creates a project plan. The project plan includes an estimate of how long the project will take to complete, an outline of the steps involved, and a list of deliverables. Deliverables are documents, services, hardware, and software that must be finished and delivered by a certain time and date.

DESIGNING THE SYSTEM

A project is ready to move into the design stage once the project team has approved the plan, including the budget. The design process begins with the writing of the documentation, which covers functional and design specifications. In most cases, the project team creates the functional specifications, describing what the system must be able to do.

Student Name | Confidential

IMPLEMENTATION

The project can move into the next phase, implementation, once the development team and the systems house develop the design specification and approve the plans. This step is where the actual work of putting the system together is completed, including creating a prototype and completing the programming. In most cases, implementing the new system is the longest, most difficult step in the process.

SUPPORT STAGE

A system goes into the support stage after it has been accepted and approved. A support contract normally allows users to contact the systems house for technical support, training, and sometimes on-site troubleshooting. Even if the system was designed in-house, the responsible department often operates as an independent entity—sometimes even charging the department acquiring the system. The support stage continues until a new information system is proposed and developed, usually years later. At that point, the existing system is retired and no longer used.

Student Name | Confidential

Case Study Apply Your Skills

Part 1

You work in the Training Department at Hart International and your department is responsible for preparing training material and training employees on how to use software applications within the company. Your supervisor asked you to help her prepare a Microsoft Word training manual. She wrote a portion of the manual and had you add training information and format the manual. (If you completed Part 1 of the Case Study for Chapter 7, you should have a document saved in your Word2010L2C7 folder named **WL2-C7-CS-HITraining.docx**.) Open **WL2-C7-CS-HITraining.docx** from the Word2010L2C7 folder on your storage medium and then save the document with Save As in your Word2010L2C8 folder and name it **WL2-C8-CS-HITraining**. Move the insertion point to the end of the document and then insert the document named **HIManual.docx** located in your Word2010L2C8 folder. (Insert the file with the Object button in the Text group in the Insert tab.) If you do not have **WL2-C7-CS-HITraining.docx** in your Word2010L2C7 folder, open **HIManual.docx** from your Word2010L2C8 folder and then save the document with Save As and name it **WL2-C7-CS-HITraining.docx**. Add additional information to the document on how to insert the following buttons on the Quick Access toolbar: Quick Print, Open, Close, Spelling & Grammar, and Thesaurus. Apply formatting to the document and then save the completed document.

Part 2

Your supervisor has decided that options on company computers should be modified and wants you to determine the steps to make the modifications and then include the steps in the training manual. Open the Options dialog box and then determine how to make the following modifications:

- Change the color scheme to *Black*. (General)
- Change the grammar writing style to *Grammar & Style*. (Proofing)
- Change the minutes for saving AutoRecover information to 5 minutes. (Save)
- Change number of recent documents that display at the Recent tab Backstage view to *15*. (Advanced)

With **WL2-C8-CS-HIManual.docx** open write the steps on how to make each of the customizations listed above. Save the document.

Part 3

Prepare the document for distribution by inspecting the document and then restricting editing to only comments. Save, print, and then close **WL2-C8-CS-HIManual.docx**.

Performance Assessment

Word2010L2U2

Note: Before beginning unit assessments, copy to your storage medium the Word2010L2U2 subfolder from the Word2010L2 folder on the CD that accompanies this textbook and then make Word2010L2U2 the active folder.

Assessing Proficiency

In this unit, you learned features for referencing a document such as footnotes, endnotes, citations, and bibliographies; you learned how to insert tables of contents, figures, and authorities, as well as indexes; and features for sharing and distributing documents such as inserting comments, tracking changes, comparing and combining documents; and restricting access to documents.

Assessment 1 Sort Text

1. Open **SHSSort.docx** and then save the document with Save As and name it **WL2-U2-A1-SHSSort**.
2. Select the five clinic names, addresses, and telephone numbers below *SUMMIT HEALTH SERVICES* and then sort the text alphabetically in ascending order by clinic name.
3. Sort the three columns of text below *EXECUTIVE TEAM* by the extension number in ascending order.
4. Sort the text in the table in the *First Half Expenses* column numerically in descending order.
5. Save, print, and then close **WL2-U2-A1-SHSSort.docx**.

Assessment 2 Select Records and Create Mailing Labels

1. Use the mail merge feature to create mailing labels using the **SHS.mdb** data source file (located in the Word2010L2U2 folder). Before merging the data source file with the mailing labels document, sort the records alphabetically by last name.
2. Merge the sorted data source file with the labels document.
3. Save the merged labels document and name it **WL2-U2-A2-Lbls1**.
4. Close the document and then close the labels main document without saving it.
5. Use the mail merge feature to create mailing labels using the **SHS.mdb** data source file. Select records from the data source file of clients living in the city of Greensboro and then merge those records with the labels document.
6. Save the merged labels document and name it **WL2-U2-A2-Lbls2**.
7. Close the document and then close the labels main document without saving it.

Assessment 3 Insert Footnotes in a Desktop Publishing Report

1. Open **DTP.docx** and then save the document with Save As and name it **WL2-U2-A3-DTP**.
2. Create the first footnote shown in Figure U2.1 at the end of the second paragraph in the ***DEFINING DESKTOP PUBLISHING*** section.
3. Create the second footnote shown in Figure U2.1 at the end of the fourth paragraph in the ***DEFINING DESKTOP PUBLISHING*** section.
4. Create the third footnote shown in Figure U2.1 at the end of the second paragraph in the ***PLANNING THE PUBLICATION*** section.
5. Create the fourth footnote shown in Figure U2.1 at the end of the last paragraph in the document.
6. Keep the heading INITIATING THE PROCESS together with the following paragraph of text.
7. Save and then print **WL2-U2-A3-DTP.docx**.
8. Select the entire document and then change the font to Constantia.
9. Select all of the footnotes and change the font to Constantia.
10. Delete the third footnote.
11. Save, print, and then close **WL2-U2-A3-DTP.docx**.

Figure U2.1 Assessment 3

Fellers, Laurie, *Desktop Publishing Design*, Cornwall & Lewis Publishing, 2010, pages 67-72.

Moriarity, Joel, "The Desktop Publishing Approach," *Desktop Publishing*, August 2012, pages 3-6.

Wong, Chun Man, *Desktop Publishing with Style*, Monroe-Ackerman Publishing, 2011, pages 89-93.

Rushton, Andrew, *Desktop Publishing Tips and Tricks*, Aurora Publishing House, 2012, pages 103-106.

Assessment 4 Create Citations and Prepare a Works Cited Page for a Report

1. Open **DesignWebsite.docx** and then save the document with Save As and name it **WL2-U2-A4-DesignWebsite**.
2. Format the title page to meet MLA requirements with the following changes:
   a. Make sure the *Style* option is set to *MLA Sixth Edition*.
   b. Select the entire document, change the font to 12-point Cambria, the line spacing to 2.0, and remove the spacing after paragraphs.
   c. Move the insertion point to the beginning of the document, type your name, press the Enter key, type your instructor's name, press the Enter key, type the title of your course, press the Enter key, and then type the current date.
   d. Insert a header that displays your last name and the page number at the right margin, and change the font to 12-point Cambria.
3. Press Ctrl + End to move the insertion point to the end of the document and then type the text shown in Figure U2.2 (in MLA style) up to the first citation [the text (*Mercado*)]. Insert the source information from a journal article written by Claudia Mercado using the following information:

> *Author =* **Claudia Mercado**
> *Title =* **Connecting a Web Page**
> *Journal Name =* **Connections**
> *Year =* **2012**
> *Pages =* **12-21**
> *Volume =* **5**

4. Continue typing the text up to the next citation [the text *(Holmes)*] and insert the following source information from a website:
   > *Author =* **Brent Holmes**
   > *Name of Web Page =* **Hosting Your Web Page**
   > *Year =* **2011**
   > *Month =* **September**
   > *Day =* **28**
   > *Year Accessed =* (type current year)
   > *Month Accessed =* (type current month)
   > *Day Accessed =* (type current day)
   > *URL =* **www.cmcp.net/webhosting**

5. Continue typing the text up to the next citation [the text *(Vukovich)*] and insert the following information from a book:
   > *Author =* **Ivan Vukovich**
   > *Title =* **Computer Technology in the Business Environment**
   > *Year =* **2011**
   > *City =* **San Francisco**
   > *Publisher =* **Gold Coast Publishing**

6. Insert the page number in the citation by Ivan Vukovich using the Edit Citation dialog box.

7. Type the remaining text in Figure U2.2.

8. Edit the Ivan Vukovich source by changing the last name to *Vulkovich* in the *Master List* section of the Source Manager dialog box.

9. Create a new source in the document using the Source Manager dialog box and include the following source information for a journal article:
   > *Author =* **Sonia Jaquez**
   > *Title =* **Organizing a Web Page**
   > *Journal Name =* **Design Techniques**
   > *Year =* **2012**
   > *Pages =* **32-44**
   > *Volume =* **9**

10. Type the following sentence at the end of the last paragraph in the document: **Browsers look for pages with these names first when a specific file at a website is requested, and index pages display by default if no other page is specified.**

11. Insert a citation for Sonia Jaquez at the end of the sentence you just typed.

12. Insert a citation for Claudia Mercado following the second sentence in the first paragraph of the document.

13. Insert a works cited page at the end of the document on a separate page.

14. Format the works cited page to meet MLA requirements with the following changes:
    a. Select the *Works Cited* title and all the entries and click the *No Spacing* style.
    b. Change the font to 12-point Cambria and change the spacing to 2.0.
    c. Center the title *Works Cited*.
    d. Hang-indent the works cited entries.

15. Save and then print **WL2-U2-A4-DesignWebsite.docx**.

16. Change the document and works cited page from MLA style to APA style.
17. Save, print page three, and then close **WL2-U2-A4-DesignWebsite.docx**.

Figure U2.2 Assessment 4

One of the first tasks in website development is finding a good host for the site. Essentially, a web host lets you store a copy of your web pages on the hard drive of a powerful computer connected to the Internet with a fast connection that can handle thousands of users (Mercado). Hosting your own website is possible but is feasible only if you own an extra computer that can be dedicated to the role of a web server, have a high-speed Internet connection, and feel confident about handling the job of network security and routing (Holmes). Most people's situations do not fit those criteria. Fortunately, several free and fee-based web hosting services are available.

As you plan a website, decide what types of content you will include and then think about how all of the pages should link together. Most websites consist of a home page that provides the starting point for users entering the site. "Like the top of a pyramid or the table of contents of a book, the home page leads to other web pages via hyperlinks" (Vukovich 26). Most home pages have the default name index.html (or sometimes index.htm).

Assessment 5 Create an Index and Table of Contents for a Desktop Publishing Report

1. At a blank document, create the text shown in Figure U2.3 as a concordance file.
2. Save the document and name it **WL2-U2-A5-CF**.
3. Print and then close **WL2-U2-A5-CF.docx**.
4. Open **DTPDesign.docx** and then save the document with Save As and name it **WL2-U2-A5-DTPDesign**.

5. Make the following changes to the document:
   a. Apply the Heading 1 style to the title and apply the Heading 2 style to the two headings in the report.
   b. Apply the *Simple* Quick Styles set.
   c. Mark text for an index using the concordance file **WL2-U2-A5-CF.docx**.
   d. Insert the index at the end of the document.
   e. Apply the Heading 1 style to the title of the index.
   f. Insert a table of contents at the beginning of the document.
   g. Make sure the Heading 1 style is applied to the title of the table of contents.
   h. Number the table of contents page with lowercase Roman numerals.
   i. Number the other pages in the report with Arabic numbers and start the numbering with 1 on the page containing the report title.
6. Make sure the table of contents and index display the correct page numbers. If not, update them.
7. Save, print, and then close **WL2-U2-A5-DTPDesign.docx**.

Figure U2.3 Assessment 5

message	Message
publication	Publication
design	Design
flyer	Flyer
letterhead	Letterhead
newsletter	Newsletter
intent	Design: intent
audience	Design: audience
layout	Design: layout
thumbnail	Thumbnail
principles	Design: principles
Focus	Design: focus
focus	Design: focus
balance	Design: balance
proportion	Design: proportion
contrast	Design: contrast
directional flow	Design: directional flow
consistency	Design: consistency
color	Design: color
White space	White space
white space	White space
Legibility	Legibility
headline	Headline
subheads	Subheads

Assessment 6 Create Captions and Insert a Table of Figures in a Report

1. Open **SoftwareCareers.docx** and then save the document with Save As and name it **WL2-U2-A6-SoftwareCareers**.
2. Move the insertion point to the line above the first table and create the caption *Table 1: Software Development Careers*. **Hint: Change the** Label **option at the Caption dialog box to** Table. (Change the paragraph spacing after to *0 pt*.)
3. Move the insertion point to the line above the second table and create the caption *Table 2: Application Development Careers*. (Change the paragraph spacing after to *0 pt*.)
4. Move the insertion point to the beginning of the document and then insert a section break that begins a new page.
5. With the insertion point below the section break, number pages at the bottom center of each page and change the starting page number to 1.
6. Move the insertion point to the beginning of the document and then insert the *Automatic Table 2* table of contents.
7. Press Ctrl + Enter to insert a page break. (If your insertion point does not move to the new page, continue to Step 8 and the insertion point will move to the new page when you start typing *Tables*.)
8. Type **Tables**, press the Enter key (your insertion point may not move down to the next line), and then insert a table of figures using the *Formal* format.
9. Apply the Heading 1 style to the title *Tables*.
10. Move the insertion point to the beginning of the document and then change the numbering format to lowercase Roman numerals.
11. Update the entire table of contents.
12. Make sure the table of figures displays the correct page number. If not, update it.
13. Save, print, and then close **WL2-U2-A6-SoftwareCareers.docx**.

Assessment 7 Insert Comments and Track Changes in an Online Shopping Report

1. Open **OnlineShop.docx** and then save the document with Save As and name it **WL2-U2-A7-OnlineShop**.
2. Type the word **Source** at the end of the first paragraph in the report, select the word, and then insert the comment **Include the source where you found this definition.**
3. Type the word **Examples** at the end of the paragraph in the *ONLINE SHOPPING VENUES* section, select the word, and then insert the comment **Include at least two of the most popular online shopping stores.**
4. Turn on tracking and then make the following changes:
   a. Delete the comma and the words *and most are eliminating paper tickets altogether* that display at the end of the last sentence in the second paragraph.
   b. Edit the heading *ADVANTAGES OF ONLINE SHOPPING* so it displays as *ONLINE SHOPPING ADVANTAGES*.
   c. Bold the first sentence of each of the bulleted paragraphs on the first page.
   d. Turn off tracking.
5. Display the Word Options dialog box with *General* selected and then change the *User name* to **Trudy Holmquist** and the *Initials* to **TH**.

6. Turn on tracking and then make the following changes:
   a. Delete the words *the following* in the first paragraph in the *ONLINE SHOPPING ADVANTAGES* section.
   b. Insert the following bulleted text between the third and fourth bulleted paragraphs on the second page: **Keep thorough records of all transactions.**
   c. Turn off tracking.
7. Print the document showing markups.
8. Display the Word Options dialog box with *General* selected and then change the *User name* back to the original name and *Initials* back to the original initials.
9. Accept all of the changes in the document *except* the change deleting the comma and the words *and most are eliminating paper tickets altogether.*
10. Save, print, and then close **WL2-U2-A7-OnlineShop.docx**.

Assessment 8 Combine Documents

1. Open **Software.docx** and then save the document with Save As and name it **WL2-U2-A8-Software**.
2. Close **WL2-U2-A8-Software.docx**.
3. At a blank screen, combine **WL2-U2-A8-Software.docx** (the original document) with **Software-CL.docx** (the revised document) into the original document.
4. Save **WL2-U2-A8-Software.docx**.
5. Print the document showing markups.
6. Accept all changes to the document.
7. Make the following changes to the document:
   a. Change the style set to Modern.
   b. Apply the Concourse theme.
   c. Apply the Elemental theme colors.
   d. Insert the Mod (Odd Page) footer.
8. Save, print, and then close **WL2-U2-A8-Software.docx**.

Assessment 9 Restrict Formatting in a Report

1. Open **InterfaceApps.docx** and then save the document with Save As and name it **WL2-U2-A9-InterfaceApps**.
2. Display the Restrict Formatting and Editing task pane and then restrict formatting to Heading 1 and Heading 2 styles. (At the message that displays asking if you want to remove formatting or styles that are not allowed, click No.)
3. Enforce the protection and include the password *report*.
4. Click the <u>Available styles</u> hyperlink in the Restrict Formatting and Editing task pane.
5. Apply the Heading 1 style to the title of the report and apply the Heading 2 style to the four headings in the report.
6. Close the Styles task pane.
7. Close the Restrict Formatting and Editing task pane.
8. Save the document and then print only page one.
9. Close **WL2-U2-A9-InterfaceApps.docx**.

Assessment 10 Insert Document Properties and Save a Document in a Previous Version of Word

1. Open **KLHPlan.docx** and then save the document with Save As and name it **WL2-U2-A10-KLHPlan**.
2. Make the following changes to the document:
   a. Apply the Heading 1 style to the three headings in the document (*Plan Highlights*, *Quality Assessment*, and *Provider Network*).
   b. Change the style set to Modern.
   c. Apply *Foundry* theme colors.
3. Move the insertion point to the end of the document and then insert the document named **KLHPlanDiagram.docx**.
4. Display the document information panel and then type the following information in the specified text boxes:
   a. Title = **Key Life Health Plan**
   b. Subject = **Company Health Plan**
   c. Keywords = **health, plan, network**
   d. Category = **Health Plan**
   e. Comments = **This document describes highlights of the Key Life Health Plan.**
   f. Close the document information panel.
5. Save the document and then print only the document properties.
6. Inspect the document and remove any hidden text.
7. Save and then print **WL2-U2-A10-KLHPlan.docx**.
8. Assume that the document will be read by a colleague with Word 2003 and run the compatibility checker to determine what features are not supported by earlier versions of Word.
9. Save the document in the *Word 97-2003 Document (*.doc)* format and name it **WL2-U2-A10-KLHPlan-2003format**.
10. Save, print, and then close **WL2-U2-A10-KLHPlan-2003format.doc**.

Writing Activities ■■■■■■■ ■■■■ ■■■■ ■

The following writing activities give you the opportunity to practice your writing skills along with demonstrating an understanding of some of the important Word features you have mastered in this unit.

Activity 1 Prepare an APA Guidelines Document

You work for a psychiatric medical facility and many of the psychiatrists and psychiatric nurses submit papers to journals that require the papers to be formatted in APA style. Your supervisor has asked you to prepare a document that describes the APA Guidelines and then provides the steps on how to format in Word a document in APA style. Find a website that provides information on the APA style and include the hyperlink in your document. (Consider websites for writing labs at a local college or university.) Apply formatting to enhance the visual appeal of the document. Save the document and name it **WL2-U2-Act1-APA**. Print and then close **WL2-U2-Act1-APA.docx**.

Activity 2 Create a Rental Form Template

You work in a real estate management company that manages rental houses. You decide to automate the standard rental form that is normally filled in by hand. Open **LeaseAgreement.docx** and then save the document with Save As and name it **WL2-U2-Act2-LeaseAgreement**. Look at the lease agreement document and determine how to automate it so you can fill in the document using the find and replace feature in Word. Change the current *Lessor* and *Lessee* names to *LESSOR* and *LESSEE*. Save the document as a template named **LeaseForm** to the Word2010L2U2 folder on your storage medium. Open the **LeaseForm.dotx** template and then complete the following find and replaces. Use your judgment about which occurrences should be changed and which should not.

> DAY = 22nd
> MONTH = February
> YEAR = 2012
> RENT = $950
> DEPOSIT = $500
> LESSOR = Samantha Herrera
> LESSEE = Daniel Miller

Save the document and name it **WL2-U2-Act2-Lease1**. Use the **LeaseForm.dotx** template to create another rental document. You determine the text to replace with the standard text. Save the completed rental document and name it **WL2-U2-Act2-Lease2**.

Internet Research ▪▪▪▪▪▪▪▪▪ ▪▪▪▪▪▪▪▪▪

Create a Job Search Report

Make sure you are connected to the Internet and then use a search engine to search for companies offering employment opportunities. Search for companies offering jobs in a field in which you are interested in working. Locate at least three websites that interest you and then create a report in Word about the sites that includes:

- Site name, address, and URL
- A brief description of the site
- Employment opportunities

Create hyperlinks from your report to each of the three sites and include any other additional information pertinent to the sites. Apply formatting to enhance the document. Save the document and name it **WL2-U2-Act3-JobSearch**. Print and then close **WL2-U2-Act3-JobSearch.docx**.

Job Study ▪▪▪▪▪▪▪▪▪▪▪▪▪▪▪▪▪▪▪▪▪▪

Format a Guidelines Report

As a staff member of a computer e-tailer, you are required to maintain cutting-edge technology skills, including being well-versed in the use of new software programs such as Office 2010. Recently, your supervisor asked you to develop and distribute a set of strategies for reading technical and computer manuals that the staff will use as they learn new programs. Use the concepts and techniques you learned in this unit to edit the guidelines report as follows:

1. Open **Strategies.docx** and then save the document with Save As and name it **WL2-U2-JS-Strategies**.
2. Turn on tracking changes and then make the following changes:
   a. Change all occurrences of *computer manuals* to *technical and computer manuals*.
   b. Format the document with appropriate heading styles.
   c. Insert at least two comments regarding the content and/or formatting of the document.
   d. Print the list of markups.
   e. Accept all of the tracked changes.
3. Turn off tracking changes.
4. Insert a table of contents.
5. Number pages in the document.
6. Create a cover page.
7. Save, print, and then close **WL2-U2-JS-Strategies.docx**.

Index

printing, 191
viewing and editing, 192–194
Format Picture dialog box, 17, 20, 21, 23
Format Shape dialog box, 23
formatting
   bibliography, 204–205
   chart design, 37–38
   chart layout, 38
   defining numbering, 9–10
   restricting, 295–296
   with styles, 138–142
   works cited page, 204–205
Full Screen Reading view, 275

G

General Options dialog box, 299, 300
grammar checker, 53, 58
grammar checking, 58–59
   changing options, 59
graphic, linking using, 148, 149–150
graphs, 35

H

hang indents, 6
Header button, 25
header gallery, saving content to, 93, 95–96
headers
   creating different first page, 28–29
   creating for different sections, 30–32
   creating odd and even, 29–30
   defined, 25
   inserting elements in, 25–26
   positioning, 26–28
   tab settings in, 26–27
hyperlinks
   inserting, 146–150
   inserting cross-references as, 150–151
   linking to email address, 149
   linking to file in another program, 148, 149–150
   linking to new document, 148, 149–150
   linking to place in document, 147
   linking using graphic, 148, 149–150
   navigating using, 147
   purpose of, 146

I

I-beam marker, display of bookmark as, 144
Ignore Rule button, 58
images
   applying advanced formatting to, 20–21
   inserting and customizing clip art, 19–20
indents, 6
   hang indents, 6
index, 233–238
   inserting, 237–238
   inserting, using concordance file, 241
   marking text for, 233–236
   updating and deleting, 241–242
Index dialog box, 237
information
   changing user, 263–264
   researching, 66–67
Info tab Backstage view, 302, 305, 316, 317
Insert Chart dialog box, 35
Insert Hyperlink dialog box, 146
inserting
   clip art image, 19–20
   comments, 255–261
   comments in Reviewing Pane, 256–258
   custom building blocks, 97–99
   custom numbers, 6–8
   elements in headers and footers, 25–26
   fields, 104–106
   hyperlinks, 146–150
   index, 237–238
   multilevel list numbering, 13–16
   nonbreaking space, 185
   photographs, 21–23
   table of contents, 219, 220–221
   works cited page or bibliography, 202–203
Insert Picture dialog box, 25

K

Keep lines together option, 33

L

layout, customizing, 17–20
Layout dialog box, 17, 18

Horizontal section in, 18
Vertical section in, 18
line break, inserting in list, 11
list
   changing level of bulleted, 11
   inserting line break in, 11
   multilevel, defining, 14–16
   multilevel, typing, 14–16

M

Mail Merge Recipients dialog box, 178, 179, 181
Mark Index Entry dialog box, 233–234
marking document as final, 305–306
Mark Table of Contents Entry dialog box, 226
markup, showing, 265–266
master document, 278
   creating, 278–279
merging documents, 273–275
Microsoft SharePoint Server 2010, 251
minimizing the ribbon, 107
Modern Language Association (MLA) style, 194, 202
modifying building blocks, 99–101
Modify Style dialog box, 222
multilevel lists
   defining, 14–16
   inserting numbering, 13–16
   typing, 14–16

N

navigating, 142–146
   between comments, 258
   with cross-references, 151
   using bookmarks, 144–146
   using hyperlinks, 147
   using Navigation pane, 142–144
   using table of contents in, 219
   to tracked changes, 267
Navigation pane, navigating using, 142–144
New dialog box, 188, 189
New from Existing Document dialog box, 188
New tab Backstage view, 188
Next Sentence button, 58
nonbreaking space
   finding and replacing, 186–187
   inserting, 185
Normal.dotm template, 130